Scottish
Business Law

TEXT, CASES & MATERIALS

This book is dedicated to the memory
of Elizabeth Willett

Scottish Business Law

TEXT, CASES & MATERIALS

Second edition

Chris Willett LLB(Hons)

Lecturer in Law, Warwick University

and

Aidan ODonnell BA, LLB

Lecturer in Law, Glasgow Caledonian University

BLACKSTONE PRESS LIMITED

First published in Great Britain 1991 by Blackstone Press Limited,
9–15 Aldine Street, London W12 8AW. Telephone 0181-740 1173

© C. Willett and A. ODonnell, 1991

First edition, 1991
Second edition, 1996

ISBN: 1 85431 440 8

British Library Cataloguing in Publication Data
A CIP catalogue record for this book is available from the British Library

Typeset by Style Photosetting Ltd, Mayfield, East Sussex
Printed by Ashford Colour Press, Gosport, Hampshire

Contents

1.1 The legal regulation of business: rationale and general nature
1.2 The resolution of disputes 1.3 Legal advice

2.1 Legal nature 2.2 Legal formalities 2.3 Choice of business form

3.1 Introduction: rules, planning, philosophy and context 3.2 Nature of
contract 3.3 Offer, withdrawal of offer, and acceptance 3.4 Intention to create
legal relations 3.5 Gratuitous obligations 3.6 Certainty of terms 3.7 Void,

voidable and unenforceable contracts 3.8 Contractual formalities 3.9 Capacity to contract 3.10 Legality and public policy 3.11 Contractual terms
3.12 Agreement improperly obtained 3.13 Unfulfilled expectations: error
3.14 Frustration 3.15 Discharge, breach of contract and remedies
3.16 Quasi-contract

4   Delictual Rights and Duties   111

4.1 Function, nature and extent of delict 4.2 Negligence: duty of care
4.3 Negligent acts and economic loss where property involved 4.4 Negligence: breach of duty 4.5 Proof of negligence 4.6 Causation and remoteness
of damage 4.7 Defences to negligence claims 4.8 The Consumer Protection
Act 1987 4.9 Nuisance 4.10 Injury on the premises: occupiers' liability and
breach of statutory duty 4.11 Economic delicts

5   The Law of Agency   155

5.1 Contractual capacity 5.2 Becoming an agent 5.3 The relationship
between principal and agent 5.4 The relationship between agent, principal
and third party 5.5 Termination of agency

6   The Law Relating to the Sale and Supply of Goods   174

6.1 Aims, values and sources 6.2 Sale and supply of goods — types of
contract and sources of regulation 6.3 Subject matter and price 6.4 Capacity
and formalities 6.5 Stipulations as to time 6.6 Implied terms 6.7 The passing
of property 6.8 Transfer of title 6.9 Performance of the contract 6.10 Breach
of contract

7   Consumer Credit   204

7.1 Legal controls on credit 7.2 Types of credit 7.3 Types of agreements
7.4 Licensing 7.5 Seeking business 7.6 Formalities 7.7 Liability of suppliers,
creditors and dealers 7.8 Termination and default 7.9 Extortionate credit
bargains

8   The Law of Employment   229

8.1 The distinction between contracts of service and contracts for services
8.2 The form of the contract of employment 8.3 Obligations of employer and
employee 8.4 Termination of the contract of employment 8.5 Unfair dismissal 8.6 Redundancy payments 8.7 Equal pay 8.8 Discrimination on
grounds of sex or marital status 8.9 Racial discrimination 8.10 Maternity
rights 8.11 Health and Safety at Work Act 1974

Preface

This second edition continues to deal with topics which are important elements of most law courses and which tend to form the core of 'business law' courses. We try to show the ways in which the rules are relevant to commercial activity and highlight the way in which law can be used to plan behaviour. However, the book is not a 'practice guide' which seeks to guide practitioners and businesses through the law and practice of transactions. This would involve discussion of drafting, types of official documents, court procedures etc. These are beyond the scope of a book which aims primarily to provide an analysis for students and academics. Clearly it is relevant to such an analysis to draw attention to the law's role in planning transactions. It is also important to give readers an insight into some of the values and policies which underly the rules, and this is something which we have sought to give more emphasis to in this second edition.

In many chapters (and/or in the Cases and Materials) we have either expanded discussion of particular topics (e.g., the European Union, wrongful trading, director's duties, negligence) or added discussions which were not there previously (e.g., on ombudsmen, the banking code of practice, the new laws on unfair terms product safety, contractual formalities and the economic delicts.

We would like to acknowledge the help and advice of Professor Kenny Miller (University of Strathclyde) and Ruth Cameron (Glasgow Caledonian University). Special thanks to Owen McIntyre (Manchester University) for his article in the Materials on the European Union. Responsibility for errors of law or expression lies, of course, with ourselves.

C. Willett
A. ODonnell

Preface to the First Edition

The aim of this book is to explain and critically analyse the key legal principles which affect commercial activities in Scotland. We hope that our analysis will provide students, practitioners and business people with a clear framework of principles, along with a sense of the dynamic and controversial nature of law.

There are very few rules of law which do not, in some way, impact on commercial activities. A book of this kind must select the common law and statutory principles which form the basis of a host of more specialised rules. For this reason we think it is crucial that a grasp of the law of contract delict, sale of goods, consumer credit, agency and employment should come first and foremost. We also feel that it is important to explain the basic principles governing the operation of partnerships and companies, so that the reader may draw conclusions as to the suitability of alternative business forms, in different circumstances.

The cases and materials are intended to provide access to primary materials which the reader would otherwise be required to seek out from specialised sources. They are also intended to help the reader develop the ability to deal with the raw material of law — the cases and statutory provisions. The excerpts from articles hopefully provide access to a broader range of perspectives than are normally available in a traditional textbook.

We would like to thank all of the staff at Blackstone Press for their constant support throughout the project. Our appreciation also to Professor Pat Leighton (Anglia Higher Education College); Kenny Miller and Alistair Clarke (Strathclyde University) and Con McMahon (Glasgow Polytechnic) who made helpful comments on draft chapters. Responsibility for errors of law or expression lies, of course, with ourselves.

C. Willett
A. ODonnell

Acknowledgments

The authors and publishers would like to thank the following for permission to reproduce copyright material:

Basil Blackwell: extracts from *Modern Law Review*.

Barry Rose Publishing: extracts from the *Anglo-American Law Review*.

Butterworth Law Publishers Ltd: *All England Law Reports*.

Sweet and Maxwell: extracts from *Journal of Business Law* and *Law Quarterly Review*.

T & T Clark Ltd and the Scottish Council of Law Reporting: extracts from Session Cases.

W. Green & Son Ltd: *Scots Law Times; Green's Business Law Bulletin*.

The Incorporated Council of Law Reporting for England and Wales: *Weekly Law Reports; Law Reports Appeal Cases*.

Industrial Relations Services Eclipse Group: *Industrial Relations Law Reports*.

Lord McCluskey: extracts from *Law, Justice and Democracy* (1987).

Table of Cases

EUROPEAN CASES

Table of Statutes

TABLE OF STATUTORY INSTRUMENTS

TABLE OF EUROPEAN
LEGISLATION

CHAPTER ONE

Introduction to the Law and its Role in the Business World

1.1 THE LEGAL REGULATION OF BUSINESS: RATIONALE AND GENERAL NATURE

In a modern industrialised society, commercial and industrial activities directly or indirectly affect the lives of virtually all of the members of that society. Clearly such activities must be subject to some form of control; not least because they are a central feature in the competitive acquisition of wealth. As law is a major means of social control generally, so it has adopted a similar role in the business world. This is not to say that law is the only means by which standards are kept at a level which society finds acceptable. Businessmen may also be guided by personal values of trust and honour, or by the ethics of their profession. They will also wish to avoid disputes where at all possible, and, as such, attempt to find common ground with those with whom they come into conflict. However, there may be no common ground, or it may be that price, greed or self-esteem make it difficult to recognise such that there is. So, while the purchaser of goods may be bitterly disappointed in their quality, the manufacturer or seller may be equally disappointed that the purchaser expects too much. While an employer may feel unable to afford to continue to employ someone who is slow and unproductive, the employee in question probably believes that more patience and training should be given. The law has therefore been required to develop principles and formulate rules to regulate the relationships between sellers and purchasers of goods, between employers and employees and between all those who play a part in, or who are affected by, the world of business. These principles and rules form part of what is generally known as the *civil* law.

As well as mediating between individuals in this way, society may feel moved to say that certain types of behaviour pose a more serious threat to society generally and should be punished as *criminal* offences. So, for example, certain statutes have made it an offence to make statements which mis-describe goods and services (see Chapter 9). The parties responsible may also be liable under the civil law to compensate those who have suffered loss in reliance on such statements, (see Chapters 3 and 4). In addition, as we become more sophisticated in maintaining acceptable standards, the realisation dawns that prevention is better than cure, i.e. it may be preferable to erect regulatory, *administrative* frameworks which promote the safety, fair dealing or openness which is desired. Examples of such administrative regulation of business include:

(a)   The function of the Health and Safety Executive in the promotion of safety through publicity and training and the investigation of hazardous situations (see Chapter 8, para. 8.11.2).

(b)   The power of the Director General of Fair Trading to seek assurances from traders that they will discontinue conduct which is contrary to consumer interests (see Chapter 9, para. 9.3.1).

(c)   The requirement that those running a limited liability company should register as public documents their memorandum and articles of association, (see Chapter 2). This is an example of what might be described as a 'disclosure culture'. It is based on the notion that in return for the privileged legal status accorded to limited companies, these companies should be open with the public, at least in relation to such fundamental matters as the kind of business in which they will engage.

(d)   The powers of regulators of the utility industries to require the industries to meet certain performance standards (see Chapter 9).

Of course, these administrative frameworks are not wholly divorced from traditional civil and criminal law regulation. If an employer chooses to ignore exhortations, e.g., from the Health and Safety Executive, to educate his staff on matters of safety, he may be committing an offence under the Health and Safety at Work Act 1974. Equally, if someone is injured as a result, the employer may be liable to compensate that person in civil law for breach of contract or negligence (see Chapters 3, 4 and 8).

The whole process of setting standards to prevent harm occurring and/or to resolve disputes also provides a framework within which businesses and private individuals can plan their activities in the knowledge of their rights and duties. So a businessman may consider the rules on misrepresentation when drafting advertisements, and the rules on offer and acceptance (see Chapter 3) when considering his procedures for taking or placing orders. He will also consider the rules on product liability when considering his quality management and design systems (see Chapter 4), and the rules on unfair dismissal if he is thinking of dismissing an employee (see Chapter 8). These rules may not always tell him precisely what is acceptable, but he will be nearer to understanding the pitfalls.

1.1.1   The law and changing values

The standards which a society sets to control the commercial activities of its members act as a useful barometer of the economic and political values of that society. During the nineteenth century, the dominant economic philosophy was that of laissez-faire. The theory was that market forces are the best means of controlling business activities and setting standards. Business should be allowed to develop untrammelled by state intervention. Parties should be free to contract with one another on whatever terms they wish, as long as they are not illegal and as long as those involved are mature and sane enough to understand the nature of their obligations.

This philosophy was enshrined in the doctrine of freedom of contract. During the twentieth century, however, with the rise of the consumer society, the belief became prevalent that it was unrealistic to assume that parties negotiated equally for goods or services. The practice had become established of traders offering goods and services to consumers on the basis of standard form contracts, weighted heavily in their own favour. It seemed that any 'choice' that the consumer had was illusory, as all traders dealt on similar terms. It was thought to be equally naive to assume that employees or tenants, for instance, could negotiate equally with their employers or landlords. As Lord Devlin has said 'the courts could not relieve in cases of hardship and oppression, because the basic principle of freedom of contract included freedom to oppress' (*The Common Law, Public Policy and the Executive*, p.10).

The law's response was to allocate guaranteed rights to those perceived to be the weaker parties, e.g., rights as to the quality of goods and services and the safety of the workplace and the habitability of rented accommodation (see Chapters 3 and 8 below). Along with these protections came criminal sanctions, to protect against poor standards of safety both generally (e.g., the Health and Safety at Work Act 1974) and in specific industries (e.g., the Food Safety Act 1990). The radical, market-orientated philosophy of the present government has, however, seen a perceptible return to laissez-faire standards in business. This is exemplified by a diminution in the statutory protection afforded in respect of job security (see Chapter 8).

The public sector reforms of the last 15 years, particularly those involving the contracting out and privatisation of services, have also to some extent been motivated by a belief in the benefits of a market-orientated economy. This market-driven approach has been seen as a more efficient way of delivering improved public services than the allocation of ever-increasing resources and/or the promulgation of citizens' rights to good quality service. (See discussion by Rawlings and Willett in Willett (Ed.) *Aspects of New Public Sector Regulation* (forthcoming) Elgar, (1995).)

It is important to recognise, therefore, that when Parliament, or the courts or some other law-making agency are deciding whether to have any given rule or how it should be applied, the decision is likely to be informed by value judgements of the sort described above. When deciding whether to test the fairness of the terms contained in contracts made by consumers, it is important to ask why we think this is necessary. The argument is basically that consumers are so ill-informed about the terms of standard form contracts and the risks they involve that it is difficult for them to make rational choices or to negotiate with sellers. This means that the terms may not be disciplined by market forces, and so it is argued that we are justified in applying standards of fairness (Chapter 3). But of course, even if these arguments are valid, every time we interfere with a market transaction by picking it apart it is clear that there are costs as well as benefits. Sellers will be unsure whether their terms will stand and may have to take out higher insurance against risks, and pass this on to the consumer in higher prices. The same sort of arguments apply in the employment context, where we must weigh up the benefits of rules which give job security and the right to withdraw labour against the costs to the employer, who may respond by employing fewer staff.

Even issues of safety are not immune from such considerations. The level of safety which is insisted upon and the stringency of the measures used to enforce these levels are influenced by considerations of this 'cost-benefit' nature. The benefits of a very high safety standard are that most who are injured will be compensated: the costs are that the price of products may rise, some firms may be unable to continue to compete, and so the choice of products available to consumers may be reduced. For example, the Consumer Protection Act 1987, says that manufacturers and others are strictly liable if a product is defective and causes injury to a consumer (Chapter 4); on the other hand, there is a defence available if the manufacturer can show that the state of scientific and technical knowledge was not such as to make it reasonable for him to have known of the defect. So while the law wishes to compensate whenever a consumer is injured, it also wishes to encourage advances in technology.

The response of the law is often to find balances such as this between the different goals which a modern industrialised society has. So, e.g., job security might be available only after a certain period of employment (see Chapter 8). In the unfair terms context it might be said that only terms *other than* the price and main subject matter may be tested for faults — so we enforce the basic free market exchange but disallow 'fringe' risks which are unfair e.g., certain types of exemption clause (see Chapter 3).

1.1.2   Law and other factors

It is not only formal legal rules which govern and regulate commercial, political and private behaviour. We know from common sense and empirical study, for example, that relationships between businesses are often heavily influenced by factors such as trust, cooperation and the wish to do business again (see Beale and Dugdale in the Cases and Materials section for Chapter 1). So just because Company A could enforce a contractual term against Company B (e.g., giving a remedy for late payment, delivery or whatever), does not mean it will do so. B may be a good customer, or even a friend, whom A does not wish to lose; it may be too costly to go to court; the ethics of the trade sector in question may frown on parties taking legal action against one another, so that A's reputation with other traders would be damaged by taking action. In other sorts of relationships there may be different sorts of restraints on enforcing formal legal rights. For example, consumers may not understand either that they have rights when products do not live up to their expectations, or what those rights are (see Willett, 'The Unacceptable Face of the Consumer Guarantees Bill,' 54 MLR 552, Willett, 'The Quality of Goods and the Rights of Consumers' 44 NILQ 218 and discussion of problems enforcing consumer rights in Willett, *Unfair Terms in Consumer Contracts*, Chapter 10).

In recent years especially, the limitations of formal legal rules have been more clearly recognised. So businesses agree to take their differences to arbitration; forthcoming 1996 codes of practice are drawn up to define the standards of service and types of warranties which businesses in a particular sector will offer to customers, and to define a process for informal redress through the company or a trade association, if there is dissatisfaction; 'ombudsmen' schemes proliferate in banking, insurance, building society and funeral services to provide cheaper, more accessible redress for customers. Often these processes provide not only such redress, but also better rights than the formal law would have insisted upon. This happens partly due to a genuine desire by the industry to set high standards, but partly also due to a concern to ensure that government will not impose formal regulation, or (as the case may be) more formal regulation (see the discussion of codes of practice in the Cases and Materials section for Chapter 3).

It is important to be conscious of the relationship between formal rules, problems of lack of information, lack of resources to take action, and the fact that taking formal legal action may be in no one's interest, etc. Such a perspective enriches our understanding of what rules aim to achieve and are capable of achieving, and how to use legal and other instruments (e.g., codes of practice) to achieve our policy goals. However, an awareness of the instruments, other than formal rules, which have already developed to regulate the commercial world is also important from a practical point of view. A book of this length and nature cannot delve into every sector of the economy and set out the various systems in place, but a flavour of some of these systems is given in the Cases and Materials section for Chapter 3.

1.1.3 Classifications of law

1.1.3.1 Private and public law Private law regulates the relationships between individuals and provides a remedy where one individual (or a body recognised as such by law, e.g., a company) infringes the rights of another individual. Private law therefore regulates the rights of parties who enter into contractual relations (see Chapter 3). It also regulates what will happen where the behaviour of one individual affects the rights of others. For example, the law of delict holds that we must guard against causing harm to those whom it is foreseeable our actions will affect, e.g., by the manufacture of dangerous products. The law of delict also requires that the property rights of others are respected, e.g., liability for nuisance, (see Chapter 4).

Public law regulates the relationship between the state and private citizens. It therefore governs constitutional matters (e.g., the conduct of government and the civil liberties of private citizens); administrative law (e.g., the activities of regulatory agencies such as the Health and Safety Executive and the Office of Fair Trading) and criminal law (the punishment of behaviour deemed by government to be socially dangerous or unacceptable).

1.1.3.2   Civil and criminal law   This is the most important means of classifying law. From the discussion thus far, it is possible to draw certain conclusions. First, the rationale of the two types of law is different. Civil law seeks to remedy and perhaps compensate for a wrong (such as a breach of contract) committed by A against B. It provides a system of civil courts (see 1.3.1.1 below) through which B can personally proceed with an action. B would be known as the *pursuer* and A as the *defender*. The purpose of such an action is not to *punish* A, but to recover from him the losses he has caused. Criminal law seeks to prohibit certain conduct and punish it when detected. The action will be taken by the state in the criminal courts (see 1.3.1.2 below). The types of behaviour may range from serious crimes, such as murder or rape, to behaviour which offends against standards of commercial morality, e.g., the misdescription of goods under the Trade Descriptions Act 1968 or the sale of foods of inferior quality under the Food Safety Act 1990, ss. 1-3 (see Chapter 9). Such behaviour may *also* amount to a breach of contract, or the commission of a delict, for which compensation may be sought separately in the civil courts.

For example, if A is sold contaminated food in B's supermarket, A will probably have an action against B in contract law for breach of the implied term that goods be of satisfactory quality, (see Chapter 6 below). If the contamination amounts to a 'defect' within the meaning of the Consumer Protection Act 1987 (see Chapter 4) there may be an action for compensation against the producer and possibly others in the chain of supply. Finally, the local authority may choose to prosecute B under the Food Safety Act 1990 for selling food which is unfit for human consumption and injurious to health.

The other main distinction between civil and criminal law is the standard of proof which is required to succeed in one's action. The civil law requires one to prove, *on the balance of probabilities*, that the alleged behaviour took place. The criminal law, however, requires that the wrongful conduct be proven *beyond all reasonable doubt*. This is a much higher standard of proof and it is utilised largely because the liberty of the accused may well be at stake.

1.1.3.3   Classification by source   Another traditional way of classifying law is by reference to its source, i.e., legislation, common law, custom, etc. This cuts across the distinction between public and private and civil and criminal law. Both civil and criminal law, for example, are made up of a mixture of principles of common law statutory provisions and the other sources of law.

The main sources of law in Scotland are statute, delegated legislation, judicial precedent, the institutional writers and custom, but, especially in the business sector, the law of the European Union, which sometimes has direct effect, (see Cases and Materials, Chapter 1) is increasingly important.

Statute law   Statute law or legislation is the main source of law today. Statute law is law which has been formally enacted by Parliament. Parliament consists of two chambers; the House of Commons, which is an elected body, and the House of Lords, which consists of life peers, spiritual peers, the law Lords and hereditary peers. Parliament, under the unwritten British Constitution, is the supreme law-making body. Legally, there is nothing that Parliament cannot do. Whatever law Parliament enacts, will, by definition, be lawful, no matter how unfair or unpopular.

This ability of Parliament to do as it pleases is known as the doctrine of Parliamentary supremacy or sovereignty. (For a discussion of this, see Munro, *Studies in Constitutional Law*, Chapters 5 and 6.) Parliament can repeal Acts passed by earlier Parliaments. Theoretically, it could repeal all earlier legislation, but it is unlikely to have the time or the inclination to do so. Most legislation takes effect from some date after it has been given the Royal Assent, but in exceptional cases, legislation is passed with retrospective effect. An example would be the War Damage Act 1965, which was passed following the decision of the House of Lords in *Burmah Oil Company Limited v Lord Advocate* 1964 SLT 218.

Most legislation is initiated by the government, although there is provision for Private Members' Bills to be initiated by individual members of Parliament. There are two ways in which an individual member may introduce proposed legislation. The 'ten minute rule' allows a member to introduce a Bill, and speak on it for ten minutes. A further ten minutes is allowed for speeches for those opposed to the proposals. A vote is then taken. Bills introduced under the rule are used more as a way of bringing an issue to the attention of fellow members, than as a serious attempt at legislation. Better known is the Private Members' Ballot. This involves the drawing of lots by members. Those who draw one of the top 20 or so numbers have the opportunity to propose legislation. This legislation will be debated on a set number of Fridays which are specially set aside for such bills. The reality is that as the government is in charge of the overloaded Parliamentary timetable, it will ensure that only those bills of which it approves will pass through the required Parliamentary stages. The government may make use of the Private Members' Ballot to introduce 'social' legislation with which it does not wish to be forever associated. Examples include the decriminalisation of abortion and of male homosexual intercourse.

When a Private Member's Bill is enacted, it is sometimes rather misleadingly described as a Private Member's Act, although it has the same force as any other Act of Parliament.

For a Bill to become an Act it must pass through five stages in both Houses of Parliament and receive the Royal Assent (see the Cases and Materials section for Chapter 1). With the exception of financial legislation (e.g., the Finance Bills which seek to enact the Chancellor's Budget proposals), Bills can start their lives in either the Commons or the Lords. The stages in both Houses are a first and second reading, a committee stage, a report stage, and a third reading.

The first reading is purely formal and amounts to no more than the reading of the Bill's title and its subsequent printing. The second reading is a debate on the main points of the Bill. At the committee stage, the Bill is scrutinised in minute detail and amendments made. The committee will report back to the Commons or Lords (as appropriate). At the report stage, further amendments will be made. The third reading is the final vote on the Bill. If passed, the Bill then goes through the same procedure in the Commons (or Lords).

Other types of Acts which are specially labelled are consolidating Acts, codifying Acts, public and general Acts and private Acts. A consolidating Act is one which gathers existing legislation into one single Act, the Employment Protection (Consolidation) Act 1978 being a good example. A codifying Act is one which enacts all the law on a topic, both common and statute in a single Act, e.g., the Partnership Act 1890 or the Sale of Goods Act 1893. Public and general Acts are the vast majority of Acts which could apply to anyone and which have general application; private Acts are those which have limited application and purpose, such as the creation of special powers for a local authority; they are usually sponsored by the local authority or other large organisation which seeks to benefit from their provisions.

Not all Acts of Parliament apply to Scotland. If it does not, this will be stated in the Act (usually in the last section). Some Acts apply only to Scotland. They will have the word 'Scotland' in brackets, e.g., Debtors (Scotland) Act 1987.

Other Acts will contain provision for the application of the main provisions to Scotland with certain changes or modifications contained in specific sections.

For an example of an Act of Parliament, with annotations as to its constituent parts, see the Cases and Materials section for Chapter 1.

Delegated legislation   Parliament's appetite for enactment is greater than the time available. The increasing involvement of government in the life of the citizen, as compared with the beginning of the century, has led to an explosion in the use of delegated legislation. This involves the delegation of Parliament's law-making power to some other body or person, such as a local authority or a government minister. Examples include local authority by-laws and ministerial regulations such as those made under the Fair Trading Act 1973. Delegated legislation is akin to a system of sub-contracting. Those to whom the authority to legislate is delegated can act only within the parameters of a 'parent' or enabling Act, which will usually delimit their powers. Should they exceed their delegated powers they will be held to be acting *ultra vires* (beyond their powers). It is really another form of statute law; it was described by Lord Hewart, the Lord Chief Justice of England, as the 'New Despotism' on the grounds that delegated legislation usurped the hard-won legislative powers of Parliament.

While this is true to some degree, given the pressure of time and the technical complexity of much modern legislation, delegated legislation is inevitable and necessary. There are parliamentary and judicial controls to prevent the possibility of abuse of delegated legislation. For example, the enabling Act (i.e. the Act which creates the power for such legislation to be made) may require the measure to be laid before Parliament; the provision in question may qualify for scrutiny by special parliamentary committees; or, where an issue of public importance is involved, a special parliamentary procedure involving a local inquiry and/or a petition to Parliament may be required (see Statutory Orders (Special Procedure) Acts 1945 and 1965 and provisional orders under the Private Legislation Procedure (Scotland) Act 1936).

The courts may declare delegated legislation to be *ultra vires* if

(a) it did not follow the procedure prescribed in the enabling Act, or
(b) it is substantively objectionable, e.g., because it removes fundamental rights (*Attorney General* v *Wilts United Dairies* [1921] 39 TLR 781, HL); and in the case of by-laws it is repugnant to the general law; or it is unreasonable or uncertain.

Interpretation of statutes Lord Hailsham estimated that 'nine cases out of ten which come before the House of Lords depend, in the end, upon the interpretation of a statute'. It is one of the tasks of the judiciary to interpret and construe the words used in an Act in the event of a dispute as to their meaning. It would often be impractical, indeed impossible, to ask Parliament what the words mean (but see *Pepper* v *Hart* [1992] 3 WLR 1032 where the Lords sought help from *Hansard*) and, where there is any doubt as to the meaning, the judges will use one of three recognised approaches to statutory interpretation.

The Literal Rule is where the judge gives the words used their normal or literal meaning, no matter what the absurdity of the result. An example of such potential absurdity is the English case of *R* v *Harris* (1836) 7 C&F 416, where the accused had bitten off the end of his victim's nose. He was charged under an Act which made it an offence to 'unlawfully and maliciously stab, cut or wound any person'. Nobody would equate biting someone's nose off with any of the above. Harris was therefore, after applying the Literal Rule found not guilty of the offence. Although this approach used to hold sway in many cases, particularly those involving income tax statutes (see *I R C* v *Hinchey* [1960] AC 748), the modern trend has been to pay greater heed to the consequences of any given interpretation.

The Golden Rule will be used where the Literal Rule tends to absurdity or injustice. Where a word has alternative meanings, the meaning resulting in the least absurd consequence will be chosen. The most famous example here is the case of *R* v *Allen* (1872) LR 1 CCR 367. Allen was accused of an offence under the Offences Against the Person Act 1861, s. 57 of which provided: 'Whosoever being married, shall marry any other person during the life of the former husband or wife . . . shall be guilty of [bigamy]'. Allen, while married to Ann, married Harriet. He was charged under s. 57. He argued that he was not guilty because, as he was already married to Ann, he had not 'married' Harriet at all. The court's solution to this was to give to the word 'marry' its secondary meaning of going through the form and ceremony of marriage. Allen was therefore found guilty.

The Mischief Rule places emphasis not so much on the words used, but on the intention of Parliament when the Act was passed, i.e. what mischief was the Act passed to remedy. It is most appropriate where the language is inherently ambiguous and Parliament's intention needs to be unearthed. An example is *Leadbetter* v *Hutchinson* 1934 JC 70, where the accused was charged with salmon poaching. The Tweed Fishing Act under which he had been charged allowed the court to forfeit any boat, cart, basket or carriage. The court held that 'cart' included a motor cycle combination. This allowed the court to 'cope with the mischief'.

Many Acts also contain an interpretation section which defines the meaning of words used in the Act. An example we will come across later is the Sale of Goods Act 1979, s. 61(1) (see Chapter 6). The Interpretation Act 1978 also provides a useful guide, laying down basic rules of interpretation.

Statutory interpretation is a complex area, and it is impossible to do it justice in such a small space. The recent decision in *Pepper* v *Hart* [1992] 3 WLR 1032 has focused attention on the topic. For a full analysis, see Walker, 'Discovering the Intention of Parliament' 1993 SLT 121 which discusses the House of Lords break with a long standing tradition in their attempt to interpret statutes. The dissenting judgment of Lord Mackay in *Pepper* is worth reading as it would seem to reflect the view that the financial cost of seeking Parliament's intention from Hansard is something that must be considered before using this approach.

Judicial precedent   In spite of the dominance of statute as a source of law, judicial precedent still has a very important role to play. It depends on the use of previous judicial decisions to assist a judge. It was only in the nineteenth century that the strict doctrine of judicial precedent, or *stare decisis* came to be applied in Scotland, as it had been for many years in England. The doctrine of judicial precedent recognises the hierarchical nature of the Scottish court system with, in civil matters, the House of Lords at its head (see 1.3.1.1 below).

The core of the doctrine is that what a judge says in a particular case is, in some circumstances, binding on judges in future cases. Basically, all courts are bound to follow the previous decisions of courts which rank above them. Decisions of the House of Lords on matters of Scots law would therefore be binding on all other Scottish civil courts; a decision of the Inner House of the Court of Session would be binding on the Outer House and on the sheriff courts. The doctrine is, however, not as strong in the criminal courts as it is in the civil courts.

In the course of his judgment a judge will cover a lot of ground; he will relate the facts, he may refer to other cases that are similar but not, to his mind, the same. The only part of his judgment that will be binding will be the *ratio decidendi* (the reason for the decision). Other statements, known as *obiter dicta* (things said by the way) will not be binding. They may, however, be persuasive – not lightly to be ignored if made by prominent judges in the higher courts. It is difficult to give a definitive conception of the ratio of a case. One description is that it is that part of the judgment which was necessary to dispose of the facts of the case. Cases may, however, have more than one ratio; these may be broad or specific and may be mixed up with *obiter dicta.* In appeal cases in the Court of Session, there will be more than one judge, perhaps even 'the hale fifteen'. Each may give a different reason for his decision (a classic example of this is the House of Lords decision in *British Railways Board* v *Herrington* [1972] AC 877). The question as to which is the true ratio in such circumstances is, at best, tortuous and, at worst, unanswerable.

In addition to binding precedents, there are also persuasive precedents. These are the decisions of lower courts or those of other jurisdictions, e.g., English courts. Before 1966, the House of Lords felt bound by its own previous decisions, but, since the 1966 Practice Statement, it no longer regards itself as bound to follow them; nevertheless, it has rarely departed from precedent (a notable recent example being *Murphy* v *Brentwood D C* (see Chapter 4)). A party who wishes the House of Lords to use its power to depart from a previous decision must make this clear in the appeal documents.

Those in favour of precedent argue that it makes for certainty, uniformity and a degree of flexibility, which allows the law to develop to meet changing social and economic circumstances. Critics say it makes for rigidity, which prevents the development of the law and leads to judges furiously looking for some means of evading a precedent that would normally bind them. The physical difficulty of disovering precedents has been alleviated somewhat by the introduction of Lexis and Lawtel, computer databases holding details of decisions and judgments.

For a discussion of the way judges make decisions see the extract from Lord McCluskey in the Cases and Materials section for Chapter 1.

The institutional writers Gloag and Henderson (*Introduction to the Law of Scotland*, 9th edn, p. 14) say 'a writer on law is not in any proper sense an authority during his lifetime, unless he is raised to the Bench'. Those writers whose works are regarded with this authority are known as 'Institutional Writers'. Their works will either have covered the whole of Scots law or substantial areas of it. The most important institutional writers are Stair, Erksine, Bankton and Bell and, in the field of criminal law, Hume and Alison.

The courts will not have recourse to these writings, unless the cupboard of statute and precedent is bare. Notwithstanding this, Professor Walker considers that the statement of an institutional writer is equal in authority to a decision of the Inner House of the Court of Session. In any event, the great value of these writers is that their views have been considered in past cases and have been endorsed by judicial comment or precedent.

Custom Custom may, in some areas, still be a source of law. In mercantile law, the courts will recognise customs operative in particular trades. Also, local customs may be important in determining property rights, or in deciding on the validity of some particular method of governing a burgh. For a local or general custom to be recognised as a rule of law, it must be: (1) generally acquiesced in as having the force of law for a substantial, although undefined time; (2) definite and certain; (3) fair and reasonable (see *Bruce* v *Smith*

(1890) 17 R 1000); and (4) not inconsistent with legal principle. Although it will, by necessity, vary from the general rules of common law, it must not conflict with them or with statute law. Given these conditions, custom as a source of law has but a limited potential.

Equity   Equity, in the sense of implicit fairness or equality before the law, is also a source of Scots law. It must be distinguished from equity in the English sense, which refers to the body of rules and principles laid down by the former Court of Chancery. More specifically, equity in Scotland can refer to the equitable power available to the Court of Session and the High Court of Judiciary to provide a remedy where none is otherwise available. This is known as the *Nobile Officium* of the Court and is rarely exercised.

The European dimension   Since the United Kingdom joined the European Economic Community in 1973 and the passing of the European Community Act 1972, Community legislation has applied to Scotland. The increasing importance of the European dimension justifies a discussion which looks not merely at European Union law as a source of law, but also at the European Union's history and institutions. (See the Materials for Chapter 1 where there is such a discussion.)

1.2   THE RESOLUTION OF DISPUTES

No matter what precautions are taken, sooner or later the businessman will be involved in a dispute of some sort or another. He may have difficulty in supplying goods as he contracted to; he may have a client who cannot, or will not pay; or he may fall foul of some statutory provision. After prevention, the best and cheapest way of dealing with disputes is negotiation, e.g., through the services of the Arbitration, Conciliation and Advisory Service where industrial disputes are concerned. In the event that the dispute cannot be settled, then recourse may have to be had to the courts, or perhaps to some form of arbitration.

1.2.1   The courts
Courts in Scotland are either civil courts or criminal courts. Civil courts concern themselves with disputes between ordinary citizens, or between the citizen and the state. The criminal courts concern themselves with punishment of those persons who engage in acts which the state has seen fit to prohibit. While civil actions are brought by an individual, criminal actions are brought (except in the rarest of cases) by the Crown, in the name of the Lord Advocate who is the government's senior law officer in Scotland and head of the Crown Office.

The Lord Advocate's representatives throughout Scotland are the procurator fiscals, legally qualified civil servants who bring almost all prosecutions in District Courts and sheriff courts (see below at 1.2.1.1). The procurator fiscal service is organised on a sheriffdom basis. Each sheriffdom has a regional procurator fiscal, assisted by depute procurator fiscals. Prosecutions in the

High Court of Justiciary may be undertaken by the Lord Advocate or by the Solicitor General for Scotland (the government's second senior law officer). This will happen only rarely however. Most prosecutions are brought by advocates depute, of whom there are at any one time about 15. They are advocates employed to present cases on behalf of the Crown.

Although private prosecutions are theoretically possible, there have been only three this century. Prosecutions may also be brought by a regulatory agency such as a local authority or the Office of Fair Trading. In the commercial world this latter sort of prosecution is the most likely, e.g., for an alleged offence against food safety or trade description laws, or for failure to adhere to an assurance given to the Director General of Fair Trading (see Chapter 9).

Both civil and criminal courts rise in ascending order of importance from courts of first instance to courts having appellate jurisdiction. A court of first instance hears a case for the first time, whereas courts with appellate jurisdiction will hear cases on appeal from other courts.

1.2.1.1 Civil courts

Court of Session The principal civil court in Scotland is the Court of Session which sits in Edinburgh. It consists of an Inner House of mainly appellate jurisdiction (which is divided into First and Second Divisions presided over by the Lord President and the Lord Justice-Clerk respectively); and an Outer House which is a court of first instance. The Court of Session consists of 25 judges, currently assisted by eight temporary judges. The 25 permanent judges are known as Senators of the College of Justice (or Lords Commissioners of Justiciary when hearing criminal cases). The senior judge is the Lord President, assisted by the Lord Justice-Clerk.

The terms Inner House and Outer House have their origin in the physical location of the courts when they heard cases in the Tolbooth.

Those eligible for appointment as judges are, advocates, sheriff-principals or sheriffs of five year's standing, or solicitors who have had right of audience in the Court of Session or High Court of Justiciary for not less than five years.

Eight judges sit in the Inner House; the remainder, known as Lords Ordinary, sit in the Outer House, which consists of a number of courts having jurisdiction over all civil matters which are not expressly excluded. The Outer House also deals with a variety of administrative matters.

In particularly important or difficult appeal cases, there is provision for the whole Court of Session to sit, although this would be extremely unusual; normally only the judges of *either* the First *or* Second Division will hear appeals which are made from decisions of the Outer House or the sheriff courts.

House of Lords Appeals from the Court of Session may lie to the House of Lords, the supreme Court of Appeal for Scottish civil cases. The role of the House of Lords as an appeal court is distinct from its role as a legislative body. It consists of the Lord Chancellor, the eleven Lords of Appeal in Ordinary and those peers who have held high judicial office. The quorum for hearing a case is three, but usually five sit.

Where an appeal from the Court of Session is being heard, there will almost always be at least one of the two Scottish Lords of Appeal in Ordinary present, although this is not compulsory.

Sheriff Court   In terms of volume of business, the most important civil courts in Scotland are the sheriff courts. The jurisdiction of the sheriff courts is very wide, although a sheriff cannot hear some actions, e.g. those involving status or for proving the tenor of a lost document. Sheriff courts' jurisdiction over persons is laid down in the Sheriff Courts (Scotland) Acts 1907 and 1913. Generally speaking, jurisdiction is limited to matters arising within the locality of the sheriffdom. Some actions are exclusively reserved for sheriff courts. (This is known as the sheriff courts' privative jurisdiction.) Scotland is divided into six sheriffdoms, each with a sheriff-principal and about ten full-time sheriffs; in the Sheriffdom of Glasgow and Strathkelvin, there are more.

Actions in the sheriff courts may be either summary causes or ordinary causes. The former are much less formal and the value of the actions must not exceed £1,500. Ordinary causes are actions involving a value of more than £1,500, or a decision other than an award of money. In addition to these traditional causes of action, there is now a simplified small claims procedure which makes it easier and cheaper to raise an action worth less than £750. It is doubtful if the small claims procedure has achieved its aims of increasing access for the ordinary citizen, and of deformalising procedure. As far as the former is concerned, almost all cases are brought by public utilities and large corporations against ordinary citizens. For the latter, the degree of informality and consequent user-friendliness of the procedure would seem to depend solely on the individual sheriff. (For a comparative analysis of the small claims procedure in Scotland, England and Wales see, Ervine, 'The Importance of Small Claims Courts' [1995] *Consumer Law Journal* 24. An extract describing the operation of the Scottish system is in the Cases and Materials section for Chapter 1.)

From the sheriff, an appeal may be made to the sheriff-principal on a point of law only, if the action was under summary cause procedure. He has the discretion to allow a further appeal to the Inner House of the Court of Session. Where ordinary causes are concerned, appeals can go either to the sheriff-principal and then to the Inner House, or directly to the Inner House.

1.2.1.2 Criminal courts   The criminal courts are concerned not with the resolution of disputes, but with the punishment of those whose wrongdoing is perceived to be a threat to society. Criminal jurisdiction may be *solemn*, which will involve a jury trial and is reserved for the more serious offences heard in a sheriff court or the High Court. In a jury trial it is for the jury of 15 to decide on the verdict. The judge plays no part in this. He is there to advise on the law, and if necessary to decide on the sentence. The jury plays no part in sentencing, although there have been suggestions that juries and victims should be involved in the sentencing process. Alternatively, criminal jurisdiction may be *summary*. Summary jurisdiction involves the judge sitting alone and is reserved for less serious offences in sheriff courts and district courts.

In criminal cases the Crown must prove its case 'beyond reasonable doubt'. This is a higher hurdle to clear than the pursuer having to prove his case on 'the balance of probabilities' in the civil courts. Scotland differs from other jurisdictions in that there are three verdicts available to the judge or jury. The accused my be found guilty, not guilty, or not proven. This last has been the subject of heated debate and attempts have been made to have the verdict abolished. Opinion on the matter would seem to be finely divided. Much of the criticism of the verdict is founded on the belief that juries do not understand it fully. An accused person who is found not proven is in the same position as one found not guilty, i.e. he cannot be tried again for the same offence.

High Court of Justiciary The supreme criminal court is the High Court of Justiciary which consists of the same judges as the Court of Session. The court sits in Edinburgh, but there is a provision for it to go 'on circuit' around Scotland, as required. The High Court has exclusive jurisdiction in cases of murder, treason, rape and incest. Normally, one judge sits with a jury of 15. In addition to sitting as a court of first instance, the High Court acts as an appeal court for the lower criminal courts. When acting as an appeal court, three judges usually sit.

Sheriff court Sheriff courts may exercise jurisdiction in both solemn and summary criminal procedure. In solemn proceedings, the maximum possible sentence is three years and an unlimited fine; in summary proceedings, it is six months and a fine of £5,000.

District Court The District Courts were provided for by the District Courts (Scotland) Act 1975. There are District Courts in all but one of the local authority and islands areas (Orkney). The judges are either Justices of the Peace who sit with a *legally* qualified assessor, or, (in Glasgow only) they are stipendiary magistrates. Stipendiary magistrates, who are paid and must be solicitors or advocates of five years' standing, have the same powers as the Sheriff in summary proceedings (see above). Justices of the Peace may impose a fine of £2,500, or 60 days' imprisonment. The District Courts deal with almost 50 per cent of all criminal proceedings.

1.2.1.3 Miscellaneous courts and tribunals Other courts which might be used by the businessman, or against him, include the Lands Valuation Appeal Court, the Restrictive Practices Court and the Employment Appeal Tribunal. The last one has the equivalent authority within its area of jurisdiction as does the Court of Session. Appeals may be made from it on a point of law to the Court of Session and the House of Lords.

There are also many tribunals which have been established for the speedier, cheaper and less formal resolution of disputes over matters such as employment, rent, social security, etc. For the businessman, the most important of these are industrial tribunals.

An industrial tribunal consists of a legally qualified chairman and two 'wing men', one a representative of employers' organisations and the other a representative of trade unions. Appeals may be made from their decisions to the Employment Appeal Tribunal and on to the House of Lords.

1.2.2 Arbitration

Another means of resolving disputes is the use of arbitration. Arbitration is used widely in the construction industry. It will often be the case that a contract between parties will specifically provide that, in the event of a dispute, it will be submitted to an arbiter who may or may not be named. If arbitration is chosen, the jurisdiction of the courts will be excluded. The main advantages of arbitration are seen to be speed, cost and privacy. A dispute will almost certainly be resolved more quickly than it would be in the court system. Another advantage is that the arbiter will be a specialist in the area under dispute, which might be highly technical.

1.2.3 Ombudsmen

Consumers of services such as banking and insurance may be able to make use of the industry ombudsman as an alternative to taking court action (see the Cases and Materials section for Chapter 3).

1.3 LEGAL ADVICE

The businessman or consumer who is faced with a problem which involves the need for legal advice has a variety of sources from which he can seek assistance.

1.3.1 Advocates and solicitors

Unlike some other countries, e.g., the United States and Canada, the legal profession is divided into two branches: advocates and solicitors, each with their own field of expertise and jurisdiction. Advocates are specialist court pleaders and until recently they alone had the right of audience in the superior courts (apart from the parties themselves). As well as appearing in court, advocates will often be asked for their 'opinion' by solicitors on some area of law, perhaps as a preliminary to litigation, or to test the chances of likely success in litigation. Clients may not engage an advocate directly, but must use the services of a solicitor to do this. Advocates, unlike solicitors, practise on their own and are not permitted to form partnerships. Solicitors, on the other hand, are allowed to form partnerships and can be approached directly by those requiring advice or assistance. Many of them will spend their time in office-based work and never, or rarely, appear in court. The traditional Scottish solicitor was seen as a 'man of business', who would carry out a wide range of tasks for his clients, e.g. drafting wills, conveyancing, forming companies, giving tax advice, etc; this remains the case today. Since the Admission as a Solicitor with Extended Rights (Scotland) Rules 1992 came into force, qualified solicitors who qualify under the Rules may appear as solicitor advocates in the Court of Session and High Court of Justiciary.

1.3.2 Other sources of advice

Apart from the legal profession itself, there are other sources of legal advice available, such as Citizens' Advice Bureaux and one of the few law centres. These would tend to be used by the consumer rather than by the businessman.

Advice on legal matters affecting their particular area of specialisation would also be available from Health and Safety Inspectors (see Chapter 8) and Trading Standards Officers (see Chapter 9), amongst others. Most businessmen will be members of an employers or trade association, where advice and assistance will be available, while the individual who is a member of a trade union may be able to call on the services of the union's legal department, particularly if the problem is employment related.

Further reading
Gloag and Henderson (1987), *Introduction to the Law of Scotland*, 9th edn, W. Green Ltd, Chapters 1 and 2.
The Laws of Scotland Memorial Encyclopaedia, vol. 6.
MacQueen (1993), *Studying Scots Law*, Butterworths.
Paterson & Bates (1993), *The Legal System of Scotland*, 3rd edn, W. Green Ltd.
Walker (1988), *Principles of Scottish Private Law*, 4th edn, Clarendon Press, Chapter 1.
Walker (1992), *The Scottish Legal System*, 6th edn, W. Green Ltd.
White & Willock (1993), *The Scottish Legal System*, Butterworths.

CHAPTER TWO

Types of Business Organisation

Scots law permits businesses to be structured in a variety of different ways, to suit everyone from an ice-cream salesman to a multi-national company. The most common types of business organisation recognised by Scots law are the sole trader, the partnership, and the limited company. Those forms of business organisations carry with them a variety of different legal rights and duties with regard to setting up the organisation, the members of the organisation, and those who deal with the organisation by buying or selling from it, or lending money to it. These rights and duties define what must be done for the business to be validly constituted (see 2.2 below), the financial protection which can be achieved by members of the organisation (see 2.1 below) and the remedies which outsiders or other members may have against those involved in running an organisation (see 2.1 and 2.3 below).

From a practical point of view, it is clear that businesses must consider these rules when deciding what form their business should take; how money should be raised; how outside organisations should be dealt with, etc. It is also clear that consideration of these rules tells us much about the way in which the law chooses to balance the various interests, e.g., those of majority and minority shareholders, directors, creditors, etc.

Of course, the law will be relied upon only sometimes. For example, if a company owes money to the bank, a shareholder may pay the money from his personal resources rather than hide behind the corporate veil. The shareholder may well consider it to be in his interests to do this if he wishes the company to obtain credit on another occasion. Other rules in this area are more prescriptive, and must always be adhered to, e.g., the obligations on companies to file certain documents with the Registrar of Companies (see 2.2.3 below).

One of the first and most important decisions which a businessman will have to make will be as to which legal form his business should take. The purpose of this chapter is to examine the basic legal nature of the three business forms to outline the formalities required before each may commence trading, and to discuss how these, and other factors, may lead to a prudent investment or choice of business form. By focusing on the impact of the rules upon choice of business form, we hope to highlight the law's role in regulating the exercise of power in organisations (see 2.3.1 below), as well as the distribution of financial risks as between members and third parties (see 2.3.2–2.3.4).

This chapter is intended to provide only an introduction to some of the most important of these rules, and readers who are interested in areas not covered should consult the further reading section at the end of the chapter.

2.1 LEGAL NATURE

2.1.1 Sole trader

A sole trader is a one man or one woman business which may or may not also engage employees. The individual *is* the business and in this sense the law applying to the business is the same as that applying to the individual in his or her private affairs. The main practical consequence of this is that he or she will not be responsible to anyone else for running the business. The sole trader will reap all the rewards and pay all of the debts personally.

2.1.2 Partnership

The law relating to partnerships was codified by the Partnership Act 1890, although this must be read alongside the general principles of contract, delict and agency which apply to the partnership and its relationship with third parties.

Section 1 of the Act defines a partnership as 'persons carrying on a business in common with a view of profit'. Although there is a basic principle that a partnership cannot have more than 20 members, solicitors, accountants and stockbrokers are exempt from this restriction and the Secretary of State may exempt other trades or professions (Companies Act 1985, s. 716). Exemption has been granted to valuers, estate agents, land agents, actuaries, consultant engineers, building designers and loss adjusters.

In the absence of any express agreement in the partnership contract itself, all partners are entitled to an equal share in the property and profits of the partnership, and equal participation in management.

2.1.2.1 Legal status of the partnership The partnership has a separate legal personality from its members (see Partnership Act 1890, s. 4(2)). This means that the firm may own property; commit delicts (see Chapter 4 and *Mair* v *Wood* 1948 SC 83); enter contracts (through the agency of the individual partners); and sue or be sued by the individual partners. It does not mean, however, as is the case with limited companies, that the individuals are protected from liability for the firm's debts (see below).

2.1.2.2   Partners' duties to each other   Partners must disclose to each other matters within their knowledge relating to the partnership; account to each other for profits gained by virtue of being a partner; not compete with the partnership; and exercise care and diligence in partnership affairs (Partnership Act 1890, ss. 28 to 30).

2.1.2.3   Liability of individual partners and of the firm   Each partner is jointly and severally liable for the debts of the firm (Partnership Act 1890, s. 9). This means that if a two man partnership owes £1,000 for office equipment which they purchased as a firm, the supplier is entitled to sue one of the partners for the full amount of the debt. Such a partner would then be entitled to proceed against the other to recover the latter's share of the debt (Partnership Act 1890, s. 4(2)). However because, in such a case, the debt is primarily that of the firm (which is a distinct legal person from the individual partners) the creditor must first seek payment from the firm. Where the firm fails to pay, the partners become liable.

The firm will be bound to honour transactions carried out in its name by any of the partners provided these were within the ordinary course of the partnership's business (Partnership Act 1890, s. 5). This is because the partners are viewed in law as the agents of the firm (see Chapter 5, para. 5.2). This rule will apply notwithstanding the firm's internal arrangements as to management responsibility, unless the third party knows that the partner has no authority to carry out the act in question, or does not know or believe him to be a partner. The intention is to protect third parties who legitimately believe that an individual partner is acting on behalf of the firm.

For example, A and B might run a travel agency and purchase their office furniture from C who owns a furniture warehouse. If one day A decides he would like a four-poster bed and contracts to buy one from C, C would not be entitled to recover the cost of the bed from the firm, but would have to pursue A individually. This is quite obviously because C should know that a four-poster bed is unlikely to play any part in the running of a travel agency business. If, on the other hand, A had chosen to buy an office carpet, this sale would bind the partnership. This would be the case even if A and B had expressly agreed between themselves that only B should purchase carpets. The reason again is simply that from C's perspective the purchase of an office carpet would be a perfectly normal transaction for a travel agency. In such circumstances, A would, if necessary, have to reimburse B for the loss caused to the firm by his (A's) breach of the partnership agreement.

2.1.3   Limited companies

The bulk of the law relating to limited companies is to be found in the Companies Act 1985, which consolidated previous legislation. Important amendments in relation to company objects are made by the Companies Act 1989. Companies will of course also be affected by other legislation, e.g., the Insolvency Act 1986 and the Financial Services Act 1986, and by the law of contract, delict and crime.

2.1.3.1 Limited liability   One of the most important principles of company law is the limited liability of the shareholders. This means that the liability of the shareholders is limited to the amount, if any, unpaid on their shares. The main purpose of this rule is to encourage investment and enterprise, and its origins may be traced to a Select Committee Report in 1850 which said that changes in the law should 'give additional facilities to investors of capital which their industry and enterprise is constantly creating and augmenting . . . if such measures were carried out a stimulus would be given to the industry of the community'.

2.1.3.2 Separate legal personality   Another important feature of a company is its separate legal personality. The company is a distinct legal person in its own right. This concept is closely linked to the concept of limited liability. The dual operation of these principles is illustrated by the case of *Salomon* v *Salomon* [1897] AC 22 HL.

Salomon was a sole trader who formed a limited company to take over his business. Salomon, his wife and his five children took one share each and the company paid Salomon £39,000 for the business. This sum was made up of £9,000 in cash, £20,000 in £10 shares and £10,000 in debentures (a debenture is simply a document which proves that the company owes someone, in this case Salomon, a certain sum). When the company became insolvent it was held that the company was a separate legal person from Salomon and that his liability on winding up was limited to the value of his shares. Salomon himself was a creditor of the company and having security (in the form of his debentures) he was entitled to the only remaining assets of £6,000, in part payment of the £10,000 which was owed to him by the company (see also *Grierson, Oldham and Co. Ltd* v *Forbes, Maxwell & Co. Ltd* (1895) 22 R 812).

2.1.3.3 Lifting the corporate veil   The courts may be prepared to lift or 'pierce' the corporate veil and look at the true management or control which is in operation. This may be done to detect tax evasion, or to determine whether the managers of the company are actually enemy aliens (see *Daimler Co Ltd* v *Continental Tyre & Rubber Co Ltd* [1916] 2 AC 307). It will also happen where incorporation is being used to facilitate fraud. For example, in *Gilford Motor Co Ltd* v *Horne* [1933] Ch 935, a managing director of a company agreed not to solicit customers from his employers after leaving his present employment. On leaving the company's employment he formed a company to solicit customers. This intention was, of course, to find a means of circumventing his aforementioned contractual obligation. The Court of Appeal held that the veil could be lifted and an order granted to restrain what was effectively his action as an individual.

In certain circumstances, the courts have viewed a group of connected parent and/or subsidiary companies as a single economic unit (see *DHN Food Distributors Ltd* v *Tower Hamlets LBC* [1976] 1 WLR 852). The reasons for this were appropriately summed up by Templeman LJ in *Re Southard & Co Ltd* [1979] 1 WLR 1198 CA, where he said that:

it is not surprising that when a subsidiary collapses, the unsecured creditors wish the finances of the company and its relationship with other members of the group to be narrowly examined, to ensure that no assets of the subsidiary company have leaked away; that no liabilities of the subsidiary company ought to be laid at the door of other members of the groups, and that no indemnity from a right of action against any other company, or against any individual is by some mischance overlooked.

The Scottish courts have taken a more restrictive view on lifting the veil in such circumstances. In *Woolfson* v *Strathclyde Regional Council* 1978 SLT 159, Lord Keith (in the House of Lords) approved the view of the Court of Session to the effect that 'it is appropriate to pierce the corporate veil only where special circumstances exist indicating that it is a mere facade concealing the true facts'.

One of the major problems in this area of law is the vagueness and uncertainty which prevails. Although the law must clearly evaluate fact situations as they are presented, the lack of coherent principle ill serves commercial interests. This lack of coherence is typified in the following excerpt from a judgment in the recent decision of *City of Glasgow DC* v *Hamlet Textiles Ltd* 1986 SLT 415 (at 416):

> . . . it has been recognised that in certain circumstances the court is entitled to 'lift the corporate veil' and have regard to the realities of the situation . . . It is not easy to define in what circumstances the court will lift the corporate veil, and until the facts have been established in this case, it is not possible to say whether the circumstances are sufficiently special to justify piercing the veil.

The corporate veil can also be lifted by virtue of certain statutory provisions:

(a)   Where a person knowingly operates a company as its sole member for more than six months; in such circumstances, the individual is jointly and severally liable with the company for debts incurred after the six month period has expired (Companies Act 1985, s. 24). But see Companies (Single Member Private Co.) Regulations 1992.

(b)   Where a person is concerned directly or indirectly in the management of a company while an undischarged bankrupt or while disqualified by court order from so acting; such a party incurs personal liability for debts incurred during the relevant period (Company Directors Disqualification Act 1986, ss. 11(1) and 15(1) to (4)).

(c)   Where a person, without leave of the court, is involved directly or indirectly with a company bearing the same or a similar name to that borne (in the previous twelve months) by a company with which he was involved and which went into liquidation; such a person is personally liable for the debts incurred by the company during any period of his involvement which occurs for the next five years (Insolvency Act 1986, s. 217).

(d)   Where there has been fraudulent trading (see 2.3.3 below).

(e)   Where there has been wrongful trading (see 2.3.3 below).

2.2 LEGAL FORMALITIES

The formalities which the law will require for the formation and management of a business will vary depending on whether it operates as a sole trader, a partnership or a limited company.

2.2.1 Sole trader
There are no special formalities required for an individual who chooses to operate as a sole trader. A sole trader may, of course, be required to obtain a licence for the sale of particular goods such as alcohol, or apply for planning permission to materially change the use of premises (see the Town and Country Planning (Scotland) Act 1972). A sole trader who trades in any business name is also bound by the provisions of the Business Names Act 1985 (see 2.2.4 below).

2.2.2 Partnership
It is not necessary to enter into a formal partnership contract. In the absence of such a formal agreement the various rights and duties imposed by the Partnership Act 1890 will apply (see 2.1.2 above). It is common practice, however, and very wise to draw up a formal contract regulating the relationship. This will cover such matters as the name of the business; how the business is to be financed; the management of the premises; the distribution of profits and remuneration of partners; accountancy procedures and the financial year; the rights and duties of the partners; and the resolution of disputes between the partners.

The Business Names Act 1985 also applies to partnerships and imposes certain requirements on them (see 2.2.4 below).

2.2.3 Companies
A far greater degree of formality is required to set up a company than applies in the case of either sole traders or partnerships.

Certificate of incorporation It is not possible to trade as a registered company until a certificate of incorporation has been issued (Companies Act 1985, s. 13). This is effectively the company's birth certificate and it will not be issued until certain detailed particulars are sent to the Registrar of Companies (in Edinburgh or Cardiff).

Particulars for registration The documents which must be registered are the memorandum of association, the articles of association, the names and particulars of the directors and the company secretary and the intended address of the registered office; a statutory declaration that all of the requirements of the Companies Acts have been complied with must also be delivered. The most important of these documents are the memorandum and the articles which we will examine in greater depth.

Memorandum of association This contains the name of the company, the country where the registered office is situated, the objects clause, a statement that the liability of the members is limited and a statement of the share capital.

The most important of these is the objects clause which outlines the purpose for which the company has been formed. The company may not engage in any activities which do not fall within these stated purposes. If it does so these activities are said to be *ultra vires* (beyond the powers) of the company. However, the significance of this rule has been greatly reduced by the amendments made to the Companies Act 1985 by the Companies Act 1989, ss. 108 to 110 (see Cases and Materials for Chapter 2). First, s. 110 allows a company's memorandum to state that its objects are to carry on business as a general commercial company; if such objects are given there is no restriction on the type of business which may be done. Secondly, the *ultra vires* rule is now apparently purely a matter of internal corporate concern; s. 108 states that the validity of an act done by a company shall not be questioned on the ground of lack of capacity. There is therefore no longer any question of transactions with innocent third parties being set aside. Shareholders who are aggrieved by rash and speculative activities are therefore left to pursue an action for breach of directors' duties. Their right to do so is expressly preserved by s. 108. It is of course open to a majority of the shareholders to ratify any act or transaction by special resolution in general meeting (see 2.3.1 below).

Articles of association   The articles regulate the internal management of the company and represent a mutual contract between the shareholders and the company (Companies Act 1985, s. 14). However, this only gives rights to individuals in their capacity as members, and not in other capacities, e.g., as prospective employees. This means that a clause in the articles to the effect that an individual shareholder is to be employed as a solicitor or accountant would not be enforceable (see *Eley* v *Positive Life Assurance Co* (1876) 1 Ex D 88).

2.2.3.1   Public or private company   If a company is to be public its registered name must end with the words 'public limited company', the share capital must be no less than the statutory minimum (at present this is £50,000) and it must have at least two members. A public company cannot commence business or borrow money until it has been issued with a trading certificate by the Registrar. A private company is every company which is not a public company. It must have at least one member, although there is no prescribed minimum share capital, and its shares need not be paid up. It does not require a trading certificate to commence business, however it may not offer shares to the public, as a public company can.

2.2.4   Business names

Wherever a business, whether that of a sole trader, a partnership or a company, trades under a name other than its own (i.e., the surname or surnames of a sole trader or partnership or the corporate name of a company), it is bound by the provisions of the Business Names Act 1985. Certain additions, such as forenames and initials are permitted, but certain types of names, such as those giving the impression that the business is connected with the government, may not be used and certain other business names require the permission of a government department or other body before they may be used. Where a business name is used, for example, where a sole trader chooses to trade as 'Blooms', a florists, then, under the Business Names Act 1985, s. 4, the sole trader's name and business address must be displayed clearly on all business letters, invoices, receipts and written orders for goods and at his place of business. A similar requirement applies in the case of companies and partnerships; in the latter case, the name of each partner must be displayed except where there are more than 20 partners and the business keeps a list of partners' names for inspection at its office. Section 5 makes it a criminal offence to fail to comply with these requirements. It also gives the courts discretion, where it is just and equitable, to refuse to enforce contracts against people dealing with a business which has failed to comply with s. 4 where this has caused loss to such people.

2.3 CHOICE OF BUSINESS FORM

The choice as to the most appropriate form of business organisation will clearly depend on a whole range of factors – legal, personal and financial. However it may be useful to analyse the criteria for this choice under the following headings. These criteria are not exhaustive and the weight which is attached to any factor will vary with individual circumstances.

2.3.1 Involvement in management and power to make decisions

If this took priority over all other criteria, the most appropriate business form would clearly be sole trader. The only restraints on business policy on a sole trader are those which he either voluntarily adopts, in the form of contractual obligations to employees and fellow traders, and those imposed by delict and statute as to the safety of his premises and his products. A partner also suffers these restrictions, along with the obvious need to consult fellow partners to the extent dictated by the Partnership Act or the contract of partnership. A shareholder in a limited company is limited by contractual, delictual and statutory obligations, as well as the limitations inherent in the value of his shareholding. Indeed a minority shareholder has very limited rights to participate in the management of the company. The basic principle is that of majority rule, with the company itself being the only party entitled to raise an objection to mismanagement (see *Foss* v *Harbottle* (1843) 2 Hare 461 and *Edwards* v *Halliwell* [1950] 2 All ER 1064). If the company is controlled by those who are accused of the mismanagement, it is obviously unlikely that they will be prepared to bring an action against themselves. It is however open to minority shareholders to take a derivative action on behalf of the company where there has been fraud by the controlling majority (see *Prudential Assurance* v *Newman Industries* [1982] 1 All ER 354 and Paterson, 'The Derivative Action in Scotland', 1982 SLT (News) 205). The most common example of fraud would be personal appropriation of corporate assets by those in control (see *Cook* v *Deeks* [1916] 1 AC 554). Other options open to aggrieved minority shareholders are:

(a) The right to take a personal action for breach of personal rights guaranteed by the articles of association. This would cover such rights as the

right to vote or the right to have a dividend paid in cash (see *Pender* v
Lushington (1877) 6 ChD 70 and *Wood* v *Odessa Waterworks Co* (1889) 42
ChD 636). However it would not extend to rights to force directors to retire
in accordance with the articles or to have a poll taken (see *Mozley* v *Alston*
(1847) 1 Ph 790 and *MacDougall* v *Gardiner* (1875) 1 ChD 13 CA).

(b)   The right to insist on a special majority decision on an issue of policy
for which such a majority is required by the articles (see *Edwards* v *Halliwell*
[1950] 2 All ER 1064 CA).

(c)   The right to raise an action against directors and majority shareholders who take action and enter transactions which are beyond the capacity
of (*ultra vires*) the company. This is not compromised by the fact that since
the Companies Act 1989, the company will almost invariably be bound by
such transactions. Indeed, minority shareholders may be more strongly
inclined to take action for damages against the majority where they find the
company saddled with unwanted and unexpected commitments to other
traders. However, their ability to do so may have been curtailed by the
decision in *Smith* v *Croft (No. 2)* [1988] Ch 114, where it was held that a
company may resolve by ordinary resolution not to pursue a claim for
damages in the interests of the company. Such a resolution will bind minority
shareholders and prevent them taking action.

If shareholders are aware of the fact that directors intend to bind the
company to a transaction which is *ultra vires* they may seek in interdict to
restrain them so doing (see Companies Act 1989, s. 108 in the Cases and
Materials section for Chapter 2). The difficulty is that such action is often
only discovered once it has been taken. If this is the case the company is
bound and the aggrieved shareholder is left to take the course of action
described in the previous paragraph (see generally Companies Act 1989,
ss. 108–110 in the Cases and Materials section for Chapter 2).

(d)   The right to raise an action restraining the company from acting
contrary to the Companies Act 1985 or the general law, e.g., calling a general
meeting without the requisite notice or issuing equity shares without giving
priority to the statutory preferential rights of existing equity shareholders (see
the Companies Act 1985, ss. 89(1), 90(6), and 94(5)). This right of action
is subject to the same restriction as applies to (c) above, i.e. that the company
may pass an ordinary resolution to the effect that no action will be taken (see
Smith v *Croft (No. 2)* above).

(e)   The right under the Insolvency Act 1986, s. 122, to have the company
wound up on the grounds that it is just and equitable to do so. The court will
only make a winding-up order if there appears to be no other remedy and if
there will be surplus assets available for the petitioners after the creditors have
been satisfied (see *Re Ochery Construction Ltd* [1966] 1 All ER 145). This
remedy will normally be granted in circumstances commonly known as a
'quasi-partnership', where the company has been based from the outset on
mutual confidence and personal trust. Typically this trust will have generated
a legitimate expectation in all parties to share in management. Once that trust
has broken down, and one or more parties is suffering prejudice, those parties
may wish to withdraw their money from the company. However, they may

find it difficult to sell their shares. This is because it is common for the articles of private companies to restrict the rights of members to transfer shares without the permission of other members (see *Ebrahimi* v *Westbourne Galleries Ltd* [1973] AC 360). A remedy under s. 122 offers an escape route for such parties.

(f) The right to seek a remedy under the Companies Act 1985, s. 459 based on the 'unfairly prejudicial conduct' of the majority (see the Cases and Materials section for Chapter 2 where s. 459 is reproduced in full). This has the advantage over the previous remedy that it is less drastic. The court may 'make such order as it thinks fit for giving relief in respect of the matters complained of'. This may involve appointing or removing directors; restraining the company from doing a particular act; authorising civil proceedings to be brought on behalf of the company; or providing for the purchase of the aggrieved member's shares. The final two options may be the more effective in remedying unfairly prejudicial conduct. The right to take civil proceedings may enable the aggrieved minority to take action to enforce directors' duties of reasonable care and skill. This obviously goes further than simply being entitled to take action in cases of fraud. The possibility of ordering the purchase of shares belonging to the aggrieved minority enables them to 'escape' from the company where the articles may otherwise prevent this.

Recent decisions suggest that it may amount to unfairly prejudical conduct if a member is unreasonably excluded from the decision making process (see *Re A Company* [1986] BCLC 376). This is of course most likely to apply in small companies of the 'quasi-partnership' type mentioned above. It is in these cases that the minority shareholders can most readily be said to have a legitimate expectation to participate in the management of the company. (For a full discussion of minority rights see Hollington, *Shareholder's Rights*, 1990, Sweet and Maxwell and also Bouchier, 'Yet Another Attempt to Remedy Unfair Prejudice', 1991 JBL 132.) The issue of minority rights is only one issue important to the relationship between shareholders and those in control of companies. A number of other issues relating to common law and statutory responsibilities of directors are discussed in the Cases and Materials section for Chapter 2.

2.3.2 Raising capital and obtaining credit

The ability of sole traders and partnerships to raise capital and obtain credit for goods will depend on the creditworthiness of the individuals. This is also true to some extent of those running a limited company. Financial institutions who lend money to companies will wish to protect themselves from the limited liability rules and will tend to take personal guarantees from directors who borrow on behalf of the company. Indeed, the Companies Act 1985, s. 36 provides for directors to be personally liable on contracts made *prior* to incorporation. So any party who lends money or supplies goods or services to a 'director' prior to a company's formation will not require to insist on a personal guarantee as they will be protected by s. 36. Directors may expressly exclude such responsibility. However, to use the phrase 'for and on behalf of the company' does not constitute such an exclusion (see *Phonogram Ltd* v *Lane* [1981] 3 All ER 182). Only a rather imprudent lender or supplier will entertain a director in a pre-incorporation situation who expressly excludes personal liability.

2.3.2.1 Floating charges and Romalpa clauses The most significant advantage which a company has in raising money is its ability to create a floating charge as security for a loan; this is provided for by Part XII of the Companies Act 1985 and Chapter II of Part III of the Insolvency Act 1986. This option is not open to partnerships and sole traders (but see the proposals to allow these forms of business to create such charges — these are discussed in the Cases and Materials section for Chapter 2). The attractive feature of this form of security is that the charge does not attach to any particular property belonging to the company, until the company is wound up or a receiver is appointed. This enables the company to continue trading in property over which the charge 'floats'. The company and its prospective lenders may prefer this to the creation of a fixed charge which attaches immediately to plant, machinery or buildings, and restricts the uses to which they may be put. However, if the company becomes insolvent, holders of fixed charges have priority over holders of previously created floating charges, unless the floating charge has already 'crystallised' by the time the fixed charge is created, or unless a 'negative pledge clause' has been used by the holder of the floating charge. This is a clause restricting or prohibiting the future creation of a subsequent fixed or floating charge ranking prior to or equally with the charge in question. Section 140 of the Companies Act 1989 clarifies the law on this point.

It is clear that from the company's perspective a floating charge is a very attractive and flexible means of providing security. However, it is a form of security of which other traders and suppliers must be wary. A company may appear to have considerable assets, which are in fact compromised by floating charges, enforceable at any time. On the strength of this apparent wealth, suppliers may give credit. If the company becomes insolvent, these unsecured creditors may find that the assets of the company are out of their reach, having been cleared out by the floating charge holders. A supplier giving credit terms should check the Companies Register for floating charges; they must be registered within 21 days of their creation under the Companies Act 1985, s. 410.

Trade suppliers have, however, developed another form of protection against losing out to charge holders. This is known as a retention of title or Romalpa clause (see *Aluminium Industrie Vassen BV* v *Romalpa* and *Armour* v *Thyssen* and other cases in Chapter 6, para. 6.7.4.). Its intended effect is that the ownership (title) in goods should not pass to the purchaser until he has paid for them. The effectiveness of such clauses seems to depend on what happens to the goods once the purchaser had them in his possession, i.e. whether they are used in manufacturing processes and or resold. In a straightforward case, where the goods in question are still in the possession of the purchaser in their original state, the clause means that the seller has a more effective form of security than floating charge holders and other unsecured creditors because the goods in question never legally became the assets of the company. They cannot therefore be distributed by the liquidator to other creditors, but have to be returned to the seller. Other lenders, particularly banks, have become increasingly reluctant to lend money on the strength of a floating charge, where a form of silent security, like a retention of title clause, could be lurking. This diminishes the benefit to companies of being able to create floating charges.

2.3.3 Insolvency and recovery of debts from directors

As mentioned above creditors can pursue the personal assets of a sole trader or the partners in a firm to satisfy their debts. There is the added advantage in the case of a partnership of being able to choose to sue one partner, who will be jointly and severally liable for the debts of the firm (see 2.1.2.3 above).

To this extent these business forms are inherently more attractive to a potential lender or creditor, than is a limited company. With the latter, the creditor cannot *prima facie* sue the shareholders for anything more than the amount unpaid on their shares. However, the framework for corporate insolvency provides two exceptions to this principle.

First, where, at some time before the commencement of the winding-up of a company a director knew or should have known that the company could not avoid going into insolvent liquidation and he did not then take every step to minimise the potential loss to the company's creditors, a court may order him to contribute to the company's assets (Insolvency Act 1986, s. 214). This is known as *wrongful trading*. Secondly, there is a remedy against directors (and, in certain cases, other parties) where a company's business is carried on with intent to defraud creditors or for any fraudulent purpose (Insolvency Act 1986, s. 213). This is known as *fraudulent trading* and, again, a court may order a contribution to be made to the company's assets.

An account of recent case law is given in the Cases and Materials section for Chapter 2.

The difficulty with fraudulent trading is that it is virtually impossible to prove, as it requires actual dishonesty. Wrongful trading under s. 214 effectively asks whether the director acted reasonably diligently given his particular knowledge, skill and experience, i.e. it judges a subjective individual objectively. The most likely targets of this provision are directors who run under-capitalised companies. Given that a private company is not obliged to have a minimum share capital, it is important to discourage directors from running companies where the level of capital does not match the scale of operations and level of commitments.

These rules do not, however, alter the basic conclusion that creditors will have more success recovering debts from solvent sole traders and partners whose businesses have become insolvent than they will from solvent but honest directors whose company has failed.

2.3.4 Use of the enterprise's money

A sole trader has absolute freedom as to how he disposes of resources which are effectively his own personal property. A partner has a *pro indiviso* share of the firm's assets, and may take such money from the firm as is agreed with the other partners. Neither partners nor company directors are permitted to take secret profits from transactions entered into by virtue of being a partner or director. This is grounded on basic principles of agency (see Chapter 5, para. 5.3.2.5) and more specifically, in the case of directors, on their fiduciary duty to the company.

This fiduciary duty extends to requiring a director to disclose any financial interest which he has in a transaction in which the company intends to become involved (see the Companies Act 1985, ss. 310 and 317). A further restraint is imposed on directors by the Companies Act 1985, s. 330, which prohibits the making or guaranteeing of loans by a company to one of its directors.

2.3.5 Nature of the market
The nature of the proposed market might play a significant part in the choice of business form. On the one hand, if one is uncertain whether a product or service will sell, the best protection for an initial investment would be the limited liability provided by incorporation. Conversely if it is important to take advantage of a seasonal market, acting as a sole trader or partnership might be chosen to avoid delay and formalities.

Further reading
Bourne and Pillans, (1996) *Scottish Company Law*, Cavendish.
Cuisine and Forte, (1987), *Scottish Cases and Materials in Commercial Law*, W. Green Ltd, Chapter 6, pp. 302–363.
Gloag and Henderson, (1987), *Introduction to the Law of Scotland*, 9th edn, W. Green Ltd, Chapters 24 and 25.
S. Mayson, D. French and C. Ryan, (1995), Mayson, French and Ryan on Company Law, 12th edn, 1995-96 Blackstone Press.

CHAPTER THREE

Business Contracting: General Principles

3.1 INTRODUCTION: RULES, PLANNING, PHILOSOPHY AND CONTEXT

Commercial enterprises of all kinds, from market traders to multi-nationals, enter into a variety of transactions simply in order to facilitate their daily business. For example, money is borrowed, lent and invested; goods and premises are bought, sold, hired or rented; insurance is taken out and staff are hired. Such transactions take place because one person has something that someone else wants. An employer, for instance, requires someone with a particular skill to make his operation more efficient. He is unlikely to find someone who will donate this skill on a purely altruistic basis. He is more likely to encounter someone who wishes to make use of the skill which he has, and be paid for it. If the two can come to a mutually acceptable arrangement about wages, terms and conditions, etc., then they can do business. The scope which exists for negotiation on these issues, will of course depend on the sort of transaction involved. In some contexts there will be considerable negotiation, e.g., in a complex engineering contract with many detailed design requirements, time specifications and very high costs. In other contexts there will be virtually no negotiation, e.g., where a salesman buys a lunch on the company account he is unlikely to haggle over the prices on the menu.

In most transactions, large and small, each party will carry out his side of the bargain to the satisfaction of the other. In a small minority of cases, however, there may be disagreement about what exactly was agreed and expected; how much it was to cost, and what was to happen if one of the parties did not carry out his side of the bargain. In many instances such disagreements may be resolved by referring to some written agreement which the parties have signed but it would be totally impractical to put in written form many of the everyday transactions which are effected, such as the buying of a meal or newspaper.

The response of the law to this problem has been to develop a common set of rules to regulate all or significant numbers of commercial, consumer and private transactions, and more specialised rules to govern specific types of transaction, e.g., sale, hire and insurance. These common principles have become known as the general principles of law of contract and are the subject of this chapter. This chapter and the corresponding materials also contain some discussion of principles relevant to contracts for services generally and to contracts of insurance in particular. Later chapters deal with some other specific types of contract, e.g.: contracts for the sale of goods; contracts financed by credit; contracts negotiated by an agent and contracts of employment.

What is the practical significance of contract law to business? Why does the law of contract matter to those who transact *as* businesses, or *with* businesses as other businesses or as private individuals/consumers? The most obvious reason is that transactions of all types have the potential to give rise to the sort of disputes mentioned above. For example, what exactly can each party hold the other party to? The law provides the basis of an answer to this by the rules on agreement, promise, intention to create legal relations, certainty, capacity and formalities (see 3.2–3.9 below). Suppose A (a manufacturer) is selling audio equipment to B (a retailer). These rules tell us when they reached an agreement (if indeed at all), which the law will hold them to. Perhaps there were certain important matters (e.g., the price or the terms of payment) which were never really agreed upon (see 3.3.3.2). Even if these matters were agreed, perhaps the law will not hold parties to the agreement because of insanity or intoxication (although we are sure that this would be an unlikely situation to arise in the business world!).

There are other rules which may intervene to prevent agreements being enforceable as contracts. Many of these are simply reflections of the tactics which business people and private individuals sometimes use to achieve transactions which are profitable. For example, advertising literature may exaggerate in varying degrees the facilities which a hotel has or the benefits which a particular washing powder can bring; a sub-contractor may tell a main contractor that he cannot finish the job for the agreed price and must get more if he is to complete it; a lawyer or bank manager may encourage a client to enter an agreement with him or her which is very unwise for the client. These sorts of tactics are respectively regulated by rules on misrepresentation, duress and undue influence (see 3.12). They are clearly relevant to the party who may be tempted to use such tactics — they tell him or her what he or she can get away with, e.g., how exaggerated the advertising claims can be, how the suggested renegotiations of contract should be approached. The rules are also, of course, relevant to the party on the receiving end of the tactics, enabling him to determine whether he can avoid the transaction.

Other rules tell the contracting parties which terms may be held to be not binding because they are unreasonable or unfair (see 3.11 below), thereby enabling parties to consider their terms in this light and to consider the possibility of challenging another party's terms. There are also the rules on remedies, which define the steps which can be taken to enforce contractual rights.

This brief discussion has tried to answer the question raised above as to the usefulness of rules on contract law to business and those it transacts with; it has tried to show the potential for the rules to be used to plan behaviour at the contracting and dispute stage. However, there is another angle on contract law. What value systems does it follow? Is it simply about enforcing market transactions as they occur, however disparate the bargaining strengths of the parties may be, or however burdensome the terms for one of the parties may be? Will it, on the other hand, take a more welfarist approach which recognises that disparities of intelligence, education, skill, sophistication or bargaining options may limit the ability of one of the parties to protect his interests; or that certain contractual terms are objectively unfair, or unfair in the sense that they overburden a party who is poor, ill or who has just lost his job? [See the discussion of welfarism by Brownsword et al. (1994), *Welfarism in Contract Law*, Dartmouth and Brownsword et al. and Willett, in Willett (ed.), *Fairness in Contract Law*, forthcoming, (1996) Elgar.

As a starting point, it can be said that there are no general principles with such a sweeping power to intervene, or at least no general principles which would be likely to intervene unless a very extreme form of inequality of bargaining power existed, or the terms deviated very markedly from what would typically expected in the market in question (see below at 3.12.5). However, the idea that contract law simply enforces market transactions, without heed to other values, must be qualified in a number of respects.

First, the rules on formalities are based, at least in part, on a concern that contracts such as those for the purchase of land, which involve a considerable investment, should not be undertaken lightly.

Secondly, there are controls on contracts made by those with no capacity or limited capacity, e.g., minors. There is clearly a concern here to protect those who are less able to bargain on their own behalf from burdens which they are not in a position to bear.

Thirdly, there are the rules on misrepresentation, error, duress, undue influence, etc., Here there is a concern that the full and rational consent of one of the parties is inhibited, either by tactics used by the other, or due to certain types of error. On the basis of this the contract may be set aside.

Effectively, therefore, the law is regulating the bargaining environment, saying that certain tactics are unacceptable, whether positive deception, coercion or influence, or taking advantage of an error made by the other party. Indeed, what will count as a misrepresentation will often take account of the relative knowledge and expertise of the parties (see 3.12.1.1 below). Of course the doctrines are of limited application, but within their sphere of operation they clearly regulate the bargaining environment leading up to a contract and the substantive burdens the contract imposes.

It might be said that rules which are concerned with remedying situations where full and rational choice has been undermined, are simply attempts to reinforce true liberal values. However, there is also clearly an attempt to make values of free choice work a bit better for certain contracting parties. The law could, after all, say that a misrepresentation deprives someone of choice only because that person makes the choice not to verify all information. But the law does not expect contracting parties to verify all information, and does provide a remedy for the misrepresentations of others.

Next there are those rules (e.g., on collateral contracts, and implied terms) which add to the obligations/liabilities of one or both of the parties. These may well be obligations/liabilities which the party in question was not planning to undertake (certainly he has not made the commitment in the formal contractual document). However, the law says that the commercial context, the relative expertise of the parties, the importance placed on certain matters by the other party, should help to create obligations and liabilities (see 3.11.1.3–3.11.2.4).

There is a fifth category of rules which go even further, by setting standards for the validity of certain sorts of terms. Some of these rules (e.g., those on restraint of trade and penalties) apply to all contracts (although restraint of trade is clearly relevant only to some). There are clear agendas here, despite what the contract might say, to promote the freedom to ply one's trade and to control the burdens which one party may impose on another for breach of contract (see below at 3.10 and 3.15.5.5). So again, contract cannot be used to achieve just any end chosen by the parties. This is further illustrated by the controls on exemption clauses in consumer and commercial contracts; and on unfair terms generally (excepting price and main subject matter) where consumer contracts are concerned (see below at 3.11.3–3.11.8). In both these cases there is the protection of various reasonable expectations and fairness norms in favour of parties who might be unable to assert their interests in the normal market circumstances. It is often the case that these controls are justified, at least partly, by a perception that where standard form contracts are used, the other contracting party may have limited opportunity to make a full and rational choice about the risks; and that this may, in turn, mean that those classes of contractors who deal on the others' standard terms cannot realistically be expected to effect market pressure for better terms. Recognition of this problem seems, once again, to be an example of an attempt to make the market work more effectively for its 'weaker' parties than a wholly 'freedom of contract' regime will do.

This idea was introduced in Chapter 1 (see 1.1.1). However, it was also pointed out that regulating the market had to be done carefully. There is the need to promote certainty and efficiency in market transactions, neither of which is necessarily encouraged by rules which refuse to enforce what the parties agree to. The problems with such rules are several. First, they may unduly protect parties who are capable of looking after, or who should be encouraged to look after, themselves. It is for this reason that we often find different levels of protection being given to those who contract as businesses and those who contract as consumers (see below at 3.11.6.2 and 3.11.6.4) Secondly, any rule which might overturn what parties agree involves a degree of uncertainty for the parties, who may have to take other steps to be sure their interests are protected. For example, if a supplier is unsure whether a clause limiting his liability for defects will be upheld, he must insure against the risk of the clause not being upheld and/or improve his quality management systems, so that the risk of supplying defective products is reduced. It is important, therefore, that, in the interests of efficiency and certainty, when the law does regulate the market it does so via rules which are as predictable in their application as possible. So, for example, it should be as clear as possible what features of a term and the bargaining environment in which it is agreed are likely to make it fair (see 3.11.6, 3.11.8 and discussion of the test of unfairness in the Unfair Terms in Consumer Contracts Regulations in the Cases and Materials for Chapter 3); it should be as clear as possible what will make a term a penalty. Judges have a large role to play here, in setting out the criteria which are important in the application of rules. However, legislative bodies can use tactics which give considerable guidance on criteria, e.g., an annex of terms regarded as indicatively unfair (see 3.11.8 below).

We now turn to a different sort of point about rules of contract law. A proper understanding of contract, as a means of planning business behaviour and/or as a regulator of the market, always requires a recognition of the wider context. As we said in Chapter 1, businesses and consumers do not litigate every time the other uses a misrepresentation or an unfair term, or breaks the contract. Whether use is made of the formal rules through the formal courts will depend on the knowledge and resources of the parties; how important the issue is to the parties; the existence of other means of settling the dispute, e.g., arbitration, negotiation, an ombudsman hearing, etc.

3.2 NATURE OF CONTRACT

A contract is basically any agreement which has the binding force of law. There are many reasons why not all agreements are given the binding force of law. For example, as has been said above, the law may consider the promise not to have been seriously intended (see further 3.4); it may disapprove of the tactics used by one of the parties to force the other to agree (see 3.12 below); the parties may not be considered mature enough to understand the nature of the agreement being entered into (see 3.9 below); the terms may be regarded as unfair or unreasonable, (3.11); or the agreement may be to do something which is illegal or immoral, e.g., to rob a bank or to hire a hotel room for acts of prostitution (see 3.10 below). Our first task is to examine the circumstances in which the law considers there to be an agreement. The rules on agreement represent the law's basic threshold requirement for the enforceability of private and commercial transactions as contracts (except where gratuitous obligations are concerned, where there need not necessarily be an 'agreement' at all (see 3.5 below)). Having considered agreement, we will then examine the other various factors which can affect the enforceability of agreements, and lastly turn to the sanctions which are available for breach of enforceable agreements.

3.2.1 Why agreement?

The businessman must know when the law considers him to have made an agreement if he is to plan and execute his activities with certainty and be safe from litigation. For example, a manufacturer might mistakenly believe that negotiations for the sale of computer equipment have not resulted in a binding agreement. Consequently he might sell the equipment to someone else. The result is that (subject to the agreement being binding in all other aspects) he is bound to sell the same thing to two people. If he only has one piece of equipment he will have to fulfil his obligation to one buyer and compensate the other buyer for breach of contract.

3.2.2 How is agreement recognised?

Often common sense will inform as to when an agreement has been struck. One party presents his terms and the other signals his assent by a nod, a signature, or a handshake. However, as negotiations become more complex and are conducted through so many different mediums (face to face, telephone, telex, fax, post etc.), the law must provide consistent principles which can determine the existence or otherwise of an agreement. The model which the law has adopted to test for agreement is that of offer and acceptance. To determine whether two or more parties have agreed to carry out a certain obligation or set of obligations the law will seek a clear offer from one party which sets out specific terms and a clear unqualified acceptance of that offer from the other party. When an offer has been duly accepted, there is a binding contract.

An offer is an expression of willingness to be bound on certain specific terms, should those terms be accepted by the other party. A crucial distinction must be drawn between this and the kind of statement which simply expresses a willingness to negotiate or a statement which requests or supplies information, e.g., as to availability or price. Only an offer can be converted into an agreement by acceptance. In *Philip & Co.* v *Knoblauch* (1907) SC 994, K sent a telegram to P stating 'I am offering today Plate linseed. . . . and have pleasure in quoting you 100 tons at 41/3, usual Plate terms. I shall be glad to hear if you are buyers and await your esteemed reply'. P wired an acceptance but K refused to supply him, alleging that his telegram was a 'quotation'. It was held however that its terms were clear and unequivocal enough to be an offer. As such there was a binding contract.

In *Harvey* v *Facey* [1893] AC 552, however, the defendants responded to an inquiry by stating the lowest price which they would accept for a farm. The plaintiffs 'agreed' to buy at this price and considered themselves to have entered a binding contract. The court held that an indication of the lowest price which would be considered was not an offer which could be converted into a binding contract by 'acceptance'.

3.2.3 Offer and invitation to treat

The type of statement which merely indicates a willingness to negotiate or to listen to offers is generally known as an invitation to treat. Often, as in *Harvey* v *Facey*, the language used will indicate whether a statement contains the requisite degree of commitment to make it an offer or whether it is no more than an invitation to treat. However, all business is not conducted by such 'conversational negotiation', directed verbally or in writing to a specific party. For example, goods and services may be advertised to the public, or put on display in shops or at an auction; tenders may be invited for the execution of a specific piece of work; alternatively situations may arise whereby there is no appreciable negotiation as such and yet there is a contractual relationship, e.g., where a motorist enters a car park or a pedestrian boards a bus. In all such circumstances the law is required to decide when agreement has taken place, e.g., is it when goods are taken from the supermarket shelf or is it when they are paid for? In the case of a bus, is it when you board the bus or when you pay the conductor? This question is important because it determines whether, for example, the shopper could replace goods before they have been paid for or whether the bus user could alight with impunity before being apprehended by the conductor! If, in these instances, there was no binding agreement until the encounter with the shop assistant or the conductor, then the answer would be in the affirmative. This might appear reasonable and representative of the intentions of the respective parties in the case of the shopper in the supermarket. However the same could hardly be said of the latter case, unless one supposed that we lived in a world of extraordinarily altruistic bus companies!

So how are we to judge in such situations the point at which the parties intend themselves to be bound contractually? The answer seems to be that intention should be judged by a combination of commercial convenience, fairness and policy. The interplay of these factors may be illustrated by an examination of the typical circumstances in which the problem arises.

3.2.3.1 Advertisements and displays   These are generally construed as being invitations to treat. The offer is taken to be made by the customer who responds to the advertisement, takes the goods to the cash desk or requests them from the shopkeeper, e.g., as in the case of cigarettes kept behind the counter. It is then for the advertiser or shopkeeper to decide whether to accept or reject the offer. Obviously in the vast majority of cases he or she is unlikely to refuse to sell but the theory is that the choice must be available.

The argument in the case of the shop is that a shop is a place for bargaining and not compulsory sale and also that 'it would be wrong if a shopkeeper was obliged to sell goods to a man he hated or a barber to cut the hair of a filthy person merely because his window display or price list was an offer' (Smith & Street, *The Consumer Adviser*, Institute of Trading Standards, 1978, p. 63). The more general argument against holding displays or advertisements to be offers is that there would automatically be a contract when the consumer indicated his wish to buy, and that advertisers or shopkeepers would be in breach of contract to every customer when they ran out of stock. This is not entirely convincing as it would be possible to imply a term into the offer to the effect that it only stayed open as long as stocks lasted. Indeed if the seller did attempt to 'haggle' over the price he would probably be guilty of a criminal offence for giving a 'misleading price indication' under the Consumer Protection Act 1987, s. 20.

Notwithstanding these arguments, the general rule has been applied so that a shelf display in a self-service chemist (*Pharmaceutical Society of Great Britain* v *Boots Cash Chemist* [1953] 1 QB 401), the display of a flick-knife in a shop window (*Fisher* v *Bell* [1961] 1 QB 394) and the advertisement of wine by a circular (*Grainger* v *Gough* (1896) AC 325) have all been held to be invitations to treat. Other kinds of displays and advertisements, such as restaurant menus and holiday brochures, would presumably be classified in the same way. So the guest would make a selection and be considered to be offering to buy that particular meal or holiday. The restaurant/travel agent/ hotel could then accept or reject the offer depending on availability. This does not of course mean that there is no responsibility for things said in the menu/brochure (see para. 3.12) but simply that the contract does not take place until a representative of the establishment has sanctioned it.

3.2.3.2.   Advertisements and displays: exceptions to the general rule

Reasons of practicality   The above analysis may be suitable where there is an identifiable party to accept or reject the customer's offer. However, in cases where no such person is available it would be impractical and potentially unfair to refuse to recognise a contract until such a person materialises. For example the display of deckchairs on a beach or the mere presence of a vending machine or bus would probably be treated as offers. The acceptance would be deemed to take place by sitting on the chair, placing money in the machine or boarding the bus. If it were otherwise, and the consumer was perceived to be making the offer, then there would be no completed contract until some later time or, in the case of the vending machine, never. It would mean, for example that, despite a consumer having deposited coins in a machine, the machine could refuse to supply the commodity, because no contract had yet been made. The machine would simply be rejecting the offer made by the consumer.

Reliance caused by unambiguous promise   The courts have also shown willingness to depart from the general rule where its application would enable the businessman to escape liability where certain clear and unambiguous advertisements have induced reliance by the other party. For example, in *Carlill* v *Carbolic Smoke Ball Co* [1893] 1 QB 256, an advertisement to the effect that £100 would be paid to anyone who used the company's product in the prescribed manner and caught influenza was held to be an offer to the world at large, which could be accepted by anyone who followed the instructions (see also *Petrie* v *Earl of Airlie* (1834) 13 S 68). To constitute an offer 'to the world at large' the terms of such an advert must clearly promise something if someone performs specified acts. Such an unequivocal promise is often difficult to distinguish from advertising 'puff'. For instance, what is the effect of a statement which says, 'we guarantee satisfactory use of our product'? Probably such a statement is too vague to be enforceable. Where a statement is very clear, it may well be that it can be regarded in Scotland as an enforceable gratuitous promise, which requires neither acceptance nor consideration by the other party (see 3.5 below).

3.2.3.3   Auction sales   The advertisement of an auction is seen merely as an invitation to treat and *not* as an offer to hold the sale, which is accepted by

everyone who turns up (*Harris* v *Nickerson* (1873) LR 8 QB 286). To classify the advertisement as an offer would mean that anyone who cancelled a sale would be liable in breach of contract and consequently for the travelling expenses of all those who turned up.

In the case of an auction advertised as 'without reserve' the position in English law is that such an advertisement is an offer which is accepted by the highest bona fide bidder. A refusal to sell to such a person, or the imposition of a 'reserve' price would amount to a breach of contract (*Warlow* v *Harrison* (1859) 1 E & E 309). It seems however that in Scots law there is no contract until the auctioneer has accepted the highest bid (*Fenwick* v *Macdonald, Fraser and Co* (1904) 6 F 850). Professor Walker has suggested that there should be implied into every such advertisement 'an actionable promise to allow every lot to be sold and not to withdraw it merely because the highest bid was deemed inadequate' (*Law of Contracts and Related Obligations*, 2nd edn, p. 114). Even in the absence of such an implied promise it is arguable that it constitutes misrepresentation to advertise 'without reserve' and then reject an offer. This would entitle the bidder to recover damages.

At the auction itself the request for bids is merely an invitation to treat and any offers may be accepted or rejected by the auctioneer. The Sale of Goods Act 1979, s. 57(2) stipulates that acceptance is represented by the fall of the hammer or in another customary manner and that until acceptance any bid may be withdrawn.

3.2.3.4 Tenders A request for tenders for work to be done, or goods to be sold or supplied, made, for example, by a local authority, is classed as an invitation to treat. The offer is made by the various hopeful contractors and it is for the local authority to accept or reject such offers as they see fit. There is no obligation to accept the cheapest tender (or indeed the highest offer) for something which you are buying or selling by this means in the absence of express language to the effect that this is intended (e.g., 'highest bid secures'). Where such language *is* used this constitutes what is known as a 'standing offer', which is accepted by the first bidder to meet its terms (see *Spencer* v *Harding* (1870) LR 5 CP 561).

There can be problems in such situations where standing offers are met by 'referential bids', i.e. bids which are stated to be '£X or £1 above any other bid'. This tactic was adopted in *Harvela Instruments Ltd* v *Royal Trust Co of Canada Ltd* [1985] 2 All ER 966, in response to a request for sealed bids. The House of Lords decided that in the absence of the offeror specifically allowing for such bids they were invalid. The reasoning was that if all parties used referential bids the bargaining process would be undermined completely.

3.3 OFFER, WITHDRAWAL OF OFFER, AND ACCEPTANCE

As indicated earlier (see para. 3.2.2 and 3.2.3 above), business negotiations take place through a range of different mediums both in terms of the means of communication and complexity. Such negotiations can present the law with a number of problems. For example, is the offer still able to be accepted in the eyes of the law when the offeree purports to accept it? Also, even if it is still able to be accepted, has the so-called 'acceptance' actually accepted precisely what was on offer?

In either case the situation may be complicated by negotiation for the sale of the same thing to a third party. For example, A is negotiating with B for the sale of his car. B has sent a letter to A indicating that he will pay the price asked. Before A receives the letter he sells the car to C. B and C will both feel, with some justification, that they are entitled to the car. The rules of offer and acceptance attempt to provide a consistent formula to be applied to such a situation.

3.3.1 Offer

An offer, by whatever means it is communicated, is not effective until it is received by the person to whom it is addressed (the offeree) (*Adams* v *Lindsell* (1818) 1B & Ald 681).

3.3.2 Termination of offer

The five modes of termination are dealt with below.

3.3.2.1 Death and Insanity An offer may be terminated by the subsequent death or insanity of the offeror (*Bell Comm*, I, 344) or the offeree (*Thomson* v *James* (1855) 18 D, 1) unless the unfortunate individual was only an agent, e.g., a purchasing manager.

3.3.2.2 Lapse of time An offer ceases to be effective after any final date specified for acceptance, or after a reasonable time.

What is reasonable depends on the type of goods, the condition of the market and all of the circumstances. Where the goods in question tend to fluctuate in price, e.g., shares or gold, it will be unreasonable to expect the offer to stay open for very long. In *Wylie and Lochead* v *McElroy & Sons* (1873) 1 R, 41 an offer to carry out iron work was not accepted for five weeks by which time the price of iron had risen sharply. It was held that there was no valid contract. Alternatively the type of communication, (e.g. fax), or the language used ('I must hear immediately') might indicate urgency. In such circumstances, as with dealings in commodities and shares, a reasonable time might be measured in hours or less.

3.3.2.3 Revocation An offer may be revoked, i.e. withdrawn, by the offeror at any time until it is accepted (*Bell Comm*, I, 343), subject to any promise to keep the offer open for a specified period. Such a promise is not binding in English law unless supported by consideration (*Dickinson* v *Dodds* (1876) 2 ChD 463), but the absence of such a rule in Scots law (see 3.5 and *Littlejohn* v *Hawden* (1882) 20 SLR 5) enables the offeree to feel secure that he has a certain deadline and is not subject to the caprice of the offeror. The English Law Commission has recommended that English law be brought into line with Scots law on this point and that a promise to keep an offer open for a specified period should be enforceable. The recommendation has not however been taken up and this should be borne in mind when business is being conducted in England or whenever the proper law of the contract is English.

A revocation does not take effect until received by the offeror. (*Thomson* v *James*). This is in sharp contrast to the rule that an acceptance by post is sometimes effective when posted (*Adams* v *Lindsell, Holwell Securities* v *Hughes* [1974] 1 All ER 161 and 3.3.3.3 below). The operation and interaction of these two rules is often crucial in determining whether there is a binding contract.

3.3.2.4 Revocation provided for in terms of offer An offer may lapse on the occurrence or non-occurrence of an event specified or implied in the offer. In *Financings Ltd* v *Stimpson* [1962] 3 All ER 386, an offer to buy a car from a hire-purchase company was held to have lapsed when the vehicle was no longer in a reasonable condition at the time of the purported acceptance.

3.3.2.5 Attempted revocation: what is its status? An offer is probably withdrawn if communication of attempted withdrawal does not come to the offeree's notice purely as a result of his own carelessness, e.g., where a letter is received or a message left on an answering machine or fax during normal business hours, but the letter is not opened or the machine not turned on. Although there is no direct authority on this point it would seem unfair to hold otherwise because to do so would mean that an offeree could carelessly or conveniently ignore reasonable attempts to withdraw an offer. He could then accept the offer and secure a binding contract contrary to the wishes of the other party.

It is uncertain in Scots law whether an offer is effectively withdrawn if the offeree hears from a source other than the offeror that the offer has been withdrawn. It was held in the English case *Dickinson* v *Dodds* (1876) 2 ChD 463 that if the offeree heard from a reliable third party then this could constitute a valid withdrawal. This would appear to put both offeror and offeree in a rather precarious and uncertain position. As Professor Walker has said 'People cannot conduct business in reliance on gossips or rumours'. (*Law of Contracts and Related Obligations*, 2nd edn, London, Butterworths, 1985, p. 121.) If an offer is accepted before being revoked there is a binding contract.

3.3.3 Acceptance

Acceptance is the means by which the offer becomes a contract 'and this acceptance may be either in words, or by writing, or by doing what is required as the counterpart of the offer' (*Bell Comm*, I, 343). An acceptance, therefore, could vary from a formal written intimation, to placing coins in a vending machine or boarding a bus.

There are three key principles guiding the law in this area: first that the acceptance must be made in response to the offer; secondly that it must match the terms of the offer and thirdly that it must be communicated to the offeror. These principles require closer examination.

3.3.3.1   Acceptance must be in response to offer   One cannot validly accept an offer of which one is unaware. Parties cannot be said to be 'agreeing' if one of them is unaware that the other has anything on offer. So if A offers a reward for anyone who finds his lost dog, B cannot claim the reward if he only hears of the reward when he delivers the dog (see *R* v *Clarke* [1927] 40 CLR 227). This rule also means that if A and B make identical offers to each other simultaneously by post there is no contract. Although this appears harsh it has been justified as promoting certainty (*Tinn* v *Hoffman* (1873) 29 LT 271), parties need only feel in danger of being bound when they have participated in at least some bargaining. It is thought that in the case of 'cross offers' such as these, the slightest indication of positive acquiescence (by words or action) would be taken to seal the agreement.

In addition, it should be noted that if a communication from one party could be construed as an enforceable gratuitous promise (see 3.5 below), then it may be enforceable as it stands, whether or not the beneficiary is aware of it.

3.3.3.2   Acceptance must match the terms of the offer   Clearly there cannot be said to be an agreement between A and B if A offers to sell his car for £1,000 and B offers to buy it for £900. Indeed an 'acceptance' which does not unequivocally accept all of the terms of the offer is not an acceptance at all, but a counter-offer which requires to be accepted by the original offeror if there is to be a binding contract. In *Hyde* v *Wrench* (1840) 3 Beav 334, Hyde offered to sell at £1,000; W offered £950 and when this was refused he 'agreed' to pay £1,000. The offer of £950 was held to be a counter-offer which rejected the original offer, rendering it no longer capable of being accepted. (See the Cases and Materials section for Chapter 3 for an extract from the recent Outer House decision *Avintair* v *Ryder Airline Services* 1993 SCLR 576, in which the facts revealed a lack of consensus.) The courts do draw a distinction however between a rejection and a request for further information, e.g., as to whether the offeror would accept credit terms (see *Stevenson* v *McLean* (1880) 5 QBD 346). It also appears, from *Roofcare Ltd* v *Gillies* 1984 SLT (Sh Ct) 8, that a qualified verbal acceptance will not operate as a counter-offer where the final contract is to be reduced to writing. *Objective offer and acceptance*   It is quite obvious in a case like *Hyde* v *Wrench* that the 'acceptance' as expressed does not match the terms of the offer. However, it is often the case that, although on the face of it the parties have similar intentions, one or both may allege that they have misunderstood or been misled about the import or detail of the agreement. Where one party is at fault in misleading the other party or taking advantage of an obvious erroneus expression of the terms, the contract may be invalidated under the law of error or misrepresentation (see 3.12 and 3.13 below). However, in the absence of unconscionable behaviour by one party, the contract will be enforced according to what the parties appear *objectively* to have agreed. As Lord President Dunedin stated in *Muirhead and Turnbull* v *Dicksons* (1905) 7 F 686:

> Commercial contracts cannot be arranged by what people think in their inmost minds. Commercial contracts are made according to what people say.

So if A believes he is offering to buy B's 1989 Escort XR3i and B believes he is offering to sell his 1980 Escort 1.3L we must ascertain which is the most reasonable interpretation of the circumstances. In the absence of evidence as to what has been spoken or written, such reasonable interpretation can most probably be gleaned from the price. A would find it difficult for example, to be taken seriously in his belief if the price was £1,000 as would B if the price was £8,000 (see generally *Stuart v Kennedy* (1886) 13 R 221; *Duran v Duran* (1904) 7 F 87; *Morrison Law v Paterson* 1985 SLT 255; and see the discussion of error, at 3.13).

Silence generally not acceptance   It is generally not competent to stipulate that if no response is made to an offer it will be taken to have been accepted. In *Felthouse v Bindley* (1872) 11 CB (NS) 869 A indicated that he would consider a horse sold to him if he heard nothing to the contrary from B. It was held that B's silence on the matter did not amount to an acceptance of the offer. This rule is generally rationalised as intended to protect B in such circumstances from having an obligation imposed on him to either reject the offer or be saddled with a contract. In this light it is perfectly fair. However, it might appear less attractive where B happily assumed that he *would* have a contract if he did not reply. This is most likely to occur where there has been a course of dealing to this effect between the parties. In such a situation it seems that silence might be construed as acceptance (*Bell Comm* I, 344, *Barry Ostlene & Shepherd Ltd v Edinburgh Cork Co* 1909 SC 1113). It is less clear what the position would be where there was no course of dealing but B simply takes A at his word and assumes that there is a binding contract when the requisite time has passed. It could be argued that to apply the basic rule from *Felthouse v Bindley* would frustrate the perfectly reasonable espectations of B.

Unilateral contracts – offer and acceptance   Most contracts made by business people will involve an exchange of commitments similar to that seen in the cases discussed so far. A offers to buy a product for £X and B accepts this offer. A is committing himself to buy at this price and B is committing himself to sell at the same price. There may be circumstances in which no such mutual (or bilateral) commitment can be found, but the law takes the view that the commitment of one party should nevertheless be enforceable.

This can arise in two ways. First, in a wholly gratuitous promise or contract where A promises to do something for B, expecting nothing in return, e.g., a promise to make an annual contribution to charity. The problems associated with this kind of situation are discussed below (see 3.5). Secondly, A may promise that if B performs a certain act, e.g., finds his lost dog or rides a penny farthing bicycle from Glasgow to Edinburgh, he will give him something or perform him a service. It should be noted that B generally is not committing himself to *do* anything. If however, he chooses to perform the requisite act, he will be entitled to the reward. He may have accepted the offer by *saying* that he will carry out the activities in question, and in such circumstances he is bound from this point.

Often, however, B is taken to accept A's unilateral offer by performing the act in question. This is of most relevance to the businessman where he chooses to enhance sales by offering a 'free gift' if a certain quantity of his goods are purchased. No one is under any obligation to purchase anything. However, if they do purchase the specified quantity, they become entitled to the gift. Alternatively, as in *Carlill* v *Carbolic Smoke Ball Co* (see 3.2.3.2 above), a business may attempt to inspire confidence in their product by making claims about its qualities and backing these claims up by certain promises. In this case the Smoke Ball Co claimed that their product was a means or preventing influenza (in addition to numerous other ailments) and that if it was used in the prescribed manner for a certain period and the user caught influenza the company would pay the user £100. Having followed the instructions religiously Mrs Carlill caught influenza and successfully recovered her £100 on the basis that by using the ball as prescribed she had accepted the offer, and had become entitled to the £100.

This latter situation may be able to be construed as an enforceable promise (see 3.5 below). If so, then although the beneficiary must carry out the condition attached to the promise, this condition is not an 'acceptance', as no acceptance is needed where a promise is concerned. In addition, the promise is just that, a promise, not an offer, so that it is irrevocable and there can be no question of it being withdrawn before the condition is fulfilled.

3.3.3.3 Acceptance must be communicated The general principle is that acceptance is not effective until it is communicated to the offeror, i.e. until it 'impinges on the consciousness of the offeror'. This will apply where the parties are in each others presence or may be treated as such, i.e. where they deal by telephone or telex. In such circumstances there is no acceptance until it comes to the notice of the offeror. So if a spoken acceptance was drowned by noise it would not be effective. Equally if a telex message accepting an offer is sent from London to Vienna it does not take effect until received in Vienna. (*Brinkibon* v *Stahag Stahl* [1983] 2 AC 34; see also *Entores* v *Miles Far East Corporation* [1955] 2 QB 327).

The postal rule However if the parties have been negotiating by post and this remains a reasonable means of communication in the circumstances then the acceptance is effective when posted (*Adams* v *Lindsell* (1818) 1B & Ald 681; *Jacobson Sons & Co* v *Underwood & Sons Ltd* (1874) 21 R 654). In *Byrne* v *Van Tienhoven* (1880) 5 CPD 344, VT posted on the 1st of October an offer to sell B 1,000 boxes of tin plates. On the 8th of October he sent a letter revoking his offer. On the 11th B telegraphed acceptance, and he confirmed by letter on the 15th. On the 20th B received VT's letter of revocation. It was held that there was a contract from the 11th when acceptance was posted. The revocation, which did not take effect until the 20th (see 3.3.2.3 above) was too late. If, however, as in the case of *Holwell Securities Ltd* v *Hughes* [1974] 1 All ER 161, the offeror indicates that he wishes to actually receive the acceptance, then postal rule will not apply. Such an intention might be gleaned from language such as 'notice in writing', 'to arrive first post Friday morning', etc. It was also indicated in *Holwell* by Lawton LJ that the postal rule should not operate in any case where it would cause 'manifest . . . absurdity'. The Scottish Law Commission has proposed that an acceptance should not be valid until it is received, although the offer should be able to be withdrawn only up to the time the acceptance is dispatched (Scot Law Com. No 144, *Report on the Formation of Contract*, 1993, at p. 34).

(The judgment of Lawton LJ in *Holwell* is reproduced in the Cases and Materials section for Chapter 3.)

Authority to communicate acceptance For an acceptance to be effective it must have been communicated by someone with authority to do so. In *Powell* v *Lee* [1908] 99 LT 284 a candidate for a headmastership was told informally by one of the interviewing board that he had been appointed. When the board changed their decision, there was held to be no breach of contract because the board member had not been authorised to communicate acceptance to the candidate. This case emphasises the importance of seeking official confirmation of 'acceptances' before acting upon them.

Withdrawal of acceptance In theory it should be impossible to withdraw acceptance, because once there has been acceptance there is a binding contract. This is certainly the case where the acceptance has actually 'impinged on the consciousness' of the offeror. However, in *Countess of Dunmore* v *Alexander* (1830) 9 S 190, it was apparently held that a postal acceptance may be withdrawn before it reaches the offeror by means of another communication. It has been argued that this case was really decided on the grounds that what was being withdrawn was an offer and not an acceptance at all (see Cheshire, Fifoot & Furmston, *Law of Contract*, London: Butterworths 11th edn, 1986). This view may be difficult to sustain on the facts of the case. It may in fact be more sensible to view the case as one where strict application of the postal rule would cause 'manifest . . . absurdity' (see above). This explanation appears rational on the facts of the case. The acceptance letter, although posted first, arrived at the same time as the withdrawal of acceptance. It is inconceivable, therefore that the recipient had any opportunity to place reliance on the acceptance in any way.

3.3.4 Has agreement been reached?: problems of standardised contracting

Whether agreement has been reached really depends on the question as to whether the acceptance matches the terms of the offer (above 3.3.3.2). However this issue is often rather simplistically expressed as simply a question of concurrence as to price or product. The problem tends to arise in more complex circumstances, though, such as negotiation by standard form contract.

3.3.4.1 Standard form contracts: battle of the forms A great deal of modern business is conducted through the medium of standard form contracts. These are contracts which the business organisation in question will generally use with all of their customers or suppliers. They represent a highly cost effective means of negotiating because they avoid the need to draft new terms and conditions for every fresh transaction. They have also been prepared in the light of the prevailing law and with a view to the avoidance of conflict and litigation; this is not to say that many standard form contracts do not contain clauses of more than dubious legality (see 3.11.3–3.11.6), often on the realistic expectation that the psychological advantage of a term weighted heavily in one's favour outweighs the very slight danger that the other party will go so far as to challenge it in court.

In any event if one was to examine the standard terms of a buyer and a seller in a particular industry there would clearly be differences on a range of issues such as quality, delivery, and penalties for non-compliance. The process of negotiation will often involve orders and supplies in the form of, or associated with, such standard terms. In most cases the transaction will come to a satisfactory conclusion and the parties will not be interested in how either or both sets of terms would fare if tested in court. Indeed, even if there is a dispute, research shows that businessmen are less concerned with who would win a legal battle and more with reaching a mutually acceptable settlement. Beale and Dugdale's research into contracts between business-men (a summary of which is reproduced in the Cases and Materials section for Chapter 3) revealed that:

> there was a considerable awareness of the fact that in many cases an exchange of conditions would not necessarily lead to an enforceable contract . . . Legal enforceability seemed secondary to reaching a common understanding.

However if a great deal stands to be lost or gained it may be that litigation is thought to be the only solution. This has happened with price variation or escalation clauses which are used by sellers or suppliers, especially where there is considerable delay between formation of the contract and delivery/ payment. Such clauses purport to entitle the seller or supplier to increase the contract price in accordance with inflation. What will normally happen is that both parties will proceed with the contract, happily believing/trusting that their own terms have prevailed and not expecting a major price rise to bring the clause into play. Should the unexpected happen and the issue be litigated, the courts have adopted several approaches based on offer/acceptance prin-ciples. These are exemplified in the following cases.

In *Butler Machine Tool* v *Ex-Cell-O Corp* [1979] 1 All ER 965, the sellers offered to sell a machine to the buyers. Their standard conditions included a price variation clause and a provision that their terms were to 'prevail over any terms and conditions in the buyers' order'. The buyers placed an order on a form containing conflicting terms (in particular there was no price variation clause). At the bottom of the buyers' order was a tear-off confirma-tion slip expressly subject to the buyers' terms which the sellers completed and returned. It was held that the sellers were unable to alter the contract price. The contract had been completed by the sellers' acceptance (in filling out the tear-off slip) of the buyers' counter-offer (constituted by sending their terms and conditions). The sellers' original offer and all its terms had been rejected by the buyers' counter-offer. This finding was based on the *Hyde* v *Wrench* approach which effectively holds that the legal effect of each com-munication is negated by a subsequent contradictory communication.

A similar approach was adopted in *Uniroyal Ltd* v *Miller & Co Ltd* and in *Chitton Bros Ltd* v *S Eker Ltd* (8 July 1980 (unreported) (OH)). In the latter case, a fabric supplier sent a customer an order form with a tear-off acknowledgement slip. The customer ignored this form and sent his own order. A provision on this order conflicted with the supplier's terms, but the supplier dispatched the fabric. The court held that the supplier's order form was an offer. It had been met by a counter-offer from the customer and this counter-offer was accepted by the supply of the goods. (See also *Continental Tyre and Rubber Co Ltd* v *Trunk Trailer Co Ltd* 1987 SLT 58 and *Gordon Adams and Partners* v *Ralph Jessop* 1987 SCLR 735).

The lesson for those conducting business negotiations is to be wary of acting on negotiations if it is possible that the other parties, terms are at that point prevailing. This is because such actions will generally be seen as acceptance of whatever terms are taken to be on the table at the time. If it is important to act quickly, then action should be accompanied by a re-assertion in writing of one's own terms. However this may result in a situation where there cannot be said to be a concluded agreement. For example, in *BSC* v *Cleveland Bridge & Engineering Co Ltd* [1984] 1 All ER 504, the defendants requested delivery in a particular sequence. The plaintiffs refused to supply on the basis of any conditions other than their own, but they began to manufacture and supply the product. It was held that there was no concluded contract between the parties. However, the defendants had to pay a reasonable sum for the goods supplied. The payment of this sum was based on quasi-contractual principles (see 3.15 below).

A recent decision illustrates the operation of the typical problem in the special context of a contract for the sale of land. In *Rutterford Ltd* v *Allied Breweries Ltd* 1990 SCLR 186 an offer (by A) in relation to land was met by a qualified acceptance (from B). The difference between the parties was over the holding of a sum of money and remedies in circumstances of dissatisfaction. It was held that it was not open to B at a later date to withdraw their qualifications and accept A's original offer. This offer had died when met with a qualified acceptance i.e. a counter-offer. It was also held that, although in some cases the negotiations following the qualified acceptance might indicate that A did not treat it as a counter-offer, this was not possible in this case: the mere fact of continued negotiations was not enough to raise this inference.

This decision reiterates the judicial preference for certainty in negotiations. (For a discussion of the status of 'letters of intent', and whether they amount to concluded contracts see 'Conditional Acceptances and Letters of Intent', J. A. K. Huntley, 1990 SLT 121.)

3.4 INTENTION TO CREATE LEGAL RELATIONS

Once it has been established that the parties have made an agreement, the question which traditionally is asked next is whether the parties intended to create legal relations. Normal social intercourse generates numerous promises many of which would never be thought of by the parties as involving a legal commitment to do anything, e.g., promises made in jest, agreements to meet for a drink or a meal. In this respect the business person need not be overly concerned as these are not the type of agreements which particularly interest him. He is far more concerned with agreements of a commercial nature, and the law presumes that in such agreements the parties do intend to create legal relations. This is clearly a vital presumption to make if the law is to provide any kind of support for market transactions. Commercial parties cannot be expected to *prove* that commercial agreements were made seriously. The presumption in favour of serious intent will apply if the contract is made in a business setting, unless the parties clearly express a contrary intention. Such contrary intention is occasionally expressed by the use of a 'binding in honour only' clause (see *Rose & Frank* v *Crompton* [1925] AC 445).

Whatever the particular language used, it must be a clear and unambiguous statement that legal relations are not intended. The courts place a heavy onus on a contracting party who alleges that legal relations were not intended in a commercial context. For example, in the English case *Edwards* v *Skyways Ltd* [1964] 1 All ER 494, the defendants argued that their reference to a promised payment as 'ex gratia' indicated that they did not intend legal relations. The court held that the strong presumption in favour of intended legal relations had not been rebutted. The same view was taken in the Scottish case *Wick Harbour Trs* v *The Admiralty* 1921 2 SLT 109. However, in the recent decision *Kleinwort Benson* v *Malaysian Mining Corp* [1989] 1 All ER 785, a 'letter of comfort' to a bank, which stated a parent company's 'policy' of ensuring that the debts of its subsidiary would be paid, was held not to have been intended to be legally binding. The statement was treated as one of present intention, an intention which might well change if the circumstances altered radically. The circumstances *did* change radically when the tin market collapsed, resulting in a large liability for the subsidiary company to the bank. The decision was also based on the fact that the parent company's refusal to give a formal guarantee itself indicated that there was no intention to be legally bound.

In a non-commercial setting the presumption is that the parties did not intend to create legal relations. This applies where agreements are made between family or friends or between any parties where a party stands to gain or lose financially from the agreement. The latter type of situation is best exemplified by agreements relating to the membership of clubs, societies and voluntary religious bodies (see *Anderson* v *Manson* 1909 SC 838; *Forbes* v *Eden* (1867) SM (HL) 36). These will generally not be enforceable unless they involve a right to payment or to hold a particular office. Parties to a social or domestic agreement may be able to show that they intended to be legally bound, particularly if there is a financial interest involved. Examples include an agreement to live apart which includes an agreement as to aliment (*Campbell* v *Campbell* 1923 SLT 670); an arrangement between two family members and a lodger to contribute to a newspaper competition which carried a prize (*Simpkins* v *Pays* [1955] 3 All ER 10); and a house-sharing agreement between two families (*Parker* v *Clark* [1960] 1 All ER 93).

3.4.1 Collective agreements

Under the Trade Union and Labour Relations Act 1974, s. 18, collective agreements between employers and trade unions are conclusively presumed not to have been intended to create legal relations unless the agreement is in writing and contains a provision to the contrary.

3.5 GRATUITOUS OBLIGATIONS

All of the examples discussed thus far have involved contracts with a commitment from both parties to do something. Scots law also recognises what is known as a gratuitous obligation where only one party makes any kind of commitment. An example of such an obligation may be seen in the case of *Mortons Trs* v *Aged Christian Friend Society of Scotland* (1899) 2 F 82 when M offered to become personally responsible for 50 life pensions of £6 each. This offer was accepted by the defenders and it was held that a valid contract had been constituted and the money was payable. In English law such gratuitous contracts are not recognised as being enforceable unless contained in a deed under seal. This is because of the doctrine of consideration which requires 'something of value' to be either given or received by both parties (*Currie* v *Misa* (1875) LR 10 Ex 153). This has led to some practical difficulties in English law, particularly in regard to the renegotiation of contracts.

In Scots law these difficulties do not arise because gratuitous obligations are enforceable.

Scots law, historically at least, recognises a distinction between a gratuitous promise (not requiring acceptance) and a gratuitous contract. Most gratuitous obligations appear to be analysed as contracts now. It used to be the case that gratuitous promises and possibly gratuitous contracts also could only be proved by writ or oath. The Requirements of Writing (Scotland) Act 1995 has abolished the writ or oath rule in relation to all contracts to which it applies (see 3.8.2 below), and gratuitous obligations in the course of a business need be neither constituted in writing, nor proven by writ or oath. However, those made outside the course of a business must be constituted in writing s. 1(2), and see also the Scot Law Com No 112 at p. 10; see also discussion by MacBryde, 'Promises in Scots Law', 42 ICLQ, 48. Professor MacQueen has pointed out the numerous gratuitous obligations which take place in a commercial contract (see the Cases and Materials section for Chapter 3 for an extract from his article).

The reform means that these important commercial promises, whose enforcement simply reflects the reasonable expectations of the parties, are now provable by normal means. On the other hand, non-commercial promises, which are less likely to be made seriously, would have to establish their seriousness by being constituted in writing. This approach steers a sensible course, recognising on the one hand that gratuitous obligations have an important role to play in commercial transactions, and that obstacles should not be placed in the path of enforcement; while also recognising that outwith a commercial contract a more important priority is to ensure that a gratuitous obligation was really seriously intended.

3.5.1 Jus Quaesitum Tertio

Two contracting parties may confer a benefit on a third party by the creation of a *jus quaesitum tertio* (right in favour of a third party). For this to arise the parties must clearly have intended to confer a benefit on a named third party. However, unless the benefit has been expressed as irrevocable then the two original contracting parties may change their position later (see *Carmichael* v *Carmichael's Executive* 1920 SC (HL) 195).

Although third parties may, on these conditions, benefit from a contract, they may never be subjected to liabilities under it, as they have never given consent to the arrangement. They may, however, choose to agree or consent at some future date to having rights or liabilities under a contract assigned to them. (For a detailed discussion of the rules relating to assignation see Gloag and Henderson, *Introduction to the Law of Scotland*, Chapter 10.)

3.6 CERTAINTY OF TERMS

Gloag said that 'in order to create a contractual obligation an agreement must be reasonably definite. Vague general understandings cannot be enforced' (*Contract*, 1985, p. 11).

The law is faced with a difficulty in this context in that businessmen do not necessarily talk in the same precise language as that used by lawyers. The law must, however, try to ascertain the intention of contracting parties and not frustrate their wishes because they have been slightly imprecise or vague. So, for example, the courts will look for trade usages or customs, or may attempt to imply terms which make business sense of the contract. Indeed the Sale of Goods Act, s. 8(2) provides that if the price of goods has not been fixed by the parties, a reasonable price may be fixed. It would be commercially impractical for the law to take a hard line on certainty.

On the other hand the courts will not 'thrust on the words meanings which they cannot bear' (C.B. Burns, *The Commercial Law of Scotland*, p. 1). In one case the court refused to enforce a contract for the prohibition of 'unseemly buildings' because this phrase was not clear enough to bear any definite meaning (*Murray Trs* v *St Margaret's Convent Trs* (1907) SC (HL) 8). Also, in *Scammell & Nephew* v *Ouston* [1941] 1 All ER 14, the parties agreed to transfer a van 'on hire-purchase terms'. This was held to be too vague. The court concluded that:

> the parties never in intention, nor even in appearance, reached an agreement . . . They did, indeed, accept the position that there should be some form of hire-purchase agreement but they never went on to complete their agreement.

(For a contracting case in which what was certain about the agreement outweighed what was vague, see *Scottish Wholefoods Ltd* v *Raye Investments, Barclays Bank PLC* 1994 SCLR 60.)

In *Australian and New Zealand Banking Group* v *Frost Holdings* [1989] VR 695 the parties were negotiating over the sale of calendars. It was held that there was no binding contract unless and until the parties agreed on matters of price, quality, size, style and design. These, said the court, were not merely specifications, but constituted the subject matter of the negotiations.

Even where no contract can be found the court may order a reasonable price to be paid for any goods or services which have been delivered. (See for example the case discussed above (see 3.3.4.1), *BSC* v *Cleveland Bridge & Engineering Co Ltd*, where the contractual negotiations broke down. The reasonable sum payable in such circumstances is based on quasi-contract and will be due only if the goods or services have been beneficially transferred to the other party (see 3.16 below). Note that in the *Avintair* case (referred to at 3.3.3.2 above and contained in the Cases and Materials section), in which no consensus was found, it does not appear that a quasi-contractual claim for the services was made. Perhaps this was because they did not benefit the other party.

3.7 VOID, VOIDABLE AND UNENFORCEABLE CONTRACTS

Despite the existence of agreement on relatively certain terms with the clear intention to create legal relations it may be that some other factor operates to affect the contract's validity. Such factors may operate either to make a contract void, voidable or unenforceable.

3.7.1 Void contracts
A void contract is a legal nullity and is considered never to have happened. No rights can arise under such a 'contract' either in favour of the parties who made the agreement or in favour of any third party who may innocently have become entangled in the relationship. So if a contract for the sale of goods by A to B is void, then no ownership or title to the goods passes to B. B is therefore unable to pass a good title to the goods to an innocent third party buyer, C. This is because of the rule (*nemo dat quod non habet* – see Chapter 6 below) that no one can pass a better title to goods than he himself possesses (see *Morrisson* v *Robertson* discussed below at 3.13.1.4). The result is that, in such circumstances, A may recover the goods from C and C's only remedy is to maintain an action for breach of contract against B. The problems associated with this type of situation are discussed in more detail below. Among the transactions which are void are certain contracts with those under the age of majority (see 3.9.1 and 3.9.2); contracts with insane persons (see 3.9.4 below) and contracts entered into under essential error, e.g., as to the identity of the other party (see 3.13.1.4). The law holds only a very narrow category of contracts to be void, as it is commercially undesirable to pick apart transactions. This causes uncertainty and is inefficient.

3.7.2 Voidable contracts
A voidable contract is one which gives rise to rights and obligations but which may be set aside if challenged. Where contracts are voidable it is usually because the law recognises that consent has been improperly obtained, e.g., by misrepresentation, undue influence or duress (see 3.12 below), or because

particular formalities which the law requires have not been adhered to (see 3.8 below). A voidable contract is distinguished from a void contract in that with the latter the vitiating factor is considered to be so fundamental that the parties can never be taken to have agreed or consented in the first place. The right to set the contract aside is lost: (1) where *restitutio in integrum* is not possible, i.e. where the parties cannot be returned to their original position, e.g., where building work is involved (see *Boyd & Forrest* v *Glasgow SW Ry Co* 1912 SC (HC) 93; (2) where one or both parties have acted on an agreement which is defective in its formalities (see 3.8.1 below); (3) where the party seeking to set the contract aside is barred through lapse of time (see *Leaf* v *International Galleries* [1950] 2 KB 86; (4) where property transferred under a voidable contract is sold to a third party who buys in good faith and without notice of the seller's defective title (see 3.12.1.6 below).

We can see that even where the law is prepared to hold a contract voidable (e.g., because of distaste for the way it was induced), there is a concern to mitigate the implications of picking transactions apart. The four cases in which the right to set aside a voidable contract is lost are all cases in which commercial certainty and/or the legitimate expectations of third parties may be adversely affected by setting the contract aside.

3.7.3   Unenforceable contracts

Unenforceable contracts are in all respects valid and productive of rights and obligations, although the law chooses for various reasons not to allow them to be enforced. This may be in any of the following situations:

(a)   Where the parties state an intention not to be legally bound (see 3.4 above).

(b)   Where the obligation cannot be proved.

(c)   Where the contract is unreasonably in restraint of trade (see 3.10.3 below).

(d)   Where the contract is a gaming contract (see *Robertson* v *Balfour* 1938 SC 207 per L J C Aitchison at 211 and *Kelly* v *Murphy* 1940 SC 96 per Lord Wark at 117). This does not, however, apply to contracts between the competitors in and organisers of a competition where a prize is at stake. In such circumstances the courts will enforce a claim for the prize (see *Graham* v *Pollok* (1848) 10D 646 and *O'Connell* v *Russel* (1864) 3 M 89).

3.8   CONTRACTUAL FORMALITIES

Although where practical, it is wise to reduce contracts to writing, this is not a general prerequisite of validity in Scots law, Requirements of Writing (Scotland) Act 1995, s. 1. Such a requirement would of course be totally impractical in many of the everyday transactions which are vital to commercial and domestic life, e.g., the purchase of a meal, a drink or the weekly shopping. A reqirement of writing imposes costs on contracting parties — the seeking of advice, the reduction to writing, the exchange of documents, etc. The general rule, therefore, is that contracts may be entered into orally or in writing or may be inferred from the actions of the parties. What is more, any dispute as to formation may be resolved by written or oral ('parole') evidence.

3.8.1 Writing required for valid constitution

Writing is required by certain statutes for certain specific types of contract (see e.g., hire purchase agreements in Chapter 7, employment contracts in Chapter 9 and cheques under the Bills of Exchange Act 1882). The Requirements of Writing (Scotland) Act 1995 s. 1(2) says that writing is also required for:

(a)   the constitution of—

(i)   a contract or unilateral obligation for the creation, transfer, variation or extinction of an interest in land;

(ii)   a gratuitous unilateral obligation except an obligation undertaken in the course of business; and

(iii)   a trust whereby a person declares himself to be sole trustee of his own property or any property which he may acquire;

(b)   the creation, transfer, variation or extinction of an interest in land otherwise than by the operation of a court decree, enactment or rule of law; and

(c)   the making of any will, testamentary trust disposition and settlement or codicil.

However sections 1(3) and (4) say that,

Where, a contract, obligation or trust mentioned in subsection (2)(a) above is not constituted in a written document complying with section 2 of this Act, but one of the parties to the contract, a creditor in the obligation or a beneficiary under the trust ('the first person') has acted or refrained from acting in reliance on the contract, obligation or trust with the knowledge and acquiescence of the other party to the contract, the debtor in the obligation or the truster ('the second person')—

(a)   the second person shall not be entitled to withdraw from the contract, obligation or trust; and

(b)   the contract, obligation or trust shall not be regarded as invalid,
on the ground that it is not so constituted, if the condition set out in subsection (4) below is satisfied.

(4)   The condition referred to in subsection (3) above is that the position of the first person—

(a)   as a result of acting or refraining from acting as mentioned in that subsection has been affected to a material extent; and

(b)   as a result of such a withdrawal as is mentioned in that subsection would be adversely affected to a material extent.

These provisions apply to contractual *variations* as well as to the *creation* of contractual obligations (s. 1(5)).

In order for the contracts which require writing for constitution to be properly executed they must be subscribed by both parties (s. 2(1)).

If a document bears to have been described by the grantor of it and is signed by a person as a witness to the grantor's signature, then the document is presumed valid as long as the name and address of the witness is included and there is nothing in the document to suggest that it has not been signed and witnessed as described, (s. 3(1)).

Where there is no such presumption of validity, the court may, on application by one of the parties or anyone with an interest, endorse the document; or if it has already been registered in *Books of Council and Session* or *Sheriff Court* books, the court may grant a decree to this effect, (s. 4(1) and (2)).

The new Act abolishes the rules on *rei interventus* and homologation as far as the constitution of contracts is concerned. However the new rules on detrimental reliance (see ss. 1(3) and (4) above) will have a similar effect, and the old case law will remain useful for example and analogy. So where buyers or sellers act upon a defective agreement (e.g., by doing work, spending money etc.), and the other party knows and acquiesces, then the contract will be enforceable as long as the action taken is significant enough (typically a matter of value) to affect the actor materially, and mean he would be materially compromised if the contract was not enforceable.

The new Act also abolishes the rules on proof by writ or oath (s. 11).

3.9   CAPACITY TO CONTRACT

Despite the appearance of all the appropriate requisites of validity, the law may classify a contract as void or voidable because one or more of the contracting parties does not have the requisite legal capacity. Capacity to contract is limited in the case of young persons under 18, insane persons, aliens, and corporate bodies. The rules relating to corporate bodies are discussed in Chapter 2, para. 2.2.3.

3.9.1   Young persons under the age of 18

The common law rules that regulated the legal capacity of persons under 18 years old were radically altered by the passing of the Age of Legal Capacity (Scotland) Act 1991. The Act is a useful example of private members' legislation being used to enact Law Commission proposals (the legislation was introduced by the late Sir Nicholas Fairbairn). The Act basically divides under-18s into two groups:

(a)   under 16;
(b)   16–18.

3.9.1.1   Under 16   Section 1 of the Act begins by stating that persons under the age of 16 lack the capacity to enter into any transaction. The word 'transaction' is not synonymous with contract but extends to making a will, bringing or defending a civil action, or making a gratuitous promise (s. 9). The effect of this section is to render any such transaction entered into by an under 16-year-old void.

The Act recognises, however, the increasing economic sophistication of this group by providing exceptions to the total lack of capacity suggested by s. 1. Under-16s will have contractual capacity provided that:

(a)   the transaction is one which would commonly be entered into by a *person of his age* and circumstances; and
(b)   the terms of the contract are not unreasonable (s. 2).

So the courts must consider whether it is common for a child of a certain age to enter a particular sort of contract; and whether this contract is common for someone of the standard of living which the child enjoys; and whether the terms are reasonable (typically that they are worse than the market norm). It is likely that many of the older common-law based cases will be mined for guidance (see, e.g., *Nash* v *Inman* [1908] 2 KB 1).

3.9.1.2   Persons aged 16 and 17   Effectively, such persons have the same legal capacity as those who have attained the age of majority. The old common law rules made provision for the setting aside of contracts on the basis of 'lesion' or disadvantage to the minor. Section 3 gives statutory force to these rules by making provision in certain circumstances for the setting aside of transactions which in the view of the sheriff court or Court of Session are held to be 'prejudicial'. A transaction is defined as prejudicial if it was one which an adult exercising reasonable prudence would not have entered into, and which has caused or is likely to cause substantial prejudice to the young person. The young person must apply to have the contract set aside before the age of 21. He cannot have contracts set aside which he either ratified after reaching 18, or which he entered into in the course of his own business or where the young person misrepresented some fact, e.g., his age.

To some extent, therefore, the new rules, like the old, offer little comfort to the beleaguered business, which faces the possibility of contracts entered into with 16 and 17-year-olds being set aside during this 5-year period. In most cases, however, this 'time bomb' will be a dud. In addition, for the avoidance of doubt the Act provides for proposed transactions to be ratified, at the request of the parties, by a sheriff. Once the decision has been ratified it cannot later be challenged. It is difficult to imagine much use being made of this procedure.

3.9.2   Insane persons
Insane persons have no contractual capacity and any 'contract' which they make is void (*Stair* I, 10, 3). They must pay a reasonable price for necessaries (Sale of Goods Act 1979, s. 3). Contracts of an ongoing nature are not necessarily avoided by supervening insanity. However, with partnership, for example, it is a ground on which dissolution may be sought from the court.

3.9.3   Intoxication
To vitiate a contract drunkenness must have been such that the party could not be said to be capable of consenting to an obligation, i.e. he simply does

not know what he is doing. In such circumstances a contract would be voidable but it may only be avoided if appropriate steps are taken immediately on the recovery of senses.

3.9.4 Enemy aliens
In time of war, residents of an enemy country have no contractual capacity, and it is a criminal offence to contract with any such person.

3.10 LEGALITY AND PUBLIC POLICY

We have said above (at 3.1) that the law will often lay down certain rules or standards in relation to the sorts of contracts which may be made, or the terms which may be used. The first example of this which we will now consider is the law's position on illegal contracts and contracts which are contrary to public policy as being in restraint of trade. In both cases, what appear to be freely entered into market transactions or terms come under scrutiny, because they offend against certain societal values and norms.

Contracts which are in some respect tainted by illegality are known as *pacta illicita* (illegal agreements). As indicated above, the law may object to a contract on various grounds. However, it is generally recognised that a contract may either be illegal under statute or at common law.

3.10.1 Statutory illegality
The effect of a contract which is illegal by virtue of an Act of Parliament depends on what Parliament's intention is adjudged to have been in any particular case. There are, however, two guiding principles. First, a contract or contract term declared void will never be enforced. An example of such a term would be one which attempted to exclude or restrict liability for death or personal injury caused by negligence in a business context (see Unfair Contract Terms Act 1977, s. 16 and 3.11.6.1 below). Terms tend to be void because they represent a departure from a legal norm — in the example given, liability for death or injury caused by fault — which departure it is thought should not be allowed via a formal document over which the injured party would have a limited opportunity to negotiate. However, if the contract is not illegal in any other respect the courts may give effect to rights arising on performance, e.g., the right to be paid a reasonable sum for services or goods (see *Jamieson* v *Watts Trs* 1950 SC 265 and *Cuthbertson* v *Lowe* (1870) 8 M 1073). In other words, the law will try to limit the extent to which it interferes with the consequences of the parties' transaction. It would generate uncertainty and inefficiency if every term in every contract which contained a void term was unable to be enforced. Secondly, where a statute, without declaring a contract to be void, imposes penalties on those who enter into it, it is a matter of construction of the statute whether the contract was intended to be treated as void. It may be, for example, that the provision is purely for administrative convenience or for revenue purposes. In such circumstances the contract may be enforced. However, the general presumption is that if a contract imposes penalties, the intention is that the contract is not to be enforceable.

3.10.2 Common law

There is a general distinction between contracts which are illegal at common law because they involve moral turpitude and those which are illegal because they are contrary to public policy. Those falling into the former category include contracts to commit a crime, perpetrate a fraud or further immorality. For example, in *Pearce v Brooks* (1886) LR 1 Ex 213, a contract for hire of a coach by a prostitute was not enforceable, because it was to be used 'as part of her display to attract men'. Contracts contrary to public policy include contracts with an enemy state or its citizens (*Regazzoni v K.C. Sethia (1944) Ltd* [1958] AC 301; contracts for smuggling (Bell, *Prin.* 42); contracts which interfere with the administration of justice; and contracts involving an unreasonable restraint on personal liberty. The final category has generated an enormous amount of litigation, much of which has been focused on restraint of trade clauses (see 3.10.3 below).

The general effect of illegality at common law is to render a contract void; and as such, productive of no legal rights or remedies for either party. This is expressed in the maxim *ex turpi causa non oritor actio* (out of an immoral situation an action does not arise). This rule is subject to exception, particularly where the parties are not equally culpable (*in pari delicto*), one party perhaps having suffered fraud or undue pressure from the other to enter into the contract. In such circumstances the court will assist the innocent party, if appropriate. Again we see the law attempting to take a subtle approach, refusing to allow contract to be used to enforce wrongful behaviour but not wishing to allow this to unsettle the whole agreement or prejudice an innocent party. The most common instance of this is where a bankrupt makes a secret payment to a creditor. Despite the fact that this is an illegal agreement and cannot be enforced to the creditor's advantage, the court will order repayment of the sum to the bankrupt. The presumption is that the beleaguered bankrupt has been taken advantage of by the unscrupulous creditor, who aims to jump the queue for payment (see *MacFarlane v Nicoll* (1864) 3 M 237).

It may also be possible for the innocent party to obtain redress in the case of an illegal contract by claiming on another ground of law, e.g., breach of collateral contract or recompense. The former would apply where A is induced by B to enter a contract which turns out to be illegal and void. He may be able to establish that B has effectively promised and contracted that the agreement would be valid. In *Strongman v Sincock* [1955] 2 QB 525, the architects had promised the builders that they would obtain the necessary building licences for the work in question. When they failed to do so, rendering the work illegal, the builders successfully sued for breach of the architect's collateral warranty that licences would be obtained. Although this is an English authority there seems no good reason in principle why it should not apply to Scots law.

A claim for recompense is quasi-contractual (see 3.16 below) and operates on the equitable principle that a party should receive reasonable payment for work done. For example, in *Clay v Yates* 1856 2S LJ ex 237, Clay recovered a payment for the work he had done in preparing a book for printing, despite the fact that he refused to publish it because of its defamatory content.

3.10.3 Contracts in restraint of trade

Agreements which restrict the right of one or more parties to work or trade come in a variety of forms. The most common are:

(a)   those imposed by an employer which restrict an employee's right to work for any other employer in a certain area for a specified period after leaving the original employment;

(b)   similar clauses aimed by the buyer of a business at the seller;

(c)   franchise or sole agency agreements where one party commits himself to taking all his supplies from a particular manufacturer;

(d)   agreements between manufacturers to limit output or maintain the selling price of goods at a certain level.

Such agreements present the law with something of a dilemma in that they have a tendency to restrict free trade, competition and individual liberty but to control them is to control freedom to contract, a principle which was traditionally central to the law of contract. Having said this, the reference to 'freedom' of contract requires some qualification. It seems likely that an element of the law's suspicion of these sorts of terms emanates from the fact that they tend to be contained in standardised contracts, which may offer little opportunity for negotiation or bargaining. With a lower degree of what might be called 'real consent' based legitimacy, it may be thought more acceptable to question terms which impose a restraint on the right to work or trade. The approach in the case of (a), (b) and (c) has been to hold that such restraints are enforceable, unless they can be shown to have been unreasonable both as between the parties and in the public interest (*Nordenfelt* v *Maxim Nordenfelt Guns and Ammunition Co Ltd* [1894] AC 535). The treatment of contracts falling within paragraph (d) has been largely overtaken by statutory and European Union control (see 3.10.3.5 below). Where the bargaining power of the parties is particularly disparate, the courts may impose a heavier onus on the party relying on the clause to prove that it is reasonable. This may happen when one party has imposed a standard form contract on another. For example, in *Macauley* v *A Schroeder Music Publishing Co. Ltd* [1974] 1 WLR 1308, a 21-year-old songwriter was contracted to give his exclusive services for five years; full copyright vested in the company; when royalties exceeded £5,000 the agreement was to be extended for a further five years and the publishers could terminate the agreement with one month's notice. The House of Lords held that the publishers had not been able to justify such a one-sided agreement and that it was accordingly contrary to public policy and void. It should be noted that Lord Diplock placed stress on the issue of inequality of bargaining power rather than the question of restriction on free trade.

As we have said, the tendency to control restraint of trade clauses is probably motivated not only by the substantive nature of these clauses, but also by the suspect bargaining conditions in which they are 'agreed'. However, most judges do not, as Lord Diplock did, actually focus upon 'relative bargaining power' as part of the test. Rather they concentrate on the substantive features of the term – nature of restraint, geographical scope, etc.

3.10.3.1 Protectable interests: employer/employee and purchaser/seller restraints
In both cases reasonableness as between the parties is to be assessed by measuring the nature of the interest protected against the scope of the restraint and deciding whether the latter is unnecessarily wide to protect the former. If so the clause will not be enforced.

Employers/employees An employer is entitled to protect himself against his trade secrets being divulged and his customers being enticed away from him.

In *Bluebell Apparel Ltd* v *Dickinson* 1978 SC 16, a management trainee was held to a clause which restrained him from working for a competitor of his ex-employers anywhere in the world for two years after leaving his employment. His employers manufactured 'Wrangler' jeans and he had left their employment and gone to work for Levi Strauss & Co. The clause was upheld on the basis of the trade secrets which he possessed and might feasibly pass on to his new employers.

This was also the ground of the decision in *SOS Bureau Ltd* v *Payne* 1982 SLT (Sh Ct) 33, where a person working for an employment agency was interdicted from working for a competitor within a quarter of a mile for one year. The employee in question was said to possess important knowledge of work systems and rates of commission. This decision would appear to give employers an alarmingly wide power of restraint. It is difficult to see how it can be appropriate to interpret 'trade secrets' so widely. After all, if an employee does not know his employers system of work, he must find it difficult to carry out his duties. It must, however, be conceded that the reasoning in *Payne* appears to be supported by that of Lord Cowie in *A & D Bedrooms Ltd* v *Michael* 1984 SLT 297. This appears to be a departure from the approach taken by Lord Atkinson in the leading English case *Herbert Morris Ltd* v *Saxelby* [1916] AC 688, where he said that an employee:

> violates no obligation express or implied arising from the relation in which he stood to the [employers] by using in the service of some persons other than them the general knowledge he has acquired of their scheme of organization and methods of business.

In *Geo. A Moore & Co Ltd* v *Menzies* [1989] GWD 568, an employee of furniture manufacturers was held to a clause which prohibited him (after leaving his employment) from soliciting or dealing with any person or company who had, to his knowledge, dealt with his employers in the previous two years.

Purchasers/sellers The purchaser of a business is entitled to protect the interest or goodwill in the business he has acquired. This does not mean that he can prevent competition *per se*. He may do so only in so far as the competition affects the goodwill of the business, for which, of course, he has paid. In *Vancouver Malt & Sake Brewing Co Ltd* v *Vancouver Breweries Ltd* [1934] AC 181, although a company was licensed to brew beer, they only ever brewed sake. When they sold the business they covenanted not to brew beer for fifteen years. It was held that as the company did not brew beer there was no goodwill to be passed to the purchasers. The covenant was simply a restriction on competition *per se*, and was accordingly void.

3.10.3.2 Scope of restraint The geographical extent of a restraint of trade clause and the length of time for which it is to operate are key factors; the view taken by the court may depend on how densely populated an area is, the type of business in question, and the extent to which the employee or seller would be in a position to interfere with the employer's or purchaser's legitimate interests. So, in a thinly populated area of Scotland with a limited range of customers, 20 miles was not an unreasonable restriction to place on a photographer's assistant to prevent him enticing customers from his ex-employer (*Stewart* v *Stewart* 1899 1 F 1158). In another case, however, it was held to be unreasonable to restrict a local canvasser from working within 25 miles of such a densely populated area as London (*Mason* v *Provident Clothing & Supply Co Ltd* [1913] AC 724. In *Fitch* v *Dewes* [1921] 2 AC 158, the close contact which a solicitor had with clients during his training in a smallish town, justified a restriction on working within seven miles of the Town Hall.

The importance of the nature of the business and where it is carried on is highlighted by contrasting the decisions in *Nordenfelt* v *Maxim Nordenfelt Guns and Ammunition Co Ltd* (above) and *Dumbarton Steamboat Co Ltd* v *MacFarlane* (1899) 1 F 993. In the former case it was not unreasonable to place a 25-year worldwide restraint on the seller of a cannon manufacturing business because of the highly restricted market, consisting solely of national governments. In the latter, a restriction affecting the whole of the United Kingdom applied in relation to a carrier's business which only operated in Glasgow and Dumbarton was held to be unreasonable.

3.10.3.3 Severability and drafting policy It may be that a contract contains several restrictions some of which are reasonable and others not. If such clauses are clearly distinct from one another the courts will strike out the unreasonable one (by the 'blue pencil rule') and allow the reasonable one to stand, as in *Mulvein* v *Murray* 1908 SC 528, where it was reasonable to restrict an ex-employee from canvassing customers but not to prevent him from selling or travelling in any of the towns travelled in by his ex-employer. The courts will not, however, water down a clause to make it reasonable. So, in *Empire Meat Co Ltd* v *Patrick* [1939] 2 All ER 85 CA, the court would not prevent a butcher opening up next door to his ex-employer and taking his customers, because the five mile restriction was too wide. Had the restriction been more reasonable in the circumstances it would probably have been upheld but as it was the clause either stood or fell on its own terms.

The lesson here is clear in respect of drafting restraint of trade clauses. One must look at all relevant factors, conclude what might be considered reasonable and enforceable and draft an appropriate clause. If desired, clauses which are more onerous in other respects may be drafted in the expectation that they will not be challenged. However they must be clearly separate and distinct from the reasonable clause, lest they should taint it and render it unenforceable.

3.10.3.4 Franchise or sole agency agreements The courts' attitude towards such arrangements can vary tremendously from a case like *Schroeder* where they will look very carefully at the fairness of the bargain, to a situation where the parties may be seen as operating on a more equal commercial footing. For example, in *Esso Petroleum Co Ltd* v *Harper's Garage (Stourport) Ltd* [1968] AC 269, the House of Lords upheld a clause under which the garage was bound to sell only Esso petrol for four years and five months and disallowed a clause which imposed a 21-year restriction. The court found support for allowing the shorter restriction in a Monopolies Commission Report in 1965 which recommended a five-year limit in such cases, and also in their own wish to follow 'the habitual inclination of the courts not to interfere with business decisions made by businessmen authorised and qualified to make them'.

3.10.3.5 Retail price maintenance agreements These are agreements under the terms of which an agent or retailer undertakes not to sell goods below list prices. Although they have been challenged at common law (see *Dunlop Pneumatic Tyre Co* v *New Garage and Motor Co Ltd* [1915] AC 79) and are prima facie void, it seems generally accepted that the courts will not set them aside unless they offend against the public interest (*McEllistrim* v *Ballymacel-ligott Co-Operative Agricultural & Dairy Society Ltd* [1919] AC 548 (HL)).

Such agreements are now mainly regulated by statute. The Resale Prices Act 1976 prohibits individual resale price maintenance agreements except where they can be shown to the Restrictive Practices Court to be in the public interest, in which case an order may be made exempting that class of agreements. Breach of the provisions of the Act give rise to a civil claim for interdict or damages on the basis of breach of statutory duty.

Anti-competitive practices generally are also regulated by Articles 85 and 86 of the Treaty of Rome. A detailed discussion of these provisions is a matter for a text on competition law. Briefly the effect of the articles is to prohibit:

all agreements between undertakings, decisions by associations of under-takings and concerted practices which may affect trade between Member States and which have as their object or effect the prevention, restriction or distortion of competition within the common market.

Article 86 lists agreements which will typically fall under the provision, including those which fix prices or control production. However the Commission retains the right to grant exemption where the agreement in question has economic benefits. Any alleged benefits must extend in their effect to consumer interests.

3.11 CONTRACTUAL TERMS

The previous section dealt with a particular type of contractual term which is of importance in certain types of contract. The nature, scope and subject matter of the terms which might make up the substance of the obligations under any given contract are infinite. In attempting to define the boundaries of the parties' contractual obligations in any given case we must ask ourselves several key questions. How does the law interpret what the parties have said or done or written? What will the law add to the parties' expressed wishes, either to make more sense of the agreement or to protect one party?

3.11.1 What the parties say, do or write

Whether the agreement is oral, written, to be inferred from the actions of the parties, or a combination of all of these, the cardinal principle underlying what may be taken to have been agreed is that it should be judged objectively. This means that if two people appear, *from all the evidence*, to have committed themselves in a certain way then they cannot successfully allege that this was not their true intention (see 3.3.3.2 above). The law will not look at their innermost minds but only at what they can bring in evidence to illustrate the objective face of the agreement (see 3.13.1.1 below).

With this point in mind, we must examine the rules used by the law to interpret what has happened. We use 'interpretation' in two senses. First in its 'technical' sense, i.e. what does a word or expression mean? Secondly to describe the court's task of determining: (i) the differing degrees of import-ance which the parties may place on their contractual obligations; and (ii) in the context of often complex and protracted negotiations, which statements, promises etc should form part of the contractual obligation?

3.11.1.1 Technical interpretation Our intention is to state the basic principles.

(a) Words and phrases should be given their clear everyday meaning.

(b) Ambiguous words should be interpreted so as to give effect to the contract. Businessmen are not expected to be as precise as lawyers in what they say or do, but if their agreement is so vague as to be uncertain it cannot be enforced (see 3.6 above).

(c) The rules of statutory interpretation discussed in Chapter 1 (see para. 1.2.3.1) are applied to contracts to clarify any uncertainty.

(d) Contracts which restrict freedom, e.g., a restraint of trade clause or a burden on land, are construed strictly. Unless they are expressed with the utmost clarity they will be unenforceable.

(e) Standard form contracts and exclusion clauses are construed *contra proferentem* (against the offeror). This basically means that any ambiguity will be interpreted in favour of the party who is not relying on the term in his action.

(f) If there is a written contract, oral or documentary evidence cannot be brought to add to, vary or contradict the written terms. However it seems that acquiescence by one party in the modification or non-observance of written terms may be proved by oral evidence. This would excuse the non-observance of a contractual term (*Taylor* v *Duffs Inns* (1869) 7 M 357) but would not constitute a modification for the future (*Kirkpatrick* v *Allanshaw Coal Co* (1850) 8 R 327).

3.11.1.2 The relative importance of contractual terms The first stage in such a determination is to recognise the varying levels of status that parties may accord their obligations under a contract. Parties may elect that their obligations arise automatically or that they are to be dependent on some external factor such as a specified future event. As amongst these obligations they may say that some are material and others not, the former justifying rescission if broken and the latter only damages (see 3.15.3 and 3.15.5 below). In the absence of any express intention by the parties, the court will make a decision as to materiality based on the commercial importance of the term to the innocent party and the extent to which the breach affects the fundamentals of the contract. In certain contexts, such as shipping, particular terms are traditionally classified as material, e.g., the capacity of a ship for a particular cargo or the date of expected readiness to load.

Scots law does not have the rigid classification of conditions and warranties, which is operated in English law and roughly corresponds to the Scottish classification of material and non-material. As such English cases on this area, although useful for example and analogy, must be treated with care. One of the main problems faced by the English courts has been how to treat a term which is labelled a 'condition', but the breach of which may or may not have serious consequences. Some judges feel that if a term is called a condition it must be assumed that the parties thought of it as being a material term and intended a breach to result in repudiation of the contract. Others are more inclined to take a position nearer to Scots law and examine the seriousness of the consequences (see *Hong Kong Fir Shipping Co Ltd* v *Kawasaki Kisen Kaisha Ltd* [1962] 2 QB 26).

3.11.1.3 The extent of the contractual obligation It may be that before we even reach the stage of assessing the relative importance of contractual obligations, the circumstances are such that it is unclear as to which statements, promises etc actually form part of the contract. This arises most typically in the case of statements which are made by sellers about the product which they are trying to sell. Such statement may be made before or at the time of an agreement, which could be oral or written. The law must decide on the status it wishes to accord to such claims and assertions, so that if they turn out to be false or exaggerated the aggrieved party will know how to frame his action.

This basic distinction is between statements, promises etc which are regarded as terms of the contract and those which are regarded as non contractual representations. The criteria operated by the courts seems to depend on the importance placed on the statement by the person at whom it was directed (*Bannerman* v *White* 1861 10 CBNS 844); the lapse of time between the making of the statement and the final contract (*Routledge* v *McKay* [1954] 1 All ER 855); and the expertise of the party making the statement (*Oscar Chess Ltd* v *Williams* [1957] 1 All ER 325, *Dick Bentley Productions Ltd* v *Harold Smith (Motors) Ltd* [1965] 2 All ER 65). The greater importance a pursuer has placed on a statement, particularly if made by an expert seller, and the closer in time to the contract, the more likely it is that the statement will be a contractual term (allowing recovery for breach of contract if the statement is false).

3.11.1.4   Damages for breach of a collateral contract   Another approach which
was developed by the courts to this type of statement was to construe it as a
collateral contract. The idea is that it is not a term of the main contract,
rather it is on the strength of that statement that the main contract has been
made. As such it is thought to be of sufficient signficance to be given
contractual force. This device is often used in hire-purchase sales, such as in
Brown v *Sheen & Richmond Car Sales Ltd* [1950] 1 All ER 1102, where the
salesman promised that the car would give 'thousands of trouble free miles'.
On the strength of this false statement, the customer entered into a hire-
purchase agreement with a finance company. That statement was treated as
a collateral contract and the customer was entitled to damages for breach of
this contract.

3.11.1.5   Damages for misrepresentation   If a statement is not a term but a
non-contractual representation and it is made negligently and it induces the
other party to contract there is now a remedy in damages under the Law
Reform (Miscellaneous Provisions) (Scotland) Act 1985, s. 10(1).

3.11.1.6   Reasonable expectations   The rules just described are examples of
the law not being content with the formal terms of a contract as definitive of
the obligations being placed on the parties. So remedies are given in respect
of pre-contractual statements, and the expectations they generate, when the
'formal' contractual terms may purport to be offering lesser commitment. It
is clear that if there was no concern over the protection of reasonable
expectations the law could construe contractual intention just to cover the
formal document, thereby not allowing for enforceability of pre-contractual
statements. Reasonable expectations also play a role in the control of
exemption clauses, controlled partly because they depart from reasonable
expectations as to the other party's obligations and the remedies available for
breach of these obligations.

In one provision, UCTA 1977 speaks *explicitly* of terms which depart from
the reasonable expectations of the customer or consumer (see s. 17(1)(a) at
3.11.6.4. below and set out in the Cases and Materials section for Chapter
3). Other sections control exemption of liability for the sort of reasonable
expectations enforced by the above rules on pre-contractual statements. This
is done by the control of terms exempting liability for breach of contract,
which includes a collateral contract (s. 17(1)(a) at 3.11.6.4), and the control
of terms exempting liability for negligent misrepresentation (s. 16, 3.11.6.1
below, and see Cases and Materials section for Chapter 3).

3.11.2   Implied terms

In addition to what the parties say or do in the context of their agreement,
the law may decide that other terms should be added to the contract. This
may be done for a number of reasons. However, the aim is generally either
to give recognition to the customs of a particular trade; to give effect to
normal expectations in certain recognised relationships; to generally give the

contract business efficacy; or to set a standard for goods and services. Again it seems that there is a concern to reflect the reasonable expectations of the parties. The law could easily take a narrow view of contractual intention and simply enforce what the parties take the time and effort expressly to articulate. However, it chooses to add to this to reflect reasonable expectations. Although there must be actual agreement or consent for core elements of the agreement, it is difficult to speak of many of the implied terms below being based on agreement.

3.11.2.1 Terms implied by custom or trade usage If a custom in a particular trade or profession is reasonable, clear and well established it is binding on parties dealing in that trade or profession, whether or not they are aware of it.

3.11.2.2 Terms implied in particular relationships Subject to express contrary agreement, the courts will imply standard terms into established categories of contract. For example, the employer's duty to remunerate his employee for work carried out under a contract of employment does not require to be explicitly spelled out in any written or verbal agreement.

3.11.2.3 Terms implied to give business efficacy The courts will imply terms which are necessary to make sense of a contract. In *Moorcock* (1889) 14 PD 64, the contract provided for a vessel to come alongside a jetty to discharge her cargo at low water. When she did so she was damaged by coming to rest on hard ground when the tide ebbed. The court implied a term to the effect that it was safe for her to come alongside the jetty at low tide.

The courts will also imply terms which it is established were so obvious to the parties that they felt no need to state them expressly. This is done by means of the 'officious bystander' test. The nature of this test was described in the famous judgment by MacKinnon LJ in *Shirlaw* v *Southern Foundries Ltd* [1939] 2 KB 206, where he said:

> Prima facie that which in any contract is let to be implied and need not be expressed is something so obvious that it goes without saying; so that, if, while the parties were making their bargain, an officious bystander were to suggest some express provision for it in their agreement, they would testily suppress him with a common 'Oh, of course!'

It is worthy of emphasis that the matter in question would have to be something non-contentious, otherwise both parties are unlikely to agree with the officious bystander. For example, in *Spencer* v *Cosmos Holidays, The Times*, 24 November 1989, the defendant tour operators sought to incorporate a term in their contract of booking with the plaintiff. This was to the effect that if the hotel should wrongly eject the plaintiff the defendants would not be responsible unless they were at fault. The court held that if the officious bystander had suggested such a term to the parties the plaintiff would have replied 'No fear!' The term was consequently not implied.

3.11.2.4   Terms implied in contracts for the supply of goods and services to set standards   Parliament has imposed obligations as to title, quality, fitness and description in contracts for the sale of goods (see Chapter 6 below). Exclusion or limitation of these obligations is controlled by s. 20 of the Unfair Contract Terms Act 1977 (see below). In contracts for the supply of services (*locatio operis faciendi*) where professional or technical skill is involved (doctors, lawyers, tradesmen, builders, repairers, etc.), there is a duty to exercise reasonable care and skill in the performance of a service, although not necessarily to bring about a particular result (see Bell, *Comm.* 1, 489, *Prin* 153; *Fish* v *Kapur* [1948] 2 All ER 176). So a lawyer must recognise the authorities relevant to his client's case that a reasonably competent lawyer would notice; a doctor must recognise symptoms and make a diagnosis as astutely and accurately as would the average doctor; but neither (in the performance of the reasonable care and skill duty) is committed to securing success. The lawyer need not win the case, the doctor need not cure the patient — unless any reasonably competent lawyer or doctor would have done so, e.g., where there is so little evidence for a conviction that only an objectively incompetent defence would have failed to secure an acquittal. Exclusion or limitation of the duty of care and skill is controlled by the Unfair Contract Terms Act 1977, s. 16 (see below).

If no fee has been agreed a reasonable fee will be payable, unless there is evidence that gratuitous services were intended (*Mackersy's Exors* v *St Giles Cathedral Board* [1904] 12 SLT 391).

Apart from general principles such as these, the law has also developed rules to deal with specialised problems of particular relationships. For example, problems of disclosure and warranties in insurance contracts; confidentiality and presentation of cheques in banker-customer contracts; passing of property and risk in building contracts; loading, deviation from route, delivery, delay, etc. in contracts of carriage. We do not have the space necessary to examine these rules in detail, and readers are referred to Walker, *Private Law*, vol. 2 (1988), Butterworths, v284–501 for an encyclopaedic summary. Those especially interested in banking services should refer to Wallace and McNeil, *Banking Law*, (1991), W. Green Ltd. However, we have taken the opportunity to include in the Cases and Materials section for Chapter 3 some discussion of rules specific to insurance contracts and also discussion of codes of practices and ombudsmen applicable to banking and insurance services. We felt this to be important, not only because these services are important in a modern economy, but also because the provisions in question provide interesting case studies of the increased consumer protection which codes and ombudsmen can often bring to the consumer.

3.11.3   Exemption clauses

This section is concerned with a particular species of contract term; one which attempts to exclude or restrict the liability of the supplier of goods and services for liability for defective performance. As has been said above, the defective performance may often be a failure to meet the consumer's or customer's reasonable expectations, as well as a failure to adhere to express terms. Such terms are commonly known as exemption clauses and some are controlled by the Unfair Contract Terms Act 1977 (see 3.11.4 to 3.11.8 below for full discussion; they are also now controlled, as are most consumer contract terms, by the Regulations on Unfair Terms in Consumer Contracts (see 30.11.9 below). Before the 1977 Act need even be brought into play, however, it is important to determine whether the clauses or terms in question form part of the contract between the parties. If they do not then they are of no effect on this ground alone, irrespective of what may be said by the 1977 Act.

It is also necessary to decide whether the clause in question uses language which is effective to exclude the particular liability which has arisen (see 3.11.3.3 below). However, before asking either of these questions the first step must be to decide on the liability which arises in the absence of the exemption clause.

3.11.3.1 Liability arising in the absence of the clause The possibilities are endless, but the most common types of liability would be for failure to deliver goods or services of the standard fixed by the above rules as to quality, reasonable care and skill, etc.; for late or wrong delivery; or generally for failure to perform adequately a term of the contract.

It is vital to clarify, at the outset, the liability or liabilities potentially involved for two reasons:

(a)   without doing so it is impossible to know whether the language of the exemption clause covers this liability;

(b)   without doing so it is impossible to apply the provisions of the Unfair Contract Terms Act. The application of this Act depends on the type of liability being excluded.

3.11.3.2 Enforceability of exemption clauses: incorporation in the contract The second question we may ask is 'can the clause be taken to have been incorporated in the contract?'. This really means asking whether the parties, or more importantly the party who is prejudiced by the clause, may be taken to have agreed to it. Such agreement will normally be inferred in circumstances where a document containing the terms has been signed, even if the terms had neither been read nor understood (*L'Estrange* v *F Graucob Ltd* [1934] 2 KB 394), unless the signatory has been misled about the effect of the clause (*Curtis* v *Chemical Cleaning & Dyeing Co* [1951] 1 KB 805). This objective analysis of the evidence may be subject to exception where the clause is so unusual or onerous or prejudicial to the rights of the signatory that it should have been specially drawn to his attention. So it has been held recently (*Interfoto* v *Stilletto* [1988] 1 All ER 348) that a clause stipulating for extremely high compensation where photographs were not returned to a library on time was invalid because it had not been specifically drawn to the attention of the borrower. This approach is clearly based on a suspicion of the extent to which customers are really consenting to small print terms. However, the rule in question only goes so far as to require disclosure. If this is done then the term passes the test even if the bargaining environment is otherwise unfair (e.g., because there is disparity of bargaining strength or no alternative and better terms are on offer) and despite the degree of substantive unreasonableness of the term. These broader fairness issues can, however, be looked at under UCTA 1977 or the Directive on Unfair Terms in Consumer Contracts (see 3.11.8 below). The *Interfoto* approach will be most helpful to commercial parties who are burdened by terms which are not exemption clauses (like the clause in the case itself), and which are not therefore covered by UCTA 1977.

Returning now to what common-law controls there are on exemption clauses (on top of what UCTA 1977 provides), there is some doubt as to the applicability of *Interfoto* to exemption clauses. It cannot be said with certainty that the court would have taken the same approach if the clause had been one excluding or restricting liability. The other authority on this point is *Thornton* v *Shoe Lane Parking* [1971] 2 QB 163, where it was held that a notice excluding liability for personal injury required a more explicit warning than that given. However this authority must be qualified in two respects. First it did not relate to a clause in a signed document but to a notice on display in a car park. Secondly it had already been decided by the court that the clause did not form part of the contract because it had not been drawn to the customer's attention at the time the contract was made.

Whatever the precise extent of the *Interfoto* special prominence rule, in all cases the question is whether the clause has been adequately drawn to the attention of the other party at the time when the contract was made. This really depends on two factors. First whether sufficient prominence has been given to the clause either in the signed document or wherever it is to be found, e.g., on a ticket or notice. The clause may be referred to on such notice or ticket as long as the reference itself is given sufficient prominence. So the reference may be on the face of the ticket and say 'See back for conditions', or it may be that a notice on packaged goods refers to 'conditions of contract currently in force and obtainable on request'. These are lower requirements than the *Interfoto special* prominence rule. *Sufficient* prominence is given to a collection of terms which are reasonably clear and available, or even which are clearly referred to via a chain of reference of the sort described, which involves only providing a ticket which clearly draws attention to the existence of conditions. This is far from specially drawing attention to a particular term. Secondly, prominence must be given to the clause at the time when the contract was made. So, in *Olley* v *Marlborough Court Hotel* [1949] 1 KB 532, a notice was prominently enough displayed in a hotel bedroom. However, the contract for the let of the room had clearly taken place at the reception desk. The notice could therefore not in any sense be seen as a term of the contract. Similarly, if goods have been ordered and delivered, an exclusion of liability which arrives with the goods is not a term of the contract for the sale of goods. It is clear therefore that the question will often turn on when (chronologically) the agreement may be said to have been finalised (see offer and acceptance and the 'battle of the forms' – 3.3 above). In keeping with the prevailing philosophy that agreements should be analysed objectively, it will not normally matter that subjective factors affecting one party at the time, e.g., blindness, illiteracy or inadvertence, mean that he did not in reality have notice of the terms. However, where it can be shown that the party relying on the clause is aware of the ignorance or misunderstanding, it may be that a greater effort must be made to give notice to the other party.

It is possible to infer notice of a clause where the clause has been used in a well established and consistent course of dealing between the parties. This may be appropriate where, in the particular circumstances, notice of the clause has not been given or comes too late. In *Spurling* v *Bradshaw* [1956] 2 All ER 121, a receipt containing an exemption clause was delivered after the contract was made. In previous dealings the plaintiff had often received a similar document and had not troubled to read it. The clause was held to be incorporated into the present contract by virtue of the previous dealing. Presumably a similar decision would have been made in *Olley* v *Marlborough Court* (see above) if the guest in question had stayed at the hotel on a number of previous occasions. In *McCutcheon* v *David McBrayne Ltd* 1964 SC HL 28, however, the course of dealing had been inconsistent and therefore the failure of the shipping company to ask the customer to sign the risk note was fatal to its incorporation in the contract. (See *Wm. Teacher & Sons Ltd* v *Bell Lines Ltd* 1991 SCLR 130 (OH) for a recent discussion of these issues.)

A further factor to be considered may be whether the document which contains the clause is one which a reasonable man might assume to contain contractual terms. The question is whether it could be taken to form an integral part of the contract or rather simply was an acknowledgement or receipt for payment or advertising literature. In *Chapelton* v *Barry UDC* [1940] 1 KB 532 a ticket for the use of a deckchair was held to be no more than a receipt for payment and, as such, words which appeared on it could not be treated as contractual terms. In *Taylor* v *Glasgow Corp* 1952 SC 440, a ticket for entry to public baths was seen in the same way. However, transport tickets tend to be seen differently, and to be construed as contractual documents on which passengers can expect to find conditions or a reference to conditions (*Thompson* v *London Midland & Scottish Rly Co* [1930] 1 KB 41).

3.11.3.3 Enforceability of exemption clauses: what liability is excluded? The third question to be asked is 'does the clause cover the particular type of liability in question?' This should be a simple question of the language used in the clause. However, because the courts have traditionally felt that exemption clauses were unduly burdensome on the weaker party to the bargain, they developed certain rules of construction which were intended to limit the circumstances in which a clause would be effective to cover the liability in question.

The most basic and general principle was the application of the *contra proferentem* rule (see 3.11.1.2 above), which involves interpreting any ambiguities in favour of the party who is prejudiced by the clause.

A complicated body of case law has developed around clauses excluding or restricting liability for negligence. The first clear principle is that if there is liability for breach of contract and negligence, a generally worded clause (e.g., which refers simply to 'no liability') will be construed only to cover the breach of contract liability, and not the negligence liability (*White v John Warwick & Co* [1953] 2 All ER 1021). However if the language used is sufficiently clear and unambiguous then negligence will be covered along with breach of contract. An example of such a clause is afforded by *Ailsa Craig Fishing Co Ltd v Malvern Fishing Co Ltd* 1982 SC (HL) 14, where the clause limited liability in the case of 'any liability . . . under the express or implied terms of this contract or at common law, or in any other way'.

A generally worded clause will usually cover liability for negligence if such liability is all that arises in the circumstances. For example, in *Alderslade v Hendon Laundry Ltd* [1945] 1 All ER 244, liability for 'lost or damaged articles' in a contract to launder some handkerchiefs was limited to twenty times the contract price. This was held to be sufficient to cover loss caused by negligence as negligence was the only type of potential liability in the circumstances.

Even where there is a fundamental breach of contract, liability for such may be covered if the clause is clear enough. This was clarified by the House of Lords in *Photo Production Ltd v Securicor* [1980] AC 827. This case involved a contract whereby an employee of the defendants was to patrol the premises of the plaintiff to prevent burglaries or fires. The defendants' patrolman deliberately started a fire on the premises causing damage of £615,000. This clearly amounted to a fundamental breach of contract on the part of the defendants. However, they successfully argued in the House of Lords that their exemption clause covered such circumstances. The clause had stated Securicor not 'to be responsible for any injurious act or default by any employee . . . unless such act or default could have been foreseen and avoided by the exercise of due diligence'. The Court of Appeal had held that an exclusion clause could not protect a party from liability for fundamental breach of contract. This had been in line with the Court of Appeal's view in a series of cases (*Karsales (Harrow) Ltd v Wallis* [1956] 2 All ER 866, *Harbutt's Plasticine Ltd v Wayne Tank & Pump Co Ltd* [1907] 1 QB 447). Such an approach was clearly intended to impose a limitation on the use of exemption clauses where it was felt that their application could effectively negate one party's responsibilities under a contract.

The House of Lords, however, affirmed the position taken in *Suisse Atlantique Société d'Armement Maritime SA v Rollerdamsche Kolen Centrale NV* [1967] 1 AC 361 and felt unable to interfere with the right of contracting parties to allocate risks as they saw fit. Lord Wilberforce made specific reference in his judgment to the (then new) Unfair Contract Terms Act 1977 (see 3.11.4 below), which he said was evidence of Parliament's wish to intervene in certain types of contract (consumer and standard form) and either outlaw exemption clauses or impose a test of fairness. He concluded that in respect of contractual terms not covered by the Act, the courts should be slow to interfere with the parties' right to apportion risk as they saw fit.

(For detailed discussion of these rules, see Willett, *Unfair Terms in Consumer Contracts*, forthcoming, (1996), Chapter 4.)

3.11.4 The effect of the Unfair Contract Terms Act 1977

The Unfair Contract Terms Act 1977 was passed in response to the Law Commission's *Second Report on Exemption Clauses*. This report sympathised with the judicial suspicion of exemption clauses, pointing out that they were usually to be found on complex standard form contracts. Such a contract would be presented to a consumer on a 'take it or leave it' basis, and even if he appreciated what it contained he would be unlikely to appreciate the manner in which it affected his rights. It has been argued elsewhere that this may make for a lack of real choice for individual consumers and customers. Also, if only small numbers of buyers appreciate the degree to which their expectations are being undermined, or even that there is in theory the opportunity to bargain, the mass market of buyers is unlikely to be able to exert market pressure for improved terms: Willett, *Unfair Terms in Consumer Contracts*, forthcoming, (1995) Chapter 2. The Commission said that:

The result is that the risk of carelessness or of failure to achieve satisfactory standards of performance is thrown on to the party who is not responsible for it or who is unable to guard against it. Moreover by excluding liability for such carelessness or failure the economic pressures to maintain high standards of performance are reduced.

The title of the Act is misleading, as it suggests that the Act provides general protection against the use of 'unfair' terms in contracts. Were this the case, any term could be set aside if it was thought unfair or prejudicial to the interests of the weaker party in the contract. This might potentially include price variation clauses, restraint of trade clauses, clauses stipulating for an unreasonably high security or charging an unreasonably high price for goods, exemption clauses and innumerable other types of term. A general test of unfairness, applying to most terms in *consumer* contracts, is contained in the Unfair Terms in Consumer Contracts Regulations (see 3.11.9 below).

3.11.5 The provisions of the Unfair Contract Terms Act 1977

The full text of the relevant sections is reproduced in the Cases and Materials section for Chapter 3. In particular these are intended to give practice at dealing with complex statutory material.

3.11.5.1 The scope of the Act The attention of the Act is focused mainly on exclusion or restriction of various types of liability arising within and beyond the scope of a contract (see 3.11.6 below). (The types of contract to which the Act does and does not apply are listed in s. 15, which is reproduced in the Cases and Materials section for Chapter 3.) The approach of the Act depends on whether the contract is a consumer contract, a standard form contract or a contract freely negotiated between the parties (see

3.11.6.2–3.11.6.4 below). More sections apply to the first two categories than to the third. A consumer contract is one where one party does, and the other does not, make the contract in the course of a business (or hold himself out as doing so), and the goods are of a type ordinarily supplied for private use or consumption. The onus is on the party alleging that the contract is not a consumer contract to prove this (s. 25(1)). It has been held in *R & B Customs Brokers Co Ltd v UDT Ltd and Saunders Abbot (1980) Ltd* [1988] 1 All ER 847 that there can be a consumer contract between two businesses if the purchaser is neither integral to the business nor a one-off trade venture. The case involved the sale of a used car to a 'two-man' company of shipping brokers who clearly were not in the business of buying cars and were therefore no different to a private buyer when it came to this type of purchase.

A standard form contract is any contract (whether a consumer or a commercial contract) in which the customer deals on the other party's written terms (s. 17(3). These terms may wholly written or partly written and partly oral, including a set of fixed terms which the party in question applies without material alteration (see *McCrone v Boots Farm Sales* 1981 SC 68). Presumably, therefore, if a purchaser was to extract concessions on material terms from a seller's standard form contract, it would cease to be classified as such, and would be seen as freely negotiated. The key significance of the contract being standard form is that s. 17 will apply even where the contract is not a consumer contract (see 3.11.6.4 below).

3.11.5.2 The effect of the Act   The keystone of the Act's approach is to render certain exemption clauses void and others subject to a test of reasonableness (see s. 24 and 3.11.6 below). Where the latter applies the onus is placed on the party relying on the clause to prove that it is reasonable. In *Continental Tyre & Rubber Co Ltd v Trunk Trailer Co Ltd* 1987 SLT 58, the Court of Session held that the party in question should make specific averments, addressing himself if appropriate to the criteria specified in the Act as being relevant. Section 24 starts by stating that in determining whether it was reasonable to incorporate a clause in a contract regard is to be had to the circumstances which were, or ought reasonably to have been, in the contemplation of the parties when the contract was made. Section s. 24(3) says that the courts should have particular regard to the resources available to the party relying on the term to meet the liability in question and how far it would have been open to that party to cover himself by insurance. Where the clause attempts to *limit* liability as opposed to excluding it completely or where the clause attempts to exclude or restrict liability for breach of the implied terms as to description, fitness or quality under the Sale of Goods Act 1979. Section 24(2) says the court should have particular regard to the criteria in sch. 2 to the Act. These are:

(a)   the strength of the bargaining positions of the parties relative to each other, taking into account (among other things) alternative means by which the customer's requirements could have been met;

(b)   whether the customer received an inducement to agree to the term, or in accepting it had an opportunity of entering into a similar contract with other persons but without having to accept a similar term;

(c)   whether the customer knew or ought reasonably to have known of the existence and extent of the term (having regard, among other things, to any custom of the trade and any previous course of dealing between the parties).

(d)   Where the term excludes or restricts any relevant liability if some condition is not complied with, whether it was reasonable at the time of the contract to expect that compliance with that condition would be practicable;

(e)   whether the goods were manufactured processed or adapted to the special order of the customer.

The approach of the courts to the reasonableness test will be discussed in greater depth below (see 3.11.7 below).

3.11.6   Types of clauses subject to control

The main types of clauses subject to control are dealt with in turn below.

3.11.6.1   Clauses excluding or restricting liability for breach of duty   Section 16 of the Act provides controls on exemption from liability for breach of duty for things done in the course of a business; it applies whether the breach of duty is contractual or delictual, and where it is contractual whether it is a consumer contract, a standard form contract or a freely negotiated contract. The duty in question may be a duty under a contract to exercise reasonable care and skill in the performance of a service such as repairing a car or laundering someone's clothes; a duty to exercise reasonable care and skill at common law (e.g., in the manufacture of products duties are owed to those with whom the manufacturer has no contractual relationship, such as consumers); or a duty to take reasonable care under a statute, such as the Occupiers' Liability (Scotland) Act 1960 (which deals with the safety of those visiting one's premises).

A term or notice clause which attempts to exclude or restrict liability for breach of any such duty will be void if it relates to personal injury or death and subject to the test of fairness and reasonableness if it relates to other types of loss. Section 16 covers the type of clause which attempts to restrict or exclude the *existence* of a duty in the first instance. This point has been confirmed in the decisions on negligent valuations (*Smith* v *Bush* [1989] 2 WLR 790 and *Harris* v *Wyre Forest DC* [1989] 2 WLR 790). The effect of this section on common law duties and duties arising under the Occupiers' Liability (Scotland) Act 1960, which may arise outwith the contractual nexus, is really the province of Chapter 4, which deals with delict, and will be discussed there. The main impact of the section on contractual liability relates to the term implied in a contract for the performance of a service that it will be carried out with reasonable care and skill (see 3.11.2.4 above). There have been several decisions on the application of the reasonableness test to clauses which exclude or restrict liability for the negligent execution of a service. There are no specific statutory reasonableness guidelines for this type of liability. However, if the clause places a financial *limit* on the compensation payable (e.g., the contract price) then the courts may look at the two criteria in s. 24(3) which relate to the resources of the party relying on the clause and the extent to which it would have been feasible to cover himself by insurance.

In *Waldron-Kelly* v *BRB* 1981 CLY 303 and *Wright* v *BRB* 1983 CLY 424, the courts had to consider the reasonableness of a clause used by BRB, which limited liability for failure to deliver goods to a sum calculable by reference to the weight of the goods. In the former case the clause was held to be unreasonable. In the latter, however, the clause was upheld on the grounds that BRB had no means of knowing the true value of the goods. The owner had this knowledge and was in a better position to insure against loss (see s. 24(3)). A further reason given was that BRB's competitors in the carriage of goods offered terms which were often less generous to the consumer. This consideration is one of those contained in sch. 2 to the Act, which is intended to guide the court under s. 20 (clauses excluding or restricting liability for breach of implied terms as to description and quality in sales and hire-purchase contracts). However, it is clear that the courts do not feel restricted in the factors they will consider. This is further evidenced by the sch. 2 criteria considered in *Woodman* v *Photo Trade Processing Ltd* 17 May 1981 (unreported) and *Warren* v *Truprint Ltd* [1986] BTLC, Luton County Court. In *Woodman* a clause limiting liability to the cost of a replacement film was held to be unreasonable.

The following factors were considered relevant:

(a)   the clause offered no insurance facility and no advice was given to insure;

(b)   the customer's attention was not specifically drawn to the clause (from sch. 2);

(c)   the Code of Practice for the Photographic Industry recommended a two-tier service with total exclusion of liability in the case of normal service, and full acceptance of liability in the case of the more expensive special service. The special service was not offered in this case.

On all of these grounds the clause was held to be unreasonable.

In *Philips Products Ltd* v *Hyland* [1987] 2 All ER 620 the negligent driver of a hired excavator damaged the hirer's factory. The clause in question purported to place responsibility on the hirer. It was held to be unreasonable on the grounds that the hirers did not regularly hire plant and drivers, exercised no control over the drivers and had little opportunity to arrange insurance.

We can see that two particular factors, i.e. the degree of choice available to the consumer and who is best able to insure against the loss, are always of interest to the courts. In *Smith* v *Bush* (see above) the House of Lords said that these factors should always be looked at, along with the relative bargaining strengths of the parties and the difficulty of the task in respect of which liability is being excluded or limited.

These factors are also relevant to application of the test under s. 16 and ss. 20 and 17 below. One point which emerges is that in both consumer *and* commercial cases the courts tend to take the view that sellers and suppliers should insure on the basis of the liability norm in question (unless this is impractical or prohibitively expensive), rather than using an exemption clause. This is especially the case where it would be difficult for the other party to insure and/or where the seller or supplier is trying to avoid liability for negligence in itself or a breach of contract which took place negligently (see *Phillips* v *Hyland* above and *Mitchell* v *Finney Lock Seeds* below). The objection to avoiding liability for negligence reflects the attitude of the Law Commission (see above), to the effect that exemption clauses should not be a way of reducing pressures to maintain high standards. This point apart, offering a chance of full liability at a higher price (which will of course help pay for the supplier's insurance if the consumer takes up this option) will clearly assist a supplier's case (see *Woodman* v *Photo Trade Processing* above) where the consumer opts for the limited liability service and then challenges the clause.

3.11.6.2   Clauses excluding or restricting liability for breach of implied terms as to title, description, quality, and fitness for purpose   (See Chapter 6 for a full discussion of these terms.) Section 20 of the Act provides controls on the exemption from liability for breach of these implied terms.

Such exemption clauses are totally void in all contracts (whether standard form or freely negotiated) for the supply of goods (contracts of sale, exchange, hire-purchase, hire and work and materials) to the extent that they relate to title, e.g., a clause under which a seller excludes liability should it transpire that the goods are not his to sell would be void and of no effect (although the implied term as to title itself applies only to a limited extent where a contract of hire is concerned). To the extent that such clauses refer to the terms as to quality, description, or fitness for purpose, they are void in consumer contracts (whether standard form or freely negotiated) and subject to a test of reasonableness in other contracts, whether between businesses or private individuals and whether standard form or freely negotiated. However, it must be borne in mind that the implied terms as to quality and fitness only apply in the first place where the sale is in the course of a business (ss. 20 and 21).

In these contracts, the courts are pointed specifically in the direction of the sch. 2 guidelines for assessing reasonableness. They may of course look at the special factors relevant to limitation clauses, where appropriate (see s. 24(3)), and at whatever other factors are relevant in the circumstances. In *Mitchell* v *Finney Lock Seeds Ltd* [1983] 2 AC 803, liability for the sale of defective cabbage seeds was limited to the contract price. The House of Lords took into account the following factors in holding the clause to be unreasonable:

(a)   the ease and cheapness of insurance available to the defendants;
(b)   the negligence of the defendants;

(c)   the failure to follow past practice and negotiate a settlement with the purchaser in excess of the limitation imposed.

In *Knight Machinery (Holdings) Ltd* v *Rennie* 1995 SLT 166, it was held that the very least expected of a clause excluding or restricting this type of liability was that its effect be clear (see the Cases and Materials section for Chapter 3). Of course, this is a threshold requirement, and a term can easily fail the test on other grounds.

It is more likely that a clause in a freely negotiated contract would be more reasonable than one in a standard form contract.

3.11.6.3 Chains of responsibility   The combined provisions of the Unfair Contract Terms Act 1977 and the Sale of Goods Act 1979 may leave a retailer in a very precarious position where defective goods are supplied to a consumer. It will be impossible for him to avoid responsibility under the Sale of Goods Act (see 3.11.6.2 above). However, when he turns to his supplier to recover his losses he may find that any exemption clause in their contract is upheld. This is because the clause, being contained in a non-consumer contract, would not be void, but subject to the reasonableness test. It may be, however, that since the introduction of strict manufacturer's liability for defective products (Consumer Protection Action 1987, see 4.8 below), the consumer will choose to take action against the manufacturer, especially where he is more readily identifiable as 'being to blame'. This would reduce the burden on retailers who have traditionally been in the front line of liability to consumer buyers.

The Consumer Protection Act could however only be used where the product had caused injury or damage to property, and not where it was simply of poor quality (see Chapter 4, para. 4.8). The Consumer Guarantees Bill 1990, which failed to become law, sought to introduce remedies against manufacturers for poor quality products (for a discussion of the proposed 'consumer guarantee' see Willett, 'The Unacceptable Face of The Consumer Guarantees Bill' 54 (1991) MLR 552). It is likely that the European Union will soon introduce such a remedy (see Beale, in Willett (ed), 'Fairness in Contract', forthcoming, Elgar, 1996).

3.11.6.4 Clauses excluding or restricting liability for breach of contract   Not all breaches of contract by suppliers of goods and services relate to the implied terms as to fitness, quality, title, and description. For example, goods may be lost or not delivered or work may not be done to specification. The possibilities are endless and it is important that fitness, quality, title, and description are seen as only one category of contractual obligation.

Exemption clauses which relate to other types of obligation and the breach thereof, are covered by s. 17. The section applies where one of the contracting parties is a consumer or where the contract is on one party's written standard form contract. Any clause in such a contract which excludes or restricts liability for breach of a contractual obligation to a consumer or customer is subject to the test of reasonableness. So too is a clause which, in respect of a contractual obligation, claims to be entitled to render no performance or a performance substantially different from that which the consumer or customer reasonably expected from the contract (see the Cases and Materials section for Chapter 3, where a case decided under s. 17 is discussed).

These two limbs of s. 17 appear to be aimed at different types of clause. The first simply focuses on exclusion or restriction of liability for breaches such as non-delivery or late delivery of goods or failure to meet design specifications. The second limb focuses on the type of clause which attempts to water down the obligation undertaken below a level which a consumer would reasonably anticipate.

The *Zinnia* [1987] 2 Lloyds Rep 211 was decided on the English equivalent of the first limb. The clause in question sought to exclude liability for economic loss which arose after the wrong materials were used to repair a ship. The clause was held to be reasonable, particularly in view of the relatively equal bargaining position of the parties.

3.11.7 Criminal sanctions

It is a criminal offence, under the Consumer Transactions (Restrictions on Statements) Order 1976, to use void written exemption clauses. This would cover notices in shops such as 'no refunds' or 'sale goods may not be returned', which would clearly be void under s. 20 (see 3.11.6.2 above). It would also cover notices which attempt to restrict or exclude liability for negligence by a supplier of a service, e.g., a notice at a swimming pool which reads 'no liability for death or injury howsoever caused'.

3.11.8 Unfair Terms in Consumer Contracts Regulations 1994

These regulations were passed to implement the EU Directive on Unfair Terms in Consumer Contracts (93/13/EEC of 5 April 1993). The Directive is based upon a similar idea as UCTA 1977 in the UK, i.e. that consumers (the Directive applies only to consumer contracts) have little real choice in the face of a supplier's terms. As such terms can justifiably be tested for fairness. The Regulations contain an annex to indicate the sort of terms which may be regarded as unfair (Regulation 4(4), Sch. 3). Many of these are exemption clauses which would be covered by UCTA 1977, and again we might say that part of the unfairness lies in the idea that they depart from the consumer's reasonable expectations as to the supplier's obligations and liabilities.

However, any term can be tested for fairness under the Regulations as long as it does not define the price or the main subject matter of the contract. Even then it can be tested if it is not plain and intelligible language (regulation 3(2)). The annex contain terms which are clearly not exemption clauses, e.g., those which involve the imposition of an unreasonable burden by the supplier on the consumer (term (e)), or which involve a burden or obligation being placed on a consumer when the supplier does not bear proportionate obligations or burdens (see terms (d) and (f)). Another theme of unfairness in the annex involves terms which give unilateral control to the supplier to alter, terminate, etc. the relationship (see terms (g), (j) and (k)). Some of these terms might already be caught by UCTA 1977, especially by s. 17(1)(b). However, whether or not this is the case is possibly incidental, because the test of unfairness in the regulations applies *in addition* to the UCTA controls and any other common-law controls which may apply (e.g., as to disclosure under the *Interfoto* rule — see 3.11.3.2. above). Under the regulations a term is unfair if, 'contrary to the requirements of good faith it causes a significant imbalance in the rights and obligations arising under the contract, to the detriment of the consumer' (Regulation 4(1)). It is possible that this test is more favourable to consumers than the reasonableness test under UCTA 1977. If a term is unfair it will not be binding upon the consumer, but the remainder of the contract will continue to be binding if this is possible without the unfair term (Regulation 5). The regulations also require that terms be drafted in plain and intelligible language, and say that ambiguities will be construed in favour of the consumer (regulation 6). In addition, the regulations give a power to the Director General of Fair Trading to seek an interdict to prevent the use of unfair terms (regulation 8). This seeks to implement Article 7 of the Directive, which requires adequate and effective means to be used to control unfair terms (other than the right of individual consumers to challenge terms in their own contracts). The adequate and effective means is supposed to include the right to take action being vested in those having a legitimate interest in protecting consumers (Article 7(2)). It is open to some question as to whether it is sufficient to give this power to the Director General. Article 7(2) may require a right of action to be given to bodies such as the Consumers' Association and the National Consumer Council. The Consumers' Association is currently seeking judicial review of the decision not to give them access to the courts.

The Cases and Materials section of Chapter 3, contains an extract written by one of the authors on the test of unfairness (for further analysis see Willett, *Unfair Terms in Consumer Contracts*, forthcoming 1996; Willett, 'Unfair Terms in Consumer Contracts' (1994) *Consumer Law Journal*, vol. 2, No 4, 114; Willett, 'Unfair Terms & Redistribution of Power' (1994) 17 *Journal of Consumer Policy* Nos 3–4, 471; Willett, 'Plain Language in Consumer Contracts' (1995) 210 *SCOLAG* 28).

3.12   AGREEMENT IMPROPERLY OBTAINED

The agreement of one of the parties to a contract may have been obtained in a manner of which the law disapproves in some respect, e.g., by false or misleading promises (misrepresentation), the exertion of unfair pressure (duress), or by taking advantage or either one's own dominant position or the particularly weak position of the other party (undue influence, facility and circumvention). The general effect of such impropriety is to render the contract voidable (see 3.7.2 above).

There are at least two ways of contrasting these rules with those on the fairness and reasonableness of terms at 3.11 above. First, the above rules apply to specific types of contract or contract terms, while the rules discussed below apply to all terms. So it is only a consumer who can rely on the protection of the Unfair Terms Regulations, and then only where the term is not the price or main subject matter; but if a party is misled or coerced by another then no matter whether he is a consumer or any other purchaser, or indeed a seller, the contract (including main subject matter and price terms) will be voidable. A second distinction is that the rules to be discussed below are concerned with specific instances of advantage taking in which the innocent party's real choice is in some way limited. The rules on terms, on the other hand, tend to be grounded in a much more general suspicion of the extent to which certain transactions ever involve real choice in respect, at least, of some of the terms. This is allied with a concern to regulate those terms by reference to some notion of fairness (see discussion above).

3.12.1 Misrepresentation

The sellers of goods, services and property will inevitably make a wide range of promises and assertions in relation to what they are trying to sell. Where such statements are relied upon by the buyer and turn out to be false, the buyer may be able to have the contract set aside for misrepresentation. He may also be able to claim damages. An understanding of this area requires two central questions to be addressed. First, when will a particular statement justify an action in misrepresentation? Second, what remedies are available? In answering these questions we can often draw conclusions as to the deeper principles and interests which are being advanced and balanced with each other. The predominance of certain of these interests mean that the remedies for misrepresentation have certain limitations which are of considerable practical significance.

3.12.1.1 Actionable misrepresentation To be actionable, a statement must be an inaccurate statement of past or present fact, of a material nature, and it must have induced the other party to contract. It is important to distinguish between a statement of fact and various other types of statement, such as the following, which would not ground an action.

Sales puffs? Sales puffs are statements whose truth cannot be judged by any objective standard, e.g., 'a desirable residence', 'fertile and improvable land', or 'a magnificent view'. If a product is described as 'Top Class Coffee' it need not be top class, but it must be coffee. The latter is clearly a statement of fact. Equally if the sales puff purports to have the support of verifiable evidence, e.g., 'statistics show that . . . ', it will be treated as a statement of fact.
Opinion A subjective and personal opinion, e.g., that a piece of land will support a certain number of sheep (*Bissett* v *Wilkinson* [1927] AC 177), is not a misrepresentation, should it prove untrue. However, a stated opinion which is not honestly held will be a misrepresentation. An example would be a seller saying 'I *think* this is a Rembrandt', when, in fact, he does not think so at all. In addition, an 'opinion' given by someone with expertise is more likely to be viewed as a statement of fact (see *Esso Petroleum* v *Mardon* [1976] QB 801).
Statement as to the future. A statement of future intention, e.g., 'I plan to increase this company's profitability' is not a misrepresentation if the

intention does not come to fruition. It is a misrepresentation, however, if the intention does not in fact exist. For example, if an airline takes a booking knowing that the flight in question may be overbooked, then the ticket holder has effectively been misled as to the availability of seats (see *British Airways Board* v *Taylor* [1976] 1 All ER 65).

Silence or concealment   It will not generally be misrepresentation to fail to bring to the attention of the other party some fact which is material to the contract, e.g., that the mine which a person is selling is in fact rich with coal and worth much more than the seller is charging. However this principle is subject to exception in contracts *uberrimae fidei* (of the utmost good faith). These include contracts of insurance, contracts of partnership, and contracts for the purchase of shares in a company – there is also a duty to disclose where the parties stand in a fiduciary relationship toward each other (as do parent and child, trustee and beneficiary, agent and principal, and partners *inter se*). In such circumstances if one of the contracting parties is aware of information which would affect the other's view of the contract, he must disclose it.

In the context of insurance contracts, failure to disclose a material fact makes the contract voidable (*The Spathari* 1925 SC (HL) 6), even where the non disclosure is irrelevant to the claim. However, self-regulation has gone some way to limit the harshness of this rule for a private consumer who obtains insurance cover. The Statement of Insurance Practice, used voluntarily in the industry, instructs members to indicate to potential customers the matters which they regard as important. In addition, the Insurance Ombudsman has tended to depart from the strict legal position, saying that the claim allowed should be reduced only to the extent that the failure to disclose was relevant to it (see discussion by Rawlings & Willett, 'Ombudsmen in Financial Services in the UK', in the Cases and Materials section for Chapter 3).

Silence may also be held to constitute a misrepresentation where it positively misleads, whether as to the truth of a previous or current statement or the way in which particular actions will be understood. For instance, it would be misrepresentation to fail to correct a previous statement about the profitability of a business when, due to illness, such profitability was no longer enjoyed at the time of the actual sale (*With* v *O'Flanagan* [1936] 1 All ER 727 CA). It has also been held to be misrepresentation to refrain from pointing out that a gun barrel had deliberately been plugged in order to conceal a serious manufacturing defect (*Horsfall* v *Thomas* (1862) 1 H&C 90), and to fail to disclose that reconditioned cash registers were not in fact new (*Gibson* v *NCR* 1925 SC 500).

The false statement of fact must relate to a material matter, meaning that it would have induced a reasonable man to enter the contract (see Lord Carmont in *Ritchie* v *Glass* 1936 SLT 591, at pp. 593–4).

3.12.1.2   Was the misrepresentation actually acted upon?   Even if the misrepresentation is material, i.e. would normally influence a person, it will only render the contract voidable if it has been acted upon and served to induce the contract in question. This will generally be assumed where it is material.

However, if the other party is ignorant or indifferent to the misrepresentation or has exercised his own judgment in entering into the contract then the validity of the contract will not be affected. For example, in *Horsfall* v *Thomas* (see 3.12.1.1 above), although there was a deliberate attempt to mislead the purchaser of the gun, the latter did not even inspect the barrel and was clearly uninfluenced by the seller's machinations. In *Attwood* v *Small* (1838) 6 C&F 232, the seller of a mine exaggerated its earning capacity, but had little or no influence on the buyer who only entered into the transaction after relying on a report from his own agent that the seller's claims were true.

3.12.1.3 Actionable misrepresentation — rationale Although parties are normally bound to the agreements that they make, the concepts just discussed indicate that the law qualifies this where the agreement has been induced by material false statements relied upon by the other party, so that the reliance on the falsehood undermines the extent to which the representee is making a really free agreement. However, the full significance of this is seen only by looking at remedies and the limits on their use.

3.12.1.4 Remedies for misrepresentation and other options Misrepresentation renders a contract voidable and, as such, may allow the innocent party to set the contract aside. There may also be a claim in damages. However, these remedies are sometimes of limited assistance in practice to a party who has been misrepresented. This can be illustrated as follows.

The law classifies misrepresentation, for remedies purposes, according to the blameworthiness of the defender. If the statement is deliberately intended to mislead the other party or illustrates a reckless disregard for whether or not he is misled, then the statement is classified as a fraudulent misrepresentation (*Derry* v *Peek* (1889) 14 App. Cas. 337). If, on the other hand, the statement is made carelessly or negligently in circumstances which make it reasonable for the recipient of the statement to rely on its truth, the statement is a negligent misrepresentation (or misstatement) (*Hedley Byrne & Co.* v *Heller & Partners Ltd* [1964] AC 465); negligent misstatement is fully discussed in Chapter 4. In both cases the misrepresentation amounts to a delict, for which damages are payable. The Law Reform (Miscellaneous Provisions) (Scotland) Act 1985 confirmed that a party who has been induced to enter into a contract by a negligent misrepresentation may claim damages from the misrepresentor (see 4.2.4.2 below). However, if a misrepresentation is neither fraudulent nor negligent it is classed as innocent. This might be the case where a seller has reasonably placed faith in information given to him or contained in a brochure and has no reason to suspect that the statement might not be true. In such circumstances no delict has been committed and, as such, there is no claim for compensation. It may also be that the innocent recipient of the statement is unable to have the contract set aside because one of the circumstances exists which prevents the voidable contract being set aside. i.e. the parties cannot be restored to their original position; where a reasonable time has lapsed; or where property transferred under the voidable contract has now passed to a third party (see 3.7.2 above). These rules apply to protect the security of transactions and avoid the 'unravelling' of chains of contracts which may affect the rights of an unsuspecting third party who has since acquired the goods (see below). However, they mean that the misrepresentee may lose his right to rescind the contract. In *Boyd & Forrest* v *Glasgow & SW Ry Co* 1912 2 SC (HL) 93, a railway company misrepresented the hardness of the subsoil to the builders of the railway. This resulted in the cost of the work for the railway being approximately £136,000 more than was originally expected. Because of the nature of the contract, the parties could obviously not be restored to their original position and so the contract had to stand. Also, because the misrepresentation was seen as innocent, there could be no damages in respect of it. A similar problem would arise in a situation like a holiday booking contract which has been induced by a misleading claim about a hotel's facilities. The remedy of rescission is unavailable because the holiday clearly cannot be 'given back', in any sense. A similar problem will arise in any case where the subject matter of the contract is a service or goods which have been consumed or resold or in any other case where the right to recission has been lost (see 3.7.2 above).

In the search for some redress the party who has been misled in such circumstances has several options. One option is to attempt to have the representation construed as a term of the contract or as a collateral contract, and thereby obtain damages for breach of contract (see 3.11.1.3–3.11.1.4 above). Another option would be to argue that the maker of the statement *was* in fact negligent in not checking the information before passing it on and is therefore liable to pay damages under the 1985 Act (see above). That may be difficult in Scots law, not least because it first must be proved that a duty of care not to make careless statements was owed by the other party. It must then be proved that the other party did not take reasonable care in making the statement, i.e. it seems that the Scots remedy is still grounded in the *Hedley Byrne* common-law duty of care, which has simply been statutorily extended to apply as between contracting parties. The problems of establishing a duty of care and breach of the duty are discussed in relation to delict (see Chapter 4, para. 4.3). The position of the party relying on a misrepresentation and entering a contract was greatly improved in English law by the Misrepresentation Act 1967 which eradicated the need to prove the existence of a duty of care. All that is required to be shown is that the statement has induced the contract and was untrue (Misrepresentation Act 1967, s. 2(1)). The onus is then on the maker of the statement to prove that he took reasonable care in checking stated facts. This brings more statements within the ambit of control as there will always be circumstances where A has suffered from relying on statements but is unable to prove that they were made negligently; at the same time B may, if asked to prove the contrary, find it impossible to do so. This encourages parties to take greater care in making pre-contractual claims and assertions. There will never be any need for an English misrepresentee now to use the *Hedley Byrne* route to damages for negligent misstatement, as long as it was a misstatement which induced a contract.

Indeed, English misrepresentees have two further advantages. First, damages under s. 2(1) of the 1967 Act are assessed as if the misrepresentation had been made fraudulently (i.e. unforeseeable losses are recoverable — see *Royscott Trust Co Ltd* v *Rogerson* [1991] 2 QB 297, [1991] 3 All ER CA — such losses would not be recoverable under the common law negligence principles which the Scottish 1985 Act is based on). Secondly, English misrepresentees may, at the discretion of the court, obtain damages in lieu of rescission if rescission would have been available. This may be useful if rescission is unprofitable for the buyer, who wishes to sell the product on.

3.12.1.5 Restrictions on remedies reviewed Although the law formally recognises the idea that it is wrong to mislead another party in such a way as to induce him to enter a contract, it also places importance on the security of transactions and the rights of third-party purchasers and consequently restricts the misrepresentee's right to rescind. Scots law is also markedly less ready to award damages for non fraudulent misrepresentation than is English law, adhering to the requirement of a special relationship between the parties giving rise to a duty of care, and the need for the pursuer to establish a breach of duty.

We can now consider the impact of the rescission rules on the particularly problematic situation where goods have been obtained by an innocent third party from a party, or via a party, who has obtained them from an original owner by misrepresentation.

3.12.1.6 Misrepresentees versus innocent third parties This problem arises mainly because of the rule that the right of the innocent party to have the contract set aside usually is lost if the goods have been sold to a third party who buys in good faith (see 3.7.2 above). This principle is most aptly illustrated by cases where a crook (A) fraudulently obtains goods on credit by misleading the seller (B) as to his creditworthiness or ability to pay. Typically the fraud will have been effected by the use of a stolen cheque book (*MacLeod* v *Kerr* 1965 SC 253) or by claiming to be a person of moral and financial substance whom the seller feels he can safely give credit to (see *Phillips* v *Brooks* [1919] 2 KB 243, where the buyer claimed to be 'Sir George Bullough' and was given a ring on credit by the jeweller; or *Lewis* v *Averay* [1971] 3 All ER 907, where the purchaser obtained goods on credit by claiming to be Richard Greene, the actor of 'Robin Hood' fame). The next stage is for the crook to sell the goods to an innocent third party (C) who has no knowledge of the prior dealings. If A discovers the fraud which has been perpetrated he must act to set the contract aside immediately (e.g., by contacting the police and/or the Automobile Association in the case of a car (see *Car & Universal Finance* v *Caldwell* [1965] 1 QB 524 where this was considered to be sufficient to avoid the contract. However, in *MacLeod* v *Kerr* it was held that contacting the police was not an act sufficient to avoid the contract (see Chapter 6 below para. 6.8). If the contract is set aside before B sells to C, then B cannot pass title to the car to C and A will be able to recover it from C or any subsequent buyer. However, if, before the voidable contract is set aside by A, C buys the car from B in good faith, then C will obtain title to the car. In such circumstances A will not be able to recover 'his' car. The problem with the obvious alternative of A bringing an action for damages against B is that B is likely to be unavailable, whether absconded or imprisoned, or insolvent. A (the original seller) is the most likely loser in such circumstances as he normally has not been able to set the original contract aside before B has sold the goods to C. A's only other option is to contend that B's misrepresentation induced a fundamental error in his mind about the contract, i.e. he thought he was dealing with another person entirely, e.g., the true owner of the cheque book or with whatever other person B may have claimed to be. If A can prove this, the conract will be wholly void, B will not be able to pass title to C, and A will therefore be able to recover the goods. The doctrine of error is discussed below (see 3.13.4). However, it should be recognised that the chances of such an action succeeding are very slim. If this does happen C is left to pursue B for breach of the implied term (s. 12, Sale of Goods Act) that he will pass good title to the goods. The practical chances of success against a crook such as B are slim to say the least. However, as has been said, it is normally the original owner who is the loser, the law regarding protection of the legitimate expectations/property rights of innocent purchasers as more important than those of misrepresentee sellers who part with their goods without security.

It may be that if the original owner has transferred his goods by barter rather than by sale, then fraud by the buyer will make the contract void rather than simply voidable, and he will be able to recover the goods from a third-party purchaser (*O'Neil* v *Chief Constable, Strathclyde* 1994 SCLR 253).

3.12.2   Force, fear and duress
A contract induced by violence or threats of sufficient magnitude which cause such fear as to overcome the will of a reasonable man will render a contract void (*Stair* I, 9,8; *Earl of Orkney* v *Vinfra* (1606) M 161 1). The key seems to be that the threat itself is illegitimate, in the sense of being a threat to do something unlawful (e.g., commit violence or blackmail), and that the consequence is that the other party is put in a position that he has no real choice. There clearly *is* a choice, i.e. to suffer the consequences. However, when it is said that the person's will has been overcome what is really meant is that the alternative is so unpleasant that a reasonable man would be persuaded. There is an exception in the case of a bill of exchange, e.g., a cheque. If a holder can establish that he gave value for the bill without any notice of objection, he may enforce it (Bills of Exchange Act 1882, ss. 29, 30, 38).

Threats of physical violence will clearly be rare in the legitimate business world, and as such there is a dearth of modern case law (see, however, the Australian case *Barton* v *Armstrong* [1975] 2 All ER 465, where one company director threatened to kill another if he would not buy him out). Nevertheless, the doctrine appears to be wide enough to accommodate cases where the threat is to break a contract (*Gow* v *Henry* (1899) 2 F 48), or carry out some other wrongful act. If this is the case then it would cover what is known in English law as economic duress, which seems to make a contract voidable. This normally involves the making of any illegitimate threat, e.g., to break a current contract between the two parties, in order to force a renegotiation of the terms. The dilemma for the law is to decide whether the other party agreed to the renegotiation because he genuinely felt that there was no alternative (e.g., because of pressure from his own creditors as in *D & C Builders* v *Rees* [1966] 2 QB 617), or whether he made a rational commercial decision (see discussion of these issues in *North Ocean Shipping Co* v *Hyundai* [1979] QB 705; *Pao On* v *Lau Yiu Long* [1979] 3 All ER 65; *The Siboen and The Sibotre* [1976] 1 Lloyds Rep 293; and *Atlas Express* v *Kafco* [1989] 1 All ER 641). Again, for the doctrine to operate, the threat must be illegitimate. So it cannot amount to duress (or force and fear) if what is being threatened is perfectly lawful, e.g., to take bankruptcy proceedings against a party unless he makes a payment or gives security for his debt (see *Hunter* v *Bradford Property Trust* 1977 SLT (notes) 33 and *Hislop* v *Dickson Motors (Forres)* 1978 SLT (notes) 73.

3.12.2.1 Setting the contract aside   Where the contract is voidable the key is to take action immediately after the contract to set it aside. Otherwise one might be held to be barred from withdrawing, due to lapse of time. In the *Atlantic Baron* [1978] 3 All ER 1170, where a contract was entered under economic duress, the innocent party took no steps to set the voidable contract aside until eight months after it was finalised. The contract was held to have been affirmed and the right to avoid the contract was lost. It is thought that a similar approach would be taken by the Scottish courts.

Again we see that there are two principles in a conflict of sorts. On the one hand, the law disapproves of contracts being made other than by normal market forces, i.e. it disapproves of threats of a physical or economic nature which would undermine the real choices of a reasonable man. On the other hand, at least where economic duress is concerned, there is a concern to protect security of transactions by saying that the contract is merely voidable. If the innocent party does not act quickly enough the contract must stand. This protects the other party from being left in limbo for too long. In addition, the law will not allow a voidable contract to be set aside where the parties cannot be restored to their original position, or where an innocent third party has acquired rights. Again we see that reluctance to unravel transactions and the wish to protect the reasonable expectations of innocent buyers (see 3.7.2 and 3.12.1.4 above).

3.12.3 Undue influence
The doctrine of undue influence has its origins in the English law of equity. In Scots law, a contract is voidable on the grounds of undue influence where one party naturally reposes trust and confidence in another (e.g., parent and child, doctor and client (patient), solicitor and client, or banker and customer) and the stronger party takes advantage of this trust to obtain a transaction which is disadvantageous to the weaker. We will normally see the disadvantage in the fact that the transaction departs from the market norm, e.g. a car is sold by a parishioner to his priest or minister for less than its market value. The best way of showing that no advantage was taken of the

weaker party is to show that he obtained independent advice. This is not necessarily conclusive, the real question being whether the party alleging undue influence acted freely and voluntarily. So like misrepresentation and duress, the law is concerned to regulate situations in which 'real' consent is undermined by conduct of the other party.

Scots and English law differ in that Scots law does not presume undue influence in certain recognised relationships (see Cheshire, Fifoot & Furmston, *Law of Contract*, at pp. 316–7). In Scots law, the undue influence must be proved on the facts of each individual case. However, there is no doubt that in the context of certain relationships, if a transaction appears to be one-sided and the disadvantaged party has not taken independent advice, the court will look very closely for the abuse of a position of trust. Examples of undue influence include a heavily indebted client agreeing to pay over his full business account plus £1,000 to his solicitor (*Anstruther* v *Wilkie* (1856) 18 O 405); a 17-year-old agreeing to convey the family home to his mother in life rent (*Allan* v *Allan* 1961 SC 200); and an elderly farmer remortgaging his home beyond what was prudent, to secure his son's business debts to the bank which he also was a long-time customer and in which he placed great trust (*Lloyds Bank* v *Bundy* [1974] 2 All ER 757).

Again, there are the limitations on setting aside a contract which is merely voidable, so the innocent party must act quickly before, e.g., the guilty party sells goods to an innocent third party, or the law holds too much time to have lapsed (see 3.7.2. above).

3.12.4 Facility and circumvention

A contract is also voidable if there is shown to have been facility and circumvention. Facility refers to the weak mental or physical state of one of the parties, and circumvention to the advantage taken of this state of affairs by the other party. The facility could be caused by old age, sickness, or a generally nervous disposition (see *Hope LJC* in *Clinic* v *Stirling* (1854) 17 D 15), and the more extreme it is, the less is required in terms of circumvention (see Lord Ormidale in *Munro* v *Straus* (1894) OT 1039 at 1047). The transaction must be to the lesion (or disadvantage) of the facile party.

in *Mackay* v *Campbell* 1966 SC 237, it was pointed out that the facility, circumvention and consequent disadvantage were obviously closely interrelated, and although all three were required it was often difficult to identify the issues separately. A further complicating factor is that there may be a very fine line to be drawn between facility and insanity, and between circumvention and fraud. The latter distinction is of limited importance as they have the same effect on the contract, i.e. rendering it voidable. In fact fraud and circumvention are often pleaded together. However, in respect of the former distinction, insanity renders a contract wholly void, whereas facility and circumvention render it only voidable. As such, it could be vital to know the mental state of the party in question, especially if property passed with the contract and has subsequently been resold. If the contract was merely voidable for facility and circumvention, it would not be recoverable whereas, if the contract was void for insanity, it would.

English law might cover cases of facility and circumvention by its rules on undue influence, which do not only cover relationships of mutual trust and confidence, but also other situations in which there is unacceptable influence or pressure, e.g., where a party signs a contract when in a state of severe ill health. There is an overlap here with the rules on unconscionability which have been used to set aside contracts because one of the parties is poor and ignorant or is vulnerable, because he is inexperienced and is about to inherit money (see *Fry* v *Lane* (1888) 40 Ch D 312, and *Buckley* v *Irwin* [1960] NI 98. There do not appear to be comparable authorities in Scotland, (but see 3.12.5 below).

3.12.5 General inequality of bargaining power
All of the above (misrepresentation, duress, undue influence, and facility and circumvention) involve circumstances which effectively mean that one party is in a stronger bargaining position than the other. This inequality has either been created by deception or duress, or it has been nurtured by the abuse of a situation where one of the parties is vulnerable. However, there are clearly countless other circumstances in which one party is, *per se*, in a stronger bargaining position than the other, whether by virtue of greater skill, expertise or whatever. Indeed, as we have seen, the law may regard supplier–consumer, landlord–tenant or employer–employee relationships as being inherently dogged by inequality of bargaining, e.g., because one of the parties can use standard form contracts which allocate the rights and duties, but which present themselves in ways which make it very difficult for individual negotiation to take place or for the 'invisible hand' of the market to bargain on the weaker party's behalf. The response to these sorts of problems has been to erect tests of unfairness which tend to focus on an examination of departure from certain substantive fairness norms and the fairness of the bargaining environment. In other words, how much liability has been excluded and did the consumer have any real choice or opportunity to bargain? (See above at 3.11.5–3.11.8). There is even, as we have seen, control of terms exempting liability in standard form commercial contracts, partly justified by the lack of opportunity for bargaining in these contexts.

However, what about contracts or terms which are not covered by these straight controls on unfairness, e.g., contracts between private individuals, or non-exemption clauses contracts between commercial parties or the terms in consumer contracts covering the main subject matter and the price? If there is alleged to be inequality of bargaining power, can the law do anything? For example, A, who has a limited understanding of the complexity of the computer market, sells equipment to B, who is an expert, for much less than it is worth. Does A have a remedy? A may, of course, be able to establish a case under one of the specific doctrines, e.g., if A is particularly weak-minded, or if the tactics used by B amount to misrepresentation or duress. It is clear that the breadth of these doctrines, e.g., when silence amounts to a misrepresentation, or who is regarded as weak-minded, says a lot about the law's readiness to protect the weaker party from market rigours, i.e. how welfarist it is prepared to be (see Willett, 'Unfair Terms in Consumer Contracts' forthcoming, 1996). As has been said at 3.12.4 above, English law may give protection, not only where there is undue influence in the Scottish sense of abuse of trust and confidence, but also where there is undue pressure more generally, or where one of the parties is poor, ignorant or an expectant heir. But is there in either jurisdiction a general principle of inequality of bargaining power which will cover situations not covered by the rules mentioned? This is perhaps more important in Scotland because the specific rules do not appear to cover as many types of inequality as the English rules do (see above at 3.12.4).

There is authority in Erskine that Scots law does recognise such a general principle:

> All bargains which from their very appearance discover oppression, as an intention of any of the contractors to catch some undue advantage from his neighbour's necessities, lie open to reduction on the head of dole or extortion, without the necessity of proving any special circumstances of fraud or circumvention on the part of that contractor.

However, there seem to be no modern authorities. It appears that if such a rule is still recognised it would require a very clear disparity of bargaining strength (e.g., our seller of computer equipment being very naive as compared to the buyer), along with a significant departure from the market value in terms of the price paid or the value received.

In English law, such an example might be covered as a unconscionable transaction. However, the English courts have refused to recognise a general principle of inequality of bargaining power (see *National Westminster Bank* v *Morgan* [1985] 1 All ER 821, per Lord Scarman at 830, where he criticised such a suggestion by Lord Denning in *Lloyds Bank* v *Bundy* [1976] QB 326).

3.13 UNFULFILLED EXPECTATIONS: ERROR

Once parties have made apparently binding agreements, the expectation is that they will be carried through to a mutually beneficial conclusion. However, a myriad of different circumstances may arise or come to light which preclude the realisation of this expectation. It may be that the facts were not as one or both of the parties supposed at the time the contract was made (e.g., in relation to the type of goods on sale, their price or quality). So a buyer may believe that he is buying a Jaguar when in fact it is a Metro; a seller may believe that his land is worth £50,000 when in fact it is worth considerably more because of the presence of valuable mineral deposits; a party borrowing money may believe that he is signing an unsecured loan when in fact it is a loan secured on his property — the possibilities are endless. If the error in question has been induced by the other party there may be a remedy in misrepresentation (see 3.12.1 above). However, there may also be a remedy based on the fact that the contract has been entered into under essential error as to its terms. This is only allowed where the error or mistake is seen as striking at the very heart of the bargain (see 3.13.1.1 below).

Another possibility is that the circumstances change *after* the contract is made, e.g., the goods are lost or stolen or one of the parties falls ill and is unable to carry out his side of the bargain. The parties may have provided for such eventualities in their contract, allocating the various risks and insuring accordingly. However, it is often impractical to plan for all possible eventualities and the law has had to develop principles to deal with unforeseen changes in circumstance. These rules revolve around the doctrine of frustration (see 3.14 below).

Finally, one of the parties may decide not to fulfil his obligations under the contract, i.e. to breach it. In such circumstances the law must decide which remedies should be available to the innocent party, as well as trying to place a financial value on his lost expectation of performance (see 3.15 below).

For the moment, we must turn our attention to the consideration of error. This is an extremely complex area of the law, not least because of the very numerous types of error or mistake that may be made in relation to a contract and the various ways in which such errors may be brought about.

One critical distinction is between the situation where A and B are not in subjective agreement, i.e. once again the argument is that one or both is not really agreeing to the terms (mutual or unilateral error as to the true facts); and the situation where A and B are in agreement but are both mistaken (in the same sense) as to the true facts (common error). We will deal with these in turn.

3.13.1 Mutual/unilateral error

A basic problem is posed by the question whether there are certain issues to which an error or mistake must always relate, or sometimes relate or never relate to be operative, i.e. is there some kind of threshold rule which says that a buyer's error, as to the quality or quantity of goods, or a seller's error, as to the value of his property, is never operative? Are there certain matters to which the error or mistake must relate as a threshold requirement before it can be of any relevance? (This is often suggested by English commentators on the English rules, who say that mistakes as to terms, subject matter and identity are relevant, but not as to quality; but this may be misleading because, e.g., mistake as to identity is not always enough (see below), and if the mistake as to quality is as to the quality which the other is actually offering, then it may be operative.) We take the view that the issue as to what one is mistaken about is not generally a question, the answer to which in itself determines whether a claim based on error will succeed.

It is true that in Scots law a traditional starting point for discussions of this area is identification of the five matters about which there could be error which could be regarded as essential or as error in substantialibus. These were identified by Bell as:

(a) error as to the nature of the contract (e.g., the belief that one is signing a contract of insurance when in fact it is a contract of guarantee);

(b) error as to the identity of the other party (believing one is buying a computer from A when in fact the seller is B);

(c) error as to the subject matter of the contract (believing oneself to be buying a computer when in fact what is being sold is a video recorder);

(d)   error as to the price or consideration (a buyer believing the price to be £10 when it is in fact £100, or a seller believing it to be £100 when it is in fact £10);

(e)   error as to the quality, quantity or extent of the subject matter (a buyer believing that land or goods are worth more than they are, or a seller believing that they are worth less than they are).

If we use 'error' in a layperson's sense then these categories obviously exemplify most of its likely manifestations, and in this sense form a useful starting framework. However, it is quite clear that Scots law will not in all circumstances set aside contracts due to such errors. Indeed, unless such errors have been induced by misrepresentation it will be on very rare occasions that they will be operative. The real issue is what criteria are used to decide when any given error will be operative. As a general rule this is determined by considerations relating to the mutual understandings of the parties as to the issue in question and the way the courts view those understandings. Relevant issues which we will discuss further below are whether the parties could objectively be said to be agreeing to anything clear at all; whether, even if they were agreeing objectively (i.e. on reasonable appearances) to X, the party who contests that he believed differently believes differently because of a failure properly to express his own intentions, or possibly due to a misunderstanding as to the terms offered by the other, or whether his error or mistake is simply as to the value of what is being bought or sold, or some other matter affecting how good a bargain he has made; and whether the party who is not mistaken knew or could be taken to have known of the error. We will deal with these issues in turn.

3.13.1.1   *Objective appearance of agreement*   As stated above, the law will generally say there is an agreement to X where there objectively appears to be one, irrespective of the fact that one of the parties believes that the agreement is something different from X.

Suppose that A believes himself to have contracted to sell his Ford Granada to B, but B believes himself to have bought A's Mercedes, and both are ignorant of each other's error (known as mutual error). Suppose the price to be understood by both to be £6,000. The law's first question is which version of events represents what an objective bystander would regard the parties as having intended to take place (see above at 3.3.3.2). The answer may be that neither understanding is preferable, in the sense that there is no evidence (whether documentary, on oath, or as to price, custom, etc.) which points unequivocally to one interpretation of the agreement being the more reasonable, i.e. the agreement is inherently ambiguous. In such circumstances the law may say that the lack of agreement as to the essentials means that there is no contract.

In *Stuart & Co.* v *Kennedy* (1885) 13 R 221, stone coping was sold at a price per foot, one of the parties believing the measure to be the linear foot and the other believing it to be the superficial foot. There was no contract, although the price had to be paid on principles of quasi contract (see below

3.16). In *Raffles* v *Wichelhaus* (1864) 2 H & C 906, two ships of the same name sailed from the same port in successive months. One of the parties intended the cargo they were contracting for to go on one ship, while the other party had in mind the other ship. It was held to be open to the defendant to show that the contract was ambiguous and that he intended to use the October ship. This case simply provides an example of mutual error that might potentially be fatal to the existence of an agreement. The case did not actually go to the jury. If a court had to decide such a case today, the bottom line remains whether there was an agreement on objective appearances.

3.13.1.2 Unilateral error If the court is faced with a situation where A believes the agreement to be X and B believes it to be Y, and it concludes that on reasonable objective appearances the agreement is X, then we say that B has made a unilateral error. The position seems to be that if the error is as to terms of the contract and A knows of B's error then the contract may be able to be set aside where it is a form of error of expression. An error of expression involves a situation where prior negotiation indicates that the agreement *was* originally Y but B has wrongly expressed himself as agreeing to X. So, for example, in *Angus* v *Bryden* 1992 SLT 884, a seller of fishing rights intended to convey only the river fishings and not the sea fishings which he also owned. This mistake was held to be able to invalidate the contract. This is a slightly broader form of error of expression than that discussed at 3.13.3 below where the error of expression must have taken place through the medium of a written document. This is probably not necessary here, although it will very often be the case.

Another illustration is *Steuart's Trs* v *Hart* (1875) 3R 192 (approved in *Angus* v *Bryden*), where the seller of property mistakenly thought that the feuduty was nine pounds 15 shillings rather than the 3 shillings which it actually was. The purchaser knew of the error, and the court set the contract aside on the basis that he should not be able to take advantage of the seller's error on this essential matter. This approach was preferred in *Angus* v *Bryden* to the approach taken in *Spook Erection (Northern) Ltd* v *Kaye* 1990 SLT 676, where Steuart's Trs was not followed. The refusal to follow *Steuarts Trs* in *Spook Erection* was based on reading *Stewart* v *Kennedy* (1890) 17R HL 1, and Lord Watson's judgment to be saying that there could *never* be a remedy where there was a unilateral error which was not induced by the other party (for a discussion of *Spook Erection*, see Willett, 'Uninduced Misapprehensions in Contract Law' (1992) 7 JCL. However, *Angus* v *Bryden* seems now to have confirmed that a contract can be set aside where there is an essential error of expression as to terms which is known to the other party. The position seems to be the same in England, where in *Smith* v *Hughes* (1871) KR 64B 597, it was held that if A is mistaken as to what terms he is agreeing to then the contract can be set aside if B knows of the mistake. This principle can be seen at work in the decision, which said that wrongly believing the oats to be of a certain quality was not enough to set the contract aside; however, it would be enough if the mistaken belief was that the other party was actually agreeing to that level of quality. We must elaborate on this distinction. When two people make a contract they have a range of expectations as to the benefit they will gain, e.g., a car which is red, which is fast, which can do 40 mpg and 100 mph, which will retain a very good resale value, or for which there is a special market in which sale can bring a big profit. Only some of these expectations will be enshrined as contractual promises, and it is, of course, the task of the rules on agreement to decide precisely which ones. So it may have been expressly agreed that the price would be £5,000, the engine capable of 40 mpg, but not that the car would depreciate in value by only a certain amount per year. Nevertheless, the buyer may have mistakenly believed that it would depreciate only by this amount when in fact the depreciation rate is much greater. This is not a mistake as to what was contractually promised but only as to peripheral expectations. Of course, there might have been a promise on this issue, and if so then such a mistake as to what was promised, which was known to the seller, would be enough to set the contract aside.

So the sale of a piece of land or a product will stand notwithstanding that the seller is unaware (and the buyer is aware) that it contains valuable mineral deposits or is a valuable antique; but the sale will not stand if the seller believed mistakenly that the buyer was promising as a term of the agreement that the land was useless or the product was not an antique. This might occur because there had been prior negotiations in which the buyer had indicated that this was his view, although he had never formally promised this as a term of the contract. Of course in such circumstances there might well be a misrepresentation which would make the contract voidable. So relative to a complete freedom of contract approach, which holds a mistaken party to the correct letter of the agreement, the law is providing a degree of protection. However, the law will go no further and protect from bad bargains generally.

A further illustration of the rule is provided by the English case *Hartog* v *Colin & Shields* [1939] 3 All ER 566. The seller mistakenly offered his product for sale at a price 'per pound' when it was clearly intended (and the buyer knew this) that it should be offered at the same price 'per piece' (which made the product more expensive). This was a mistake as to the terms on which the seller himself was offering to sell the product, and was capable of setting the contract aside.

3.13.1.3   Error as to nature of obligation   There is some doubt as to whether the same rules apply where the mistake is as to the nature of the obligation itself, e.g., one of the parties believes himself to be signing a mortgage document when in fact it is a guarantee, i.e. a different obligation. This happened in *Royal Bank of Scotland* v *Purvis* 1989 GWD 1190. It was held that as long as the mistaken party knew that some sort of obligations were being undertaken, they must stand. Surely, however, this would not apply if the bank had known that the other party had never intended to commit to a contract of this nature? (Cf J. Thomson, 'Error Revisited', 1992 SLT 215.)

3.13.1.4   The identity of the other party   Where personal identity is essential, a contract may be void where one party is mistaken as to the identity of the other. This typically arises where a party obtains property on credit by lying as to his identity in order to give the impression of creditworthiness. Here the error or mistake has been induced so that the contract is at the very least voidable. The issue tends to be how fundamental the error was, measured by how important identity was to the party who claims to be mistaken. This is what dictates whether the contract will be void. We have seen in the discussion on misrepresentation (see 3.12.1.6 above) that the courts are reluctant to go beyond holding the contract voidable for misrepresentation in which case the seller may lose title to the goods when they are sold to an innocent third party purchaser (see 3.7.2 and 3.12.1.6). To be held void the circumstances must be such that it is clear that the deceived party had no intention of dealing with anyone other than the person that the deceiver claimed to be, i.e. identity must be crucial.

This is virtually impossible to prove where the parties are dealing face to face. In such circumstances there is a powerful presumption that the seller intended to deal with the individual standing in front of him, notwithstanding that he was deceived as to his creditworthiness. In the two cases mentioned already (*Phillips* v *Brooks* and *Lewis* v *Averay*) the seller was not able to rebut this presumption, despite there having been a degree of verification of identity in both cases which might have emphasised the importance of the other party's identity to the seller. In *Phillips*, the seller checked the phone book for the claimed name 'Sir George Bullough' and, in *Lewis*, the crook masquerading as the Robin Hood actor produced a Pinewood Studios card. However, in neither case was this sufficient to establish that identity was vital.

The seller is likely to be in a stronger position if he knows the person whose identity has been assumed by the crook or if he knows someone for whom he claims to be acting. For example, in *Morrisson* v *Robertson* 1908 SC 332, M sold cows on credit to Telford on the strength of his claim to be the son of Wilson (whom M had dealt with in the past). Telford then sold the cows to R, and absconded. It was held that the contract between M and Telford was void, as M never intended to deal with anyone other than the son of someone he knew and trusted (Wilson). As the initial contract of sale was void, no title could be passed to R, and M was able to recover the cows.

Where the parties do not deal face to face it may be easier to establish that the identity of the other party is crucial, particularly where the persona adopted by the crook is someone well known in the trade (compare *Cundy* v *Lindsay* (1878) 3 App Cas 459, with the contrasting decision *King's Norton Metal Co Ltd* v *Edridge, Merrett & Co Ltd* (1897) 14 TLR 98).

It is unfortunate that the competing interests of the innocent seller and the innocent third party have to be adjudicated by means of this rather tortuous distinction between identity and creditworthiness. Having said this it does seem more appropriate to place a greater burden of inquiry on the seller, who is in a better position to ensure against this kind of thing and who is not obliged to give credit in the first place.

3.13.1.5 Unilateral error where obligation gratuitous   A unilateral error can be relied on to set aside an obligation which is gratuitous, even where it has not been induced, is not known by the other party and does not go to an essential issue such as the terms of the contract or the identity of the other party. The only requirement would seem to be that the error is material to the obligation in question (see *Hunter* v *Bradford Trust* 1977 SLT (notes) 33 and *Security Pacific Finance* v *Filshie's Trustee* 1994 SCLR 1100).

3.13.2 Common error

The circumstances in which this type of error will invalidate the contract have been very narrowly construed by the courts. One view that has been put forward is that a contract will be invalidated only where the thing being contracted for is totally different from that which the parties believed it to be (see the judgment of Lord Atkin in *Bell* v *Lever Bros* [1932] AC 161). However, this has often been said to extend only to circumstances where the error is as to the existence of the subject matter; it has not been taken to cover errors as to quality, e.g., the mistaken belief that a painting is an old master, when in fact it is a copy (see *Leaf* v *International Galleries* [1950] 2 KB 86), or a failure to appreciate that a book was in fact a valuable rarity (see *Dawson* v *Muir* (1851) 13 D 843). However, in such circumstances, the party who loses out may still have a remedy in misrepresentation or breach of contract. For example, A and B may both believe that a painting is an old master because A (the seller) has told B (the buyer) that this is the case. If A has been honest and yet careless in making this error, then B may have a remedy for negligent misrepresentation (see above at 3.12.2.1). If he was totally innocent B still may be able to contend that A has effectively made a contractual promise to the effect that the painting was an old master, and borne the risk of it not being one (see above discussion of contractual terms and collateral contracts at 3.11.1.2 to 3.11.1.4). This approach was taken in the Australian case *McRae* v *Commonwealth Disposals Commission* [1950] 84 CLR 377 where the defendants contracted to give salvage rights to the plaintiffs on a reef which did not exist. It was held that the defendants had undertaken the risk of non-existence, and impliedly promised that the reef did exist. They were accordingly liable for breach of contract.

A difficult question for the doctrine of common error is whether non-existence of the subject matter can extend to a situation where the subject matter is so *qualitatively* different that it does not exist in the sense that it was thought to. The authority of Lord Atkin's judgment in *Bell* v *Lever Bros* is that the doctrine does not extend to such qualitative errors. However, *obiter dicta* in *Ferguson* v *Wilson* (1904) 6 F 779 suggest that if a business is represented to be profitable and it is not, then the subject matter (a profitable business) does not exist. Also, in the recent decision *Associated Japanese Bank* v *Credit du Nord* [1988] 3 All ER 902, the subject matter of a guarantee contract was a contract for the supply of industrial machines. This contract clearly existed, but, due to the fraud of the third party, the machines did not. Steyn J held that the contract was subject to an implied condition precedent that the machines existed and that the guarantee was void for common mistake (the English equivalent of error).

This may signal an extension of what comes within the ambit of common error. It would be of most help where, as in the above case, there is no opportunity to allege misrepresentation or breach of contract against the other party. Rather one wishes to avoid an obligation which, due to neither contracting party's fault, is not as it seemed. The practical question for the court in such a case appears to be who should bear the risk of things not being as they seemed, and a broad conception of common error to cover qualitative matters may help the party who is not to be taken to have borne the risk in question, by making the contract void and thereby releasing him from his obligations. However, there is quite a distinct problem associated with an analysis of common error which is prepared to hold the contract void. This may be appropriate in the *Japanese Bank* case, or in a situation like *Leaf* v *International Galleries*, where we might wish to say that the Galleries should bear the risk of things not being as they seemed. Holding the contract to be void means that the party who was more innocent avoids its obligations; but what if there is a contract for goods which are later discovered not to exist, but a proper construction of the contract suggests that the buyer was taking this risk i.e. buying the 'chance' that the goods existed. If, as is often suggested in England, the law is that such a contract is void, the buyer may escape the consequences of a risk which he undertook in that he will not have to pay. It is certainly the case that in the more limited circumstances where goods have perished at the time the contract is made the contract is void, apparently irrespective of whether the buyer could properly be said to be taking such a risk (s. 6, Sale of Goods Act). However, it may be the case that in Scots law in cases falling outside s. 6, the overriding issue is who has borne the risk of the circumstances in question, whether this be as to existence, quality, or whatever. The appropriate remedy (whether avoidance, breach of contract, etc.) will then follow.

3.13.3 Error of expression involving writing
This occurs where the parties have come to an agreement and then reduced it to writing but the writing does not properly express what was agreed originally, e.g., due to clerical error.

A well known example of this is *Krupps* v *Menzies* 1907 SC 903 where a clerical error misstated the salary of a hotel manageress as one-fifth rather than one-twentieth of the hotel's profits. A proof of the facts was allowed to determine if reduction was justified.

Under s. 8 of the Law Reform (Miscellaneous Provisions) (Scotland) Act 1985, the court now has the power in such circumstances to order rectification of the document so that it expresses the original common intention of the parties; rectification can have retrospective effect. (For an illustration of the operation of this section, see *Bank of Scotland* v *Brunswick Developments (1987) Ltd, Raymond Ellis Blin* 1994 SCLR 102.)

3.14 FRUSTRATION

This section is concerned with a situation where parties' contractual expectations cannot be fulfilled because of events which occur *after* the contract has been made, e.g., destruction of the subject matter or death of one of the parties.

In commercial contracts the parties will often go to great lengths to plan for such contingencies. *'Force majeure'* clauses are used to define who should bear the risk of unforeseen events interfering with performance. In the knowledge of such risk allocation, the parties may insure accordingly. However, where no provision has been made for such eventualities the law provides a framework within which disputes may be resolved; the doctrine of frustration.

3.14.1 Nature and effect of frustration

Frustration has been defined in the following terms by Lord Radcliffe in *Davis Contractors Ltd* v *Fareham UDC* [1956] 2 All ER 145:

> frustration occurs whenever the law recognises that, without default of either party, a contractual obligation has become incapable of being performed because the circumstances in which performance is called for would render it a thing radically different from that which was undertaken by the contract.

The modern basis of the doctrine is that the circumstances have changed so materially that the parties may not be said to have promised to do what is now required of them. This may be because what is now required is impossible or 'radically different' from what was originally promised. In either case the effect of frustration is to discharge the parties from their contractual obligations.

The courts' task is to ascertain the extent to which the parties may be said to have borne the risk of changing circumstances altering their commitments. Where there is no written provision, the courts must take it that normal foreseeable exigencies such as increasing costs and travel delays are to be expected; on the other hand, wholly improbable occurrences, such as death or outbreak of war, would not have been contemplated.

3.14.2 Changed circumstances due to the fault of one of the parties

Essentially, frustration may only result from an event which is beyond the control of either party. Therefore, if the party pleading frustration can be shown to bear some responsibility for the event, then the contract is not frustrated. In *Maritime National Fish Ltd* v *Ocean Trawlers* [1935] AC 524, MNF, who had four trawlers, chartered another one from OT. Trawling required a licence from the Canadian government. MNF applied for five licences but were awarded only three and claimed the charterparty with OT was frustrated. The Privy Council held that MNF's own election to attach the licences to their own trawlers was responsible for the failure of the common object of the charterparty. The frustration was self induced and amounted to wrongful repudiation by MNF.

However, there are clearly degrees of fault, and a small element of blameworthiness may not prevent the doctrine applying.

3.14.3 Recognised categories of frustration

Certain types of situation have come to be recognised as likely to frustrate a contract. These are as follows:

(a) destruction of subject matter rendering performance impossible;
(b) death or illness of one of the contracting parties rendering performance impossible;
(c) change in circumstances rendering the attainment of the object of the contract impossible; and
(d) State action rendering performance of the contract impossible or illegal.

3.14.3.1 Destruction of subject matter rendering performance impossible The most famous example of this is *Taylor* v *Caldwell* (1863) 3 B&S 826. C agreed to let T use a music hall for four concerts in the summer of 1861. Six days before the first concert the music hall was destroyed by fire. The fire was the fault of neither party. T sued for damages for breach of contract as the premises were unusable. The court held that C was not liable in damages. The contract was frustrated by the occurrence of the fire.

The Sale of Goods Act 1979, s. 7 makes special provision for the sale of specific goods. It states that if they have perished before property has passed to the buyer, the contract will be frustrated. The difficulty with s. 7 is that it begs the question whether the same principle applies to non-specific or unascertained goods (see Chapter 6, para. 6.2.2). On the general principle of frustration as expressed in *Taylor* v *Caldwell,* there seems no reason why unascertained goods should not be covered, unless, of course, there is reason to believe that either party was taking the risk that goods would perish.

3.14.3.2 Death or illness of one of the contracting parties rendering performance impossible Death or serious illness will frustrate the contract, as long as the personal contribution of the unfortunate party is material to the contract. For example, in *Condor* v *Barron Knights Ltd* [1966] 1 WLR 87, a member of a pop group was advised by his doctor that his health would be seriously endangered if he continued to fulfil the group's demanding schedule of events. His contract was held to be frustrated. It is unlikely, however, that, for example, a contract with a firm of builders would be frustrated because of the death of the proprietor, if other members of the firm would be competent to carry out the work.

3.14.3.3 Change in circumstances rendering the attainment of the object of the contract impossible In *Krell* v *Henry* [1903] 2 KB 740, Henry hired rooms in Pall Mall on the route of the coronation procession of Edward VII. The licence agreement was limited to the proposed day of the coronation and the price of the hire was very high. The King caught pneumonia and the coronation was cancelled. Krell sued for the hire charge. The court held that viewing the coronation procession was the sole object of the contract and the contract was frustrated.

However, in *Herne Bay Shipping Co* v *Hutton* [1903] 2 KB 683, a pleasure boat was hired 'for the purpose of viewing the naval review and a day's cruise round the fleet'. The review by the King was cancelled but it was still possible to cruise round the fleet. The court held that the contract had two purposes, one of which was still capable of performance. The contract was not frustrated.

It seems that the courts would be highly reluctant in modern times to hold that a contract had only one purpose. The risk of parties avoiding bargains simply because they have become less profitable is apparently too high. For example, in *Amalgamated Investment & Property Co Ltd* v *John Walker & Sons Ltd* [1977] 1 WLR 164, a contract for the sale of a warehouse for £1,700,000 was entered into. Both parties contemplated that the warehouse would be demolished and the price reflected its development potential. AIP (the buyers) enquired before the contract was made whether the building was listed as being of historical or architectural interest. JW (the sellers) replied truthfully that it was not. Contracts were signed on 25 September 1973. On 26 September, the Department of the Environment announced that the building had been listed and could not be demolished. Without development potential, the warehouse was worth only £200,000. AIP refused to complete, claiming rescission of the contract *inter alia* on the basis of frustration. The Court of Appeal held that, although the listing of the building was a supervening event which rendered the property much less valuable, it did not make performance impossible. It could have been said that the sole object of the contract was to lease a warehouse with development potential. The fact that the court chose not to construe the contract in this way shows that they wish to apply frustration of object as narrowly as possible. The courts will tend to find (as in the *Herne Bay* case) that there was more than one object to the contract. Indeed with most commercial contracts, it is very likely that there *will* be more than one object. However, in some circumstances it might be very difficult to say that there were collateral objects. For example, if A's uncle has booked A's wedding function at B's hotel, and A is left standing at the altar, in the absence of specific contractual provision, would the contract be frustrated or would the uncle have to pay for the function?

3.14.3.4 State action rendering performance impossible or illegal Such state action might arise for instance in the form of a declaration of war; in the requisitioning of land, materials or manpower; or by making the transactions in question illegal.
Declaration of war In *Vinelvet AG* v *Vinava Shipping Co Ltd* (*The Chrysalis*) [1983] 2 All ER 658, a ship was trapped in the Shat Al Arab river by the outbreak of the Iran-Iraq war on the 22 September 1980. It was not known how long the war would last or how long neutral ships using the river would be affected. In an arbitration, the arbitrator held the contract had become frustrated by 24 November 1980. From that date, hire charges ceased to be payable. The court upheld the arbitrator's decision. The question as to whether the 1991 Gulf conflict would frustrate contracts affected by it is discussed by McBride and Scobbie, 'The Iraq and Kuwait Conflict: The

Impact on Contracts', 1991 SLT 39. The authors make the important point that the individual contractual circumstances should be carefully construed.

State requisitioning   In *Metropolitan Water Board* v *Dick, Kerr & Co Ltd* [1918] AC 119, the materials being used to build a reservoir were requisitioned, and the labour force was conscripted. The contract was held to be frustrated.

Supervening illegality   Where it becomes illegal to trade with the other party, because they come from an enemy country in war time, the contract will be frustrated. Also a particular transaction may be made illegal after the contract has been made. In *Denny, Mott & Dickson* v *Fraser* [1944] AC 265, wartime regulations made a contract for the sale of timber illegal. It was held that this frustrated the contract.

3.14.4   Leases and frustration

A lease can be frustrated through destruction of the subject matter (rei interitus), or through constructive destruction, e.g., where a 14-year lease of salmon fishings could not be used because of its use by the RAF as a gunnery and bombing range (see *Tay Salmon Fisheries Co.* v *Speedie* 1929 SC 593). This approach takes much more cognisance of the reasonable expectations of the tenant than the English rules, which are far less likely to allow frustration of a lease (see *National Carriers Ltd* v *Panalpina Ltd* [1981] AC 675).

3.14.5   Delay and impracticality

The attitude of the courts to circumstances which cause delay and/or impracticality in performance is rather difficult to state clearly. Parties are apparently not relieved of their obligations by fluctuating economic conditions such as shortages of labour and materials. In *Davis Contractors Ltd* v *Fareham UDC* [1956] 2 All ER 145, Davis Contractors Ltd agreed to build 78 houses in eight months for £92,000. Because of serious shortages of labour and materials the work took 22 months and cost £18,000 more than had been estimated. Davis Contractors Ltd claimed the contract was frustrated and thus they were not bound by the original price. They sued on a *quantum meruit* basis (i.e. for the value of the work done). The House of Lords held that the additional hardship involved in performance did not frustrate the contract. In such circumstances commercial contractors would normally try to guard against this problem by inserting a price variation clause in the original contract but Davis Contractors had not done so.

In cases of delay caused by war the courts are often reluctant to see the situation as permanent. In *Tamplin SS Co* v *Anglo-Mexican Petroleum* [1916] 2 AC 397 a ship was requisitioned for war service in February 1915. Its charter had three years to run. The court held that it seemed likely in February 1915 that the interruption in the charter would only be temporary and it was held not to have been frustrated. However, in *Embiricos* v *Sydney Reid Ltd* [1914] 3 KB 45, a Greek ship was chartered for a voyage through the Dardanelles. War broke out between Greece and Turkey and the charterers claimed the charter was frustrated. The court accepted the plea of frustration, although a little later the Turkish authorities unexpectedly announced a guarantee of safe passage through the straits for a limited period.

The position appears to be that impossibility of performance is required for frustration to take effect, and that this is not satisfied by impracticality. The courts will normally view delay as no more than impracticality. For example, in *The Eugenia* [1964] 1 All ER 161, a charterparty provided for a voyage from Genoa via the Black Sea to India. It was assumed that the voyage would be made through the Suez Canal. The charterers claimed that the contract was frustrated by the closure of the Suez Canal. It was held that the contract was still possible as the ship could have sailed the long way round, via the Cape of Good Hope. However, Lord Denning's judgment suggested that a more substantial diversion might have been sufficient to frustrate the contract. There is some support for this view that severe impracticality may frustrate a contract in later Court of Appeal decisions (see *Staffordshire Area Health Authority* v *South Staffordshire Waterworks Co* [1978] 3 All ER 769 and *Pole Properties Ltd* v *Feinberg* [1982] 43 P&CR 121). These are, of course, only of persuasive authority in Scotland.

3.14.6 Effect of frustration
Money paid in advance for a service which is not rendered due to frustration is recoverable. In *Cantiere San Rocco* v *Clyde Shipbuilding Co* 1923 SC (HL) 105, a contract for the construction of engines for an Austrian company was frustrated by the outbreak of war between the UK and Austria. After the war the Austrian firm were able to recover their deposit. However, where one contracting party confers a gain on the other by work done in pursuance of the frustrated contract, he may be able to recover compensation under the quasi-contractual principle of recompense (see 3.16.2 below).

3.15 DISCHARGE, BREACH OF CONTRACT AND REMEDIES

Where frustration is pleaded unsuccessfully, the normal conclusion is that the party relying on it is in breach of contract. However, it must be remembered that most contractual relationships do not come to a head in such a dramatic fashion. Before considering breach of contract it is appropriate to summarise the various means by which contractual obligations may be discharged or extinguished.
Acceptilation or discharge This happens where a creditor discharges his rights under a contract without seeking any (or further) performance. This is in effect a type of gratuitous promise (see above para. 3.5.1).
Payment Payment in legal tender may be insisted upon, if there is no agreement to the contrary. Bank notes issued by Scottish banks are not legal tender. If a cheque is accepted it is treated as conditional payment, and should the cheque be dishonoured the debt revives itself.
Compensation or set-off If one party is both debtor and creditor of the other party under separate obligations, there is a right, under the Compensation Act 1592, to set off the debt owed against the debt due. However, this can only be done if both debts are 'liquid' (i.e. presently payable). So if A owed B £100 for services rendered, A cannot set against this £50 which it is claimed B is liable to pay in respect of faulty goods which did not fulfil A's requirements. This is because the £50 claim is 'illiquid', i.e. B's liability has

yet to be established. However if the liquid and illiquid debts relate to the same transaction, set-off is allowed. So, in the above example, if A's complaint was that the services in relation to which the debt arose were defective, the right of set-off may be exercised.

Novation Novation applies where the parties mutually substitute a new debt or liability for the previous one. This typically happens in the case of the renewal of a bill of exchange. Novation may take the specialised form of 'delegation', where a new debtor is substituted. However, in a case where a new debtor assumes liability, the presumption is that the original debtor is still liable (see *McIntosh v Ainslie* (1872) 10 M 304). It should be made very clear that the new debtor is intended to take over the whole responsibility for the debt.

Confusion Confusion discharges a debt in the situation where the obligation to pay money and to be paid the same money become vested in the same person (*Stair I*, 18, 9). This may happen in the case of succession where the debtor succeeds as heir to his creditor.

Lapse of time Contracts, such as employment contracts or partnership agreements, may be entered into for a defined period. When this period ends the obligations are generally discharged. However, in the case of leases, employment and partnership, the relationship is renewed on its old terms by tacit relocation, if neither party takes steps to terminate the agreement (see *Stair II*, 9, 23).

3.15.1 Definition of breach of contract

A breach of contract arises when one of the parties refuses or fails without legal justification to perform satisfactorily one of the express or implied terms of the contract. The law provides the innocent party with a range of possible remedies in such circumstances. These remedies are dealt with below.

3.15.2 Specific implement

Specific implement takes the form of a decree *ad factum praestandum* which orders the party in breach to carry out obligations under the contract, e.g., to deliver the goods or complete the building work. The decree can be demanded as of right except in the following cases:

(a) Where the obligation in question is the payment of money. The appropriate remedy in such a case is diligence.

(b) Where the intimate relationship involved would make specific implement inappropriate. For example, it is undesirable to force someone to work for or with someone (in a contract of employment or partnership) if he does not wish to do so. The appropriate remedy in this type of case would be damages.

(c) Where it would be impossible to comply with the decree. For example, where a builder has failed to fulfil a term that he would obtain planning permission, it is pointless to decree that he should fulfil his obligation to build a house on the land.

(d) Where the court cannot enforce the decree, e.g., because the party in breach of contract is not subject to the jurisdiction of the Scottish courts.

(e)   Where there is no *pretium affectionis*. In the case of a sale of an article which can be obtained on the open market, the appropriate remedy for a purchaser where the seller does not deliver is to buy the goods elsewhere, and claim any difference in price in damages from the seller.

These 'exceptions' cover a huge number of very typical cases, and it begins to become rather unrealistic to speak of specific implement as a typical way of 'enforcing' a contract.

3.15.3   Rescission

Rescission is the right of the innocent party to refuse to perform his future obligation under the contract, on the material breach of it by the other party. This might be appropriate where a product is of poor quality or unsuitable for its purpose. The right of rescission could be exercised by handing back the product and refusing to pay for it.

3.15.3.1   Justification of rescission: materiality   An innocent party may rescind a contract where the other party is in breach of a material term of the contract or where the breach is of a material nature. Factors relevant to whether a term is material include what the parties expressly or impliedly agreed and any provision made by law.

Express or implied provision made by the parties   The parties may expressly state any term to be material, indicating that breach of it will justify rescission. If such an intention is clear then it will be given effect no matter how trivial the term appears to be.

The terms of a contract may clearly indicate the importance the parties intended to ascribe to them; in such circumstances it may be implied that a term was or was not material. Such an implication is most readily made where the term clearly does or does not 'go to the root' of the contract. For example, it would clearly be material to a contract for the sale of a car that what was delivered was a car not a bicycle; it might not be material that a car radio had been promised but not installed. The appropriate remedy in the first case would be rescission, in the latter it would be to seek compensation (damages).

In less clear cut cases it can be difficult to decide on the importance that the parties may be taken to have placed on the term. In *Wade* v *Waldon* 1909 SC 571, a comedian contracted to perform in a theatre on a date one year subsequent to the contract. One of the terms of the contract was that he should give a fortnight's notice of his intention to appear, along with bill matter, before his appearance. He failed to do so and the manager of the theatre refused to fulfil his engagement. It was held that, although the comedian was in breach of contract and the theatre was entitled to recover damages, they were not entitled to repudiate the agreement, because the term in question was not material.

In *Graham* v *United Turkey Red Co* 1922 SC 553, an agent for the sale of goods agreed not to sell the same type of goods if they were supplied by anyone else. This was held to be a material term the breach of which entitled the principals to repudiate the agreement.

Provision by law as to effect of breach   Certain statutes imply terms into contracts of a particular class. In so doing they may indicate whether the implied term is to be treated as material to the contract. The best known examples of this are the implied terms as to fitness for purpose, merchantability, description and title contained in the Sale of Goods Act 1979. The effect of s. 15B of that Act is to classify these as material terms of a contract of sale where the sale is to a consumer (see 6.6 below). Where the buyer is not a consumer it is for the court to decide on the circumstances in question whether the breach is material.

It has been affirmed in a recent Court of Session case that materiality generally is a question of the facts and circumstances of each individual case (see *Blyth* v *Scottish Liberal Club* 1982 SC 140 which is included in the Cases and Materials section for Chapter 3).

3.15.3.2   Conditions and warranties: English law   Although English case law may occasionally provide good examples of the relative importance of contractual terms (see *Bettini* v *Gye* [1876] 1 QBD 183 and *Poussard* v *Spiers* [1876] 1 QBD 410), they must be treated with caution. This is because English law has traditionally adopted a rather rigid classification of terms into conditions (material) and warranties (non-material) with little attention being paid to the effects of breach. Although this has changed to some extent and the English courts will sometimes examine the effects of a breach (see *Hong Kong Fir Shipping Co Ltd* v *Kawasaki Kisen Kaisha Ltd* [1962] 2 QB 26), the position is not at all certain.

3.15.3.3   Remedy where breach not material   Where the breach is not of a material term or where its effect is not considered to be serious enough, the innocent party may not repudiate, but can claim damages (see below for a full explanation of the principles applicable to damages for breach of contract).

3.15.4   Retention and lien

Retention and lien are closely linked. They both involve the right to withhold performance of one's own contractual obligations in response to a breach by the other party. They are appropriate where the breach is not of a material term, where the breach is not material enough to justify rescission or where rescission is of no practical use, i.e. because the contract has been substantially performed.

A typical instance of retention would be refusal to pay a debt in response to the creditor's breach. This breach may have been, for example, the delivery of goods or services of insufficient quality. This remedy may only be exercised where the creditor's breach relates to the same contract. This is because any claim which exists against the creditor is 'illiquid' and as such may only be used as an excuse for retention where it arises under the same contract as the liquid debt.

Lien is the right of one party to a contract to retain the property of a party in breach, as security for performance of an obligation. For example, an employee has a lien over any of his employer's property which was placed in his prior possession until he is paid for work carried out (Bell, *Prin* 1411, 1419).

3.15.5 Damages

Most commercial and consumer contracts are entered into with the expectation of gain. This anticipated gain may be the making of a profit or the enjoyment of a product or service. The purpose of according damages for breach of contract is to give effect to this expectation of gain by placing the innocent party in the position that would have existed had the contract been performed. This includes pecuniary losses, e.g., loss of profit, and non pecuniary losses, e.g., disappointment, irritation, etc. which flows from a holiday which does not live up to expectations (see *Jarvis* v *Swan Tours* [1973] 2 QB 233). This is to be contrasted with the purpose of damages in delict which is to place the injured party in the position that would have existed had the delict not been committed.

The role of damages in compensating lost expectations is exemplified by the following three examples:

(a) A is a builder who contracts with B, an entrepreneur, to build an open-air swimming pool. The pool is to be complete by 1 May (the start of the summer season). If A is a month late in completing the work, what damages should he pay? B's expected gain from the contract was to make a profit over the summer season; he has lost one month's profit as a result of A's breach of contract and he should receive this in compensation.

(b) X books a holiday with Heatspot Tours in Spain. X had been assured that the hotel was a five minute walk from the beach and that there were tennis and golf facilities. In fact he discovers on arrival that the hotel is a half hour walk from the sea and there are no tennis or golf facilities. What damages should Heatspot pay him? Let us say that he paid £500 for the holiday. If the value of the holiday he actually got could be estimated at, say, £250, he should apparently receive the difference between what he got (£250 worth of holiday) and what he paid for (£500 worth of holiday). However, he might object that if he had wanted a £250 holiday he would have booked one. The law's response is to award extra compensation for the disappointment suffered at having his annual holiday ruined (see *Jarvis* v *Swan Tours*, above).

(c) A agrees to supply B (a farmer) with ten tons of fertiliser on 1 June at a cost of £30 per ton. Payment is to be made on delivery. If A fails to deliver, B's entitlement to compensation will again be an amount which recognises his lost expectation of profit. Specific provision is made in the Sale of Goods Act 1979 for failure to perform contracts of sale. Section 51 stipulates that the damages payable should be the difference between the contract price and the market price on the date delivery was due. This is intended to reflect the fact that a purchaser would expect to have a product which he could then sell on the open market if he wished. In this case if we suppose that the market price was £50 per ton, the damages are calculated by deducting £30 from

£50 leaving £20 and multiplying by the number of tons contracted for (10). This gives a figure of £200.

The above examples must be qualified in the light of two key principles – remoteness of damage and mitigation of loss. Both of these principles control the liability to which the guilty party can be subjected.

3.15.5.1 *Remoteness of damage*

3.15.5.1 Remoteness of damage The leading case on this issue is *Hadley* v *Baxendale* (1854) 9 Exch 341, in which carriers were in breach of contract by failing to return a broken crankshaft to a mill on time. However, damages for loss of profits were not recoverable because the carriers could not be taken to know that the mill owners had only one crankshaft. The court stated two guiding principles upon which entitlement to damages should be based:

(a)   that the innocent party may recover damages, 'such as may fairly and reasonably be considered as arising naturally, i.e., according to the usual course of things'; *or*
(b)   that the innocent may recover damages 'such as may reasonably be supposed to have been in the contemplation of both parties, at the time they made the contract, as the possible result of the breach of it'.

The first principle effectively provides for a situation where the losses would be the natural consequence of the breach, foreseeable to anyone without the need to have knowledge of any special circumstances. All of the examples given above would fall into this category. A recent example of recovery of such loses is afforded by *Grant* v *Ullah* 1987 SLT 639 (OH). Purchasers pulled out of a house sale and the owners had to sell three months later for less money. They recovered damages to cover the difference in price, the cost of insurance and rates remaining payable until the new owners moved in, interest on their building society loan, and their estate agent's and solicitor's fees resulting from the failed contract.

The second principle anticipates a situation where, although the losses could not be said to be foreseeable in normal circumstances, the party in breach knows of special circumstances which make them foreseeable. For example, if the carriers had known of the fact that there was only one crankshaft they would have been able to foresee the losses which occurred and they would have been liable for them. In the first example given above, if B had also lost a valuable contract to host the area swimming championships then A would be liable for damages in respect of that loss, if, at the time of contracting, B had told him of that liability. The lesson for contracting parties is to be clear about special circumstances in negotiations with suppliers, builders, etc.

The two principles were developed and applied in *Victoria Laundry (Windsor) Ltd* v *Newman Industries Ltd* [1949] 1 All ER 997. Victoria Laundry ordered a new and larger boiler for their business in order to expand. Newman Industries agreed to supply and install it by a certain date. Full installation was delayed for five months. Victoria Laundry sued for breach claiming: (i) £16 a week loss of profit on the extra capacity they would have had; (ii) £262 a week they would have earned on special dyeing contracts with the Ministry of Supply. The Court of Appeal held that only (i) was recoverable as there was no knowledge of the special dyeing contracts. Asquith LJ merged the *Hadley* v *Baxendale* rules into a single principle of foreseeability. The loss should be foreseeable as something 'liable to result' from the breach. Clearly, losses which are not naturally foreseeable in this way must have been made foreseeable when the contract was made. In *The Heron II* [1967] 3 All ER 686, shipowners were nine days late in arriving at a Mediterranean port with a cargo of sugar. There was a sugar market at the port and in those nine days the market price of sugar had fallen. The shipowners knew of the existence of the market but not that the charterers wished to sell the cargo there. The House of Lords held that the loss of profit was recoverable. The test used was also based around foreseeability, although a number of different approaches were taken to it — the judges varied from thinking that the loss should be foreseeable as 'liable to result', 'likely to result', 'not unlikely to result', 'a real danger' and 'a serious possibility'. It seems clear, however, that they believed the test to be more onerous for the pursuer than the test of remoteness in delict, which requires only that losses arise 'naturally and directly' from the delictual act. This was confirmed by Orr and Scarman LJJ in *Parsens (Livestock) Ltd* v *Uttley Ingham & Co Ltd* [1978] QB 791. Their Lordships said that it must have been within the contemplation of the parties as a serious possibility that a defective feeding device for pigs might injure the pigs. Denning MR was in the minority, believing that in the case of physical damage the test was just as liberal as the *English* test in tort (this is less liberal than the Scottish delict test (see 4.6.2 below) but still more liberal than the contract approach being advocated by the other judges).

In *Balfour Beatty Construction* v *Scottish Power plc* 1994 SLT 807 it was held that the defenders could not reasonably have foreseen that the pursuers required a non stop supply of electricity for the fulfilment of their separate building contract, as this would require a very high degree of technical knowledge of the construction industry.

3.15.5.2 Mitigation of loss Even where losses are foreseeable they will be recoverable only to the extent that the innocent party has taken reasonable steps to mitigate his loss, for example, taking steps to buy replacement goods where the seller has failed to deliver. However, the innocent party is not expected to go to extraordinary lengths to cut his losses. In *Gunter* v *Lauritzen* (1894) 31 SLR, a seller of a quantity of hay failed to deliver and, when sued for damages, claimed that the buyer could have got a substitute quantity by buying small parcels here and there throughout the country. It was held that the buyer was not expected to go to such lengths to minimise his loss. Similarly, a holidaymaker whose two star hotel has been overbooked would not be expected to walk for hours with heavy baggage in the search for alternative accommodation which is precisely comparable in price. On the other hand if he immediately booked into a five star hotel, without making any effort to find something more modest, he would be unlikely to recover the extra cost.

The mitigation principle means that there will often be no damages claimable where the product or service is alternatively available, or, where the breach is by a customer, where alternative customers are easily found. The mitigation principle is effectively a requirement of good faith incumbent upon the innocent party, to the effect that he should not take the easy course and sit back and claim damages, but that he should try to avoid suffering a loss.

3.15.5.3 Mitigation and anticipatory breach The principle of mitigation of loss is compromised where one party is in anticipatory breach of contract, i.e. where he indicates prior to the due date for performance that he does intend to fulfil his obligations. The law gives the innocent party the choice as to whether to accept the repudiation and sue for damages immediately or to hold out for performance. Clearly, by exercising the latter option one may not be mitigating loss but adding to it. This problem was exemplified in *White & Carter (Councils) Ltd v McGregor* [1962] AC 413, where a garage owner repudiated a contract to have his garage advertised on litter bins on the day the contract was made. The advertisers chose to proceed with the preparation of the material, and sue for damages when they were not paid. The House of Lords held they were entitled to do so. Lord Reid, however, suggested that this right to hold out for performance might not be open where performance of the contract required cooperation between the two contracting parties or where the innocent party had no legitimate interest in performing the contract rather than claiming damages. Again we see a good faith principle being asserted as incumbent upon the innocent party.

In *Clea Shipping Co v Bulk Oil International (The Alaskan Trader)* [1984] 1 All ER 129, a ship was time-chartered for 24 months. After nearly a year, the vessel suffered a serious engine failure and was taken for repair which would last several months. The charterers repudiated but the owners repaired the ship and re-delivered it. The charterers declined to accept it but the owners kept it at the disposal of the charterers for the remaining eight months of the charter. The charterers contested their liability for the hire charges for the final eight months of the charter and the High Court held that the ship owners had no legitimate interest in continuing with the contract. They should have accepted the repudiation and mitigated their loss. The charterers were thus not liable for the hire charges for the final eight months.

In *Salaried Staff London Loan Co Ltd v Swears & Wells* 1985 SLT 326 tenants made an anticipatory breach of a 34-year lease five years into the lease, but the landlord was held entitled to sit back and require performance. However, it was accepted that there might be circumstances in which the landlord would be expected to take steps to mitigate, i.e. by looking for another tenant.

3.15.5.4 The innocent party's choice The innocent party may feel that by holding out for performance he is keeping the contract alive, there being the possibility that the other party will change his mind and perform. However, care should be taken when deciding to hold out for performance, for, if any supervening factor rendered the contract frustrated in the interim, both the right to rescind and the right to claim damages would be lost. In *Avery* v *Bowden* [1855] 5 E&B 714, Bowden chartered Avery's ship and agreed to load her with a cargo at Odessa within 45 days. The ship went to Odessa and, before the 45 days had elapsed, B told the ship's captain that he would not be loading a cargo. The ship stayed on in the hope that Bowden might change his mind. Before the expiry of the 45 days, the Crimean war broke out rendering performance of the contract illegal. Thus the right to rescind was lost.

3.15.5.5 Penalty damages clauses Contracting parties often include clauses in written contracts which stipulate for a certain sum to be payable in the event of any or certain breaches of contract. As long as such sums represent a reasonable pre-estimate of the loss which would flow from the breach in question such clauses are perfectly enforceable. They tend to be referred to as *liquidated damages* clauses in such circumstances. However, if they make no attempt to pre-estimate the loss and are in reality simply a fine or penalty they are not enforceable. This is because the purpose of damages for breach of contract is to compensate actual foreseeable loss and not to impose penalties. So the law is limiting the extent to which the parties can impose burdens upon each other, insisting that damages should represent the estimated real losses of the innocent party (for a discussion of control of agreed remedies, see Collins, 'Control of Agreed Remedies' in Willett (ed.), *Fairness in Contract,* forthcoming, Elgar, (1996)).

The leading case on this issue is *Dunlop Pneumatic Tyre Co* v *New Garage & Motor Co Ltd* [1915] AC 79 where the House of Lords laid down rules for the construction of these clauses. The relevant parts of the judgment are reproduced below in the Cases and Materials section for Chapter 3.

One factor which strongly indicates a penalty as opposed to liquidated damages is the imposition of the same penalty in the event of different types of loss, some serious and some trifling. For example, in *Dingwall* v *Burnett* 1912 SC 1097, an agreement for the lease of an hotel contained obligations of varying importance, with a provision for payment of £50 for breach of any of them. This was held to be a penalty clause. On the other hand the circumstances may be such that it is very difficult to estimate loss. If this is the case the courts will not take such a harsh view of clauses which fix a sum. In *Clydebank Engineering Co* v *Castaneda* (1904) 7 F (HL) 77 the contract stipulated a payment of £500 per day to the Spanish Government during delayed delivery of torpedo boats. This was upheld on the ground that accurate estimation of the loss was impossible at the time of contracting.

3.15.6   Bars to enforcement
Parties may be barred from enforcing their contractual rights.

The right to enforce an obligation where one party is in breach of contract is limited by the Prescription and Limitation (Scotland) Act 1973, which relates to the case where an action in both contract and delict is barred by the passage of time. The relevant sections are set out in the Cases and Materials section for Chapter 4.

The right to set an agreement aside or not to perform it, e.g., as a result of the other party's misrepresentation may be restricted by the rules on setting aside voidable contracts (see 3.7.2 above).

3.16 QUASI-CONTRACT

Quasi-contract imposes obligations on parties who have not undertaken any contractual obligation. These obligations are similar to those flowing from contract in that they may relate to the paying of money or the returning of property. They are imposed for reasons of equity. For example, where contractual negotiations have broken down or where a contract has been frustrated, one or both parties may have incurred expense in pursuance of the transaction. This expense may be recoverable under principles of quasi-contract. Domestic quasi-contract (excluding general average and salvage) may broadly be classified as follows.

3.16.1 Restitution
Restitution requires a party who has no title to goods to restore them to their true owner. This covers cases where goods are delivered by mistake; stolen goods are found or purchased; a period of hire comes to an end; or money has been paid under mistake of fact. Where stolen goods are concerned, the bona fide purchaser is liable for any profit he makes on a re-sale if the original owner cannot recover the goods.

3.16.2 Recompense
This principle is defined by Bell as follows:

> where one has gained by the lawful act of another, done without any intention of donation, he is bound to recompense or indemnify that other to the extent of the gain (Principles, 538).

This definition does not make it clear that, for the principle to operate, it is also necessary that the pursuer should have suffered some loss and that he had no other legal remedy open to him. The doctrine is equitable and, as such, each case must be examined on its own merits. Its most typical application will be to a situation where goods have been supplied or work done but the price cannot be recovered under an orthodox contractual claim, e.g., because the contract is frustrated. It is important to bear in mind that the amount recoverable in recompense is not what has been expended, but rather a sum to take account of the gain conferred on the other party. So, if a great deal of time was expended on a construction which was destroyed, it is unlikely that there would be a claim in recompense. Equally, while the defender must have been enriched in some manner, the pursuer must have suffered a loss of some kind. It is not sufficient that the defender should simply have benefited incidentally from something which the pursuer has done for his own purposes. For example, in *Edinburgh Tramway Co* v *Courtenay* 1905 SC 99, the pursuers had let to an advertising contractor the right to display advertisements on their vehicles. Under the terms of the agreement, the contractor had to supply the fittings. The company obtained new vehicles which had suitable fittings. The contractor therefore did not need to supply fittings. The company was unable to recover any recompense from the contractor because they (the company) had lost nothing from the contractor's gain.

3.16.3 *Negotiorum gestio*

A *negotiorum gestor* is someone who intervenes to manage someone else's affairs, where the latter is unable to manage them himself. Although no authority has been given for the intervention, it is assumed that if it had been possible to ask for authority it would have been granted. The *negotiorum gestor* is entitled to recompense for expenditure incurred in the course of managing the other person's affairs. This principle will typically apply where a person is suddenly incarcerated as a result of imprisonment or insanity or where, for some other reasons they cannot be contacted when action must be taken. *Negotiorum gestio* is closely related to the doctrine of agency of necessity (see Chapter 5, para. 5.2.4). Both will apply rarely in modern times when ease of communication is the norm.

Further reading
Gloag and Henderson, (1987), *Introduction to the Law of Scotland*, 9th edn, W. Green, Chapters 3–15.
D. M. Walker, (1995), *The Law of Contracts and Related Obligations in Scotland*, 3rd edn, T&T Clark.
Woolman (1994) *Contract*, 2nd edn, W. Green.

CHAPTER FOUR

Delictual Rights and Duties

4.1 FUNCTION, NATURE AND EXTENT OF DELICT

Chapter 3 examined the nature of obligations undertaken by contractual processes. Such obligations are traditionally said to give rise to 'personal rights', i.e. the right to expect the other party to perform his side of the bargain. Such enforceable obligations and rights are clearly integral to commercial relationships but could never form the full picture. This is because individual and business interests are capable of being promoted and at the same time prejudiced by such an infinite class of people and by equally infinite means. The vast majority of these people will never have 'promised' in a contractual sense to behave or not behave in a certain way.

For example, I clearly do not 'promise' not to drive carelessly and injure other road users. However, no one would imagine that if I do so I will not be liable in some way. In fact, I will probably be criminally liable for the offence of reckless or careless driving but I will normally also be liable in civil law to compensate those to whom I have caused injury. This liability rests on principles of 'delict' or 'reparation' (known in English Law as 'tort'). Similarly a manufacturer would not normally be taken to have 'promised' anyone other than employees or immediate customers that his products will be safe, or that his operations will not cause offence (by way of smell, noise or fumes, for example). Again the redress for those affected who find themselves outside of the contractual nexus lies in the law of delict.

In other words delict may be said to extend the range of people whose interests must be respected. The right to have interests protected in this sense is said to arise from law, (as opposed to rights and obligations in contract which arise from agreement between two or more parties); such rights are generally termed 'real rights'. The essence of a real right is that once established it is enforceable against anyone whose actions interfere with its exercise. The right, for example, to safe passage on the highway or to good reputation may be vindicated against all those who interfere by means of careless driving or defamatory statements. It should, however, be borne in mind that many contractual obligations (although arising within the context of a relationship which has been voluntarily undertaken) have in reality been fixed by law.

4.1.1   Delict, business and social values
One of the key purposes of the law of delict is therefore to determine the extent to which obligations are owed to those to whom no contractual commitment has been made. In a business context, this is of most relevance in determining liability for the manufacture of products, the provision of services and the use of premises (see below).

Liability in delict is traditionally determined by asking whether A has suffered loss as a result of a legal wrong committed by B. This is encapsulated in the maxim *damnum* (loss) *datum* (caused) *injuria* (legal wrong). This begs several questions. First, how is one to know which acts or omissions are deemed 'wrongful'? Secondly, what type of 'loss' is seen as compensatable?

From a practical point of view, businesses and those whose lives they affect must know what behaviour, in what circumstances, and with what consequences will give rise to liabilities. When will there be liability for a product which injures a consumer or for advice which is ill-conceived? With some sense of the answers to such questions businesses can plan their activities. They can stay sufficiently abreast of research into product risks as to be able to make out a credible 'development risks' defence (see 4.8.4.5 below). They can structure the format and substance of advice so that it is less likely to fall below the law's standards (see 4.2.4 below).

As we did with contract, it is appropriate to stand a little further back from delict and consider the social and economic choices which it must make. It is in the business of protecting certain interests, which the parties have not protected via the autonomous act of contracting with the defender in question, i.e. delict will protect even where protection has not been 'bought' by a contract with the defender. This is fundamentally because it is recognised that it is unrealistic to expect private and individual protection to be taken against all of those who might cause us prejudice and who may be in much the stronger position to prevent the loss occurring or to protect against the burdens it causes.

For example, the recipient of a gift will not find it easy to obtain a contractual warranty or guarantee as to safety from the party who manufactured it or sold it, to the party now donating it; the pedestrian or the party entering temporarily into premises will find it impossible to obtain contractual protection from the driver or owner against injury. Even the purchaser of unsafe goods may find that his claim against the retailer in contract (see 6.6. below) is useless because the retailer is insolvent.

On the other hand, the driver or the manufacturer is in a strong position to prevent harm occurring through careful driving, good quality management, etc. He (or his insurer) also knows how likely the problem is to occur and can therefore insure against liability. However, quite apart from wishing to protect people against losses which they could not take autonomous steps to protect themselves from, there may be some forms of prejudice which society finds unacceptable and wishes to control, not only in the interest of the particular individual who was injured but also in the interests of society. So the law of delict wishes to discourage and deter negligent conduct, because such conduct is economically inefficient as well as socially harmful.

At the same time, when we speak of negligent conduct which affects others, the law will normally impose liability only where the defender can foresee the potential for harm to the pursuer and the parties stand in such a relationship of proximity that it is reasonable to expect the defender to prevent harm being caused to the pursuer; and there is a causal link between the negligence and the loss, and the damage caused is not too remote (see 4.2, 4.3 and 4.6 below).

Other behaviour which is difficult for an injured party to protect against contractually, and which is socially and economically undesirable, is intentional acts by others which are intended to cause economic/commercial harm, and which go beyond free and fair competition, marketing etc. (see 4.11 below); and use of one's property in ways which interfere with the peaceful enjoyment of property by others (see 4.9 below). Both of these sorts of activities are regulated by delict. Indeed, in the case of nuisance, which regulates interference with the comfortable enjoyment of the property of others, only a small degree of fault or negligence is required, probably because of the large degree of control which we normally have over activities likely to cause such injury to others' property, and the limited control which the other party has. If I own domestic, commercial or industrial property then I am in a strong position to know what risks are likely to emanate from it, while the owners of neighbouring property which may be affected by such risks are less well-informed. It is clear who is best able to prevent the risk materialising into a loss, or to protect against the loss by insurance. For these reasons a high level of liability is placed on the owner, against which he can then take out insurance. In the case of products which injure consumers, the law also imposes liability without proof of negligence, on the basis of the considerable control which the producer has over the safety of his products.

Where personal injury or damage to property is concerned, the law will generally impose at least a negligence standard of care (see 4.2 below), and is very reluctant to see the risk passed back to the party suffering the loss (see 3.11.6 above), i.e. we are not typically expected to protect ourselves contractually or by insurance against the foreseeable consequences of the negligence of others. However, when it comes to economic loss, not flowing from physical injury or damage to property (and not intentionally caused), although the same duty of care test is theoretically used, the law is much more inclined to be unsympathetic to pursuers (see 4.2.3–4.3 below). There are a number of reasons for this. First, it tends to be easier to cause economic loss, whether by the production of a defective product or by the carrying out of a defective service. A disappointed expectation in terms of quality is much more common than actual injury or damage to property. It is true that the negligent party is still in a better position to prevent the problem arising than is the party affected. However, the potentially large number of claims may prompt us to say that there is an unacceptable burden on defenders if they must compensate for such losses. There clearly is an argument that the loss is morally of a less significant nature than damage to person or property, and that if protection against such a loss is desired it should be contracted for with the party likely to cause the loss, or via a separate insurance policy. At the same time it may be difficult to obtain such protection, because the party likely to cause the loss simply refuses to give such protection, or the protection from whatever source is extremely costly. It may also be that the party likely to cause the loss is responsible for raising expectations as to the standard of the product or service he offers, such that there is a strong element of reliance that there will not be quality problems. In deciding upon the recovery of economic loss these are the sorts of considerations which must come into play (see 4.2.4–5 below; for further discussion of the social and economic policy choices facing the law of delict, see Howells & Weatherill, *Consumer Protection* (1995), Dartmouth; Canaghan & Mansell, *The Wrongs of Tort* (1993), Pluto; Bernstein, *Economic Loss* (1993), Longman).

The remainder of this chapter will consider the principles of delictual liability which most affect commercial activities such as the supply of goods and services, the use of business premises and the intentional interference with business relations of others. We will start with delictual liability for negligence, which is of the broadest significance to commercial activities.

4.2 NEGLIGENCE: DUTY OF CARE

Negligence developed as the main means of extending liability beyond the contractual nexus. It is traditionally taken to require the establishment of three factors – the existence of a duty of care, breach of that duty, and consequent damage.

The question as to whether a duty of care is owed by one party to another may depend on a multitude of factors. However, the application and inter-relation of these factors can only properly be understood if one key premise is appreciated. This is that the law is basically struggling to define the range of people to whom duties are owed; the range of activities which may be subject to duties; and the types of interest which one owes a duty not to interfere with (e.g., physical injury, damage to property, financial loss).

The issue of loss requires brief elaboration at this stage. The general test for establishing a duty of care tends to be easier to pass where the loss involves physical injury to or damage to the property of the pursuer. If financial loss (e.g., loss of earnings) results from this, then there is no more difficulty than there would have been if the damage had simply been to person or property. The test becomes more difficult to satisfy when there is pure economic loss, i.e. loss which does not flow from physical or property damage (see, e.g., loss caused by negligent misstatement, which is usually purely financial, at 4.2.4 below, and where pure economic loss is caused by a negligent act, at 4.3. below). As has been said above, this is because liability for such losses is often felt to be too burdensome for defenders, there being a greater expectation that pursuers should protect themselves against such losses.

4.2.1 The neighbour principle

Until 1932 there was no generalised concept of duty of care in negligence. However, in *Donoghue* v *Stevenson* 1932 SC (HL) 31, Lord Atkin sought to rationalise and develop the older case law into a coherent principle, the 'neighbour principle'. The facts of the case are well known. The pursuer drank a bottle of ginger-beer manufactured by the defender which had been purchased for her by a friend. The bottle containing the ginger-beer was opaque, it was opened by the shopkeeper (who supplied it) and an amount of the drink was poured into a glass. The pursuer's friend thereafter poured the remainder of the ginger-beer into the glass, when a decomposing snail which had been in the bottle emerged. The pursuer claimed that she had suffered shock and illness and sued the manufacturer in negligence. She was not able to sue the café owner for breach of the implied terms of the Sale of Goods Act as to merchantability and fitness for purpose, because she was not in a contractual relationship with him. She therefore sued in delict, arguing that the manufacturer of a product owed a duty to her as the ultimate consumer of the product to ensure that there was no injurious element in it.

The House of Lords held that the manufacturer of products, which he sells in such a form as to show that he intends them to reach the ultimate consumer in the form in which they left him, with no reasonable possibility of intermediate examination being cognisant of the risk of injury to life or property, owes a duty to the consumer to take reasonable care. The defender had failed to take reasonable care and was therefore liable to the pursuer for the injury which she sustained.

In the course of his judgment, Lord Atkin took the opportunity to place the manufacturer's duty to the consumer in the context of the neighbour principle, which he described in the following terms:

> The rule that you are to love your neighbour, becomes, in law, that you must not injure your neighbour; and the lawyer's question, Who is my neighbour?, receives a restricted reply. You must take reasonable care to avoid acts or omissions which you can reasonably foresee would be likely to injure your neighbour. Who, then, in law is my neighbour? The answer seems to be – persons who are so closely and directly affected by my act that I ought reasonably to have them in contemplation as being so affected when I am directing my mind to the acts or omissions which are called in question.

4.2.2 Activities to which the neighbour principle applies

The neighbour principle and its subsequent development and qualification by the courts has helped to define the various circumstances in which duties are owed in respect of products and services. In the context of production, it will apply in the case of all manner of dangerous defects in goods, structures or installations which may have been caused by careless workmanship, design defects or simply poor quality control. It might also apply to a failure to withdraw a product from the market where it is known to be potentially harmful. Although in *Donoghue* v *Stevenson* the duty applied to the manufacturer, it can extend to anyone whose failure to take care might be foreseen to result in harm to another. So, in circumstances where retailers play a part in the manufacturing process, e.g., where a hotel prepares food, or in a situation where retailers might be expected to notice a manufacturing defect, they too could be held to owe a duty of care. The duty of care could also extend to those responsible for the marketing or assembling of goods, whose failure to detect or warn of a defect could lead to damage or injury, e.g., sales and marketing managers, sub-contractors, assemblers, packagers and bottlers, wholesalers, distributors and those who let goods on hire.

In the context of the provision of services, the duty may be owed by professionals and others who carry out treatment, give specialist advice or do specialist work which they expect will be relied upon, or by anyone who carries out skilled or manual labour of some kind for the benefit of others. It may also be owed by public authorities who have policing or regulatory functions to protect the public interest in some way. The significance of potential liability in all such cases is again the extension of responsibility for one's activities beyond the contractual nexus. For instance, an accountant might be liable for giving a negligent and exaggerated picture of a company's profitability, which has induced investment by another party (see *J E B Fasteners* v *Marks Bloom & Co* [1983] 1 All ER 583 and *Caparo Industries PLC* v *Dickman & Others* [1990] 1 All ER 568 para. 4.2.4 below). Similarly where A contracts with B to have his factory re-fitted, B may sub-contract for the services of a range of specialists, e.g., plasterers and electricians. If one of these specialists is negligent and causes damage to the factory, he may be liable to A in negligence, which may be a valuable recourse for A where B has protected himself from contractual responsiblity by an exemption clause, or where he has gone out of business.

This section has looked very generally at the sort of activities that *might* be covered. However, we must now examine the rules developed to define precisely *who* duties can extend to.

4.2.3   Who is one's neighbour?

The original *Donoghue* v *Stevenson* type 'neighbour' was a person who one could reasonably be foreseen or 'contemplated' as likely to be affected by one's actions such that they would suffer injury or damage to their property. However, the precise circumstances must always be considered. In *Bourhill* v *Young* 1942 SC (HL) 78, a motorcyclist negligently overtook another vehicle and caused an accident. A woman who arrived on the scene suffered from shock when she saw the aftermath of the accident. It was held that no duty of care was owed to her by the motorcyclist because she could not have been in his contemplation. In this way she could be distinguished from those whom he might have struck with his motorcycle or even those who might have been struck by flying metal in the wake of the collision. Such injurious consequences for those immediately at the scene could clearly be contemplated but the nervous reaction of someone who only later arrived on the scene could not.

It is not necessary to have foreseen precisely what happened for there to be a duty of care, as long as the type of injury is reasonably foreseeable — see *Hughes* v *Lord Advocate* 1963 SC (HL) 31, where it did not matter that negligent workers who left paraffin lamps beside a manhole covered only with tarpaulin could not have foreseen that a child would take the lamp, climb into the manhole and fall, burning himself. They could foresee that there was a risk of danger by fire in a general sense, and this was enough for there to be a duty of care. This idea of reasonable foreseeability of a general type of harm has helped to allow a duty of care to apply to those who negligently allow third parties to cause harm to the pursuer by, for example, allowing borstal boys under one's supervision to escape and damage a yacht (*Home Office* v *Dorset Yacht Co* [1970] AC 1004); not properly securing premises one is working on so that thieves obtain entry via those premises to an adjacent jeweller's shop (*Squire* v *Perth & Kinross DC* 1986 SLT 30); supplying an alarm system which fails and thereby aids a burglary (*Frys Metals Ltd* v *Aurative Ltd* 1991 SLT 689); but, again, the final harm caused must have been a type foreseeable, so that this test is not met where failure to secure premises leads not only to a break in, but to a fire, when neither the building nor the contents were especially inflammable (*Maloco* v *Littlewoods* 1986 SLT 272).

4.2.3.1 Foreseeability and the other factors — the current position It seems now to be the case that for any duty of care to arise there must, along with foreseeability, also exist a relationship of proximity between the parties, and it must be fair and reasonable to impose a duty in the circumstances; but this is far from saying that all types of pursuer, defender, pursuer-defender relationships, types of loss, etc. should be looked at in the same way. Rather, different areas should develop in recognition of the different problems raised by different categories of case (especially economic versus physical loss — for further discussion, see below). This overall approach is exemplified in Lord Bridge's judgment in *Caparo Industries* v *Dickman* [1990] 1 All ER 568, at 572–4:

In determining the existence and scope of the duty of care which one person may owe to another in the infinitely varied circumstances of human relationships there has for long been a tension between two different approaches. Traditionally the law finds the existence of the duty in different specific situations each exhibiting its own particular characteristics. In this way the law has identified a wide variety of duty situations, all falling within the ambit of the tort of negligence, but sufficiently distinct to require separate definition of the essential ingredients by which the existence of the duty is to be recognised . . . What emerges is that, in addition to the foreseeability of damage, necessary ingredients in any situation giving rise to a duty of care are that there should exist between the party owing the duty and the party to whom it is owed a relationship characterised by the law as one of 'proximity' or 'neighbourhood' and that the situation should be one in which the court considers it fair, just and reasonable that the law should impose a duty of a given scope upon the one party for the benefit of the other. But it is implicit in the passages referred to that the concepts of proximity and fairness embodied in these additional ingredients are not susceptible of any such precise definition as would be necessary to give them utility as practical tests, but amount in effect to little more than convenient labels to attach to the features of different specific situations which, on a detailed examination of all the circumstances, the law recognises pragmatically as giving rise to a duty of care of a given scope. Whilst recognising, of course, the importance of the underlying general principles common to the whole field of negligence, I think the law has now moved in the direction of attaching greater significance to the more traditional categorisation of distinct and recognisable situations as guides to the existence, the scope and the limits of the varied duties of care which the law imposes. We must now, I think, recognise the wisdom of the words of Brennan J in the High Court of Australia in *Sutherland Shire Council* v *Heyman* (1985) 60 ALR 1 at 43-44, where he said:

> It is preferable, in my view, that the law should develop novel categories of negligence incrementally and by analogy with established categories, rather than by a massive extension of a prima facie duty of care restrained only by indefinable 'considerations which ought to negative, or to reduce or limit the scope of the duty or the class of person to whom it is owed.

One of the most important distinctions always to be observed lies in the law's essentially different approach to the different kinds of damage which one party may have suffered in consequence of the acts or omissions of another. It is one thing to owe a duty of care to avoid causing injury to the person or property of others. It is quite another to avoid causing others to suffer purely economic loss.

In *The Nicholas H* [1994] 3 All ER 686, it was held that the *Caparo* requirements of foreseeability, proximity, and fairness and reasonableness of imposing a duty should be applied in all negligence cases, whatever the type of loss concerned. However, as we shall see below, the courts continue to look to specific concepts and solutions to respond to particular problems.

4.2.3.2 A note on terminology These labels (i.e. foreseeability, proximity, etc.) are fairly vague and open-ended, and they give the courts a fair degree of flexibility. They will, from now on, be the hurdles which a pursuer must cross to establish a duty of care. However, they will be interpreted strongly by reference to the tests which have evolved over the years for different categories of case, e.g., negligent misstatement causing economic loss, and negligent acts causing economic loss. Indeed, the focus on categories of case is made clear by Lord Bridge's remarks in *Caparo* (see above). The language used by the cases over the years to express the test they were applying will clearly not fit neatly into the three-prong test now applying. There has always been, and there remains, the foreseeability requirement. However, what has been spoken of as proximity, reliance, special relationships etc. probably roughly equates to the other two requirements of proximity and fairness/reasonableness.

4.2.4 Negligent misstatement causing economic loss

The duty of care principle has developed through various categories of case, one of them being where the negligence is in the making of a statement, the preparation of a report or the giving of advice, all of which might be relied upon by the other party, causing economic loss. As has been said, the law takes a more restrictive approach where recovery for economic loss is concerned, looking for a significant degree of reasonable reliance by the pursuer on the defender to justify imposing a duty.

In *Hedley Byrne & Co Ltd* v *Heller & Partners Ltd* [1964] AC 465, Heller & Partners were bankers to Easipower Ltd, which was a client of advertising agents, Hedley Byrne & Co. Through their own bank, the plaintiffs made an enquiry to the defendants as to the financial standing of Easipower Ltd, mentioning an advertising contract for £100,000. The reply was headed 'Confidential. For your private use and without responsibility on the part of the bank or its officials'. The letter said that Easipower was a 'respectably constituted company, considered good for its ordinary business engagements. Your figures are larger than we are accustomed to see'. Relying on this, the plaintiffs incurred expenditure on behalf of Easipower and lost £17,000 when the company went into liquidation. The plaintiffs alleged that the reference had been made carelessly and that the defendants owed them a duty to take reasonable care in giving them information. The House of Lords agreed that in the appropriate circumstances there could be such a duty although the defendants were not liable on the facts, because of the disclaimer of responsibility.

4.2.4.1 The 'special relationship' and reasonable reliance The duty of care in such circumstances was held to arise in the context of a 'special relationship'. Lord Reid said that this arose:

> where it is plain that the party seeking information or advice was trusting the other to exercise such a degree of care as the circumstances required, where it was reasonable for him to do that, and where the other gave the information or advice when he knew or ought to have known that the enquirer was relying on him. . . . [where a person] is so placed that others could reasonably rely upon his judgment or his skill or upon his ability to make careful inquiry, [and] a person takes it upon himself to give information or advice to, or allows his information or advice to be passed on to, another person who, as he knows or should know, will place reliance upon it, then a duty of care will arise.

What seems to be necessary is reliance, which the maker of the statement knows or ought to know about and which is reasonable. The maker of the statement is thereby assuming responsibility for the statement. In *Henderson and others* v *Merrett Syndicates Ltd and others* [1994] 3 All ER 506, Lord Goff said that:

> an assumption of responsibility coupled with the concomitant reliance may give rise to a [delictual] duty of care.

So one is said to assume responsibility for statements (and possibly professional or expert work generally), to those with whom one has such a close and special relationship as to visualise that they will reasonably place reliance on the statement's work in question (see J. M. Thomson, 1995, SLT 139).

One of the most difficult questions is when reliance can be said to be reasonable. It would not be reasonable to rely on opinions expressed on social or informal occasions, or even in a professional or business context, unless it was clear that the pursuer was seeking considered advice (see *Mutual Life & Citizens' Assurance Co Ltd* v *Evatt* [1977] AC 793, CA).

In *Howard Marine & Dredging Co Ltd* v *Ogden & Sons (Excavations) Ltd* [1978] 2 All ER 1134, Lord Denning did not consider it reasonable to rely on an opinion given 'off the cuff' over the telephone. However, in *Chaudhry* v *Prabhakar & Another* [1988] 3 All ER 718, CA, the defendant, at the request of a friend, found a second-hand car for sale and advised the friend to buy it, knowing that she was relying on his skill and judgment. The Court of Appeal held that the defendant owed to the friend a duty of care and would be liable to her for any negligent misstatement concerning the car if she relied on it and thereby suffered loss.

It seems that even where a businessman is not in the business of giving advice the duty may arise when an enquirer consults the businessman in the course of his business and makes it plain that he is seeking considered advice and intends to act on that advice. If the businessman chooses to give advice without any warning or qualification, he will be under a duty to take such care as is reasonable in the circumstances. In *Esso Petroleum Co Ltd* v *Mardon* [1976] QB 501, although the defendants were not in the business of giving advice, they were experienced and had special knowledge and skill in estimating the petrol throughput at a filling station, whereas the plaintiff did not. As such they were responsible for the negligent estimation given by their agent to a prospective purchaser.

4.2.4.2 Negligent statements and contracts A further significance of the *Esso* case was that it involved two parties who subsequently, and as a result of the statement in question, entered into a contractual relationship. This gave plaintiffs in England a useful course of action where they were misled by the other contracting party as to the benefits of entering a contract. However, pursuers in Scotland could not (until recently) claim damages in such circumstances, unless the other party had been fraudulent (see *Manners* v

Whitehead (1898) 1 F 171). Such a course of action is, however, now enshrined in the Law Reform (Miscellaneous Provisions) (Scotland) Act 1985. Section 10(1) provides for damages to be recoverable by a party who has been induced to enter into a contract by a negligent misrepresentation made by or on behalf of the other party to the contract. It should be noted that the pursuer will still be required to prove the existence of a special relationship giving rise to a duty on the maker of the statement to take care and a breach of that duty. This still places Scottish pursuers in a far less favourable position than their English counterparts. For the latter, the Misrepresentation Act 1967 abolishes the need to prove a special relation-ship/duty of care as between contracting parties and places the burden of proof on the maker of a false statement to prove that he had reasonable grounds for believing it, i.e. he was not negligent (see *Howard Marine* v *Ogden* above).

4.2.4.3 Professional activities and statements Professionals such as account-ants, solicitors, architects and surveyors, by the preparation of a document or report, may affect a range of people, e.g., clients, potential investors and potential property purchasers. If they carry out this service negligently, the question arises as to whether they are liable to compensate those affected. The criterion for deciding on this question is effectively the same as that applied to negligent misstatements generally, i.e., is there a special relation-ship which justifies reliance by the pursuer on the defender that the work will be undertaken and/or the advice given with a reasonable degree of care and skill? The defender is then said to have 'assumed responsibility' to the pursuer. However, we find that the law is reluctant to impose a duty where the number of potential pursuers is large. The concern to limit the range of potential pursuers then finds its way into assessments of proximity/fairness and reasonableness (see *Caparo*, below).

In *JEB Fasteners Ltd* v *Marks Bloom & Co.* [1983] 1 All ER 583, it was held that auditors who prepared a company's accounts, knowing that the company was in difficulty and needed finance, ought to have foreseen that a takeover was a possible source of finance, and that someone contemplating a takeover might rely on the accounts. Accordingly, in preparing the accounts, the auditors owed a duty of care to a person who did so. Their duty would not extend, however, to 'strangers of whom they have heard nothing and to whom their employer without their knowledge may choose to show their accounts'. A similar decision was reached in *Twomax Ltd* v *Dickson, McFarlane and Robinson* 1984 SLT 424.

The significance of these decisions may have been severely restricted by the *Caparo* case already quoted from at 4.2.3.1 above, in which the concern to limit the range of pursuers is evident.

In this case Caparo purchased 100,000 shares in Fidelity plc in June 1984. Several days later Fidelity's accounts for the year ending 31 March 1984 were issued to shareholders, including Caparo. Relying on these accounts Caparo purchased a further 50,000 shares and subsequently made a successful takeover bid for Fidelity. In July 1985 Caparo brought an action against, *inter alia*, Touche Ross, the auditors of Fidelity, alleging negligent over-valuing of stock and insufficient provision for after sales credits. Caparo alleged it would not have paid what it did for the shares if it had seen an accurate report. It was argued that Touche Ross owed a duty of care to investors and potential investors; that they ought to have known that Fidelity's profits and share price had fallen and Fidelity required financial assistance; and that, therefore, they ought to have foreseen that Fidelity was vulnerable to a takeover bid and persons such as Caparo might rely on its accounts for deciding whether to make such a bid and might suffer loss if the accounts were inaccurate.

The House of Lords held that no duty was owed to Caparo in its capacity as an investing shareholder. The view was taken that a relationship giving rise to reasonable reliance arises only where the plaintiff knows that the defendant belongs to a determinate class of people who will be shown the material, and can thereby be expected to rely on it for the purposes of a particular type of transaction. The idea seemed to be that there are too many shareholders who could use the information for too many reasons to impose liability. The facts were distinguished from those arising in *Smith* v *Bush* and *Harris* v *Wyre Forest DC* [1989] 2 WLR 790, HL (where plaintiffs recovered losses suffered by purchasing property in reliance on a negligent valuation), on the basis that in these cases the negligent valuer knew that the valuation report would be passed to a prospective purchaser who would base his decision to buy on its contents, i.e. a specific transaction was in the offing. The conclusion on this category of cases seems to be that it is these sorts of factors which will decide whether the general requirements of foreseeability, proximity and fairness and reasonableness are satisfied (see above). The terminology may come in slightly different forms to suit the particular circumstances.

These concepts of foreseeability, proximity, assumption of responsibility, etc. are clearly very open-textured, and it is important to recognise that they are applied with strong reference to the social and economic realities of the various relationships and the results which these realities suggest as reasonable or fair. These realities involve the choices which parties may or may not have as to the risks to take; the protection which can be taken against such risks (whether by taking independent advice, taking out insurance or taking out a contractual form of protection from some party); whether there is a large class of potential pursuers who might be able to claim if they were affected — this means possibly opening the floodgates of liability and unfairly prejudicing potential defenders; and the implications of the imposition of a duty for allocations of risk which have already been made by other parties (e.g., an auditor may have excluded liability to those parties whom he thought would rely on the advice, but not in relation to the pursuer).

One distinction between *Caparo* and *Smith* and *Harris*, for example, is that potential investors of the *Caparo* sort are much more in the risk game than are first-time house buyers with limited resources, who would be hard pushed financially to seek the extra protection of a full survey.

Other recent cases in this area include *James McNaughton Papers Group Ltd* v *Hicks Anderson & Co* [1991] 1 All ER 134 and *Morgan Crucible Co plc* v *Hill Samuel Bank Ltd* [1991] 1 All ER 148. See also the discussion in J. G. Logie,

'Liability in Negligence', 1991 SLT 169 at 170 and the judgment in *Smith* v *Carter* 1994 SCLR 539, where the Caparo test is applied (reproduced in the Cases and Materials section for Chapter 4).

4.2.5 Negligent misstatement, valuations and exclusions

It has now been confirmed in England that valuers may owe a duty of care to prospective house purchasers in circumstances such as those which applied in the cases of *Smith* and *Harris*. In *UCB Bank plc* v *Dundas Wilson, CS* 1989 SLT 243, it was held that a similar duty might arise in Scots law. An attempt to exclude or restrict liability for breach of this duty of care will be subject to control under s. 16 of the Unfair Contract Terms Act 1977 (see 3.11 above).

4.2.6 Non-reliance economic loss involving professional or expert defenders

The above strains of the neighbourhood principle – i.e. those relating to advice, statements, reports etc. involving professionals and experts – have in common, *inter alia*, the requirement of reasonable reliance by the pursuer on the defender in the making of the statement or the preparation of the report. However, a distinct approach was taken in the English case, *Ross* v *Caunters* [1980] Ch 297, where an intended beneficiary under a will was held entitled to recover damages from a solicitor whose negligence had nullified her entitlement. The rationale of this decision seems to be that the execution of the will was intended to confer a benefit on the plaintiff. Therefore, although she had not contracted with the solicitor and could not be said to be taking action on reliance on him as such, she had a reasonable expectation of gain, which had been frustrated. It is also rather difficult to speak of the defender 'assuming a responsibility' to someone he has not even met, if assuming responsibility is akin to promising to be liable. This decision was specifically approved by the House of Lords in *White* v *Jones* [1995] 3 WLR 187 (HL). The Outer House, however, in the next case refused to follow *Ross* v *Caunters*. In *Weir* v *J.M. Hodge & Son* 1990 SLT 266, Lord Weir said that he was bound by a nineteenth-century House of Lords decision *Robertson* v *Fleming* (1861) 4 Macq. 167, according to which a professional lawyer employed by one party to do work for the benefit of another cannot be liable to the latter for loss due to his negligence (but see *MacDougall* v *Clydesdale Bank Trs* 1993 SCLR 832, in which the Outer House expressed sympathy with *Ross* v *Caunters*).

If *Ross* v *Caunters and White* v *Jones* are ultimately accepted as part of Scots law, then it would be necessary to think of reliance as only being one way in which liability can arise where the defender is professional or has expertise of some kind. *Ross* and *White* suggest that where a professional or expert stands in such a close (or 'special') relationship to another as to have power over the attainment of the other's expectations, then there may be a duty. Here we see the limitations of concepts such as reliance and assumption of responsibility when it comes to trying to cover all of the different ways in which pursuers may be so 'closely and directly affected' by the actions of defenders as to justify a duty. Basing duty on whether one is closely and directly affected goes back to the first principles of *Donoghue* v *Stevenson* (Lord Atkin at p. 580 and above at 4.2.1). It is submitted that this still provides a realistic starting point, allowing the courts to deal with the many different ways in which A can impact B. Looking to the current test the courts can decide if there is a situation of close and direct impact. If so, they can hold there to be foreseeability and proximity. It is still open, however, to say that there is no duty under the third criteria of fairness and reasonableness — perhaps because the pursuer belongs to a large class of potential pursuers and there is the danger of opening the floodgates, or because the pursuer could have bargained for alternative protection.

4.2.7 Non-reliance economic loss caused by statements

Spring v *Guardian Assurance plc* [1994] 3 All ER 129 also provide an example of a case in which one party (in this case an employer) was in a position to closely and directly affect the fate of an ex-employee by the sort of reference which he provided. The employer provided a negligent reference, accusing the ex-employee of fraud when in fact he had merely been incompetent. The employee clearly had not acted in reliance upon the reference, and although Lord Goff talked of the employer having assumed responsibility this also seems slightly unreal. He was, however, held to owe a duty of care, by both Lord Goff and three of the other judges. The other three preferred the broader approach of the *Caparo* test, saying that there was, on the facts, foreseeability, proximity and factors making it fair and reasonable to impose a duty. It should also be noted that this case also lacks the element of the defender who, in making the negligent statement, or doing the negligent act, is exercising some sort of professional expertise. So it is clear that the professional status of the defender, (just like the reliance of the pursuer or the assumption of responsibility by the defender) is not always necessary.

4.2.8 Overview

In the above cases we either find a statement or act by a professional or expert involving reliance or having some other impact, or a statement by someone who is not professional or expert which involves reliance or impacts another. The category of cases now to be considered involve *acts* rather than statements, and need not involve a professional or expert.

4.3 NEGLIGENT ACTS AND ECONOMIC LOSS WHERE PROPERTY INVOLVED

In many cases of liability for defective acts, all or part of the claim will represent damage to property (e.g., where negligent rewiring results in an explosion which damages plant and machinery), and/or alternatively personal injury. If such loss or injury leads in turn to financial loss, e.g., because a business has to close down until its machinery is operative or someone injured by a defective product has to take time off, then such financial loss is recoverable. Financial loss is also potentially recoverable when it arises as a result of the sort of situation described above. It is usually, of course, the primary type of loss in such cases.

There are also some cases in which the qualitative defectiveness of property or damage to property can cause economic loss to a party. Sometimes this is recoverable.

4.3.1 Types of property related economic loss
A negligent act might cause an economic loss of the following types:

(a) The supply of goods or of heritable property which is defective, either in a purely qualitative sense or because it is unsafe, although as yet it has caused no physical injury or damage to other property. By supply of a product we are not including only the party who supplied it to the pursuer under a contract, but also someone further up the chain of supply who may have been negligent in causing it to be defective. This type of loss has also been claimed against those engaged in the carrying out of an act or function which may stop such a product or heritable property from being defective, but which, if carried out negligently, will contribute to the defectiveness (e.g. the regulatory functions of local authorities in securing compliance with building regulations).

(b) A negligent act which damages something other than the property of the pursuer, but which damage causes an economic loss to the pursuer, e.g., damage to an electricity cable which feeds the pursuer's premises, damage to a bridge which is vital to the pursuer's business (see the *Norsk* case at 4.3.3.2 below), damage to property for which the pursuer is contractually responsible, or damage to property in the possession of a buyer who does not yet have legal ownership.

Category (a) is now generally seen as pure economic loss. There was never any doubt of this in cases where the product supplied was simply defective. However, the problem of classification proved difficult where the defect was dangerous to the pursuer or to other property belonging to the pursuer. This has been clarified by *Murphy* v *Brentwood DC* [1990] 2 All ER 908, at least to a point. The plaintiff purchased a house from a construction firm and after 11 years discovered cracks which were dangerous and would have cost £45,000 to correct. He sold the house at a price £36,000 lower than its market value would have been without the defects. It was held that the cost of remedying a dangerous defect was pure economic loss which was not in these circumstances recoverable.

By reaching this decision, the House overturned the decision in *Anns* v *Merton London Borough* [1977] 2 All ER 492, HL. The facts in that case were similar. The local authority had negligently approved plans to build maisonettes on inadequate foundations and it was held that in such circumstances an occupier could recover the cost of remedying the defects.

The position now is that unless the negligence in question leads to *actual* personal injury or damage to property other than the product or structure to which the negligence related, it is classed as pure economic loss. So the possessor of a dangerous product is in the same position as the possessor of a shoddy product as far as the classification of loss is concerned. This position was confirmed in *Department of the Environment* v *Thomas Bates & Son* [1990] 2 All ER 943, where the remedial work was required due to a builder's negligence. Again it was held that until actual physical injury or damage to other property took place the loss was purely economic. There are, however, still several issues in relation to which the position is uncertain. The first relates to how the law should define 'property other than the product' for the purposes of knowing whether or not physical or economic loss has been suffered.

In *D & F Estates* v *Church Comm. for England* [1988] 2 All ER 992, HL, it was suggested by Lord Bridge that if property was constituted by a 'complex structure' (e.g., a building) then damage to one part caused by negligent construction of another part could qualify as damage to other property, i.e. physical and not purely economic loss. However, it was decided in *Murphy* that, where the property was the work of one contractor, the component parts could not be viewed separately. This would suggest that if a car is supplied with a defective tyre which causes the car to crash, the loss is purely economic (in the absence of physical injury) – see discussion of a similar problem in the context of the Consumer Protection Act 1987 at 4.8 below.

It was accepted in *Murphy* that if one part of the structure had come separately, it might be viewed separately. So if a car tyre was supplied separately, or the wiring for a house carried out as a distinct contract, there might be liability if damage was caused to another part of the car or house.

The second problem is the suggestion by some of the judges in *Murphy* that if a defect in property needed to be remedied to prevent injury to a third party, the cost of remedial action might not be economic loss. The position is unclear.

The second category of loss, i.e. where the damage is to property not belonging to the pursuer, but upon which he is financially dependent or for which he is financially responsible, has always been categorised clearly as economic loss.

4.3.2 In what circumstances might economic loss be allowed?

Prior to *Junior Books* v *Veitchi Co* (below), it was not believed that either category of economic loss was recoverable (see *Dynamco Ltd* v *Holland Hannen & Cubitts (Scotland) Ltd* 1972 SLT 38, and Rodger, 'Some Reflections on *Junior Books*' in Birks (ed.), *The Frontiers of Liability*, 1994). However, the development of the duty of care concept in the *Junior Books* case suggests that there may be some scope for a wider range of claims in both categories.

In *Junior Books* v *Veitchi Co* 1982 SLT 492, the pursuers, who owned a factory, contracted with Ogilvie Builders for the laying of a new floor. The pursuers' architects nominated Veitchi Co as specialist sub-contractors. The floor was laid negligently and the pursuers successfully recovered the cost (economic loss) of remedying the situation. The specialist expertise of the Veitchi Co, along with the fact that they were nominated by the architects and were seen as being in a near to contractual relationship with the pursuers, were the main factors weighing in favour of there being sufficient proximity for a duty to arise. However, in *Muirhead* v *Industrial Tank Specialities* [1985] 3 All ER 705, a similar claim was refused. In this case, the defendants had manufactured pumps unsuitable for the British mains electricity system. Having passed down a chain of supply, involving at least four intermediary companies, the pumps were fitted in the plaintiff's lobster farm to re-circulate the water in the tanks. When the pumps failed, the plaintiff claimed for the loss of the lobsters and the economic loss, including loss of profit, on intended sales. The former claim was allowed but not the latter. It was held that a claim for economic loss was allowable in such circumstances only where there was very close proximity between the manufacturer and the ultimate purchaser and real reliance by the latter on the former (as there had been in *Junior Books*). In *D & F Estates* v *The Church Commission* [1988] 3 WLR 368, Lord Bridge said (at p. 381) that *Junior Books* was a unique case depending on the near contractual relationship which existed between the pursuer and the defender. It should not, he said, be taken as a statement of principle on the recoverability of economic loss.

The most recent decision to reach the House of Lords is *Murphy* v *Brentwood DC* (see 4.3.1 above for the facts) where Lord Keith appeared to confirm that once a loss is classed as economic it is virtually never recoverable outside *Hedley Byrne* type cases. Lord Oliver, on the other hand, said that the classification of the loss was not conclusive. It was, he said, a question of having regard to all of the factors to see if there was a sufficient relationship of proximity to give rise to a duty to prevent the type of loss in question (whatever it may be). He did indicate, however, that a closer degree of proximity would be required where the loss was economic.

The Scottish courts appear to tend towards Lord Oliver's approach. However, they seem to be ambivalent as to whether the existence of a series of contracts of which both parties form a link should contribute to, or detract from, any proximity argued for. There is also the question raised by damage to moveable property neither owned nor possessed by the pursuer in which the pursuer has an economic interest (i.e. the second category discussed at 4.3.1 above). The courts seem to say that where there is no proprietary or possessory title there can be no recovery (see the *Scott Lithgow* and *Landcatch* cases below).

In *Scott Lithgow Ltd* v *GEC Electrical Projects* 1989 GWD 1770, the pursuers sought damages in delict for negligent wiring carried out by sub-contractors which had caused economic loss, i.e. the need to replace the wiring. The Outer House (Lord Clyde) held that:

(a)   A claim for economic loss was not to be assessed on the basis of remoteness of damage rules.

(b)   The type of loss was not conclusive but only a factor in deciding whether a duty of care existed.

(c)   *Junior Books* had depended heavily on the close proximity between the parties, however there *might* exist proximity without the nomination of, or reliance on, sub-contractors, as in that case.

(d) It was significant that the parties had chosen to structure their relationship in a contractual chain and separate themselves by a main contractor. This indicated that no duty of care should be owed as between those (the pursuers and the sub-contractors) who had chosen not to make contractual commitments to each other.

(e) In *Junior Books* the pursuers had owned the defective property. The pursuers in the present case had failed to make averments on this matter. This was fatal to their claim.

This case was cited with approval in *Landcatch Ltd* v *Gilbert Gilkes* 1990 SLT 688, where Lord Morton had to decide on the recoverability of economic losses caused by negligent failure to maintain a proper supply of sea water to a fish farm. He focused on:

(a) Whether the pursuers could be said to have relied on the expertise of the defendants who had manufactured the water turbine generators. The answer was in the negative, it being more reasonable to rely on the consulting engineer.

(b) The fact that the pursuers had not nominated the defenders to do the work.

(c) The fact that the pursuers had no interest in the defective articles.

(d) The importance of the existence of a contractual claim to the existence, or otherwise, of a duty. The pursuers had not made the position clear, thereby fatally weakening their case.

In *Norwich Union Life Insurance Society* v *Covell Matthews Partnership* 1987 SLT 452, Lord McCluskey looked at reliance, the existence of a contractual chain and the general questions of proximity and foreseeability in holding the pursuer's claim to be relevant.

The pursuers in *Parkhead Housing Association* v *Phoenix Preservation Ltd* 1990 SLT 812 were also successful. This case involved a claim by an employer in a building contract against a specialist sub-contractor in respect of a defective damp-proof course installed during a renovation project. Lord Prosser looked at the same factors as those considered in the above cases, making the point that *D & F Estates* did not overrule *Junior Books*. However, in upholding the pursuer's claim, he also said that the contractual chain in question actually brought the parties into proximity, rather than separating them. In *Comex Houlder Diving Ltd* v *Colne Fishing Co Ltd (No 2)* 1992 SLT 89, Lord Prosser again thought that the existence of a contractual structure could help to establish proximity; although he was ambivalent as to whether the making of a commitment by A to B, in the way of an indemnity for defective performance, should indicate that A is in a relationship of proximity with C to whom A's performance is also important, or whether the failure to give an indemnity to C too should indicate that A is signalling the full extent to which he regards himself responsible.

4.3.3 Implications for specific categories of loss

4.3.3.1 Category (a) It seems that if there is a close enough relationship of proximity, there can probably be liability for the supply of a defective piece of property which ultimately reaches the pursuer. The pursuer's loss is that the property is worth less than it would have been had it not been defective. (See Willett, 'Economic Loss in the UK After Murphy', Spring 1991 NILQ and Stapleton, 'Duty of Care and Economic Loss: A Wider Agenda', (1991) 107 LQR 24.9.)

The analysis of *Junior Books* by Professor Thomson (*Delictual Liability*, pp. 75–81) would restrict its applicability to a situation where the parties are connected by contracts existing at the time of the negligence of the defender, and the defender knows the specific identity of the pursuer. The idea is that the defender is performing a contract for X, knowing that careless perform-ance of it (e.g., by laying a defective floor, providing a defective product, etc.) will mean defective performance of X's contract with the pursuer, which will cause the pursuer loss. There may be no liability if exemption cluases or other terms in the contracts indicate an intention to exclude it. Professor Thomson regards this as a species of wrongful interference with contract, i.e. the defender by his negligent performance of his contract with X wrongfully interferes with X's contract with the pursuer. This is clearly a situation in which the sort of reliance/proximity talked of in *Junior Books* might well exist; and *Junior Books* and the other cases discussed above could be read as wrongful interference with contract. However, it must be said that the discussion in the above cases of the role of contractual structures does not unambiguously make a contractual chain between pursuer and defender, which exists at the time of the defender's negligence and involves knowledge by the defender of the specific identity of the pursuer, a requirement of *Junior Books* liability.

An analysis which does involve such requirements certainly means that the range of those who may claim, and those against whom they may claim, is restricted in a way which may make it attractive. It may be thought that if *Junior Books* is an extension of general negligence liability, or of the delict of wrongful interference with contracts effectively to allow delictual recovery for poor quality property, then the restrictions imposed by Professor Thomson's model are appropriate. Clearly one of the problems in this area is to restrict the numbers of potential pursuers and defenders.

Another problem, of course, is to give a reasonable degree of recognition to losses suffered as a result of negligent acts, where there is justified reliance on the negligent party by the party who has suffered or where the pursuer is 'closely and directly affected' by the defender's act. These circumstances may occur in such a way as to argue that there is proximity and that it is fair and reasonable to impose a duty (thereby satisfying the difficult elements of the *Caparo* test). There may well be circumstances where this occurs outside Professor Thomson's paradigm of liability. For example, a manufacturer's reputation may be such (or his domination of a market may be such) that those who choose his products from a seller who bought from the manufac-turer (or who have no choice but to so choose his products) may reasonably be able to claim reliance on adequate quality, especially if they are a small specialised market of buyers. There may be an effective exclusion clause (only possible if the final buyer is a commercial party — (see 3.11.6.2 above) which prevents a contractual remedy against the middleman, or alternatively the middleman may be insolvent or be unable to be sued for some other reason.

This situation may not be covered by the approach to *Junior Books*, which sees parties as being proximate only if the defender knows that negligent performance of his contract will lead to defective performance of an existing contract to which the pursuer is party. This is because in the situation described, the pursuer's contract, i.e. to sub-buy the goods, will often not exist when the defender's contract is made. It may nevertheless be the case that the position of the defender in the market, his reputation, the general structure of the market, and the inability of the pursuer to bargain for alternative protection means that there is a close and direct relationship of proximity. It may also be that the pursuer belongs to an identifiable and small class, so that it is fair and reasonable to impose a duty to members of such a class, there not being a 'floodgates' danger.

4.3.3.2   Category (b)

The problem with category (b) loss is that there is no possessory or proprietary title in the goods vesting in the pursuer; and it seems from the *Landcatch* and *Scott Lithgow* judgments that this is crucial. Indeed, in *Nacap v Moffat Plant Ltd* 1987 SLT 221, the defenders damaged a pipeline which the pursuers did not own but were working on for the owners, British Gas. The pursuers suffered loss, due to their inability to complete their contract with British Gas on time. The pursuers' lack of proprietary or possessory title to the pipe meant that they could not sue the defenders.

It seems fairly clear that if a *Junior Books* duty of care is seen as resting upon traditional negligence principles then the law has set its face against this sort of claim, where there is no proprietary or possessory title to the property. However, Professor Thomson's argument that wrongful interference with contract is the basis of *Junior Books* may provide a chink of light for pursuers if it could be said that this remedy does not require possessory or proprietary title. There would arguably be an acceptable control on the number of potential claims because this form of the liability could most legitimately require that the defender should know that his actions are likely to interfere to the detriment of the particular pursuer, with a particular contract to which the pursuer is currently a party (e.g., by putting the pursuer in breach of that contract as in *Nacap*; or by depriving the pursuer of the opportunity to benefit from the contract by using a bridge to transport goods, or using a pipeline to transport oil — see *Norsk Pacific Steamship Co Ltd v CNR* (1992) 91 DLR (4th) 289 and *Caltex Oil Ltd v The Dredge Willemstad* (1976–77) 136 CLR 529 respectively). It *does* seem necessary in category (b) cases that the defender knows of particular contracts, because he is not a defender like the one in category (a) who knows that distribution of his products is inevitable when he contemplates what will happen if he is negligent. The two cases, *Norsk* and *Caltex*, are Canadian and Australian decisions where the pursuers had contractual rights to use the bridge and the pipeline respectively, which they could not benefit from due to the defenders, who were not party to the contracts, damaging these structures. The success of the pursuers was not on the basis of wrongful interference with contract, but simply on the basis of general principles of negligence, the proximity being found in the fact that the pursuers were part of a small, identifiable class who used the bridge and the pipe.

The wrongful interference with contract approach (as a category of negligence) would be narrower than the *Nosk* and *Caltex* approaches to the extent that particular contracts would have to be known of by the defender. We would also, of course, have to find the requisite proximity on the particular facts. If this is still a strain of negligence then proximity is necessary and will not exist simply because A negligently affects B's contact with C. This time it is less appropriate to speak of the pursuer having *relied* upon the defender, i.e. he has not entered a contract in reliance on the defender's reputation, expertise, etc. The issue here, rather, is reasonable expectation. How reasonable was the expectation of the pursuer that the defender would take special care to avoid damaging his contractual interests? As we have said, the defender must know of the contractual relationship between the pursuer and the other party, and in this category the relationship clearly must exist at the time of the defender's negligence (pursuers might consider making sure potential defenders do have such knowledge). It might also be said that the defender should be someone whose knowledge and expertise of the task in question, and perhaps the geography of the area, where relevant, means that it is reasonable for pursuers to expect a certain level of care. We would suggest that the fact that the defender was in a contractual relationship with one of the parties could strengthen the pursuer's argument, but should not be a prerequisite. It will also be relevant to ask why the pursuer did not protect himself contractually from the type of loss in question. Was the risk at all foreseeable? Given the bargaining strengths of the .parties, and the customs and structure of the market, was it reasonably practicable for contractual protection to be sought from the other contracting party, or collaterally from the defender or via insurance? In the *Norsk* case, the commercial user of the bridge was actually offered contractual protection by the owner of the bridge, so that even if the negligent party knew of the contract between the bridge owner and the user there must be a serious doubt that the user could have established proximity on the approach we have been describing. How can it be reasonable for a business to rely upon third party's not being negligent when contractual protection was explicitly offered in the context of a contractual relationship? Perhaps the position would be different where a private consumer is involved and the ability to bargain for cheap alternative protection is limited (see the discussion by Stapleton of these sorts of factors underlying decisions as to duty of care in the Cases and Materials, Chapter 4).

4.3.4 Other difficult duty of care issues

There are a number of other very difficult areas in which the decision as to whether to impose a duty of care raises a number of policy problems for the law. There is no space to deal with them here. However, good accounts can be found in Thomson, *Delictual Liability* (1994), Butterworths, pp. 62–6, and

Bailie, 'Nervous Shock', 1994 SLT 297; Stewart, *Delict* (1993), W. Green Ltd, at pp. 105–9 (where liability of public authorities is concerned), and Thomson, 'Delictual Liability between Parties to a Contract', 1994 SLT 29 (the issue speaks for itself).

4.4 NEGLIGENCE: BREACH OF DUTY

4.4.1 Standard of care and the reasonable man

A defender is not liable simply on the ground that he owes a duty of care to a pursuer. The second requirement is that he must have broken this duty. Breach of duty takes place when the defendant falls below the standard of care which is expected of a reasonable man finding himself in the circumstances in question.

Alderson B stated in *Blyth* v *Birmingham Waterworks Co Ltd* (1856) 11 Ex, 781 that:

> Negligence is the omission to do something which a reasonable man, guided upon those considerations which ordinarily regulate the conduct of human affairs, would do, or doing something which a prudent and reasonable man would not do.

The 'reasonable man' can be characterised as 'Mr Average' who would be neither over prudent nor over confident.

4.4.2 The objective standard

This standard makes no allowance for subjective factors such as stupidity, inexperience or disability. For example, in *Nettleship* v *Weston* [1971] 3 All ER 581, the defendant was a learner-driver who crashed into a lamppost injuring the front seat passenger. At first instance, the plaintiff's claim was dismissed because the defendant had been doing her best to control the car. The Court of Appeal held that the standard of care required for a learner-driver is the same as that required of any other driver, namely that of a reasonably competent and experienced driver. The defendant's driving had fallen below this standard, and it was irrelevant that this was due to her inexperience.

If a person chooses to hold himself out as competent in something in which he is not officially skilled he may be judged by the standards of a skilled practitioner in this field. In *Wells* v *Cooper* [1959] 2 QB 265, a DIY carpenter was judged by the standards of a reasonably competent carpenter.

4.4.3 The reasonable businessman or professional

The reasonable businessman behaves as would the average practitioner in his business, trade or profession. Being a reasonably competent member of a trade or profession probably involves keeping up to date with developments in safety and technology, and following the standard procedures of the industry or profession. All manner of other factors may be relevant, including the particular circumstances of the individual and the business context. Most cases will turn on expert evidence as to what it is reasonable to expect in the circumstances. If standard practices and procedures have been followed a finding of negligence is unusual.

In *Bolam v Friern Hospital Management Committee* [1957] 1 All ER 118, McNair J took the view that 'a doctor is not guilty of negligence if he has acted in accordance with a practice accepted as proper by a responsible body of medical men, skilled in that particular art'. It can be said, therefore, that a doctor is not negligent when acting in accordance with recognised medical practice and that this is so even if there is a body of opinion that takes a contrary view. This approach has been approved by the House of Lords in *Maynard v West Midlands Regional Health Authority* [1984] 1 WLR 634 and *Whitehouse v Jordan* [1981] 1 All ER 267 and applies not only to diagnosis and treatment but also the disclosure of information by doctors to patients (see *Sidaway v Bethlehem Royal Hospital Governors* [1985] 1 All ER 643).

However, the courts may exceptionally decide to raise the standards of behaviour and competency in a particular business or profession by holding a standard practice to be negligent (see *Lloyds Bank Ltd v E B Savory & Co* [1933] AC 201, HL, where a bank's practice of not asking for details of a customer's husband's employment, when an account was being opened, was held to be negligent). If there is a legitimate division of professional or commercial opinion as to how a service should be carried out or the safety of a product ensured, a defendant will not be negligent for following one of the two strands of opinion and mistakes and errors of judgment are allowable up to a point. For example, in *Wooldridge v Sumner* [1963] 2 QB 43, a showjumper who misjudged the speed of his horse and collided with a photographer was held not to be negligent. However, an error of judgment will amount to negligence where it shows 'a lapse from the standard of skill and care required to be exercised to avoid a charge of negligence' (per Lord Roskill in *Whitehouse v Jordan* [1981] 1 All ER 267)'. This basically means no more than that the error of judgment is not necessarily negligence in itself but may provide strong evidence of negligence.

4.4.4 Setting the standard

The standard to be expected of the reasonable layman or businessman must be determined in the context of a number of competing influences. On the one hand, he will be expected to do what is possible to minimise the risk of injury to another party. On the other hand, this expectation must be qualified by practical considerations such as cost and the importance of the activities in which he is engaged. To take a simple example: the risk of accidents involving motor vehicles would clearly be reduced if their use was prohibited or if the national speed limit was 30 mph, but the impracticality and financial cost to business and society of such a prohibition or reduction is such that a driver is not held to be negligent for driving over 30 mph.

The decided cases reveal that the following factors are taken into account when considering whether the requisite standard of care has been broken.

4.4.4.1 The likelihood of harm occurring If a particular danger could not reasonably have been anticipated, the defendant has not acted in breach of his duty of care, because a reasonable man would not take precautions against an unforeseeable consequence.

This does not mean that liability will be automatically imposed whenever it might conceivably have crossed the mind of a normal person that the occurrence of damage was a possibility. Lord Dundedin, in *Fardon* v *Harcourt-Rivington* [1932] All ER 81 (at p. 83), took the view that 'people must guard against reasonable probabilities, but they are not bound to guard against fantastic possibilities'.

The law takes account of the degree of probability of the consequence occurring; probability being measured by reference to knowledge at the time of the event. In *Roe* v *Minister of Health* [1954] 2 All ER 131, during the course of an operation, the plaintiff was paralysed by anaesthetic which had become contaminated by disinfectant. The anaesthetic had been kept in glass ampoules which were stored in the disinfectant and became contaminated by seepage through invisible cracks in the glass. At the time of the accident in 1947 this risk was not known. The Court of Appeal held that the hospital authorities were not liable because the danger was not reasonably foreseeable. Lord Denning said that the court 'must not look at the 1947 accident with 1954 spectacles'. However, it would clearly have been negligent to adopt the same practice in 1954.

The general principle in relation to the likelihood or risk of harm was well expressed by Lord Oaksey in *Bolton* v *Stone* [1951] AC 850, HL (at p. 863):

> The standard of care in the law of negligence is the standard of an ordinarily careful man, but in my opinion, an ordinarily careful man does not take precautions against every foreseeable risk. He can, of course, foresee the possibility of many risks, but life would be almost impossible if he were to attempt to take precautions against every risk which he can foresee. He takes precautions against risks which are reasonably likely to happen. Many foreseeable risks are extremely unlikely to happen and cannot be guarded against except by almost complete isolation.

4.4.4.2 The seriousness or gravity of the potential harm Even where the likelihood of harm occurring may be relatively low its potential for injury or damage, should it occur, may be very high. In such a case the defender will be expected to have taken account of the potentially grave consequences, in carrying out any activities and a greater degree of precaution is expected. As Lord Macmillan has said 'Those who engage in operations inherently dangerous must take precautions which are not required of persons engaged in the ordinary routine of daily life' (see *Muir* v *Glasgow Corporation* 1943 SC (HL)). In *Paris* v *Stepney Borough Council* [1951] AC 367, (HL), the defendants knew that the plaintiff employee was blind in one eye. In the course of the plaintiff's work a chip of metal entered his good eye blinding him completely. He alleged that the defendants were negligent in failing to provide goggles, although it was not usual to do so for that type of work. In the House of Lords the defendants were held liable. The duty of an employer was owed to each individual employee and in determining the requisite

degree of care an employer must have regard to the gravity of the consequences of the potential injury to each person rather than to people generally.
The consequences of an accident to this employee were total blindness as
opposed to partial blindness. Thus a higher degree of care was owed.

4.4.4.3 The social value or utility of the defendant's conduct The social utility
of the defendant's activity may justify taking greater risks than would
otherwise be justified. In *Daborn v Bath Tramways Motor Co Ltd* [1946] 2 All
ER 333, it was held that it was not negligent to use a left-hand-drive vehicle
as an ambulance in wartime, when there was a shortage of vehicles for the
task, even though it was difficult to give hand signals and this had caused an
accident. Asquith LJ (at p. 336) said that, in assessing what is reasonable
care, the risk must be balanced against the consequences of not assuming the
risk and that the purpose to be served, if sufficiently important, justifies the
assumption of abnormal risk. Similarly, in *Watt v Hertfordshire County Council*
[1954] 1 WLR 835, the plaintiff was a fireman called out to an emergency
where a woman was trapped under a lorry. A vehicle designed to carry a
heavy lifting jack was not available so the jack was taken on an ordinary lorry
with three firemen steadying it. The jack slipped, injuring the plaintiff. His
employers were not liable. The risk had to be balanced against the end to be
achieved.

4.4.4.4 The cost of preventative action It is true that some risks are unavoidable and others can be eliminated or reduced only at great expense. The law
must determine the point at which the cost of precautions would justify a
reasonable man in not taking them. In *Latimer v AEC Ltd* [1953] 2 All ER
449, the defendant's factory was flooded after a heavy rainfall, and water
became mixed with oil leaving the floor very slippery when the flooding
subsided. Sawdust was spread over the surface but there was not enough to
cover the entire area. A workman slipped on the uncovered part and was
injured. The trial judge held the defendants liable for failing to close down
that part of the factory. The House of Lords agreed that this might be
necessary if the risk to employees was sufficiently grave, but that had not been
the position in this case.

Generally, it can be said that, where a large reduction of risk can be
obtained by minimal expenditure, the defendant has acted unreasonably if he
does not take precautions. Conversely, where considerable expense would
produce only a minimal reduction in risk, it is reasonable for the person to
do nothing.

In *Overseas Tankship (UK) Ltd v Miller Steamship Co Pty Ltd (The Wagon
Mound I)* [1967] 1 AC 617 (PC), a large quantity of bunkering oil was spilled
in Sydney harbour as a result of the carelessness of the defendants' engineer.
This is a high flash-point oil and very difficult to ignite in the open. However,
it did catch fire (probably as a consequence of hot metal falling to the water
from welding operations carried out on a wharf) and caused extensive
damage. The Privy Council concluded that a reasonable engineer would have
foreseen the possibility of the oil catching fire though the likelihood of it doing

so was extremely small. However, all that was needed to stop the discharge was the closing of a valve and it was held that a reasonable man would not ignore even a small risk 'if action to eliminate it presented no difficulty, involved no disadvantage and required no expense'.

When precautions are not practicable, then the risks of continuing the activity have to be weighed against the disadvantages of stopping the activity altogether. In *Withers v Perry Chain Co Ltd* [1961] 1 WLR 1314, it was not possible to give an employee, who was susceptible to dermatitis, work which did not involve a risk of contracting the disease. It was held that the employers were not liable as there were no further precautions that the employers could have taken, short of dismissing the plaintiff.

4.5 PROOF OF NEGLIGENCE

The burden of proving negligence rests generally on the pursuer, who must do so on the balance probabilities. It is clear that a person who is injured by a defective product or service will not always succeed in proving negligence or fault in the face of the above criteria. The law of negligence, by its very nature, focuses on the behaviour of the defender and asks whether it falls below a certain standard. This distinguishes it generally from the law of contract which focuses on the expectations of the parties as defined by the express or implied terms of the contract, so, for example, a seller may be liable for defective goods without being in any sense 'at fault'. This traditionally meant that injured parties who were not in a direct contractual relationship with the supplier had a more difficult task to recover compensation than those who were in such a relationship.

For example, in *Daniels & Daniels v R White & Sons Ltd and Tarbard* [1938] 4 All ER 258, a husband and wife both suffered injury when they consumed lemonade which was contaminated with caustic soda. The bottle had been purchased by Mr D from Mrs Tarbard's pub, having been manufactured by Whites. Mr D was able to recover from Mrs Tarbard for breach of contract but Mrs D, having no contract with Mrs Tarbard, had to try to prove that the manufacturers were negligent in allowing the lemonade to become contaminated, which, on the particular facts, she was unable to do. This would be the result wherever reasonable precautionary methods and good quality control could be shown. In other words where an unsafe product is simply one which has 'slipped through the net', then so long as this net is reasonably carefully constructed the manufacturer will not be liable in negligence. A consumer who is injured by a defective product now has an alternative remedy in the form of the Consumer Protection Act 1987 which does not require proof of fault (see 4.8 below).

4.5.1 *Res ipsa loquitur*
The difficulty of proving negligence is mitigated to some extent by the operation of the principle *res ipsa loquitur* (the thing itself speaks).

In circumstances where the accident seems inexplicable other than by the negligence of the defendant, the defender may be required to disprove negligence under the doctrine of *res ipsa loquitur*. It is important that the pursuer could have no way of knowing the precise cause of the accident. If he does have the means of proving negligence, then he must do so. The doctrine will apply, according to Erle CJ in *Scott* v *London and St. Katherine Dock Co* (1865) 3 H & C 596, 'where the thing is shown to be under the management of the defendant or his servants, and the accident is such as in the ordinary case does not happen if those who have the management use proper care'. In *Elliott* v *Young's Bus Service* 1945 SC 445, Cooper LJC described it as:

> the policy of the law that intervenes to relax the logical stringency of proof and so invert the normal onus in order to avoid denial of justice to those whose rights depend on facts incapable of proof by them, and often exclusively within the knowledge and control of their opponent.

The principle was applied in *Scott*, where heavy sacks of sugar fell from a loading bay and injured the plaintiff. More recently, it was applied in *Ward* v *Tesco Stores Ltd* [1976] 1 WLR 810 (CA), where yoghurt was spilt on the floor of the defendant's store. The yoghurt was not wiped up and the plaintiff slipped on it and was injured. There was no explanation as to how the yoghurt came to be on the floor of the shop. *Res ipsa loquitur* was held to apply, the defendants were unable to discharge the burden of disproving negligence and were consequently held liable.

4.6 CAUSATION AND REMOTENESS OF DAMAGE

The third and final stage in determining whether a defender is liable in negligence is to ask whether the breach of duty has caused damage which is not too remote to be compensated.

4.6.1 Causation

Causation involves two related questions. First, was the breach of duty in factual terms a cause of the damage? Causation must be proven by the pursuer on the balance of probabilities and it is judged, 'by applying commonsense standards. Causation is to be understood as the man in the street, and not as either the scientist or the metaphysician would understand it' (per Lord Wright in *Yorkshire Dale SS Co* v *M.O.W.T.* [1942] AC 691). This inquiry is often described as the search for 'cause in fact'.

Secondly, it is important to decide, where there are several potential causes, which of them should be regarded as the legal cause of the damage – the 'cause in law'. This inquiry may arise either where there are simultaneous but independent causes or where a subsequent act intervenes between the defendant's negligence and the damage. There is considerable case law on this second point, particularly in relation to intervening acts.

Although we will address cause in fact and cause in law under separate headings, they are very closely related, and probably really address the same question – was the damage the natural and probable consequence of the negligent act?

4.6.1.1   Cause in fact   A useful means of determining whether the breach of duty may be described as a material cause of the damage is to ask whether the damage would or could have occurred otherwise. This is known as the 'but for' test – would the damage have arisen 'but for' the negligence? If so the negligence is not a material cause. In *Barnett* v *Chelsea Kensington Hospital Management Committee* [1969] 1 QB 428, a doctor in a casualty department sent a patient away without treatment, telling him to see his own doctor. The patient died from arsenic poisoning. It was held that the doctor's conduct was negligent, but the expert evidence indicated that the patient was beyond help and would have died in any event. Therefore the doctor's negligence did not cause the death. Similarly, in *Robinson* v *The Post Office* [1974] 2 All ER 737, a doctor's omission to test for an allergic reaction to an anti-tetanus vaccination was not causally related to the patient's subsequent reaction, because the test would not have revealed the allergy in time.

It is often difficult to draw conclusions using the 'but for' test. This is because the court has to speculate as to what might have occurred had the defendant behaved in a different way. In *McWilliams* v *Sir William Arrol & Co Ltd* 1962 SC (HL) 70, a steel erector who was not wearing a safety belt fell to his death. His employers were in breach of a statutory duty to supply safety belts, but the House of Lords held that they were not liable because it was probable that the deceased had rarely, if ever, used a safety belt in the past and so it was a natural inference that he would not have worn a belt on this occasion. Lord Reid commented that it would not be right to draw such an inference too readily because people do sometimes change their minds unexpectedly, but the evidence in this case was 'overwhelming'.

4.6.1.2   Proof   Where it is difficult or impossible to ascertain the precise cause of damage it may be virtually impossible for the pursuer to succeed even where the existence of negligence is not in doubt. This is illustrated by the recent decision in *Wilsher* v *Essex Area Health Authority* [1988] 2 WLR 557, HL, where the plaintiff was born prematurely and placed in a special care baby unit at a hospital managed by the defendants. If he was to survive, he needed extra oxygen and to ensure that the correct amount was administered it was necessary to insert a catheter into an umbilical artery so that his arterial blood oxygen levels would be accurately read on an electronic monitor. A junior doctor mistakenly inserted the catheter into the umbilical vein with the result that the monitor gave a lower reading and the mistake was not immediately corrected. The following day, it was realised that the plaintiff had been supersaturated with oxygen for a period of about 8 to 12 hours and, within 30 hours of the plaintiff being received into the special unit, the mistake was rectified. The plaintiff developed retrolental fibroplasia, a condition of the eyes which resulted in blindness. A likely cause of the condition, but not a definite or only possible cause, was that too much oxygen had been administered within the first 30 hours after birth or at a later stage. The plaintiff claimed damages from the defendant health authority for the negligent medical treatment he had received in their special care baby unit.

In the House of Lords, it was held that the plaintiff's injury was attributable to any one of a number of causes, although the evidence was insufficient to establish the particular cause. In such circumstances, negligent conduct which enhanced an existing risk of injury did not raise a presumption, or entitle the court to make an inference, as to causation, in favour of a particular cause. The onus remained on the plaintiff to prove on a balance of probabilities that the cause alleged led to the injury. The House of Lords ordered a re-trial.

In the earlier case of *Kay* v *Ayrshire and Arran Health Board* [1987] 3 WLR 232, HL, the pursuer was given an overdose of penicillin and became deaf, but it could not be established on the balance of probabilities that the deafness was caused by the overdose, rather than the meningitis for which the penicillin was initially administered. However, in *Bryce* v *Swan Hunter Group plc and Others* [1988] 1 All ER 659, the deceased was employed for most of his working life from 1937 until 1975 in shipyards owned by the three defendant companies. In the course of his employment the deceased was exposed to asbestos dust which caused him to contract mesothelioma, from which he died in 1981 at the age of 60. His widow, as administratrix of his estate, brought an action against the defendants claiming damages in respect of his death. She contended, *inter alia*, that the methods of work and the processes employed by the defendants had caused the release of asbestos dust into the deceased's working environment which had resulted in him contracting the disease. The defendants contended that even if they had been in breach of the duties they owed as the employers of the deceased there was no evidence that those breaches had caused the disease and therefore the plaintiff had failed to discharge the burden of proof. However, it was held that the defendants owed the deceased a duty not to use methods of work and processes which created or increased a risk that the deceased would contract that disease. If they were in breach of that duty and the deceased had in fact contracted the disease, they were to be taken to have caused the disease by their breach of duty.

The *Bryce* decision follows the authority of *McGhee* v *NCB* 1973 SLT 14 to the effect that there is a causative link between the negligence and the harm if the former materially increases the likelihood of the latter occurring. However, this approach will be taken only if the negligence in question is accepted on the balance of probabilities as being capable of having caused the injury (albeit that actual cause is on the balance of probabilities difficult to establish) In *McGhee* and *Bryce* it was clear that dust *could* cause the injuries in question. In *Kay*, it was never proven that an overdose of penicillin could cause deafness.

4.6.1.3 Cause in law: effect of novus actus interveniens The law may operate to break the chain of causation where an act of the pursuer or a third party intervenes between the defender's negligence and the pursuer's injury. Such a 'new cause which disturbs the sequence of events' (per Lord Wright in *The Oropesa* [1943] 32 is known in law as a *novus actus interveniens* (a new intervening act).

The act of the pursuer will operate as a *novus actus* if it is unreasonable in the circumstances. For example, in *McKew* v *Holland & Hannen & Cubitts*

(Scotland) Ltd [1969] 3 All ER 1621, HL, the defenders negligently injured the pursuer's leg, which as a result was liable to give way without warning. Without asking for assistance, he attempted to descend a steep flight of stairs without a handrail and he fell suffering further injuries. The House of Lords held that the defenders were not liable for his additional injury because the pursuer's conduct was unreasonable and constituted a *novus actus*. However, in *Wieland* v *Cyril Lord Carpets Ltd* [1969] 3 All ER 1006, the plaintiff had to wear a surgical collar as a result of the initial injury. This restricted the movement of her head which reduced her ability to use her bifocal glasses. Eveleigh J held the defendants liable for further injuries sustained in a fall down some steps, on the basis that it was foreseeable that one injury may affect a person's ability to cope with the vicissitudes of life and thereby be a cause of another injury. The distinction from McKew (above) seems to be that it was *not unreasonable* in the present case for the plaintiff to attempt to descend the stairs.

If the actions of the pursuer are on the whole reasonable, then a negligent mode of execution will not break the chain. However, it may reduce the damages payable, on the basis of contributory negligence (see 4.7.1 below). In *Sayers* v *Harlow UDC* [1958] 1 WLR 623, the plaintiff was trapped in a public lavatory by a faulty door lock. After calling for assistance without response, she decided to climb out, but fell when she placed her weight on a toilet-roll holder which gave way. It was held that it was reasonable to attempt the escape, although she had been careless in the manner of its execution. The chain of causation was not broken, but she was held contributorily negligent.

4.6.2   Remoteness of damage: natural and direct consequences
In *Malcolm* v *Dickson* 1951 SC 542, Thomson LCJ said (at 547):

> a wrongdoer is not held responsible for all the results which flow from his negligent act. Practical considerations dictate, and the law accepts, that there comes a point in the sequence of events when liability can no longer be enforced. This rule of convenience and commonsense is enshrined in the maxim *causa proxima remota spectatur*.

This policy finds expression in the principle that a defendant is liable only for losses which arise naturally and directly from his wrongful act; directly means simply that the chain of causation must not have been broken (see 4.6.1 above), naturally, however, has been held to mean 'according to the ordinary, usual or normal course of things' (per Lord Haldane in *SS Baron Vernon* v *SS Metagama* 1928 SC (HL) 21 (at 25)). This is probably more generous to the pursuer than the English foreseeability test (see the *Wagon Mound No 1* [1961] AC 388). For example, it will allow recovery for all medical expenses incurred as a natural and direct consequence of an injury even where certain of the treatment has been wrongly (but not negligently) prescribed (see *Rubens* v *Walker* 1946 SC 215). It is unlikely that this would be held to be 'foreseeable' in an English court.

In a more recent case, *Campbell* v *F. and F. Moffat (Transport) Ltd* 1992 SCLR 551, 1992 SLT 962, a person who was injured in a road accident was able to recover the redundancy paymnts which he would have been paid by his employer if he had still been employed when the employer's business ceased. He was not employed at that time because the defender's negligence in causing his injury led to his employment being terminated two years prior to the closure/redundancies. The loss of redundancy payments was a *type* of loss (financial, relating to lost employment) which was foreseeable, and as such a duty of care existed in respect of it (see *Hughes* v *Lord Advocate*, at 4.2.3). It may not in itself have been foreseeable, and so would possibly not be allowable in England. However, it did arise *naturally* and *directly* from the negligence and was therefore recoverable in Scotland.

4.6.2.1 Liability for a victim's particular sensitivities Once it is established that the type of injury suffered by a victim arose as a natural and direct consequence of the wrongdoing the defender will be liable for the full extent of this injury. This will apply even where a particular sensitivity of the pursuer leads to an abnormal degree of injury. This principle is normally expressed by the maxim that a wrongdoer 'must take his victim as he finds him'.

In *Smith* v *Leech Brain & Co Ltd* [1962] 2 QB 405, the plaintiff's husband was burned on the lip by a piece of metal. The burn was treated and it healed, but due to a premalignant condition the burn promoted a cancerous growth which ultimately led to his death. Parker CJ held the defendants liable for the death, taking the view that:

> The test is not whether these (defendants) could reasonably have foreseen that a burn would cause cancer and that the plaintiff would die. The question is whether these [defendants] could reasonably foresee the type of injury he suffered, namely the burn. What, in the particular case, is the amount of damage which he suffers as a result of that burn, depends upon the characteristics and constitution of the victim.

In *Robinson* v *Post Office* [1974] 1 All ER 737, the plaintiff was injured as a result of the defendant's negligence. He suffered a serious allergic reaction to an anti-tetanus injection given to him at the hospital. The Court of Appeal held the defendants were liable for this injury, stating that a person who could reasonably foresee that the victim of his negligence may require medical treatment is liable for the consequences of the treatment, even though he could not reasonably foresee those consequences or that they would be serious.

4.7 DEFENCES TO NEGLIGENCE CLAIMS

The most significant potential defences for delicts involving negligence are contributory negligence and *volenti non fit injuria*. These might also be pleaded in answer to a claim for breach of statutory duty, or in response to an action under the Occupiers' Liability (Scotland) Act 1960.

4.7.1 Contributory negligence

This defence is provided for in the Law Reform (Contributory Negligence) Act 1945. If the defendant can show that the pursuer contributed by his own negligence to his loss or injury, the court will reduce the damages to take account of this.

For example, in *Stone* v *Taffe* [1974] 1 WLR 1575, Mr Stone was a committee member of a society which regularly met at a public house owned by a brewery and managed by their employee Taffe. Taffe agreed to allow the society, of which he was also a member, to use an upstairs room at the public house for a social occasion. Drinks were served to members of the club by Taffe until the early hours of the morning, without any extension having been granted by the licensing magistrates. Mr Stone, when leaving the premises by a narrow unlit staircase at approximately 1.00 am, fell and was killed. The widow of Mr Stone sued both Taffe and the brewery for damages *inter alia* under the Occupiers' Liability Act 1957 (the English equivalent of the Occupiers' Liability (Scotland) Act 1960). They were held liable, but Mr Stone's contributory negligence reduced the award of damages by 50 per cent.

It would probably also be contributory negligence to take a lift in a car knowing that the driver was drunk (see *McCaig* v *Langan* 1964 SLT 121), or to misuse a defective product. Recently there was held to be contributory negligence on the part of a drunk pedestrian who was run over by a negligent driver (*Malcolm* v *Fair* 1993 SLT 342, where damages were reduced by 50 per cent).

The court will take into account all of the circumstances of the case in order to ascertain whether the pursuer acted reasonably and prudently in the circumstances. Allowance is made for inadvertence caused by necessary haste or fatigue and also for emergency action which has been necessitated by the negligence of the defendant. (See *Laird Line* v *U.S. Shipping Board* 1924 SC (HL) 37.)

4.7.2 *Volenti non fit injuria*

The essence of this plea is that the pursuer has, with full knowledge of the facts, voluntarily assumed the risk of injury. The defender must establish that the pursuer actually 'consented' to run the risk in question. This argument is accepted very rarely, particularly where the presence of the pursuer at the locus of the incident is virtually unavoidable or is at the behest of the defender. So it cannot be said that a tenant consents to run the risk of dangerous premises simply through knowledge of the danger and continued habitation, while waiting for the landlord to repair them (cf. *Shields* v *Dalziel* (1894) 24 R 849, which is now of doubtful authority). It might be different if the tenant knows there is a risk but does nothing himself and does not inform the landlord.

The plea of *volenti* tends to fail in cases of injury sustained at work. The typical assertion by an employer will be that the employee consented to the risk inherent in the work by continuing to do it. Usually, however, employees are seen as simply following orders and, as such, not truly consenting.

The plea succeeded in *Sylvester* v *Chapman Ltd* (1935) 79 SJ 777, where the plaintiff was mauled by a leopard, having gone behind a barrier to extinguish a cigarette end. *Volenti* will also succeed where clear warning notices are ignored (see 4.10.1.4 below).

4.7.3 Prescription and limitation

Actions in negligence will be defeated where too long a time elapses between the act or omission which constitues negligence and the bringing of the court proceedings. The law's provisions on this subject are now contained in the Prescription and Limitation (Scotland) Act 1973. The relevant sections are reproduced in the Cases and Materials section for Chapter 4.

4.8 THE CONSUMER PROTECTION ACT 1987

This Act came into force in March 1988 and implements in large part the 1985 EEC Directive on product liability (Dir. No. 85/374/EEC). It imposes strict liability on producers of defective products which cause loss or damage to property, or death or personal injury. The new rules are based on the premise that producers or products should in certain circumstances bear the risk of their products being defective and causing loss or injury, without the injured party having to prove negligence. The theory is that producers benefit generally from the sale of their products, control the process of production and are capable of insuring against isolated losses at minimal expense. The accompanying memorandum to the Directive stated that 'the compensation paid forms part of the general production costs of the product. The increase in cost is reflected in the pricing. The damage is thus, from an economic point of view, spread over all the products which are free from defects'. This is felt to be preferable to allowing the cost to fall on the unfortunate consumer who is not in a position to insure, and who may find it difficult to prove negligence.

4.8.1 Who is liable?

Four categories of people may be liable.

Producers.   Under s. 1(2), the 'producer' includes the manufacturer, those who have won or abstracted a product (e.g., minerals and natural gas) and those who process food, e.g., by freezing it or canning it.

'Own branders'.   For example, a supermarket which puts its own name on a product and does not reveal the name of the manufacturer.

Importers of products into the EEC.   Thus, a French company which buys goods from Sweden (a non-EEC country) and sells them to British suppliers may be liable under the Act.

Suppliers.   Suppliers of goods may be liable where they are asked by an injured party to identify one of the above parties in the chain of supply and fail to do so within a reasonable time.

Section 2(4) exempts from liability those who supply game or agricultural produce which has not undergone an industrial process. This produces the rather strange result that if, for example, there is an inherent defect in vegetables (due to chemical contamination from the soil) which causes injury, an importer may be liable if the vegetables have been canned or frozen, but not if they are fresh.

4.8.2   What is a defect?

Section 3 classes a product as defective where 'the safety of the product is not such as persons generally are entitled to expect'. Section 3(2) outlines the criteria to be used in measuring such consumer expectations, they cover such factors as who the product is aimed at (children/adults, experts/amateurs); safety of packaging; adequacy of instructions and warnings; the reasonably anticipated use to which a product will be put; and what standards prevail at the time of supply (a product will not be unsafe simply because subsequent means are found to make it safer).

In the case of manufacturing defect, the move away from negligence is clear. There will no longer be any need to establish that the manufacturer had any reason to know of the defect. The focus is on the defect and the extent to which it does not measure up to the consumer's reasonable expectations. The reasonableness or otherwise of the manufacturer's actions is irrelevant; a consumer could no longer fail to succeed in a case like *Daniels* v *Tarbard* (see 4.5 above).

In the case of a design defect, however, it has been suggested in some American decisions that if such defects could not reasonably have been discovered (i.e., there is no negligence), then the manufacturers should not be liable. It is submitted that this is incorrect as a general proposition. The development risks defence discussed at 4.8.4.5 (which is only about the reasonableness of having discovered defects given scientific and technical constraints, not the reasonableness of discovering defects in the context of financial or systemic constraints) stands as the only excuse based on having behaved as a reasonable manufacturer, i.e. having been devoid of fault or negligence. The position which will be adopted by the United Kingdom courts is yet to be seen, although it should be remembered that the European Court is likely to interpret provisions which aim at encouraging cross-border shopping as needing to instil a high level of consumer confidence.

Although s. 3(2) makes the use of warnings a relevant criteria in assessing defectiveness, it is submitted that this should not be taken to mean that a product is not defective simply because its dangerous propensities have been pointed out. It may of course be dangerous to use any product in certain ways but, if a product is used reasonably and normally and proves unsafe, the use of a warning should not prevent it being held to be defective.

4.8.3   What is damage?

Section 5 sets out rules for determining what damage can be claimed for under the Act. The sweep of the provisions as regards death and personal injury is broad and covers, by virtue of s. 45, any disease or other impairment of a person's physical or mental condition (e.g., nervous shock).

There can also be a claim for damage to property.

There are four key restrictions to claims for damage to property under the Act.

First, there is no liability for loss of or damage to the defective product itself (s. 5(2)). This includes the property self-destructing but causing no other damage, or being simply of very poor quality. The possibilities for recovery of such 'category (a)' economic loss in negligence are discussed at 4.3.2. above and are fairly limited. Of course, if one has bought under a contract of sale there is a remedy for poor quality goods under the Sale of Goods Act 1979 (see 6.6.3 below). The most vulnerable parties are those who have been gifted the goods and those purchasers whose seller is insolvent or otherwise unsueable. Section 5(2) rules out a remedy for poor quality under the Consumer Protection Act, and a remedy in negligence will not be easy.

Secondly, there is no liability for loss or damage to any property supplied with the product in question comprised in it (s. 5(2)). This is simply regarded as another type of quality defect or economic loss, the two pieces of property being seen as one qualitatively defective product because the defective part was contained in the rest of the structure when supplied. So, if a car is supplied with a defective tyre, which causes the car to crash, there is no liability for damage to the car. Neither, of course, is there liability for damage to the tyre itself, but if a supplier happened to have provided a new tyre after the vehicle was purchased, there would be liability for the damage to the car because the new tyre would not have been supplied 'comprised in' the property which it damaged.

Thirdly, only damage to property ordinarily intended and actually intended in the particular case for private use or consumption is recoverable (s. 5(3)). This provision requires the court to look at the nature of the property and its intended use in the particular case. Clearly, tractors are not ordinarily for private use, so if A's tractor is damaged by his engine oil there can be no claim. A car *is* ordinarily for private use, but there will be no claim if the damaged car is used for business purposes.

Finally, damage to property must exceed £275 in value in order to be allowable (s. 5(4)).

4.8.4 Defences
Section 4 outlines the various defences available under the Act. Section 6(4) also applies the defence of contributory negligence to claims under the Act.

4.8.4.1 Statutory or EEC authority Section 4(1)(a) exonerates anyone whose supply of a defective product was attributable to compliance with a statutory or community obligation. This seems likely to arise only exceptionally.

4.8.4.2 Mistaken identity or stolen goods Section 4(1)(b) provides a defence where a supplier is either wrongly identified as such or the goods have been stolen from him and subsequently supplied.

4.8.4.3 Private supply There will be no liability on a party who supplies goods privately or with no intention of making a profit, e.g., where a car is sold privately or a cassette recorder is given as a present or where food and drink is prepared for a charity function (s. 4(1)(c)).

4.8.4.4   No defect at the relevant time   No party in the chain of supply will be liable where the defect occurred further down the production chain; caused, for example, by adaptation or alteration, removal of warnings or labels. This defence, though generally very sensible, appears to produce the rather strange result that, if a retailer tampered with goods and made them defective, he could not be liable under the Act since his only liability depends on failing to identify a producer who would otherwise be liable. Of course, such a retailer will be liable in contract to purchasers and in negligence to anyone to whom he owes a duty of care.

4.8.4.5   Development risks defence   This is the most controversial and problematic of the defences. Section 4(1)(e) exonerates a defendant producer where:

> the state of scientific and technical knowledge at the relevant time was not such that a producer of products of the same description as the product in question might be expected to have discovered the defect if it had existed in his products while they were under his control.

The central question here is the ability to *discover defects by scientific and technical research*. It is probably intended to afford a defence to those in high risk industries which rapidly expand their product development their knowledge and appreciation of risks. If a manufacturer of pharmaceuticals, for example, can show that awareness of serious side effects emerged only after he supplied the drug in question, it seems that the defence would be available. If, on the other hand, the side effects were known of at the time of supply, the defence may not be available. The key question is whether the average producer of such products should know of the defect. We are therefore dealing with a negligence standard, but only with regard to knowledge that the defect exists. This is the substantial difference between the standard imposed by the Act and that imposed by the law of negligence. Under the law of negligence, the producer might still have been able to escape liability where he knows of the defect if it could not be shown by the pursuer that, measuring risk against cost, a reasonable producer would still supply the drug. Now the defender must show that it was reasonable not to know of the defect. If he knows of it, he cannot argue that it was too costly to eradicate. So it should no longer be a defence to a claim for injury or damage caused by a defective product to say that it was impractical and costly to eliminate a risk (e.g., by improved quality control). It should only avail a producer to establish that the likelihood of a defect was not within the realms of the scientific or technical knowledge of those selling such products. A final point to note is that this may prejudice small producers whose scientific and technical expertise is not as well developed as their larger competitors. This is because the defence makes no reference to the degree of knowledge any individual producer might be expected to have of the latest developments in knowledge.

4.8.4.6   Component parts   A manufacturer of a component part of a defective product has a defence where the defect is wholly attributable either to a design defect in the finished product, or to compliance by the component part producer with instructions provided by the producer of the finished product (s. 4(1)(f)).

4.8.5 Liability for defective products: causation

Whatever changes may have been made in respect of standard of care by the Act, it is clear that the injury must still have been *caused* by the defective product. This will involve the same difficulties as already apply in establishing negligence claims (see 4.6 above). For a full discussion of product liability in Scotland see Powles, 'Product Liability – A Novel Dimension in Scotland', in *Obligations in context*, (1990), W. Green Ltd; and see also Howells, *Comparative Product Liability* (1993), Dartmouth and Stapleton, *Product Liability* (1994) Butterworths.

Prescription and Limitation relevant statutory provisions are reproduced in the Cases and Materials section for Chapter 4.

4.9 NUISANCE

Nuisance is defined by *Bell* in the following terms:

Whatever obstructs the public means of commerce and intercourse whether on highways or navigable rivers; whatever is noxious, or unsafe, or renders life uncomfortable to the public generally or to the neighbourhood; whatever is intolerably offensive to individuals in their dwelling houses, or inconsistent with the comfort of life, whether by stench, by noise or by indecency is a nuisance.

This rather grandiose definition is clearly capable of covering a wide range of activities carried out on business premises. However, its main application will be to activities which cause injury or discomfort to those occupying neighbouring property. Typical instances are incursions by smoke (*Crump* v *Lambert* (1867) 15 LT 600), destructive animals (*Farrer* v *Nelson* (1885) QBD 258), unreasonable noise (*Christie* v *Davey* (1893) 1 Ch 316), vibration (*Hoare* v *McAlpine* [1923] 1 Ch 167), water, smell, fumes, gas, heat, electricity and vegetation. Recent examples include the noise caused by the erection of scaffolding for seating at a military tattoo (*Webster* v *Lord Advocate* 1984 SLT 13); the building of an extension which obstructed the light to a neighbour's windows (*Carr-Saunders* v *Dick McNeil* [1986] 1 WLR 922) and noise from road-breaking operations (*Strathclyde RC* v *Tudhope* 1983 SLT 22).

4.9.1 Interference with comfortable enjoyment

The key to liability in nuisance is that the pursuer's right to comfortable enjoyment of his property has been interfered with. This takes paramountcy over considerations as to whether the defendant's use of the property was reasonable, a specific consideration in English Law (see *Watt* v *Jamieson* 1954 SC 56). However, notwithstanding the principle that the circumstances are to be seen from the point of view of the victim, it is clearly relevant to question the reasonableness of the complaint in the circumstances. What would be classed as a nuisance in a residential district would not necessarily be so in an industrial district, but an addition to pre-existing discomfort may amount to a nuisance (*St Helens Smelting Co v Tipping* (1865) 11 H&C 642).

It is also relevant to examine the duration of the interference and the sensitivity or otherwise of the persons or property affected; both provide evidence as to whether there has been an unacceptable interference with the pursuer's comfortable enjoyment of his property. As to duration, the cases turn to a large extent on their own facts and circumstances. A lengthy interference is more likely to be held to be significant. However, it may be that its trivial and infrequent nature will cause the action to fail. In *Bolton v Stone* [1951] AC 850 (HL), for example, cricket balls were hit onto the highway from a pitch six times in thirty years and this was held not to constitute a nuisance. However, in *Castle v St Augustines Links* [1922] 38 TLR 615, a nuisance was constituted by golf balls being continually struck onto the highway. Although unusual, it is possible for a single, isolated interference to constitute a nuisance as long as it has been caused by a more permanent condition related to the property, e.g., where an explosion is caused by an accumulation of gas over a period (*Midwood v Manchester Corp* [1905] 2 KB 597).

It is no defence to an action for nuisance to show that the pursuer knew of the nuisance when he moved to the area (*Fleming v Hislop* (1886) 13 R (HL) 43); or that the nuisance is being contributed to by other parties (including the pursuer) (*Duke of Buccleuch v Cowan* (1866) 5 M 214). or that the public benefits from the activities which cause the nuisance (*Shotts Iron Co v Inglis* (1882) 9 R (HL) 89). It is therefore not open to a manufacturer to defend a claim for nuisance caused by noxious fumes by claiming that he employs a large number of people and is a valuable asset to the local or national economy. However, operations which might otherwise constitute a nuisance may be legalised by statute, e.g., the Civil Aviation Act 1949, ss. 40 and 41.

4.9.2 Nuisance, negligence and recoverable losses

Although nuisance does require some degree of fault (*culpa*) for there to be a claim in damages (see *RHM (Scotland) Bakeries v Strathclyde Regional Council* 1985 SLT 3 in the Cases and Materials section for Chapter 4), it is still a distinct delict from negligence. This may be important for two reasons.

First, in a negligence action, the initial consideration is whether the defendant owes the pursuer a duty of care. The extent to which the duty concept can restrict the range of liability is discussed at length above. However, such a duty is not required to establish liability for nuisance. Secondly, nuisance protects against interference with the comfortable enjoyment of interests in land. So there may be a claim for damage to the land and buildings or to one's enjoyment thereof as a domestic occupier but, if the interest in the land which is affected is purely economic, such pure economic loss would also be recoverable, e.g., where a hotel lost custom due to building operations as in *Grosvenor Hotel Co v Hamilton* [1894] 2 QB 836. Given that the status of a claim for pure economic loss based on negligence is tenuous (see 4.3 above), it might be advantageous to frame a claim in nuisance where an economic interest in land can be said to have been prejudiced.

4.9.3 Remoteness
Of course any claim for economic loss, physical injury or damage to property will be subject to the same rules as to remoteness of damage as those which apply to a claim in negligence (see 4.6.2 above).

4.9.4 Interdict
In addition to, or in lieu of, claiming damages, the pursuer may seek an interdict to prohibit the continuation of the nuisance. This will obviously be most appropriate in the case of an ongoing interference, e.g., a process of manufacture which emits smoke and fumes, as opposed to a serious but isolated interference, e.g., a gas explosion.

4.9.5 Prescription and personal bar
The right to sue in respect of a nuisance is lost if no objection is raised for 20 years, i.e., the period of the negative prescription (see Prescription and Limitation (Scotland) Act 1973, s. 7. However, the period will start to run again if there is an increase in the extent of the nuisance. The right to sue may be lost after a shorter period if it can be shown that the pursuer has consented to the nuisance or has acted in such a way as to be personally barred from raising an objection now.

4.9.6 Defences to nuisance actions
A claim that an action is carried out with statutory authority is potentially the most important defence to an action in nuisance, given the range of industrial activities carried out in the public and private sector which are authorised by statute, e.g., the operation of utilities such as gas, electricity and water or the construction and maintenance of roads. However, it is unusual for the statutory authority in question to be absolute, it is normally granted provisionally, i.e. on the express or implied condition that the activity in question will be done without injury to others. The scope of statutory authority as a defence is also limited by the rule that if the nuisance is due to negligence and without negligence the activity would have been innocuous, the statutory authority affords no defence (see *Metropolitan Asylum District* v *Hill* (1881) 6 App Cas 193).

It is also possible that it would be a defence to a claim for nuisance to allege that the nuisance was caused either by an act of God or by the act of a third party, of which the defendant had neither actual nor constructive notice (see *Sedleigh-Denfield* v *O'Callaghan* [1940] AC 880).

4.10 INJURY ON THE PREMISES: OCCUPIERS' LIABILITY AND BREACH OF STATUTORY DUTY

Nuisance does not protect those who are caused loss or injury while on the offending premises. This is because liability for nuisance depends on the

interference with a right in land. Where injury is caused to those present on
the premises the action must lie in negligence, occupiers' liability or breach
of statutory duty. Liability for negligence depends on the established principles of breach of duty, caution and foreseeability of damage (see 4.2 to 4.8
above), the two other forms of potential liability are discussed below.

4.10.1 Occupiers' liability

Occupiers' liability is based on the Occupiers' Liability (Scotland) Act 1960
which imposes a standard of care, of the type applying in negligence, on a
person who has occupational control of premises towards those who come
onto the premises. (Sections 1 and 2 of the Act are reproduced in the Cases
and Materials section for Chapter 4.)

The party deemed to have occupational control will, of course, normally
be the party who physically occupies the premises as heritable proprietor or
tenant. However, occupational control may be deemed to vest in parties other
than the physical occupiers. For example, a brewery may be deemed to share
occupational control of a tied public house, with the publican (see *Stone* v
Taffe [1974] 3 All ER 1016). In a recent case, it was decided that a local
authority did not have occupational control of property simply because they
had issued a control of occupation order under the Housing Act. Lord
Dervaird said that 'control' for the purposes of the Occupiers' Liability
(Scotland) Act 1960 was such 'control as entitles the person having it to take
the steps desiderated to make the premises safe'. This did not exist in the
circumstances of the case, where the effect of the order was to render guilty
of an offence anyone who permitted the premises to be occupied (*Feely* v
Co-operative Wholesale Society Ltd 1990 SLT 547).

The dangers which an occupier must guard against are those caused by:

(a)   the state of the premises, e.g., structural defects and slippery floors; or

(b)   anything done on the premises, e.g., the operation of machinery or
wiring or the keeping of a dangerous animal (see *Smithers* v *Boyd* (1886) 14
R 150); or

(c)   anything omitted to be done on the premises, e.g. a failure to fence
or mark hazards or, as in *Stone* v *Taffe*, a failure to light a staircase properly.

4.10.1.1 Standard of care The standard of care owed depends on the
position of the occupier and that of the injured party (see Lord Reid's
judgment in *McGlone* v *BRB* 1962 SC (HL) 1). The standard is effectively
fixed by the foreseeability or likelihood of a person of the type injured being
so injured by the prevailing conditions. This may involve taking greater
precautions against the natural curiosity of children. On the other hand it may
also mean that a lower standard is expected in respect of a trespasser. In
McGlone v *BRB* a boy was injured while climbing an electric transformer. It
was held that the defendant's duty had been discharged by the erection of a
barrier which could only be overcome by a deliberate act intended to defeat
its clear function. Lord Guthrie said that 'the liability of an occupier
cannot fairly be made to depend on the outcome of a conflict between his

precautions to exclude entry and the ingenuity and agility of a youthful and determined trespasser'. See also the more recent decision in *Titchener* v *BRB* 1984 SLT 192. The pursuer's claim must actually specify in what respect there is a breach of the standard of care. In *McGuffe* v *Forth Valley Health Board* 1991 SLT 231, the pursuer slipped on snow on the defender's premises. The claim failed for lack of specification as to what would have been a reasonable period within which to remove the snow.

4.10.1.2 Exclusion of liability The Act permits occupiers to extend, restrict, exclude or modify obligations under the Act by written or verbal contract. This right, as far as it relates to any dilution of the obligations, is severely restricted by the Unfair Contract Terms Act 1977 (see Chapter 3, 3.11.6.1). Any contract term which attempts to exclude or restrict liability for personal injury or death is void. It is probably also an offence, under the Consumer Transactions (Restriction on Statements) Order 1976 (see Chapter 9, para. 9.3.1) to attempt to exclude or restrict liability in this way. A contract term which attempts to exclude or restrict liability in respect of other loss or damage (e.g., to property) is subject to the test of reasonableness laid down in the Unfair Contract Terms Act; it is clear from the decided cases that it will rarely be reasonable to exclude liability in such circumstances as against a consumer.

4.10.1.3 Contributory negligence Where the pursuer has contributed to his own loss or injury, the damages payable will be reduced accordingly under the Law Reform (Contributory Negligence) Act 1945, s. 1. There might be contributory negligence where the pursuer tampered with some device or frequented a part of the building where he should not have been and the workings of which he did not understand (e.g., a guest who entered a hotel kitchen). On contributory negligence generally see 4.7.1 above.

4.10.1.4 Volenti Non Fit Injuria The voluntary assumption of risk by the pursuer, e.g., by going to a part of the building from which he is specifically excluded, will amount to a good defence, but such an exclusion would have to be clear and unequivocal, as the courts are reluctant to allow this defence nowadays (see 4.7.2 above).

There is clearly a difference between a notice which prohibits entry and one which exempts liability for the consequences of entry. The former, if accompanied by reasonable precautions (such as a locked door if the danger is great) is probably sufficient to put someone on their guard; should they choose to ignore it they may be taken to have voluntarily accepted the risk. The latter is no more than an attempt to exclude or restrict liability and as such is subject to the Unfair Contract Terms Act.

4.10.2 Breach of statutory duty

Where a statutory duty is imposed on a public or private sector industry, the normal sanction for its breach is criminal liability (see e.g., the Factories Act 1961 and the Health and Safety at Work Act 1974). However, if a breach of statutory duty causes injury to an individual, he may have a claim in delict for this breach alongside whatever liability there may be for negligence, nuisance, under occupiers' liability or, in the case of employees, for breach of contractual duties. Liability for breach of statutory duty will arise where the statute is aimed to protect the class of people from which that person comes and if the injury is of the type which the statute was designed to prevent. Whether this is the case can only be determined by reference to the specific language of the statute in question.

In *Groves* v *Wimborne* (*Lord*) [1898] 2 QB 402, an employer failed in his statutory duty to fence dangerous machinery. An employee who was injured as a result was able to recover damages, as the aim of the provision was clearly to protect employees. In *Gorris* v *Scott* [1974] LR 9 Ex 125, the plaintiff's sheep were washed overboard because the defendant failed in his statutory duty to provide pens on the ship's deck. There was no action in delict for this breach of duty because the purpose of the duty was to prevent the spread of disease and not to prevent sheep being washed overboard. In *McNeill* v *Roche Products* 1989 SLT 498, it was held that the purpose of the Factories Act, s. 14 (requiring the fencing of dangerous machinery) was to avoid the risk of accident caused by inadvertence. It was therefore no defence to an action for breach of this statutory duty to say that the pursuer had contributed to his own injury by inadvertently putting his hand too close to the blade of a cooling fan. He could not have done so if the machinery had been properly guarded.

The modern trend is for statutes to state explicitly whether an action for breach of statutory duty is to be available or not. For example, the Sex Discrimination Act 1975, s. 66 and the Race Relations Act 1976, s. 57 both specify that breach of the duties not to discriminate may ground an action for breach of statutory duty. The Consumer Protection Act, s. 41 confers a remedy for breach of statutory duty in the event that breach of any obligation imposed by safety regulations causes loss or injury.

4.11 ECONOMIC DELICTS

There are a number of delicts which involve intentonal (i.e., not just negligent) interference with the business activities of others. These are important, apart from anything else, because they are essentially concerned with placing limits on the extent to which socio-economic power can be used to effect gain for one's self and inflict economic detriment on others. As we have seen above, the law is very reluctant to impose liability for negligently caused economic loss, i.e. loss resulting from a breach of a duty to take care. Indeed, to put this more accurately, the law is very reluctant to *impose a duty* to take care to prevent economic loss. But what about *intentional* conduct which affects the economic interests of others? We do not have the space to do anything other than give the briefest summary of the law's approach. However, we hope that this summary can point to the sorts of policy problems the law is faced with and where to look for more detail as to how it responds.

The first basic prinicple is that if A acts intentionally and even maliciously, but nevertheless lawfully, to harm B's economic interests then there is no liability. So if A encourages X (by appealing to his longstanding friendship, or by threatening not to buy his goods again, which he has not yet contracted to do anyway) to stop doing business with B, then A is not liable to B, assuming that X is not being told to do something unlawful to B, e.g., breach a contract (see *Allen* v *Flood* [1898] AC 1, HL). However, in circumstances which A's tactics are still lawful (i.e. they do not involve a threat to injure X, or break a contract with him or commit a delict against him) the law will nevertheless hold A liable if what he induces or procures is for X to break a contract with B, or if he wrongfully interferes with a contract between X and B. So A might have encouraged X not to fulfil his contract to supply B with goods. If this puts X in breach of contract there is the delict of inducement to breach of contract. If X is not in breach of contract because of an exemption clause in his contract with B, there is nevertheless the delict of wrongful interference with business (see *BMTA* v *Gray* 1951 SC 586, *Rossleigh* v *Leader Cars Ltd* 1987 SLT 355, the latter emphasising that A must know of the existence of the contract between X and B for A to be liable; and *Torquay Hotel Co Ltd* v *Cousins* [1969] 2 Ch 106). In effect, therefore, A's freedom to act freely in the marketplace becomes controlled when he begins to interfere with the norm that says contracts should be performed, even if there is technically no liability for breach due to an exemption clause.

There also now seems to have developed a delict — wrongful interference with business — in which the intentional harm caused by A to B is of a broader, less clearly defined nature than interfering with or causing the breach of contracts to which B is a party. So in *Lonrho plc* v *Fayed* [1990] QB 490, the loss to Lonrho was that they were forestalled from making bids for Harrods while the Monopolies & Mergers Commission (MMC) reported; while Fayed, as a result of fraudulent misrepresentations to the DTI about his reputation, avoided having his bid referred to the MMC, and was able to bid before the MMC reported. This, it was held, could amount to wrongful interference with Lonrho's business. However, for this delict to exist the means used by the defender must have been unlawful, e.g., fraudulent misrepresentation as in this case, so that the law, while expanding the type of injury that may be claimed for, is placing a constraint on claims by requiring unlawful means to have been used.

There are two other interesting delicts in which there is no requirement that what A gets X to do to B should be unlawful in the sense of being a breach of contract. First there is conspiracy. There is a delict because either:

(a) although the means used would not have been unlawful if carried out by individuals (e.g., persuading others to undercut B), there is a conspiracy of two or more people *and* the predominant motive is to harm B (see *Crofter Handwoven Harris Tweed Co* v *Veitch* 1942 SC (HL) 1); or

(b) unlawful means (e.g., breaches of contract, commission of a delict, breach of a statutory obligation) are used by conspiring parties A and X and there is an intention to harm B, perhaps only by undercutting him (here there is no need that the intention to harm B should be the predominant motive: see *Lonrho* v *Fayed*).

The second delict in which the harm caused to B need not be in itself unlawful is where A induces X to commit the harm by an unlawful threat to X. This is called intimidation (see *Rookes* v *Barnard* [1964] AC 1129).

4.11.1 Passing Off

The delict of passing off involves misrepresentation (whether by language, labelling, presentation of products, advertising, etc.) which is made in the course of trade to prospective customers, which is calculated to injure the business or goodwill of another, and actually has caused or will probably cause such damage (see Lord Diplock in *Erven Warwick BV* v *J. Townend & Sons (Hull) Ltd* [1979] AC 731 at 742). This delict will typically be committed by passing off one's products as those of someone else, thereby riding on their reputation and causing them loss (for a full discussion see J.M. Thomson, (1994), *Delictual Liability*, Butterworths, pp. 25-8, and H. McQueen, 'Wee McGlen and the Action of Passing Off', 1982 SLT (News) 225).

Further reading

W. J. Stewart, (1993), *An Introduction to the Scots Law of Delict*, 2nd edn, W. Green Ltd.

J. M. Thomson, (1994) *Delictual Liability*, Butterworths.

D. M. Walker, (1988), *Principles of Scottish Private Law* (vol. II), 4th edn, Clarendon Press, Parts 6 and 7.

CHAPTER FIVE

The Law of Agency

Agency is a threeway relationship. It involves an agent, a principal and a third party. The function of the agent is to bring the principal and the third party together in a contractual relationship. The agent is a type of business matchmaker. An agent may be an employee of his principal, e.g., a sales assistant, or an independent contractor, e.g., an estate agent. Not all employees will be agents for their employers, only those whose job it is to bring third parties into a contractual relationship with the employer. Checkout operators in a supermarket will therefore be agents for their employer whereas employees who fill shelves will not be. The need for agents is obvious. Physical and temporal limitations dictate that a businessman cannot deal with all his customers alone. Even in a small shop the owner will usually need help. The task of this assistant may be perceived purely as selling things to people. However, selling (or buying) involves entering into a contract and thus in law the function of the sales assistant is to effect a contract between the customer (who is the third party) and the employer (who is the principal).

The distinctive characteristic of agency is that, although an agent has the authority to effect a binding contract between the principal and the third party, the agent will not generally be a party to that contract and will thus acquire neither rights or liabilities under it.

The main issues in agency are those of authority and trust. These are of concern in the general law of contract, but are more so in agency contracts because of the physical separation that will usually exist not only between the actual contracting parties, but also between the principal and agent. As far as authority is concerned the third party needs to know the extent of the agent's authority (either his actual authority or that authority that will be implied by the courts). Without knowing this he is likely to be wary of dealing with the agent, which would of course frustrate the whole purpose of the agency. A principal needs to trust the agent to carry out the agency with the principal's best interests in mind: the agent needs to trust the principal to indemnify and pay him as agreed. The legal rules relating to these core elements have been developed over many years by the courts. Agency is an area of law which is dominated by the common law; there has been relatively little statutory intervention (but see the Prevention of Corruption Acts 1906 and 1916, the Partnership Act 1890 and the Estate Agents Act 1979). Agency is also an area of Scots law where decisions of the English courts have had a strong influence on the development of the law. This influence has been given judicial recognition and approval (see Lord Moncrieff in *Rederiaktiebolaget Nordsyjernan* v *Salvesen & Co* (1903) F 64 at 76.

Although there are many different kinds of agents, all agents fall into one of two general categories.

General agents. A general agent has the authority to carry out any of the duties which a person of his trade or profession usually carries out, e.g., a solicitor, or the captain of a ship.

Special agents. A special agent has much more limited authority. He will usually only have authority to act on his principal's behalf in a particular transaction, e.g., bidding at an auction.

The *extent* of the authority of the agent is all important and is discussed below (5.4.1). This chapter examines how the principal/agent, relationship is formed; the obligations of these two parties and their respective relationship with third parties.

Not every person whom the law regards as agents will necessarily so describe themselves, e.g., a director is an agent for the company, a partner for the partnership, and some employees for their employers. To make matters slightly more confusing many who describe themselves as agents are not agents in the eyes of the law. For example, a car dealer may be described as a BMW agent. The car dealer is not, however, acting on behalf of BMW when he sells a car but on his own behalf. The contractual relationship is between the customer and the car dealer. There has been, of course, a separate contractual relationship under which BMW supplied the car to the dealer.

5.1 CONTRACTUAL CAPACITY

There may be a contract between the agent and the principal. If there is, then both agent and principal must have the necessary contractual capacity. The function of the agent generally, however, is to bring principal and third party together in a contractual relationship to which the agent will not be a party. In this role therefore the absence of contractual capacity on the part of the agent may well be irrelevant.

Gow in his *Mercantile and Industrial Law of Scotland* (at page 516) gives the example of a father sending his pupil son into a shop to buy a bottle of lemonade. There is no contract between father and son. They are in law, however, principal and agent. It is the capacity of the principal that matters;

so a principal who lacks contractual capacity cannot increase his capacity by employing an agent of full capacity.

5.2 BECOMING AN AGENT

There are several ways in which a person can become an agent.

5.2.1 Express appointment of agent
The express appointment of an agent may be made orally or in writing. The written contract need not be probative. A written appointment may be made by granting a power of attorney or a factory and commission. The advantage for both principal and agent of a written appointment is that it will be easier to prove the extent of an agent's authority in the event of a dispute. In the event of a dispute about the existence or extent of an agent's authority parole evidence can be used.

5.2.2 Implied appointment of agent
The relationship of agency may arise by implication. For example, the appointment of a partner will make the partner an agent of the partnership and of the other partners where partnership business is concerned. Equally, many employees will be agents by implication. Whether or not an employee is an agent will depend on the employee's role. In *MacKenzie* v *Cluny Hill Hydro* 1908 SC 200, it was held that an hotel manager was an agent by implication. Theatre and shop managers have also been held to be their employer's agents but, in contrast, it has been held that a hotel gardener, a stage assistant and a store security guard are not agents by implication. In the recent case of *Lord Advocate* v *Chung* 1995 SLT 65, the court was faced with deciding whether or not the relationship of father and son *per se* gave rise to an agency. It held that it did not.

5.2.3 Ratification of agency
Becoming an agent by ratification differs from the previous two methods in that the principal may not have authorised the agent to act at all, or may have authorised the agent to act in one particular transaction but the agent has exceeded that authority and contracted in a different transaction. Ratification comes, if at all, when the 'principal' decides to effectively condone the lack of authority and retrospectively bind himself to the transaction in question. If, however, he chooses not to do so the agent is left with personal liability under the contract.

There are limits on the appointment of an agent by subsequent ratification. Before there can be agency by ratification, the following criteria must be satisfied:

(a)   The agent must have claimed to be acting on behalf of a principal and to have named him. An undisclosed principal cannot ratify, e.g., in *Keighley, Maxstead & Co* v *Durant* [1901] AC 110, an agent, R, acted without authority in the purchase of wheat. R contracted in his own name but the purchase was intended by him to be a joint one with the plaintiffs. D, the seller of the wheat, was not aware of this fact. KM later agreed to take the wheat but in the event R and KM refused delivery of the wheat. When D tried to sue KM for damages arising from this breach the House of Lords held he could not do so. KM's purported ratification of R's unauthorised act (by agreeing to take the wheat) was ineffective as R had disclosed neither the name nor the existence of his principal.

(b)   The principal must have been legally capable of doing the act in question both when the agent made the contract and at the date of purported ratification. In *Goodall* v *Bilsland* 1909 SC 1152, Lord President Dunedin held that, where a solicitor had purported to act for parties in an appeal case (although they had not asked him to do so), they could not subsequently ratify his actions because, at the date of the supposed ratification, the ten-day statutory limit for making appeals had run out. (See the Cases and Materials section for Chapter 5.)

(c)   The principal must have been in existence both at the date of the contract and the ratification. As is evident from the case of *Kelner* v *Baxter* (1866) LR 2CP 174, this can cause problems for company promoters and indeed anyone who purports to contract on behalf of a *company* before its incorporation. In *Kelner*, the plaintiff sold wine to the defendant, who said he was acting on behalf of a company which was about to be formed. On incorporation, the company sought to ratify the contract made by the defendant. It was held that it could not do so as it (the company) was not in existence at the time the contract was made (see also *Tinnevelly Sugar Refining Co Ltd* v *Mirlees, Watson and Yaryan Co Ltd* (1894) 21 R 1009, in the Cases and Materials section for Chapter 5).

(d)   The principal must ratify the act in time. There may be a period laid down as in *Goodall* v *Bilsland* (see above). If not, the ratification must occur within a reasonable time and what is reasonable will depend on the circumstances. For example, in the English case of *Grover & Grover Ltd* v *Matthews* [1910] 2 KB 401 CA, a contract of insurance had been taken out by an agent on his principal's behalf but without his authority. The principal did not ratify the contract until after the insured property had been destroyed by fire. The Court of Appeal held that the ratification was too late and was ineffective as was therefore the insurance policy. The Marine Insurance Act 1906, s. 86 provides that contracts of marine insurance are an exception to this rule.

(e)   The principal must have had full knowledge of all the relevant facts unless he indicates that he is happy to ratify no matter what the circumstances.

There is no clear authority in Scotland as to whether there can be ratification where the agent ostensibly deals as principal. English law does not permit ratification in such a situation. Lord McNaughton said (in *Keighley*) that the basis for this rule was that civil obligations cannot be created or founded upon undisclosed intention. Gloag says (at p. 143), the rule should be followed in Scotland.

5.2.4 Agency by necessity

The concept of agency arising through necessity is strictly speaking an English one but it is a form of the Scots doctrine of *Negotiorum Gestio* (management of affairs). The term agent of necessity is, however, in common use in Scotland. Agency by necessity arises where, because of an emergency, one party acts on behalf of another although he has not been asked to do so. Agency of necessity will only arise where the interests of one party are at stake, he cannot be contacted, and some action is taken in good faith on his behalf.

In *Great Northern Railway* v *Swaffield* (1874) LR 9 Ex Ch 132, the defendant sent an unaccompanied horse by rail from London to Bedfordshire. Upon arrival, there was nobody to collect the horse. The station staff had no way of contacting the defendant so they had the horse stabled. Swaffield objected to paying the 6d stabling charge on the grounds that he had not authorised it. The dispute dragged on until the stabling bill was £17. The railway company paid this, delivered the horse to Swaffield and claimed that they had acted as agents of necessity and should therefore be reimbursed for their outgoings. The court held that they had acted as agents of necessity. There was an emergency, they could not contact Swaffield, and had acted in his best interests. Agency by necessity arose quite frequently in the past, for example, where perishable goods were delayed in transit and were sold on the owner's behalf before they became worthless. Improved communications mean that it is much less likely to arise today but it could arise in more mundane circumstances than in *Swaffield*. If your neighbours were climbing in the Himalayas and you had a vandalised window of theirs repaired you would be an agent of necessity and could claim that your neighbours reimburse you the cost of the glazier's bill.

5.3 THE RELATIONSHIP BETWEEN PRINCIPAL AND AGENT

In most cases the relationship between the two and their specific obligations, one to the other, will depend on the contract between them. Such a contract, as we have seen, may be written or oral, or may arise by implication or necessity. To avoid, or at least lessen, the opportunity for dispute, it is preferable that the contract is embodied in some form of written document no matter how informal. Agent and principal are free to agree whatever terms they wish provided they are not unlawful; the relationship is after all a consensual one.

Where commercial agents are concerned, regard should also be had to the Commercial Agents (Council Directive) Regulations 1993 (SI 1993 No 3053). These regulations became operative on 1 January 1994 and implement Council Directive 86/653/EEC. They apply to self-employed commercial agents and their principals, and deal with remuneration and the conclusion and termination of the agency contract. (See also Commercial Agents (Council Directive) (Amendment) Regulations 1993, SI 1993 No 3173.)

There are, however, terms implied by common law into the relationship. As with all contracts, there are rights and obligations due and owed by each party one to the other.

5.3.1 The rights of the agent

5.3.1.1 Remuneration Whether or not the agent is entitled to a fee or commission will depend on the express or implied terms of the contract. Generally speaking mercantile agents, such as auctioneers, stockbrokers, shipbrokers and insurance brokers, are entitled to be paid but this presumption can be rebutted as in the case of *Dinnesmann v Mair* 1912 1 SLT 217. In that case, it was held that, by custom of trade, the agent had to rely for his remuneration on the proceeds of sale of the herrings which had been consigned to him. In short, if he sold no herrings he would not be entitled to any commission.

The agent's right to remuneration will, of course, arise only when he has carried out the task he was retained to do. Whether or not he has done this may be a matter of dispute. One of the areas where disputes will most frequently arise will be where an estate agent has been used to effect the sale of a house. The principal (seller) may claim, perhaps with justification, that the resultant sale owed more to the principal's efforts than to the agent's.

In general, the courts will examine the circumstances to discover if the result achieved can be attributed to the efforts of the agent and, if it can be, then will be entitled to be paid (see *Walker, Fraser & Steele v Fraser's Trustees* 1910 SC 222 (see the Cases and Materials section for Chapter 5).

In the absence of express provision as to remuneration, the customary rate should be paid, e.g., fees determined by a professional body. If there is neither an express provision nor an implied one, the agent will be paid on the basis of *quantum meruit* (as much as he has earned). This is a quasi-contractual remedy (see Chapter 3, para. 3.16).

5.3.1.2 Relief The principal must relieve the agent of all losses, liabilities and expenses incurred by the agent in the course of the agency. *Dinnessman v Mair* would suggest that the agent is entitled to deduct his expenses from the proceeds of goods he has sold on his principal's behalf. The principal need not indemnify an agent who has acted illegally or carelessly and without skill and care. For example, in *Davison v Fernandes* (1889) 6 TLR 73, the plaintiff was a stockbroker who sold shares for the defendant after having quoted a wrong selling price which induced the defendant to sell. When the defendant discovered the error he repudiated the contract. In accordance with Stock Exchange rules the plaintiff had to compensate the would-be purchaser. He then sought to be relieved of this liability by the defendant but the court held that his negligence in quoting the wrong price barred him from any right of relief. *Tomlinson v Liquidators of Scottish Amalgamated Silks Ltd* 1935 SC (HL) 1 is authority for there being no right of relief where an agent has incurred expenses in defending himself against criminal charges. Tomlinson was a promoter and director of Scottish Amalgamated Silks Ltd. The company went into voluntary liquidation. Tomlinson was charged and tried for fraud on the basis that he had issued a fraudulent prospectus and had misapplied company funds. In the event, he was acquitted and sought to recover from the liquidator the expenses incurred in his defence which amounted to some £11,500. He based his right of relief both on common law and more specifically on the articles of association of the company, which provided for the indemnification of any director against all costs, losses and expenses which he might incur by reason of any act done by him as a director. It was held that he was not entitled to be relieved of this liability either at common law or under the articles as the expenses were incurred in 'a mere personal misfortune which overtook him' and not as part of his duties as a director.

5.3.1.3 Lien The agent has a right of lien over any of the principal's property which is in his possession as a result of the agency. A lien is the right to retain possession of goods until a debt has been paid. The agent can exercise this right until the principal has paid the agreed remuneration and expenses and relieved him of any liabilities arising out of the contract.
Lord Kinnear said in *Glendinning* v *Hope* 1911 SC (HL) 73 (at 78):

> every agent who is required to undertake liabilities or make payments for his principal, and who in the course of his employment comes into possession of property belonging to his principal over which he has power of control and disposal, is entitled, in the first place, to be indemnified for the monies he has expended, or the loss he has incurred, and, in the second place, to retain such properties as come into his hands in his character of agent.

The right of lien does not allow the agent to sell the principal's goods and it is lost if the agent parts with possession of the goods. The agent will usually have a general lien, that is the right to retain the principal's property until any sums due by the principal have been paid, i.e. the goods retained need not be specifically related to the payments due. It is recognised that solicitors, bankers, and factors have a general lien but the decision in *Findlay (Liquidator of Scottish Workmen's Insurance Co Ltd)* v *Waddell* 1910 SC 670 would suggest that an auditor or accountant has no comparable general lien. Auditors and accountants may, however, have a special lien (see below). The attitude of the courts is that they do not favour the extension of general liens beyond the established categories. A special lien is the right to retain property until any sums owing on that particular piece of property have been paid, e.g., a garage could hang on to your car until you have paid for repairs to it. It would, however, have no right of lien against luggage in the car.

5.3.2 The duties of the agent
If there is a contract between principal and agent it may set out the agent's duties. If, however, there is no contract, or if it is silent, there are agent's duties which are implied by law. These duties will apply unless the contract makes express provision for their exclusion. The relationship of principal and agent is one which involves a special degree of trust. It is what is known as a fiduciary

relationship. The principal entrusts his affairs to the agent; the principal must, therefore, be able to rely on the agent. This sense of trust could be said to lie at the heart of the principal-agent relationship. The agent must put his principal's interests before his own. This will obviously create tension at times.

It may be that the contract between them will expressly prohibit the agent from acting as an agent for other principals, but if that is not expressly mentioned then it will not be implied (*Lothian* v *Jenolite* 1969 SC 111). It would, therefore, be permissible for an insurance broker to sell the policies of several different companies unless expressly prohibited from doing so. Indeed in *Kelly* v *Cooper* [1992] 3 WLR 936 PC, the court held that a term *was* to be implied that in the ordinary course of business an agent was entitled to act for other principals, and to keep confidential from each principal information obtained from other principals. This will surely be true only as long as there is no breach of the duty of good faith (see below at 5.3.2.5). The following duties will be implied in the absence of any express provision to the contrary.

5.3.2.1 Duty to obey instructions

The agent must carry out his principal's instructions provided that they are lawful and reasonable. The exact form of these instructions will depend on the nature of the relationship between the parties. For example, someone who wishes to buy or sell a house and uses the services of a solicitor to do so will only give very general instructions often amounting to no more than 'sell my house'. In such a case, the solicitor must act according to the general established customs of the profession. In the absence of express instructions, the agents must exercise their best judgment provided that they act with the standard of care that would be expected of a competent member of their trade or profession.

Lord McLaren said in *Fearn* v *Gordon & Craig* (1893) 20 R 352 (at 358):

A law agent is not an artificer to carry out mechanically the instructions of his client. He is a legal adviser as well as an executant. The client, in general, is no more capable of telling his lawyer how to proceed in the business for which he is employed, than a patient is able to tell his physician or surgeon how to operate. Accordingly, when a purchaser employs a conveyancer, he is not expected to tell the solicitor what deeds he is to prepare, and what enquiries regarding previous transactions are necessary. It is for the solicitor to tell him what is necessary.

An agent who neglects to carry out his principal's instructions will be liable to the principal. In *Turpin* v *Bilton* (1843) 5 M G 455, B, an insurance broker, agreed to effect an insurance policy on T's ship. He failed to do so and when the ship sank uninsured it was held that B was liable in damages to T for the loss. In *Gilmour* v *Clark* (1853) 15 D 478, G instructed to take a consignment of goods from Edinburgh to Leith docks and put them on board *The Earl of Zetland*. The goods were, however, put aboard another vessel *The Magnet*. *The Magnet* sank. It was held that C was liable to G for the value of his lost cargo.

5.3.2.2 Duty to exercise reasonable care   All agents are under a duty to exercise reasonable skill and care. Bell (Bell's Principles § 221) said they must act with 'the care and diligence of a man of common prudence'. Where the agent is a member of a particular trade or profession, he must exercise the appropriate standard of skill and care. More skill is expected of a professional person acting in his professional capacity than is expected of a layman acting for a friend. It does not matter that the agent acts gratuitously, he is still obliged to exercise reasonable care. An agent who acts gratuitously is known as a mandatory. The mandatory's duty to exercise reasonable skill and care can be seen in *Copland* v *Brogan* 1916 SC 277 (see the Cases and Materials section for Chapter 5). Brogan, a carriage hirer, had acted as a messenger for Copland, a schoolteacher, on several occasions. He acted gratuitously. On the occasion in question Copland had asked Brogan to cash some cheques for him. Brogan did this but on the way home he lost the money. There was no imputation of dishonesty on Brogan's part. It was held that Brogan had to make good the loss to Copland. The mere fact of the loss without any satisfactory explanation was evidence that Brogan had failed to exercise reasonable care. Reasonable care was defined as being, 'such care as a man of common prudence generally exercises about his own property of like description' (Lord Justice Clerk Scott Dickson quoting from Bell's *Principles* in *Copland* v *Brogan* at p. 282).

Older English authorities suggested that a gratuitous agent (mandatory) was liable only if gross negligence could be shown. This duty was discussed in the recent English case of *Chaudhry* v *Prabhakar and Another* [1988] 3 All ER 718 (see the Cases and Materials section for Chapter 5), where C had asked P to buy a car on her behalf. He was not a mechanic but had bought and sold several cars in the past. He was not to be paid. C stipulated that she did not want a car that had been involved in an accident. P bought a one year old car the bonnet of which had been crumpled and repaired, but he made no enquiries of the seller. The car was discovered to be unroadworthy having been previously written off. C sued both P and the seller, who had already admitted liability under the Sale of Goods Act 1979, s. 14(2) and had abandoned his appeal. Stuart-Smith LJ said (quoting Ormerod LJ in *Hough-land* v *R R Low (Luxury Coaches) Ltd* [1962] 2 All ER 159 (at 161):

> I have always found some difficulty in understanding just what was 'gross negligence' because it appears to me that the standard of care required . . . is the standard demanded by the circumstances of that particular case . . . The question we have to consider in a case of this kind (if it is necessary to consider negligence) is whether in the circumstances of this particular case a sufficient standard of care has been observed . . .

Stuart-Smith LJ went on to say that whatever standard of care was required of an unpaid agent, the defendant, in buying a car that was so obviously suspect, had fallen below it. The court held, with some doubts expressed by May LJ, that a gratuitous agent owes his principal a duty of care to exercise the degree of care and skill which could reasonably be expected of him in all the circumstances, that degree of care and skill being measured objectively and not subjectively. The defendant was held to be liable in damages to the plaintiff. The approaches of Scott Dickson LJC and Stuart-Smith LJ are complementary and in no way contradictory.

The Supply of Goods and Services Act 1982, s. 13, affirms the common law position of both Scotland and England by making the exercise of reasonable skill and care an implied term of all contracts of agency. The section does not, however, apply to Scotland.

5.3.2.3 Duty to act in person The relationship of agent and principal is one which involves a high level of trust and, therefore, the agent is under a duty to act personally. He must, *prima facie*, carry out his tasks by himself. He must not delegate the performance of his duties to someone else. This is expressed by the maxim *delegatus non potest delegare* (a delegate cannot delegate). This maxim does not mean that the agent is prohibited from employing clerical and other assistants and has 'almost been eaten up with exceptions' (Gow, *Mercantile Law of Scotland*, p. 530). Much will depend on whether the agent has been chosen for his own particular and unique personal qualities. If this element of *delectus personae* (choice of person) is present then there will be a presumption against delegation. The contract between principal and agent may expressly provide for delegation or it may be implied by custom of trade or profession. Thesiger LJ said in *De Bussche v Alt* (1878) 8 ChD 286, 'the exigencies of business do from time to time render necessary the carrying out of the instructions of the principal by a person other than the agent originally instructed for the purpose . . .'. If delegation is permitted, then there will be a contractual relationship between principal and sub-agent similar to that between principal and agent. However, if the sub-agent fails to carry out his duties then *MacKersey v Ramsay Bonar & Co* (1843) 2 Bell's App. 30 is authority for any liability falling on the original agent.

An architect has been held to be impliedly authorised to delegate some of his duties to a surveyor (*Black v Cornelius* (1879) 6 R 581). The danger of implied authority can, however, be seen in a similar case some years later, *Knox & Robb v Scottish Garden Suburb Co Ltd* 1913 SC 872. In that case, it was held that the architect agent had no implied authority to delegate. Whether or not a solicitor has authority to delegate, e.g., to an advocate, will depend on whether the principal knows that the litigation involves an advocate's services. A solicitor has no implied right to instruct an advocate if a case goes to appeal even where the solicitor himself has no right of audience. However, in *Robertson v Faulds* (1860) 22 D 714, it was held that a country solicitor had authority to delegate the handling of Court of Session business to Edinburgh agents.

5.3.2.4 Duty to keep accounts The agent is under a duty to keep his property and that of the principal separate, e.g., he must not pay money received as agent into his own bank account. In addition to the common law rules on keeping accounts, there may be additional statutory provision, such as the Solicitors Accounts (Scotland) Rules. It is, of course, in the interests of the agent as well as the principal that clear and concise accounts are kept. The accounts must reflect any discounts received. The principal and not the agent is entitled to any interest gained from the deposit of money due to the principal (*Brown* v *IRC* 1964 SC (HL) 180). In the event of any deficiency which cannot be explained the agent is bound to make good the loss to the principal. In *Tyler* v *Logan* (1904) 1 F 123, T owned a number of shoe shops and L was the manager of the Dundee branch. There was a discrepancy of some £62 which L could not explain. The court held that even although there was no suggestion of dishonesty, or even negligence, L had to make good the money to T.

5.3.2.5 Duty to act in good faith Whatever the agent does must be done in good faith for the benefit of his principal. He must not allow his personal interests and those of his principal to conflict. If there is, or is likely to be, any such conflict of interests, the agent must make the circumstances known to the principal. It will then be up to the principal to give or refuse his consent. What amounts to a conflict of interest will depend on the express or implied terms of the contract, for it is possible to be agent for more than one principal. In *Lothian* v *Jenolite Ltd* 1969 SC 111, it was held that, where the contract of agency was in writing, there is no implied condition that the agent will never, without the principal's consent, act so as to bring his and his principal's interests into conflict, Lord Milligan said (at 120):

> The proposition which the defenders invite us to affirm is that in all agency cases there is an implied condition that the agent will not without the permission of his principal act, even in an outside matter, in such a way as to bring his interests into conflict with those of his principal. There is admittedly no case in which such a proposition has been affirmed . . . , If the defenders had wanted to restrict the activities of the pursuer, they could have asked him to agree to their proposed restriction . . . they cannot now seek to rectify the position by attempting to discover an implied condition.

In *Kelly* v *Cooper* (above 5.3.2), Cooper, an estate agent, was instructed by Kelly to sell a house. The owner of an adjacent house also instructed Cooper to sell his house. This adjacent house was sold first. The purchaser then offered to buy Kelly's house (through Cooper). Cooper made no mention to Kelly that he had handled the sale of the adjacent house. Both sales were completed. Kelly claimed that Cooper had breached his duty by failing to disclose information and that there had been a conflict of interest. The court disagreed. The reasoning of the Privy Council was similar to that of Lord Milligan in *Lothian* v *Jenolite*. The decision in *Kelly* is also judicial approval that the circumstances of estate agency contracts give rise to an implied contract term that the normal duty of disclosure is displaced.

There are several aspects of the duty to act in good faith:

(a)   the duty not to make a secret profit;

(b)   the duty not to misuse confidential information; and
(c)   the agent's duty when buying and selling property.

These are dealt with in turn below.

Duty not to make a secret profit   The agent must not use his position to make a profit for himself over and above the remuneration paid to him by the principal. Not all profits earned over and above the remuneration from the principal will be a secret profit. Many agents will by custom receive money over and above what they receive from their principal. A waiter in receipt of tips might be the most obvious example; he is entitled to keep them unless there is some express arrangement or custom that dictates otherwise. The agent will, in many circumstances, find himself faced with the choice of competing third parties all anxious to contract with the principal. He may be offered some form of inducement and, if he accepts it, he must credit the principal with the amount.

In *Ronaldson v Drummond & Reid* (1881) 8 R 956, a solicitor, who was acting on behalf of trustees, engaged an auctioneer to arrange the sale of some furniture. The auctioneer paid some of his commission to the solicitor. Lord Craighill described this practice as 'a most reprehensible one' and hoped it would be the last he heard of it. It was held that the solicitor had to account for the payment to the trustees. It was argued in this case that this custom of split commissions was a custom of trade which presumed the principal's implied consent. The court said that even if this was so it was no defence.

Secret profits, or secret commissions as they are sometimes known, also include what are known more colloquially as bribes. A bribe is a payment made to an agent by a third party who knows that the agent is acting on his principal's behalf. The payment is kept secret from the principal. There is a very thin dividing line between a secret profit and a bribe. To quote Lord Denning on another matter altogether 'you will recognise one [a bribe] when you see one'. If it can be proved that a secret commission was paid or received corruptly then both donor and recipient will be guilty of a criminal offence under the Prevention of Corruption Acts 1906 and 1916. In addition to criminal consequences there are consequences under civil law. The principal may dismiss the agent, recover commission paid and refuse to pay any due. Payment of secret commissions is a civil wrong, so the third party may be liable in damages to the principal who may refuse to peform the contract. The agent is of course entitled to commission earned during the period when there was no breach of faith (see *Graham v United Turkey Red Co* 1922 SC 553). In *Kelly v Cooper* (above) the court held *obiter* that an agent who committed an innocent breach of fiduciary duty could recover any commission otherwise payable. The principal need not show that any loss has been suffered from the agent receiving a secret commission: it is enough to show that the agent has made a profit over and above the agreed remuneration.

Duty not to misuse confidential information   In the course of an agency an agent may come into possession of a wide range of information which is commercially sensitive and confidential. Agents must not use this information for any purpose other than that of their principal. This duty may last beyond the termination of the agency. For example, in *Liverpool Victoria Friendly Society* v *Houston* (1900) 3 F 42, Houston had been an agent of the Society but had been dismissed by them. He then gave a list of the Society's members, which had come into his hands while an agent, to a competitor, who used it to canvas for business. The court held that the lists were confidential and Houston was not entitled to use them and could be interdicted from so doing. Lord Pearson said 'the law implies a contract that the information shall not then or afterwards be ultroneously disclosed to a third party'.

Duty when buying and selling principal's property   It will often be the function of the agent to buy and/or sell property, either heritable or moveable, for the principal. Agents may not sell their own goods to their principal without the principal's consent. In *Armstrong* v *Jackson* [1917] 2 KB 822, A employed J, who was a stockbroker, to buy shares for him. J already owned some of those shares and he sold them to A. When A discovered this, he sought to rescind the contract. It was held that he could do so. There was a conflict of interest. As a buyer the agent's aim is to buy goods at the lowest price while as a seller his aim is to get the highest possible price. It was immaterial that the shares were sold at the market price. The principal should have been told.

This element of full disclosure also applies where the agent seeks to buy property from his principal. In *McPherson's Trustees* v *Watt* (1877) 5 R (HL) 9, W was an advocate in Aberdeen who acted as a broker in the sale and purchase of estates. He acted as law-agent (solicitor) for the trustees. They asked him to arrange the sale of four houses and he sold the houses to his brother, with whom he had made a prior arrangement that he would pay half the price in return for two of the houses. When the trustees discoverd this they sought to rescind the contract. W claimed specific performance but the House of Lords held that the contract was invalid and it was immaterial that the contract price was a fair one. Lord Blackburn said:

> we do not inquire whether it was a good bargain or a bad bargain before we set it aside. The mere fact that the agent was in circumstances which made it his duty to give his client advice puts him in such a position that, being a purchaser himself, he cannot give disinterested advice — his own interests coming in contact with his client's; that mere fact authorises the client to set aside the contract, if he chooses so to do.

5.4   THE RELATIONSHIP BETWEEN AGENT, PRINCIPAL AND THIRD PARTY

The function of the agent is to link his principal and the third party in a contractual relationship which will impose rights and obligations on each of them. The agent should ideally obtain no rights and have no obligations imposed on him under the contract. He will have, as it were, dropped out of the picture. He may incur liability to the third party, however, if he has been fraudulent or negligent irrespective of whether the fraud or negligence was authorised by the principal or whether the principal has been bound. The principal may also be liable for losses caused by the agent's fraud if the fraudulent act is within the agent's apparent authority. In *Lloyd* v *Grace, Smith & Co* [1912] AC 716, the defendants were a firm of solicitors who had given their managing clerk, S, general authority to conduct the conveyancing business of the firm. S fraudently induced the plaintiff, a widow, to make over some property to him and he sold it for his own benefit. It was held that the solicitors were liable to her because S had been acting with apparent authority (see below).

5.4.1 Agent's authority

Whether or not an agent succeeds in linking principal and third party in a contractual relationship will depend to a large extent on whether the agent has exceeded the authority given by his principal . If that authority has been exceeded, the principal will not be bound and the agent will be liable to the third party for breach of warranty of authority (see *J. M. & J. H. Robertson* v *Beatson Macleod & Co* 1908 SC 921). In such cases, as we have seen earlier (see 5.2.3 above), the principal may choose to ratify the agent's unauthorised act; thus relieving the agent of liability. The authority possessed by the agent will, if disputed, be a question of fact in each case. The authority possessed by the agent may be expressly specified in the contract between them, or may be implied from the circumstances, trade, custom, etc (actual authority).

In addition to actual authority which is authority expressly conferred either in writing or orally, the agent has implied authority to do anything necessary for and ordinarily incidental to the carrying out of his duties. General agents have the implied authority that is generally recognised in their particular trade, business or profession. For example, a ship's captain has authority to employ a shipbroker and an architect in certain circumstances has authority to employ a surveyor. However that authority is limited to what is necessary or expected, for example, a general agent has no implied power to borrow money and a solicitor has no implied authority to appeal to a higher court.

Another type of authority is ostensible or apparent authority. This is authority which has been neither expressly nor impliedly conferred but which the agent appears to have because of the conduct of principal and agent and the representation by the principal that the agent is acting on his behalf. An example can be seen in *Hayman* v *American Cotton Oil Coy* (1907) 45 SLR 207, where the 'principal' advertised in the *Glasgow Herald* indicating that H was his agent. He also allowed H to so indicate on H's letterheads, and wrote to customers indicating H's agency. The doctrine of personal bar by holding out will operate here unless the third party knew that the agent did not in fact have the apparent authority, or could be taken as knowing that the authority was lacking. Where the third party knows that the agent would not normally have authority, but he chooses to rely on the agent's (false) assertions that he does have authority, the principal will not be bound (but see below). It may be, for example, that a principal has withdrawn actual authority from an agent, but has failed to notify third parties of this, or that a principal has placed some restriction on an agent but has not made this known to third parties. In both these situations, the third party (unless aware of the reality) is justified in believing that the agent has the necessary authority to act on the principal's behalf. Statutory applications of ostensible authority can be seen in the Partnership Act 1890, s. 36(1) and the Factors Act 1889, s. 2(1).

In *Freeman & Lockyer (a firm)* v *Buckhurst Park Properties Ltd* [1964] 2 QB 480, Diplock LJ said 'it is upon the apparent authority of the agent that the contractor normally relies in the ordinary course of business. In *Watteau* v *Fenwick* [1893] 1 QB 346, the defendant had appointed H to manage a public house. H had been expressly forbidden to buy cigars on credit but, in spite of this prohibition, bought cigars on credit from the plaintiff. It was held that the principal/defendant was liable to pay for the cigars as it was within the ostensible or apparent authority of a pub manager to buy cigars on credit.

Two recent English cases would seem to indicate a division of opinion by the judiciary where ostensible authority is concerned. The cases — *Armagas Ltd* v *Mundogas SA (The Ocean Frost)* [1986] 1 AC 717 and *First Energy (UK) Ltd* v *Hungarian National Bank* [1993] 2 *Lloyds Rep* 94 — are analysed by Reynolds in (1994) 110 LQR 21, at 23–25 (see the Cases and Materials section for Chaper 5). In *Armagas*, the House of Lords restated the principle that where the third party knows that the agent would not normally have the authority and there is nothing beyond the agent's own false assertion that he has authority then the principal is not bound. However, in *First Energy (UK) Ltd* the court held that where the agent (a bank manager) had no authority to grant a loan and the third party knew this, an offer of such a loan was binding on the principal (the bank). In *Dornier* v *Cannon* [1991] SC 310, the court said that the more extraordinary the transaction then the less likely it was that the agent had authority to enter into it. It would be a question of fact and degree as to whether the agent's actions were within his apparent or ostensible authority. (See also Brown (1995) JBL 360 'Agent's Apparent Authority: Paradigm or Paradox'.)

For further illustrations of what constitutes ostensible authority, see the Cases and Materials section for Chapter 5, where an account of the case *International Sponge Importers* v *Watt & Sons* 1911 SC (HL) 57 is to be found. (See also *British Bata Shoe Company* v *Double M Shah Ltd* 1980 SC 311.)

Another type of authority is presumed authority, which is the authority which the law presumes the principal would have given had he been consulted. An example of presumed authority is s. 35 of the Companies Act 1985. Agency of necessity is no more than an example of presumed authority.

5.4.2 Agent's liability

Agents are liable to indemnify their principals if they have acted outwith their actual authority. In addition, if agents acting beyond their authority have made a contract with a third party, which their principal refuses to ratify, they will be liable to the third party for breach of warranty of authority.

Whether agents have exceeded their authority or not they may still incur liability in certain circumstances. Liability (if any) will depend on how the agent has contracted with the third party. The agent may have disclosed the fact of his agency and either named his principal or refused to name him (often one of the reasons for using agents is anonymity), or the agent may not have disclosed the fact of his agency at all.

Where the agent has acted fraudulently, the principal will not be liable unless he has made the fraud possible or had benefited from it. The same principle has been held to apply where the agent deliberately fails to communicate material facts to his principal (*Muirs Exrs* v *Craig* 1913 SC 349). However, where the agent has acted negligently the principal may have to bear the loss for the agent's defaults (*Laing* v *Provincial Homes* 1909 SC 812).

5.4.2.1 Agent for named principal As a general rule the agent will incur no liability. There are, however, some exceptions to this:

(a) where the agent expressly and in writing incurs liability (to avoid this situation the agent must always make it clear that he is merely an agent and incurs no personal liability);

(b) where his liability is implied by trade custom (*Neil* v *Hopkirk* (1850) 12 D618;

(c) where the principal has no contractual capacity, e.g., a contract made on behalf of an unincorporated body which has no separate legal personality (see also *Kelner* v *Baxter* at 5.2.3 above).

5.4.2.2 Agent for an unnamed principal This is an area where there is little Scottish authority. Normally the same general principles apply as apply where the principal is named. There is, however, a presumption that the third party would have been unwilling to contract with someone whose identity was unknown to him. As a result, the personal liability of the agent will be more readily inferred in construing the contract but this will depend upon the exact circumstances of the case. The agent may be liable by trade usage or custom or, Gow has suggested (at p. 524), because he does not name his principal within a certain time or within a reasonable time. The case Gow relies on is *Brydon* v *Muir* 1869 7 M 603. It seems clear from the case, however, that the agent's liability arose because he did not disclose the name of the *third party* to the principal, thus making it impossible for the principal to recover money owed. In *The Santa Carina* [1971] 1 Lloyd's Rep 478, it was held that even if a trade custom can make the agent personally liable then the custom's existence has to be proved. Lord Denning said (at 481):

I know that in many trades there is a custom by which the broker is liable. Those cases rest on a custom of the trade. There was no such custom alleged or proved (in this case). It seems to me that, in the circumstances of this case, the proper inference is that the agents were, when they gave the telephone message, giving it as agents only.

5.4.2.3 Principal undisclosed Where the agent acts for an undisclosed principal, both principal and agent are liable. The third party will obviously first look to the agent for performance and hold him liable for breach. The principal may, however, disclose himself (or be disclosed), and is then liable. In *Armstrong* v *Stokes* (1872) LR 7 QB 598 at 603, Blackburn J said:

... it is too firmly established that where a person employs another to make a contract for him, he as principal is liable to the seller, although the seller had never heard of his existence and entered into the contract solely on the credit of the person whom he believed to be the principal though in fact he was not. It is established law that if on the failure of the person with whom the vendor believed himself to be contracting, the vendor discovers there is an undisclosed principal behind, he is entitled to take advantage of this unexpected godsend.

This view has recently been echoed by Lord Jauncey in *Boyter* v *Thomson*. (*The Times*, 16 June 1995.)

The third party will have to choose whether to sue the agent or the principal, but cannot sue both. Once he has made the choice it is final (*Ferrier* v *Dodds* (1865) 3 M 561).

5.5 TERMINATION OF AGENCY

If there is a contract of agency the normal rules as to termination of contracts will apply. The contract of agency may specify that the relationship is to terminate after a particular task has been accomplished or on the expiry of an agreed period of time or the contract may be terminated by agreement between the parties, by unilateral action or by the operation of a rule of law.

5.5.1 Termination by principal or agent

Provided there was no agreed period for which an agency was to run, either the principal or agent may terminate it at any time. An unjustified termination before the expiry of the agreed period of an agency will render the party terminating the agency liable in damages. On termination, the principal remains liable to pay the agent any unpaid remuneration and is under a continuing duty to indemnify the agent in respect of liabilities incurred in the course of the agency. Where a principal terminates an agency, the agent must be allowed to complete any transaction in which he is engaged. A principal is entitled to continuing access to the agent's records (after termination), relating to acts done in the principal's name, unless that right was expressly excluded by the contract (*Yasuda Fire & Marine Insurance Co. of Europe, Re* [1995] 2 WLR 49).

If the agent is a *procurator in rem suam* (known in England as an agent with an interest), the agency is irrevocable unless reasonable cause can be shown for its revocation. In *Galbraith & Moorhead* v *Arethusa Shipping Company* (1896) 23 R 1011, brokers took 500 shares in a ship on condition that they be appointed sole chartering brokers. The condition was accepted but some five years later the company sought to terminate the agency agreement. It was held that they could not do so. Lord Adam said 'I have great difficulty in holding that an agreement for which consideration has been given could be terminated at will by the other contracting party'.

5.5.2 Termination by operation of a rule of law

The relationship will be terminated by any of the following:

(a) By the expiry of the relevant period of time; this may have been expressly agreed or may be by trade custom, e.g., the authority of a stockbroker terminates at the close of the current account (*Lawford* v *Harris* (1896) 12 TLR 275).

(b) When its object is accomplished; if the agent is authorised to act as agent in a specific piece of business once he has performed it, the relationship is terminated.

(c) Where the object of the contract has become impossible, e.g., if the agency was established for the sale or purchase of a specific article and this has been destroyed. Other examples of impossibility have included the agent being called up for military service (*Marshall* v *Glanvill* [1917] 2 KB 87), or war making one of the parties an enemy alien (*Boston Deep Sea Fishing and Ice Co Ltd* v *Farnham* [1957] 3 All ER 204).

(d) The death of the agent will terminate the relationship because the relationship is a personal one and hence the individual identity and existence of the agent is of the essence. *Friend* v *Young* [1897] 2 Ch 421 suggests that even if there is a joint agency the death of one agent ends the authority of the other. The death of the principal also normally terminates the agency provided the agent was aware of the principal's death (*Campbell* v *Anderson* (1829) 3 WES 5L 384, which would seem to be an exception to the rule that death is a public fact of which no notice need be given: see also *Life Association of Scotland* v *Douglas* (1886) 13 R 910. After the principal's death, the agent may complete any transactions in which he is engaged.

(e) Bankruptcy of the principal has the same effect as death. Bankruptcy is deemed to be a public fact of which no notice need be given but the agent may complete any transaction. The bankruptcy of the agent need not terminate the agency. It would seem to depend on whether there is an express provision to that effect in the contract. In *McCall* v *Australian Meat Co Ltd* (1870) 19 WR 188, it was held that the bankruptcy of the agent did not terminate the agency, however, in *Hudson* v *Grainger* (1821) 5B 3 Ald 27, the bankruptcy of the agent, a factor, terminated the relationship. It should be noted that the court in *Hudson* felt that the agent's continued solvency was an implied contractual term.

(f) Insanity of the agent terminates the relationship, as does the insanity of the principal, provided it is permanent. The effect of the insanity of the principal is the same as that of death or bankruptcy, i.e. the agent may complete transactions in which he is engaged.

5.5.3 Notice to third parties
Upon termination of an agency, it is advisable for a principal to give notice to all persons who have had dealings with the agency of its termination. If the principal fails to do so, any contracts entered into by third parties in the bona fide belief that the agent still had the principal's authority will bind the principal. A principal should contact all existing customers and advertise the fact of the termination to others. In the case of a partnership, the Partnership Act 1890, s. 36 imposes a duty on the firm to do this.

Further reading

Cuisine and Forte, (1987), *Scottish Cases and Materials in Commercial Law*, Butterworths, Chapter 6, pp. 271–301.

Fridman, (1990) *Law of Agency*, 6th edn, Butterworths.

Gloag (1929) *The Law of Contract*, 2nd edn, W. Green Ltd.

Gloag and Henderson, (1987), *Introduction to the Law of Scotland*, 9th edn, W. Green Ltd.

Gow, (1994), *Mercantile and Industrial Law of Scotland*, W. Green Ltd.

Markesinis & Munday, (1992), *Outline of the Law of Agency*, 3rd edn, Butterworths.

McEwan, (1986), *The Laws of Scotland Stair Memorial Encylopaedia*, pp. 247–80.

Marshall, (1992) *Scots Mercantile Law*, 2nd edn, W. Green Ltd, Chapter 1.

Stone, (1995), *Law of Agency*, Cavendish Publishing.

Walker, (1989), *Principles of Scottish Private Law*, W. Green Ltd.

CHAPTER SIX

The Law Relating to the Sale and Supply of Goods

6.1   AIMS, VALUES AND SOURCES

Chapter 3 examined the principles of contract law which apply to all contracts. This chapter considers the specialised rules which have been developed to regulate contracts for the sale and supply of goods. These are very important contracts in a modern economy. The general principles discussed in Chapter 3 apply to contracts for the sale and supply of goods and provide the answers to problems of formation, incorporation of terms, misrepresentations, error, breach, etc. However, the rules contained in this chapter often give a specialised solution which replaces these general principles or adds to them. For example, the legislation on supply of goods implies terms as to quality, description, fitness for purpose and title into these contracts, while the general principles will imply terms only where it is necessary for business efficacy. Clearly, a contract for the supply of goods could survive without implied terms on quality and the other matters so that a strict freedom of contract approach would find it unacceptable to imply such terms. For reasons of social policy the law has decided that, nevertheless, buyers should have rights in respect of quality and the other matters without having to bargain for them. We also find specialised solutions to problems which arise only in sale or supply of goods, i.e. passing of property and transfer of title.

   Of course, rules such as these are vitally important in the planning and execution of business activities, and in the negotiation or litigation of disputes.Suppliers must know their obligations and potential liabilities in respect of poor quality goods if they are to draft terms which suit their interests, whether by minimising the scope of the obligation or the degree of liability, or whatever. Inevitably there are controls on terms excluding or limiting obligations and liabilities, and these must also be considered (see 3.11.3 above).

The rules on passing of property also provide a good example of rules which are vital to the planning of transactions. These rules determine the point at which ownership and risk of loss or damage passes from the seller to the buyer of goods. A buyer may find that the goods are at his risk while they are still in the possession of the seller. If this is going to be the case, he may wish to negotiate a term which alters this rule and says that the goods are not at his risk until he has possession. Alternatively, he may wish to insure against loss which occurs when the goods are still with the seller.

The specialised rules in this chapter also help us to develop a clearer picture of the values of the law of contract. We said in Chapter 3 that there were a number of rules which regulated the bargaining environment and the terms of the contracts. Thus, although the basic aim of the substantive law of contract was to enforce the agreements made by the parties, it was also prepared to protect the parties from certain sorts of burdens and losses and to carry out a degree of regulation of the bargaining environment within which contracts are made. Many of the specialised rules on supply of goods and services also introduce standards on various issues such as title, quality, description, fitness for purpose of goods, obligations to deliver and accept goods, remedies for non performance, etc. These standards apply even where the parties have said nothing on such matters. In other words, the law fills out what are perceived to be the reasonable expectations of the parties on these important matters. So the law is not, in this respect, enforcing only what has been expressly agreed to, what the parties have chosen to bargain for. Often the parties have agreed only to the basic gist of an exchange, i.e. product or service X for £Y; they may have said nothing on matters such as quality, delivery, etc. The rules on these issues provide a legally defined standard for the risk in question. Without them, and in absence of express agreement on any given matter, one of the parties would lose out, at least relative to what the legal rules say. For example, in the absence of rules implying terms as to quality, the buyer (in the absence of an express term) could not hold the seller to account. In the absence of rules placing an obligation of acceptance on buyers they might be able to refuse goods capriciously.

Indeed, the rules often have a significance even where the parties have agreed terms on those matters. Although the basic principle is that the parties can agree to whatever terms they wish, this is subject to severe qualification. The terms on quality, fitness and description can never be overruled in consumer sale or supply, and may be overruled in commercial sale or supply only if reasonable (see 3.11.3 above and below at 6.6). The implied terms as to title can never be overruled by agreement. Agreements to compromise the duty to deliver might also be subject to the reasonableness test (see 3.11.6 above and below at 6.9.1).

The rules on the seller's rights and remedies (e.g., to demand acceptance by the buyer, to sue for the price, to stop goods in transit, etc.) are most vulnerable to contrary agreement, it being doubtful that such contrary agreement would be subject to the reasonableness test (see 3.11.6 above and below at 3.6.6). This indicates that the law is more concerned to protect the perceived reasonable expectations of buyers from exclusion or restriction by formal agreement than it is to protect the expectations of sellers (see discussion above at 3.11.3 and below at 6.6.5).

The rules on passing of property (see 6.6.7 below) and transfer of title (see 6.6.8 below) perform different sorts of functions. The former are partly concerned with the problem of goods being lost, stolen, destroyed or damaged after the contract of sale but before the buyer takes physical custody, i.e. while they are still with the seller, in transit etc. The law must fix a point when ownership, and with it risk, passes. Roughly speaking the approach seems to be to say that ownership passes when, even though physical delivery may not yet have taken place, the transaction is final in all other respects (see 6.6.7 below). While it might be argued that the seller should bear total risk until physical transfer, the law's view seems to be that this is too great a burden, and that the risk should generally pass before this point unless the parties agree otherwise.

The rules on transfer of title are basically about mediating the conflict of interest between an original owner of goods who has lost possession of them and an innocent purchaser who acquires them from someone else. Although the law asserts a general principle (the *nemo dat* rule, (see below at 6.8, 6.8.1) to the effect that good title can be passed only by the original owner, a number of exceptions ensure that innocent purchasers generally get title. One reason for this is that the law wishes to protect the security of transactions. It does not wish to unravel a series of sales simply to protect the property rights of an original owner.

6.2 SALE AND SUPPLY OF GOODS — TYPES OF CONTRACT AND SOURCES OF REGULATION

At 6.1 we discussed the problems which rules on sale and supply of goods must resolve — problems of arguments over title, when ownership is to pass, the buyer's expectations as to quality, fitness, etc. Many of these problems are relevant to a range of different types of contract under which goods are transferred from one party to another. For example, the issue of quality of goods might arise in contracts of hire, sale, exchange, hire-purchase, and indeed in any contract under which A transfers goods to B. The problem of fixing a time for the passing of ownership will be relevant to contracts of sale, hire-purchase and other transactions in which legal ownership is to pass from A to B, but is irrelevant to contracts such as hire where the seller always remains the legal owner.

Most of the law in this area is either in the legislation covering contracts of sale (the Sale of Goods Act (SGA) 1979), or is closely modelled on it. As such this chapter will take the SGA 1979 as its main focal point and make reference to other contracts for the supply of goods where appropriate.

We must distinguish contracts of sale (covered by the SGA from other contracts for the supply of goods (which are not covered by the SGA).

However, it must be remembered that the rules governing these other contracts are normally of the same effect as the rules under the SGA. It is nevertheless important to recognise that the source of these rules is not the SGA, but rather the Sale and Supply of Goods Act 1994 and the Consumer Credit Act 1974, where the implied terms as to quality of fitness, etc. are concerned, and the common law where other issues are involved.

A contract of *sale* of goods is a contract whereby the seller transfers or agrees to transfer the property in goods to the buyer for a money consideration called the price (s. 2(3)). Where under such a contract the property (i.e. the legal ownership) in the goods is transferred from the seller to the buyer the contract is called a sale (s. 2(4)). This would include a credit sale (i.e. one where the price is to be paid by instalments), as long as the property is indeed transferred at the time of the contract (a credit sale is also regulated by the Consumer Credit Act 1974, sec 7.2.3 below). Where the transfer of the property in the goods is to take place at a future time or subject to some conditions later to be fulfilled, the contract is called an agreement to sell. This would include what is known as a conditional sale. In a conditional sale the seller retains ownership until some condition (typically payment of all due instalments) is fulfilled.

A conditional sale must be distinguished from a hire-purchase (HP) agreement, which looks strikingly similar from a practical point of view in that the customer in an HP agreement obtains goods and pays up over a period, with the option of becoming the owner, normally on making the last payment. However, it is this option which makes the difference. Unlike under a conditional sale (i.e. an agreement to sell under s. 2) the buyer under a hire-purchase agreement, is not promising to buy, although of course, in practice, he will almost invariably do so. He is, in theory, hiring the goods up until the point when he exercises the right to buy. The Consumer Credit Act regulates HP agreements and conditional sales if credit is involved. Specifically it applies the same implied terms as to description, quality, etc. as apply to the contract of sale (these are discussed at 6.6 below). The Consumer Credit Act also controls the supplier's remedies against the consumer in circumstances where the consumer is in default (see 7.8 below). Furthermore, along with the common law, it covers disputes over ownership of the goods as between the hire-purchase company and a purchaser who has bought from the hirer (see 6.8.1 below). As far as other problems are concerned, i.e., duties to deliver and accept goods, and remedies for breach of these duties, the courts would probably apply similar rules to HP agreements as they do to agreements for sale (below at 6.10).

There are a number of other contracts under which goods will be supplied from one party to another. One possibility is a contract for work and materials, e.g., where a painter paints and sells a portrait using his own materials, or a mechanic installs parts in the course of a service to a vehicle. Whether the goods are regarded as being transferred under a contract of sale, rather than as part of a contract for work and materials, will depend upon whether the parties intended to contract principally for skill and labour or principally for the transfer of the goods (see generally *R&J Dempster Ltd v*

Motherwell Bridge & Engineering Co Ltd 1964 SC 308, *Robinson* v *Graves* (1935) 1KB 579, *Pollock* v *Macrae* 1922 SC 192 (HL) and *Lee* v *Griffin* (1861) 1 BES 272). If there is a contract for the sale of goods the SGA applies; otherwise the Supply of Goods and Services Act 1994, s.6 and sch.1 apply the same implied terms as to description, quality, etc. to the goods which are transferred. The common law position on matters such as delivery, acceptance and payment, and passing of property is broadly analogous.

Another possibility is the contract of hire under which there is never any intention to transfer anything other than possession, i.e. ownership always remains with the lessor. Clearly here there will never be any issue as to transfer of property/ownership. The Sale and Supply of Goods Act 1994 applies the same implied terms as in sale. A more recent aspect of business practice is the leasing contract under which items such as cars, photocopiers, computers, etc. are 'leased' either to private consumers or to businesses. This practice has become attractive for the lessor because it amounts to an income rather than a capital acquisition, and also for tax reasons. There is no legally recognised category involving the lease of moveable property. As long as there is no binding arrangement that the customer should buy *or* have the option to buy at the end of the lease, then the contract is effectively one of hire. However, if the customer has a legally binding option to buy the contract is one of hire-purchase. If there is actually an agreement from the outset that the customer will buy at the end of the lease, then the 'lease' is actually an agreement to sell under s. 2(5) of the SGA.

Another possible arrangement is barter or exchange, where the consideration is not money but goods (see generally *Urquhart* v *Wylie* 1953 SLT (Sh G) 87, *Widenmeuyer* v *Burn Stewart & Co Ltd* 1967 SLT 129 and *Sneddon* v *Durant* 1982 SLT (Sh ct) 39). These do not qualify as sales because of the lack of money consideration (see definition above); however, the typical 'part exchange' where an old car and money are exchanged for a new or newer car is a sale (see *Sneddon*, above, where Sheriff Bell approved such a view expressed by Professor Walker). If the contract is one of exchange or barter the Sale and Supply Goods Act 1994 applies the same implied terms on description, quality, etc. and the common law applies rules analogous to sale on obligations to deliver, accept and pay (see below at 6.9).

6.3   SUBJECT MATTER AND PRICE

6.3.1   Goods
Goods are defined in s. 61(1) of the SGA as 'in Scotland all corporeal moveables except money; and in particular "goods" includes emblements, industrial growing crops, and things attached to or forming part of the land which are agreed to be severed before sale or under the contract of sale'.

Noticeably absent from the definition of goods are heritable property and incorporeal property. The SGA does not therefore apply to the sale of houses or shares. The exclusion of money from the definition of goods is not absolute; money which is not treated as currency may be 'goods'. This would cover antiques or collectors' coins and money which is used solely as a foreign exchange commodity. In *Moss* v *Hancock* [1899] 2 QB 111, for reasons that need not concern us, the court had to decide whether a gold coin which had been stolen and resold was goods. It held that it was.

Goods may be existing or future goods. The former are those owned and possessed by the seller, the latter those to be manufactured or acquired by the seller after the contract is made s. 5(i). So where future goods are concerned the initial contract will be what was described at 6.2 above as an 'agreement to sell'. Existing goods may be ascertained, specific or unascertained. Ascertained goods are those goods identified and agreed upon at the time the contract of sale is made, e.g., the red Ford Sierra, registration number C25 LGB; unascertained goods (undefined in the Act) are purely generic goods, e.g., five tonnes of coal or an unidentified part of a larger whole, e.g., a packet of cigarettes from behind a newsagent's shelves. Unascertained goods could also be future goods which have still to be manufactured or acquired by the seller.

These categories are important, particularly in relation to the question of the passing of property and risk, (see 6.7 below).

6.3.2 Price

Section 8 of the Act deals with price. The price for the goods must always be in money. If there is no money involved the contract is one of barter and common law rules apply. The price may be fixed by the contract, may be left to be fixed in a manner agreed by the contract or may be determined by the course of dealing between the parties. Where none of these apply the buyer must pay a reasonable price; what is reasonable is a matter of fact in each case. Usually, it will be the market price.

An important issue raised by non-agreement on price is the means which are to be adopted to determine a reasonable price.

6.3.2.1 Market value/reasonable price? In *Wilson* v *Marquis of Breadalbane* (1859) 21 D 957, negotiations took place as to the sale of cattle. Wilson sent the cattle to Breadalbane, saying the price was £15 per head. Breadalbane took delivery of the cattle but wrote back saying the price agreed had been £13 per head. He remitted payment based on this amount to Wilson. Inglis LJC said in this case there was no agreement as to price and normally there would be no contract but as the buyer had taken delivery of the cattle he must pay the market value (reasonable price). This was shown to be £15 per head. In *Stuart* v *Kennedy* (1885) 13 R 221, there was confusion between seller and buyer as to how the price of the goods was to be computed; the market value method of establishing a reasonable price was apparently confirmed. However, in *Glynwed Distribution Ltd* v *S. Koronka & Co* 1977 SLT 65, the pursuers delivered hot rolled steel to the defenders. Koronka took delivery thinking it was 'British steel' at £103.50/tonne. Glynwed thought they had sold 'foreign steel' at £149/tonne. The Sheriff said that a reasonable price need not be the market price and he fixed a price of £135/tonne. Lord Kissen said (at 68) that 'the reasonable price must be fair and just to both parties' and Lord Leechman (at 70) also stressed that while the 'market value' test had been used in the past there must now 'be introduced . . . the element of what is fair and just to both parties.'

6.3.2.2 Trade custom Trade customs may be such that they operate automatically. Those who do not wish to be bound by them must make express provision to this effect; for example in *Duthie & Co* v *Merson & Gerry* 1947 SC 43, a case involving the sale of fish, a trade custom which allowed the deduction of a 3d per £1 discount on purchases was withdrawn by the sellers. They intimated this change to the purchasers who continued however to deduct the 3d per £1 when settling their accounts. When the sellers brought an action to recover the unpaid discount, the purchasers claimed in their defence that there was a custom of trade with regard to the discount which the sellers were not entitled to terminate without the consent of the buyers. The court held that, by intimating the withdrawal of the discount to the purchasers, the sellers had made clear that they no longer wished to be bound by the previous practice of selling at a discount.

6.3.2.3 Third party valuation It may be that the price is to be fixed by the valuation of a third party, e.g., Sothebys. If the third party either cannot or does not fix a price then the agreement is cancelled. Where the goods, or some of them, have already been delivered to the buyer, the buyer will have to pay a reasonable price (s. 9(1)). If the failure to have the goods valued is the fault of buyer or seller, that party may be liable in damages to the party not at fault (s. 9(2)).

6.4 CAPACITY AND FORMALITIES

Under s. 3 of the SGA, capacity to buy and sell is regulated by the general law concerning capacity to contract (see Chapter 3, para. 3.8). These rules also apply to other contracts for the supply of goods.

Unless there is some provision to the contrary there are no special formalities required either for the constitution or proof of a contract of sale. In *McConnachie* v *Geddes* 1918 SC 391, Lord Salvesen said (at 398), 'So far as I know, the only form of property, the sale and purchase of which must be constituted by writing is heritage'. The sale of a ship therefore may be carried out without formalities although the conveyance of title to the ship will require a bill of sale in statutory form to be executed by the transferor, witnessed and registered.

6.5 STIPULATIONS AS TO TIME

Unless a different intention appears from the terms of the contract, stipulations as to time of payment are not of the essence of a contract of sale (s. 10). So a breach of such a stipulation will not give the innocent party the right to rescind the contract but simply to claim damages. The word stipulation has no technical meaning. It denotes any term of the contract. If time *is* an essential part of the contract and one party is in breach of the stipulation, the other party will be entitled to rescind the contract. It was said in *Paton* v *Payne*

(1897) 33 SLR that time will normally be considered to be of the essence in contracts between commercial parties.

6.6 IMPLIED TERMS

Sections 12–15 of the Sale of Goods Act imply in to contracts of sale terms which protect the most important of buyer expectations The same terms are implied into contracts of hire-purchase by Part III of the Consumer Credit Act 1974; into contracts for the transfer of property in goods by the new s. 11A–E of the Supply of Goods and Services Act 1982; and into contracts for the hire of goods by the new s. 11G–K of the 1982 Act. Both of these new sets of provisions come as part of a new Scottish section of the 1982 Act added by the Sale and Supply of Goods Act 1994, sch. 1. These terms have always applied in England under Pt I of the 1982 Act, and were previously only implied at common law in Scotland.

The focus is on title (the seller's right to sell); the description of the goods, and their quality and fitness. Whether a seller has title to what he purports to sell is considered to be so vital to the security of transactions that the Unfair Contract Terms Act 1977 does not allow the implied term that the seller will pass good title to be excluded in any circumstances. The other implied terms may not be excluded where the purchaser is a consumer and where the purchaser is a commercial party, they may only be excluded if it is reasonable in the circumstances (see 3.11.6.2 above). This distinction is intended to reflect the weaker bargaining position of consumers.

6.6.1 Implied terms as to title

Under s. 12, the seller is taken to guarantee that, in the case of a sale, he has the right to sell the goods and, in the case of an agreement to sell, he will have such a right at the time the property is to pass. He also undertakes that the goods are free and will remain free from any charges or encumbrances (third party rights) which have not been made known to the buyer before the contract is made, and that the buyer will enjoy quiet possession of the goods. It has been held that the seller was in breach of the provisions of s. 12 when he supplied goods that carried a label which constituted a breach of a third party's trademark, and which the buyer could not resell without risking legal action. Anyone who 'sells' stolen goods will be in breach of the term implied by s. 12 and an innocent purchaser could in theory sue for breach of that term. Such an innocent party will obtain no title to the goods as the sale of stolen goods does not fall under one of the exceptions to the *nemo dat* rule (see 6.8). In practice those who sell stolen goods are unlikely to be around to defend an action or have the money to compensate the buyer, and rights are worthless unless they can be enforced.

The implied term as to title cannot be excluded in any contract (Unfair Contract Terms Act, s. 20(1)(a), as amended by SGA, s. 63(1) and sch. 2).

6.6.2 Implied terms as to description

In a sale of goods by description, there is an implied term that the goods will correspond with the description, and, in a contract of sale of goods by sample as well as description, there is a condition that the goods must correspond with both sample and description. A sale can be by description even though the goods are selected by the purchaser e.g., a tin of beans is 'sold by description' as the buyer cannot see the contents. More obvious examples of sales by description would be a purchase from a mail order catalogue or newspaper advertisements. It seems that the greater the expertise of the purchaser the less likely the sale is to be seen as a sale by description; the assumption being that the expert purchaser has not relied on the description given. In *Harlingdon and Leinster Enterprises Ltd v Christopher Hull Fine Arts Ltd* [1990] 1 All ER 737 it was held that the fact that a description was applied to goods either in the course of negotiations or in the contract itself did not necessarily make the contract one for the sale of goods by description for the purposes of s. 13(1) of the 1979 Act, since for the sale to be 'by' description the description had to be influential in the sale so as to become an essential term of the contract. Here it was held that a statement by one art dealer to another as to who had painted a particular painting was not a sale by description, as one art dealer would not usually rely upon a description by another. If it *is* in fact decided that goods *have* been sold by *description*, the next question is whether they comply wth the description.

Description can cover size, quantity, weight, method of manufacture etc. It is always a question of fact whether goods comply with their description. It would seem that any deviation, no matter how slight, from the description given will be a breach of the implied term. In *Arcos v E A Ronassen & Son* [1933] AC 470 a quantity of $\frac{1}{2}$ inch thick timber staves were ordered. The staves delivered varied in thickness from $\frac{1}{2}$ inch to $\frac{5}{8}$ inch. The timber was acceptable for the buyer's purposes but despite this the buyer was held entitled to rescind the contract. Lord Atkin said (at 479) 'A ton does not mean about a ton, or a yard about a yard. Still less when you descend to minute measurements does half an inch mean about half an inch . . . the right view is that the condition of the contract be strictly observed'. Also in *Re Moore & Co Ltd and Landauer* [1921] 2 KB 529 it was held that a consignment of fruit packed in cartons of 24 instead of 30 as specified in the contract was a breach of the term as to description (even though the correct total was supplied). However, in *Reardon Smith Line Ltd v Yngar Hansen-Tangen* [1976] 1 WLR 989 Lord Wilberforce said (at p. 998) that the test was 'excessively technical and due for re-examination'. The law may therefore be ready to take a more liberal view of compliance with description. The main significance of this will be in relation to consumer contracts, where breach of the implied term has always been regarded as a material breach giving rise to a right to reject the goods (see 6.9 below). If the courts take a more liberal approach to compliance then capricious rejection for minor breaches will be controlled. Where commercial contracts are concerned, there can now be rejection in Scots law only where the breach is actually material i.e., not just deemed to be so, so that even if a hard line is taken on what is compliance with description, there can be only a damages claim if the breach is small. The damages will compensate for actual loss only so they may be insignificant where the breach is slight. (See 6.6.5 below).

Further guidance as to the nature of the concept of description can be gleaned from *British Steamship Co Ltd* v *Lithgows Ltd* 1974 SLT (Notes) 20, where a contract for the building of a bulk carrying vessel specified the exact power requirements of its engine. After delivery and commissioning, there was repeated trouble with the vessel, owing (it was alleged) to failure in one part of her main engine. The pursuers in an action for breach of contract averred that the defenders were in breach of the implied term as to description in s. 13(1). Lord Maxwell distinguished between 'capacity' (of the engine), a matter of description, and 'reliability', a matter of quality; as there was no question that the engine could not deliver the required horsepower and revolutions then the question of description did not arise. The pursuer might have been able to succeed if he had argued under s. 14 (but see Lord Maxwell's *dicta* (at 22)). In *Ashington Piggeries* v *Christopher Hill Ltd* [1972] AC 441, Lord Wilberforce said 'The test of description, at least where commodities are concerned, is intended to be a broader, more common sense, test of a mercantile character ... leaving more delicate questions of condition, or quality, to be determined under other . . . sections of the Act'.

The major advantage for buyers of the implied term about description is that it applies to private sales as well as sales in the course of a business. It therefore affords some protection when buying goods from private individuals. The more recent decisions indicate a reluctance to allow the obligation as to description to be used as a guarantee of quality; quality being the province of s. 14 (below). This approach (which focuses on identity as being synonymous with description) must cast considerable doubt not only on *Re Moore* but also on *Arcos* v *Ronassen* (see above).

6.6.3 Implied terms as to quality and fitness

Section 14 of the SGA is perhaps the best known section of any Act of Parliament. It starts off by paying lip service to the old idea of *caveat emptor* but then goes on to make major inroads into it. Section 14(1) provides 'except as provided by this section and section 15 and subject to any other enactment, there is no implied condition or warranty about the quality or fitness for any particular purpose of goods supplied under a contract of sale'. But s. 14(2) goes on to imply a quality obligation where there is a sale in the course of a business. This obligation was that goods be 'merchantable quality'; However, the Supply of Goods and Services Act 1994, s.1, has replaced the old s. 14(2) of the SGA with a new provision which implies an obligation of 'satisfactory quality'. Section 14(2) now reads:

(2)   Where the seller sells goods in the course of a business, there is an implied term that the goods supplied under the contract are of satisfactory quality.

(2A)   For the purpose of this Act, goods are of satisfactory quality if they meet the standard that a reasonable person would regard as satisfactory, taking account of any description of the goods, the price (if relevant) and all the other relevant circumstances.

(2B)   For the purposes of this Act, the quality of goods includes their state and condition and the following (among others) are in appropriate cases aspects of the quality of goods —

(a)   fitness for all the purposes for which goods of the kind in question are commonly supplied;

(b)   appearance and finish;

(c)   freedom from minor defects;

(d)   safety; and

(e)   durability.

(2C)   The term implied by subsection (2) above does not extend to any matter making the quality of goods unsatisfactory.

(a)   which is specifically drawn to the buyer's attention before the contract is made;

(b)   where the buyer examines goods before the contract is made, which that examination ought to reveal; and

(c)   in the case of a contract for sale by sample, which would have been apparent on a reasonable examination of the sample.

The first obvious point is that this section, unlike s. 13 above, applies only to contracts made in the course of a business. Next it should be noted that there is now a general test (s. 14 (2A) above) and a list of factors which are relevant to its application (s. 14(2B) above). These factors should always be read in the light of the general test, to which they contribute. We are being told by s. 14 (2B), what is relevant to the general test; we are not being told that simply because a product has, for example, a minor defect (see s. 14 (2A)(c) it is necessarily of unsatisfactory quality. All the factors must be set in the scales to determine if the goods meet the standard that a reasonable person would regard as satisfactory.

Safety may be an exception to this, as it surely must be the case that goods fail the test if they are unsafe. There will be many other circumstances in which it is very clear that products fail the test, e.g., by not being able to perform their function at all or hardly at all. For example, a car that will not start or will rarely start; a washing machine that does not clean clothes at all or hardly at all; an umbrella which is full of holes, or one which collapses constantly or with the slightest wind.

The problem, of course, comes with the less clear-cut cases, e.g., where the car, washing machine or umbrella is erratic rather than nearly useless. Here the criteria in the test are really put to use. A lower than average price might indicate a lower standard, although, as Ervine as pointed out, the reduction may have been to induce a quick sale rather than to indicate inferior quality (see Ervine, 'The Sale and Supply of Goods Act 1994' 1995 SLT 1). Of course the price may have been reduced for *both* of these purposes, e.g., where meat is 'reduced for quick sale' in a supermarket. This lowers the standard such that the meat need not, perhaps, be as tender as usual. Of course it must not give the purchaser food poisoning or it clearly will not be of satisfactory quality. Description is also very important and can raise or lower the level that a reasonable person thinks is satisfactory. For example, a description which speaks in glowing terms of how a product has been manufactured to the highest standards of design is likely to help to make unsatisfactory a product which turns out not to be useless, but to be erratic.

Although none of the factors listed in (s. 14(2B) is conclusive, aspects (a) to (c) and (e) probably go some way to making the satisfactory quality standard higher than the merchantability standard was. Aspect (d) (safety) makes no difference, as products would have been unmerchantable if they were unsafe, just as they will be unsatisfactory if they are unsafe.

Aspect (a) is relevant because the idea of 'fitness for purposes' is altered in two important respects from the old s. 14(2). First, there is no longer a reference to fitness for 'any of the purposes' for which such goods are commonly supplied; now the reference is to fitness for 'all purposes' for which such goods commonly supplied. This means that there is less room for a seller to argue that, even although a four wheel drive truck does not perform well on rough terrain, at least it performs satisfactorily on the road (see *AswaN Engineering Establishment* v *Lupdine* (1987) 1 WLR 1). Of course, if the buyer has a purpose in mind which is not 'common' to all (e.g., to inflate hot water bottles with his lungs as part of a strongman act) then failure to fulfil this purpose is unlikely to make the goods unsatisfactory. In such a case a buyer should make his purpose known, and he may have a remedy under s. 14(3) (6.6.3.3 below) if the goods do not make the grade.

Aspect (a) is also important in that (unlike the previous s. 14(2)) there is no reference to the fitness for purpose being measurable by reference to what it is 'reasonable to expect'. It may be that the courts occasionally thought that it was reasonable to expect minor defects (see especially *Millars of Falkirk* v *Turpie* 1976 SLT 66).

The reference to appearance and finish (s. 14(2B)(b)) and freedom from minor defects (s. 14(2B)(c)) is important, because it emphasises that the standard is concerned with factors other than the functionality of the product. This had been in doubt in the case of the old definition due to the decisions in cases such as *Millars of Falkirk* v *Turpie*. However, the case of *Rogers* v *Parish (Scarborough) Ltd* (1987) 2 All ER 232, seemed to confirm that even the old definition required that at least a *new* (in this case) car should be capable of being driven 'with the appropriate degree of comfort, ease of handling and reliability and . . . of pride in the vehicle's outward and interior appearance' (Mustill LJ). We now have statutory confirmation of this which is likely to be most useful from a buyer's point of view, enabling him to point to this criterion on the list of aspects in s. 14 (2B) thereby pressing home his claim to the seller.

The inclusion of durability as a criterion in s. 14(2B)(e) is again probably most important from the point of view of emphasis. The old definition probably required that goods be durable in the sense that they were in a state at the time of the delivery such that they would last for a reasonable time (see *Lambert* v *Lewis* (1982) *AC* 225, and Ervine, 'Durability, Consumers and the Sale of Goods Act' 1984 JR 147). However, buyers may have been uncertain on this point and this uncertainty could easily be exploited by sellers (especially against consumer buyers, who may have a very limited understanding of their rights'. (See on this point and on the background to the new law Willett, 'The Unacceptable Face of the Consumer Guarantees Bill (1991) 54 MLR 552 and Willett, 'The Quality of Goods and the Rights of Consumers' (1993) 44 NILQ 218.)

6.6.3.1 Second-hand goods The standard for second-hand goods will clearly be lower than for new goods, the price will be lower and there will be more of an expectation of minor defects. An important measure (as with new goods) will be how the goods in question compare with similar goods in a similar market at a similar price. The less well the quality compares the more likely the goods will be unsatisfactory.

6.6.3.2 Defects and examination Turning now to s. 14(2C), two points are of importance. First, para. (a) refers to defects *specifically* pointed out. It is no good for a seller to get a buyer to sign or acknowledge a statement that says 'all defects are acknowledged', or something akin to this. If a seller is to be excused from a particular defect that would make the goods unsatisfactory, he must point that defect out. Secondly, the buyer *need not* examine goods, but if he does he must find what a reasonable person would find, otherwise he cannot complain.

6.6.3.3 Private sales If one buys something in a private sale and it is defective or unsuitable there is no claim under s. 14 because s. 14(2) states that the section only applies to 'sales in the course of a business'. There may of course be a claim under s. 13 if the goods do not conform to description. Under the Business Advertisement Order 1977 (S.I. 1918), it is an offence for a business seller to masquerade as a private seller in order to attempt to evade the s. 14 obligations. In small ads for cars etc, a trader should include the designation '(T)' to make it clear that it is a sale in the course of a business. It is however not uncommon for unscrupulous traders to pose as private sellers and to operate from addresses with which they have no connection.

6.6.3.4 Fitness for particular purpose Where the seller sells goods in the course of a business and the buyer expressly, or by implication, makes known to the seller any particular purpose for which the goods are being bought there is an implied term that the goods supplied under the contract are reasonably fit for that purpose whether or not that is a purpose for which such goods are commonly supplied, except where the circumstances show that it is unreasonable for him to rely on the skill or judgment of the seller (s. 14(3)).

In order to qualify for protection under s. 14(3), buyers must show that they told the seller, either expressly or by implication, of the purpose to which they intended to put the goods. In most cases this will be done by implication; a television is usually only bought with one purpose in mind and the same will apply with most consumer items. In such cases there is no need for the buyer to specify the particular purpose for which the goods are required. In *Priest v Last* [1903] 2 KB 148, Priest, who had no special knowledge of hot water bottles, bought one from Last who regularly sold them. Priest asked Last whether he could fill the bottle with boiling water and was told he could not but that he could use hot water. Priest did not say why he wanted the bottle. The fifth time the bottle was filled with hot water it burst, burning Priest's wife. Evidence showed that the bottle was defective. It was held that Priest had relied on the skill and judgment of Last in selecting his stock and there was a breach of what is now s. 14(3); there was no need for Priest to have mentioned the intended purpose of the bottle as it was an obvious and normal one.

However, where a buyer has special needs, which the goods must cater for, then these must be drawn to the seller's attention if the section is to apply. For example, in the case of *Griffiths* v *Peter Conway* [1939] 1 All ER 685 a lady with particularly sensitive skin bought a Harris Tweed coat which aggravated her condition. It was held that, as she had not told the seller of her condition, she could not rely on s. 14(3).

In *Frost* v *Aylesbury Dairy Co Ltd* [1905] 1 KB 608 CA, milk containing typhoid germs was supplied to the plaintiff's household which led to his wife catching typhoid fever from which she died. The milk was unfit for human consumption and s. 14(3) applied. The case illustrates that the liability under SGA is strict; it was no defence to say that there was no way the defendants could have discovered the presence of the germs. (See also *Grant* v *Australian Knitting Mills Ltd* [1936] AC 85 and contrast, *McCallum* v *Mason* 1956 SC 50, both of which are to be found in the Cases and Materials section for Chapter 6.)

6.6.3.5 Reliance on seller's skill and judgment Once the buyer has intimated his purpose it is presumed that he relied on the seller's skill and judgment. In the case of *Grant* v *Australian Knitting Mills Ltd* it was said that by going into a retail shop the buyer relies on the seller's skill and judgment in selecting his stock. If the seller also happens to be the manufacturer of the goods it will be particularly difficult for him to argue that the buyer did not rely on his skill and judgment. This would seem to be the case even in situations where the buyer has supplied the specifications (see *Ashington Piggeries Ltd* v *Christopher Hill Ltd* [1972] AC 441).

6.6.3.6 Satisfactory quality and fitness for purpose In many cases both s. 14(2) and s. 14(3) will apply. If a car will not go because it lacks an engine it is clearly neither of satisfactory quality nor fit for its purpose. If, however, a car is scratched and dented it may well be fit for its purpose but not of satisfactory quality (see *Rogers* v *Parish* above). On the other hand, if the buyer asks for a car that is capable of towing a caravan and is supplied with a Mini, then the car may well be of satisfactory quality, but not fit for its purpose.

6.6.3.7 Sale by sample A contract of sale is a sale by sample where there is an express or implied term to that effect in the contract. Section 15 specifies three implied conditions in a sale by sample:

(a)   that the bulk will correspond with the sample;

(b)   that the buyer will have a reasonable opportunity of comparing the bulk with the sample;

(c)   that the goods shall be free from any defect rendering them unsatisfactory which would not be apparent on a reasonable examination of the sample.

The application of s. 15 can be illustrated by *Godley* v *Perry* [1960] 1 All ER 36. Godley, a six-year-old boy was blinded in one eye when firing a stone from a plastic toy catapult which broke. He had bought the catapult from Perry. He sued Perry for breach of the implied conditions in s. 14. Perry had bought the catapult by sample from a wholesaler. His wife had tested it by pulling back the elastic, but no defect had been revealed. Analysis of the plastic showed it to be of poor quality and unsuitable for the purpose. Perry brought the wholesaler into the action claiming a breach of the conditions in s. 15. The wholesaler had bought the catapults from another wholesaler who had obtained them from Hong Kong. The first wholesaler brought the second wholesaler into the action, alleging a similar breach of s. 15. It was held that:

(a)   the defendant (Perry) was in breach of s. 14, because the catapult was neither merchantable nor fit for its purpose.

(b)   Perry could recover from the first wholesaler who was in breach of s. 15(2)(c), because the catapult had a defect which rendered it unmerchantable and this defect was not apparent on examination. The first wholesaler could recover from the second wholesaler on the same grounds.

6.6.4   Limits on the protection offered by the implied terms
The protection of the implied terms is limited in the fact that they only protect an immediate buyer as against his seller. This is because they are implied terms of the contract of sale, i.e. they are relevant only as between the parties to the contract. There is no redress under s. 14 for a consumer against a manufacturer with whom he did not directly contract. Neither is there redress for someone who subsequently purchases from a consumer buyer. This is because the consumer buyer is not selling in the course of a business (see 6.6.3 above) and the subsequent purchaser has no contractual relationship with anyone else.

The best alternative in any of the above circumstances is for the injured user of the defective product to pursue an action under the Consumer Protection Act 1987 (see 4.8 above). However, such action will succeed only if the defective product damages other property or injures someone. So although the Act extends protection for defective products beyond the contractual nexus it does not extend to purely qualitative defects, e.g., a car which simply will not work.

6.6.5   Remedies for breach of the implied terms
Where there is a breach of any of the above implied terms, the buyer can claim damages and, if the breach is material, reject any goods delivered and repudiate the contract (SGA, s. 15B as inserted by the Sale and Supply of

Goods Act 1994, s. 5). The damages which can be claimed are such as to compensate for the loss directly and naturally resulting in the ordinary course of events from the breach (SGA s. 53A(1) as inserted by the Sale and Supply of Goods Act 1994, s. 5(3)). Where the breach is as to quality and the buyer keeps the goods the damages will, prima facie, be the difference between the value of goods at the time of delivery and the value they would have had if they had fulfilled the contract (SGA, s. 53A(2)).

As far as rejection and repudiation are concerned, a breach of the implied terms will always be deemed to be material, thereby giving a right to reject and repudiate, where the buyer is a consumer (SGA, s. 15B(2)). It was not absolutely clear, before this section was inserted by the 1994 Act, that any buyer *always* had a right to reject and repudiate in Scotland. The confusion was caused by the fact that general principles of Scots contract law allow rejection and repudiation only where the breach is material. However, the SGA classified the implied terms as condition and appeared to import into Scotland the English condition/warranty rules under which breach of a condition automatically gives a right to reject. It is now clear that the implied terms are not pre-classified in this way in Scotland (see sch. 2 of the 1994 Act, amending the references to 'conditions'). It is also clear that materiality of breach is the issue. However, deeming all breaches to *be* material in consumer cases is intended to make the law clear and user-friendly where consumers are concerned. Consumers will often be in a weaker position than commercial buyers, perhaps being uncertain of the nature or existence of their rights and having limited resources to pursue them. A clear right to reject is important. The view has been taken, on the other hand, that commercial buyers should be able to reject only where the breach is material. This is clearly intended to prevent bad faith rejection by commercial buyers for slight breaches of contract. This may happen where the contract has become unprofitable for the buyer, e.g., because the market for resale has collapsed. As was said above, this rule may or may not always have applied in Scotland. Certainly it did not always apply in England, where all buyers had a right to reject where there was a breach of any kind. The English position has now been amended so as to say that English commercial buyers can reject only where the breach is not so slight as to make it unreasonable (new s. 15A of the SGA).

6.6.5.1 Loss of the right to reject Even where a breach is material or deemed to be material, the right to reject applies only if the buyer is not taken to have 'accepted' the goods within the meaning of SGA, s. 35. The buyer is deemed to have accepted the goods when he intimates to the seller that he has accepted them, or when the goods have been delivered to him and he does any act in relation to them which is inconsistent with the ownership of the seller, or when, after the lapse of a reasonable time, he retains the goods without intimating to the seller that he has rejected them (s. 35(1), (4)).

The buyer cannot lose his right to reject by intimation or by an inconsistent act until he has had a reasonable opportunity of examining the goods to ascertain that they conform to the contract (s. 35(2)). Whether a reasonable opportunity for examination has been enjoyed is also a relevant factor in deciding whether a reasonable time has elapsed (s. 35(4)). These rules aim to strike a fair balance between the legitimate interest of the buyer in escaping from a contract in which he has lost confidence, and the legitimate interest of the seller and the market generally of maintaining a degree of commercial certainty.

The right to an opportunity for examination has been given a higher profile in the reformed s. 35 (amended by the Sale and Supply of Goods Act 1994, s. 2). Previously the right to examine operated only as a qualification to acceptance by intimation. This change tips the balance slightly in favour of buyers. However, the Scottish courts have, it seems, always taken account of the patency or otherwise of a defect and how reasonable it was for the buyer to have discovered it in determining when a reasonable time has elapsed (see discussion by Ong in the Cases and Materials section for Chapter 6 and also Willett, 'The Quality of Goods and the Rights of Consumers' 44 NILQ 218). Buyers are also favoured by the new s. 35(3) and (6). Section 35(3) says that a consumer cannot lose his right to examine as a precondition if being held to accept by intimation or inconsistent act, by agreement, waiver or otherwise. This should mean that signature of a note which deems an examination to have taken place will be of no effect. Section 35(6) says that no buyer accepts merely because he asks for or agrees to a repair, or disposes of the goods under a sale or other disposition.

6.7 THE PASSING OF PROPERTY

In every contract of sale there will be a moment when the legal ownership or 'property' in the goods passes from seller to buyer. The identification of this moment is important for the following reasons:

(a) In the event that the buyer becomes bankrupt, with or without possession of his goods, then only if property has passed, will the goods form part of the estate in sequestration.

(b) Section 20 of the Act says that *prima facie* risk, (e.g., of loss or damage), passes with property (ownership), although there are exceptions to this in s. 20(2) and (3).

(c) When property has passed, the seller can demand payment.

(d) If property has passed, sellers normally have no right to deal in the goods, even where they remain in possession (but see 6.8.3 below for an exception).

Under the common law of Scotland, the property in the goods did not pass until the goods were delivered, in the sense of being physically handed over. Since the passing of the SGA, however, property can pass independently of delivery.

Having decided that the goods are ascertained the question becomes, what was the intention of the parties. If this is not clear from the contract, a number of rules are used as a supposed surrogate for the parties' intentions.

These rules are not guided by when physical delivery or transfer takes place, but rather by when the contract appears to be complete in the sense that it is unconditional and the goods are in a deliverable state.

6.7.1 Ascertained or unascertained goods: intention of the parties

Ascertained goods are goods which are identified and agreed upon when the contract is made. Unascertained goods are goods defined only by a description which applies to all goods of the same class, or goods which form part of a larger consignment, or future goods. Section 16 provides 'no property is passed unless and until the goods are ascertained'.

In *Hayman & Son* v *McLintock* 1907 SC 936, McNairn & Co were flour merchants who had a large number of sacks of flour in Hayman's store. McNairn sold 250 sacks to McConnell and 100 to Stewart and in implementation of these sales, McConnell and Stewart were given delivery notes addressed to Hayman. He sent them acknowledgements that he held the sacks, subject to their instructions. He did not, however, separate the sacks from the others, nor were they labelled in any way. McNairn & Co were sequestrated. Who did the 350 sacks in the store belong to? It was held that the trustee in sequestration (McLintock) was entitled to all the sacks stored for McNairn, including the 350 for McConnell and Stewart. They were unascertained and, under s. 16, no property in them had passed to McConnell or Stewart. The situation would have been different if the flour had been labelled for McConnell and Stewart or even set aside separately (see also *Healy* v *Howlett* [1917] 1 KB 337).

Where the goods are ascertained, then 'the property in them is transferred to the buyer at such time as the parties to the contract intend it to be transferred' (s. 17(1)). Thus the seller may make provision in the contract that he reserves the right of disposal of the goods in the event, for example, of the purchaser's bankruptcy (see s. 19). Section 17(2) says that to ascertain the intentions of the parties regard must be had to their conduct, the terms of the contract and the circumstances of the case.

In *Woodburn* v *Andrew Motherwell Ltd* 1917 SC 533, the pursuer sold hay to the defender. The pursuer was to place the hay at the defender's disposal for baling. The pursuer was to cart the hay to the railway station for weighing and the weight was to determine the price. Some bales of hay were destroyed in the farmyard by fire. Whose hay? Woodburn's or Motherwell's? It was held that entry to the farm and bailing were acts inconsistent with the seller remaining the owner (see s. 35 at 6.9.3 below). The circumstances of the case disclosed an intention that the property should pass at that point. The hay therefore belonged to Motherwell.

6.7.2 The intention of the parties and the rules in s. 18

It will often not be clear, either from the contract, the conduct of the parties or the circumstances of the case, what the intentions of the parties were.

Section 18 lays down five rules to be used in ascertaining the intention of the parties. These will only apply where there is no intention discernable from the contract, the parties' conduct or the circumstances. As the Lord President said in *Woodburn* v *Andrew Motherwell* (at 538), 'The rules in section 18 are merely intended to be a guide in ascertaining the intention of the parties . . . if the intention of the parties is quite plain . . . then the rules of section 18 do not come into play at all'.

6.7.2.1 Rule 1 Where there is an unconditional contract for the sale of specific goods in a deliverable state, the property passes when the contract is made and it is immaterial whether the time of payment or the time of delivery, or both, be postponed. Goods are in a deliverable state if they are in such a state that the buyer would, under the contract be bound to take delivery. In *Tarling* v *Baxter* (1827) 6 B&C 360, Baxter purchased a haystack, but, before he could take it away, it was destroyed by fire. Once again, the question was, whose haystack had gone up in flames. It was held that Baxter had to pay. The property had passed (in the absence of any contrary intention) at the time the contract was made. The fact that he had neither paid nor taken delivery was immaterial. A consumer who bought a particular car could experience this type of situation. If the car were left on the seller's premises until insurance cover was arranged, the buyer would be the owner of the car, but would not be in possession of the car. If the car were to be damaged by vandals, the loss would fall on the owner, a rule expressed by the maxim *res perit domino* (a thing perishes to the disadvantage of its owner). The seller has a duty (s. 20(3)) to take proper care of the buyer's goods if they remain in his possession, but this duty is not absolute and it is conceivable that, if the property had passed, the buyer would be left without a remedy.

6.7.2.2 Rule 2 Where there is a contract for the sale of specific goods and the seller is bound to do something to the goods for the purpose of putting them in a deliverable state, the property does not pass until the thing is done and the buyer has notice that it has been done.

Thus, if the seller has agreed to fit a radio cassette to a car, then the property will not pass until the radio cassette has been fitted and the buyer informed. In *Brown Bros* v *Carron Co* (1898) 6 SLT 231 (OH), the pursuers contracted to sell a steam crane to the defenders. The contract provided that Brown should make some modification to the crane while erecting it. Carron, who no longer wanted the crane, refused to take delivery and the court held that as the property had not passed at the time of the breach, then Brown's only remedy was damages. He could not claim the contract price under s. 49(1) (see 6.10 below). See also *Underwood* v *Burgh Castle Syndicate* [1922] 1 KB 343.

In *Gowans ('Cockburn's Trustee)* v *Bowe & Sons* 1910 2 SLT 17, Cockburn, a farmer, had sold the whole of a growing crop of potatoes (specific goods) to the defender. The farmer was to grow, lift, pit and transport the potatoes to harbour. The farmer was sequestrated. At the date of the sequestration of the farmer, the potatoes had been grown, lifted and pitted at the farm. Both the trustee in bankruptcy and the defender claimed ownership of the potatoes. The defender argued that the goods were in a deliverable state when they were pitted (stored in pits). This argument was accepted; the carting of the goods was not necessary to make them deliverable, it was, said Lord Cullen, 'only a facility for their removal'.

6.7.2.3 Rule 3 Where there is a contract for the sale of specific goods in a deliverable state, but the seller is bound to weigh, measure, test or do some other act or thing with reference to the goods for the purpose of ascertaining the price, the property does not pass until the act or thing is done and the buyer has notice that it has been done.

An example would be where a customer asks for a piece of meat in a butchers. The butcher will have to weigh it in order to ascertain the price. If a dog runs off with the meat before it is weighed, the loss is the butcher's; if it has been weighed, then the loss is the customer's. Ownership will only pass when the meat has been weighed and the buyer has been told the price.

6.7.2.4 Rule 4 When goods are delivered to the buyer on approval or on sale or return or other similar terms, the property in the goods passes to the buyer:

(a) when he signifies his approval or acceptance to the seller or does any other act adopting the transaction;

(b) if he does not signify his approval or acceptance to the seller, but retains the goods without giving notice of rejection then, if a time has been fixed for the return of the goods, on the expiration of that time and, if no time has been fixed, beyond a reasonable time.

A sale on approval might involve the consumer ordering goods on 'fourteen days approval'. He will usually not have seen the goods, merely a picture of them, or read a description of them. Sale or return would cover a situation where, e.g., wine is needed for a party. In order to avoid the possibility of running short, one might order more than is thought to be needed, with the proviso that unused bottles may be returned without payment. Similarly, a retailer might acquire goods from a wholesaler on this basis, e.g., newspapers are generally supplied to newsagents on sale or return terms. Sale or return situations do not initially involve a sale at all; the customer is merely being supplied with goods which he may or may not elect to buy.

Approval, acceptance, or adoption Approval or acceptance of the transaction will normally be constituted by keeping the goods and sending off payment. This might be classed as express approval or acceptance. The buyer may, however, signify his approval or acceptance by implication; i.e. by doing 'any other act adopting the transaction', e.g., he might use the goods in such a way that his actions are held to constitute acceptance. Examples would include using wool supplied on approval to knit a jumper, selling, gifting, or pawning the goods in question, or making notes in a book so supplied.

A reasonable time Property in the goods may also pass to the buyer in such situations if he retains the goods beyond the limit stated in the 'approval' or 'sale or return' agreement. It may well be, however, that no time is stated. The relevant time will, in such circumstances, be 'a reasonable time'. *Poole* v

Smith's Car Sales (Balham) Ltd [1962] 1 WLR 744 gives some indication of what a reasonable time might mean. Poole left his car with the defendant on 'sale or return' terms in August 1960. After several requests, the defendant returned the car in November 1960 in a badly damaged condition due to misuse by the defendant's employees. It was held that as the car had not been returned within a reasonable time, the property in the car had passed to the defendant and he was liable to pay the price agreed.

6.7.2.5 *Rule 5*

Where there is a contract for the sale of unascertained or future goods by description and goods of that description and in a deliverable state are unconditionally appropriated to the contract, either by the seller with the assent of the buyer, or by the buyer with the assent of the seller, the property in the goods then passes to the buyer. Such assent may be express or implied and may be given either before or after the appropriation is made.

In *Hayman & Son v McLintock* (above), the sacks of flour at issue were not set aside or marked in any way, although the order was marked in the seller's books and warehouse records. It was held that the property had not passed, but remained with the sequestrated seller. A general acknowledgement that goods had been sold did not constitute appropriation. Goods will be held to be unconditionally appropriated to the contract when they are separated, set aside and earmarked for a particular buyer.

A delivery to the buyer, or to a carrier or other custodier (whether named by the buyer or not) for the purpose of transmission to the buyer, without reserving a right of disposal, is deemed to be an unconditional appropriation to the contract.

In *Wardar's Import and Export Co Limited v Norwood & Sons Limited* [1968] 2 QB 663, there was a purchase by the plaintiff of 600 cartons of kidneys held in a cold store. The purchaser's carrier arrived to take delivery. He found the cartons on bogies on the pavement outside the cold store. The carrier handed over a delivery note authorising release of the cartons. The carrier began loading the cartons at 8.00 a.m. At about 10.00 a.m. he noticed that the kidneys were thawing. However, he continued loading, finishing at 12 noon. The kidneys were later found to be unfit for human consumption and had to be destroyed. It was held that there had been no passing of property when the contract was made, because the kidneys were still unascertained (s. 16 – see 6.7.1 above). Transfer of property took place when the delivery note was handed over and the carrier was allowed to begin loading. That amounted to unconditional appropriation and both property and risk passed at that stage to the plaintiff.

In *Badische Anslin Fabrik v Basle Chemical Works* [1898] AC 200, it was held that posting goods in response to a buyer's order amounted to unconditional appropriation to the contract. The goods therefore became the property of the buyer upon posting. Buyers by post should therefore note that, unless they stipulate otherwise, they bear the risk of loss in transit.

6.7.2.6 *Sale of goods which have perished*

If there is a contract for the sale of specific goods and the goods without the knowledge of the seller have perished at the time the contract is made, the contract is void (s. 6). This means that the seller has no obligation to deliver and the buyer has no obligation to pay. It should be noted that this section applies only where the goods have 'perished', i.e. they must have been in existence in the first place but have perished by the time the contract was made. As has been pointed out, it is not clear what the position is where the goods have never existed. It may be that it is open to the court to hold that the buyer has no remedy because he bought a chance and must pay for it, or that the seller must deliver because he warranted the existence of the goods. However, it seems more likely that the common law position is that such a contract is void for common error, meaning there is no obligation on either party.

A quite separate issue arises if the goods are destroyed or perish *after* the contract is made but *before* it is performed. Here the contract is frustrated under s. 7 (see 3.14 above) for the rules applying to a frustrated contract).

6.7.3 Reservation of the right of disposal

The s. 18 rules will apply only where the intention of the parties is unclear. Otherwise, s. 17 will apply and the property in the goods will pass when the parties intend it to pass. The seller may therefore choose to reserve the property in the goods until certain conditions are fulfilled; the most common condition applied is that property will not pass until the buyer pays the price, so goods can be delivered to the buyer, but still belong to the seller.

Section 19 makes provision for the mechanics of the seller reserving rights in the goods. Where there is a contract for the sale of specific goods, or where goods are subsequently appropriated to the contract, the seller may, by the terms of the contract, or appropriation, reserve the right of disposal in such goods until certain conditions are fulfilled; and in such a case, notwithstanding the delivery of goods to the buyer, or to a carrier or other handler or custodier for the purpose of transmission to the buyer, the property in the goods does not pass to the buyer until the conditions imposed by the seller are fulfilled. This right under s. 19 is a reflection of the right existing in the common law of contract to make a sale under a suspensive condition.

The use of such a suspensive condition under SGA was recognised by Gloag and Irvine, *Rights in Security*, p. 241: 'It would seem to be competent, both at common law and under the Sale of Goods Act (1893) for a seller of goods to deliver them at once to the purchaser and yet to retain the right to them as his property on the bankruptcy of the purchaser, if the sale is made under the express condition that the property is not to pass until after the expiry of a certain period, or until some act is done'. Sellers will be tempted to take advantage of this conceptual device so that they can recover the property in question should the buyer become insolvent. If the property has become that of the buyer then its value will have to be distributed amongst a number of creditors. If the seller does not expressly retain title then it is likely to pass to the buyer in most cases by virtue of rule 1 (see 6.7.2.1 above).

6.7.4 Romalpa clauses

Contractual clauses based on SGA, s. 19 are known as retention of title clauses or, more commonly, Romalpa clauses, after the case in which they first came to prominence in the United Kingdom. In *Aluminium Industrie*

Vassen BV v *Romalpa Aluminium Ltd* [1976] 2 All ER 552, AIV sold aluminium foil to Romalpa under the following terms:

(a) the ownership of the foil would pass to Romalpa only when they had paid all outstanding debts to AIV;

(b) Romalpa would store the foil separately;

(c) if the foil was used to make new objects (which was, of course, the purpose for which it was bought), those objects would be stored separately and be owned by AIV as security for payment;

(d) Romalpa could sell the new objects, but until they had discharged their debt to AIV, they should hand over to AIV the claims for payment that they had against purchasers.

Romalpa got into financial difficulties and a receiver was appointed under powers contained in a debenture held by a bank. At the time the receiver was appointed, Romalpa owed AIV £122,000. In order to recover some of that, AIV sought to recover foil valued at £50,000 and the proceeds of foil sales which amounted to a further £35,000. This £35,000 was the sum of receipts since the appointment of the receiver and he had kept it separate from Romalpa's other monies. It was held that AIV were entitled to recover the foil and the proceeds of the sale thereof, because the effect of the terms of the contract was that Romalpa were agents and bailees (custodiers) for AIV. Property in the foil had never passed to Romalpa. AIV's success meant that they could salvage £85,000 of the £122,000 owed to them, instead of the money being used to satisfy the other creditors.

It was argued for Romalpa that the retention clause created a charge which required registration under the Companies Act 1985 and, as the charge had not been registered, the retention clause was inoperative. The Court of Appeal said that as the requirement to register was confined to charges over the company's property and the property in the aluminium had not passed to Romalpa, it did not apply. It should be noted that, in Scotland, a fixed security over corporeal moveables other than ships or aircraft, does not have to be registered (Companies Act 1985, s. 410).

6.7.5 Further developments of Romalpa

It should be noted that AIV did not seek a decision on clause (c) of their contract with Romalpa. Problems have, however, arisen in situations where the buyer has mixed the goods bought in a manufacturing process. In *Borden (UK) Ltd* v *Scottish Timber Products Ltd* [1979] 3 All ER 961, the plaintiffs supplied resin which was to be used in making chipboard to the defendants. The contract included the following terms:

property and goods supplied hereunder will pass to the customer when:

(a) the goods, the subject of this contract, and,

(b) all other goods, the subject of any other contract between the company and the customer which, at the time of payment of the full price of the goods, sold under this contract, have been delivered to the customer, but not paid for in full,

have been paid for in full.

The defendants went into receivership and Borden sought to trace their resin into chipboard made from the resin and also to trace the proceeds of the sale of chipboard.

The Court of Appeal held that the defendants were not bailees (custodiers) of the resin. Borden knew that the resin would be used almost immediately as part of the manufacturing process and would cease to exist, except as a constituent part of the chipboard over which there was no contractual charge. Thus there was no fiduciary relationship.

It would seem that in England, following *Borden* and subsequent cases, for a retention of title clause to be effective over mixed goods, it must be registered under the Companies Act 1985, s. 395 as a charge over the assets of the purchasing company. In Scotland, it is thought that a clause which purports to give the seller rights over goods which have been manufactured from the goods and from other materials which were never the seller's property would be ineffectual as an attempt to create a security without possession (see Gloag and Henderson, 'Introduction to the Law of Scotland', at 205).

In Scotland it has been held that a straightforward clause in the contract which states that the property in the goods will only pass to the seller when the goods have been paid for will be given effect by the courts. In *Archivent Sales and Development Ltd* v *Strathclyde Regional Council* 1985 SLT 154, Lord Mayfield said that a simple retention of title clause was merely a sale made under a suspensive condition (which condition the courts would enforce). Until recently, difficulties have arisen where the retention of title clause provides that the title to the goods will not pass to the buyer until he has paid all sums owed by him to the seller. The use of such clauses (known as 'all sums retention clauses') was discussed in *Deutz Engines Ltd* v *Terex Ltd* 1984 SLT 273. The contract at issue contained a condition that title to the goods would remain with the seller until all sums due to them from the buyer had been paid. This clause was held to be invalid as a covert security without possession and caught by the provisions of s. 62(4), which meant that SGA did not apply and any case based on it would be unsuccessful. Lord Ross distinguished between 'price only' retention clauses, which, he said, were acceptable and 'all sums' retention clauses which were not. His view was followed in several other Scottish cases, including *Archivent* (above).

The recent House of Lords decision in *Armour* v *Thyssen Edelstahlwerke* 1990 SLT 891 has settled academic unease at the correctness of the decision in *Deutz Engines*, which it overruled. The decision in *Armour* would seem to strengthen the position of apprehensive sellers in an uncertain economic climate, as it specifically covered an 'all sums' provision, as opposed to a 'price only' provision. Lord Kerr said 'the parties clearly expressed . . . their intention that the property in the steel should not pass . . . until all debts . . .

had been paid. In my opinion there are no grounds for refusing to give effect to that intention'.

For a full discussion of the complex issues arising from some of the above cases, see the articles by Gretton and Reid in the *Scots Law Times* (1985), at p. 329, (1989) (NEWS) 185 and by Clark SLT (1991) 155.

6.8 TRANSFER OF TITLE

As a general rule, a buyer cannot acquire ownership of goods from another party unless that party is either the owner or acting with the owner's authority. This is expressed by the maxim *nemo dat quod non habet*. Roughly translated, this means that you can't give what you haven't got. A thief, for example, will have no title in the goods he has stolen, thus he cannot pass on title to anyone who buys the goods from him. An owner of stolen goods can recover them from anyone into whose hands they have fallen, however far removed that person may be from the thief. The general rule also applies to 'sales' by someone who has found goods, or where an original transaction relating to the goods was void. All such goods are tainted by a *'vitium reale'* (inherent fault). Anyone who purchases such goods and has to return them to their true owner may claim against the seller under s. 12 (see 6.6.1 above), but, as we have seen, this is likely to be of little practical use, as the seller is, in most cases, a fraudulent person, who has obtained the goods dishonestly, resold them and absconded (see 3.12.1.2 above).

As with all good rules, the *nemo dat* rule is subject to a number of exceptions and these can be found in ss. 21 to 26. Where sales of goods are concerned the general policy behind these exceptions is to give the buyer the confidence that, at least in certain circumstances, his title is a valid one. An unqualified application of the *nemo dat* rule would render invalid a whole chain of transactions and make business and consumer contracting intolerably uncertain. The exceptions are described below.

6.8.1 Exceptions to the *nemo dat* rule
Section 21 provides that:

> Subject to this Act, where goods are sold by a person who is not their owner, and who does not sell them under the authority or with the consent of the owner, the buyer acquires no better title to the goods than the seller had, unless the owner of the goods is by his conduct precluded from denying the seller's authority to sell.

Section 21 in itself introduces a statutory operation of the doctrine of personal bar (see Chapter 3, para. 3.7.3). An example would be where the person selling is either an agent or employee of the owner of the goods and the buyer is therefore justified in believing he had the authority to sell. It will, however, be very rare for a true owner to be prevented by the doctrine of personal bar from exceeding his rights (see *Central Newbury Car Auction* v *Unity Finance Ltd* [1957] 1 QB 371).

A good title can be obtained when goods are sold under a court order, e.g., guns, cars, etc. used in the commission of a crime and forfeited by the court (s. 21(2)(b)). Also a pawnbroker can pass good title to unredeemed pledges (Consumer Credit Act 1976, ss. 74, 120(1)(b)), and a chief constable can, after certain steps have been taken, pass title to lost or abandoned goods (Civic Government (Scotland) Act 1982, ss. 67 to 79).

Where the seller has a voidable title to the goods, the position under SGA, s. 23 is exactly the same as under the common law of contract, i.e. the buyer will acquire a good title to the goods, provided that he buys them in good faith and without notice of the seller's defective title (see *Macleod v Kerr* and *Car and Universal Finance Co Ltd v Caldwell* in the Cases and Materials section for Chapter 6 which discuss ways in which the original owner can set aside the contract before the goods can be sold to the sub-buyer. However, even where this is possible the sub-buyer will probably be protected by s. 25 (see below).

The other major exceptions to the *nemo dat* rule are to be found in SGA, ss. 24 and 25. Both sections use the term mercantile agent. A mercantile agent is defined in the Factors (Scotland) Act 1890, s. 1 and is any person who normally has authority to deal with goods by way of buying, selling, consigning for sale, or using them as security. Examples would include salesmen, auctioneers and brokers (see *T. Graham & Sons Ltd v Glenrothes Development Corpn.* 1967 SC 284). If such a person is in possession of goods or documents of title to goods with the consent of the owner then any sale, pledge or disposition by him in the ordinary course of business is as valid as if it were authorised by the owner, as long as the buyer acts in good faith with no notice of the agent's lack of authority. A typical scenario will be where A gives his car to a dealer to sell, but the dealer sells it contrary to some condition set by A, e.g., that it be sold for over £5,000. The buyer will get title. However, this section requires the agent to be in possession of the goods *in his capacity as a mercantile agent*, not, for example, as someone who has simply hired the goods or who is repairing them for the owner.

Section 24 deals with the situation where a seller remains in possession after a sale in which ownership has already passed (e.g., the sale is unconditional and the goods are deliverable — see Rule 1 above at 6.7.2.1 — but the seller has not physically delivered) and the situation where a dealer sells goods to a finance company to raise money but retains possession. Such persons can transfer ownership under s. 24.

Section 24 states that:

where a person has sold goods and continues or is in possession of the goods, or of documents of title to the goods, the delivery or transfer by that person, or by a mercantile agent acting for him, of the goods or documents of title under any sale, pledge, or other disposition thereof, to any person receiving the same in good faith and without notice of the previous sale, has the same effect as if the person making the delivery or transfer were expressly authorised by the owner to make the same.

In *Pacific Motor Auctions* v *Motor Credits Ltd* [1965] 2 All ER 105, dealers sold cars to the plaintiffs, but remained in possession of them for display purposes. The dealers subsequently resold the cars to the defendants, who were unaware of the previous sale. It was held that the defendants obtained good title under an Australian equivalent of s. 24.

Section 25 has similar provisions in respect of someone who, having bought or agreed to buy goods (not including someone under a conditional sale or a hire-purchase agreement) obtains possession of them. This possession must be obtained with the owner's consent and a third party will get good title only if the disposition takes place in such a way that he is entitled to assume that the seller is acting as a mercantile agent, even if he is not actually a mercantile agent. It does not matter if the situation is one in which the buyer has only a voidable title and this title has been avoided by the seller. The buyer can still pass title as a 'buyer' in possession to a sub-buyer. In *Newtons of Wembley Ltd* v *Williams* [1965] 1 QB 560, the plaintiffs sold a car to a conman who paid with a cheque which was dishonoured. The plaintiffs rescinded the agreement by taking all reasonable steps to trace the conman and the car through informing the police. The conman sold the car to a third party, who bought in good faith at an established second-hand car market (i.e., the rogue sold in the way a mercantile agent would be expected to do). The third party buyer obtained good title to the car by operation of s. 25; had he bought the car privately, the assumption that the conman was acting as a mercantile agent would not have applied and the original owner (Newtons) could have recovered the car in accordance with *Car and Universal Finance Co Ltd* v *Caldwell*.

The rules as to transfer of title have been criticised by the Crowther Committee in the following terms:

> Unfortunately, statutory protection for the bona fide purchaser has developed in a haphazard and piecemeal fashion and some of the relevant principles have been so drafted and interpreted as to make their application depend, not upon principles of equity and justice, but on fine technicalities which have little rhyme and less reason.

The bemused consumer would no doubt agree.

One final point remains on the transfer of title. Where goods are hired under a hire-purchase contract, any resale by the hirer will not normally allow a good title to be passed. However, under the Hire-Purchase Act 1964, Part III (as substituted by the Consumer Credit Act 1974, sch. 4), a private purchaser who buys a car in good faith and for value will obtain a good title to that car even if it is still subject to a hire-purchase agreement or conditional sale agreement.

The Department of Trade and Industry have suggested two important reforms to the law in this area (DTI, *Transfer of Title: A Consultation Document*, 1994). First, that the rules should be relaced by a general rule which allows title to be passed by *anyone* who has the goods through the acquiescence of the owner or because the owner has entrusted them to him.

This would include all the above categories *and* those holding goods under hire-purchase agreements or conditional sale agreements, and long-term hiring and leasing, although more short-term possession, such as for repair or weekend or week-long car hire, would possibly not be covered. In addition, the sale by the party not having title would have either to be in the course of a business, or appear to be so to the third party purchaser, who, as now, would have to buy in good faith. It is suggested that the burden of establishing good faith should be shifted to the third party purchaser, whereas at the moment it lies with the original owner except where the Factors (Scotland) Act is concerned (see above). Such a reform would shift the law considerably in favour of innocent purchasers, especially where the party selling to them holds the goods under hire-purchase, conditional sale, lease, etc., but would clearly reduce the security value of these arrangements for original owners.

The second proposal is simply to reform Part III of the Hire-Purchase Act 1964 (see above) to extend its protection to purchasers who buy any product, even where they are business buyers and even where the party selling holds the goods under a lease or bill of sale. This would probably do nearly as much as the first proposal, although the precise extent of the first is unclear.

6.9 PERFORMANCE OF THE CONTRACT

The basic duties of a seller and buyer are quite simple. The seller must deliver the goods and the buyer must accept and pay for them unless the contract indicates otherwise. Normally, the two obligations are concurrent. It should be noted that a breach of either obligation does not give the innocent party a right to rescind the contract, unless specific provision has been made for this (ss. 27 and 28).

6.9.1 Delivery

The term 'delivery' is defined in s. 61(1) as 'the voluntary transfer of possession of the goods from one person to another'. Whether it is for the buyer to take possession of the goods or for the seller to send them to the buyer is a question to be determined in the light of the express or implied terms of the contract between the parties (s. 29(1)).

In the absence of agreement to the contrary the place of delivery is the seller's place of business if he has one and, if not, his residence; except that if the contract is for the sale of specific goods, which, to the knowledge of the parties when the contract is made, are in some other place, then that place is the place of delivery (s. 29(2)). Where, under a contract of sale, the seller is bound to send the goods to the buyer, but no time for sending them is fixed, the seller is bound to send them within a reasonable time. Where the goods at the time of sale are in the possession of a third party, there is no delivery by seller to buyer unless and until the third person acknowledges to the buyer that he holds the goods on his behalf.

Demand or tender of delivery may be treated as ineffective unless made at a reasonable hour; what is a reasonable hour is a question of fact. Unless otherwise agreed, the expenses of and incidental to putting the goods in a deliverable state, must be borne by the seller. The seller is free to include terms which depart from these general rules on delivery. However, if such terms depart from what the buyer's expectations were, then the terms may be controlled under s. 3 of the Unfair Contract Terms Act 1977 (see above at 3.11.5).

6.9.2   Delivery of the wrong quantity

Where the seller delivers to the buyer a quantity of goods less than he contracted to sell, the buyer may reject them if the shortfall is material, but if the buyer accepts the goods so delivered, he must pay for them at the contract rate (s. 30(1)). Where the seller delivers to the buyer a quantity of goods larger than he contracted to sell, the buyer may accept the goods included in the contract and reject the rest, or he may reject the whole, but only if the excess is material (s. 30(2)(D)). Where the seller delivers to the buyer the goods he contracted to sell, mixed with goods of a different description not included in the contract, the buyer may accept the goods which are in accordance with the contract and reject the rest, or he may reject the whole (s. 30(4)) (see *Re Moore & Co* v *Landauer & Co* at 6.6.2 above). These rules are subject to any usage of trade, special agreement or course of dealing between the parties (s. 30(5)).

It should be noted that these rules as to rejection differ from the rules in relation to the implied terms as to description, quality, etc. In the case of implied terms, consumers always have a right to reject (the breach always being deemed to be material — see 6.6.5 above). Here the breach must *actually* be material for even a consumer to be able to reject. There is, of course, always a right to damages for breach.

6.9.3   Instalment delivery

Unless otherwise agreed, the buyer of goods is not bound to accept delivery of them by instalments (s. 31(1)). Where there is a contract for the sale of goods to be delivered by stated instalments, which are separately paid for, and the seller makes defective deliveries in respect of one or more instalments, or the buyer neglects or refuses to take delivery of or pay for one of the instalments, it is a question, in each case, depending on the terms of the contract and the circumstances of the case, whether the breach of contract is a repudiation of the whole contract, or whether it is a severable breach, giving rise to a claim for compensation and the right to reject that instalment, but not to a right to treat the whole contract as repudiated (s. 31(2)). For example, in *Warinco A G* v *Samor S P A* [1977] 2 Lloyd's Rep 582, there was a contract for the sale of Italian rape-seed oil in two instalments. The first instalment was rejected as not conforming to contract. The buyers wished to repudiate the whole contract but it was held that they could not do so. A dispute about one instalment did not entitle the buyers to repudiate the whole contract. The test depends upon two factors: first, what ratio the breach bears in a quantitative sense to the whole contract, and, secondly, the likelihood of the breach being repeated in later instalments (see *Maple Flock Co* v *Universal*

Furniture Products (Wembley) [1934] 1 KB 148). Of course, even to have a right to reject the defective instalment, the breach must be material.

6.9.4 Delivery via a carrier

Where the seller is authorised or required to send the goods to the buyer, then delivery of those goods to a carrier, whether named by the buyer or not is prima facie deemed to be a delivery of the goods to the buyer. The seller must make a reasonable contract with the carrier, having regard to the nature of the goods, e.g., if they are perishable, he must arrange for them to be delivered speedily. If the goods are sent by sea, the seller must inform the buyer of this so as to give him the opportunity to insure them, otherwise the risk is with the seller (s. 32).

Where the seller agrees to deliver goods at his own risk, at a place other than where they were sold, the buyer takes the risk of the goods deteriorating unless it has been otherwise agreed (s. 33).

6.9.5 Acceptance

The buyer is bound to accept the goods which the seller delivers in accordance with the contract. Section 37 provides that where the seller is ready and willing to deliver the goods and requests the buyer to take delivery but the buyer does not do so within a reasonable time, then he is liable to the seller for any loss arising and for storage charges.

6.10 BREACH OF CONTRACT

Should either party fail to perform his duties under the contract, the other party has certain remedies available to him. These remedies vary, according to the circumstances of the case, the nature of the breach and so on.

Part V of the SGA (ss. 38 to 48) lays out the rights the seller has against the goods which are the subject of the contract, whereas Part VI (ss. 49 to 54) lays out the personal remedies the seller has against the buyer and vice versa. These sections, with comments, are contained in the Cases and Materials section for Chapter 6.

Further reading
Atiyah, (1995), *Sale of Goods*, 9th edn, Pitman.
Cuisine and Forte, (1987), *Scottish Cases and Materials in Commercial Law*, W. Green Ltd, Chapter 1.
W.C.H. Fruine, (1995), *Consumer Law In Scotland*, W. Green Ltd.
Furmston, (1994), *Sale and Supply of Goods*, Cavendish.
Gloag and Henderson, (1987), *Introduction to the Law of Scotland*, 9th edn, W. Green & Son Ltd, Chapter 17.
Marshall, (1992), *Scots Mercantile Law*, 2nd edn, W. Green Ltd, Chapter 4.
Walker, (1988), *Principles of Scottish Private Law*, 4th edn, Oxford University Press.

CHAPTER SEVEN
Consumer Credit

Credit in its many manifestations is very much a fact of life in modern day Scotland despite its general unacceptability to previous generations. We are surrounded by exhortations to borrow or buy goods on credit. The terms vary from 'interest free' to rates that would shame the most reviled usurers of the past; in a series of cases several years ago involving illegal moneylending, we have heard of interest rates which in percentage terms run to millions. Despite legitimate interest rates in the United Kingdom being among the highest in the western world, an insatiable appetite for credit remains, although somewhat blunted by the excesses of the 1980s.

Few of us will never make use of credit; there are few who can afford to buy their homes without the benefit of a secured loan from bank or building society; cars are more often than not acquired through a dealer-arranged loan, a bank loan or a hire-purchase agreement; most people carry a purse or wallet full of plastic credit cards; even students have been asked to make use of credit to finance undergraduate education through the Student Loans Scheme. Credit will typically fall under one of two headings: (i) borrowing money, e.g., from a bank or credit card company, to be spent on goods and services; (ii) paying for goods and services over a period of time.

Another dimension is therefore added to such traditional conceptual notions as the sale and supply of goods and services. These traditional relationships are, of course, regulated by established common law and statutory rules which may hold parties liable for misleading or untrue promises, defective performance etc. We have already pointed out that in all contractual relationships, of which creditor–debtor is another example, the law must find a balance between the protection of parties from overreaching by their contracting partners, the desire to maintain high standards in the supply of goods and services (see 3.1), the need for certainty and security in market transactions, and the importance of transactions not being too costly for the parties, etc. Where the credit dimension is added the law must decide on the extent to which this element raises particular reasons why those who provide it should be controlled. They clearly have the ability, through advertising, to influence the consumer to commit to the primary transaction. They also benefit from this transaction through interest payments. What legal burdens should they suffer in the interests of consumer protection?

Again, there are difficult policy choices. Credit may involve a large, long-term commitment for the debtor, and the law may wish to ensure that this is not undertaken lightly and that the supplier's skills and resources in presentation, persuasion, etc. are not abused, and that consumers can escape from agreements without unacceptably heavy burdens being imposed or the creditor obtaining a windfall. On the other hand, creditors must find it worthwhile to be in business, so they must be able to enforce agreements freely entered into by consumers.

With these policies in mind the law has set down a complex framework which licenses those entitled to offer credit; imposes requirements in relation to advertisements and the terms upon which credit is offered, so that the consumer makes as rational a choice as possible; allows consumers, in restricted circumstances, to cancel agreements and also to terminate at a later stage, with controls on the liabilities they can suffer, and places responsibilities upon creditors for breach of contract by the suppliers of goods and services.

7.1 LEGAL CONTROLS ON CREDIT

Credit has a long history but the post-war explosion in its use, coupled, of course, with lower levels of personal saving and the vulnerable position of debtors have led to calls for its availability to be restricted. Those who call for government intervention may be unaware that the legislature has controlled credit for many years, with a radical reform in the early 1970s, which led to the passing of the Consumer Credit Act (CCA) 1974.

Before 1974 the law relating to credit was to be found in different Acts of Parliament, e.g., the Hire-Purchase Act 1964, the Moneylenders Acts, and the Pawnbrokers Acts. The Acts regulating credit were different according to the status of the creditor and the type of credit. No one government department was in overall control of enforcing the provision of the different Acts and the fact that the rules were to be found in different Acts made them more inaccessible than they should have been, and meant there was widespread ignorance of the provisions.

During the late 1960s and early 1970s the Crowther Committee was authorised to examine the whole field of consumer credit. Their report was issued in 1971 and some of their recommendations became the framework for the Consumer Credit Act 1974. The Act received the Royal Assent on 31 July 1974, but the process of change, given the complexity of the task and the replacement of various schemes by one comprehensive one, meant that change was gradual. Indeed some sections of the Act only came into force in

May 1985, some 14 years after the Crowther recommendations were made. The Act replaced the previous piecemeal provision with a comprehensive framework for the regulation of consumer credit and consumer hire agreements (see 7.3.1 and 7.3.3 below). The provision of any kind of financial accommodation to individuals (including unincorporated businesses) is covered, but credit and hire agreements where both parties are corporate bodies are not (s. 189(1)).

7.2 TYPES OF CREDIT

The Act defines credit as including a cash loan and any other form of financial accommodation (s. 9(1)). In practical terms this wide definition covers all of the following common arrangements and other less common transactions.

7.2.1 Loans

The main source of loans are the banks, and the finance houses. Money is also lent by moneylending firms. The rates of interest charged by these will be usually much higher than that charged by the banks. Some retail stores, e.g., Marks and Spencer have recently expanded their financial services to include loans which are not linked to the purchase of their goods. Since the passing of the Building Societies Act 1986, the building societies have become major providers of loans for the purchase of consumer goods and services, in addition to their traditional house purchase loans.

There are various ways in which money may be borrowed from banks and finance houses.

Overdrafts Overdrafts are offered by banks and other organisations that issue cheque books. They involve the lender agreeing to honour the customer's overspending by means of cheques drawn on his or her account. The customer should normally agree a limit to this 'overspend'. If this is done the rate of interest charged will be approximately 4 per cent over the usual base rate. If the customer, however, overdraws without prior arrangement, the rate of interest charged will be much more, perhaps 15 per cent over base rate. Overdrafts are usually arranged for fixed periods but are theoretically repayable on demand which can cause difficulty. An overdraft will normally require no security and is one of the cheapest ways to borrow. This had led to lenders increasingly directing applicants for overdrafts towards personal loans (see below) where the interest rate will generally be higher, and therefore more in the lender's interest.

Ordinary loans These apply where the customer borrows a fixed sum from a bank and repays that sum plus interest over an agreed period of time. The rate of interest charged will fluctuate during the period of the loan, in line with changes in the bank's base rate. The rate of interest will generally be more than for authorised overdrafts. Ordinary loans are only available from banks and then only to existing customers.

Personal loans These are similar to ordinary loans, but available from other institutions and to both customers and non-customers. They too involve borrowing a fixed sum over an agreed period. The rate of interest is, however, fixed at the outset and remains constant over the period of the loan. This can be an advantage as the customer knows exactly how much he has to repay each month. It will not be an advantage however if interest rates fall drastically. The customer would be 'tied in' at the previous higher rate. The rate of interest will be higher than that for ordinary loans. Personal loans are available from banks, building societies, finance houses, and some retailers.

Budget accounts Budget accounts are designed to smooth out the customer's cash flow. Domestic bills such as electricity, gas, council tax, etc. seem to have a nasty habit of all landing on the mat at the same time. A budget account, or revolving account, involves the customer working out his expenditure for the year, the bank adds a service charge to this of approximately 1 per cent and this total figure is divided by twelve; the resulting amount is transferred by standing order from the customer's current account to the budget account each month. A separate cheque book is issued to pay bills as they fall due. Interest is charged in months when the account is in debit. The rate of interest charged is similar to that for ordinary loans. Accounts of this type are run mainly by the banks. It is, in effect, another form of overdraft facility.

Secured loans With some loans, the borrower may be required to provide security for the loan in the event of default. Security may take the form of a heritable security on property or may relate to particular goods (e.g., pawning goods). Security is normally required where the loan relates to property, e.g., where it is advanced for the purchase of a property or major repairs and improvements to a house. Many larger loans from finance houses for the purchase of cars and other major consumer goods are secured on property. However, since the Act covers only agreements where the amount of credit does not exceed £15,000, most loans for the purchase of houses are not covered by the Act; in any event, many consumer credit agreements secured by heritable security are exempt from the provisions of the Act (see 7.3.4 below).

7.2.2 Hire-purchase

A hire-purchase agreement is defined in the Act, s. 189(1).

> A hire purchase agreement means an agreement, other than a conditional sale agreement, under which—
> (a) goods are hired in return for periodical payments by the person to whom they are hired; and
> (b) the property in the goods will pass to that person if the terms of that agreement are complied with and one or more of the following occurs—
> (i) the exercise of an option to purchase by that person,
> (ii) the doing of any other specified act by any party to the agreement,
> (iii) the happening of any other specified event.

Some analysis of this definition is required. Strictly speaking, when the consumer enters into a hire-purchase agreement, he agrees to *hire* the goods

concerned, not to buy them. He has the option to buy but no obligation to
do so. The reality is somewhat different. The consumer who enters into such
an agreement will have no wish to hire the goods at all; he wants to buy them.
Nor does the retailer or finance company wish to hire out the goods; they
want to sell them and make a loan respectively. There would seem therefore
to be a gulf between the letter of the law and what happens in real life. Given
that most people do not read documents which they sign, few will even be
aware that the agreement talks of 'hiring'.

The reason for the form of hire-purchase agreements is an historical one.
One of the problems faced by creditors had been that of default on the part
of the debtor, but most people at whom credit was aimed had nothing to offer
as security for the credit advanced. Once the creditor lost possession of the
goods he was faced with the possibility of the debtor selling the goods and
vanishing, leaving the creditor with a loss. Moreover, if the property in the
goods had passed to the debtor then the creditor could not simply take the
goods back if the debtor defaulted, because they no longer belonged to him
but to the debtor. Court action for the recovery of the amount outstanding
was required, and this was expensive, time-consuming, and, in the case of an
insolvent or obstinately reluctant debtor, often unsuccessful. Various methods
of creating security over goods were tried and were found deficient in one way
or another. Eventually what is in essence our current form of hire-purchase
agreement was devised and its theoretical basis was given judicial approval in
1895 in the case of *Helby* v *Matthews* [1895] AC 471 HL. It became
increasingly popular, to such a degree that the term 'hire-purchase' is often
(wrongly) used by both debtors and creditors as a generic name for all forms
of credit. The advantage of hire-purchase to the debtor was that he obtained
immediate possession and use of the goods. The advantage to the creditor
was that, as he remained the owner of the goods, he could repossess them in
the event of default in payments and, as seen in *Helby* v *Matthews*, he could
recover them from an innocent third party into whose hands they had fallen.
This power to repossess the goods in the event of default (often minor) led
to abuse and subsequently to the imposition of statutory constraints (e.g.,
Hire Purchase Act 1938). An extract from the case of *Helby* v *Matthews* is to
be found in the Cases and Materials section for Chapter 7.

The typical hire-purchase agreement today involves the cost of the goods
and the cost of the credit being added together. The total is divided by the
number of payments, either weekly or more commonly monthly. It will only
be on the payment of the last monthly/weekly payment that the goods will
become the property of the hirer. Before then he can not lawfully sell them
or give them away. The reality will be, however, that the goods are frequently
given away (e.g., as a present). The creditor will be unaware of this, and in
any event has no practical interest in the matter provided that payment is
made as agreed. A similar situation will also apply where conditional sales are
involved (see 7.2.3). The ability to repossess goods has diminished in
importance. The process is time-consuming and the repossessed goods will
usually be worth only a small percentage of their original value. Repossession
will be more useful where high value goods (e.g., cars) are concerned. Of

more importance than actual repossessions is the coercive effect of the right to repossess.

7.2.3 Conditional sale and credit sale

A conditional sale agreement means an agreement for the sale of goods or land under which the purchase price or a part of it is payable by instalments and the property in the goods or land is to remain with the seller (notwithstanding that the buyer is to be in possession of the goods or land) until such conditions as to the payment of instalments or otherwise as may be specified in the agreement are fulfilled (s. 189(1)). It differs from hire-purchase in that it is specifically a contract of sale. The seller, however, operates a reservation of title clause whereby the ownership of the goods remains with the seller until the conditions in the agreement are met. The key and indeed only condition will normally be the payment of the price of the goods and agreed interest charges. The debtor is not free to sell the goods or dispose of them in any other way until the conditions are complied with. Although hire-purchase and conditional sales are theoretically different the Act treats them as being the same.

A credit sale agreement is 'an agreement for the sale of goods under which the price or part of it is payable in instalments, but which is not a conditional sale agreement' (s. 189(1)). In credit sales the ownership of goods passes to the buyer/debtor upon the contract being made. He is therefore free to sell them or otherwise dispose of them. He is, of course, obliged to pay the agreed instalments. As in hire-purchase and conditional sale agreements, the price of the goods and the cost of credit are added together. The buyer/debtor then repays this over a period of months. The interest rate is fixed at the outset. The creditor in this situation is in effect making an unsecured loan. He may feel that the advantages of reserving the property in the goods is slight, given that they may be of relatively minor value and will involve time and effort to resell.

7.2.4 Credit cards, charge cards and vouchers

Credit cards are plastic cards issued by banks and credit card companies to individuals (and companies) which allow the holder to charge the purchase of goods to the bank, or whoever issued the card, who then bills the customer in a monthly accounting period. The customer may settle the account in full by the agreed date, in which case no interest need be paid on the balance. The customer may however choose to use the credit option and pay a minimum of 5 per cent of the balance with the unpaid balance being carried forward to the next monthly accounting period. Interest will be charged when the account is not paid in full. The issuer of the card will have agreed a credit limit with the card holder which may be varied from time to time. The issuer will also enter into agreements with retailers, restaurants, garages, etc. whereby those organisations agree to accept the cards in lieu of cash or cheques. They will pay a percentage of the transaction price to the card issuer.

The consumer has the advantage of not having to carry cash which might be lost. In the event that the card is lost, the liability of its holder is limited (by s. 84) to £50 and there is no liability for any losses arising after the issuer is informed of the loss; the credit card agreement must contain the name, address and telephone number of the person to be contacted in the event that a card is lost (s. 84(4)). The holder is also free of the need to arrange credit for each transaction and is able to spread the cost of major purchases over a period of many months.

The retailer has the advantages of having less cash to handle and so reducing the risk of theft, of being able to accept the custom of people who are restricted to spending, or wish to spend, via the card, and of being free of the need to deal with administration of individual credit transactions, with all the risks attached. There is moreover, a belief that the consumer is apt to spend more when not handing over cash. Some argue, however, that the use of credit cards pushes up the cost of goods because the commission paid to the card-issuer has to be financed.

Recent legislative changes mean that retailers can now charge less for cash sales but it is felt that dual pricing of this nature will more usually mean that a higher price will be charged when a credit card is used. It was of course always open to someone paying cash to ask for a discount, e.g., the amount that would be paid in commission to the card company but, despite our reputation, this would not seem to be the Scottish way. After completion of a credit card sale, the retailer submits the sales slips to the card issuer who settle the amount less the commission. The rate of commission is believed to be 3–4 per cent but it is of course open to negotiation. The current APR for the consumer on credit cards ranges from 14 per cent to 30 per cent approximately. (On APR, see 7.5.5 below.)

Credit cards are issued mainly by banks and building societies. The issuers will belong to a clearing organisation such as Visa or Mastercard. These cards may be used in any establishment that carries the Visa or Mastercard logo. Some retailers issue their own 'in house' version of such cards which operate on the same principles, e.g., Marks and Spencer Chargecard and Frasercard, but they have the disadvantage for the consumer that they can only be used in certain shops. The advantage for the retailer is that commission charges are avoided and a database is available if the retailer decides to expand into different sectors, e.g., financial services. Retailers' charge cards tend to have a slightly higher APR. Most issuers charge no fee for the card but recently some have begun to charge a fee ranging from £6 to £12. There may in some cases be a choice of whether or not to pay a fee, if a fee is paid the APR charged will usually be slightly less.

Examples of charge cards, which used to be known as travel and entertainment cards, are those issued by American Express and Diners Club. Most banks now issue their own version of charge cards (usually in the form of 'Gold Cards'). The customer uses them as he would a credit card and the arrangement between retailer and card issuer is similar. There are, however, several key differences. The card holder has to pay a membership fee annually, as well as a fee on the issue of the card. Also, the account has to be paid in full each month. In this sense there is no 'credit' involved, apart from the period between purchase and payment, i.e. there is no 'financial accommodation' involved. Unlike the credit card, there is theoretically no credit limit. In practice one would be imposed if it was felt the cardholder was living beyond his means. Normal charge cards are exempt from the provisions of the Act, because there is no provision for extended credit (s. 16). 'Gold' charge cards are, however, covered by the Act because they include a credit facility in the form of an unsecured overdraft, usually at preferential rates.

Companies like Provident, Caledonian and Shopacheck supply vouchers to their customers. These vouchers can be used in stores that have an agreement to accept them. As with credit and charge cards, the shop requires payment from the issuing company. The shop pays commission to the company. The customer repays by means of weekly payments which are collected by an agent of the company. This type of credit is much more expensive than the others mentioned above, partly because of the cost of collection and the perceived lower credit-worthiness of the debtors.

7.2.5 Store budget accounts
Store budget accounts are operated by many retailers, particularly clothes stores, or are operated for them by finance companies. The retailer and the customer agree a monthly payment and the customer is given a credit limit which is a multiple of that amount. Normal multiples are 12 or 24, so if a customer agrees to pay £20 per month there will be a credit limit of £240 or £480, depending on which multiple is applied. The customer can spend up to the credit limit and, as repayments are made, is free to spend again. An example of this type of credit is the Personal Account available in Burton Group stores.

Interest is charged on the outstanding balance at the end of the month. This type of credit tends to be more expensive than a credit card. A normal APR might be approximately 34 per cent, with some retailers charging as much as 40 per cent.

7.2.6 Credit unions
Credit unions are self-help financial organisations which are formed and run by people with a common bond, e.g., working or living in the same place. Members agree to make regular savings. These savings are then used to lend money to members who need it at much lower rates of interest than would be charged commercially. Because of the low interest rates charged, loans from credit unions are exempt from the provisions of the Act. They are governed by the Credit Unions Act 1979. The first Scottish credit union was established in Drumchapel (Glasgow) in 1970. The largest is that run by the employees of Strathclyde Regional Council.

7.3 TYPES OF AGREEMENTS

As we saw earlier, the Act regulates the provision of financial accommodation to individuals (including unincorporated businesses and associations). It applies only to regulated agreements and to agreements where the amount of credit available is less than £15,000. A regulated agreement is defined in s. 189(1) as a consumer credit agreement or a consumer hire agreement other than an exempt agreement. The limit of £15,000 applies only to the amount of credit granted, not to the total cost of the goods or services which may be higher. For example, the total amount payable under an agreement may be £17,500 but, if this includes a deposit of £1,000 and interest of £2,000, the amount of credit given originally is only £14,500 and the agreement will be covered by the Act.

7.3.1 Consumer credit agreements

A consumer credit agreement is a personal credit agreement by which the creditor provides the debtor with credit not exceeding £15,000 (s. 8(2)). A personal credit agreement involves the extension of credit from the creditor to an individual debtor (this it should be recalled, includes unincorporated businesses and associations).

Sections 10 and 11 provide legal definitions of the various forms that such credit might take and the various terms used.

7.3.1.1 Running account credit and fixed sum credit Running account credit is defined as a facility under a personal credit agreement whereby the debtor is enabled to receive from time to time (whether in his own person or by another person), from the creditor or a third party, cash, goods and services (or any of them) to an amount or value such that, taking into account payments made by or to the credit of the debtor, the credit limit (if any) is not at any time exceeded (s. 10(1)(a)). Examples would include bank overdrafts and credit cards. To prevent attempts to avoid the provisions of the Act by either setting a limit above £15,000 or no limit at all s. 10(3)(b) contains anti-avoidance provisions.

Fixed sum credit is defined as 'any other facility under a personal credit agreement whereby the debtor is enabled to receive credit, whether in one amount or by instalments (s. 10(1)(b)'. Examples include hire-purchase, conditional sale and credit sale agreements and bank loans.

7.3.1.2 Restricted use credit and unrestricted use credit A restricted use credit agreement is defined by s. 11(1) as

a regulated consumer credit agreement,

(a) to finance a transaction between the debtor and the creditor, whether forming part of that agreement or not, or
(b) to finance a transaction between the debtor and a person (the supplier) other than the creditor, or
(c) to refinance any existing indebtedness of the debtor's, whether to the creditor or another person.

Examples include hire-purchase, credit sales, conditional sales and shop budget accounts.

Unrestricted use credit is defined as 'a regulated consumer credit agreement not falling within s. 11(1)'. Examples include overdraft facilities and cheque cards.

If credit is supplied which is intended by the creditor to be restricted use but the money is paid directly to the debtor, then the agreement will be one for unrestricted use credit. An example would be where credit is advanced to install central heating in the debtor's house. If the cheque is made out to the installer then the credit is restricted use. If, however, the cheque is made out to the debtor it will be unrestricted use even if the debtor does in fact use it to pay for the central heating. We shall see the significance of this later.

7.3.1.3 Debtor–creditor–supplier agreement and debtor–creditor agreements
Section 12 provides that:

A debtor–creditor–supplier agreement is a regulated consumer credit agreement being—

   (a)   a restricted use credit agreement which falls within section 11(1)(a), or
   (b)   a restricted credit use agreement which falls within section 11(1)(b) and is made by the creditor under pre-existing arrangements or in contemplation of future arrangements between himself and the supplier, or
   (c)   an unrestricted use credit agreement which is made by the creditor under the pre-existing arrangements between himself and a person (the supplier) other than the debtor, in the knowledge that the credit is to be used to finance a transaction between the debtor and the supplier.

There are two possibilities here. The creditor may be the person who supplies the goods or services, (a two party debtor–creditor–supplier) or he may be someone who has an arrangement with the supplier (a three party debtor–creditor–supplier).

An example of the first situation would be where a retailer finances his hire-purchase credit and conditional sales from his own resources. Another example is where the retailer sells the product to the creditor who then supplies both product and credit to the customer. This is the classic car hire-purchase situation; although there appear to be three parties involved, in law, the car dealer has dropped out by selling the car to the finance company. The latter then acts as supplier and creditor.

An example of the second situation is where the retailer has an arrangement with a money-lender or credit card company, whereby the latter finances the purchase of goods by the debtor from the retailer.

A debtor–creditor agreement is defined in s. 13. Basically, it is any regulated credit agreement that is not a debtor–creditor–supplier agreement. Examples would include bank loans, overdrafts, indeed any loan where there is no connection between the creditor and the supplier, in the sense that the loan is not tied to a specific purpose.

The significance of distinguishing whether or not an agreement is a debtor–creditor or debtor–creditor–supplier agreement is that, under the Act, the creditor in a debtor–creditor agreement incurs no liability for the quality of the goods supplied. However, in a debtor–creditor–supplier agreement, the combined effect of ss. 56 and 75 is to render creditors liable for the misrepresentations and breaches of contract of the retailer (see 7.7 below).

7.3.2 Credit-token agreements
A credit token agreement is defined in s. 14(2) as a regulated agreement for the provision of credit in connection with the use of a credit-token. A credit token is defined in s. 14(1) as:

> a card, check, voucher, coupon, stamp, form, booklet or other document or thing given to an individual by a person carrying on a consumer credit business which undertakes—
>
> (a) that on production of it (whether or not some other action is also required) he will supply cash, goods and services (or any of these) on credit; or
> (b) that where on production of it to a third party (whether or not any other action is also required) the third party supplies cash, goods or services (or any of them), he will pay the third party for them (whether or not deducting any discount or commission) in return for payment to him by the individual.

Some examples of credit-tokens are credit cards, shopping checks and bank cash cards when the customer has an overdraft (s. 14(4)), but cheque guarantee cards are not credit-tokens. The reason for their exclusion from the definition is that the bank is not paying the supplier of the goods or services but merely honouring its guarantee of payment of the cheque.

7.3.3 Consumer hire agreements
The Act controls consumer hire agreements because it was appreciated that a hire agreement often amounts to the giving of a 'financial accommodation'. A consumer hire agreement is defined by s. 15(1) as:

> an agreement made by a person with an individual (the hirer) for the hiring of goods to the hirer, being an agreement which—
>
> (a) is not a hire-purchase agreement, and
> (b) is capable of subsisting for more than three months, and
> (c) does not require the hirer to make payments exceeding £15,000.

It should be noted that this definition requires that the agreement must be capable of lasting for more than three months, not that it has to do so. The Act does not apply therefore to short term hires, e.g., a car for the annual holiday or a paint stripper when decorating.

7.3.4 Exempt agreements

An exempt agreement is not regulated by the Act. An exempt agreement is defined in s. 189(1) as 'an agreement specified in or under s. 16'. Those specified by s. 16 (as amended by the Consumer Credit (Exempt Agreements) Order 1989 SI 1989/869) are:

(a) Consumer credit agreements where the creditor is
  (i) a local authority or building society, or
  (ii) an insurance company, friendly society, organisation of employers or employees, a charity, land improvement company or body corporate named or specifically referred to in any public general act,
and the agreement is secured by a heritable security (mortgage). For the agreement to be exempt, the organisations in (ii) have to be specified in the Consumer Credit (Exempt Agreements) Order 1989.

(b) Debtor–creditor–supplier agreements where the number of payments by the debtor does not exceed four, provided the agreement is not a hire purchase agreement or conditional sale agreement. This would cover normal trade credit given, for example, by a grocer, milkman or newsagent.

(c) Debtor–creditor–supplier agreements for running account credit where the whole of the outstanding credit has to be paid off, e.g. American Express, Diners Club (see 7.2.4 above).

(d) Low cost credit agreements, that is debtor–creditor agreements where the maximum interest rate does not exceed whichever is the higher of 13 per cent or one per cent above the highest base rate set by the London and Scottish clearing banks within 28 days of the agreement being made.

(e) Certain agreements which have a connection with a country outside the United Kingdom.

(f) Consumer hire agreements for the hire of meters for gas, electricity or water and the hire of telephones.

The Consumer Credit (Exempt Agreements) (Amendment) Order 1995 SI 1995, No 1250 has amended the 1989 Order by adding the names of six bodies corporate to the list of bodies named or specifically referred to in Orders made under provisions of the Housing Act 1985 (in Scotland the Housing (Scotland) Act 1987). Where such a body is named the CCA does not regulate certain of the agreements under which that body advances money on the security of a dwelling house.

7.3.5 Partially regulated agreements

Certain agreements that are neither totally exempt nor totally regulated.
Non-commercial agreements. A non-commercial agreement is defined as 'a consumer credit or consumer hire agreement not made by the creditor or owner in the course of business carried on by him' (s. 189). It would cover, for example, a loan between friends. Such agreements are exempt from the provisions of the Act regarding formation and cancellation (see 7.6 below).
Small agreements. A small agreement is defined (by s. 17(1)) as 'a regulated consumer credit agreement, for credit not exceeding £50, other than a

hire-purchase or conditional sale agreement; or a regulated consumer hire agreement which does not require the hirer to make payments exceeding £50, being an agreement which is unsecured or secured by a guarantee or indemnity only (whether or not the guarantee of indemnity is itself secured)'. Small agreements are exempt from most of the provisions of the Act on formation and cancellation (see 7.6 below). There are provisions in s. 17(3) and (4) to prevent attempts to split up a larger transaction into several smaller transactions so as to avoid the Act's provisions.

7.4 LICENSING

The first major control imposed by the Act was a licensing system. There had been a licensing system under the Moneylenders Acts but enforcement was practically non-existent and, provided that the moneylenders did not infringe the criminal law, they were left to their own devices. The Act provided that licensing was to be centralised at the Office of Fair Trading. The Director General of Fair Trading was to be responsible for the issuing of licences. In addition to this central control, the Act requires trading standards officers to enforce the Act at local level.

A licence is needed to carry on a consumer credit or consumer hire business or an ancillary credit business. However, under the Consumer Credit Act (Commencement No. 4) Order 1977 there is a deferment (to a date to be appointed) for a credit brokerage business conducted by an individual which is confined to introductions resulting in credit under debtor-creditor-supplier agreements not exceeding £30. Local authorities and bodies empowered by a public general Act to engage in credit or hire are exempt from these requirements (e.g., Scottish Power who rent electricity meters to customers). A licence is not needed if you are a private lender, e.g., a father lending a son money to buy a house, (see also *Wills* v *Wood* (1984) SJ 222), or someone who only occasionally enters into transactions belonging to a business of that type, e.g., a solicitor who makes occasional bridging loans to clients.

The following categories of business require a licence:

(a) Consumer credit businesses, e.g., banks, finance companies and firms offering loans to employees;

(b) Consumer hire businesses, e.g., television rental and car rental companies;

(c) Credit brokerage, e.g., insurance agencies, car dealers, solicitors, accountants, estate agents and shops, indeed anyone who introduces clients or customers to someone who is in the business of consumer credit or consumer hire;

(d) Debt adjusting and debt counselling, i.e. anyone negotiating or advising hirers or debtors, e.g., Citizens Advice Bureaux;

(e) Debt collecting;

(f) Credit reference agencies, i.e. agencies which store the personal records of individuals from information obtained by them from previous lenders.

Any person who carries out any of these activities for which a licence is required commits an offence if he does not have one (s. 39). Any agreements which have been entered into while the requisite licence was not held are only enforceable on a validating order of the Director General.

7.4.1 Applying for a licence

Two types of licence are issued. A standard licence is issued to a single named person. A single person includes a company, a partnership, or an unincorporated association. It must be granted if the applicant satisfies the Director that he is a fit person to engage in activities covered by the licence and that the name on the licence is not misleading or otherwise undesirable.

A group licence covers such persons and activities as are described in the licence and may be issued only where it appears to the Director that the public interest is better served by so doing than by obliging the persons concerned to apply separately for individual licences. The Law Society of Scotland and the Institute of Chartered Accountants are examples of bodies who have been issued with a group licence.

Applications for a licence must be in writing, in the proper form and provide such information as is specified. The application must be accompanied by the correct fee. The current fee for a sole trader is £80, plus £10 for each additional category of business applied for. The fee for all others is £150, plus £10 for each additional category. When the licence is issued it states the categories covered. Registered loan societies, friendly societies and credit unions do not have to pay any licence fee. Standard licences and group licences previously were issued for 15 years. As from June 1991, the standard licence period is five years (Consumer Credit (Period of Standard Licence) Regulations 1975, SI 1975 No 2124, as amended by SI 1991 No 817). They can be withdrawn at any time (Consumer Credit (Termination of Licences) Regulations 1976 and 1981).

7.4.2 Refusal of a licence

The decision on whether to grant a licence is based on information provided by the applicant and from other sources such as trading standards officers. If the Director General wishes to refuse a licence or to revoke an existing one, he must inform the applicant that he is 'minded to refuse' or 'minded to grant it in terms different from those applied for', and issue the appropriate notice as provided by s. 27(1)(a). This notice will specify the Director General's reasons and allow the applicant to present his case. If the applicant is unsuccessful in persuading the Director General to change his mind and issue a licence, he can appeal to the Secretary of State and from him he can appeal on a point of law to the Court of Session. The Director General will pay particular attention to criminal convictions for fraud, dishonesty or violence, convictions under the Trade Descriptions Acts, and other improper and unfair practices, e.g., restricting the consumer's legal rights. The most frequent refusals have arisen in the motor trade and the finance trade.

An illustration of the judicial approach to the granting of licences can be seen in the dicta of Sheen J. in *North Wales Motor Auction* v *Secretary of State for Trade* (1981) CCLR 1. He said 'the granting of a licence is a privilege and it is a privilege which is to be granted only to those who are thought fit by the Director General on proper evidence to be fit persons'.

(For more on licensing, see D. B. Williams, 'Licensing Appeals Under the Consumer Credit Act 1974' (1987) 84 LS 250.)

7.5 SEEKING BUSINESS

One of the primary objectives of the Act was to create a climate of 'truth in lending' whereby consumers could make informed choices where credit was concerned. They could only do this if there was some control exercised over the information supplied to them. There was also the need for some standard means of measuring the cost of borrowing. Three main areas of seeking business are covered by the Act; advertising, canvassing and quotations.

7.5.1 Advertising

Section 44(1) of the Act empowers the Secretary of State to make regulations about the form and content of credit advertisements. Advertisements are defined widely in the Act. Under s. 43(1), they include 'any advertisement published for the purposes of a business carried on by the advertiser, indicating that he is willing to provide credit, or to enter into an agreement for the hiring of goods. Section 43(1) is very widely drafted but there are exemptions in s. 43(2) to (4), which have the effect of limiting the Act's provisions on advertising to consumer credit and consumer hire business, and also to businesses which provide credit which is secured on land (see also Consumer Credit (Exempt Advertisements) Order 1985). Section 189(1) defines advertising very broadly. It includes advertising in publications, on television and radio, and by notices, signs and labels. The regulations which have been made pursuant to s. 44(1) are the Consumer Credit (Advertisement) Regulations 1989, SI 1989 No 1125. These regulations are both detailed and complex.

Advertisements are divided into three categories, simple, intermediate and full. A simple advertisement must contain the name of the creditor, his postal address, telephone number, logo, and occupation. An intermediate advertisement must contain the above information and in addition there must be warning notices (e.g., 'Your home is at risk if you do not keep up repayments on a loan') for loans secured on land and for foreign currency mortgages, information about any other security requirements, insurance, deposit requirements, information about credit brokers' fees, information about terms of business, the cash price for debtor–creditor–supplier agreements, and the APR where the cash price is given. If no APR is given, there must be a statement that the total amount payable is no greater than the cash price. If the APR is not fixed, there must be a statement that it is variable. A full advertisement must contain all the above, plus details of advance payments, the amount and frequency of repayments, the total amount payable, and details of all other payments or charges. It is an offence to contravene the advertising regulations (s. 167). It is also an offence to advertise extended use credit facilities relating to goods or services unless the goods or services are available for cash (s. 45). Under s. 46, it is an offence to convey information which is in a material respect false or misleading. Section 47(1) states that where the advertiser commits an offence, the publisher, the deviser of the advertisement and any person who procured publication will have committed an offence. Defences available to the publishers are contained in s. 47(2) and 'due diligence' defences are contained in s. 168(1). The defences are almost identical to those in s. 24, Trade Descriptions Act 1968 (see Chapter 9).

(For more on advertising, see P. Circus, 'The New Advertising Regulations' (1990) 15 LS Gaz 20.)

7.5.2 Canvassing

The Act contains provisions, in ss. 48 to 51, to control the doorstep selling of credit. Under s. 49(1), it is an offence to canvass debtor-creditor agreements off trade premises; basically this means anywhere other than business premises. Canvassing involves soliciting the consumer to enter into a regulated agreement by making oral representations during a visit which has not been previously arranged. It will not be an offence provided that the visit is made in response to a signed request. Section 49 does not apply to debtor-creditor-supplier agreements; these can be canvassed off trade premises provided the supplier of the creditor has the appropriate licence (s. 23(2)).

Under s. 50, it is an offence to send to young persons under eighteen, with a view to financial gain, any document which invites them to borrow money; obtain goods on credit or hire; obtain services on credit, or apply for information on any of the foregoing. It is also an offence (under s. 51) to deliver or send by post an unsolicited credit token (see 7.3.2 above) to a person. When credit cards were first introduced in Britain, the issuer sent them out to customers whom they knew had bank accounts. These customers had not asked for the cards and many did not want them. This is now an offence. To be 'solicited' the consumer must have applied in writing for the card. It is not an offence to send unsolicited renewal credit tokens e.g., a new visa card (see *Elliot* v *Director General of Fair Trading* in the Cases and Materials section for Chapter 7.

7.5.3 Quotations

Section 52 authorises the making of regulations as to the form and content of quotations to customers by a person who carries on a consumer credit or consumer hire business, or a business in the course of which credit is provided to individuals, secured on land. The regulations are in the Consumer Credit (Quotations) Regulations 1989. They are similar to the regulations governing advertisements. Quotations must include specific information, e.g., as to the APR, amount of credit, the amount, number and frequency of payments and a comparison of cash and credit transactions.

7.5.4 Credit status enquiries

Creditors will obviously need to know as much as possible about the financial history of potential debtors. Only then will they be able to make an informed decision. This is usually done by using the services of a credit reference agency. There are several of these in the UK, the best known being CNN, which has built up a substantial database of credit transactions. A credit reference agency is defined as 'a person carrying on a business comprising the furnishing of persons with information relevant to the financial status of individuals, being information collected by the agency for the purpose, (s. 145(8), CCA). Banks' status enquiries are not covered by the definition. Banks, however, after initial resistance, are increasingly using the services of these agencies.

The Act makes provision for debtors (potential or actual) to access information that relates to them. Potential creditors must disclose if they have used an agency when assessing an applicant's financial status. They need do this only if so requested by the applicant. They are required to supply the address of the agency (s. 157, CCA). The applicant can then apply for a copy of the file held on him by the agency. He does this in writing, paying a fee of £1. Provided that there is enough information supplied to identify the applicant, the agency must comply with the request. The copy of the file must be 'in plain English' (s. 158, CCA). There is provision for the applicant to correct false or outdated information (s. 159, CCA). In the event of a dispute the matter will be resolved by the DFT, if either party so requests. Breach of any of the above duties is a criminal offence punishable by a fine.

7.5.5 Annual Percentage Rate [APR]

One of the ways in which the Act seeks to promote a climate of truth is by creating a standard measure of the cost of credit, which will enable the consumer to compare like with like and make an informed judgment as to who is offering the best deal. A standard measure was required because in the past creditors could present their interest rates in different ways, e.g., per annum or per month. The standard measure adopted is the annual percentage rate or APR. The APR removes the problems faced by the consumer in the past when attempting to compare rates calculated in different and often deliberately confusing ways. Creditors must calculate the APR according to standard formulae which are laid down in regulations made under the Act (Consumer Credit (Total Charge For Credit) Regulations 1980, SI 1980 No 51, as amended by SI 1985 No 1192 and SI 1989 No 596). In addition to interest charged, account must also be taken of any other cash forming part of the transaction such as an arrangement fee or compulsory insurance or any fee charged for the issue of a credit card, e.g., the annual fees announced by most credit card issuers over the last few years have to be taken into account when calculating the APR.

7.6 FORMALITIES

The Act regulates the form and content of individual credit or hire agreements. The rules do not apply to non-commercial agreements; debtor-creditor agreements for overdrafts on current accounts or small debtor-creditor-supplier agreements for restricted use credit. (See 7.3.5 above). An example of the form which a credit agreement complying with the Act's provisions might take is to be found in the Cases and Materials section for Chapter 7.

7.6.1 Prospective agreements
Section 55 enables regulations to be made requiring specified information to be disclosed in a prescribed manner to the debtor or hirer before a regulated agreement is made. If the regulations are not complied with the agreement will be improperly executed. No regulations have as yet been made.

Sections 57 and 58 make provision relating to antecedent negotiations and the right to withdraw from a prospective agreement and make an agreement void if it purports to bind a consumer to enter into a regulated agreement at some time in the future (s. 59(1)).

7.6.2 Form and content of agreements
Under s. 60(1), the Secretary of State is required to make regulations as to the form and content of regulated agreements. The aim of the regulations is to ensure that the debtor or hirer is made aware of his rights and duties under the agreement, the remedies available to him and the amount and rate of the total change for credit (if applicable). The Consumer Credit (Agreements) Regulations 1983 (as amended) provide that the agreement must:

(a)   be legible;
(b)   state the amount of credit or credit limit;
(c)   state the total charge for credit;
(d)   state the amounts and frequency of payments;
(e)   state the APR;
(f)   state if any security has been provided;
(g)   in the case of a cancellable agreement, contain details of the debtor's right to cancel; and
(h)   be signed personally by the debtor and by or on behalf of the creditor.

7.6.3 Copies
Sections 62 and 63 contain provisions as to the debtor's right to receive a copy (or copies) of the agreement. Usually the customer will sign the agreement in the creditor's premises but it will only be signed by the creditor once the customer's credit status has been established. The customer in this situation must be given a copy when signing, and be supplied with another copy when it is signed by the creditor, thus making the agreement an executed one. This second copy must be given to the customer within seven days of the agreement being made. If both debtor and creditor sign at the same time, the agreement is an executed one at that time and the customer is entitled to only one copy.

Breach of any of the requirements of ss. 62 and 63 means that the regulated agreement is improperly executed and can be enforced against the debtor or hirer only with the authority of a court order (see 7.8.4 below).

7.6.4 Notice of cancellation rights
Sections 67 to 74 provide debtors or hirers with the right, in certain circumstances, to change their minds after signing an agreement. These

provisions are a recognition that, faced with a professional high pressure salesman, people sign agreements which on reflection they wish they had not. A regulated agreement may be cancelled by the debtor or hirer if there were antecedent negotiations which included oral representations made in the customer's presence by an individual acting as or on behalf of the negotiator, and the agreement was signed by the customer at a place which was not the permanent or temporary trade premises of the creditor, owner or negotiator or any party to a linked transaction. Negotiations which are made by telephone are not made 'in the presence of' the customer so, if you sign an agreement at home and all the antecedent negotiations were by telephone, the agreement is not a cancellable one. If the agreement is cancellable under the Consumer Credit (Cancellation Notices and Copies of Documents) Regulations 1983 as amended it must indicate the right of cancellation, explain how and when this is to be done and to whom such notice of cancellation is to be intimated.

Notice of cancellation must be given before the end of the fifth day following the day on which the debtor or hirer received the second statutory copy of the agreement, or, if no second copy was required (see 7.6.3 above), the statutory notice of his cancellation rights. This period is known as the cooling-off period. For example, if the debtor or hirer signs an unexecuted agreement on 11 December and receives his second copy on 17 December, then the cooling off period during which he can cancel ends at midnight on 22 December. The cancellation must be in writing; no special form is laid down for giving notice of cancellation but there is an optional form prescribed by the Consumer Credit (Cancellation and Copies of Documents) Regulations 1983. The notice of cancellation must be served on:

(a)   the creditor or owner; or
(b)   the credit-broker or supplier who negotiated the contract; or
(c)   any person specified in the notice of cancellation rights; or
(d)   any person who in the course of a business carried on by him, acted on behalf of the debtor or hirer in any negotiations for the agreement.

Cancellation is effective as soon as posted, whether or not it arrives. In the event of non arrival, the debtor would have to prove that he had posted the notice of cancellation.

7.6.5   Effects of cancellation

The effect of cancellation is to cancel both the agreement and any linked transactions. It is as if the agreement had never been entered into. The consumer is entitled to have returned to him any deposit paid and any trade-ins (these must be returned within 10 days, failing which an allowance, equal to their 'trade-in value', must be paid). The consumer has a lien on any goods in his possession until this is done. The consumer may send such goods back but he is not obliged to do so. Until they are collected he must take reasonable care of them, although even this duty ceases 21 days after the notice of cancellation is served.

7.7 LIABILITY OF SUPPLIERS, CREDITORS AND DEALERS

The supplier of goods owes various duties either under the common law of contract or delict or under statutue (e.g., the Sale of Goods Act) to his customers. Breach of these may lead to the supplier being sued for breach of contract or negligence. Sometimes (in three party debtor–creditor–supplier cases), the supplier (e.g. the car dealer) is a distinct person from the creditor (the finance company). In other cases (two party debtor–creditor–supplier cases), the dealer (having convinced the customer to make a purchase) does not actually supply the car direct but sells it to the finance company who then supply it to the customer on hire-purchase or similar credit terms.

Section 56(2) provides that in the case of a debtor–creditor–supplier agreement, negotiations 'shall be deemed to be conducted by the negotiator' in the capacity of the agent of the creditor, as well as his actual capacity, and the creditor is therefore responsible for misrepresentations made by a supplier. Any agreement which seeks to exclude liability under s. 56(2) is void (s. 56(3)). This means that in both types of situation mentioned above, the creditor will be responsible for the misrepresentations of the dealer.

Section 75 makes the creditor in a three party debtor–creditor–supplier agreement jointly and severally liable with the supplier for misrepresentation and breach of contract. This section applies only to the three party situation and not to a two party case of hire-purchase, where the finance company (having purchased the car) acts as both supplier and creditor to the purchaser. This latter situation is however well covered by s. 56. Section 75 is concerned only with a situation where the creditor (e.g., a finance company) and the supplier (e.g., the car dealer) are two distinct parties. A creditor who is sued under s. 75 has a right of indemnity against the supplier. The rationale for s. 75 was explained in the Crowther Report. They saw the lender and supplier as being engaged in a joint venture, and therefore that it would not be right that the lender could disclaim all responsibility for goods supplied and still insist on the payments being maintained.

In most cases, the aggrieved customer could pursue an action against the dealer independently. For example, if the dealer is the supplier of the item, then he would clearly be personally liable for his breach of contract or misrepresentation. Equally, he may be liable for breach of collateral warranty where his statements have sparked the chain of events which leads to the customer being supplied with both the goods and the credit by the finance company. The attraction of ss. 56 and 75 is that they jointly provide an alternative means of redress. This protection also applies where the consumer buys goods or services which are charged to a credit card, provided that the value of the transaction is over £100, but s. 75 does not apply to transactions charged to American Express green cards or Diners Club, because they make no provision for extended credit. This right will be useful if the supplier has, for example, gone into liquidation; s. 75 was heavily utilised against the credit card companies after the collapse of Laker Airways. However, because s. 75 only came into effect on 1 July 1977 it does not cover cards issued before that date. Some card issuers have agreed to extend the s. 75 protection to these cards also, but this is voluntary and could be withdrawn.

There is increasing pressure on the government to repeal s. 75, or at least to limit its scope. Card issuers have argued that they have no liability in any case under s. 75, unless they recruited the supplier, or if the transaction took place outside the UK. (Both these issues are fully discussed by Graham Stephenson in 'Joint and Several Liability of Creditors and Suppliers under s. 75, [1994] CLJ 174.) Goode has argued that the card issuers' position is unsustainable. The Director General of Fair Trading in his second report on Connected Lendee Liability has rejected calls from card users to abolish 'joint and several liability'. Issuers' liability should, however, be limited to the amount of the credit involved (it is currently unlimited). Agreement has also been reached with the card issuers that they will meet claims relating to transactions outside the United Kingdom. This agreement runs until December 1996. Any changes to s. 75 will probably be introduced by regulations made under the European Communities Act 1972, as the United Kingdom already needs to take action to implement EU law on consumer credit. In the case of a unilateral contract established by a running credit agreement, there is a separate acceptance of the creditor's continuing offer each time the facility is used, so that on each occasion when the debtor uses the card a distinct contract is generated, governed by the terms of the running account agreement (R. Goode, *Consumer Credit Law*, paras. 677, 1076).

An extract from the case of *United Dominions Trust* v *Taylor* 1980 SLT 28, which considers a claim under s. 75, is to be found in the Cases and Materials section for Chapter 7.

7.8 TERMINATION AND DEFAULT

A regulated agreement may be terminated either by the debtor or creditor. Early settlement of the amount due under an agreement is governed by s. 94 and the Consumer Credit (Rebate on Early Settlement) Regulations 1983, which provide that the creditor must in most instances pay the debtor a rebate of the interest charges. The formula for calculating the rebate is set down in the regulations. The rebates formula makes allowance for the fact that the creditor has had the setting up and administration charges to pay at the start of the agreement, generally by taking the settlement date as two months later than it actually is.

7.8.1 Termination by debtor or hirer

It should be noted that settlement and termination are not necessarily the same. The debtor may at any time before the final payment is due give written notice to terminate the agreement. The debtor's liability is to pay:

(a)   all sums accrued due;
(b)   any additional sum required to bring the total paid up to one half of the total price, or such lesser amount as may be specified in the agreement.

The goods must be returned to the creditor and the debtor may be liable in damages if he has failed to take reasonable care of them (s. 100(4)).

Under s. 100(3) the court has the discretion to mitigate the debtor's liability on any of the above counts to whatever extent will adequately compensate the creditor.

The hirer under a regulated hire agreement may terminate the agreement by giving written notice. The right to terminate does not arise until the agreement has been in existence for 18 months, unless there is provision for a shorter period. The period of notice is the lesser of one instalment period or three months. There is no right under the Act to terminate a consumer hire agreement where the hire payments exceed £900 per year, or where the goods are hired for a business and are chosen by the hirer from a supplier, before any hire agreement is made, or where the hirer intends to re-hire the goods to someone else.

7.8.2 Termination by creditor

The agreement may make provision for termination by the creditor in a number of circumstances, however, in the great majority of cases, the reason for the creditor wishing to terminate will be that the debtor is in breach of the agreement. The most common form of breach is failure to make payments as specified. The Act provides some protection for the debtor. Prior to the passing of the Hire Purchase Act 1938, it was not uncommon for a debtor who was unable to make payments to have the goods repossessed by the creditor even where the breach was small and the payments had nearly all been made. The modern law is more sympathetic to the defaulting debtor.

7.8.2.1 Default When a debtor defaults on an agreement, the creditor cannot terminate it until a default notice has been issued to the debtor (s. 87). The notice must specify the nature of the breach and the action required to remedy it or, if it cannot be remedied, what sum if any is required as compensation (s. 88). The debtor or hirer must be told of the consequences of failure to comply with the default order and must comply within seven days. If the debtor complies, the breach is treated as having never happened (s. 89). In the event that there is no compliance, the creditor may pursue any remedies laid down by the agreement provided these have been specified in the default notice (s. 88(4)).

A debtor who is served with a default may, under s. 129, apply to the court for a time order. Basically, if granted, it gives the debtor a breathing space in which either to remedy the breach and/or pay the arrears. In *First National Bank* v *Syed* [1991] 2 All ER 250, CA, the court gave some guidance as to the factors that should be considered before issuing a time order. It was essential to consider the position of both creditor and debtor. In *Syed*, the debtor's poor repayment record and the likelihood that it would continue weighed heavily with the court in refusing the time order. The court also has the power in the case of hire-purchase and conditional sale agreements to change the pattern of payments. The decision in *Southern and District Finance plc* v *Barnes and Another, The Times,* 19 April 1995, is the first decision of a Superior Court which was faced with the question of whether if a time order has been applied for under s. 129, the court is also entitled to reduce the contractual interest rate under the provisions of s. 136 (which allowed the court to amend any agreement). The Court of Appeal held they could. Although the decision is not binding in Scotland, it will be highly persuasive. The decision in *Barnes* is the opposite to that reached in *Murie McDougall Ltd v Sinclair*, 13 June 1994, unreported. If the Court of Appeal's view is followed in Scotland, debtors will be able to apply for a time order under s. 129 and also in certain circumstances to apply for a reduction in interest rate under s. 136. (For a full discussion of the issues raised by *Barnes*, see O'Carrol Scolag, June 1995, p. 87.)

7.8.2.2 Repossession of the goods The reason for the popularity of hire-purchase and conditional sale among creditors was the security they had either by reserving title or by only hiring the goods. Abuse of these rights led to the introduction of provisions in the Hire Purchase Act 1938 which reduced their applicability and gave a measure of protection to the debtor. While it may be said that the ability to repossess goods is of questionable value as the goods may well have decreased in value, it is likely that the fact that the debtor knows he may suffer the loss of the goods may spur him on to pay the outstanding instalments. The 1974 Act, s. 90 builds on the earlier protective provisions. It states that where a debtor is in breach of a regulated hire-purchase or conditional sale agreement but has paid to the creditor one-third or more of the total price of the goods, although the property in the goods remains with the creditor, there is no right to recover the goods without a court order. Goods covered by s. 90 are known as protected goods.

Section 92(1) further provides that the creditor is not entitled to enter any premises to take possession of goods unless he has obtained a court order. This is a useful protection if the goods do not come under the protection of s. 90.

There are severe penalties for breaches of s. 90 — the agreement will terminate, the debtor is released from all further liability and will in addition be entitled to recover all he has already paid. Entry to premises in contravention of s. 92(1) is actionable as a breach of statutory duty (see Chapter 4).

7.9 EXTORTIONATE CREDIT BARGAINS

Under the Moneylenders Acts 1900 and 1927, the courts had the power to reopen any transaction falling under the Acts where it was felt to be harsh and unconscionable. The Moneylenders Act 1927 said that if the rate of interest exceeded 48 per cent per annum it would be presumed to be harsh and unconscionable unless the contrary could be shown. The court could reopen the transaction and give relief to the debtor. These provisions have been replicated and expanded on in ss. 137 to 140 of the Act. The provisions apply not only to regulated consumer credit agreements but to all agreements between debtor and creditor except hire agreements. There are no maximum financial limits. Where the debtor alleges that a credit bargain is 'extortionate' it is for the creditor to prove to the contrary (s. 171(7)).

Under s. 138, a credit bargain is 'extortionate' if:

(a) it requires the debtor or a relative of his to make payments (whether unconditionally or in certain contingencies) which are grossly exorbitant; or
(b) it otherwise grossly contravenes principles of fair dealing.

Section 138 contains guidelines which the court should use in determining whether or not the bargain is extortionate, i.e. interest rates when the agreement was made; the age, business experience and state of health of the debtor, together with the financial pressure he was under; the degree of risk accepted by the creditor, and his relationship with the debtor. The courts will also wish to know if an inflated cash price was quoted in order to give the assurance of a lower interest rate. Indeed they can consider any factors they consider relevant. The court has sweeping powers to effectively rewrite the bargain but the amount of relief available in practice is doubtful. Francis Bennion, the draftsman of the 1974 Act, is quoted as saying 'it is likely that the courts will be sparing with relief. The bargain must after all be grossly exorbitant or unfair' (121 *Solicitors Journal*, 485).

There have not been many cases before the courts on this topic. Two English cases do however give some indication of the attitude of the courts. In *Barcabe Ltd* v *Edwards* (1983) 133 NLJ 713, the debtor who was a low paid workman responded to the plaintiff's newspaper advertisement. He had little experience of credit. He borrowed £400 at an APR of 319 per cent. The court reopened the bargain and substituted a flat rate of 40 per cent (an APR of 92 per cent!). (Funds were readily available at the time at an interest rate of 20 per cent flat rate per annum.) In *Ketley Ltd* v *Scott and Another* [1981] ICL 241 in order to finance the purchase of two flats, of one of which he was the protected tenant, Scott borrowed £20,500 from the plaintiffs. Scott's bank had rejected a loan application and he needed the money urgently. Ketley Ltd supplied the money at a few hours' notice at an interest rate of 48 per cent. Scott later claimed that the interest charged was excessive in the circumstances. The High Court did not agree. They agreed that 48 per cent was far higher than the rate charged by banks and building societies. Scott had, however, been rejected by them (he already had a large overdraft). Moreover, the lenders supplied the money within hours, without being able to check out Scott's financial position, and this exposed them to a high degree of risk. In addition, Scott was an experienced businessman who was aware of the rate charged and was, in the view of the court, under no real financial pressure to buy the houses. Reopening the transaction will not always work to the debtor's advantage, however. In *Shahabini* v *Giyahci* (1989, *Lexis*, 5 July) the Queen's Bench Division had imposed an interest rate of 15 per cent. However, on appeal this was raised to 30 per cent, as this was felt to be more equitable. (At the time the base rate was 15.5 per cent). (For more on this, see *Unjust Credit Transactions*, Office of Fair Trading, September 1991.)

Further reading
F. Bennion, (1980), *Consumer Credit Act Manual*, 3rd edn, Longman.
W.C.H. Ervine, (1995), *Consumer Law in Scotland*, W. Green Ltd.
R. Goode, (1989), *Consumer Credit Law*, Butterworth & Co.

Macleod, (1989), *Consumer Sales Law*, Butterworth & Co.

G. Stephenson, (1987), *Consumer Credit*, Collins Professional.

G. Stephenson, (1993), *Credit, Debit and Charge Cards: Law and Practice*, Central Law Publishing.

CHAPTER EIGHT

The Law of Employment

Individuals and commercial organisations will, in the execution of domestic and business affairs, enter into many contracts. The effect and significance of many of these will be short-lived, e.g., a contract to buy a beer or a newspaper; others, such as the sale or purchase of a house, will be of more lasting effect and of greater significance. One of the most important and significant contracts that most individuals will enter into will be a contract of employment.

The employment relationship has long been influenced and regulated by law, both common law and statute. This influence and regulation has grown significantly in recent years. Employment law is one area where British membership of the European Union has had a major impact. Many of the most significant changes in the law, e.g., on equal pay, sex discrimination, health and safety, and the transfer of undertakings, have had European Union or European Court of Justice parents. Under pressure from Europe, the British Government has been forced to introduce new laws on the above areas. An example of the impact of Europe can be seen in the landmark case of *Barber* v *GRE* [1990] IRLR 240. At the same time as this increase in employee rights has been going on there has also been some reduction in employee rights (a recent example would be the House of Lords decision that will allow employers to pay less to employees who refuse to give up union membership), a decision which may in Britain increase the move back to a freedom of contract approach in employment law(no matter how unrealistic). Even if this were to be the case, it is clear that law remains a powerful force in shaping the employment relationship in pursuit of certain minimum standards, particularly where the health and welfare of employees is concerned. Clearly, then, employment law is relevant to the business organisation. The duties imposed on business by law need to be taken account of, for example, when developing quality management systems or when arranging insurance cover. Employees and their advisers also need to know the law to identify the legally acceptable parameters within which they should operate.

This chapter will consider the law of employment, i.e. the law concerned with the legal relationship which exists between employer and employee and with the regulation of their respective rights and duties. The law of employment was known in the past as the law of master and servant, a term which may still be encountered from time to time. The sources of employment law are no different from the sources of law in general (see Chapter 1, para. 1.2.3). Custom, trade usage and practice and judicial precedent are of great importance but, in this field of law, legislation, UK or EU, is the principal source. Since 1963 there have been approximately 20 Acts of Parliament that have been directly related to employment law. The Employment Protection (Consolidation) Act 1978 consolidated many of the relevant provisions and is the main Act in this field, but it too has been added to and amended on many occasions, most recently by the Trade Union and Labour Relations (Consolidation) Act 1992, the Trade Union Reform and Employment Relations Act 1993 and the Employment Rights Act 1995.

8.1   THE DISTINCTION BETWEEN CONTRACTS OF SERVICE AND CONTRACTS FOR SERVICES

Before examining the law of employment in any detail, there is a conceptual hurdle to clear. The law of employment applies to the legal relationship between employer and employee; it does not apply to other workplace based relationships, e.g., that between an employer and a self-employed worker (known in law as an independent contractor). It is important for businessmen and students to be aware that the question as to whether a 'worker' is an employee or an independent contractor is of practical importance and significance for all concerned, be they employers, employees, self-employed, government departments and members of the general public.

What is the difference between them? A contract of service (also known as a contract of employment) is the type of contract that exists, for example, between the Crown and its civil servants, an education authority and its teachers, or a bank and its tellers. Crown employees exist to a certain extent in a legal limbo. They are employed under the prerogative and may be dismissed without notice. Unlike most other employees Crown employees have no remedy if they are wrongfully dismissed (i.e. if the Crown breaches its contract with them). Indeed for a long time it was the view that Crown employees did not have a contractual relationship to breach in any case, but there have been decisions which suggest that this is not the case (*Reilly* v *R* [1934] AC 176). It seems that members of the armed forces cannot sue for arrears of salary (*Mitchell* v *R* [1986] 1 QB 121) but that civil servants can (*Kodeeswaran* v *Attorney-General of Ceylon* [1970] AC 1111). The major problem in this area is that the Crown itself seems unsure. Civil Service Pay and Conditions Code paragraph 14 provides that 'a civil servant does not have a contract of employment enforceable in the courts'. This provision, it was successfully argued in *R* v *Civil Service Appeal Board, Ex parte Bruce* [1984] 3 All ER 395 was evidence that the Crown did not intend to enter into legal relations with its employees and therefore there was no contract (to break). However, in *R* v *Lord Chancellors Department, ex parte Nangle* [1991] IRLR 343 the decision in *Bruce* above was not followed, the Court being of the view that Nangle did have a contract of employment with the Crown that gave him the right to a private remedy for breach of contract. Within the field of statutory employment law s. 138 of the Employment Protection (Consolidation) Act 1978 defines Crown employment as 'employment under or for the purposes of a Government department or any officer or body exercising on behalf of the Crown functions conferred by an enactment'. There is however no mention of the existence or otherwise of a contract of employment. The position is clearly unsatisfactory as it seems to be left to the uncertainties of judicial law making. It should be noted that Crown employees can bring cases before Industrial Tribunals (see below 8.53) if they feel they have been unfairly dismissed. A contract for services, on the other hand, is the type of contract that exists between, for example, a householder and a building firm which installs a new kitchen or bathroom unit, or between household and window cleaner. The relationship between the parties in the former situation will generally be a more permanent one, although it is not the permanence or lack of it that per se distinguishes the two. The purchaser of a large property in very poor repair might have a contractual relationship that lasts over many years with the builder, but that will not make the builder an employee of the householder.

From the layman's point of view, it will often be obvious whether any particular worker is an employee or a self-employed person. We 'know' that the person who teaches our children is an employee of the education authority, just as we 'know' that the window cleaner is self-employed. Unfortunately, in law matters are not so simple. The problem is complicated by the fact that the label ('employee' or 'self-employed') that an individual may attach to himself may not, in the eyes of the courts or the Inland Revenue, be the correct one. Most of the cases where 'worker' status has been an issue have involved Government departments such as the Inland Revenue or National Insurance.

8.1.1 The implications of employee status

There are advantages and disadvantages in being an employee, just as there are advantages and disadvantages in being self-employed. Human nature being what it is, an individual may seek to combine the advantages of both while avoiding their disadvantages, e.g., people who are self-employed operate under a different Tax Schedule from employees and are entitled to more favourable allowances. This may well make self-employment an attractive option but there is a price to be paid. The price is that many statutory benefits are available only to employees e.g. redundancy payments, maternity pay, and industrial injury benefits. (See Employment Protection (Consolidation) Act 1978.)

Under the law of delict (see Chapter 4), an employer is generally liable for the acts of employees but only exceptionally for those of persons who are merely independent contractors providing services. It is in this area that a great deal of the law's attention to the distinction between employee and independent contractor has been focused.

A brief study of the nature and effect of vicarious liability should serve to illustrate some of the implications of employee status, not only for employer and worker but also for those affected by the latter's negligence or breach of duty.

8.1.1.1 Vicarious liability   Someone injured as a result of the negligence of a driver employed by Strathclyde Buses could of course choose to sue the driver, because an individual is liable for his own delicts. This is expressed by the maxim *culpa tenet suos auctores* (blame attaches to its authors). The concept of vicarious liability is an important modification of the general rule; in certain circumstances one person may find himself liable for the wrongful or negligent acts of another. Vicarious liability may arise in partnership or agency but is most frequently encountered where there is an employer/employee relationship and only rarely will an employer find himself vicariously liable for the delicts of an independent contractor or self-employed worker.

Vicarious liability involves joint and several liability. The employer will be jointly liable with the person for whose delict he is vicariously responsible. This has a twofold effect:

(a)   The pursuer may sue both the person at fault and the person vicariously liable. For example, in *Thomson & Others* v *British Steel Corporation & Another* 1977 SLT 26, a car being driven by a Mr. Ingram was involved in an accident which resulted in the death of Ingram and his two passengers. They were all employees of BSC and this action was raised against BSC *and* the widow of Ingram by the widow of one of the deceased passengers and the parent of the other passenger.

(b)   The person vicariously liable may claim from the person at fault for damages paid by virtue of vicarious liability. In *Lister* v *Romford Ice & Cold Storage Ltd* [1957] AC 555, an employee, due to his negligence, injured a fellow employee who happened to be his father. It was held that the employer could reclaim the damages payable from the negligent employee. In practice however, the employer would be unlikely to do this. Such actions would, of course, undermine the rationale behind vicarious liability, and in any case, since *Lister* employers and their insurers have had an agreement with the government not to pursue them.

To establish whether or not an employer is liable for the delicts of an employee there are several things that the pursuer must prove. First he will have to establish that the negligent party was in fact an employee of the defender. We have already seen that it may not be immediately obvious whether a person is an employee or a self-employed person. Generally speaking, for vicarious liability to exist there will have to be a contract of service between employer and worker. It will exist only very rarely where there is a contract for services.

Difficulties may arise in situations where an employee of one company is temporarily transferred to the employment of another employer. The court will examine the circumstances of the case to see if control of the worker has indeed passed to the temporary employer, or has in fact remained with the usual employer. An example can be seen in *Mersey Docks and Harbour Board v Coggins and Griffith Ltd* [1947] AC 162 where the Board hired out cranes which were operated by their employees. They hired a crane complete with operator to the defendants. Due to the operator's negligence, there was an accident and it fell to the court to decide whether the Board or the defendants were vicariously liable for the operator's negligence. In spite of the fact that the agreement between the parties said that the operator was to be regarded as the employee of the defendants, the court felt from comments made by the operator that there had been no meaningful transfer of employment and that the Board were still vicariously liable for the operator's negligence (see the Cases and Materials section for Chapter 8). Denning LJ has suggested that where a skilled employee and plant are hired out, it will be rare for vicarious liability to move from the main to the temporary employer, although it may sometimes take place with unskilled workers (*Garrard* v *Southey & Co* [1952] 2 QB 174).

Once it has been established, that a contract of employment does indeed exist, the next hurdle the pursuer must overcome is to show that the employee was acting in the course of his employment. If the employee is judged by the courts to be on what they have quaintly described as 'a frolic of his own', this will relieve the employer of legal liability. In addition, criminal acts which are for the employee's sole benefit can only saddle the employer with civil as opposed to criminal liability, unless of course the employer was party to the crime.

In deciding whether or not the activity in question was within the course of someone's employment the courts seem to have focused on four questions: *Was the employee using his employer's time for his own purposes?* We can see an example of this in the case of *Kirby* v *NCB* 1958 SC 514, where eight miners were injured when one of them lit a cigarette during a break. Statute forbade both the use of naked light and the possession of matches or cigarettes underground. The Court of Session found that the NCB were not liable for the miner's negligence. Lord President Clyde said 'if the servant uses his master's time or his master's place or his master's tools for his own purposes the master is not responsible'.

It may not, however, always be clear whether or not the employee is acting for his own purposes or in the course of his employment as in *Century Insurance Co* v *Northern Ireland Road Transport Board* [1942] AC 509. A petrol tanker driver who was delivering petrol to a Belfast garage lit a cigarette while unloading. He threw away the match which ignited some material lying on the ground. The fire spread to the tanker. Although the driver drove the tanker into the street, it exploded damaging nearby cars and houses. When the Board sought to claim from their insurers, the insurers denied liability on the ground that the driver was not acting in the course of his employment when he caused the fire. They also sought to avoid liability on other grounds which need not concern us here. Viscount Simon LC said 'every judge who has had to consider the matter agrees . . . that the driver's careless act caused the conflagration and explosion and that it was an act done within the course of his employment'. In the view of the Lord Chancellor, the driver was employed to deliver petrol and transfer it from his tanker to the storage tanks. This involved a period of waiting and it was during this waiting that he lit up. As the Lord Chancellor said, 'they also serve who stand and wait', i.e. the driver was acting within the course of his employment when he negligently discarded the match. His employers were therefore vicariously liable, and the damage was covered by their insurance.

Was the negligent employee employed to do one kind of work and did another?   This would cover a situation where a bus conductor who is employed to collect the fares, 'takes a shot' at driving the bus and, while doing so negligently, injures someone, as in the case of *Beard* v *London General Omnibus Company* [1900] 2 QB 530. In that case, it was held that the company was not vicariously liable for the negligence of the conductor as he was doing something he had not been employed to do. The employer might, however, be liable for the negligence of the driver where he has allowed the conductor to drive the bus. Another example is afforded by the case of *Alford* v *NCB* 1951 SC 248, where a miner was injured when a shot was fired by another miner who was not a shot firer. The injured miner brought an action against the NCB averring fault on the part of the unauthorised shot firer, and the vicarious liability of the NCB. It was held there was no vicarious liability as the act done was not within the scope of employment and was also expressly prohibited by statute and NCB rules.

Problems may arise where the employee's deed is incidental to the main purpose of employment. In *Neville* v *C & A Modes* 1945 SC 175, two sales assistants mistakenly stopped a person as a suspected shoplifter. The irate shopper raised an action against the store for defamation. Although the assistants were not store detectives, the court held that their actions were incidental to their main duties and the store was therefore vicariously liable.

An assault may be in the course of employment if the intention is to safeguard an employer's business (*Neville*). However, if the assault is merely an act of personal vengeance then this will not be the case (*Keppel Bus Co* v *Sa'ad Bin Ahman* [1974] 1 WLR 1082). In that case, a bus conductor employed by the appellants was rude to an elderly lady. Mr Sa'ad Bin Ahmad gallantly remonstrated with the conductor. After the lady got off, the conductor swore at the respondent, and on being asked to refrain he hit him with his ticket machine breaking his glasses and blinding him in one eye. It was held that the bus company was not vicariously liable.

What if the employee is doing what he has been authorised to do but is doing it in an unauthorised manner?   In *Kirkby* (see above), Lord President Clyde said (at p. 532):

> where the workman does some work which he is appointed to do, but does it in a way which his master has not authorised and would not have authorised had he known of it, the master is nevertheless still responsible, for the servant's act is still within the scope of his employment.

Indeed the employer may find himself vicariously liable even where the employee acts contrary to specific instructions. In *Rose v Plenty* [1976] 1 WLR 141, Plenty was a milkman whose employer was unhappy with the practice of young children being used to help deliver the milk. The milkman had been specifically instructed not to use children to deliver the milk. Plenty disregarded this instruction and employed Rose who was injured due to Plenty's negligence. Rose could and did sue Plenty but wished to establish if the employers were vicariously liable even though Plenty had disregarded specific instructions. The court held that Plenty's employer was vicariously liable because he had been acting within the course of his employment, albeit in a forbidden manner.

When does employment begin and end? In deciding whether any particular employee is within the course of his employment it may be necessary to know when employment begins and ends. Generally speaking, commuting to and from work is not within the course of one's employment; if an employee injures someone as a result of negligence on the way to or from work, there will be no vicarious liability attaching to the employer. It would seem, however, that firemen and others such as doctors who are called out to work by their employers *are* in the course of their employment while travelling to work. Additionally, employees who are travelling to and from an unusual workplace will usually be regarded as being within the course of their employment.

The House of Lords decision in *Smith v Stages and Another* [1989] 1 All ER 833 indicates that whilst the provision of a vehicle to travel to and from work does not necessarily mean that such travel falls within the course of employment, it will do so where the employee is actually paid 'travelling time', even when using his own vehicle (see the Cases and Materials section for Chapter 8).

At one level vicarious liability can be rationalised in terms of risk allocation. The employer will generally benefit from the employee's actions and therefore should be liable where loss is occasioned. More pragmatically, the employer is more likely to be able to pay any damages that may be awarded to an injured party. The employee, the actual wrongdoer, may well be 'a man of straw' and not worth suing. What actually happens is that the employer will insure against liability for the delicts of employees committed within the course of their employment.

8.1.2 Employees and contractors: pros and cons for the employer

As we have just seen, vicarious liability will generally exist only where the wrongdoer is an employee. The need to insure against liability on the part of the employer is just one of the extra expenses that have to be borne by the employer. For the businessman, it would seem that employees are expensive. If your workforce consists largely of employees there are several costs/burdens that will have to be borne in addition to the insurance mentioned above. An employer is responsible for deducting income tax from employees' income under the Pay As You Earn (PAYE) scheme and forwarding it to the Inland Revenue and there is a similar responsibility in respect of employees' national insurance contributions. The costs for the employer of administering these deductions have to be set against income. It means employing people whose main function is not tied directly to the profits/success of the business but to gathering money on behalf of the government. A rival who chooses to operate without any employees but to have a workforce of self-employed people will not have to bear any of these costs. Independent contractors (the self-employed) are responsible for their own tax and national insurance arrangements and should also bear the cost of insurance against public liability. An additional burden placed on employers whose workforce consists of employees is that an employer has a duty at common law to protect employees from foreseeable harm. This duty involves taking all reasonable steps to provide the employee with a safe place of work, proper tools for the job, adequate supervision, safety appliances etc. (see 8.11 below). This does not hold true for self-employed workers working for an employer, although the Health and Safety at Work Act 1974 does impose some similar duties.

Being the employer of employees is, therefore, an expensive and responsible business. The businessman might well ask 'why bother?'. If he uses self-employed people he saves on administrative costs and the self-employed worker enjoys the benefit of a more favourable tax regime. It would seem that nobody stands to lose except perhaps the Inland Revenue. Economic costs are not, however, the sole basis of all decision making. There are advantages to the employer in building up a more stable and permanent relationship with the workforce than may be possible by using an often more transient and temporary workforce of self-employed workers, who may feel no sense of corporate identity with the business. Indeed, as they are self-employed and thus in business on their own account, they may well place the needs and aspirations of their own business before that of the employer's business.

8.1.3 Defining employee

In spite of the many Acts of Parliament that relate to employees, the legislature has, for many years, shied away from defining 'employee'. However, in the Employment Protection (Consolidation) Act (EPCA) 1978, s. 153, an employee is defined as 'an individual who has entered into or works under a contract of employment'. A contract of employment is defined as 'a contract of service or apprenticeship, whether express or implied, and (if it is express) whether it is oral or in writing' (EPCA. 1978, s. 153(1)).

This is not particularly helpful, but in the words of Lord Denning (*Stevenson, Jordan & Harrison Ltd* v *Macdonald & Evans* [1952] 1 TLR 101), it is often easy to recognise a contract of employment when you see it, but difficult to say where the difference between it and a contract for services lies.

In the absence of any useful statutory definition of contract of employment (see above), defining the phrase has been left to the courts and tribunals. It must be said, however, that the case law on this area is often confused, confusing and contradictory (see 8.14). One definition which has often been used (and is widely accepted), is the following adopted by the Department of Social Security in relation to contracts of service, the term previously used to describe contracts of employment:

A contract of service is the legal term given to the usual arrangements made between two parties when an employer has offered employment and a person has agreed to work for him as an employee. A contract of this sort exists where there is a mutual agreement or understanding that in return for some specific remuneration in money or kind the employee shall render personal services subject to a right on the part of the employer to control and direct him in the work he does and the method of performance of his duties. Although not conclusive in itself the existence of this right of control (even if seldom or never exercised) is a strong indication that there is a contract of service.

Government departments are often involved in situations where the legal status of the worker is at issue. This is because entitlement to various benefits, e.g., unemployment benefit, and liability to be taxed under Schedule D or E will depend on the legal status of the worker. An example several years ago involved journalists with Scottish Television. The journalists operated on six- or twelve-month contracts and claimed tax allowances available only to the self-employed. The arrangement also saved the company the administrative costs and inconvenience of processing tax and national insurance contributions. The Inland Revenue ruled that they were to be regarded as staff (employees) and taxed at source on a PAYE basis. This meant that they lost their entitlement to have items such as home telephones, cars and stationery as tax-deductible expenses. It also meant, of course, that the Revenue received more tax.

8.1.4 Tests of employee status
The question of an individual's exact legal status has come before the courts on many occasions and, in the absence of any satisfactory statutory definition, it has fallen to the judges to lay down the criteria to be used in distinguishing between an employee and a self-employed person. These criteria have changed and developed to meet new social, economic and political circumstances. Over the years the courts have developed a series of tests aimed at drawing the distinction between the employed and the self-employed.

8.1.4.1 The control test It was in the context of whether or not there existed vicarious liability that the courts first had to decide whether or not a person was an employee. The core question asked revolved around the degree of control exercised by the alleged employer over the alleged employee. The matter was seen as a simple one. If the 'employer' controlled or had the right to control not only what the worker did but the manner in which he did it, then the relationship between them was that of employer and employee. In *Yewens v Noakes* [1880] 6 QB 530, Bramwell LJ summed up this view: 'A servant is a person subject to the command of his master as to the manner in which he shall do his work'.

In *Performing Rights Society Ltd v Mitchell and Booker Ltd* [1924] 1 KB 762, McCardie J said:

The distinction between 'servant' and 'independent contractor' does not seem to rest merely on the magnitude of the task undertaken . . . [it] seems, however, reasonably clear that the final test, if there be a final test, and certainly the test to be generally applied, lies in the nature and degree of detailed control over the person alleged to be a servant. This circumstance is, of course, one only of several to be considered, but it is usually of vital importance.

In contrast with an employee, an independent contractor will normally be hired to achieve a particular result but will usually have complete freedom as to how this is to be done.

The control test has its limitations, as can be seen in the case of *Hillyer* v *Governors of St Bartholemew's Hospital* [1909] 2 KB 820, where the test was taken to its logical (but absurd) conclusion when it was held that nurses working in the operating theatre were beyond the control of the hospital authorities and could not in that situation be treated as employees, i.e. for the purpose of establishing vicarious liability.

Such excessive reliance on control as a single test had been discredited as long ago as 1774 by Lord Mansfield in *Hart* v *Aldridge* (1774) 1 COWP 54, and the control test probably was never valid on its own. It is hard to imagine many situations where an employer is able to exercise close and detailed control over an employee. What, for example, about an employer who has employees in several different locations? Technological advances also began to eat away at the validity of the control test as the sole criterion to be applied in determining the status of a worker. How in any meaningful way could an employer be said to control the activities of professional and highly skilled employees such as engineers, surgeons and lawyers? Indeed it is likely that one of the reasons for their employment in the first place was the employer's deficiency in the skill possessed by the employee.

As the validity of the control test was increasingly questioned, judges began to look around for some other test. The question of control was still seen as important, although not all important. If there is an employee/employer relationship there must always be some element of control that can be exercised by the former over the latter, even though this right is seldom or never exercised or is delegated to another, for instance where, in large organisations, employees are controlled/directed by another more senior employee.

During the 1940s there were a series of cases which indicated a judicial shift. Hospitals, for example, were held to be vicariously liable for the acts of surgeons. In *Cassidy* v *The Minister of Health* [1951] 2 KB 343, Somerville LJ said:

> I would say the doctors concerned had Contracts of Service . . . they were employed, like the nurses, as part of the permanent staff of the hospital . . . and therefore, the hospital is liable if a doctor is negligent.

8.1.4.2   The multiple or economic reality test   Judges began using the control test as a starting point and adding other questions aimed at eliciting the truth about the parties' economic and legal relationship. What came to be known as the multiple or economic reality test had first raised its head in the Scottish case of *Park* v *Wilsons & Clyde Coal Company* 1928 SC 121 (see Cases and Materials section for Chapter 8). The case concerned injuries to workers underground in a colliery, and the legal thrust of the case addresses the defence of common employment which no longer exists in negligence actions.

The multiple or economic reality test came before a wider UK audience in *Short* v *Henderson* [1946] 174 LT 147, where Lord Thankerton posed the same four questions asked by Lord Hunter 18 years before in the Court of Session. In order to establish whether or not a person is an employee, the test asks whether the putative employer has:

(a) the right of selection of his employees;
(b) the right of suspension and dismissal;
(c) the right to control the method of doing the work;
(d) the obligation to pay wages or other remuneration.

If the employer has these rights and this obligation, that points to the existence of a contract of employment; if they are absent it points towards the contract being a contract for services.

In the same year the US Supreme Court also adopted the concept of an economic reality test in *USA* v *Silk* (1946) 331 US 704, where Justice Reed said 'the word employee is not a work of art but should be seen in context . . . the economic reality of the relationship was fundamental'.

The purpose of the questions is to discover the reality of the economic and legal relationship between the parties. There is no exhaustive list of questions that can usefully be asked. As was said in *Market Investigations Ltd* v *Minister of Social Security* [1969] 2 QB 173:

No exhaustive list has been compiled and perhaps no exhaustive list can be compiled of the considerations which are relevant in determining that question [employee/self-employed], nor can strict rules be laid down as to the relative weight which the various considerations should carry in particular cases. The most that can be said is that control will no doubt always have to be considered, although it can no longer be regarded as the sole determining factor.

Questions which have been asked include: Is income tax deducted at source? Is the worker obliged to provide his own tools and equipment? Not all questions are necessarily helpful. Many workers provide their own tools but that does not automatically make them self-employed. There is a world of difference between a joiner owning a basic set of tradesman's tools and being obliged to supply sophisticated and highly expensive plant or machinery. The particular circumstances will dictate the questions which are most appropriate. For example, where a worker is claimed to be self-employed it may be appropriate to ask whether he is taking a financial risk of any kind. A recent Privy Council decision gives a good illustration of the application of this type of logic. In *Lee v Chung* [1990] IRLR 236, a mason working for a building sub-contractor fell from a high stool and suffered injuries. He was entitled to compensation under the Hong Kong equivalent of the Workmen's Compensation Acts only if he was an employee. The Privy Council held that, although Mr. Lee was a skilled man who earned his living by working for more than one employer, he was not a small businessman in business on his own account with all of the attendant risks. The only risk which he ran was of being unable to find employment, a risk run by all employees.

A very full and useful illustration of the multiple/economic reality test can be seen in the case of *Ready Mixed Concrete (SE) Ltd v Minister for Pensions and National Insurance* [1968] 2 QB 497. The case concerned a company's liability to pay national insurance contributions for their workers. Liability would exist only if the workers were employees employed under a contract of employment. The workers drove lorries that delivered ready mixed concrete. These lorries were held by their drivers under hire-purchase contracts from the company. The drivers in Ready Mixed had all signed a detailed 32-page contract with the company which covered matters such as the requirement that drivers wear company uniforms, use of the lorry for other work, maintenance schedule for the lorries, how the lorry was to be painted, etc. On the surface this seemed to indicate the high degree of control that would point to employee status, but it was held that the drivers were self-employed. A major factor in the decision may have been the fact that the drivers could sub-contract the driving to others (indeed they were required to do so if they were unable to drive). The company seemed more interested in the concrete being delivered in lorries bearing its colours and by men in its uniform than it was in who wore the uniform. Also crucial to the decision was that 'the ownership of the assets, the chance of a profit and the risk of a loss in the business of carriage are [the employees'] and not the company's' (Mac-Kenna J).

The proliferation of casual workers in recent years has led to the question of status being raised in this context. Given the purportedly 'casual ' nature of the relationship between the parties, the courts appear to have felt it appropriate to examine the mutuality of obligations existing (or not) between the parties.

In *O'Kelly v Trust House Forte PLC* [1983] IRLR 369, the court had to judge on the status of 'casual' waiters who claimed to have been unfairly dismissed. The company had 'on call' a large number of casual staff due to the fluctuating nature of the banqueting business. O'Kelly was one of a well-established, long-serving group of regular casual staff who were given preferential treatment when work rotas were allocated. In theory they could refuse work but in fact never did so. If they had done so, they would have lost the coveted regular status. Similarly the company were under no obligation to offer O'Kelly work, but as he and the other regular casuals were the most experienced staff they always offered them whatever work was available. The court felt that there was no mutuality of obligation on the part of the parties. The fact that theoretically work could be refused was evidence of this lack of mutuality and, as this was seen as a prerequisite of an employer/employee relationship, without it there was not one. Curiously, in *Nethermere (St. Neots) Ltd v Taverna and Gardiner* [1984] IRLR 240, the courts applied this mutuality of obligation test, and found there to be contract of service, although the workers concerned could, like O'Kelly, refuse work. Given the increasing number of part-time, casual and homeworkers, the mutuality of obligation test as applied in *O'Kelly* is highly disadvantageous for the workforce who would almost certainly prefer the more liberal approach in *Nethermere*. The decision in *Lee v Chung* [1990] IRLR 236 may have resolved this issue. It endorsed Cooke J's approach in *Market Investigation v Minister for Social Security* (above) which said that the fundamental question is, 'Is the person who has supplied these services performing them as a person in business on his own account?'. It would seem clear that O'Kelly and his colleagues were not 'in business on [their] own account'. The decision also casts doubt on the validity of the organisation or integration test (see 8.1.4.3 below).

8.1.4.3   The organisation or integration test   Another attempt at solving the question of a worker's status had its genesis in the case of *Stevenson, Jordan and Harrison v MacDonald & Evans* [1952] 1 TLR 101 (see 8.1.3 above). The case concerned a management engineer who wished to publish a book on management. Whether he or his 'employers' had the right to copyright depended on whether or not he was an employee. Lord Denning considered that the decisive question was whether the person in question was fully integrated into the employer's organisation. This integration test had certain advantages over the control test, particularly in regard to skilled employees in respect of whom the control test is clearly inappropriate. A ship's captain, a chauffeur and a reporter on the staff of a newspaper are thus employed under a contract of service while a ship's pilot, a taxi driver and a newspaper contributor are hired under a contract for services. In the latter situation the work done is regarded not as an integral part of the business but as an accessory to it.

This test soon lost favour and was in fact applied in only a few cases. For one thing it failed to accommodate the position of business partners and company directors who are not employees but whose services are certainly an integral part of the organisation. In *Ready Mixed Concrete*, McKenna J said that the integration test posed more questions than he knew how to answer. (See also *Whittaker v Minister for Pensions and National Insurance* [1966] 3 All ER 531, and *Westall Richardson v Roulson* [1954] 2 All ER 448.)

8.1.4.4   Ordinary person test   This was used in *Collins v Hertfordshire CC* [1947] 1 All ER 633 where the question posed by the court was 'was his contract of service within the meaning which an ordinary person would give to the words'. This test was approved in *Cassidy* (8.1.4.1 above) and used in *Whittaker* (8.1.4.3 above). To submit the question to the mythical 'ordinary person' would produce even more confusion than there already is on this matter.

8.1.5 Self description

The question of how much emphasis the courts should place on the statements and intentions of the parties where they stipulate that a contract is, or more usually is not, a contract of employment has caused some disagreement. In *Ferguson* v *John Dawson & Partners (Contractors) Ltd* [1976] 1 WLR 1213, it was held that a declaration by the parties, even if it was incorporated into the contract, should be 'disregarded entirely if the remainder of the contractual terms point to the opposite conclusion'. The case concerned a building labourer working on the 'lump', a system whereby the worker, who is regarded as self-employed, is able to avoid paying tax and national insurance. Ferguson was also working under an assumed name, presumably to evade tax. While Ferguson was dismantling scaffolding, he fell off an unguarded flat roof sustaining serious injuries. As a self-employed worker he could not sue the contractors for breach of their duty of care to him, because they owed him none. If he was an employee he could sue for damages for breach of duty and claim industrial injury benefit. In spite of what the agreement between the parties had said, the court declared that the reality of the situation was that he was to all intents and purposes an employee and was therefore entitled to claim. Lawton LJ dissented saying it was 'contrary to public policy to allow a man to say he was self-employed for the purpose of avoiding the incidence of taxation, but a servant for the purpose of claiming compensation'.

Lord Denning MR followed this public policy approach in *Massey* v *Crown Life Insurance Co* [1978] IRLR 31, when he said that the worker having made his bed as self-employed must lie on it '. . . the parties cannot alter the truth of the relationship by putting a different label on it and use it as a dishonest device to deceive the revenue'. However, this approach was doubted in *Young & Woods Ltd* v *West* [1980] IRLR 201. Stephenson LJ, in the Court of Appeal, said that to hold the parties to their self description might effectively allow employees to sign away their employment status and the various rights attached to it. He said 'it must be the court's duty to see whether the label correctly represents the true legal relationship between the parties'. Such reasoning is to be preferred to that of Lord Denning as it enables the court to examine the substance of the relationship objectively.

It is clear however from *Massey* that the courts will recognise the clearly stated intentions of the parties provided the other terms of the contract are not inconsistent with that type of content. This will particularly be the case where other factors are not conclusive of the matter. (See also *Narichphy Ltd* v *Commissioner of Payroll Tax* [1984] ICR 286 QBD.)

8.1.6 A summing up

The most recent case involving worker status is *Hall* v *Lorimer* [1994] IRLR 139, which contains a useful, if somewhat colourful, summary of the current approach. The Court of Appeal said that deciding whether someone is employed under a contract of service or a contract for services 'is not a mechanical exercise of running through items on a checklist to see whether they are present in or absent from a given situation. The objective of the exercise is to paint a picture from the accumulation of detail. The overall effect can only be appreciated by standing back from the detailed picture, by veiwing it from a distance and by making an informed, considered qualitative appreciation of the whole'. This probably sums up the present approach as well as can be.

8.2 THE FORM OF THE CONTRACT OF EMPLOYMENT

There are no formalities required in Scots law for the formation of a contract except in certain limited circumstances (see Chapter 3, para. 3.7); contracts can be entered into orally, in writing or may be implied from the actions of the parties. However, there is a class of contracts known as *obligationes literis* (contracts which must be in writing). Contracts of employment for more than one year and contracts of apprenticeship fell into this class. They should therefore have been entered into in probative writing on both sides. This requirement, which often was ignored, has been dispensed with with the passing of the Requirement for Writing (Scotland) Act 1995.

Moreover, the Employment Protection (Consolidation) Act 1978, s. 1, as amended by TURERA 1993, provides that in the case of the majority of contracts of employment there is an obligation on the part of the employer to supply the employee, within two months, with a written statement detailing certain particulars of the contract (see the Cases and Materials section for Chapter 8). These particulars include the names of employer and employee; the date employment began; whether the employment is to be regarded as continuous with prior service; the rate of pay, how it is calculated, and at what intervals it is to be paid; the hours to be worked; any terms and condition relating to holiday entitlement, holiday pay, sick pay and pension arrangements; the notice period; and the job title. Reference should also be made within the document to disciplinary rules and grievances procedures.

8.3 OBLIGATIONS OF EMPLOYER AND EMPLOYEE

As with any other contract, the existence of a contract of employment will mean that each party is under certain obligations to the other. It is of course open to the parties to agree whatever terms they wish, provided they are not illegal. Employment contracts which are tainted with illegality may well be unenforceable. The employee may therefore be unable to rely on the contractual *or* statutory rights.

In *Hewcastle Catering* v *Ahmed* [1991] IRLR 473 CA, employers had instructed the employees (who were waiters) to participate in a scheme to avoid payment of VAT on meals. Kerr LJ said that the relative moral culpability of the parties may be relevant in ascertaining whether employment rights were unenforceable because the underlying contact was tainted by fraud. In this case the employees had not lost their right to complain of unfair dismissal. There is obviously a difference between a contract of employment to do something which is unlawful and a contract which is capable of being performed lawfully, was intended to be so performed, but has in fact been performed by unlawful means. The former is unenforceable, while the latter will be enforceable unless the employee stood to benefit, which was not the case in *Newcastle Catering* v *Ahmed*. In *Salveson* v *Simons* [1994] IRLR 52, part of Simons's remuneration was paid in such a way as to avoid liability to income tax. Neither the employer nor the employee knew the payment was illegal. The EAT refused to enforce a claim for constructive dismissal arising out of the contract. Lord Coulsfield said that it was not knowledge of the illegality that was important, but knowledge of what was being done — 'it is irrelevant the [the employer] did not know it was illegal. It is not necessarily inequitable that those who seek to take advantage of the tax system, . . . should not be entitled to be treated as if they were employed under a normal contract of employment'. This would seem to accord with *Ahmed*'s case. However, in reality a contract of employment does not tend to be a matter for individual negotiation. Unless the worker is of considerable stature and/or has a rare skill, he will be presented with a standard term contract, the details of which may well have been agreed between the employer or an employers' association and a trade union. This will usually be presented on a 'take it or leave it' basis. In addition to the terms agreed by the parties the law imposes obligations on both parties. Any breach of these duties will enable the employer or employee, as the case may be, to bring an action for damages if loss results. The claim may be based either on breach of contract, or in certain cases, in delict.

8.3.1 The employer's obligations at common law

The employer's *obligations* or duties may also be seen from an employee's point of view as the *rights* of the employee. We shall begin with what many employees see as the employer's most important duty, i.e. the payment of wages.

8.3.1.1 Duty to pay wages   It is possible to have a gratuitous contract where the employee agrees to work for nothing but this would be a rare event and in any event, the essence of the contract of employment is the work/wage bargain. The employer is under an obligation to pay whatever wages or salary was agreed; in the absence of agreement he must pay a reasonable sum. In deciding what is reasonable, regard would be had current pay rates in the locality/industry/profession concerned.

Holiday and sick pay   There is potential for disagreement over the question of the employee's entitlement to receive wages etc, while on holiday leave or sick leave. Most employees will, under the terms of their contract, be entitled to paid holiday leave and sick pay. Such matters should be covered either in the written contract between the parties or in the statutory written statement of particulars (see 8.2 above). In the absence of any such provision and contrary to public belief, there is no right to holiday pay implied either by common law or statute (except public holidays). There is provision for the payment of Statutory Sick Pay (SSP) to employees for up to 28 weeks in any year but this is really a case where the employer is being used to administer a state benefit which was previously dealt with (albeit in different form) by the Department of Social Security. In *Mears* v *Safecar Security Ltd* [1981] ICR

409, it was held that there was no general presumption of a right to sick pay (as opposed to SSP). Slynn J said:

> One does not begin by assuming that the term as to payment is to be implied unless the employer displaces it . . . It seems to us, accordingly, in this case, if one adopts the approach which we consider it is right to adopt in these cases, that here the term to be implied into this contract is that wages would not be paid during periods of absence due to sickness.

Itemised pay statement The Employment Protection (Consolidation) Act 1978, s. 8 gives each employee a right to an itemised pay statement which will show gross wages or salary and the amounts of any fixed or variable deductions that are made. The Wages Act 1986 makes provisions which restrict the amount which employers may deduct from employees' wages.

An obligation to provide work? At common law there is no general obligation to supply the employee with work in addition to pay. However, there are several well recognised categories of employee who must be provided with work in addition to pay. These include those whose career development depends on public exposure, e.g., actors and journalists (see *Clayton and Waller Ltd* v *Oliver* [1930] AC 209 and *Collier* v *Sunday Referee Publishing Co Ltd* [1940] 4 All ER 234); piece workers, whose remuneration depends on being provided with work (*Devonald* v *Rosser & Sons* [1906] 2 KB 728, CA and skilled employees (*Breach* v *Epsylon Industries Ltd* [1976] IRLR 180, EAT). In *Breach* it was held that there might be a right to work where the employee would quickly lose his contacts or expertise (see below).

In *Collier* v *Sunday Referee*, Asquith J stated the position 'Provided I pay my cook her wages regularly she cannot complain if I choose to take any or all of my meals out'. Given the star status accorded to some cooks today, Asquith J might, with respect, have to eat not only his words but also his meals at home.

The *Clayton and Waller* case involved an actor who had been hired to play one of the lead roles in a stage musical. In the event the appellants failed to cast him and he sued for loss of enhancement of his reputation and for the loss of publicity. Buckmaster L held that he 'was entitled to compensation because he did not appear at the Hippodrome, as by his contract he was entitled to do'. The right to work was extended to journalists in the *Collier* case which concerned the chief sub-editor of a newspaper.

The case of *Langston* v *AUEW* [1974] 1 All ER 980 raised the question whether there was a more general right to work for other categories of worker. Langston was a skilled engineer who relinquished his long-standing union membership. The employers then came under pressure from the AUEW to dismiss Langston but in the words of Pilate they 'could find no fault in him'. They sent him home on full pay trusting his absence from work would defuse what had become an industrial relations issue. When the matter came before the court, Lord Denning MR said:

> We have repeatedly said in this court that a man has a right to work, which the courts will protect . . . In these days an employer, when employing a

skilled man, is bound to provide him with work. By which I mean that a man should be given the opportunity of doing his work when it is available and he is ready and willing to do it. A skilled man takes a pride in his work. He does not do it merely to earn money. He does it so as to make his contribution to the well-being of all. He does it so as to keep himself busy and not idle.

Two years later, in the case of *Breach* v *Epsylon Industries Ltd*, Phillips J seemed to follow Lord Denning when he said:

there may well be cases which are exceptions to the general rule and where it can be said that from the nature of the employment, the circumstances in which it has to be served, and so on, there is indeed an obligation on the part of the employer to provide work. The line is a difficult one to draw.

It would seem that the courts are prepared to look at each situation on its merits.

8.3.1.2 Duty to indemnify the employee At common law there is an implied obligation on the part of the employer to indemnify or reimburse the employee in respect of losses, liabilities or expenses arising out of the due peformance of his contract. If the employee is on a 'frolic of his own', i.e. doing something outwith the course of his employment, (see 8.1 above) the duty to indemnify will not apply. Also, as we saw in the *Lister* case (see 8.1.1 above), if the employee has been negligent, e.g., in breach of his implied duty to exercise reasonable care, then the employer is under no duty to indemnify the employee but may himself claim indemnity from the employee if some third party has suffered loss or damage. Although in practice this right has rarely been exercised, the climate could change.

The law recognises joint wrongdoers, and when both employer and employee have been negligent so as to lose as against each other the right to complete indemnity, then, by virtue of s. 93 of the Law Reform (Miscellaneous Provisions) (Scotland) Act 1940, the party against whom the damages are awarded may claim a contribution from the other. For example, in *Jones* v *Manchester Corporation* [1952] 2 All ER 725, where a patient died as a result of the negligent administration of drugs, the hospital was held liable for their failure to provide adequate supervision of a recently qualified, inexperienced doctor but it was held that the hospital could recover 20 per cent of the damages awarded against them from the doctor for what was described as 'conduct inexcusable even for an inexperienced doctor'.

8.3.1.3 Duty of respect The idea that employers should treat their employees with respect is thought to be a recent development of the common law duties. It has certainly come to the fore over the last 20 years, but it has a long history in Scots law. Bell spoke of the need for the master to behave 'with gentleness and moderation in his bearing towards his servant' (Bell's *Principles* s 192). His view was further developed in *Cowdenbeath Coal Co* v

Drylie (1886) 3 Sh Ct Rep 3. In *Law of Master and Servant*, Fraser said that the duty will be influenced by the nature of the employment, the status of the employee and contemporary values. Examples of breaches of the duty have included the employer behaving in such a way as to damage the relationship of trust and confidence between the parties (*Woods* v *W.M. Car Services* (1983) IRLR 200), failing to support a senior employee (*ATS* v *Waterhouse* [1976] IRLR 386 EAT), exercising a contractual disciplinary procedure harshly or unreasonably (*Cauley* v *SWEB* [1985] IRLR 89 EAT), making false accusations of theft (*Robinson* v *Crompton Parkinson* [1978] IRLR 61). Using foul or intemperate language, or refusing time off to cope with domestic difficulties have also been held to be breaches of the duty. In *BAC Ltd* v *Austin* [1978] IRLR 332 Philips J said:

> It must ordinarily be an implied term of the contract of employment that employers do not behave in such a way which is intolerable or which employees cannot be expected to put up with any longer.

In *Dryden* v *GGHB* [1992] IRLR 469, an employee who was a lifelong smoker claimed that the introduction of a no smoking policy in the workplace was a breach of the duty of respect. The court held that there was no implied right to smoke at work (and, at least in this case, no contractual right (see 8.5.1 below)).

If the duty of respect has been reached the employee may feel that there are grounds for regarding himself as 'constructively' dismissed (see 8.5.1 below). The duty of respect does not mean that the employer is under any implied obligation to provide the employee with a reference. However, *Spring* v *Guardian Insurance plc* [1994] IRLR 460, would suggest that there is an implied term in the contract of employment that the employer who does provide a reference does so with due skill and care. It was also suggested in this case that there are some jobs where there will be an implied obligation to provide references. An example would be a job in the financial services sector where a satisfactory reference is a prerequisite to employment.

8.3.1.4 Employer's duty of care   At common law, the employer has an obligation to take all reasonable care to provide for the safety of his employees. This is not an absolute duty; reasonable care is all that is required in relation to foreseeable risks. In addition to the employer's common law duties there are many others imposed on him by statute, e.g., the Health and Safety at Work Act 1974. These statutes are part of the criminal law and will be dealt with later (see 8.11 below). The employer's common law duty of care does not extend to the employee's personal possessions, although there is statutory provision (Factories Act 1961, s. 59) that the employer should provide suitable accommodation for clothes that are not worn at work. The employer's duty is a personal one and cannot be avoided by delegating it to other employees or consultants, e.g., a safety manager or safety consultant (*Wilsons & Clyde Coal Co* v *English* [1938] AC 57).

The employer's duty of care at common law may be examined under the three headings identified by the House of Lords in *Wilson & Clyde Coal Co* v

English (above). Lord Wright said these duties were to provide competent fellow employees, to provide proper and adequate machinery, and to provide a proper system of working. We might add a fourth – the duty to provide a reasonably safe place of work (including safe access and egress). We shall examine these in turn.

Competent staff It is often the case that the greatest source of danger in the workplace is one's fellow employees, a fact that the no longer applicable doctrine of common employment (see *Park* v *Wilson & Clyde Coal* 1928 SC 121) did nothing to alleviate. The employer has a duty to pick his employees with care, as an ill-trained or incompetent employee is more likely to be accident prone. Many jobs involve team work and the unfitness or incompetence of one employee may trigger an accident which involves other employees. Incompetence might arise from increasing age, illness or perhaps an addiction problem. It may seem harsh to dismiss an employee with long service because he is not as young as he was, but, if age has blunted his ability, the employer would have to consider the potential danger to fellow employees. There is of course also a continuing obligation on the part of the employer to make sure that employees are adequately trained in matters of safety.

Employees who perform practical jokes may present more danger than others. Once an employer becomes aware of a 'joker in the pack' there may be an obligation to warn the employee concerned as to his future conduct. It would be to the employer's advantage to make it clear that any repetition of behaviour which causes danger to fellow employees will result in summary dismissal. The employer will be liable for damage unless the activity complained of is not known to him or is such that it could not be foreseen by a reasonable person.

In *Hudson* v *Ridge Manufacturing Co Ltd* [1957] 2 All ER 229, Hudson, an employee of the defendants, sustained a broken arm as a result of a practical joke by a fellow employee about whose activities there had been previous complaints. The court held that the employers were liable. In the case of *Smith* v *Crossley Bros* (1951) 95 SJ 655, two playful apprentice motor mechanics held a third (Smith) on the floor and inserted a hose into one of his orifices. Not content with this indignity, the other end of the hose was attached to a cylinder of compressed air which was then turned on. Not surprisingly, Smith was seriously injured. His claim, however, against the employer for breach of duty of care was unsuccessful. The employer was not aware of this particular prank. On the evidence the court felt that such imbecilic behaviour was totally unpredictable and could not therefore be foreseen or guarded against. (It has been said that the decision shows how little the judge knew of apprentices.)

Instances of known bullying and initiation rites are examples of activities for which the employer might be liable if he took no action to prohibit or restrict them.

Proper and adequate machinery The employer is obliged to provide and maintain suitable plant and appliances. Machinery is of course something which is being modified and updated constantly. The employer however is under no obligation to purchase state of the art equipment. At common law employers were not liable for injuries caused by defective machinery etc. which had been obtained from a reputable supplier, provided that the defect was one which the employer could not discover. While there may have been some logic to this, it meant that the injured employee would have to sue the supplier/manufacturer. This was not always easy or indeed possible especially where the latter was untraceable or out of business. This situation was altered by the passing of the Employers' Liability (Defective Equipment) Act 1969 which gives an employee injured as a result of defective equipment the right to sue the employer, who will, under the Employers' Liability (Compulsory Insurance) Act 1969, be covered by statutorily compulsory insurance.

Provision of a proper system of working A proper system of working is a safe system. It concerns not so much machinery, premises, etc., but rather the uses to which these are put. It covers the obligation of the employer to instruct and train the employees in the use of the machinery and to provide and encourage the use of safety equipment. There will be a greater burden on the employer, particularly as regards instruction and training, where the employee concerned is young or inexperienced or suffers from some known physical disability. Whether or not a safe and proper system of work exists will depend on an objective test. What would a reasonable employer have provided? The attitude of the courts can be seen in some of the following cases.

In *Brown v John Mills & Co Ltd* (1970) 114 SJ 149, the plaintiff had only recently started his job, which involved polishing brass nuts. The method he used was to wrap a piece of emery cloth round his finger. The nuts to be polished were secured in a lathe which revolved at a high speed. He held the emery cloth against the nuts and, not surprisingly, was injured. The court held that the employers were liable for failing to provide a safe system of working, and, more specifically, failing to instruct a novice as to the correct procedure.

The situation will be different where the employee concerned is experienced and aware of the risk, as in *Woods v Durable Suites* [1953] 1 WLR 857. Woods was an experienced glue spreader, an occupation in which there was a high risk of contracting dermatitis. To prevent this the employers ran a poster campaign warning of the dangers and provided barrier cream and washing facilities. Woods was also told personally about both the risk and the precautions he should take but took no precautions, contracted dermatitis, and sued his employer for failing to provide a safe system of work. The court held that the employer was not liable given that they had provided both the instructions and the facilities.

The number of hours required to be worked by the employee may involve an improper or unsafe system of working. Many jobs, e.g. security guards, involve long shifts, frequently in excess of 12 hours. If the employee is required by contract to work such hours, can this be a breach of 'the duty of care'? In *Johnstone v Bloomsbury Health Authority* [1991] IRLR 118 CA, the employee, a senior house officer, had a standard working week of 40 hours. In addition he had to be 'on call' for an average of a further 48 hours. Some weeks he was required to work 105 hours. He had little sleep and suffered, he claimed, from stress and depression. He argued that this was a breach of the employer's duty to take reasonable care for his safety. Lord Justice Stuart-Smith held that although the contract gave the employer the discretion to require the employee to work such hours, that discretion had to be exercised in the light of other contractual terms, and in particular their duty to take care for his safety. The decision in *Johnstone* would seem to be counter to the traditional common law rule that an implied contract term cannot override a contrary express term. Indeed, Lord Justice Leggat's dissenting judgment holds this still to be true. The discretionary nature of the requirement to work overtime hours was important in *Johnstone*. It was this discretion that allowed the court to imply a duty to exercise reasonable care. The majority of the court held that they would have had no power to intervene if the number of hours overtime had been prescribed.

The duty of care has been extended beyond physical damage to psychiatric damage. In *Walker* v *Northumberland CC* [1995] IRLR 35, the employee had informed his employer that the increasing workload was causing him difficulty. The problem was not addressed and the employee suffered a mental breakdown. On his return to work he was promised assistance but this was soon withdrawn. Following a second mental breakdown, he was dismissed on the grounds of permanent ill health. The High Court held that the employer was in breach of his duty of care in respect of the second mental breakdown and that an employer owes a duty to his employees not to cause them psychiatric damage by the volume or character of the work they are required to perform. This is the first decision in which the well-established principle of the employer's duty to provide a safe system of work and to take reasonable steps to protect the employee from risks which are reasonably foreseeable has been applied to find an employer liable for mental, as opposed to physical, injury.
A reasonably safe place of work The employer must take steps to ensure that the workplace is safe. Not ony must the workplace itself be safe but also the means of access and egress. Staircases and exits are therefore covered by this duty. The employer has, however, only to take reasonable steps to ensure the workplace is safe. In *Latimer* v *AEC Ltd* [1953] AC 643, there was a torrential downpour which flooded a factory floor. The rainwater mixed with oil which was already present from machinery and made the floor slippery. The employer spread several tons of sand and sawdust but some of the floor was inadvertently untreated. Latimer slipped and was injured. His claim against the employer failed because the employer had done all that he could reasonably be expected to have done. The only other action he could have taken would have been to close the factory till the floor was dry. Such drastic and costly action was not justified by the degree of risk involved (see Chapter 4, para. 4.4). The (sometimes) dynamic nature of law can be seen in the way in which the legal implications of smoking at work and the effects of passive smoking have leapt from the law reports to newspapers and television. Employers should be aware that where they permit smoking at work they may be in breach of the obligation to provide a reasonably safe place of work. (For a discussion on the issues raised by smoking at work see ODonnell, 'Smoking at Work', 1993 BUSL.B 2.5.)

8.3.1.5 Employer's obligation to bring contingent rights to the attention of employees This is a fairly novel implied term, the potential impact of which has not yet been explored fully by the courts. In *Scally and Others* v *Southern Health and Social Services Board* [1991] IRLR 478, the plaintiffs were medical practitioners in the Northern Ireland health service. They sought to sue their employers for loss sustained by them, because the board had failed to inform them of their contractual right to purchase added years of pension entitlement. The right had to be exercised within a certain time. The plaintiffs learnt of the right only after the right had lapsed. They claimed that the board were in breach of an implied term of the contract by failing to inform them of their right to purchase added years. The House of Lords unanimously upheld the plaintiffs' claim. The fact that the contract had not been negotiated individually with the plaintiffs was significant. Lord Bridge said that while he recognised that the term sought to be implied was not necessary for business efficacy, it was one which was implied as a necessary incident of a contractual relationship. He went on to say that such a term would be implied where the contract has not been negotiated with an individual employee but contains valuable rights which the employee must take steps to avail himself of, but of which he would be unaware unless they were drawn to his attention. *Scally* demonstrates yet again the dynamic nature of the common law in employment relationships and that the 'classic' implied terms are no more than a base line.

8.3.1.6 Employers' defences in cases of breach of duty of care The mere fact of loss or injury to an employee will not of course mean that the employer is at fault (unless there is strict liability under statute). At common law the concept of *culpa* or fault still exists. There are various general defences available to the employer when sued for an alleged breach of duty of care.

Exercise of all reasonable care The employer may demonstrate that he had exercised all reasonable care and therefore could not be considered to have been negligent (see *Latimer* v *AEC* above).

Time barred The employer may be able to show that the employee's right of action has become time-barred by his failure to commence proceedings within the prescribed time limits as laid down in the Prescription and Limitation (Scotland) Act 1973). Any claim made by an employee for damages allegedly caused by breach of the employer's duty of care must be made within three years of the breach. It will often be the case that the breach complained of has resulted in an obvious injury (or death). In many instances however the result of the breach may not become apparent for many years, e.g., asbestosis and exposure to radiation. In such cases, the three year period will run from the date of discovery of the disease. There is also provision to extend the limitation period if the court believes that it is equitable to do so. The relevant sections of the 1973 Act are reproduced in the Cases and Materials section for Chapter 4.

Contributory negligence The employer may be able to show that the employee himself contributed in some material way to the loss or injury suffered. This is known as the defence of contributory negligence. At common law, if the employee contributed, even slightly, to the injury, then no damages could be recovered at all. This harsh doctrine was alleviated by the passing of the Law Reform (Contributory Negligence) Act 1945. The Act provides a formula for reducing the employee's award in proportion to the degree of blameworthiness. The courts have shown that they are aware of the boredom and tedium of many jobs and seem prone to excuse what strictly speaking would amount to contributory negligence. In the case of *Caswell* v *Powell Duffryn Associates Collieries Ltd* [1940] 1 WLR 401, Lord Wright said:

> What is all important is to adapt the standard of what is contributory negligence to the facts, and to give due regard to the actual conditions under which men work in a factory or mine, to the long hours and the fatigue, to the slackening of attention which comes naturally from constant repetition of the same operation, to the noise and confusion in which the man works, to his pre-occupation in what he is actually doing at the cost perhaps of some inattention to his own safety.

Lord Wright seems refreshingly in tune here with the reality of the work experience of many. The case of *Froom* v *Butcher* [1975] 3 All ER 520 is authority for the proposition that contributory negligence extends not only to the cause of the accident/injury but to all factors that have contributed to the degree of the damage. In *Froom*, the court held that failure to wear a seat belt amounted to contributory negligence. Lord Denning MR said:

> The *accident* is caused by the bad driving. The *damage* is caused in part by the bad driving of the defendant, and in part by the failure of the plaintiff to wear a seat belt.

This attitude is important because of the many accidents where the injuries sustained are worse than they otherwise would have been had, for example, safety clothes or equipment been used (see Chapter 4, para. 4.7.1 for the general rules).

Volenti The employer may be able to show that the employee freely consented to run the risk of being injured. This is expressed by the maxim *volenti non fit injuria* (to one who volunteers there can be no injury). The word 'injury' has the legal meaning of a legally wrongful act. Originally this doctrine meant that a worker who knew of the risk attaching to a job, but continued working, had assumed the risk himself, thereby absolving the employer from liability. This was, however, seen to be a fiction which ignored the harsh economic realities of everyday life. Many jobs are dangerous but have to be done; the employee may not have true freedom to choose only a safe job and there is a world of difference between knowing of the risks and actually consenting to being injured. As was said by Scott LJ in *Bowater* v *Rowley Regis Corporation* [1944] KB 479:

> a man cannot be said to be truly 'willing' unless he is in a position to choose freely, and freedom of choice predicates not only full knowledge of the

circumstances on which the exercise of choice is conditioned, so that he may be able to choose wisely, but the absence from his mind of any feeling of constraint so that nothing shall interfere with the freedom of his will.

The fact that danger money is accepted will not on its own constitute a defence of *volenti*. The payment is merely an indication that the work carries above average risks.

On grounds of public policy the defence of *volenti* will rarely be available where there is alleged to be a breach of an employer's statutory duty. An exception can be seen in *ICI* v *Shatwell* [1965] AC 656 where George Shatwell was one of three shot firers working together. One of the others was his brother James. By statute, the employer had a duty to issue instructions that the testing of detonating wire should only be carried out from a place of safety. The statute also imposed such a duty on the employees. The cable would not reach to the shelter so the third man went to obtain more, leaving the brothers behind. In his absence, the brothers tested the circuit in the open and were seriously injured by the subsequent explosion. George Shatwell sued ICI on the grounds that they were vicariously liable to him for James's negligence and breach of statutory regulations, claiming that these had caused his injuries. Lord Reid said:

If (Shatwell) invited or freely aided and abetted his fellow servant's disobedience, then he was *volens* in the fullest sense. He cannot complain of the resulting injury either against the fellow servant or against the master on the ground of his vicarious liability for his fellow servant's conduct.

The defence of *volenti* is never available when the breach of an absolute statutory duty is involved, e.g., the failure to fence adequately the dangerous parts of a machine under the Factories Act 1961, s. 14. Were this to be allowed the effect would be to neuter the statutory protection.

Remoteness The damage suffered by an employee may be too remote a consequence of the employer's negligence because it was not reasonably foreseeable as a consequence of the negligent act or omission. The potential consequences of any breach of duty are wide-ranging. The law will not hold an employer liable for everything which flows from his breach but only those consequences that are felt to be likely. The test to be applied is that of reasonable foreseeability as a natural and probable consequence of the defence's conduct, as laid down in *Overseas Tankship* v *Morts Dock* [1961] AC 388, rather than the test in *Re Polemis 1921* (liability for all loss that results directly from the breach).

In *Doughty* v *Turner Manufacturing Co* [1964] 1 QB 518, an asbestos cover was accidentally knocked into a cauldron of molten metal. This was likely to splash and it was foreseeable that anyone in the vicinity would be injured. What did in fact happen was that there was a violent explosion caused by a previously unknown chemical reaction between the metal and the asbestos. Doughty was injured in the explosion. The employers used the defence of remoteness. Doughty argued that being burned by an explosion was much the same as being burned by splashing (which was foreseeable) and the employer was liable. The Court of Appeal said the two were very different; splashing was foreseeable and would mean liability, an explosion was not foreseeable and meant there was no liability.

The decisions in some other cases appear to be more favourable to the injured party and seem to follow Lord Reid's reasoning in *Hughes* v *Lord Advocate* 1963 SC (HL) 31. This is not an employment case but the reasoning in such cases applies equally to employment cases. He said that if 'the accident was caused by a known source of danger, but caused in a way which could not have been foreseen . . . in my judgement that affords no defence'.

In *Smith* v *Leech Brain & Co Ltd* [1962] 2 QB 405, Smith, a crane driver, was struck on the lower lip by a piece of molten metal. This resulted in a burn which was the promoting agent of a cancer, which led to Smith's death three years later. The cancer developed in tissues which had a pre-malignant condition but might not have developed (at least for many years) had it not been for the burn. The employers were held liable, the risk of the burn being something any reasonable employer would have foreseen. As was said in *McKillen* v *Barclay Curle & Co* 1967 SLT 41 'the negligent party must take his victim as he finds him'. The medical condition or particular sensitivity on the part of the injured party is no defence. However, much will depend on the circumstances of the particular case. For example, in *Cowan* v *NCB* 1958 SLT (Notes) 19, it was said that death by suicide is neither a natural nor a direct result of a moderate eye injury but it might be a result of an injury which leaves an employee severely disabled, disfigured or mentally unbalanced.

The general rules as to liability in delict and remoteness are fully discussed in Chapter 4.

8.3.2 The employee's obligations at common law
As we saw earlier the obligation of the parties may arise by agreement, by statute or they may arise from common law. It is these common law or implied duties of the employee that we shall examine next.

8.3.2.1 Duty to provide personal service A core element of the employer/employee relationship is that of personal service. If this is lacking the relationship will be something different. In practice, this means that the employee must perform his duties himself. He cannot send someone else to do his work (unless of course he has his employer's prior permission). It is difficult to imagine circumstances where this would be the case.

8.3.2.2 Duty to obey reasonable orders If the employer refuses to obey orders he may be in breach of contract and lay himself open to summary dismissal. However, employment is not serfdom, the employee only has to obey reasonable orders and, almost by definition, any orders that are unlawful will be unreasonable. Examples that spring to mind include being told to drive a vehicle that has no M.O.T. or insurance or to drive at excessive speeds. It is of course no defence to a criminal charge to claim that you were acting under an employer's orders.

The employee need only obey orders which relate to his contractual duties. The contract or list of agreed duties may include some catch-all clause like 'to assist as required'. Such a clause would not, however, oblige an employee to carry out work for which he was untrained or unqualified. In *Price* v *Mouat* (1862) 11 CB (NS), a lace buyer was ordered to card lace. This was held to be an unreasonable order which involved a lowering of the employee's status (see 8.6 below for the effect of such an order in relation to redundancy). The reality of economic life will, however, mean that an employee may think twice before disobeying an order which he sees as going beyond what he was employed to do.

We saw in *Johnstone* (8.3.1.4 above) that the requirement to work excessive hours may be a breach of duty of care on the part of the employer. What is excessive is, of course, a matter of degree. The mere fact that the employee is required to work beyond his contracted hours may not involve breach of duty of care and a refusal may well result in the employee breaching his duty to obey reasonable orders. This was the situation in *Smith* v *St. Andrews Ambulance Service* [1972] (NIRC) (unreported), where an ambulance driver had refused to pick up a seriously ill child because doing so would take him over his working day.

In *Donovan* v *Invicta Airlines* [1970] 1 Lloyd's Rep. 486 CA, an order to fly an unsafe aircraft was held to be unreasonable; in contrast, an order to firemen to cross traffic lights at red was held to be reasonable, even if not lawful at the time (*Buckoke and Others* v *GLC* [1971] ICR 655). A common source of irritation is when the employee is ordered to work at a different location. He may find this inconvenient, as in *O'Brien* v *Associated Fire Alarms Ltd* [1968] 1 WLR 1916, where the court held that men who lived in Liverpool and had been hired in Liverpool could impliedly be obliged to obey orders to work in Liverpool and its environs, but certainly not Barrow.

More than inconvenience and domestic upheaval may be at issue, as can be seen in two cases heard on the same day involving Ottoman Bank. In *Bouzourou* v *Ottoman Bank* [1930] AC 271, a Christian employee was held obliged to obey an order to work in Turkey despite the accepted hostility of the authorities there to Christianity. In contrast, in *Ottoman Bank* v *Chakarian* [1930] AC 277, an order to an Armenian employee, who had been sentenced to death by the Turkish authorities, to work in Istanbul was held to be unreasonable. The difference would seem to be that in the first case the danger was of a general nature while in *Chakarian* the risk was more specific (and indeed greater). So, in *Walmsley* v *UDEC Refrigeration Ltd* [1972] IRLR 80, an order to work in Ireland was held to be reasonable. A general fear of IRA activity did not justify refusal.

It will be to the advantage of both employer and employee if there is specific reference to mobility in the contract. However, as Government Departments have discovered in the past, even where this exists, there may be widespread refusal to move, e.g., the attempted Civil Service dispersals to Glasgow in the 1970s. Even where there is a specific reference to a mobility clause in the contract, the case of *United Bank Ltd* v *Akhtar* [1991] IRLR 507 is authority for the view that such a clause must be interpreted as including the implied requirement that reasonable notice of transfer be given, and that the employer's discretion to make relocation and other allowances be exercised in such a way as to make it possible for the employee to comply with his contractual obligation to transfer. In *White* v *Reflecting Roadstuds* [1991] IRLR 331, the EAT said that Akhtar did not imply a term that the employer should act reasonably but merely that when dealing with a mobility clause the employer should not exercise his discretion in such a way as to prevent his employee from being able to carry out this part of the contract. Mobility clauses may involve unlawful sex discrimination (see below 8.8.2.3).

An employee will also be required to obey orders which relate to new methods of working, as in *Cresswell* v *Board of Inland Revenue* [1984] IRLR 190, where the plaintiff, who was a tax officer, refused to cooperate with a changeover from manual operation to a computerised system. Walton J said that while he understood,

> all of us, being conservative (with a small c) by nature desire nothing better than to be left to deepen our accustomed ruts, and hate change . . . (nevertheless) there can really be no doubt as to the fact that an employee is expected to adapt himself to new methods and techniques introduced in the course of his employment.

A well drafted contract of employment would allow many of the changes that will obviously be required over time.

It would of course be regarded as an unreasonable order if an employee was ordered, for example, to falsify the accounts in order to cover up a discrepancy, as in *Morris* v *Henlys (Folkestone) Ltd* [1973] ICR 482. This type of situation is one which employees employed as book-keepers, accounts clerks or accountants might come across. However, in the less extreme cases of justified refusal to obey an order, it may be dangerous to do so. The only remedy if such a refusal results in dismissal is an award of damages and the giving of notice or payment of wages in lieu of notice normally satisfies liability under that head. The employee may also be able to avail himself of the protection afforded by the law on unfair dismissal (see below).

8.3.2.3   Duty to render faithful service   The employee is under an obligation to render faithful service. The employee should make no secret profits, should not accept bribes nor disclose trade secrets or confidential information to third parties. An employee must not work for trade competitors in any situation where there is likely to be a conflict of interests. The courts will enforce reasonable covenants in restraint of trade imposed by an employer upon his former employees (see Chapter 3, para. 3.9.3). These aspects of the duty of faithful service are elaborated below.

Secret profits   It will be regarded as abuse of the employee's position if he makes secret profits from the exercise of his employment. In *Boston Fishing & Ice Co* v *Ansell* (1888) 39 ChD 339 CA, Ansell, who was employed as managing director of the plaintiffs, contracted with shipbuilders for the construction and supply of vessels. He received a secret commission from the shipbuilders. This was held to be a breach of his duty to his employer.

Lord Normand summed up the situation as he saw it, in *Reading v A-G* [1951] AC 507, when he said '(A soldier) owes the Crown a duty as fully fiduciary as the duty of a servant to his master and in consequence . . . all profits gained by the use of his status are for the benefit of the Crown'.

Use of information   In the course of his employment, the employee (depending on the nature of his work) may well come across information which might be regarded as sensitive and confidential. At one extreme this might include new manufacturing processes and inventions but it would also include more mundane details like who the firm's customers are, what they buy, and how quickly they pay their bills. This type of information would be of value to the firm's competitors or indeed to an employee wishing to set up in competition with the firm. The law recognises that competition exists and must be allowed to exist and similarly that the employee may wish to better himself by moving to another employer, or indeed to set up in business on his own. An employee is not, however, allowed to do so 'on the back of his ex-employer', for example, setting up the basis of a rival company while still employed.

A *former* employee will be able to use information that he has acquired while an employee. It would of course be impossible to prevent an ex-employee from exercising skill acquired during employment in the service of another employer, e.g., in the case of an apprentice or trainee. The leading case on the matter is *Faccenda Chicken Ltd v Fowler* [1987] Ch 117 (see the Cases and Materials section for Chapter 8). The approach adopted in *Faccenda* has been followed in Scotland in *Harben Pumps Ltd v Lafferty* 1989 SLT 752. An employee who submits a tender for the future business of his employer's customers would breach the duty of faithful service (*Adamson v BEL Cleaning Services Ltd* [1995] IRLR 193).

Use of free time   Generally speaking the courts feel that what an employee does in his free time is his own affair and they are reluctant to interfere (*Nova Plastics v Froggett* [1982] IRLR 146). Normally then, an employee is allowed to 'moonlight' unless the strain of the second job leaves him unable to perform the first (*Currie v Glasgow Central Stores Ltd* 1905 12 SLT 651 OH). There may, however, be situations where the courts will interfere. An example can be seen in the case of *Hivac v Park Royal Scientific Instruments Ltd* [1946] Ch 169, where employees of the plaintiffs, who manufactured electronic components for hearing aids, worked for the defendants (who were business rivals) at the weekend. The court granted the plaintiffs an injunction because of breach of the implied duty to render faithful service.

Inventions   The position as regards inventions is governed by the Patents Act 1977 and the Copyright, Designs and Patents Act 1988. Basically this states that an invention will belong to the employer if it is made in the course of the duties for which the employee was normally employed or where it could reasonably be expected that an invention would result. So ICI would own the rights to a new wonder drug discovered by one of their research chemists if that was the work he was employed to do. However, if the drug were discovered by an office worker with no research function the invention would belong to the employee (Patents Act 1977, s. 39(1), (2) and (3)).

It is the practice for many employers to have suggestion boxes for employees, and for those suggestions that result in cost savings to earn a payment for the employee. Unless specific provision is made, it does not necessarily follow from the payment that the right to the invention passes to the employer.

In the case of *Reiss Engineering Co Ltd* v *Harris* [1985] IRLR 232, Falconer J was faced with a situation where Harris, the manager of a valve department, invented an improved valve. The judge said that 'normal duties' as laid down in the Patents Act are those you are actually employed to carry out. Harris was not employed as a designer or inventor, therefore the invention was his.

Industrial action The question of whether an employee could be said to render faithful service when he is involved in a work to rule was explored in the case of *Secretary of State for Employment* v *ASLEF (No.2)* [1972] 2 All ER 949. In that case, railway employees were working to rule and the Secretary of State had a statutory power to order a ballot or 'cooling-off' period where there was 'irregular action short of a strike'. The problem that faced the court was whether it could be argued that workers who were obeying their employer's rules in minute detail were at the same time in breach of the duty of faithful service. The court held that the work to rule was a breach of this duty.

Reporting misconduct In *Swain* v *West (Butchers) Ltd* [1936] 3 All ER 261 (CA) Greene LJ said:

> It was submitted to us that there was some general principle of law applicable to contracts of service in general . . . that a servant is under no duty to disclose the improper conduct of a fellow servant. I am unable to accept such a proposition . . . whether there is such a duty will depend on the circumstances of each particular case.

An employee who was asked a direct question would, however, be under a duty not to mislead (but see the Rehabilitation of Offenders Act 1974 below 8.5.2.2).

Much will depend on the position of the individual in the organisation. Is he, for example, a manager or supervisor? Stephenson LJ, in *Sybron Corporation* v *Rochem Ltd* [1983] IRLR 253, said that, although there might be no duty on an employer to disclose his own misconduct, he had a duty to report the misdeeds of others, especially where he was senior enough to realise that what they were doing was wrong and he was responsible for reporting on their activities. This would be the case even where such disclosure involved self-incrimination.

Duty to exercise reasonable care The employee is under an obligation to exercise reasonable care in the execution of the work in which he claims to be skilled. The employee should be able to carry out his work with reasonable proficiency. If the employee is incapable through incompetence, laziness, etc., the employer will have justification for dismissal. In *Harmer* v *Cornelius* (1858) 5 CB(NS) 236, Harmer responded to an advert for a scene painter and enclosed what he claimed to be some samples of his work. In actual fact he had never before painted scenes and this soon became evident. It was held that the employer was entitled to dismiss him without notice.

The requisite standard of care was discussed in *Superlux* v *Plaister, The Times,* 12 December 1958, it was said that an employee must take as much care of his employer's goods and interests as he would his own. (See *Secretary of State for Employment* v *ASLEF (No. 2)* above.) The defendant, who was a salesman, left 14 vacuum cleaners in his van overnight. They were stolen and it was held that he was in breach of his duty of care to the employer. The employer may seek to be reimbursed for any losses he had incurred because of the employee's breach. In *Janata Bank* v *Ahmed* [1981] IRLR 457 CA, the employer was successful in claiming the return of £34,640 which had negligently been given as overdrafts to customers who were unable to repay.

Where an employee is in breach of the duty to exercise reasonable care, the employer may use an indemnity against claims from injured third parties (see *Lister* v *Romford Ice and Cold Storage Co Ltd* [1957] AC 555). In reality this is unlikely to happen unless there is strong evidence of collusion. The *Lister* case does not lay down as a proposition of general application that every time an employee drives a vehicle during the course of his employment there is an implied agreement to indemnify the employer for any losses. In *Harvey* v *O'Dell* [1958] 2 QB 78, a storeman was asked to transport another worker on his (the storekeeper's) motorbike. Following an accident it was held that the claim for him to indemnify the employer did not exist because the storekeeper had not been hired as a driver at all.

8.4 TERMINATION OF THE CONTRACT OF EMPLOYMENT

There are several ways in which a contract of employment may be terminated. A contract of employment is just that, a contract, and therefore it can be terminated in the same way as any other contract (see Chapter 3). We shall look at some of these with specific reference to employment.

8.4.1 Termination by performance, agreement or frustration
A contract of employment may be terminated in any of the following ways.

(a) By performance of the contractual obligations. An example would be where an employee is engaged to deliver a yacht or carry out building work. The leading case is *Wiltshire County Council* v *NATFHE* [1980] IRLR 198 CA where Lord Denning said at p. 200:

> if there is a contract by which a man is to do a particular task or carry out a particular purpose, then when that task or purpose comes to an end the contract is discharged by performance. Instances may be taken of a seaman who is employed for the duration of the voyage – and it is completely uncertain how long the voyage will last. His engagement comes to an end on its completion.

Lord Denning gives another example and goes on to say:

In neither of these instances is there a contract for a fixed term. It is a contract which is discharged by performance. There is no 'dismissal'. A contract for a particular purpose, which is fulfilled, is discharged by performance and does not amount to a dismissal.

(b) By mutual agreement between the parties including the giving of notice. It will often be the case that the contract of employment will expressly provide for a given period of notice. If so it must be observed, unless it is less than the statutory minimum laid down in the Employment Protection (Consolidation) Act 1978 in which case that minimum would apply.

(c) By impossibility of performance. It may be that the purpose of the contract has become 'frustrated'. This will be for example where either employer or employee is unable to carry out their part of the contract due to circumstances beyond their control (see 3.13.1 above).

Usually frustration will arise because of the inability on the part of the employee to carry out his duties. Two situations where frustration may arise are ill health or imprisonment. In *Condor* v *Barron Knights Ltd* [1966] 1 WLR 87, Condor, who was aged 16, was employed in December as a drummer in a band on condition that he performed seven nights a week. In January he collapsed and was forbidden by his doctor from working more than four nights a week. He was dismissed and sued for wrongful dismissal but Thomson J said there was no wrongful dismissal in this case because 'at the relevant date . . . the situation was that Condor was not fit to perform his part of the contract and at that date there was no reasonable likelihood that he would in the near future become so able'. A contract will not be frustrated on account of a minor (and short lasting) illness nor will it be frustrated where there is a contractual entitlement to sick pay from the employer and it seems likely that the employee will return to work before this entitlement runs out (see *Egg Stores (Stamford Hill) Ltd* v *Leibovici* [1977] ICR 260).

Whether or not a contract will be frustrated by imprisonment will depend on the circumstances. In *O'Hare* v *Murphy Bros* [1974] ICR 603, O'Hare received a twelve month sentence for assault. It was held that although the offence itself could not be a frustrating event, because frustration must be due to an occurrence for which neither party is liable (which could not be said of the offence) the sentence, which was not self-induced, was the real frustrating event. The law would seem to be that the contract is frustrated from the time of the sentence regardless of the fact that there is an appeal (even a successful one as in (*Harrington* v *Kent County Council* [1980] IRLR 353).

Other frustrating events have included military call up (see *Morgan* v *Manser* [1948] 1 KB 184) and internment during wartime (see *Unger* v *Preston Corporation* [1942] 1 All ER 200). Generally speaking, however, there has been a reluctance on the part of the courts to hold that frustration has occurred because termination through frustration does not amount to statutory dismissal and the result may be the ability on the part of the employer to sidestep the employment protection legislation. In *Williams* v *Watsons Luxury Coaches* [1990] IRLR 164, the EAT listed the factors that should be considered in deciding if frustration has occurred. These included length of service, nature of job, nature of illness and the need for a replacement employee.

A contract of employment will also be terminated on the death of either party, which may be of some minor comfort to the employee with an unpleasant job or the employer with a troublesome workforce. Similarly it will terminate on the dissolution of a partnership but not by a mere change in the constitution of a firm (*Hoey* v *McEwen & Auld* 1867 5 M 814). The same consequences result from the compulsory winding up of a company by order of the court or a resolution for voluntary winding up on the grounds of insolvency. Straightforward cessation of business would have the same effect but the rules applying in the case of a transfer of a business have been modified by the Transfer of Undertakings (Protection of Employment) Regulations 1981 which allow for the automatic transfer of contracts in certain cases (see 8.6.4 below).

8.4.2 Termination by summary dismissal

The contract may be terminated by summary dismissal, that is dismissal without notice, or without compensation in lieu of notice. This is a very serious step to take and will be justified in only the most extreme cases. If the employer is not justified in so dismissing the employee then the dismissal will amount to wrongful dismissal and the dismissed employee may sue the employer for damages representing the loss of wages, tips and perks that would have been earned by the employee during the period of notice that ought to have been given. Actions for wrongful dismissal are a form of action for breach of contract (see Chapter 3, para. 3.14). A wrongful dismissal may also be deemed to be an unfair dismissal within the meaning of the Employment Protection (Consolidation) Act 1978 (see 8.8 below). In such cases it would almost always be more financially beneficial for the employee to claim for unfair rather than wrongful dismissal.

8.4.3 Grounds for summary dismissal

There is no simple check list of what will or will not permit summary dismissal. The exact circumstances must be taken into account. In *Sinclair* v *Neighbour* [1967] 2 QB 279, the manager of a betting shop borrowed £15 from the till replacing it the next morning, when such an act was expressly forbidden. The court said summary dismissal will be justified where the employees breach is 'incompatible with the contract of service so as to preclude further satisfactory continuance of the relationship'. Essentially there must be a loss of the basic trust and confidence that the law feels should exist between employer and employee. Grounds could include the following.

(a) Where the employee has concealed material facts at the time of being appointed (*Torr* v *British Railways Board* [1977] IRLR 185). It should, however, be noted that a contract of employment is not *uberrimae fidei* (of the utmost good faith) and the employee is not therefore obliged to disclose information that is disadvantageous, e.g., previous convictions, unless he is specifically asked (see Chapter 3).

(b)   Refusal to obey lawful and reasonable orders (see 8.2.1 above). The employer must establish that the disobedience was in response to a lawful and reasonable order. Examples would include a manager's refusal to attend a company meeting (*Lambsdale* v HMSO [1975] IRLR 239), or a nurse's refusal to attend patients (*Oxley* v *East Berkshire Health Authority* 1983 00935/LN/A) or where a hospital porter refused to empty bins (*Riley* v *Kirklees Area Health Authority* 1977 24010/77. In the last case the judge said, 'it is not uncommon to hear a stand on "principle", but it often turns out to be more a matter of obstinacy rather than a genuine principle'.

(c)   A serious breakdown in the employer/employee relationship which makes continued employment impossible. In *Pepper* v *Webb* [1969] 1 WLR 13, a gardener who had for some time been insolent and inefficient refused to plant some flowers saying he 'couldn't care less about your bloody greenhouse and sodding garden'. His summary dismissal was justified. In *Wilson* v *Racher* [1974] ICR 428, the facts were similar but the incident was a one-off and not regarded so seriously and therefore summary dismissal was unlawful. Once again the test as to whether the conduct complained of will justify dismissal has to be decided objectively i.e. there is no longer the mutual trust and confidence expected of the employer/employee relationship.

(d)   Where the employee shows gross incompetence in work in which skill was claimed. Once again much will depend on the circumstances, length of service and the previous record of the employee will be considered. In certain circumstances, one mistake may be held to be one too many, as in *Alidair* v *Taylor* [1978] ICR 445 where a pilot was dismissed for landing a plane badly and damaging it (see 8.5.2.1 below), i.e. is there no longer the mutual trust and confidence expected of the employer/employee relationship.

(e)   Serious misconduct such as fraud, theft, drunkenness and sexual immorality may all justify summary dismissal. The employee should be aware that there may be grounds for summary dismissal even where the conduct complained of occurs in the employee's own time. Except on the rarest occasions, theft or fraud at work has justified dismissal, even where the amount concerned is trifling as in *Brown* v *S.E. Hampshire Health Authority* 1983 21785/33 where 50p worth of vegetables were involved. A recent example was a cleaner who was dismissed for eating a leftover 'After Eight' mint (she was reinstated after an internal appeal). If the employer feels that the out of hours conduct of an employee will harm the business then dismissal may be justified. A university professor's affair with a student was held to be conduct which would make students think twice about applying to the university and this justified his dismissal (*Orr* v *University of Tasmania* 1957 100 CLR 856). A conviction for indecency justified dismissal in *Croffield* v *BBC* [1975] IRLR 23 and the dismissal of a bus driver because of his conviction for shoplifting was also justified (*Singh* v *London Country Bus Services Ltd* [1976] ITR 131).

In the case of serious misconduct, the test would seem to be whether the employee's conduct is detrimental to the reputation of the business or suggests that there is some weakness in him that makes him unfit for work.

It has been argued that to dismiss an employee who has been convicted of some (often) minor offence means that he is being punished twice. The employer has of course different interests to protect from those of the state. Regard should be had to the ACAS Code of Practice No 1 before deciding on such dismissals. *Securicor Guarding* v *R* [1994] IRLR 633 reinforces the code's view that the mere fact that an employee has been charged with an offence will not justify dismissal. This will be more so where (as in the case) the employee has denied the charges. The test would seem to be either unsuitability for the type of work (*P* v *Nottinghamshire CC* [1992] IRLR 363 or unacceptability to fellow employees, customers, etc. (*Bradshaw* v *Rugby Portland Cement* [1972] IRLR 46.) If unacceptability to customers is argued, the employer must be able to lead convincing evidence of this (*Grootcon* v *Keld* [1984] IRLR 302).

8.4.4 Reasons for dismissal

Until 28 February 1972, when the provisions of the Industrial Relations Act 1972 concerned with unfair dismissal first came into force, any employee dismissed with notice or with pay in lieu of notice had no legal redress whatever the reason for the dismissal. With a few exceptions, an employer had no legal obligation to give an employee any reason at all for the dismissal.

The Employment Act 1989, s. 15, now provides that an employee with not less than two years' continuous service is entitled to be provided by his employer, on request, with a written statement of the reasons for dismissal.

8.5 UNFAIR DISMISSAL

Ever since 28 February 1972 an employee (subject to certain exceptions) has had a general legal right not to be unfairly dismissed by his employer. If employees consider that they have been unfairly dismissed they may complain to an industrial tribunal. The right to claim for unfair dismissal is now contained in the Employment Protection (Consolidation) Act 1978 (EPCA) (as amended by the Employment Acts of 1980, 1982 and 1988, the Sex Discrimination Act 1986, the Trade Union and Labour Relations (Consolidation) Act 1992 and the Trade Union Reform and Employment Rights Act 1993). Section 54 of EPCA provides 'In every employment to which this section applies every employee shall have the right not to be unfairly dismissed by his employer'.

A claimant must prove his eligibility. The law on unfair dismissal only applies to employees, not to the self-employed. Claimants must establish that they have been employed by the employer in question for at least two years. The requirement of two years' service has recently been held by the Court of Appeal to involve indirect sex discrimination (see 8.8.2.3 below). The Government is, however, unlikely to better the period (which is longer than other EU states until the House of Lords have heard the Appeal. The case will almost certainly also be appealed to the ECJ. Claimants must not be over normal retiring age, members of the police service (this includes prison wardens), share fishermen, ordinarily resident outside Great Britain or employed on a fixed term contract where they have waived their rights. No claim can be made if the employment is covered by a collective agreement relating to compensation for unfair dismissal. Employees who have been dismissed for trade union related reasons may claim even if they do not have enough service and/or they are over the normal retiring age. Employees dismissed for sex or race reasons need not have the service qualification, nor do those dismissed for a reason connected with a transfer of an undertaking.

It is up to the employee to show that there has been a dismissal. Dismissal is defined for the purposes of the legislation in EPCA, s. 55(2).

... an employee shall be treated as dismissed by his employer if, but only if,

(a) the contract under which he is employed by the employer is terminated by the employer, whether it is so terminated by notice or without notice, or

(b) where under that contract he is employed for a fixed term, that term expires without being renewed under the same contract, or

(c) the employee terminates that contract, with or without notice, in circumstances such that he is entitled to terminate it without notice by reason of the employer's conduct. This is known as constructive dismissal (see 8.5.1 below).

8.5.1 Constructive dismissal

The legislation therefore covers not only cases where employers dismiss employees but also those situations where employees leave because there has been what they regard as a serious breach of contract by their employer. What we are talking about is constructive dismissal, when the employer shows by words or actions that there is no longer any intention of abiding by the implied or express terms of the agreement. Examples would include reduction in pay or status, sexual harassment, removal of privileges, and unreasonable use of mobility clauses. The onus is on the employee to show that the behaviour complained of justified leaving. This may be difficult to establish.

There are many different examples of circumstances which have entitled an employee to terminate a contract and regard that termination as equivalent to dismissal. In *Western Excavating Ltd* v *Sharp* [1978] 1 All ER 713, the employee was dismissed for taking an afternoon off work. This was reduced to 5 days suspension without pay. He asked for an advance of his holiday pay, failing which a loan; both were refused. The employee resigned to get his holiday pay and then claimed he had been constructively dismissed. The Court of Appeal found that there was no constructive dismissal saying that an employee can only argue constructive dismissal when the employer has breached the contract in some fundamental way. This was not the case here as there was no contractual entitlement to either advance holiday pay or a loan.

In *Isle of Wight Tourist Board* v *Coombes* [1976] IRLR 413, the director of the Tourist Board said in the prescence of clients that his secretary was an intolerable bitch on a Monday morning. The secretary was present. She resigned and claimed constructive dismissal. Her claim was successful as it was obvious that there was no longer trust and respect between them as evidenced by the director's remark.

Constructive dismissal was at issue in the *Dryden* case (see 8.3.1.3). The EAT found that there was no express contractual provison entitling Dryden to smoke at work. Nor could it be argued that there was an implied term relating to smoking. It had been suggested in *Wayson* v *Cooke, Webb* v *Molton* CO1T 13852/84, that the introduction of a ban on smoking was a wholly new contractual term, but Dryden conceded that the no smoking ban was a matter of work rules rather than a wholly new contractual term. Dryden submitted that the employers had acted in breach of an implied term that they should not act in such a way as to prevent her from carrying out her part of the contract. Additionally, the employers had breached the implied term that they would do nothing to damage the mutual trust and confidence between the parties. The employers argued that there had been no material breach of the contract because they were entitled to introduce a change of rules. This they had done, but reasonably, and after due consultation. The *Dryden* case was concerned with the claim that a change in rules governing behaviour (smoking) in the workplace which affects all employees is a repudiatory breach of contract in relation to one employee. The EAT were in no doubt that an employer is entitled to make rules for the conduct of employees. Further, there was no rule that where an employer introduces a rule which applies equally to all employees but has a disproportionate effect on one employee, or with which one employee cannot comply, that the introduction of such a rule would amount to a repudiation of the employee's contract. The decision in *Dryden* was based on the facts of the case and does not establish any general precedent.

It would seem from the cases where constructive dismissal has been an issue that the employer's conduct must amount to a fundamentally serious breach of contract before the employee can claim he has been constructively dismissed.

8.5.2 When is dismissal unfair?

Almost every employee who is dismissed will see his dismissal as 'unfair' because he has lost his job. Whether or not his dismissal will be 'unfair' in the eyes of the law is another matter. As Phillips J said, in *Devis & Sons Ltd* v *Atkins* [1976] ICR 196, 'The expression 'unfair dismissal' is in no sense a common expression capable of being understood by the man in the street'.

The employer has the onus of proving that the reason for the dismissal was a fair one in the circumstances of the particular case (see *Proctor* v *British Gypsum* [1992] IRLR 7). Whether or not any particular dismissal is fair or not is a matter of fact for the industrial tribunal to determine. Initially there were fears on the part of employers that under the legislation they would never be able to dismiss an employee. These fears were the result of hysteria spread by those who did not approve of the tacit acceptance the legislation gave to the property right the employee has in his job. In any case these fears proved groundless and it is questionable how effective the legislation has been. The legislation originally gave five potentially fair reasons which justify dismissal, two automatically unfair reasons, and two automatically fair reasons. These have been added to by the Trade Union Reform and Employment Rights Act 1993.

8.5.2.1 Potentially fair grounds for dismissal   For these reasons to be actually fair the tribunal must conclude that the employer acted reasonably in treating them as justifying dismissal.

Capability or qualifications   This is really two separate reasons. Capability is defined in EPCA, s. 57(4)(a) as including 'skills, aptitude, health or any other physical or mental quality'. Any other physical or mental quality would potentially cover a very wide range of employee attributes. It would seem that the employer need not prove incompetence or incapability. Lord Denning said in *Alidair* v *Taylor* [1978] ICR 445:

> Whenever a man is dismissed for incapacity or incompetence it is sufficient that the employer honestly believes on reasonable grounds that the man is incapable or incompetent. It is not necessary for the employer to prove that he was in fact incapable or incompetent.

In this case one error was held to be evidence of lack of capability. Taylor was an airline pilot who landed the plane in such a way as to cause concern to both passengers and crew. It was decided he had been negligent and he was dismissed. His dismissal was held to be fair. A warning would have been inappropriate, because there are duties in which the degree of professional skill which must be exercised and the potential consequences of the smallest departure from that high standard are so serious that one failure is enough to justify the dismissal. Normally the employer will have to show some pattern of incapability; the employee should be warned about his performance and given the opportunity to improve. This will be especially true in the case of probationary employees (*The Post Office* v *Mughal* [1977] ICR 763), although such probationers will in most cases be outwith the provisions of the legislation unless they have continuity of employment for some reason.

Ill health may also be grounds for lack of capability. The employer is allowed to consider his own business needs as well as those of the employee. In *Coulson* v *Felixstowe Dock and Rail Co Ltd* [1975] IRLR 11, Coulson was off ill for considerable periods. He was unable to carry out his normal job and was given clerical work. He was told that if he was not fit to return to his old job he would have to be regraded. He was given six months to prove his fitness. He was ill again and the employer dismissed him. It was held that the dismissal was fair.

It is unfair to dismiss an employee because of the possibility of future illness unless the nature of the work is such that it would be dangerous for the employee and fellow employees. In *Converform (Darwen) Ltd* v *Bell* [1981] IRLR 195, Bell was a works director who was off work due to a heart attack and whose employers refused to allow him back after recovery, as they were afraid he might have another attack. His subsequent dismissal was held to be unfair. It might have been different had he been, for example, an airline pilot.

Both long-term illness and persistent short-term illness may justify dismissal. Whatever the length or nature of the illness, the employers will be expected to reach a fair decision having taken all relevant circumstances into account. Some things for consideration include the needs of the business; the nature of the illness; the likely period of absence; availability of medical reports; availability of alternative work.

Qualifications are defined in EPCA, s. 57(4)(b) to mean any degree, diploma or other academic, technical or professional qualification relevant to the position which the employee held. In *Blackman v The Post Office* [1974] IRLR 46 NIRC, a telegraph officer was required to pass an aptitude test. He failed to do so after the maximum number of attempts. It was held that his subsequent dismissal for lack of qualifications was fair. Qualifications could include the possession of a clean driving licence. In *Tayside Regional Council v McIntosh* [1982] IRLR 272, McIntosh obtained a job as a motor mechanic. The advertisement specified the need for a driving licence. McIntosh had a licence at the time of appointment but he was subsequently disqualified and was dismissed because the employer had no alternative employment. It was held that his dismissal was fair because even though his contract made no mention of the need to hold a driving licence, it was clearly called for by the nature of the job (cf. *Litster v Thom & Sons Ltd* [1975] IRLR 147).

Conduct. Conduct covers a wide range which is probably why there is no statutory definition. Conduct both inside and outside working hours may be relevant. In *Thomson v Alloa Motor Co Ltd* [1983] IRLR 403 EAT, it was said that conduct within the meaning of EPCA, s. 57(2) means actions of such a nature, whether done in the course of employment or not, that reflect in some way upon the employer/employee relationship. In *Dalton v Burton's Gold Medal Biscuits Ltd* [1974] IRLR 45 NIRC, the court said that what is gross misconduct (given the absence of a legal definition) is a matter of fact to be determined by the industrial tribunal. Examples of misconduct which have been held to justify dismissal include refusing to obey reasonable orders, dishonesty, drunkenness, fighting, sexual immorality, breaches of safety regulations, absenteeism, disloyalty, and taking unlawful drugs.

In deciding whether a dismissal on grounds of conduct is fair the tribunal will examine the seriousness of the offence, and the employee's disciplinary history. In *United Distillers v Conlin* [1992] IRLR 503, the employee had been warned about his abuse of the bonus system and had received a final warning. He was accused of a similar offence shortly after. The EAT said that the dismissal was the inevitable result of the repetition of an offence soon after being giving a final warning. The fact that the value of the fraud was only £3 was immaterial. A different approach is needed depending on whether the misconduct is minor or major. While it may be fair to dismiss for acts of major misconduct, it will probably not be for acts of minor misconduct unless they are recurrent and the employee has been warned as to the consequences of his misconduct. Ideally warnings should be given and the employee should be aware of what will constitute gross misconduct. However, there will be circumstances where certain misconduct will obviously lead to dismissal. In *Ulsterbus v Henderson* [1989] IRLR 253, the Northern Ireland Court of

Appeal upheld the dismissal of a bus conductor who had failed to issue tickets in return for fares. O'Donnell LJ said 'failure to give tickets was a most serious offence . . . likely to lead to dismissal . . . obvious to any employee'. This seems sensible in that it would be impossible to list all the offences that would lead to dismissal. This is particularly true given advances in technology that increase the variety of misconduct available (see *Denco* v *Joinson* below). Conduct has been held to extend to dress. In *Boychuk* v *H.J. Symons Ltd* [1977] IRLR 395, Boychuk was a clerk who dealt with the public. She wore badges which proclaimed she was a lesbian. She was warned to remove them but refused. Her subsequent dismissal was held to be fair. The employer was entitled to take into account the feelings of the public and fellow employees. It should be noted, however, that she was not dismissed because she was a lesbian. Care should be taken with dress related dismissals lest they are discriminatory (*Smith* v *Safeway plc* [1995] IRLR 132 where it was held that the dismissal of a male employee who wore his hair in a 'pony-tail' was discriminatory). The cases that follow are some examples from the categories of misconduct already mentioned.

In *Trust House Forte Hotels* v *Murphy* [1977] IRLR 186 EAT, Murphy was a night porter who was supplied with a small stock of liquor for hotel guests. There was a stock discrepancy of £10. He admitted that he had consumed some of the liquor. The Employment Appeal Tribunal held his dismissal to be fair. In *Singh* v *London Country Bus Services Ltd* (1976) ITR 131, the employee, who drove a one man bus, was convicted of shoplifting. His subsequent dismissal was held to be fair. Also, in *Moore* v *C & A Modes* [1981] IRLR 71 the employee had been employed with C & A for 20 years. She was accused of shoplifting (which she admitted), from another store. Her dismissal was also held to be fair.

In *Neefjes* v *Crystal Products Co Ltd* [1972] IRLR 118, the employee assaulted a fellow employee at work. He was dismissed and his dismissal was held to be fair, especially in light of the fact that he had previously been warned in writing about his conduct (see also *Parsons (C & A) Ltd* v *McLoughlin* [1978] IRLR 65 EAT). In *Gardiner* v *Newport County Borough Council* [1974] IRLR 262, the employee was a lecturer in an art college many of his students were aged between 16 and 18. He was convicted of gross indecency in a public toilet. His subsequent dismissal was held to be fair (see also *Nottinghamshire County Council* v *Bowly* [1978] IRLR 252 EAT). In *Bradshaw* v *Rugby Portland Cement Co Ltd* [1972] IRLR 46, however, the employee was dismissed following a conviction for incest with his daughter. His dismissal was held to be unfair. It was, said the tribunal, 'an isolated incident, it had nothing to do with his work (he was a quarryman) and his work did not bring him into contact with female staff' (but see *P* v *Nottinghamshire CC* [1992] IRLR 363).

The dismissal of a drama teacher convicted of possessing and cultivating cannabis was held to be fair (*Norfolk County Council* v *Bernard* [1979] IRLR 220).

With the increasing use of technology in the workplace, the problem of unauthorised use of computers and connected equipment is an increasing problem. in *Denco Ltd* v *Joinson* [1991] IRLR 63, the employee gained unauthorised access to a company computer. The EAT said that unauthorised use of or tampering with computers is an extremely serious industrial offence which constitutes gross misconduct and which attracts summary dismissal. It was similar to dishonesty. Given the prevalence of computers in the workplace, employees should be made aware of the limits of permissible access. The DSS, for example, makes access of files which are not part of the employee's caseload an offence attracting automatic summary dismissal.

In *Whitlow* v *Alkanet Construction Ltd* [1975] IRLR 321, the employee was working on a house belonging to one of his managers. He had sexual intercourse with the manager's wife, both in the house and elsewhere. His dismissal was held to be fair. This seems to have been based on the view that the employee's conduct led to a loss of confidence in him by the employer.

Redundancy   The employer may show that the reason for the dismissal is one related to redundancy. This will be a potentially fair reason provided that the employer has not used redundancy to dismiss employees whose dismissal would otherwise be unfair. In *Williams* v *Compair Maxam Ltd* [1982] ICR 156, the Employment Appeal Tribunal laid down five principles of good industrial relations:

(a)   The employer should give as much warning as possible of impending redundancies so as to enable trade unions and employees to consider alternative solutions and seek alternative employment.

(b)   The employer should consult with any unions as to the best means by which the desired object can be achieved with as little hardship as possible. In particular the criteria for selection should be agreed and the actual selection should be made in accordance with that criteria.

(c)   The criteria for selection should not depend solely on the opinion of the person making the selection, but should be capable of being objectively checked.

(d)   The employer should ensure that the selection is made in accordance with the criteria, and consider any representations made.

(e)   The employer should ascertain whether there is any alternative employment which can be offered.

These principles are not rules of law, although there is a requirement to give notice and to consult trade unions (see 8.6.8 below) and a Code of Practice, they are merely guidelines and apply generally where a large, unionised employer is concerned. Indeed the use of the guidelines has been strongly criticised in Scotland. In *Simpson & Son (Motors) Ltd* v *Reid and Findlater* [1983] IRLR 401, the Scottish Employment Appeal Tribunal said that the guidelines were overworked and misapplied. In the Simpson case, two out of three employees were dismissed for redundancy without trade union involvement. Lord Macdonald said that the guidelines were not a shopping list and in *Meikle* v *McPhail (Charleston Arms)* [1983] IRLR 351, he said:

These principles must primarily refer to large organisations in which a significant number of redundancies are contemplated. In our view they should be applied with caution in circumstances such as the present where the size and administrative resources of the employer are minimal.

This apparent difference of opinion may now have been settled by the decision of the House of Lords in *Polkey* v *A E Dayton Services Ltd* [1987] 3 All ER 974. The employee was one of four van drivers. There was to be a reorganisation and three of the drivers were to be made redundant. The employee was called into the manager's office and was told that he was being made redundant with immediate effect. An industrial tribunal held that there had been a complete disregard for the provisions of the Code of Practice in not consulting with or warning the employee, but they went on to say that even if there had been consultation and warning the result would have been the same, i.e. Polkey would have still been made redundant. This finding was upheld by the Employment Appeal Tribunal and the Court of Appeal but was overturned by the House of Lords. Lord Bridge said:

> an employer having prima facie grounds to dismiss . . . will in the great majority of cases not act reasonably in treating the reason as a sufficient reason for dismissal unless and until he has taken the steps, conveniently classified in most of the authorities as 'procedural', which are necessary in the circumstances of the case to justify that course of action. . . . in the case of redundancy, the employer will normally not act reasonably unless he warns and consults any employees affected or their representative . . .

A tribunal therefore is not allowed to consider whether, if the employer had acted differently, the dismissal would have been fair; it must look not at what the employer might have done but what he actually did. Unless the employer had reasonable grounds for believing that a fair procedure would be useless, the lack of a fair procedure will inevitably lead to a finding of unfair dismissal. In *Polkey* the House of Lords has re-emphasised the importance of following fair procedures before deciding to dismiss, whether the reason is redundancy or any of the other potentially fair reasons. The decision in *Polkey* also suggests tacit approval of the principles in *Williams* v *Compair Maxam Ltd* although the case was not referred to in Lord Bridge's dicta. Procedure is therefore of major importance (and this applies to the other potentially fair reasons). This decision is of crucial importance. Effectively it means that even if the employer has a perfectly valid reason for dismissal, unless he follows the correct procedure he will be dismissing unfairly. For further material relating to the *Polkey* case, see the Cases and Materials section for Chapter 8.

In spite of the emphasis in *Polkey* on the need for procedural correctness, it seems that minor procedural lapses will be ignored by the courts, provided that they have not resulted in unfairness (see *Eclipse Blinds Ltd* v *Wright* [1992] IRLR 133). *Polkey* had specifically rejected the 'did it make any difference' test contained in *British Labour Pump* v *Byrne* [1979] IRLR 94. Balcombe L J's judgment in *Duffy* v *Yeoman & Partners Ltd* [1994] IRLR 642, would, however, seem to erode the protection afforded to employees by *Polkey*. *Duffy* would seem to suggest that less attention should be paid to what the actual employer did and more to what the hypothetical reasonable employer would have done (see Lord Bridge's judgment in *Polkey*). Balcombe LJ felt that 'there was a grave danger of this area of law becoming over-sophisticated and that there is an attempt to lay down as rules of law matters which are no more than factors which an industrial tribunal should take into account in reaching its decision whether the employers acted reasonably in the circumstances of the particular case'.

Balcombe LJ went on to say that there was no warrant for the proposition that there *must* be a deliberate decision by the employer that consultation would be useless, with the corollary that in the absence of evidence that such a decision was made, a finding by an industrial tribunal that a dismissal for redundancy is necessarily wrong *in law*. This would seem to be at odds with Lord Carlsfield's judgment in *Robertson v Magnet Ltd (Retail Division)* [1993] IRLR 512, where he said that 'if there was a failure to consult, . . . that failure made the dismissal unfair'.

Breach of statutory duty   The employer may be able to show that the reason for the dismissal was because the continued employment of the employee would be contrary to the law. The most common situation would be where an employee who is employed as a driver loses his licence. Obviously he cannot be employed as a driver until the driving ban is over but to dismiss in such circumstances may be unfair. The employer must have regard to the length of the ban, the need of the employee to drive, the possibility of moving the employee to other work, etc. The employer must act reasonably. In *Mathieson v Noble & Sons Ltd* [1972] IRLR 76, the employee who had lost his licence was willing to hire someone to drive him on sales trips but was nevertheless dismissed. It was held his dismissal was unfair. In *Appleyard v Smith (Hull) Ltd* [1972] IRLR 19, a mechanic lost his licence. It was a requirement of the job that the mechanics road tested the vehicles. His dismissal was held to be fair. The company was a small one and there was no other suitable work available. In *Gill v Walls Meat Co Ltd* HSIB 22, it was held fair to dismiss a Sikh (whose job involved working with meat) when he grew a beard. His continued employment would have breached the food hygiene regulations.

Some other substantial reason   The previous four categories are obviously not exhaustive of all the circumstances which will justify an employer dismissing an employee. This provision has been used to catch cases that did not slot neatly into the aforementioned categories. Examples of reasons in this category have been: essential business reorganisation; unreasonable refusal to agree to a change in employment terms (*St John of God (Care Services Ltd) v Brooks* [1992] IRLR 54); homosexual tendencies in an employee working with children (see *Saunders v Scottish National Lands Association* [1980] IRLR 174); and violent behaviour to fellow employees during an epileptic fit (see *Harper v NCB* [1980] IRLR 260). In *Scott Packing & Warehousing Co Ltd v Paterson* [1978] IRLR 166, the employer received an ultimatum from a major customer that the employee be dismissed. It seemed the customer suspected the employee of theft although no evidence was adduced. Such a dismissal was held to be fair on the grounds of 'some other substantial reason'. In

Gorfin v *Distressed Gentlefolk's Aid Associations* [1973] IRLR 290, it was held that to dismiss one of two incompatible employees when the resultant tension and hostility began to affect the employer's business would be fair and fell into the 'some other substantial reason' category.

Refusal to cooperate with management has also been held to fall into this category. In *St John of God (Care Services Ltd)* v *Brooks and Others* [1992] IRLR 54, employees were informed that their wages were to be reduced because of funding problems. Most accepted the need for this, but some refused and were dismissed. Curiously the EAT said that the dismissal was fair (see constructive dismissal at 8.5.1).

8.5.2.2 Automatically unfair grounds for dismissal In some cases the Act holds that a dismissal will be automatically unfair. The automatically unfair reasons are:

(a) trade union associated dismissals;
(b) pregnancy dismissals;
(c) dismissal involving 'spent convictions';
(d) dismissal connected with transfer of undertakings;
(e) dismissal involving unfair redundancy;
(f) new TURERA 1993 unfair reasons.

Trade union membership and activities A dismissal will be automatically unfair if the main reason for it was:

(a) that the employee was or proposed to become a member of an independent trade union; or
(b) that the employee had taken part in the activities of an independent trade union at an appropriate time; or
(c) that the employee was not a member of any or a particular trade union or had refused or prepared to refuse to become or remain a member (EPCA, s. 58(1)).

'Appropriate time' means time which is outside working hours, or a time within working hours at which, in accordance with arrangements agreed with or consent given by his employer. it is permissible for the employee to take part in those activities (EPCA, s. 58(2)). 'Working hours' include periods when the employee is paid but not required to work, e.g., tea and lunch breaks.

Pregnancy dismissals As the number of women who are economically active increases, greater emphasis has been placed on rights associated with maternity and childrearing. Some employment contracts may make express provision for these, but they are almost certainly still a rarity and involve very high status employees or those whose special skills puts them in an unusually strong bargaining position. Most of the rights associated with maternity are statutory and therefore are something of a *fait accompli* for the employer. This does not, of course, lessen the significance of these rights; indeed, from a human relations management viewpoint the reverse is true. As the 'rights' have not been the subject of free negotiation, there may be a tendency to forget all about them.

Under EPCA 1978, an employee who had been continuously employed for two years could complain of unfair dismissal if she was dismissed either because of pregnancy or for a pregnancy associated reason. She would be unable to complain if the employer could show:

(a) that she was unable to carry out her job; or
(b) that there was some statutory provision that precluded her working; and
(c) the employer had offered her a suitable alternative job; or
(d) that there was no suitable alternative.

The Trade Union Reform and Employment Rights Act 1993 has made significant changes to maternity rights. The rights apply to all employees (now no qualifying period of service). This will potentially have an economic impact on employers, who may therefore be tempted to avoid employing women (but see *Dekker* on not employing pregnant women). The amended EPCA, s. 60 now states that an employee shall be treated as automatically unfairly dismissed in the following circumstances:

(a) If the reason or principal reason for her dismissal is that she is pregnant or is any reason connected with her pregnancy.

(b) Her 14-week maternity leave is ended by dismissal and the reason is because she has given birth or is any other reason connected with her having given birth.

(c) Her contract was terminated after the 14-week maternity leave and the reason for her dismissal is that she had taken maternity leave or had availed herself of the benefits of maternity leave.

(d) The reason for dismissal is a requirement or recommendation referred to in s. 45 (see below).

(e) The maternity leave period is ended by dismissal and the reason is that she is redundant, but the obligation to be offered a suitable vacancy (if there is one) has not been complied with.

As we saw earlier, the employer could lawfully dismiss a woman who either was incapable of doing her job, or where continued employment would contravene some statutory provision, provided he offered her suitable alternative work (if available). TURERA 1993 has amended EPCA 1978 and has introduced new rights for women who are suspended from work because their continued employment would:

(a) be in contravention of a statutory requirement; (see Suspension from Work (on Maternity Grounds) Order 1994 SI 1994 No 2930) or

(b)   be in contravention of any provison in a code of practice issued or approved under s. 16 of the Health and Safety at Work etc. Act 1974.

Any employee so suspended has the right to be offered a suitable alternative job (see above). If there is no suitable alternative job she is entitled to be paid by her employer while suspended. Failure on the part of the employer to offer suitable alternative work or to pay wages during suspension will give the employee the right to complain to an industrial tribunal.

Spent Convictions   Convictions, like children, never leave you, they stay on file forever. There are many people in the UK with criminal convictions. For the most part these involve minor offences, usually committed in one's youth. The existence of such convictions can obviously have a negative effect on the success of job applications. The Rehabilitation of Offenders Act 1974 goes some way towards ameliorating the position of those with convictions. Basically the Act allows job applicants, etc. to ignore the existence of convictions. If the application form or interviewer asks about a criminal record, the applicant can deny he has one, i.e. he has statutory permission to lie. However, in *Torr v BRB* [1977] ICR 785 Cumming Bruce J declined to extend this protection to a denial in a job application of the existence of an unspent conviction.

There are two important points that should be noted:

(a)   The 1974 Act does not apply to all convictions. The sentence and the time that has passed since it was imposed have to be taken into account. For example, a fine will be spent and can be disregarded after five years, whereas a sentence of imprisonment of between 6 and 30 months can be disregarded only after 10 years.

(b)   Certain professions and employments are excluded from the provisions of the legislation. Among such are doctors, lawyers, accountants, social workers, judges, dentists, nurses, pharmacists, teachers (Rehabilitation of Offenders Act 1974 (Exceptions) Order 1975 as amended). A conviction which has become spent or any circumstances ancillary thereto, or any failure to disclose a spent conviction or any such circumstances, shall not be a proper ground for dismissing or excluding any person [from employment] or for prejudicing him in any way in employment. (Rehabilitation of Offenders Act 1974, s. 4(3)(b).)

It is automatically unfair to dismiss an employee who has failed to disclose the existence of a conviction unless the employment falls into one of the exempted occupations. In the latter case it will be fair to dismiss an employee who has failed to disclose the existence of a conviction.

Dismissal connected with transfer of undertakings   One of the attractions for a prospective purchaser of a business will often be the possibility of dismissing some of the staff and then offering them new, less favourable employment contracts. In response to this the EC passed Directive 77/187 (the Acquired

Rights Directive) which was designed to protect and preserve the accrued rights of an employee in such circumstances. The Transfer of Undertakings (Protection of Employment) Regulations 1981 are the UK response to the Directive. The Regulations as they stood applied only to 'commercial ventures' (which excluded many local authority services that were seen as ripe for contracting out). This has altered with the passing of TURERA 1993 and European Court of Justice decisions (see *Dr Sophie Redmond Sticthing* v *Bartol*, below). These decisions are further evidence, if any is needed, of the benefits to employees of EU law and the need for employers/managers to be familiar with it.

The Regulations apply only to relevant transfers, being a sale or other disposition of an undertaking. Significantly the concept does not cover the sale or transfer of shares, which is one of the most common ways by which control or ownership of an undertaking is transferred. Put simply, the new employer will take over all the rights, duties, powers and liabilities of the old employer. The transfer of a school from local authority control to grant-maintained status involved a transfer of undertakings, and the subsequent dismissal of the school cleaners was held to be an unfair dismissal. Any dismissal which is related to the transfer of the undertaking will be unfair unless it can be shown that the dismissal was for an 'economic, technical or organisational reason' (reg. 8(2)). It may be possible for the employer to show the reason for the dismissal is that changes in the workforce are needed, either before or after the transfer. Any dismissals in this situation will fall under the heading of dismissals for 'some other substantial reason'. Employers should note that the exception may enable them to dismiss employees, but it will not allow them to change the terms and conditions of transferred employees. Employees who have changes made to their pay, conditions, etc. may be able to claim constructive dismissal. The employer may regard this as a worthwhile investment as he could recruit new employees at lower cost. Since the sensational decision of the EAT in *Millagan* v *Securicor Cleaning Ltd* [1995] IRLR 288, employees dismissed for a reason connected with a transfer of an undertaking can bring an unfair dismissal claim even if they do not have two years' service, which limit as we saw above has also been challenged on other grounds by the Court of Appeal.

Dismissal connected with unfair redundancy It will be automatically unfair if an employee has been selected for dismissal for one of the following reasons:

(a) a trade union associated reason (see above);
(b) where the employer did not act reasonably in treating redundancy as a sufficient reason for the dismissal.

The employer may show that the principal reason for the dismissal was redundancy. Redundancy is a potentially fair reason for dismissal provided that the employer has not attempted to use a redundancy situation to dismiss employees whose dismissal would otherwise be unfair. If the dismissal is fair then the employer will of course be under an obligation to pay the relevant statutory redundancy payment. Tribunals expect employers to act reasonably (s. 57(3) EPCA) The ground rules were laid down by the Employment Appeal Tribunal in *Williams* v *Compair Maxam Ltd* [1982] ICR 156 (see 8.5.2.1)

New TURERA 1993 unfair reasons The 1993 Act has added some new automatically unfair reasons to those already mentioned above. They are contained in new ss. 57A and 60A of EPCA 1978.

Section 57A deals with situations where the employee is dismissed because:

(a)   he was carrying out designated health and safety functions; or

(b)   he was either a safety representative or a member of a safety committee and was carrying out the functions therefore; or

(c)   he left his place of work because of imminent danger; or

(d)   he took appropriate steps to protect himself or his fellow employees from the danger.

(e)   he complained to the employer about circumstances connected with his work which he reasonably believed were harmful or potentially harmful to health and safety, where there was no safety representative or safety committee, or where there was a safety representative or safety committee but it was not reasonably practicable for the employee to raise the matter by those means.

Section 60A makes it automatically unfair to dismiss an employee who has asserted that the employer has breached a statutory right. Examples of such rights are:

● right to written particulars of employment;
● right to time off for public duties;
● right to payment for time off for trade union duties;
● right to time off for ante natal care.

It is important to note that no qualifying period is required in order to claim under either of these two new sections.

8.5.2.3   Automatically fair reasons   It is automatically fair to dismiss an employee for national security reasons. Where national security is the claimed basis for dismissal the tribunal will lack jurisdiction (see *CCSU* v *Minister for Civil Service* [1985] ICR 14) or during a strike or lock-out. It would seem that the employer can fairly dismiss if at the time of the dismissal the employee was conducting a lock-out or the employee was involved in some form of industrial action, provided that all the employees are dismissed and none are re-engaged within 3 months of the dismissal. It is enough that the employer demonstrates tha dismissal and industrial action are contemporaneous. What is a strike or other industrial action may not be immediately apparent. In *Lewis & Britton* v *E. Mason & Sons* 1994 IRLR 4, Britton was sacked for refusing to drive a lorry that had no heater. A fellow driver told the employer that unless Britton was reinstated, none of the drivers would come to work. All drivers were then dismissed. The EAT said that there was no jurisdiction to hear complaints of unfair dismissal as the dismissed employees were taking part in industrial action. It would seem from this decision that refusing to obey an order may amount to industrial action. This decision surely cannot be correct as it would allow employers to dismiss such employees without fear of action. For further discussion of this see Bowers and Honeyball, *Textbook on Labour Law*, Blackstone Press, 1993 at pp. 136–141).

8.5.3 Application to an industrial tribunal: procedure

An employee who believes that his dismissal is unfair in terms of the legislation has the right to present his case before an industrial tribunal.

8.5.3.1 Procedure on application Normally an application to an industrial tribunal must be made within three months of the date of dismissal by submitting either the statutory form IT1 or a letter with the relevant information to the Central Office of Industrial Tribunals. The Tribunal has discretion to extend this period if it is satisfied that it was not reasonably practicable for the complaint to be presented within it, and the period is six months where the unfair dismissal is connected with a lockout or strike.

A copy of the application is sent to the employer (who is known as the respondent). The employee is the applicant. A copy is also sent to a conciliation officer employed by the Advisory Conciliation and Arbitration Service. The conciliation officer has a statutory duty under EPCA, s. 134 to try to settle the matter if possible. Any settlement reached through the conciliation officer is binding on the parties involved.

8.5.3.2 Pre-hearing reviews The Employment Act 1989, s. 20, provides for 'pre-hearing reviews' which can require the payment of a deposit of up to £150 before a party will be allowed to proceed.

8.5.3.3 Hearings procedure Procedure in the Industrial Tribunal is governed by the Industrial Tribunal (Constitution and Rules of Procedure) Regulations 1985. Tribunals consist of a legally qualified chairperson who must be an advocate or solicitor of seven years' standing, and two lay members, one of whom will have been nominated by employers' organisations and the other by employees' organisations. TURERA made provision for the Chairperson to sit alone and the Government has recently proposed that these powers should be extended (Resolving Employment Rights Disputes: Options for Reform 1994 HMSO 2707).

8.5.4 Orders of an industrial tribunal

If the tribunal finds that the employee has been unfairly dismissed they must decide on the remedy. The tribunal has the power to make an order for the reinstatement or re-engagement of the employee. The employee will be asked if he wishes the tribunal to make such an order. The tribunal also have power to make orders for the payment of compensation to the employee.

8.5.4.1 Reinstatement or re-engagement A reinstatement order means that the employer shall treat the employee in all respects as if he had not been dismissed. The tribunal may specify the amount of arrears of pay, and any rights and privileges which must be restored to the employee including seniority and pension rights (EPCA, s. 69(2)).

A re-engagement order means that the employer (or a successor or associated employer) must engage the employee in employment which is comparable to that from which he was dismissed or in other suitable employment. The tribunal will specify the terms of the re-engagement, e.g., pay and pension rights (EPCA, s. 69(4)).

The tribunal has discretion as to whether to make either of these orders. It will have regard to whether the applicant wishes to be reinstated, whether it is practicable for the employer to comply with such an order and whether, if the applicant contributed in some measure to his dismissal, it would be just to order his reinstatement. If the tribunal decides not to make a reinstatement order it will next consider a re-engagement order taking the same factors as above into account. If the tribunal decide to make neither a reinstatement order nor a re-engagement order then it will make an award of compensation. There are in practice very few reinstatement or re-engagement orders made. Few applicants wish such an order to be made and of those who do, few are successful. Such orders were made in only 15.7 per cent of the unfair dismissal cases that came before the tribunals in Scotland in the year to 31 March 1990.

8.5.4.2 Compensation awards Where no order for reinstatement or re-engagement is made, or where such an order is made but is not complied with, the tribunal may make an award of compensation. Where an employer fails to comply with an order for reinstatement or re-engagement, the tribunal is able to make an award, the additional award, which compensates for that failure.

The basic award This is an amount which is designed to compensate the employee for the loss of job security caused by his unfair dismissal. It is calculated in the same way as a redundancy payment (see 8.6.6 below); the same 'tapering off' provisions apply in the final year before retirement.

The maximum basic award is therefore: 20 x 1.5 x £210 (£6,300). Where the reason for dismissal is one related to membership or non-membership of a trade union the minimum basic award is £2,770.

The compensatory award This is such amount as the tribunal considers just and equitable in all the circumstances having regard to the loss sustained by the complainant in consequence of the dismissal (EPCA, s. 74(1)). There is a current maximum of £11,300. Some factors the tribunal might consider are immediate loss of wages, loss of future earnings, loss of pension rights, loss of any other benefits, and expenses incurred in looking for work.

Both the basic award and the compensatory award may be reduced if the tribunal feels that:

(a)   the employee contributed in some way to his dismissal; or

(b) the employee has not mitigated his loss by trying to find another job or unreasonably refuses an offer of reinstatement by the employer.

The additional award Such an award will be made where the employer fails to comply with an order for reinstatement or re-engagement unless he can satisfy the tribunal that it was not practicable for him to do so. The award will be calculated as follows:

(a) in an ordinary unfair dismissal case, it will be between 13 and 26 weeks' pay;

(b) in an unfair dismissal where the dismissal was an act of unlawful sex or race discrimination, it will be between 26 and 52 weeks' pay.

The current maximum wage that is taken into account is £210. The maximum award is therefore £10,920.

The special award Where the applicant requests re-engagement or reinstatement, the tribunal either refuses to make such an order or the tribunal makes the order and the employer does not comply with it, and the reason for the unfair dismissal was on the grounds of the membership or non-membership of a trade union, or on health and safety grounds then a special award may be made as follows:

(a) if no order for reinstatement or re-engagement is made the special award is one week's pay multiplied by 104; there is a minimum award of £13,775 and a maximum of £27,500 (the week's pay is not subject to the statutory limit of £210).

(b) if an order for reinstatement or re-engagement is made but not complied with the special award is one week's pay multiplied by 156; there is currently a minimum award of £20,600 and there is no maximum. There is provision for a special award to be reduced in certain circumstances (Employment Protection (Consolidation) Act 1978, s. 75A).

8.6 REDUNDANCY PAYMENTS

The Redundancy Payments Act 1965 introduced the idea that an employee had a statutory right to receive compensation in certain circumstances for the loss of his job, whether or not he had found another job. The rationale behind the Act was to overcome the resistance of employees to the changes that would be necessary as British industry attempted to adapt to changes in competition, markets, products, etc. The amount of compensation was to be related to age, length of service and the earnings (subject to a maximum) of the redundant employee. The provisions are now contained in the Employment Protection (Consolidation) Act 1978.

To be entitled to a redundancy payment, the employee must have completed at least two years' continuous service since the age of 18 with an employer. It may be the case that this limit is unlawful (see 8.5 above).

An employee who accepts a suitable alternative offer of employment is not entitled to a redundancy payment. Neither is an employee who is offered re-engagement on the same terms by his employer or an associated employer (e.g., a subsidiary company) and unreasonably refuses, or suitable alternative employment by such an employer and unreasonably refuses. Some employees are excluded from the provisions of the legislation:

(a)   Employees who have attained the age of 65 or, where there is an earlier common retiring age for men and women in their particular employment, that age.

(b)   Share fishermen.

(c)   Domestic servants in private households who are close relatives of the employer. Close relative is defined in EPCA, s. 100(2).

(d)   Employees on a fixed-term contract of two years or more who have agreed in writing to waive the right to claim redundancy payment.

(e)   Crown employees.

(f)   Employees who are ordinarily employed outside Great Britain, unless they are at the date their contract comes to an end in Great Britain on their employer's instructions.

8.6.1   The meaning of redundancy

Redundancy is defined in EPCA, s. 81(2) as the dismissal of an employee attributable wholly or mainly to:

(a)   the fact that his employer has ceased, or intends to cease, to carry on the business for the purposes of which the employee was employed by him, or has ceased, or intends to cease, to carry on that business in the place where the employee was so employed, or

(b)   the fact that the requirements of that business for employees to carry out work of a particular kind, or for employees to carry out work of a particular kind in the place where he was so employed, have ceased or diminished or are expected to cease or diminish.

Before there can be a claim for a redundancy payment there must first be a dismissal. We have already discussed the definition of dismissal (see 8.5 above). Once the employee has proved that he has been dismissed then redundancy will be presumed to be the reason unless the employer can show that the dismissal was for some other reason, e.g., misconduct. There will be no dismissal and therefore no entitlement to a redundancy payment where the employee leaves voluntarily.

The definition of redundancy covers three possible situations. The first is where the employee has ceased business altogether and therefore has no further need for employees; this situation can be easily recognised. The second situation is where the employee's business is carried out at more than one location and the location at which the employee works closes down. Whether in this second situation the employee is redundant or not will depend on the 'mobility' element in the employee's contract, and indeed whether work at a different location is offered. The third possibility is where there is a reduction in the need for employees at a particular location because, for example, of a fall in demand or mechanisation.

8.6.1.1 When the employer ceases business altogether This type of situation is easily recognisable. It does not matter what the reason for the closure is or whether it is voluntary or involuntary.

In *Gemmell* v *Darngavil Brickworks Ltd* [1966] ITR 20, the company closed down their brickworks for 13 weeks to enable essential work to be carried out. The employees were dismissed. It was held that they were redundant, as a temporary cessation of work may constitute dismissal for the purpose of the legislation (EPCA, s. 88). It may well be that the contract provides for periods of lay-off. In such a case s. 88 would not apply.

8.6.1.2 Cessation of business at employees place of employment If the employee works at a particular workplace which the employer closes then this is dismissed for redundancy, even though the employer has other workplaces still in operation. Difficulties may arise, however, where an employee's contract either expressly or by implication requires them to move. In such a situation the 'place where the employee was so employed' will not be where the employee actually worked but where he could be required to work. In *United Kingdom Atomic Energy Authority* v *Claydon* [1974] IRLR 6, Claydon was required by his contract to work anywhere in the UK or overseas. He had however worked at one location for several years. He was told the work he did was to be moved to Aldermaston. He refused to move and claimed dismissal on the grounds of redundancy. However, the court held that, since he was obliged to work anywhere in the UK and there was a job for him at Aldermaston, the requirement for workers in the place where he was employed had not ceased and his claim failed. This contractual approach to the place at which the employee is employed has been since adopted in several cases.

An employee, therefore, who has a mobility clause in his contract and refuses to move in a situation like Claydon's will find that the reason for his dismissal will be misconduct, not redundancy. For example, in *Sutcliffe* v *Hawker Siddley Aviation Ltd* [1973] ICR 560 NIRC, an aircraft technician who was stationed in Norfolk was asked to move to Scotland. His contract said he could work at any RAF station in the UK and he had already worked at several. This time he objected to moving because he had bought a house and for other family reasons. He was dismissed and claimed unfair dismissal and redundancy pay. The court held he was entitled to neither because it was a term of his contract that he should be mobile. There was nothing unfair about the request to move, and as there was work in Scotland he could not claim a redundancy payment. The decision in *Claydon* has, however, recently been doubted.

In *Bass Leisure Ltd* v *Thomas* [1994] IRLR 104, the EAT held that the place of employment was (for redundancy purposes) *not* extendable to any place where the employee could be contractually required to work, but can be decided on only after a factual enquiry 'taking into account the employee's fixed, or changing places of work, or place of work, and any contractual terms which go to define or evidence the place of employment and its extent, but not those (if any) which make provision for the employee to be transferred to another (place)'. The EAT's decision seems more sensible than the interpretation in *Claydon* which had the effect of denying the employee's statutory right to a redundancy payment by the simple insertion of a few extra words in the employment contract. (On this see also sch. 4 of TURERA 1933 implementing EEC Directive 91/533.

If there is no express provision for mobility then the courts will only rarely imply one. Lord Denning said in *O'Brien* v *Associated Fire Alarms Ltd* [1968] 1 WLR 1916 'the question whether a term is to be implied in a contract is a matter of law for the court and not a question of fact' (see 8.3.2.2 above). Mobility clauses have however been implied into the contracts of building workers and steel erectors (*Stevenson* v *Teeside Bridge and Engineering Ltd* [1971] 1 All ER 296; see also *United Bank Ltd* v *Akhtar* at 8.3.2 above), where it was held that even where there was an express mobility clause, the employer must act reasonably in implementing it). In *Meade-Hill* v *British Council, The Times*, 14 April 1995, the Court of Appeal held that a mobility clause might amount to unlawful indirect sex discrimination within ss. 1(1)(b) and 6(1) of the Sex Discrimination Act 1975.

8.6.1.3 Reduction in need for employees There are many reasons why an employer may need fewer employees. There may be a straightforward reduction in staff, work or shift patterns may be changed, or new machinery may reduce the required number of employees.

It will be redundancy within the meaning of the Act if there is a reduction or diminution in demand for employees to carry out 'work of a particular kind'. In *European Chefs (Catering)* v *Currell* [1970] 6 ITR 226, Currell was a pastry cook who specialised in making eclairs and meringues. The employer decided to make continental pastries instead and hired someone else to carry out this work. Currell was dismissed. He claimed redundancy. His claim was successful because it was held that the need for a cook of his speciality had ceased, there was therefore less demand for 'work of a particular kind'. In *Vaux and Associated Breweries Ltd* v *Ward* [1968] ITR 385, the owners of a public house decided to modernise it and turn it into a discotheque. They dismissed Mrs Ward, one of the existing middle aged barmaids as she did not fit in with the new image which called for young blondes. It was held that she was not entitled to a redundancy payment because there was no diminution of the work being done in the refurbished public house and therefore no redundancy. Mrs Ward might be more successful today as she could claim under the unfair dismissal provisions which had not been enacted at the time (see 8.5.2 above).

The courts have had to examine whether there has been a cessation or diminution 'of work of a particular kind' in the context of reorganisations.

Where the overall needs of the employer have not changed but there has merely been a change in duties and/or hours, then this has not been seen as redundancy. In *Johnson* v *Nottinghamshire Combined Police Authority* [1974] ICR 170 CA, Johnson had worked for 20 years at a police station on a five day week, Monday to Friday from 9.30 am to 5.30 pm. To achieve greater efficiency her hours were changed to an alternating shift of 8 am to 3 pm and 1 pm to 8 pm on a six day week. She refused to work these hours and was dismissed and replaced by a shift worker. She claimed redundancy. Her claim failed. In the Court of Appeal, Lord Denning said 'if the employer requires the same number of employees as before for the same tasks as before but require them at different hours there is no redundancy situation'. He expressed the same view in *Lesney Products and Co Ltd* v *Nolan* [1977] ICR 235, when he held that six machine setters were not redundant when they refused to change to double day shift working from a single day shift plus overtime. He said:

> it is important that nothing should be done to impair the ability of employers to reorganise their workforce and their times and conditions of work so as to improve efficiency. They may reorganise it so as to reduce overtime and thus to save themselves money, but that does not give the man a right to redundancy payment.

8.6.2 Transferred redundancy
This is where an employee who is made redundant in one department is moved to another department where he displaces another employee with, usually, less seniority or skill. This is known as 'bumping'. There are several decisions that support the view that the displaced employee is entitled to a redundancy payment even though there is no diminution in the work he does. The employer's overall requirements have of course diminished. There are however contrary decisions and the issue is unsettled and confused (see *Elliot Tussoma Chivers* v *Bates* [1991] UCR 218).

8.6.3 Offers of alternative employment
An employee who falls within the statutory definition of redundancy will not be entitled to a redundancy payment if he unreasonably rejects an offer of suitable alternative employment from his employer, or if he unreasonably refuses a renewal of his contract on the same terms. Such an offer may also be made by an associated employer or a new employer to whom the business has been transferred. The offer from any of these need not be in writing but it must specify the differences (if any) between the terms of the new employment and the old. The offer must be made before the end of the original contract and the new contract must begin within four weeks of that date.

8.6.3.1 Trial period If the employee is offered alternative employment which differs in terms and conditions from his old employment then the employee is entitled to have a trial period of four weeks. This trial period may be longer if the parties so agree. If the employee terminates the contract during the trial period, or if the employer terminates it, then the employee shall be treated as having been dismissed on the date on which the previous contract terminated, and for the reason that applied on that date.

8.6.3.2 Suitable offers of alternative employment In deciding whether the alternative employment is 'suitable employment', various factors must be taken into consideration, e.g., the nature of the work, the pay, the hours, conditions, and the employee's qualifications. Each case has to be looked at on its own merits. The Act says that if the employee is offered 'suitable employment' but he 'unreasonably' rejects it, then he will not be entitled to a redundancy payment. There are two separate issues here, suitability and reasonableness. However, in *Spencer* v *Gloucestershire County Council* [1985] IRLR 393, Neil LJ said that 'it was confusing to draw too rigid a distinction between suitability and reasonableness because some factors may be common to both aspects of the case'.

Some of the more important factors are illustrated in the paragraphs below.
Pay For this purpose, pay includes overtime, bonuses and fringe benefits. If the money offered in a new job is substantially lower than in the old it can be turned down. In *Sheppard* v *National Coal Board* [1966] IRLR 101, a redundant carpenter was offered a similar job which would have involved more travelling, less overtime and the loss of certain fringe benefits. It was held that the extra travelling time and loss of overtime did not make the job unsuitable but the loss of the fringe benefits did and the offer was not one of suitable employment. In *Bowman* v *National Coal Board* [1970] ITR 245, a redundant colliery worker was offered an alternative job which involved downgrading and a 20 per cent drop in wages. It was held the offer was not a suitable one.
Status An offer which involves a loss of status will not be suitable. In *Taylor* v *Kent County Council* [1969] 1TR 294, the headmaster of a boy's school was, on its closure, offered a job as a supply teacher. He would keep his salary as a headmaster. It was held that this was not a suitable offer because of the loss of status. In *Harris* v *Turner* [1973] 1CR 31, a joiner who instructed and trained apprentices was made redundant and subsequently offered an alternative job as a bench joiner. It was held that this was not a suitable offer because even though his wages remained the same he would lose the authority and status he had before.
Skill It would be highly unlikely that an offer of alternative employment that involved a skilled or semi-skilled employee taking unskilled work would ever be regarded as suitable. In *Standard Telephone* v *Yates* [1981] IRLR 21, the applicant had had a highly skilled job for ten years. She was offered an alternative job working on the assembly line. She refused and the EAT agreed that the job was not suitable, because it did not employ the skills she had developed over the previous ten years.
Place of work An offer which involves the employee in having to move to a different location or which involves extra travelling time may make the offer unsuitable. The employee may, however, be regarded as subject to an express or complied mobility clause (see 8.6.1.2 above). In *Shields Furniture Ltd* v *Goff*

[1973] ICR 187, it was held that two workers who were told to move to another factory two and a half miles away were entitled to refuse. The new job was not suitable.

Hours of work   An offer of alternative employment, which involves a change from day shift to night shift, will usually be unsuitable particularly if there will be difficulty in adjusting because of domestic circumstances etc. (*Morrison & Poole* v *Ceramic Engineering Co Ltd* [1966] ITR 404).

Nature of the work   If the alternative job is completely different from the old job then it will be unsuitable, e.g., a hospital hairdresser offered alternative work as a clerical officer (*Nairn* v *Ayrshire & Arran Health Board* [1990] Glasgow Industries Tribunal (Unreported)).

8.6.3.3   Unreasonable refusal   The suitability of the offer of alternative work must be assessed objectively. However, in assessing whether or not the employee's refusal to accept the alternative is unreasonable, regard may be had to subjective factors. The alternative job offered may be deemed suitable but the employee may not be unreasonable in refusing it and will not therefore jeopardise his right to a redundancy payment. Some factors which have been seen as reasonable grounds for refusal have included domestic difficulties, poor travel facilities and lack of educational facilities. In *Allied Ironfounders* v *Macken* [1971] ITR 109 AC, a foundry worker who turned down the offer of a suitable double day shift job because his wife was an invalid was held not to have acted unreasonably. In *Rawe* v *Power Gas Corporation* [1966] ITR 154, it was held that the employee was reasonable in refusing an alternative offer which meant a move from the south east of England to Teeside because he was afraid it would exacerbate marital difficulties. In *Collier* v *Smith's Dock Co* 1969 4 ITR 338, an employee who had worked as a shipwright for 13 years followed by seven as a chargehand shipwright was held to be acting unreasonably in refusing an alternative job as a shipwright which involved an 8 per cent loss in earnings (cf. the cases involving loss of status).

An employee may be held to be acting reasonably in refusing an offer where the job is merely temporary. However, if it is rejected on the grounds that it may not last very long, the employee may be held to be acting unreasonably and so forfeit any redundancy payment. In *Morganite Crucible* v *Street* [1972] 2 All ER 411, the employee turned down an alternative offer on the grounds that it would probably only last 12-18 months. Sir John Donaldson said her refusal was unreasonable and that no employment (with the possible exception of judicial employment) can be said to be permanent. In *Thomas Wragg & Sons Ltd* v *Wood* [1976] ICR 313 however, it was held that fear of job insecurity when combined with other factors may be reasonable grounds for refusing an offer. Wood was given notice of redundancy by his employer and obtained a new job through his own efforts. On his last day at work he was offered suitable alternative work but refused to accept it. It was held his refusal was reasonable. Lord Macdonald said:

The tribunal feels that the employee having committed himself to the new job, and having all the fears of a man of 56 who faces unemployment, and

having received the offer not too late, but . . . as late in the day as within
24 hours of the expiration of his notice, was not unreasonable in refusing
the offer, and, consequently, he succeeds in his claim.

Where an employee accepts an alternative offer whether from an existing
employer, an associated employer or a new owner of the business, then there
is no break in service for the purpose of determining continuous employment.

8.6.4 Change in the ownership of a business

One of the most common occasions for redundancy is when a business
changes hands. Where there is a change of ownership and the former owner
terminates the employee's contract but the new owner either renews it or
offers a new but suitable contract then there will be no entitlement to a
redundancy payment (EPCA, s. 94). In such a situation, the employee's
continuity of employment will also be preserved.

There is a vital difference between the transfer of a business and a transfer
of the physical assets of the business. In the former case the business is carried
on as before but the people who own it are different. Where merely the
physical assets are transferred, the new owner may use those assets in a
different business altogether. For example, in *Lloyd* v *Brassey* [1969] 1 All ER
382, one of the judges said that where a farm used for mixed farming was
sold to be used as a pig farm, this was a transfer of physical assets and not a
transfer of the business (the overall view was that it was a transfer of the
business). If in the view of the court only the physical assets of the business
have been transferred then there is no continuity of employment and the
employees can regard themselves as dismissed by reason of redundancy.

In *Woodhouse* v *Peter Brotherhood Ltd* [1972] ICR 186 CA, an employee had
worked for 34 years as a tool setter for Crossley Premier who made diesel
engines at their plant in Derbyshire. In 1965 they moved production to
Manchester and sold the plant to Peter Brotherhood Ltd. They (PB) finished
off five engines that were in the course of production and then commenced
the manufacture of spinning machines and steam turbines. There was no
transfer of trade name, customers or goodwill, the new products were quite
different from the old.

Peter Brotherhood took on the workforce but in 1971 dismissed Woodhouse for redundancy. It was held that the redundancy payment was to be
calculated on six years' service, i.e. 1965–1971, because the business hadn't
changed hands, merely the assets. Lord Denning said:

if anyone had been asked prior to August 1965: 'What business is being
carried on in the factory?' his answer would have been, 'The manufacture
of diesel engines'. And if he had been asked the same question in January
1966, his answer would have been 'The manufacture of spinning machines,
compressors and steam turbines'. If he had been asked 'Is it the same
business?' he would have said 'No'. True the same men are employed,
using the same tools: but the business is different.

Woodhouse was not entitled to a redundancy payment in 1965 because the Redundancy Payments Act 1965 had not then come into force.

In addition to the provisions of EPCA, s. 94, the Transfer of Undertakings (Protection of Employment) Regulations 1981 may also apply. These Regulations were passed to give effect to EEC Directive 77/187 and are designed to preserve the accrued rights of an employee on the transfer of an undertaking. The Regulations apply only to 'relevant transfers', which is a sale or other disposition of an undertaking; they do not cover the sale or transfer of shares which is one of the most common ways by which the control or ownership of an undertaking is transferred. Once the relevant transfer has taken place, the contracts of employees transferred as a result are deemed not to end but to continue as if made by the transferee. If an employee is dismissed after the transfer, he must look to the transferee for the redundancy payment but if he is dismissed before the transfer, he must look to the transferor. The Regulations apply only to employees employed immediately before the transfer. In *Secretary of State* v *Spence* [1986] IRLR 248, it was held that an employee who was dismissed three hours before the transfer was not employed 'immediately before' and therefore had no protection under the Regulations; 'immediately before' was to be equated with 'at the time of'. However, in *Litster* v *Forth Dry Dock and Engineering Co Ltd* [1989] IRLR 161, employees were dismissed an hour before the transfer. In order to give effect to the purpose of the Directive it was necessary to insert before 'immediately before the transfer', the words 'or would have been so employed if they had not been unfairly dismissed'. The House of Lords in *Litster* were satisfied that *Spence* was correctly decided because the reason for the dismissal in *Spence* was economic circumstances (see Regulation 8 TUPE 1981). If the reason for the dismissal is transfer related, *Lister* applies, if the dismissal is for economic technical or organisational reasons, *Spence* applies.

The decision of the ECJ in *Dr Sophie Redmond Stichting* v *Bartol* [1992] IRLR 366, is also concerned with the meaning to be given to the Directive. An undertaking includes any 'trade or business'. It has been held to cover a venture which was deliberately run at a loss (*Madden* v *University of Dundee Students' Union* [1985] IRLR 449). Prior to the *Redmond* decision, UK courts and tribunals had held that the Regulations did not cover non-commercial ventures, which would include, for example, local authority services such as catering and cleansing.

The Dr Sophie Redmond Foundation provided assistance to drug addicts. Its only source of funding was a subsidy from the local authority. The local authority decided to terminate this subsidy and transfer it to the Sigma Foundation which carried out similar work. Some of the Redmond Foundation's employees were transferred to Sigma, but some, including Bartol and three others, were not. The ECJ held that there was a 'legal transfer' for the purpose of Art. 1(1) of EEC Directive 77/187, where a public body terminates funding one legal person, as a result of which the activities of that person are terminated, and transfers the funding to another legal person with similar aims. The court had previously held in the case of *Abels* v *The Administrative Board of the Bedrijfsvereniging Voor de Metaal Industrie En de Electrotechnische*

Industrie 138/83, 7 February 1985, that the purpose of the Directive is to ensure that the rights of employees are protected in the event of transfer of their undertaking.

The court held that the Directive is applicable wherever in the context of contractual relations there is a change in the legal or natural person who is responsible for carrying on the business and who incurs the obligations of an employer towards an employee. In *Redmond Stichting* the court said that 'this Directive . . . has the object of guaranteeing the rights of employees and it applies to all employees who are covered by protection against dismissal, even if it be limited under national law'. This would clearly include, as indeed it did in *Redmond Stichting*, employees of non-commercial ventures who, as previously indicated, were specifically excluded by the 1981 Regulations. The most significant group of such employees would be employees of public sector organisations who have undergone a change of employer through the process of compulsory competitive tendering. New employers taking over compulsorily tendered contracts will be required to employ staff on existing terms and conditions. Clearly this will have major implications for local government and the future of compulsory competitive tendering. The take-over of services performed by local authorities almost always results in a change in the employment package for those employees who continue to be employed by the new employer. This is no longer possible following the *Redmond Stichting* decision and TURERA 1993. The implications for companies tendering to take over council services are clear.

In *Kenny* v *South Manchester College* [1993] IRLR 265 the plaintiff had been employed by a local education authority who provided education facilities to prisoners under a contract with the Home Office. These services were put out to tender to further education colleges which traded as private corporations. The plaintiff successfully sought a declaration that his contract would automtically transfer from the local authority to the further education college by virtue of the directive. In *Dines* v *Initial Health Care Services and Another* [1994] IRLR 336, the Court of Appeal approved and supported the decision in *Kenny* when it confirmed that the contracting out of services to another provider (following competitive tender) is a relevant transfer within the Transfer of Undertakings Regulations. Neil LJ said that decisions of the ECJ demonstrated that the fact that another company takes over the provision of certain services as a result of competitive tendering does not mean that the first business or undertaking necessarily comes to an end.

In *Porter and Nanayakkara* v *Queens Medical Centre* [1993] IRLR 486 it was held that a transfer of paediatric and neonatal services from two health authorities to an NHS trust was a transfer within the regulations.

In considering the application of the Regulations or the Directive to a transfer, this test of whether an economic unit is being transferred is used. In practice this means that it is capable of being run as a business post transfer and it has to be capable of being distinct from the other parts of the business of the transferee. In *Rask* v *ISS Kantineservice* A/S [1993] IRLR 133, Rask was employed in an in-house staff canteen providing a service to Philips employees. Philips contracted the service out to ISS who took over the responsibility for running the canteen for a fixed fee. Philips kept ownership of the catering equipment, set the price for the food, met all the running costs and determined what level of service was to be provided. The canteen was only for Philips' workers. W was dismissed because she refused to agree to a change in her pay day. She claimed unfair dismissal by ISS. ISS argued that there was no change of ownership, merely the transfer of an internal service to an outside contractor (a classic contracting out case). ISS argued that because of the restrictions placed on them by Philips, there was no change in the ownership of the service. The ECJ said that the Directive applied where 'following a legal transfer . . . there is a change in the legal or natural person who is responsible for carrying out the business . . . regardless of whether or not ownership of the undertaking is transferred'.

The transfer of a single employee falls within the scope of the directive. In *Schmidt* v *Spar und Leibkasse* (C392/92) [1984] IRLR 302 Schmidt was employed by a bank to clean one of its branches. The bank dismissed her and transferred the cleaning of the branch to the company that cleaned their other premises. She was employed by the company at a higher pay rate but to clean a larger area. The ECJ held that the directive applied. Even though the transfer involved only part of an undertaking (and an ancillary one at that), with only one employee, it fell within the scope of the directive. As the nature of the service did not change, the directive should apply.

The EAT held in *Allan and Others* v *Stirling District Council* [1994] IRLR, that a transferor employer remains liable under the Regulations for a transfer-related unfair dismissal, even although the transferee employer is also liable under them. Although the Regulations state that the transferor's liabilities are transferred to the transferee and anything done by the transferor in respect of contracts of persons employed in the undertaking is deemed to be done by the transferee, this does not exclude there being any liability on the transferor. The view of the EAT would seem to suggest some form of joint and several liability. There is an optional provision for this in Article 3(1) of the Directive but the UK did not take up this option, with the result that the transferor employer was felt to be relieved of any further liability. The Court of Session overruled the EAT (*Stirling District Council* v *Allan* [1995] IRLR 301), however, saying that if the option of joint liability under Article 3(1) has not been exercised then the transferor employer will no longer be liable. There are *obiter dicta* in the case to suggest that some form of joint liability would be sensible and desirable for the protection of employees.

8.6.5 Lay off and short-time working

There are provisions in the Act for employees who are laid off temporarily or put on short-time by the employer to claim a redundancy payment. A lay off is where no work is provided and no remuneration is paid. Short-time is where less than half the normal remuneration is earned (EPCA, s. 87(1)(2)). Unless there is express or implied provision in the employee's contract, such action by the employer will constitute dismissal on the grounds of redundancy. In *D E J McKenzie Ltd* v *Smith* [1976] IRLR 345, Smith was told by his manager on 8 February that he was being suspended for several weeks and it might be April before he was back at work. On 20 February he obtained another job. He claimed redundancy pay. Lord MacDonald said he was entitled to it; the employer's action in suspending him where there was no contractual term to that effect amounted to dismissal.

Section 88 of EPCA lays down the rather complex procedure for claiming redundancy in lay off or short-time working situations. The usual statutory definition of redundancy does not of course apply in such situations. If the employee has been laid off or put on short-time (or a combination of both) for four consecutive weeks, or six weeks in any 13-week period, he may give the employer written notice that he intends to claim a redundancy payment. This notice must be given not later than four weeks after the lay off or short-time has stopped. The employer may agree to pay the redundancy payment or within seven days may give written notice that work can resume provided he reasonably expects that within four weeks of his counter notice he expects there to be a minimum of 13 weeks without any lay off or short-time. If there is no resumption of full-time working within four weeks, the employee must claim the redundancy payment and give notice of termination. If the employer does not pay, the employee may apply to an industrial tribunal.

In *A. Dakri & Co* v *Tiffen* [1981] IRLR 57, the contract of the employee allowed temporary 'lay offs' without pay if there was a shortage of work. After four weeks the employee wrote to the company claiming redundancy pay. The following week she registered a claim with the industrial tribunal. The Employment Appeal Tribunal said she was entitled to it in spite of not having complied with the admittedly elaborate procedure. The action of the employer in laying her off for more than four weeks was not reasonable. Their conduct amounted to constructive dismissal and the employee was entitled to a redundancy payment.

8.6.6 Calculation of redundancy payments

The entitlement to a redundancy payment arises from past service, not from present or future need. The amount payable is therefore not affected by the employment situation after dismissal. The amount of the payment is calculated by reference to the employee's length of continuous service, age and weekly pay.

Continuous service This includes employment with the employer or associated employer or, where there has been a transfer of the business, employment with the transferor and transferee (see 8.6.2 above). Periods when the employee was on strike, or under the age of 18 are not counted, although they do not break continuity.

Age The amount of the redundancy payment is calculated as follows:

For each year of service while aged at least 18 but less than 22	$\frac{1}{2}$ week's pay
For each year of service while aged at least 22 but less than 41	1 week's pay
For each year of service while aged at least 41	$1\frac{1}{2}$ weeks' pay

Employees who are made redundant in the year before their 65th birthday will have the amount payable reduced by one twelfth for each month they are over 64.

The maximum number of years that can be taken into account is 20 and the maximum pay that is currently taken into account is £210. This amount is variable. The current maximum statutory payment is therefore £6,300.

Weekly pay What is a week's pay will of course vary but the principles for calculating it are laid down in EPCA, sch.14. It may be a straightforward matter to calculate the relevant weekly pay, e.g., it may in many cases be a fixed amount. There is provision for cases where there is an element of commission, bonus or piecework but overtime pay is not included unless the employer was obliged to provide it and the employee to work it.

8.6.7 Claiming a payment

An employee who believes he is entitled to a redundancy payment must make a written claim to the employer. If the employee does not or cannot pay, the employee must make a claim to an industrial tribunal within six months of the termination of the contract although the tribunal has discretion to hear claims made later provided they are made within 12 months.

8.6.8 Procedure for handling redundancies

8.6.8.1 Notification The employer has the duty, under the Trade Union and Labour Relations (Consolidation) Act 1992, ss. 188–192 as amended, to notify any recognised trade unions and the Secretary of State for Employment if he proposes to make redundancies. An employer who fails to give the required notification to the Department of Employment may be prosecuted and fined up to a maximum of £2,000. The Government has indicated (Consultation Document, April 1995) that it intends to amend TULR(C)A 1992, s. 188 to bestow rights of consultation on elected representatives of affected employees. The present provisions which give recognised independent trade unions consultation rights will still apply but in future the employee will either have to consult with them or elected representatives. There will, however, be no statutory procedure for the election of such representatives (who need not be employees). It will be left to employer and employees to devise procedures. Where the elected representatives are employees they will enjoy the same protection against dismissal as apply to union representatives. The Government has also announced that the duty to consult will only arise where the employee intends to make 20 or more employees redundant over a 90-day period. (This change is consistent with the definition of collective redundancies in Article 1(a) of EEC Directive 75/129 on Collective Redundancies.) In addition, the current law requiring employees to consult at 'the earliest opportunity' will become a requirement to consult 'in good time'!

8.6.8.2 Consultation The employer must consult with any recognised trade union if he proposes to dismiss through redundancy any of their members. This should be done at the earliest opportunity and not less than:

(a)   where he proposes to dismiss more than 100 employers at one establishment within a 90-day period, 90 days before the first dismissal takes place; or

(b)   where he proposes to dismiss 10 or more employees at one establishment, 30 days before the first dismissal takes place; or

(c)   where he proposes to dismiss fewer than 10 at one establishment, as soon as possible before the first dismissal takes place.

The employer should not issue individual notices of dismissal until consultation has begun. and these should not take effect until the end of the consultation. In *National Union of Teachers* v *Avon County Council* [1978] IRLR 55, the employers issued dismissal notices to some of their employees on 28 October. Consultation with the union began on 29 October. The Employment Appeal Tribunal ruled that this was not within the requirements of the Act and, in considering what would have happened if the beginning of consultation had preceded the dismissal notices by one day, said 'there is nothing to prevent (this) but . . . it may well (indicate) that there has never been any meaningful consultation by the employee such as is required by s. 99 in which case that will be a ground for complaint'.

The legislation originally talked about consultation (not negotiation, but see below). These are very different, but in redundancy situations the boundaries will become blurred. The employer must disclose to the trade union(s) in writing:

(a)   Reason for the proposals.

(b)   Numbers and description of those to be made redundant.

(c)   Total number of employees of each discipline employed by the employer at the establishment in question.

(d)   Proposed method of selection.

(e)   Proposed method of carrying out the redundancies with due regard to any agreed procedure, including the period over which they are to take place.

TURERA 1993, s. 34(2) now states that consultation must include ways of:

(a)   Avoiding dismissals;

(b)   Reducing the number of dismissals;

(c)   Mitigating the consequences of dismissal.

Consultation with the union must be meaningful, with a view to reaching agreement with the union. This suggests a different approach from that which applied previously. In *R* v *British Coal and Secretary of State for Trade and Industry ex parte Price* [1994] IRLR 73, the High Court said 'fair consultation involves giving the body consulted a fair and proper opportunity to understand fully the matters about which it is being consulted and to express a view on those subjects, with the consultor thereafter considering those views genuinely and properly'. Since 3 January 1995 and the repeal of EPCA

s. 59(1)(b) it is no longer automatically unfair to select for redundancy in breach of a customary arrangement or agreed procedure. It may, however, constitute unfair dismissal. The decision in *NI Hotel and Catering College* v *NATFHE* [1995] IRLR 83, holds that the employer must consult with recognised trade unions even if the union concerned has no members being made redundant at the workplace concerned.

If there is a complaint by a trade union which is upheld, the tribunal may make a protective award to the employees concerned. The maximum awards will vary depending on the amount of notice the union should have been given and what the tribunal thinks just. Maximum awards are:

(a) where the employer proposed to make 100 or more employees redundant within 90 days, the protected period shall not exceed 90 days;

(b) where the employer proposed to make 10 or more employees redundant within 30 days, the protected period shall not exceed 30 days;

(c) in any other case (fewer than 10 redundancies), the maximum protected period is 28 days.

If an award is made the employer will have to pay remuneration to the employees concerned for this protected period.

8.7 EQUAL PAY

The 1888 Trades Union Congress carried a resolution in favour of equal pay for men and women. Equal pay was the subject of a Royal Commission in 1944–46 and was adopted as policy by the International Labour Organisation in 1951. By the 1960s the issue of equal pay had become a major political issue and the 1964 Labour Government was commited to legislation on the issue. Over 40 per cent of the workforce were women yet their pay at that time was on average 66 per cent of a man's average pay. The reasons for this disparity are social, cultural and historic rather than legal. It was not unlawful at common law to discriminate against women in matters of pay and indeed in some occupations there were different salary scales for men and women even though the work carried out was similar or even identical.

The Equal Pay Act 1970 was passed in 1970 although it did not come into force until 29 December 1975. The aim of the Act is to ensure that every term in a woman's contract is not less favourable than in a man's contract in respect of pay and other conditions. It should be noted that the legislation includes men as well as women although for convenience it is framed with reference to women. This also applies to the Sex Discrimination Acts 1975 and 1986. By the time the Equal Pay Act came into force it had been amended by the Sex Discrimination Act 1975 which is aimed at eliminating discrimination in relation to non-pay matters such as selection, training, promotion and dismissal. The Equal Pay Act and the Sex Discrimination Acts operate on different principles but they are designed to be complementary and to provide a single comprehensive statutory framework for the avoidance of discrimination.

The Equal Pay Act was amended from 1 January 1984 by the Equal Pay (Amendment) Regulations 1983 following the decision of the European Court of Justice in *EC Commission* v *United Kingdom* [1982] IRLR 333. This was to the effect that the Equal Pay Act 1970 did not adequately allow for claims of equal pay to be brought on the grounds that the female employee was doing work of equal value to that done by a male employee, as provided for by Article 119 of the Treaty of Rome and as clarified by the Equal Pay Directive of 10 February 1975. EU law has had a major impact in the field of equal pay over the last decade, particularly in defining what is meant by 'pay' and where indirect pay discrimination is involved.

Article 119 states 'Each member state shall . . . ensure and subsequently maintain the application of the principle that men and women should receive equal pay for equal work'. Because Article 119 is both directly applicable and has direct effect, it is enforceable in domestic courts and allows any individual employee claiming equal pay to do so under both United Kingdom and European legislation. This can be an invaluable right as domestic legislation is narrower in its scope than European Community legislation (see *Pickstone & others* v *Freeman plc* [1988] IRLR 357). Under Article 119 pay is defined as 'the ordinary basic or minimum wage or salary or any other consideration, whether in cash or kind, which the worker receives, directly or indirectly, in respect of his employment from his employer'. Pay has been held to include post retirement travel facilities in *Garland* v *British Rail Engineering* [1982] IRLR 111, the making up of net pay to include pension contributions in *Worringham Humphries* v *Lloyds Bank* [1981] IRLR 68, the German equivalent of statutory sick pay (*Rinner-Kühn* v *FWN Spezial Gebäudereinigung* [1989] IRLR 493), redundancy payments whether statutory or *ex gratia* (*Barber* v *Guardian Royal Exchange* [1990] IRLR 240, *McKechnie* v *UBM Building Supplies Ltd* [1991] IRLR 283) and compensation for unfair dismissal (*Mediguard* v *Thane* [1994] IRLR 504). A pension paid under a contracted out private occupational pension also falls within the Article 119 definition of pay (*Barber*, above). Paid leave also falls within the definition (*Arbeiterwohl Fahet der Stadt Bellib EV* v *Botel* [1992] IRLR 423). This decision makes it clear that Article 119 can be relied upon to challenge pay-related national legislation which may have the effect of excluding women from employment protection rights.

8.7.1 Scope of the Equal Pay Act
The Act applies to all who are employed. 'Employed' is defined in s. 1(6)(a) as 'Employed under a contract of service or apprenticeship or a contract personally to execute any work or labour'. It therefore covers not only employees but in some instances the self-employed. In *Quinnen* v *Hovells* [1984] ICR 525, a self-employed salesman claimed he was paid less than women doing the same work. It was held competent for his claim to be considered.

8.7.2 The equality clause
Section 1(1) of the Act implies into every woman's contract of employment an equality clause. The effect of the equality clause is, under s. 1(2), to give a woman the same pay and conditions as a man when:

(a)   the woman is employed on like work with a man in the same employment;

(b)   the woman is employed on work rated as equivalent with that of a man in the same employment; or

(c)   the woman is employed on work which is of equal value to that performed by a man in the same employment.

If a woman in any of the above situations has any term in her contract which is less favourable than a man's, then her contract shall be modified so that it is no less favourable.

There are therefore three threads to the legislation: work, work rated as equivalent, and work of equal value.

8.7.2.1   Like work   Like work is defined, in s. 1(4), as work of the same or a broadly similar nature where any differences in the work done are not of practical importance. It should be noted that the Act does not talk of identical work, although if a woman is doing identical work to a man then there should be no difficulty. An example of broadly similar work can be seen in *Capper Pass* v *Lawton* [1977] ICR 83 where a woman worked as a cook in a company directors' dining room preparing between 10 and 20 lunches. She sought equal pay with two assistant chefs who worked in the factory canteen where they prepared some 350 meals over the day. She had a shorter working week than them and worked unsupervised whereas they were under the supervision of a head chef. The Employment Appeal Tribunal held that she was entitled to equal pay. They said that the skill and knowledge required for the job should be considered but that there was no need to minutely examine the work involved. Provided the differences that do exist are not of practical importance the work is like work.

In *Electrolux* v *Hutchinson* [1977] ICR 252, all the male employees were paid on a higher scale than all but one of the women. The employer said that this was because the men could be asked to do different work and at different times, e.g., night work. The question to be asked here was 'How often did they do so?' It was found they rarely did so. In any case the matter could have been dealt with by paying a premium at such times. It was held the work done was like work and the women were entitled to equal pay. In *Shields* v *Coomes (Holdings) Ltd* [1978] IRLR 263, the Court of Appeal took a similar line. Shields was employed as a counterhand in a betting shop. Men doing the same work were paid more because they were supposedly expected to eject troublesome customers. However, it seemed that not only had there never been trouble but the men had no training in dealing with troublemakers in any case. Shields was held entitled to equal pay.

In *Dugdale* v *Kraft Foods* [1977] ICR 48, men and women did similar work. The men however had to work a night shift. It was held that different hours did not justify a differential in the basic pay. This could be dealt with by paying the men a night shift premium. However, in *Thomas* v *NCB* [1987] ICR 757, the Employment Appeal Tribunal held that female canteen assistants who worked a day shift were not engaged in like work with a man who did the same job on the night shift. The fact that he worked alone and therefore had additional responsibilities seemed to have been an important factor. In *Noble* v *David Gold & Son (Holdings) Ltd* [1980] IRLR 252 CA, women who sorted, labelled and packed in a warehouse were held not to be doing like work with men who loaded and unloaded. Their work was lighter and there were differences of practical importance between the work they did.

8.7.2.2 Work rated as equivalent An employer may carry out a job evaluation scheme to establish if a woman's work is equivalent to a man's. Section 1(5) contains the relevant provisions. There are various ways in which this evaluation can be carried out; the most common system involves breaking each job down into separate factors like skill, effort, and responsibility, with points being awarded to each factor (see ACAS Guide No. 1). Philips J said of job evaluation schemes in *Eaton Ltd* v *Nutall* [1977] ICR 272 (at 277) for a job evaluation scheme to be legally acceptable:

> it should be possible by applying the study to arrive at the position of a particular employee at a particular point in a particular salary grade without taking other matters into account, except those unconnected with the work . . . (a scheme) which requires the management to make a subjective judgement concerning the nature of the work . . . would seem to us not to be a valid study.

Impartiality and objectiveness would seem to be the watchwords. As a result of such a scheme as that described above, it was held in this case that the female employee was not on like work. Evaluation of work done by her and a male comparator showed that he handled more expensive items and hence had greater responsibility. *Arnold* v *Beecham Group Ltd* [1982] IRLR 307 suggests that an evaluation scheme is not deemed to be complete until all the parties involved accept its validity. This would seem to effectively neuter the scheme. *Arnold* did, however, say that equal pay would apply from the moment the scheme was accepted, irrespective of whether new salary scales could be agreed. The decision by the House of Lords in *O'Brien* v *Sim-Chem Ltd* [1980] IRLR 373 was that once the evaluation scheme had been completed and accepted then equal pay applied.

8.7.2.3 Work of equal value If the provisions of s. 1(4) (like work) or s. 1(5) (work rated as equivalent) do not apply, an applicant may make a claim that her work is of equal value to that of her male comparator as provided for by s.1(2)(c). Claims are made to an industrial tribunal which has discretion as to whether or not the claim should be allowed to proceed. There is also provision for conciliation; if that fails, an independent expert will prepare a report. This report need not be accepted by the tribunal. There are limitations on the expert's access to witnesses and the workplace, although the tribunal can require the production of information and documents which it will forward to the expert. If the report recommends that the work is of equal value and the tribunal accepts the report then it will make an award of equal pay. There is provision, under s. 2(5), for this award to be back-dated.

The first and leading case on equal pay for work of equal value was *Hayward* v *Cammell Laird Shipbuilders Ltd* [1988] 2 All ER 257 (see the Cases and Materials section for Chapter 8). Hayward began work with the shipbuilders as a catering trainee and for the first three years was paid the same as various male apprentices. Thereafter her pay was less and, at the time of her initial application, she received £24 a week less than painters, joiners and insulation engineers. She claimed (in 1984), under s. 1(2)(c), that her work was of equal value to these craftsmen. Cammell Laird argued that, although the craftsmen were paid a higher basic wage than Hayward, she received additional benefits such as extra holidays, paid meal breaks and better sick pay benefits. It was agreed on the basis of an independent expert's report that her work was of equal value but the tribunal said that pay could not be looked at in isolation. Overall she was no worse off than the men when her conditions were taken into account. However, the House of Lords reversed the earlier decisions and upheld her claim to equal pay. Lord MacKay accepted the argument that, if a woman could point to any term in her contract which was less favourable than a similar term in a man's contract, then she was entitled to have the situation rectified. The word 'term' in s. 1(2) means a distinct provision or part of the contract, it does not refer to some aggregate of different terms. Pay is a distinct term, hers was less favourable, and she was entitled to have it modified.

Two weeks after the Hayward decision the House of Lords heard the appeal in *Pickstone* v *Freeman plc* [1988] IRLR 357. Pickstone and some other women were packers in a mail order warehouse. They claimed that their work was of equal value to that of a male warehouse checker who was paid £4.22 a week more than them. The employer contended that because *a* man was employed on the same work as the women and on the same pay they could not claim under s.1(2)(c). There was only one man doing the same job as the women and being paid the same money. The House of Lords said that under EEC law a woman is entitled to equal pay for work of equal value to that of a man in the same employment and that right is not defeated by there being a man who is employed on the same work at the same pay as the woman. Article 119 and the Equal Pay Directive are inconsistent with the proposition that in some circumstances discrimination which deprives a woman of equal pay may be sanctioned. Lord Keith said (at 359):

the opposite result would leave a large gap in the equal work provision, enabling an employer to evade it by employing one token man on the same work as a group of [women] . . . It is plain that Parliament cannot have possibly intended such a failure.

In *Murphy* v *Bord Telecom Eireann* [1988] IRLR 267, the European Court of Justice considered the position where women's work is rated as being of greater value then the work of higher paid men. The Court said (at 269) that the principal of equal pay for men and women:

forbids workers of one sex engaged in work of equal value to that of workers of the opposite sex to be paid a lower wage than the latter on ground of sex, it *a fortiori* prohibits such a difference in pay where the lower-paid category of workers is engaged in work of higher value.

To allow otherwise would be to have defeated the purpose of the legislation.

8.7.2.4 The comparator   In order to decide if a term is less favourable, a comparison must be made between the woman in question and a man employed by the same or an associated employer. The applicant can choose the comparator and may select male employees who work at a different location provided they enjoy common terms and conditions. 'Common terms and conditions' has been held to mean the 'same terms and conditions', not broadly similar or to the same overall effect (*British Coal* v *Smith* [1994] ICR 810). The woman need not be able to name her comparators (*Leverton* v *Clwyd County Council* [1989] IRLR 20, *Ainsworth* v *Glass Tubes & Components Ltd* [1977] ICR 347).

She may select as her comparator a predecessor. In *McCarthys Ltd* v *Smith* [1981] QB 180, Smith was employed by a pharmaceutical warehouse. She was paid £50 a week (in 1976). Her job had been vacant for five months having previously been done by a man who was paid £60 weekly. She claimed equal pay with him. The Court of Appeal held that she could not use him as a comparator. However, the European Court said that under Article 119 she could compare herself with her predecessor. What the woman cannot do is to compare herself with a hypothetical man (as can be done under the Sex Discrimination Acts).

8.7.2.5 Indirect Pay Discrimination   Unlike the Sex Discrimination Act, the Equal Pay Act does not make provision for indirect pay discrimination, i.e. where seemingly neutral criteria are applied equally to both men and women but the result is a disproportionate adverse impact on the latter. Several decisions of the ECJ have held that such indirect pay discrimination is covered by Article 119 and the Equal Pay Directive 75/117/EEC. Most recently the decision of the House of Lords in *R* v *Secretary of State for Employment, ex parte EOC* [1994] IRLR 176, which held that the hours per week qualifying thresholds that previously existed in respect of unfair dismissal and statutory redundancy were incompatible with European law, would suggest UK recognition of indirect discrimination in the field of pay. The House of Lords applied the tests laid down by the ECJ in *Bilka-Kauthaus* and *Rinner-Kuhn* (below). Lord Keith said 'while in certain circumstances an employer might be justified in paying full time workers a higher rate than part time workers in order to secure the most efficient use of his machinery (see *Jenkins* v *Kingsgate Clothing Ltd* [1981] ICR T15) that would be a special and limited state of affairs. Legislation which permitted a differential of that kind would present a very different aspect and considering that the great majority of part time workers are women would surely constitute a gross breach of the principle of equal pay... Similar considerations apply to legislation which reduces the indirect cost of employing labour' (e.g., redundancy pay and compensation for unfair dismissal).

In *Bilka-Kauthaus* v *Weber van Hartz* [1986] IRLR 317, the employer operated an occupational pension scheme for its employees. Under the rules of the scheme, part-time employees were eligible for these pensions only if they had worked full-time for at least 15 years over a total period of 20 years. Van Hartz had been employed for 15 years, the last few on a part-time basis. She was refused a pension on the grounds that she lacked the 15 years, full-time service. She claimed that the pension scheme was contrary to the principle of equal pay laid down in Article 119, because the requirement of a minimum period of full-time employment placed women at a disadvantage as they were more likely to work part-time to meet domestic obligations. The employers argued that there were objectively justified economic grounds for excluding part-timers. The ECJ held that a scheme which excludes part-time employees infringes Article 119, if that exclusion affects a far greater number of women than men, unless the employer can show that the exclusion is based on objectively justified factors unrelated to any discrimination on the grounds of sex; this may include economic grounds. In *Rinner-Kuhn* v *FEW Special Gebaudereinigung GmbH* [1989] IRLR 493, employees were paid while on sick leave, provided that they normally worked at least 10 hours a week or 45 hours a month. German law sanctioned the scheme. The ECJ held that statutory entitlement to sick pay amounted to 'pay' within the meaning of Article 119 and that a scheme which had the effect of affecting a considerably greater number of women than men is discriminatory unless the Member State can show that the legislation is justified by objective factors unrelated to any discrimination on grounds of sex. The regulations introduced following the decision in *R* v *Secretary of State for Employment, ex parte EOC* may have gone some way to clarify the issue of indirect discrimination in the field of pay.

8.7.3 Employers' defences

The employer may resist a claim on the ground that, although he accepts that the woman is employed on like work, work rated as equivalent or work of equal value, the reason for the difference in pay is 'genuinely due to a material factor which is not the difference of sex' (s.1(3)). This defence may be raised at a preliminary hearing of the tribunal. The statutory wording differs in cases of like work and work rated as equivalent from that used for cases of work of equal value. In the former, the material factor must be a material difference between the woman and the comparator while, in the latter, the material factor may be a material difference. The distinction between these is not of such importance since the decision of the House of Lords in *Rainey* v *Greater Glasgow Health Board* [1987] AC 224 (see the Cases and Materials section for Chapter 8 and below). There has been much debate as to whether market forces constitute a material factor. In *Clay Cross (Quarry Services) Ltd* v *Fletcher* [1979] ICR 1, a male clerk was employed to work alongside a long-serving female clerk. He was paid £8 weekly more than her. She claimed equal pay. The employer argued that the man would not take the job for less than he was currently earning, which was £43. Lord Denning said that market forces could not be allowed to dictate the rate for the job; that was why the Act had to be passed in the first place. However, the case of *Albion Shipping* v *Arnold* [1981] IRLR 525 held that market forces were a factor to be considered and the more recent decision in *Rainey* would seem to confirm this at the highest level.

In *Rainey*, the Health Board decided to set up its own limb-fitting service. Previously most of the work had been sub-contracted to the private sector. To get the new service up and running the Board offered higher salaries to prosthetists transferring from the private sector than they did to people who were already on the NHS salary scales. The difference was some £2,800 per annum. Rainey had been recruited onto the NHS scales. She claimed equality with the recruits from the private sector (who were all men) but failed. It was held that the reason for the difference in pay was a genuine material factor which had nothing to do with sex. The House of Lords felt that the employer had demonstrated objectively justifiable economic and administrative reasons for the difference in salary (see also *Davies* v *McCartneys* [1989] IRLR 439).

In *Enderby* v *Frenchay Health Authority* [1993] IRLR 591, the ECJ made inroads into the market forces defence in *Rainey*. Where there is evidence that a predominantly female group of workers is doing work of equal value to that of a group of male comparators but is being paid less, that will be prima facie indirect discrimnation and it will be for the employer to show that the difference in pay is justified. Whether he can justify the whole pay differential will be for the court to decide. They may feel that a proportional award should be made. It is not a defence to argue that the difference in pay arises from a collective agreement.

The decision in *Handels-Og Kontorfunkionaernes Forbund I Danmark* v *Dansk Arbejdsgiverforening* [1989] IRLR 532, demonstrates that the burden of proof rests on the employers to show that their pay practices are not discriminatory and that employees should examine the criteria used for pay increments or grading to ascertain whether they have an adverse impact statistically upon women and, if so, are they justifiable.

In addition to market forces being accepted as a genuine material factor, factors such as length of service, skill, and qualifications have been held to be genuine material factors, although these are personal to the employee.

A woman claiming equal pay may be met by the defence that the male comparator has had his earnings 'red-circled'. This is where employees have been regraded at some time in the past or have been moved because of ill health and are allowed to keep their previous pay rate even though the post they now occupy may generally be paid less. For example, in *Methven* v *Cow Industrial Polymers Ltd* [1980] IRLR 289, a female production clerk sought equality with a male production clerk who was paid some 30 per cent more than her. They both did the same work. The employers claimed that the man had been transferred from the shop floor because of age and illness but his previous wages had been preserved. It was held that this was a genuine material factor which was not due to sex.

The employer will not be able to plead 'red-circling' if the reason for it was sex-based, e.g., if the reason for the difference in pay prior to red-circling was itself discriminatory (*Snoxell* v *Vauxhall Motors* [1977] IRLR 123).

8.7.4 Enforcement

Any individual can enforce an equality clause by presenting a complaint to an industrial tribunal. The burden of proving entitlement lies with the applicant. If the employer relies on the genuine material factor defence then he must establish it. An ex-employee may bring a complaint against her ex-employer provided this is done within six months. Any award made can be back-dated up to two years from the date proceedings were instituted.

8.8 DISCRIMINATION ON GROUNDS OF SEX OR MARITAL STATUS

People are discriminated against for various reasons. While there may be a valid reason for this it is usually the result of bias and ignorance. The law does not concern itself with all forms of discrimination. It is not unlawful to discriminate against people on grounds of age or of religion although religious discrimination is unlawful in Northern Ireland, as is discrimination on grounds of political affiliation. Obviously given the dynamic nature of law and likely pressure from the post-war generation, the categories of unlawful discrimination (particularly age) may change. *The Times* (28 August 1995) reports research from the Carnegie Institute for the Third Age which indicates that most British employers would not be unhappy were there to be anti-age discrimination legislation and the Labour Party have indicated that they will introduce such legislation. The fair employment legislation in Northern Ireland, which makes discrimination on grounds of religion or political beliefs unlawful, was enacted due to pressure from the Irish-American lobby (and the fear of losing business contracts).

Common law does not concern itself with the issue of sex discrimination. The relevant law is statutory, i.e. the Sex Discrimination Acts 1975 and 1986. Although the legislation was enacted to prevent unlawful discrimination against women; it also protects men and married people. It is therefore unlawful to refuse to consider an applicant for a job because he or she is married. It is, however, still lawful to refuse to consider an applicant because he or she is not married.

8.8.1 Offering employment

It is unlawful, under the Sex Discrimination Act, s. 6(1), for a person in relation to employment by him at an establishment in Great Britain to discriminate against a woman:

(a)   in the arrangements he makes for the purposes of offering employment; or

(b)   in the terms on which he offers her that employment; or

(c)   by refusing or deliberately omitting to offer her that employment.

The word 'arrangements' has a broad meaning. It covers a wide range of techniques used to recruit employees, including advertising, (SDA, s. 38) selection procedures and questions asked at interview (see *Saunders* v *Richmond-upon-Thames LBC* [1977] IRLRL 362). Once a woman is employed, there must be no discrimination as regards promotion, training, or access to perks like cheap loans and travel facilities.

8.8.2   Forms of discrimination
There are three main kinds of discrimination; direct discrimination, indirect discrimination, and victimisation.

8.8.2.1   Direct discrimination   This is the most obvious form of discrimination and occurs when a woman receives less favourable treatment than a man solely because she is a woman. The woman must be able to establish that her unfavourable treatment is because of her sex. The legislation is concerned only with the factual and objective nature of the act not why the employer acted as he did. In *Grieg* v *Community Industry* [1979] IRLR 158, the director of the defendant company refused to employ the applicant because she would be the only woman and he felt from past experience that she would be unhappy. It was held this was unlawful discrimination, his motive was irrelevant. Similarly, in *Gubala* v *Crompton Parkinson* [1977] IRLR 10, Mrs Gubala was chosen for redundancy because her husband was working and the other potential candidate for redundancy, a man, was the only employed person in his family. No matter the motive, this was unlawful (see *Horsey* v *Dyfed CC* [1982] IRLR 395).

In *Peake* v *Automotive Products* [1978] QB 233, we see one of the earliest and still scarce claims by a man. Peake complained he was the victim of unlawful discrimination because his female fellow employees were allowed away from work five minutes before the men. The employer said the reason was safety related, to save crushing. The court accepted this and held there was no unlawful discrimination. Lord Denning said he would be disheartened if as a result of the passing of the statute 'the courtesy and chivalry that mankind gave to womankind' were to stop. Those less chivalrous than the Master of the Rolls pointed out that five minutes a day adds up to nearly three days a year! Lord Denning retreated from his much criticised position when, in the case of *Ministry of Defence* v *Jeremiah* [1980] ICR 13, he held that the requirement that women did not have to carry out dirty work that might damage their hair was direct discrimination against the men.

8.8.2.2.   Direct discrimination and pregnancy   Many discrimination cases have involved the treatment of pregnant women. The courts originally considered that a woman who was dismissed or subjected to any other detriment for being pregnant was not covered by the legislation, because there was no question of discrimination as she had no male comparator. Attempts were made to compare pregnant women with sick men (*Hayes* v *Malleable Working Men's Club* [1985] IRLR 367). The analogy was followed in several cases, but has been superseded by several decisions of the ECJ which have taken a more radical line. In *Dekker* v *Stichting Vormingscentrum Voor Jonge Volwassen* (*VJV Centrum*) *Plus* [1991] IRLR 27, D had applied for a job. She was pregnant at the time. Although she was the preferred candidate she was not employed because the employer's insurers would not reimburse them for maternity pay for Dekker (because she would already be pregnant at the time the insurance cover started). The ECJ held that refusing to employ a suitable female applicant on the grounds of the possible adverse consequences arising from employing a woman who is pregnant at the time of application is in contravention of Directive 76/207, Articles 2(1) and 3(1) (the equal treatment directive). The ECJ said 'As employment can only be refused because of pregnancy to women such a refusal is direct disrimination on the grounds of sex'.

The ECJ further held in *Handels-og Kontorfunktion-Oerernes Forbund i Danmark* [1991] IRLR 31 (the Hertz case) that the dismissal of a female worker on account of pregnancy constitutes direct discrimination on grounds of sex, although it did seem to feel that the sick man analogy applied in certain circumstances. Even with the benefit of these precedents, the House of Lords held in *Webb* v *Emo Air Cargo (UK) Ltd* [1993] IRLR 27, that it was not unlawful sex discrimination to dismiss a pregnant employee since a hypothetical sick man would have been treated similarly. The case was remitted to the ECJ for the court to determine whether a dismissal in these circumstances was discriminatory under EC law. The ECJ held that discriminatory treatment on grounds of pregnancy or maternity amounts to sex discrimination as such discrimination is gender-specific. The 'sick man' comparison may no longer be valid. The Court of Session, however, in *Brown* v *Rentokil* [1995] IRLR 211, maintains that there is still a distinction to be drawn between dismissal 'due to illness caused by pregnancy' and dismissal 'directly due to pregnancy'. The former may be acceptable; the 'sick man' has made a recovery!

8.8.2.3 Indirect discrimination This is a slightly more subtle form of discrimination. It involves applying a condition or requirement equally to men and women which the employer knows can only be complied with by a much smaller percentage of women and which cannot be justified and is to the woman's detriment because she cannot comply. For indirect discrimination to apply all four conditions must be satisfied.

An example would be to advertise for a male or female clerk, who must be six feet tall and aged between 18 and 28. No mention of sex here but the reality is that there are fewer women of this height than there are men. Unless the employer could justify the requirement, this would be indirect discrimination. The age requirement would also qualify as indirect discrimination. In *Price* v *Civil Service Commission* [1978] ICR 27, Mrs Price applied for a job as an executive officer in the civil service but was told that at 36 she was outwith the laid down age band of 17½–28. She argued that she could not have applied when she was that age because she was bringing up her children. Moreover many women would be in the same position, indicating that the proportion of women who could comply with the condition would be considerably smaller than the proportion of men. Her complaint that the requirement was unlawful sex discrimination was initially rejected on the grounds that the Sex Discrimination Act 1975, s. 1(1)(b) talks of women 'who can comply'. All women within that age band can comply since no woman is obliged to have children, and even those who do need not look after them personally. However, the Employment Appeal Tribunal said such a strict approach was 'totally out of sympathy with the spirit and intent of the Act', the condition was discriminatory. Nor could the employer justify the condition in any case.

In *Clarke v Eley [IMI Kynoch Ltd)* [1982] IRLR 131, the women applicants were among 60 women part-time workers who were made redundant in accordance with a selection procedure agreed between management and unions, which selected part-timers first. As there was a smaller proportion of women who could work full-time, this was held to be indirect discrimination. In *Home Office v Holmes* [1984] IRLR 299, the applicant, was not allowed to return to work on a part-time basis following maternity leave. She had no contractual right to work part-time. Her request was refused. She claimed indirect sex discrimination. The Employment Appeal Tribunal agreed, as the employer was unable to justify the condition that all employees were full time. The principles laid down in *Home Office v Holmes* were followed in *Wright v Rugby Borough Council* (1984) COIT 23528/44 and *Fulton v Strathclyde Regional Council* (1986) IRLIB 315.

An applicant in a sex discrimination case must be able to show that 'a considerably smaller proportion can comply' with the condition in question. The pool for comparison will be a matter for the tribunal. In *Fulton* (see above) there was a requirement that certain jobs be occupied on a full-time basis. The applicant who wished to job share claimed indirect discrimination after her request to do so was refused. Statistics showed that 100 per cent of male employees already in these posts could work full-time and 90 per cent of all women already employed in the department could work full time. It was held that that was not a considerably smaller proportion and her claim failed. Had the approach taken in *Price v Civil Service Commission* been taken by the tribunal it would have been more favourable to the applicant. It would appear from the decision in *Kidd v DRG Ltd* [1985] ICR 1 that the applicant must be able to show statistical evidence that is specific to her argument. In that case, the Employment Appeal Tribunal were content to leave the choice of the section of the community to be used as the pool for comparison to the industrial tribunal. Other cases where the issues of the pool for comparison is discussed include *Pearse v City of Bradford Metropolitan Council* [1988] IRLR 379 and *Greater Manchester Police Authority v LEA* [1990] IRLR 372.

In *Meade-Hill v British Council, The Times*, 14 April 1995, the Court of Appeal held that a clause in an employee's contract that she be required to work in such parts of the United Kingdom as her employer might require, was unlawful indirect discrimination within the Sex Discrimination Act 1975, ss. 1(1)(b) and 6(11), unless the employee could justify the requirement in the clause irrespective of the sex of the person to whom it was applied.

8.8.2.4 Victimisation Victimisation within the meaning of the Sex Discrimination Act 1975, s. 4(1) arises where less favourable treatment is given to a person because that person has brought proceedings under the legislation or has given evidence or made allegations with regard to the legislation, or intends to do any of the foregoing. Such action is not victimisation where the allegation was false and not made in good faith. (See *Aziz*, 8.9.3.)

8.8.3 Genuine occupational qualifications

There are exceptions which allow an employer to discriminate if the sex of the person required is a genuine occupational qualification. The sex of a person is a genuine occupational qualification in the following circumstances specified in the Sex Discrimination Act 1975, s. 7:

(a) The essential nature of the job calls for a man or woman for reasons of physiology or authenticity (s. 7(2)(a)). Strength and stamina are excluded here. An example would be advertising for a man to model menswear or to play Macbeth.

(b) Where decency or privacy require the job to be done by a man or woman; where members of that sex are in a state of undress or using sanitary facilities (s. 7(2)(b)). However, in a 1989 tribunal case in Glasgow it was held that being a woman was not a genuine occupational qualification for a part-time sales assistant's post in a woman's clothes shop, even though the job would normally involve working in the fitting room. It was held that the male applicant could have performed most of the duties and those he could not could be carried out by female sales assistants without inconvenience to or difficulty for the employer (*Etam plc* v *Rowan* [1989] IRLR 150). *Wylie* v *Dee & Co (Menswear) Ltd* [1978] IRLR 103 was similar. The employer alleged that being a man was a genuine occupational qualification because the employee would have to take inside leg measurements. The tribunal disagreed; it was something that was done rarely, there were seven male assistants on hand and in any case there were ways of taking the measurement without causing embarrassment.

(c) Where the job is at a single sex establishment where special care or provision is needed, all the inmates are of one sex and it is reasonable that the job be held by a person of a particular sex. Examples would be prisons or some hospitals or parts thereof (s. 7(2)(d)).

(d) Where the employee provides personal services relating to the education or welfare of individuals, and these can be most effectively provided by a person of one sex, e.g., a rape crisis centre worker (s. 7(2)(e)).

(e) Where the job involves work abroad in a country where there are restrictions or prohibitions on the employment of women, e.g. chauffeur in Saudi Arabia (s. 7(2)(g)).

(f) Where the job is one of two to be held by a married couple, e.g. club steward/ess (s. 7(2)(l)).

(g) Where the nature or location of the establishment makes it impracticable for the employee to live elsewhere than in premises provided by the employer, there are no separate sleeping or sanitary facilities, and it is not reasonable to expect the employer to alter the premises or provide alternative employment, e.g. on an oil rig or lighthouse (s. 7(2)(c)).

(h) Where the job is likely to involve the holder of the job doing his work in a private home and needs to be held by a person of one sex because objection might reasonably be taken to allowing a person of the other sex (i) the degree of physical or social contact with a person living in the home, or (ii) the knowledge of intimate details of such a person's life which is likely because of the nature and/or circumstances of the job or of the home, e.g. female companion to an elderly woman (s. 7(2)(BA).

8.8.4   Other forms of lawful discrimination

In addition to genuine occupational qualifications, the Sex Discrimination Act 1975 provides some other situations where it is lawful to discriminate:

(a)   where special treatment is afforded to women in connection with pregnancy or childbirth (s. 2(2));

(b)   where the work done is wholly or mainly outside Great Britain (s. 10(1));

(c)   in certain cases where police and prison officers are concerned discrimination is allowed in respect of height, uniform, allowances in lieu (s. 18);

(d)   where the doctrines of a faith provide that all ministers of religion be of one sex (s. 19);

(e)   where, under s. 6(4), special provision for death or retirement applies.

Section 6(4) provides that if there is a fixed age at which men retire in a particular employment there cannot be a lower age for women. Unfortunately it was still lawful to discriminate with regard to benefits under occupational pension schemes. However the decision in *Barber* v *Guardian Royal Exchange* [1990] IRLR 240 has altered this. This decision, which is arguably the most important decision made by the ECJ (as far as its impact on employers is concerned), held that occupational pensions payable under a contracted out scheme constitute 'pay' under Article 119 of the Treaty of Rome. They must therefore be non-discriminatory in their terms. This means that pensionable ages must be the same for men and women and benefits payable must be equal. UK discrimination legislation which had allowed discrimination in pension benefits and entitlements is overriden as a result of the *Barber* decision.

8.8.5   Sexual harassment

The term 'sexual harassment' is not mentioned in the Act, but it is now well established that sexual harassment constitutes unlawful sex discrimination because the harassed person is being treated less favourably 'on grounds of sex' (s. 1(1)(a)) and this may amount to a detriment (s. 6(2)(b)). Young employees (particularly females) were traditionally entitled to expect to be treated properly by their employers, and an early attempt to protect female employees can be seen in the rule that entitled a female employee whose employer tried to seduce her to rescind the contract (*McLean* v *Miller* (1832) 5 Deas Rep 270).

Porcelli v *Strathclyde Regional Council* [1986] IRLR 134 is authority for sexual harassment being a form of sexual discrimination. The applicant was one of three technicians in a school. The other two were men. She alleged that she was the victim of a campaign of harassment by the men which included lewd remarks, gestures and physical contact. Because of this she was forced to transfer to another school. She claimed that she had been unlawfully discriminated against by being subjected to a detriment contrary to s.6(2)(b). It seemed the motive behind the campaign was to make her leave. The Court of Session agreed she had suffered a detriment, which, Lord Emslie said, simply meant a 'disadvantage'. He said it must have been the intention of Parliament to restrain such degrading and unacceptable treatment.

Bracebridge Engineering Ltd v *Darby* [1990] IRLR 3 (see the Cases and Materials section for Chapter 8) is authority for the view that a single incident, provided it is sufficiently serious, can amount to detrimental treatment. Under s. 41(1), where an employee discriminates in the course of his employment, that act of discrimination is deemed to be done by the employer.

The EC has published a code of practice to combat sexual harassment, which it defines as 'unwanted conduct'. In *Insitu Cleaning* v *Meads* [1995] IRLR 4, it was again argued that a single act cannot amount to unwanted conduct because it cannot be regarded as unwanted until it is rejected. The EAT said if this was so it would amount to 'a licence for harassment'. The word 'unwanted' is essentially the same as 'unwelcome' or 'uninvited'. The view of this EAT is preferable to that of the all-male EAT in *Stewart* v *Cleveland Guest (Engineering) Ltd* [1994] IRLR 440, where it was held that it was not harassment to allow male employees to display nude female pin-ups in the workplace. They said that while S had been subject to a detriment she had not been discriminated against because a man might find them equally offensive. Michael Rubinstein, on whose proposals the EC code was based, has said that this decision essentially trivialises the effects of sexual harassment at work.

8.8.6 Enforcement

Complaints must normally be laid before the tribunal within three months of the alleged discrimination but there is a discretion to extend this period. The allegation will first be referred to a conciliation officer who will try to promote a settlement. If conciliation fails, the tribunal will hear the case. The burden of proof is on the complainant who may be assisted by the Equal Opportunities Commission in obtaining information, advice etc. If the tribunal finds the complaint well founded, it can make an order declaring the rights of the complainant and can also order that compensation be paid to the complainant. The maximum payable was until recently £11,000. However, following the decision of the ECJ in *Marshall* [1993] IRLR 445, this limit has been held to be unlawful as it breached European law. The sky would now seem to be the limit! (See Ministry of Defence cases involving the dismissal of pregnant service women.) The *Marshall* decision applied only to public sector employees, but the Government (anxious to share the misery) has introduced regulations to lift the £11,000 limit in all sex discrimination cases, whether public or private sector (Sex Discrimination and Equal Pay (Remedies) Regulations 1993, SI 1993 No 2798). The tribunal may also recommend that the respondent takes such action as seems necessary to obviate or reduce the adverse affect of the discrimination; if the recommendation is not complied with, the tribunal may award, or increase, compensation.

8.9 RACIAL DISCRIMINATION

The relevant statute here is the Race Relations Act 1976, which is modelled closely on the Sex Discrimination Act. As in that Act the legislation identifies three kinds of discrimination.

8.9.1 Direct discrimination

This is where one person treats another less favourably, on racial grounds, then he would treat someone else. If the grounds for the discrimination are racial then the actual race of the person discriminated against is unimportant. In *Showboat Entertainment Centre Ltd* v *Owens* [1984] IRLR 7, the applicant was a white man who was dismissed because he refused to exclude black youths from the premises. It was held that the applicants had been treated less favourably on racial grounds (albeit someone else's race) and there was unlawful racial discrimination.

As with direct sex discrimination, the motive of the discriminator is irrelevant. In *R* v *Commission for Racial Equality, ex parte Westminster City Council* [1985] IRLR 426 CA, a black man applied for a job as a refuse collector. This job was later withdrawn for fear of opposition from other employees. This was held to be unlawful.

8.9.2 Indirect discrimination

The provision here is very similar to that applying in sex discrimination cases (see 8.8.2.2 above). In *Panetar* v *Nestlé & Co Ltd* [1980] ICR 144, there was a prohibition against beards and long hair. It was held that this was indirect discrimination against the applicant who was a Sikh. He could in theory comply with the prohibition, however, it was not reasonable to expect him to do so because of his religion. (See also *Singh* v *Rowntree Mackintosh* [1979] IRLR 199.)

8.9.3 Victimisation

As in the Sex Discrimination Act 1975 (see 8.8.2.3 above), it will not be unlawful to accord less favourable treatment to a person who makes an untrue allegation or one not made in good faith. If the employer can show that he would have treated any of his employees (irrespective of race) in the same way as he treated the complainant then this will not be victimisation. In *Aziz* v *Trinity Street Taxis* [1988] IRLR 204 CA, the complainant made secret tape recordings of conversations with other members of his taxi owners' association. He was expelled when this was discovered. He claimed discrimination under s.2(1)(c) (i.e., victimisation).

His claim failed because the tribunal were satisfied that any other member of the association, irrespective of race, who had made such secret recordings would have been expelled. Slade LJ said 'the decision to expel him had been taken because a majority (of the association) condemned the making of the recordings as an underhand action and breach of trust'.

8.9.4   Racial grounds

'Racial grounds' are defined, in s. 3, as including colour, race, nationality or ethnic or national origins. National origins includes citizenship. The meaning of ethnic origin has caused some difficulty. In *Mandla* v *Dowell Lee* [1983] 2 AC 548, the House of Lords held that the term ethnic did not require a group to be distinguished by some fixed or inherited racial characteristic. The term 'ethnic' was wider than 'race'. The question before the House of Lords was whether Sikhs were a group of persons defined by ethnic origin. It was held they were. They were a distinct community which showed certain character-istics such as a long history, cultural tradition, common geographical origin, and common language, literature and religion. Religions as such are not covered by the Act (*Seide* v *Gillette Industries Ltd* [1980] IRLR 427). Rastafarians are not a separate group defined by ethnic origin as they lack a long history (*Dawkins* v *Department of Environment* [1993] IRLR 284).

8.9.5   Genuine occupational qualifications

An employer may lawfully discriminate where being a member of a particular racial group is a genuine occupational qualification. Section 5 specifies the circumstances in which the exception applies:

(a)   Where a member of a particular race is required for reasons of authenticity in art or photography, e.g., a black man for the role of Othello.

(b)   When the job involves working in a place where food or drink is provided to and consumed by members of the public and that place has a particular ambience. It would be lawful therefore to specify Chinese waiters for reasons of authenticity.

(c)   Where the holder of the job provides persons of that racial group with personal services promoting their welfare and those services can best be provided by a person of that racial group, e.g., a West Indian social worker in a predominantly West Indian area. In *London Borough of Lambeth* v *Commission for Racial Equality* [1990] IRLR 231, the Council advertised two jobs in their housing department, one for the assistant head of housing, the other for a group manager within the department. Over half the tenants were of Afro-Caribbean or Asian origin. The jobs were advertised as only open to Afro-Caribbeans and Asians on the grounds that the postholder would be providing members of the black community with personal services. The Court of Appeal said that as the posts would involve minimal contact with the public they could not be categorised as providing 'personal services' and that therefore the defence of genuine occupational qualification failed. In *Tottenham Green Under Fives Centre* v *Marshall (No. 2)* [1991] IRLR 162 it was held that being of Afro-Caribbean origin was a genuine occupational qualification for a post as a nursery worker within s. 5(2)(d) because an ability to read and talk in dialect was a 'personal service', even though it was not the most important attribute of the postholder.

8.9.6 Enforcement

An individual may complain to an industrial tribunal. The procedure and remedies are similar to those under the sex discrimination legislation. Following the *Marshall* decision the previous £11,000 limit on compensation (now £11,300) was removed (Race Relations (Remedies) Act 1994). The Act may also be enforced by the Commission for Racial Equality which has wide-ranging powers of investigation and enforcement.

8.10 MATERNITY RIGHTS

The Employment Protection (Consolidation) Act 1978, as amended by the Employment Act 1980, ss. 11 and 12, and the Social Security Act 1986, give employees who are absent from work due to pregnancy or confinement certain rights. These have been radically altered by TURERA as a UK response to the EC Directive on the protection of pregnant women at work (Directive 92/85 EEC), and by the Employment Rights Act 1995 (ERA).

An employee who is absent from work due to pregnancy or confinement has the right to maternity pay and leave, the right to return to work after confinement and the right not to be dismissed on grounds of her pregnancy. The legislation was described in *Lavery* v *Plessey Communications* [1983] ICR 354 as 'of inordinate complexity exceeding the worst excesses of a taxing statute; we find that specially regrettable bearing in mind that these provisions are regulating the everyday rights of ordinary employers and employees'.

8.10.1 Maternity pay

Since 1987 there has been a scheme of statutory maternity pay (SMP) payable under the provisions of the Social Security Act 1986, ss. 46 to 49 and since 1992 under the Social Security Contributions and Benefits Act 1992, ss. 164–171. The scheme replaced an earlier, more limited entitlement to maternity pay for long-serving employees and, for those who qualify for SMP, also replaces maternity allowance. SMP is paid by the employer, who is entitled to deduct the amount paid and administration costs from national insurance contributions. SMP is payable for a maximum of 18 weeks. (The maternity pay period: MPP). Payment is based on a two-tier system. The higher rate (equivalent to 90 per cent of your normal earnings) is paid for the first six weeks of the maternity pay period. The next 12 weeks are paid at a standard rate (equivalent to statutory sick pay). This at time of writing is £52.50.

8.10.1.1 Eligibility Entitlement to SMP depends on the employee having 26 weeks' continuous service with the employer at the fifteenth week before the expected week of confinement. There is no requirement to work a minimum number of hours per week. The employee must earn more than the lower earnings limit for National Insurance (currently £57 but reviewed yearly). She must provide evidence of the expected date of confinement (if requested from a doctor or a midwife within 21 days), have actually stopped work, have indicated that she will be absent on grounds of maternity (as contractually required), and have reached the eleventh week before the expected week of confinement. This last will not apply if the woman has been confined earlier than this. The woman (provided she is otherwise eligible) will be entitled to SMP whether or not she intends to return to work after the birth. Women who qualify for SMP may be excluded from receiving SMP if they are not employed by the employer during the qualifying week (see below), or are outside the EU during the first week of SMP, are taken into legal custody during the first week of the MPP or work for another employer after the confinement and during the MPP.

In *Satchwell Sunvic Ltd* v *Secretary of State for Employment* [1979] IRLR 455, the employee gave notice to leave work 12 weeks before her expected date of confinement. She stated that she intended to return to work. Her employer paid her six weeks' maternity pay. The Secretary of State refused to refund the employer on the grounds that the employee had not continued to be employed until the beginning of the eleventh week before confinement (which was then the requirement). It was held that the term 'continued to be employed' meant no more than she had a contract of employment. The Employment Appeal Tribunal said 'so long as her contract subsists it does not matter whether she is in fact at her desk or bench and the statute imposes no limitation on the reason why she may not be at work'. The contract continued until the employee resigned. The employee must not resign before going on maternity leave. However, *Hughes* v *Gwynedd Area Health Board* [1978] ICR 161 would suggest that where only a general statement by the employee that she does not intend to return to work is made, then this will not amount to resignation.

8.10.1.2 Maternity allowance Employees who do not qualify for SMP, for example because they have recently changed employers, may be entitled to maternity allowance payable under the Social Security Act 1975 as amended by the Social Security Contributions and Benefits Act 1992. In general, maternity allowance is payable for the same period and at the same rate as the lower rate of SMP.

8.10.2 Right to maternity leave

TURERA 1993 amended the previous provision by introducing a maternity leave period which applies to all employees (now contained in ERA 1995). The minimum period of leave is 14 weeks, and up to 40 weeks for those with two years' continuous service with the employer. During the period all contractual rights (except pay) will be protected. The maternity leave period begins any time after the eleventh week before the expected week of birth. The minimum 14-week period may be extended if there is some statutory prohibition on employing the woman because of her recent childbirth. To qualify the employee must inform her employer in writing at least 21 days before the maternity leave period begins (or as soon as is reasonably practicable):

(a) that she is pregnant;
(b) the expected week of childbirth.

If requested by the employer, the employee must produce a certificate from either a doctor or a midwife giving the expected week of childbirth. Many employees may in addition have a contractual right to maternity leave. They cannot exercise the two rights seperately but must choose between them (ERA, ss. 73, 80).

8.10.3 Right to return to work

Any employee who has been absent from work because of pregnancy or confinement is entitled to return to work with her employer within 29 weeks following the actual confinement, provided she satisfies the conditions for eligibility described below. She is entitled to return to the job in which she was originally employed on the same terms and conditions as she would have enjoyed had she not been absent. If it is not reasonably practicable for the employer to give her back her former job he may offer her a suitable alternative.

In *Edgell* v *Lloyd's Register of Shipping* [1977] IRLR 463, it was held that an employee whose job before confinement involved the authority to sign cheques and who reported direct to the manager of the British Division of Lloyd's Register had been offered a suitable alternative, although in her new job she no longer had the authority to sign cheques and was now expected to report to a supervisor.

An employee who unreasonably refuses a suitable alternative loses her rights. In *Bovey* v *Board of Governors of the Hospital for Sick Children* [1978] IRLR 241, the employee told the employer that she thought she would be unable to return to work full-time but would like to return on a part-time basis: part-time work attracted a lower grading and rate of pay. She claimed that these were less favourable terms and conditions. The tribunal however disagreed. They said that she had the right under statute to return to her former job on favourable terms and conditions. She, however, chose not to exercise this right by exercising a contractual right to work part-time. She could not pick the bits she liked from each, i.e. part-time from her contractual entitlement and the same pay, etc. from her statutory entitlement. The employee may elect as between the contractual entitlement (if there is one) and the statutory entitlement, but must treat whichever she chooses as an indivisible package.

8.10.3.1 Eligibility To be eligible to return to work after absence because of pregnancy or confinement, the employee must continue to be employed by her employer up to the beginning of the eleventh week before the expected date of confinement and she must then have been continuously employed for at least two years. Additionally, she must have informed the employer in writing of her intention at least 21 days before her absence begins (or as soon as practicable if that is not practicable). An employee who knows of her rights but cannot decide whether to exercise them will lose them. For example, in *Nu-Swift International Ltd* v *Mallinson* [1978] IRLR 357, it was held that the employee's indecision due to pre-natal anxiety was not a good enough reason for not notifying the employer that she wished to return to work. Under

EPCA, s. 56A, inserted by the Employment Act 1980, s. 12, if the woman works for an employer who has five or fewer employees and it is not reasonably practicable for the employer to permit her to return to work either in her old job or a suitable alternative then the employer need not do so and she will have no claim against him.

8.10.3.2 Exercise of the right to return to work The employee must give the employer at least 21 days' notice in writing of her intended date of return. The employer may postpone her return for up to four weeks, provided that she is notified before the day on which she proposed to return. The employer must tell her the reason for postponement and the day on which she may return. The employee may also delay her return beyond the twenty-ninth week after the actual confinement if she is ill. She may delay her return by a once only period of four weeks. She may also postpone her return if there is an interruption of work which makes it unreasonable to expect her to return on the stated date, e.g., a strike.

8.10.4 Ante-natal care

All women employees are entitled to time off work for ante-natal care (ERA, s. 53). There are no service qualifications required. The employer can require the employee to produce a certificate of pregnancy and an appointment card but this does not apply to the first appointment. The employee is entitled to be paid for this time off at the appropriate rate and, if she is not, she can complain to an industrial tribunal within three months. If she has been refused time off she will be entitled to compensation.

8.11 HEALTH AND SAFETY AT WORK ACT 1974

One of the most fundamental rights of the employee is the right to a working environment which is safe and free from risk to health. In addition to domestic legislation, health and safety has been heavily influenced by European legislation. Article 118A of the Treaty of Rome provides that member states should pay particular attention to encouraging improvements, especially to the working environment, as regards the health and safety of workers. Under Article 118A, the Council of Ministers adopted the Framework Directive (98/391/EEC) and five 'daughter' directives which dealt with minimum health and safety requirements in the fields of work equipment, personal protective equipment, display screen equipment, minimum workplace standards, and manual handling of loads. The Directives have been implemented in the United Kingdom by new regulations and codes of practice which came into force on 1 January 1993, i.e. the Management of Health and Safety at Work Regulations 1992, the Provision and Use of Work Equipment Regulations 1992, the Workplace (Health and Safety and Welfare) Regulations 1992, the Health and Safety (Display Screen Equipment) Regulations 1992, the Personal Protective Equipment at Work Regulations 1992, and the Manual Handling Operations Regulations 1992. It should be noted that the Management of Health and Safety at Work Regulations 1992 require employees to carry out a risk assessment exercise to determine the nature and degree of exposure that risk employees may be exposed to. Craig and Miller (1995) argue that failure to carry out such a risk assessment would be a breach of the common law requirement to provide a safe system of work. Domestic law on health and safety already covers much of that specified in the Directives, but the European Union will be a major source of health and safety law in the future. We, however, will concentrate on the provisions of the Health and Safety at Work Act 1974.

As we saw earlier an employer owes his employees a duty of reasonable care while they are in the course of their employment. This duty arises from the operation of the common law. The employer must be aware that his obligations do not stop there nor do they extend only to his employees. He must take account of the protective occupational health and safety legislation.

The first factory statute was passed in 1802 in response to concern at the conditions under which mill children were working. The Factory Act 1833 was somewhat of a turning point in that it made provision for the enforcement of the legislation by four inspectors appointed by the government. Over the next 135 years there was a piecemeal extension of protective legislation in response to specific hazards, social pressure, the trade union movement etc. By 1970 there were nine main groups of statutes and approximately five hundred statutory instruments which applied to health and safety at work, e.g., the Factories Act 1961, the Explosives Act 1875, and the Offices, Shops and Railway Premises Act 1963.

The government appointed a committee under Lord Robens to review the legislation. Once of their conclusions was 'the first and most fundamental defect of the statutory system is that there is too much law' (Robens Report 1972, para. 28). The government adopted most of the committee's proposals which became the basis for the Health and Safety at Work Act 1974 (HASWA). HASWA is what is known as an enabling Act. It lays down a framework within which changes can be made. It did not repeal the existing statutes overnight; changes will be made over a period and are unlikely to be completed by the millenium. Changes are made by the making of regulations and approved codes of practice under the 1974 Act which contain the detailed requirements.

One major change made by HASWA is that for the first time everyone who works is covered. The pre-1974 legislation did not cover many types of workplace. The only exceptions now are domestic servants (s. 51). Much more important is that HASWA extends beyond those at work to cover visitors, patients, sub-contractors etc. The basic approach of the Act is that those who control the workplace have the responsibility to make it a safer place.

It is important to realise that while breaches of the common law duties involve the civil law, breaches of the provisions of HASWA are criminal offences. The responsibility may fall on a corporate body which will not mind that it has a criminal record but as we shall see individuals may be liable under the Act and may unwittingly acquire a criminal record. Prosecution is, however, a last step, HASWA seeks enforcement through persuasion.

Section 1(1) contains a summary of HASWA's objectives:

The provisions of this Act shall have effect with a view to—

(a)   securing the health, safety, and welfare of persons at work;
(b)   protecting persons other than persons at work against risks to health or safety arising out of or in connection with the activities of persons at work;
(c)   controlling the keeping and use of explosive or highly flammable or otherwise dangerous substances, and generally preventing the unlawful acquisition, possession and use of such substances; and
(d)   controlling the emission into the atmosphere of noxious or offensive substances from premises of any class prescribed. . .

The main points to note are that the provisions extend to the welfare as well as the safety of those at work, they also cover those not at work. Mention of emissions is important. One way to make a factory less dusty or smoky is to pump the offending material outside where it affects others.

8.11.1   General duties
Sections 2 to 9 lay down a number of general duties. These apply not only to employers and employees but to the self-employed, the controllers of premises, and the designers, suppliers, manufacturers and importers of articles and substances for use at work. Most of these duties are qualified by the words 'so far as is reasonably practicable'. In *Edwards* v *NCB* [1949] 1 KB 704, Asquith LJ said (at 709):

'Reasonably practicable' is a narrower term than 'physically possible' and seems to me to imply that a computation must be made . . . in which the quantum of risk is placed on one scale and the sacrifice involved in the measures necessary for averting the risk (whether in money, time or trouble) is placed on the other, and that, if it be shown that there is a gross disproportion between them - the risk being insignificant in relation to the sacrifice - the defendants discharge the onus on them.

It would seem that where the risk of serious injury or loss of life is high then preventative action must be taken. Lord Reid said in *Marshall* v *Gotham Co Ltd* [1954] 1 All ER 937 HL (at 942) 'as men's lives may be at stake, it should not be lightly held that to take a practicable precaution is unreasonable.'
The case of *T O Harrison (Newcastle-under-Lyme) Ltd* v *Ramsey* [1976] IRLR 135 would strongly suggest that the employer cannot plead an adverse financial position as a defence as to why he did not comply with the requirements.
It is for the person who alleges he has done what is 'reasonably practicable' to establish it (HASWA, s. 40). It would seem that an employer can be required to adopt measures that are safer than those generally practised in a particular industry (*Martin* v *Boulton and Paul (Steel Construction) Ltd* [1982] ICR 366).

8.11.1.1   Duties of employers   Section 2(1) imposes a duty on all employers 'to ensure so far as is reasonably practicable the health, safety and welfare at work of all his employees'.

Section 2(2) goes on to specify different aspects of this general duty:

(a)   the provision and maintenance of plant and systems of work that are so far as is reasonably practicable safe and without risks to health;

(b)   arrangements for ensuring, so far as is reasonably practicable, safety and absence of risks to health in connection with the use, handling, storage and transport of articles and substances;

(c)   the provision of such information, instruction, training and supervision as is necessary to ensure, so far as is reasonably practicable, the health and safety at work of his employees;

(d)   so far as is reasonably practicable as regards any place of work under the employer's control the maintenance of it in a condition that is safe and without risks to health and the provision and maintenance of means of access to and egress from it that are safe and without such risks;

(e)   the provision and maintenance of a working environment for his employees that is, so far as is reasonably practicable, safe, without risks to health, and adequate as regard facilities and arrangements for their welfare at work.

It is a breach of s. 2 to make available unsafe plant even if it has not been used (*Bolton Metropolitan BC* v *Malrod Insulations Ltd* [1993] ICR 388). This case demonstrates once again the purposive approach taken by the courts to the preventative nature of the Act. (See ODonnel, 'Defective Machinery – A Cautionary Tale', 1993 BUS. L.B. 410.)

These duties are owed to employees who are defined, in s. 53(1), as individuals working under a contract of employment or apprenticeship. They are similar to the employer's common law duties (see 8.3.1.3 above). Section 2 is of course part of the criminal not the civil law.

Safety policy   Section 2(3) requires every employer, except those with less than 5 employees, to prepare and revise as often as is appropriate a written statement of their general health and safety policy. In addition to general policy it should cover the organisation and arrangements for carrying it out. This statement must be brought to the attention of the employees.

Safety representatives   Section 2(4), (6) and (7) are important in that they enable employees to be responsible for their own working environment. Trade unions can appoint safety representatives at the place of work and they must be consulted by the employer with a view to the making and maintenance of arrangements which will enable him and his employees to cooperate effectively in bringing about safe conditions of work. The employer should be notified of the appointment of these representatives, who should ideally have had two years' experience in the industry (Safety Representatives and Safety Committee Regulations 1977 as amended by the Management of Health and Safety at Work Regulations 1992; these are accompanied by an approved code of practice and non-statutory guidance notes). These Regulations allow safety representatives to investigate potential hazards and dangerous occurrences; to examine the cause of accidents; to investigate complaints relating to employees' health, safety or welfare at work; to make representation to the employer on these and on general matters affecting the health, safety and welfare of employees; to carry out inspections; to represent employees in consultation at the workplace with inspectors; and to receive information from inspectors in accordance with HASWA, s. 28(8). Section 2(4) refers to 'recognised trade unions'. If the employer does not recognise a trade union then there is no right to have safety representatives appointed. There is, however, nothing to prevent employers from allowing the appointment of safety representatives and many do. Inspections can be carried out approximately every three months, or more frequently by agreement, or in response to some specific hazard, or to determine the cause of an accident.

Safety committees If at least two safety representatives so request in writing, the employer must establish within three months of the request a safety committee. He must consult with them and representatives of the recognised trade union(s). The general function of these committees is to keep under review the measures taken to ensure the health and safety at work of the employees. Safety representatives appointed under HASWA have the right to have such time off with pay as is required to allow them to perform their functions and undergo training. If a representative is not given time off or not paid he may complain to an industrial tribunal. If the complaint is well-founded the tribunal must make a declaration and may award compensation.

Duties to persons who are not employees Section 3(1) introduced a new concept. It extended the obligations of employers to those who are not their employees. This will include the general public, contractors, visitors, and even trespassers – anyone in fact who might be affected by the employer's operations. There is no need to show that anyone has been harmed. If there is a risk of harm that will suffice (*R v Board of Trustees of the Science Museum* [1993] 1 WLR 1171). This duty can extend to taking reasonable precautions to prevent entry onto premises, e.g., building sites are both very attractive and very dangerous for young children, there are minimum standards of fencing required and guidance is published on the immobilisation of machinery and the covering of holes. Section 3(2) imposes a similar duty on a self-employed person in respect of himself and other and non-employees.

The case of *R v Swan Hunter Ltd* [1981] IRLR 403 has confirmed that employers must give full instruction and training on any specific health hazard to non-employees. General warnings and statements are not enough. This has important repercussions for those employing sub-contract labour. In 1976 eight men were killed in a fire on *HMS Glasgow*, then being built by Swan Hunter. The fire started and spread so quickly because the air was enriched with oxygen. An employee of a sub-contractor had failed to switch off the oxygen supply the previous evening. The dangers of oxygen in confined spaces was known as long ago as 1944 and had caused deaths at Swan Hunter in 1966 and 1970. As a result of these deaths Swan Hunter had prepared a booklet outlining the hazards and preventative measures. This booklet was, however, never issued to sub-contractors. Swan Hunter were charged with a breach of s. 2(2)(a) and (c) and a breach of s. 3(1), for failing to conduct their undertakings so that persons not in their employment were not exposed to safety risks.

Two recent decisions have clarified the criminal liability of employers under s. 3(1). in *R* v *Associated Octel Ltd* [1994] IRLR 3 the employer was held to be criminally liable for the negligence of an independent contractor, even although he had no actual control over how the work was done. If there is some risk of injury to the health and safety of persons not employed by the employer (e.g., contractors' employees or the public), and *a fortiori* if there is actual injury as a result of the work, then there is prima facie liability. In *R* v *British Steel* [1995] IRLR 3 it was held that an employer cannot escape criminal liability under s. 3(1) for the negligence of its employees by showing that its senior management or 'directing mind' was not involved.

Charges for safety equipment.   Section 9 provides that 'no employer shall levy or permit to be levied on any employee of his any charge in respect of anything done or provided in pursuance of any specific requirement of the relevant statutory requirements'.

Employers must not charge for safety clothing or equipment that is required by law. Section 9 applies to all personal protective equipment deemed necessary under the Personal Protection at Work Regulations. However, any safety equipment that is not required by law may be charged for, e.g., safety shoes for general labouring work. In such cases, the equipment is usually supplied at cost price and paid for by small paybill deductions over a period of time.

In *Associated Dairies Ltd* v *Hartley* [1979] IRLR 171, Associated Dairies Ltd used hydraulic trolley jacks for the handling and distribution of articles in the warehouse of Asda, Frimsby. They provided a facility whereby employees could purchase safety shoes at cost price. Employees were allowed to pay for them at £1 a week. An employee, one Mr Badger, suffered a fractured toe and other injuries when the wheel of a jack ran over his foot. The inspector issued an Improvement Notice requiring that all employees using the jacks be issued with suitable safety shoes, free of charge. Mr Badger was the first person to be so injured in five years. The cost of providing the boots free would be £20,000 initially, then £10,000 per annum. The tribunal cancelled the improvement notice because the expense of providing the free footwear was disproportionate to the risk involved to the employees, and, in any case, there was no evidence that employees would use the boots.

8.11.1.2 Duties of controllers of premises   Section 4 imposes a duty on persons who have control over premises (other than domestic premises) which are available to non-employees either as a place of work, or a place where they may use plant or substances. The duty imposed is that that the controller must take such measures as it is reasonable for a person in his position to take to ensure, so far as is reasonably practicable, that the premises and any plant or substances are safe and without risk to health. Examples of the type of place covered would be coin-operated launderettes, car washes, and self-use car service areas. However, *Westminster City Council* v *Select Managements*

[1985] ICR 353, would suggest that premises will be non-domestic where they are not in the exclusive occupation of the occupants of a private dwelling, e.g. a lift in a block of flats. This provision is the criminal counterpart of the civil liability contained in the Occupier's Liability (Scotland) Act 1960.

8.11.1.3 Duties of those in charge of prescribed premises Section 5 imposes a duty on those in charge of prescribed premises to use the best practicable means of preventing the emission into the atmosphere from the premises of noxious or offensive substances. The Health and Safety (Emissions into the Atmosphere) Regulations 1983 contain lists of both prescribed premises and noxious or offensive substances.

8.11.1.4 Duties of designers, manufacturers, importers and suppliers Section 6(1) is another general provision of considerable importance. It imposes a duty on designers, manufacturers, importers and suppliers to:

   (a)   ensure so far as is reasonably practicable that an article is so designed and constructed that it will be safe and without risks to health at all times when it is being set, used, cleaned or maintained by a person at work;
   (b)   to carry out or arrange to carry out such testing and examination as may be necessary for the peformance of the duty referred to in (a) above;
   (c)   to take such steps as are necessary to secure that persons supplied by that person with the article are provided with adequate information about the use for which the article is designed or has been tested and about any conditions necessary to ensure that it will be safe and without risks to health at all such times as are mentioned in (a) above and when it is being dismantled or disposed of; and
   (d)   to take such steps as are necessary to ensure that, so far as is reasonably practicable, persons so supplied are provided with all such revisions of information provided to them by virtue of (b) above as are necessary by reason of its becoming known that anything gives rise to a serious risk to health or safety.

Section 6(5) imposes a duty on those erecting and installing any article for use at work to ensure, so far as is reasonably practicable, that nothing about the way it is erected or installed will make it unsafe or a risk to health when used.

8.11.1.5 Duties of Employees Section 7 provides that:

It shall be the duty of every employee while at work:

   (a)   to take reasonable care for the health and safety of himself and of other persons who may be affected by his acts or omissions at work; and
   (b)   as regards any duty or requirement imposed on his employer or any other person by or under any of the relevant statutory provisions, to

co-operate with him so far as is necessary to enable that duty or requirement to be performed or complied with.

Employees who refuse to follow safety procedure or to wear safety equipment could be prosecuted, but prosecutions of employees have been rare.
Such refusal would, however, constitute a potentially fair reason for dismissal.
The employer is still, however, in charge of the workplace and has therefore
the major responsibility as regards health and safety. The Management of
Health and Safety at Work Regulations impose obligations on employers to
report dangerous situations and shortcomings in the employers' protection
arrangements.

8.11.1.6 Duty not to interfere with safety provision Section 8 makes it an
offence for any person, 'intentionally or recklessly to interfere with or misuse
anything provided in the interests of health, safety or welfare in pursuance of
any of the statutory provisions'. This, of course, includes employees and
clearly covers misuse as well as deliberate damage. The section also applies
to, e.g., visitors and trespassers.

8.11.2 Enforcement

Sections 18 to 26 concern the enforcement of HASWA. Responsibility for
enforcement is split between the Health and Safety Executive, the islands and
district councils, the Secretary of State, and specialist enforcement authorities
(e.g., for nuclear installations). The local authorities and the Health and
Safety Executive are the most important enforcement authorities. Their
powers are wide and are laid down in HASWA, ss. 20(2) and 25; they
include:

(a)   the right of entry, either alone or accompanied, to any premises to
fulfil their health and safety duties;
(b)   the right to conduct any necessary enquiry or investigation on the
premises;
(c)   the right to direct that equipment or premises be left undisturbed;
(d)   the right to seize and render harmless articles and substances;
(e)   the right to take copies of books and records.

8.11.2.1 Improvement notices Section 21 provides that if an inspector is of
the opinion that a person is contravening one or more of the relevant
statutory provisions or has contravened one or more of those provisions in
circumstances that make it likely that the contravention will continue or be
repeated, he may serve on him an improvement notice. This person may be
an employer, employee or self-employed. The notice must state the grounds
of the inspector's complaint and require the breach to be remedied within not
less than 21 days. There is the right of appeal to an industrial tribunal within
the same 21-day period. Lodging the appeal has the effect of suspending the
notice until the appeal has been dealt with.

8.11.2.2 Prohibition notice   Section 22(2) provides that:

If as regards any activities to which this section applies an inspector is of the opinion that, as carried on or about to be carried on by or under the control of the person in question, the activities involve or, as the case may be, will involve a risk of serious personal injury, the inspector may serve on that person . . . a prohibition notice.

The prohibition notice must state the grounds of complaint and the inspector may require the activity in question to cease immediately or at the end of a specified period. An appeal against a prohibition notice can be made within 21 days. However, unlike improvement notices, lodging an appeal will only have the effect of suspending the notice if the industrial tribunal so directs.

8.11.3 Offences and penalties
Section 33 lays down a wide range of offences ranging from contravening one of the statutory duties to obstructing an inspector in the course of his duties or falsely pretending to be an inspector. Prosecutions in Scotland are undertaken by the Procurator Fiscal. The maximum penalty is a fine of £5,000 for certain offences and £20,000 for others in summary proceedings. On indictment there is an unlimited fine and/or a maximum of three years' imprisonment. The average fine in 1994 was £1,400. The highest fine was £750,000. Several people have been sentenced to a suspended prison sentence, but no one has had to serve one. There are about 3,000 prosecutions each year; of these 90 per cent result in convictions.

8.11.4 Offences due to fault of another person
Section 36(1) provides that where the commission by any person of an offence under any of the relevant statutory provisions is due to the act or default of some other person, that other person is guilty of the offence. A person may be charged with and convicted of the offence by virtue of s. 36(1), whether or not proceedings are taken against the first named person.
  Section 37(1) provides as follows:

Where an offence under any of the relevant statutory provisions committed by a body corporate is proved to have been committed with the consent or connivance of or to have been attributable to any neglect on the part of any director, manager, secretary or other similar officer of the body corporate or a person who was purporting to act in any such capacity, he as well as the body corporate shall be guilty of that offence and shall be liable to be proceeded against and punished accordingly.

Section 37(1) was considered in *Armour* v *Skeen* [1977] IRLR 310 (see the Cases and Materials section for Chapter 8). Mr Armour, Director of Roads for Strathclyde Regional Council, was found guilty in the sheriff court on five charges relating to the accidental death of one of the Council's employees who fell from the Erskine Bridge while repainting it. The Council and Mr Armour were prosecuted for a breach of a number of safety provisions under the Factories Act and relevant regulations relating to the lack of a safe system of work and failure to notify the local inspector that the work was being undertaken. His prosecution was based on s. 37(1). He appealed but the High Court of Justiciary held that the sheriff had not erred in finding Mr Armour, as the Council's Director of Roads, personally liable for neglect within the meaning of HASWA, s. 37(2).

Further reading

Bowers and Honeyball, (1993), *Textbook on Labour Law* (3rd edn), Blackstone Press.

Craig and Miller, (1991), *Employment Law in Scotland*, T & T Clark.

Craig and Miller, (1995), *Law of Health and Safety at Work in Scotland*, W. Green/Sweet & Maxwell.

Davies and Freedland, (1993), *Labour Legislation and Public Policy*, Clarendon Press.

Lockton, (1994) *Employment Law*, Macmillan.

Painter, Holmes, Migdal, (1995), *Cases and Materials on Employment Law*, Blackstone Press.

Painter and Puttick, (1993), *Employment Rights*, Pluto Press.

Selwyn, (1993), *Law of Employment*, 8th edn, Butterworths & Co.

CHAPTER NINE

Administrative and Criminal Law: Regulation of Business

9.1 PURPOSE AND NATURE OF CONTROL

So far our discussion has concentrated on private law remedies for defective goods and services. However, these are not necessarily the most effective and certainly not the only form of control over business. For a start they operate after a wrong has been suffered and attempt to provide financial compensation. Vital as such compensation is, once the damage is done, it can never really change what has happened. It cannot, for example, alter the fact that a holiday which was looked forward to all year has turned out to be a miserable experience, without advertised facilities. Neither can it undo the physical injury caused by a defective product. In addition, a dissatisfied customer will often be deterred by bureaucracy and cost from pursuing the matter.

The various limitations of the private law are alleviated to some extent by the imposition of criminal sanctions for certain conduct (see 9.2 below). One advantage of criminal sanctions is that the customer does not have to take the trouble of enforcing them. Once the complaint has been made to the appropriate authority (e.g., the Trading Standard or Environmental Health Department), the matter is pursued by that authority. In addition the moral stigma attached to criminal liability may act as a deterrent and raise standards. On the other hand, criminal liability operates after the event and depends on a dissatisfied customer being aware of the possibility of taking action and the bodies to whom complaints should be made.

A more sophisticated approach is to regulate practice in the first instance, before poor standards can cause damage or injury. This may be done by giving bodies such as the Office of Fair Trading or the Health and Safety

Executive the power to oversee particular aspects of industry and commerce. Such powers may or may not be backed up with criminal penalties for non-compliance with regulations or recommendations (see 9.3 below). Of course, while both criminal and administrative regulation may provide an increased layer of protection for consumers, they also both involve costs. There is the cost of running a local or central government agency to enforce rules, and there is also the cost to business of complying with the rules. The costs of running a system of protection means that it will never be feasible to employ the number of staff or to engage in the number of inspections which might be necessary to ensure that there are never breaches of the law (see discussion of regulation of food safety by Willett, [1991] *Statute Law Review* 146).

This is one reason why the officers who enforce the rules try to encourage as much self-regulation by traders as possible. Rather than simply acting as enforcers, who react to offences by taking prosecutions, officers encourage good practice among traders, advising them how to keep within the law (see discussion by Willett, 'Emergency Food Control in the UK' in Micklitz, Röethe and Weatherill, *Federalism and Responsibility*, 1994). This process is aided by the structure of the typical trading standards or food safety type offence. There will normally be liability without proof of fault (for an exception, see 9.2.1.2 below); however, the trader will typically have available a 'due diligence' defence, which encourages good, preventative quality management by the trader in that the defence is much more likely to succeed if such a quality management system has been used (see Willett, [1991] *Statute Law Review* 146, and see 9.2.1.3 below). This sort of approach also, in some ways, reduces burdens upon traders, who know that if they have a good management system (which is in their commercial interests in any case), there is less chance of their being liable for the various offences.

Another option is to leave members of a particular trade or profession to regulate their own conduct by means of codes of practice, e.g., the *Vehicle Builders & Repairers' Association Code of Practice* or the *ABTA Code for Travel Agents*. Some codes are self-regulatory but operate within a statutory framework which can take over if the self-regulation fails to achieve acceptable standards, e.g., the *City Code on Takeovers*.

The Office of Fair Trading is probably the most significant central government institution engaged in the regulation of business, being concerned with monopolies, mergers, restrictive trade practices, and consumer interests of various kinds. The Office of Fair Trading is ultimately responsible to the Department of Trade & Industry. Other government departments also have important regulatory roles, e.g., the Home Office oversees activities involving firearms, dangerous drugs, explosives and poisons. Local authorities play the major role in enforcing the law as described in 9.2 below. The EU also has an important regulatory role in relation to business in all member states. This arises by virtue of the power of the Commission to initiate and coordinate policy, formulate and hand down regulations and directives, and enforce the terms of community treaties and rules. Recent examples of EU legislation, giving powers to regulatory authorities to regulate business, include the Unfair Terms and the Product Safety Directives (see 9.3.4 and 9.2.3 below).

9.2 CRIMINAL REGULATION

Important examples of the regulation of business by the criminal law are the prohibitions contained in the Trade Descriptions Act 1968 and the Consumer Protection Act 1987 on applying a false trade description to goods, services, accommodation or facilities or giving a false impression as to the price of goods, services, accommodation or facilities. The full text of the relevant sections is reproduced below in the Cases and Materials section for Chapter 9. However, it is useful to outline briefly the impact of the provisions (although in the interests of a full understanding the relevant sections should be considered in conjunction with the discussion below).

9.2.1 Trade descriptions

9.2.1.1 Description of goods Section 1 of the Trade Descriptions Act 1968 criminalises the application to any goods of a 'false trade description', or to supply or offer to supply goods to which a false trade description has been applied (see the relevant provisions in the Cases and Materials for Chapter 9). Anyone who offends against s. 1 is also likely to be liable to a purchaser for breach of either an express or implied term of the contract (e.g., Sale of Goods Act 1979, ss. 13 and 14, see Chapter 6, para. 6.6.2). The provisions apply to advertised goods to the extent that customers could fairly assume that the goods in question were being referred to by the advertisement.

As in the law of contract and misrepresentation, subjective advertising 'puff' which cannot be judged by any objective standard does not amount to a 'description' of goods. So to describe goods as being 'top class' when they are in fact of inferior quality, or to describe a product as giving 'extra value' when it does not, as in *Cadbury Ltd* v *Halliday* [1975] 2 All ER 226, does not amount to the application of a false trade description.

One of the most common means of committing an offence under s. 1 is by reducing the mileage shown on the odometer of a car. A report by the Director General of Fair Trading in 1978 indicated that about 50 per cent of vehicles had been tampered with in this way. The principal means which dealers have used to avoid liability is a disclaimer clause which says that no guarantee is being given as to the authenticity of the mileage. The case law on this problem has been rather confused in its import, however it seems that it is possible to draw the following conclusions. First, if a dealer has actively applied a false trade description (by clocking the car) no form of disclaimer, wherever displayed, can avoid liability. This is because the only effect that a disclaimer may have is to negate the application of a trade description. If one has already been made there can be no defence (see *R* v *Southwood* (1987) 131 SJ 1038). Secondly, even where the clocking has been carried out by a previous owner, a casual remark by the dealer or a disclaiming clause in the small print of a document is not sufficient to avoid liability (see *R* v *Southwood*). The practice in the trade is to place a sticker disclaiming liability on top of the odometer reading. This may be effective to avoid liability if it gives a clear indication that no reliance should be placed on the mileage, so the argument here is that no false statement has in fact been made.

9.2.1.2 Description of services, accommodation or facilities Section 14 of the Trade Descriptions Act makes it an offence to knowingly or recklessly make a false statement regarding certain aspects of the provisions of services, accommodation or facilities (see the Cases and Materials section for Chapter 9, where these aspects are listed in the context of s. 14). This would apply, for example, to a brochure advertising hotel rooms as having air conditioning and being furnished when in fact neither amenity was available. These were broadly the circumstances of *Wings Ltd v Ellis* [1985] AC 272, where the House of Lords also held that the false statement continued to be made for as long as the brochures remained in circulation. This meant that it was irrelevant that the defendants were unaware of the falsity of the statement when they issued the brochure; as soon as they became aware of the false description, they committed the offence. The only escape from liability would have been to seek the protection of the s. 24 defence (see 9.2.1.3 below), which they had not done.

Section 14 covers only statements of past or present fact and not promises as to the future, or statements of future intention. However, as in the law of misrepresentation, if a statement of intention is made when no such intention exists, this amounts to a false statement of present fact – the 'fact' being one's state of mind. The basic rule as to the distinction between statements of fact and statements of future intention is illustrated by *R v Sunair Holidays* [1973] 2 All ER 1233. Travel agents published a brochure advertising a Spanish hotel as having a swimming pool, childrens' push chairs and special meals for children. When the customer arrived the swimming pool was empty and the other facilities were not available. The Court of Appeal quashed the conviction on the grounds that the statements were not false statements of present fact at the time they were made.

Section 14 also applies to overbooking policies operated by hotels and airlines. In *British Airways Board v Taylor* [1975] 3 All ER 307, the airline booked a passenger on a flight to Bermuda and confirmed by letter. Although at the time of the letter the flight was not overbooked, it subsequently became so. It was held that the statement in the letter was to the effect that the booking could be confirmed and a seat could be guaranteed. This was false as an overbooking policy was being operated. Overbooking will also involve the guilty party in liability for breach of contract. In practical terms, of course, a hotel or airline which has overbooked will normally be able to placate a customer by offering an alternative and usually improved service.

9.2.1.3 Enforcement and defences Enforcement of the above provisions is the responsibility of local trading standards officers employed by the regional and islands councils. Proceedings may be brought by either summary cause or on indictment; the maximum fine is £2,000.

A defence is afforded by s. 24 which, *inter alia*, requires proof that the accused has exercised due diligence to avoid commission of the offence (see the Cases and Materials section for Chapter 9, where this defence is set out).

A good illustration of this defence is afforded by *Barker v Hargreaves* (1980) 125 Sol Jo 165, where a second-hand car dealer advertised a car as being 'in good condition throughout'. It was sold on this basis. The car had been successfully submitted for an MOT test although the certificate had contained the usual warning to the effect that the test was not evidence of the car's condition. In fact the car was badly corroded on the underside, although this was partly covered by the undersealing. On a charge of applying a false trade description under s. 1, the dealer pleaded the s. 24 defence to the effect that he had relied on the information in the test certificate. The court, however, held that the defence should fail because the corrosion could have been discovered by due diligence.

9.2.2 Misleading pricing

Misleading pricing of goods, services, accommodation or facilities is a criminal offence under the Consumer Protection Act 1987, ss. 20 and 21. The scope of these provisions is narrower than those contained in the Trade Descriptions Act in that they only apply to a transaction between a business and a consumer (i.e. ss. 20 and 21 of the Consumer Protection Act 1987).

9.2.2.1 Giving a misleading price indication The means by which a misleading indication may be given are elaborated in s. 21 (see the Cases and Materials section for Chapter 9). Examples of the type of situation covered are afforded by *Richards* v *Westminster Motors Ltd* [1975] SJ 626 and *North Western Gas Board* v *Aspeden* [1970] Crim LR 301. In the former case the quoted price for a vehicle failed to indicate that VAT was not included. In the latter case a notice advertised 'a £3 allowance when you buy any two gas fires at the same time'. As this notice was only intended to apply to hearth gas fires, the impression was given that all gas fires were £3 cheaper than they actually were. In both cases, there was held to have been a misleading price indication. (For discussion of the recent decision in *Warwickshire County Council* v *Johnson*, see Cases and Materials section for Chapter 9.)

Section 25 authorises the Secretary of State, after consultation with the Director General of Fair Trading and other appropriate parties, to approve a code of practice on misleading pricing. The Consumer Protection (Code of Practice for Traders on Price Indications) Approval Order 1988 approves the Code for this purpose. The purpose of the Code is to give guidance as to the requirements of s. 20 and promote desirable pricing practices. Although contravention of the Code will not give rise to civil or criminal liability, contravention or compliance may be relied on as evidence as to whether an offence under s. 20 has or has not been committed. The linking of a regulatory, educational Code of Practice with criminal sanctions is likely to be a powerful force for improved practice.

9.2.2.2 Enforcement and defences Enforcement is the responsibility of the trading standards authorities who have powers to test purchases and search premises. Proceedings may be brought either by summary or solemn proceedings; the maximum fine on conviction is £2,000.

Sections 24 and 25 contain available defences to prosecutions under ss. 20 and 21. The full text of these defences is reproduced below in the Cases and Materials section for Chapter 9. The Code of Practice is set out in Thomas, 'Encyclopaedia of Consumer Law', para. 2–1035.

9.2.3   Product safety: general safety requirements

Section 10 of the Consumer Protection Act 1987 imposes a 'general safety requirement' on goods (s. 10 is reproduced in the Cases and Materials section for Chapter 9). Breach of this requirement involves the trader in criminal liability. The General Product Safety Regulations 1994 (implementing the EU Council Directive on General Product Safety, 92/59) introduces a very similar standard which now co-exists with s. 10 of the 1987 Act (see discussion of this standard by Cartwright in the Cases and Materials section for Chapter 9, where the writer clearly brings out the way in which 'safety' must be defined by reference to 'acceptable' risk).

Due diligence defences are available in the case of the Consumer Protection Act and the 1994 Regulations.

Sections 13 to 18 provide an important administrative framework which allows for the use of suspension and prohibition notices; the forfeiture of goods; and for the Secretary of State to obtain information from traders in relation to the safety of their goods.

9.3   ADMINISTRATIVE REGULATION

This section will concentrate on the framework for the protection of consumers. General business regulation provisions (e.g., that relating to monopolies and mergers) are to be found in specialised works in these areas.

9.3.1   Referrals relating to unfair trade practices

The Director General of Fair Trading has a general duty under the Fair Trading Act 1973, s. 1 to keep under review commercial activities which relate to the supply of goods and services to consumers. Part II of the Act also gives the Director General the power to refer a 'consumer trade practice' to the Consumer Protection Advisory Committee on the grounds that it detrimentally affects consumer interests. After investigation and consultation with relevant parties, the committee may recommend to the Secretary of State that appropriate regulations be passed. If the Secretary of State thinks fit, he seeks the approval of Parliament and the regulation becomes law. Contravention constitutes a criminal offence. Three important references have led to the making of the following Orders.

Consumer Transactions (Restrictions on Statements) Order 1976 This Order prohibits attempts to exclude liability which would be void under the Unfair Contract Terms Act 1977 (see Chapter 3, para. 3.11.4 *et seq*). So it would contravene the Order to erect a notice excluding or restricting liability for death or personal injury caused by negligence. The Order also insists that any statement made by a retailer or manufacturer detailing a consumer's rights in respect of defective goods must be accompanied by a conspicuous declaration that the consumer's statutory rights, e.g., under the Sale of Goods Act 1979, are unaffected.

The purpose of this provision is to prevent traders giving the impression to consumers that what is said in a contract or guarantee overrides or qualifies obligations as to title, quality or description. Although no such statement can have this effect, consumers might be deterred from taking action if such a belief was induced.

Mail Order Transactions (Information Order) 1976 This Order requires mail order catalogues or advertisements to include the true name of the registered business, the name of the person carrying on the mail order business and the address from which the business is managed.

Business Advertisements (Disclosure) Order 1977 This Order prohibits advertisements which create the impression that a proposed sale is a private sale, as opposed to a sale in the course of a business.

The reason for the small number of referrals may be a reluctance to criminalise what is effectively a breach of the 'spirit' of the civil law. It may be that the alternative power, to seek assurances that certain practices will cease, will be a more effective form of regulation for the future.

9.3.2 Assurances as to detrimental conduct

Under Part III of the Fair Trading Act 1973 the Director General may seek assurances from traders that they will refrain from engaging in conduct which is a breach of either the civil or criminal law. The type of conduct concerned might relate to the safety of premises or general commercial matters, e.g., the type of conduct prohibited by the above Orders; alternatively, it might be that the trade is consistently supplying goods of poor quality or which do not conform to their description.

The advantage of this option is that the traders have the opportunity to give a written assurance that the conduct will cease. If such an assurance is not given or if it is given and broken, the Director General may take court proceedings and failure to comply with a resulting court order amounts to contempt of court. The only drawback of the option may be that the type of conduct in relation to which assurances can be sought does not extend beyond breaches of the law. It has been argued that the power to seek assurances should cover breaches of accepted standards of commercial behaviour as defined in codes of practice (*A General Duty to Trade Fairly, A Discussion Paper*, OFT [1986]), and unconscionable practices (Trading Malpractices, OFT, 1990).

9.3.3 Utilities regulation

The privatisation of utilities such as gas, electricity, telephone and water services has led to the need for regulation. Industry regulators have powers to control prices, which are much more interventionist than the powers available to the Director General of Fair Trading. There are also powers under s. 2 of the Competition and Service Utilities Act 1992, to set standards for, and require provision of information by, the utility industries. (For specialist discussion, see articles in the *Utilities Law Review*).

9.3.4 Unfair terms in consumer contracts

The Unfair Terms in Consumer Contracts Regulations 1994 discussed in Chapter 3 contain a power, vested in the Director General of Fair Trading, to seek an interdict to control the use of unfair terms in the abstract from any particular contract. The Directive which the regulations are bringing into effect (93/13/EEC) has always, since it was first discussed in 1976, regarded it as important to have some form of public control of unfair terms. It has always been recognised that individual redress by consumers will never take place in significant enough numbers to force suppliers to use fair terms (see discussion by Willett, 'Unfair Terms in Consumer Contracts', forthcoming, 1996).

9.4 SELF-REGULATION

The Director General of Fair Trading has a duty under the Fair Trading Act, s. 124(3) to encourage relevant trade and professional associations to prepare and disseminate to members voluntary codes of practice. The advantage of such self-regulation is that a code is developed specifically to meet the needs of the industry in question. It is therefore able to specify in great detail what is considered to be acceptable behaviour and may set up also suitable arbitration and informal dispute resolution mechanisms, which can provide a cheaper, speedier and less daunting option for those dissatisfied with the goods or services they have received. On the other hand, a code lacks legal enforceability; the only sanctions are expulsion from the association or an adverse notice from the Office of Fair Trading. However, bad publicity may often be as powerful a weapon in practice as legal action.

There presently exist codes of practice covering a wide range of industries including motor vehicles, electrical goods and servicing, footwear, furniture, holiday caravans, home improvement, laundry, mail order trading, package holidays, photography and postal/communication services.

Further reading
Ervine, (1988), *The Laws of Scotland, Stair Memorial Encyclopaedia*, Vol 6, Butterworths, para. 1–172.
Gloag and Henderson, (1987), *Introduction to the Law of Scotland*, 9th edn, W. Green Ltd, Chapter 18.
Harvey and Parry, (1992), *The Law of Consumer Protection and Fair Trading*, 4th edn, Butterworths.
Rowan-Robinson, Watchman and Barker, (1990), *Crime and Enforcement*, T. & T. Clark, Chapter 4.

Cases and Materials

The following section provides a range of material, consisting of cases, statutes and articles, which are intended to give the student the opportunity to study particular aspects of the law in greater depth without the need to have recourse to other works of reference and to gain an idea of the nature of the raw material, case or statute, from which the rules of law are derived. As was said in the preface, these materials could never cover all areas addressed in the text and do not try to do so. Readers should develop their understanding of areas in the text by reference not only to the materials reproduced here, but also to the articles and other materials referred to in the 'Further reading' sections and the text, which are reproduced here. The aim has been to select materials which show how Acts of Parliament are constructed, how judicial decisions are arrived at, how academic commentators view important areas etc.

It is set out in the order of the chapters in the main text for ease of reference.

CHAPTER ONE
INTRODUCTION TO THE LAW AND ITS ROLE IN THE BUSINESS WORLD

An excerpt from the Consumer Credit Act 1974 is reproduced below to illustrate many typical features of an Act of Parliament. The encircled numbers are the key to the explanatory notes below.

EXTRACT FROM CONSUMER CREDIT ACT 1974 ①

CONSUMER CREDIT ACT 1974
1974 c. 39 ②

③   An Act to establish for the protection of consumers a new system, administered by the Director General of Fair Trading, of licensing and other control of traders concerned with the provision of credit, or the supply of goods on hire or hire-purchase, and their transactions, in place of the present enactments regulating moneylenders, pawnbrokers and hire-purchase traders and their transactions; and for related matters.   [31st July 1974] ④

⑤ BE IT ENACTED by the Queen's most Excellent Majesty, by and with the advice and consent of the Lords Spiritual and Temporal, and Commons, in this present Parliament assembled, and by the authority of the same, as follows:—

PART I
DIRECTOR GENERAL OF FAIR TRADING

1. General functions of Director ⑦

(1)   It is the duty of the Director General of Fair Trading ('the Director')—

(a)   to administer the licensing system set up by this Act,

(b)   to exercise the adjudicating functions conferred on him by this Act in relation to the issue, renewal, variation, suspension and revocation of licences, and other matters,

(c)   generally to superintend the working and enforcement of this Act, and regulations made under it, and

(d)   where necessary or expedient, himself to take steps to enforce this Act, and regulations so made. ⑥

Notes

(1)   *Short Title*. This is the way an Act is commonly cited, the year being the year of publication.

(2)   *Official Citation*. Since 1963, each Statute is cited by the year in which it was passed and the chapter number of the official annual volume of statutes. 'Public General Acts and Measures of 19..'. Thus, the Consumer Credit Act 1974 is the 39th Act passed in the year 1974. Pre-1963 citations were much more complicated.

(3)   *Long Title*. This states the general purposes of the Statute. It may be used by judges as an aid to interpretation but usually the title is too truncated to give much enlightenment. Some reformers have suggested that the Long Title should be abolished and a statement of objects included as a section of the Act.

(4)   *Date of Royal Assent*. The Royal Assent has not been given in person since 1854, not refused since 1707. Under the Royal Assent Act 1967, the Assent may be simply notified to both Houses of Parliament by their respective Speakers. The Bill becomes an Act at midnight on the morning of the date of the Royal Assent. Remember though that most modern statutes contain a provision which states the date of commencement (i.e. when it comes into force) or authorises someone, usually a Minister, to make a commencement order. Thus a Minister may bring an Act into force either whole or in parts as and when he sees fit. A few Acts, such as the Easter Act 1920 have never been brought into force and are never likely to be.

(5)   *Enacting Formula*. This is the formal authorisation for the Act. The language used in this part of this Act is typical of Acts generally. The reference to the 'Lords Spiritual and Temporal' will not be made where the House of Lords has voted against a measure. This is extremely rare, however. (See the War Crimes Act 1991.)

(6)   *Sections and sub-sections*. Statutes are divided in this way and the individual parts are referred to accordingly. Smaller divisions are known as paragraphs.

(7)   *Marginal Note*. This merely indicates the contents of the section to enable the reader to scan the statute to find the part he wants. In theory, it is not part of the Act and should not normally be used as an aid to interpretation.

Notes

How many Acts of Parliament are there? Since the war there has been an unparalleled growth in legislative activity. The birth of the welfare state, a concern for law reform and an increasingly centralised state apparatus have all contributed to this situation.

The British Parliament devotes a higher proportion of its time to legislating than any other European Parliament. *Statutes in Force,*the authoritative guide, now fills some 50 volumes. Each Parliamentary session adds another 3000-odd pages to the Statute Book.

Having seen the way Acts of Parliament are structured, we will now consider the role played by judges in the process of making and interpreting law. We have selected a discussion by Lord McCluskey, not only because it gives a valuable insight into the way a judge sees his own role, but also because it emphasises the interaction of law with social and political values. (See 1.1.1, 1.2.3.4.)

EXTRACTS FROM THE 1987 REITH LECTURES
delivered by Lord McCluskey (published as *Law, Justice and Democracy*, Sweet & Maxwell/BBC, 1987)

The chill and distant heights

Even if judges are sensible enough — as I hope they are — to resist the intoxicating notion that they may be wiser, more dispassionate and sure-footed than their fellow men, others in society may seek to press them into a more intrusive, a more active role. I believe that, in a representative democracy such as ours, that would be a mistake. So I shall examine the role and character of our judiciary in the hope of assisting you to make your own judgment.

Let me start by asking: 'What do judges do?' To that question most people could offer an instant answer. After all, judges get a generous degree of media exposure as they send the wicked to prison, award large sums in damages or put an unexpected spoke in the wheel of some powerful bureaucratic machine. Occasionally, a judge attracts a degree of public attention, or even notoriety; but usually criticism is restrained, and respect freely accorded. Unlike most others who pronounce in the public domain, judges appear to offer, and to deliver, clear and definitive answers. Justice according to law is a coin which, when tossed, does not come to rest on the rim. It comes down heads or tails; it is clear who has won and who has lost. The judge gives his reasons, pronounces the result and withdraws to 'the chill and distant heights', constitutionally indifferent to the consequences. The litigants, and others, must adjust to the court's prescription, and order their affairs in accordance with it.

But the legal philosopher, the social scientist, the political activist, even from time to time the disappointed litigant, question this picture. They dare to assert, in the words of Warren Burger, lately Chief Justice of the United States, that 'unreviewable power is the most likely to self-indulge itself and the least likely to engage in dispassionate self-analysis'; and to conclude, as he did, that 'in a country like ours, no public institution, or the people who operate it, can be above public debate'.

But is ours a country like his? Do our judges wield an unreviewable power? And should the judges join in the debate about the exercise of judicial power, or should they stay above it, adopting the attitude that God presumably takes towards theology? Well, of course, the judges in England and Scotland do not see their role as being in every respect similar to that of American judges. They do not claim to exercise an unreviewable power. They engage for the most part in rendering as between one citizen and another what is due to each, at the expense of the other. True, they make occasional forays into that less private border country where the citizen comes into conflict with the state or some lesser public authority. But politics, social engineering, the constitution; these are realms which the British judge would claim to enter with reluctance, and to quit with relief, just as soon as he has done the minimum that duty requires.

But judges know perfectly well that much of what they do — though not unreviewable — is likely to be final. For most cases are won and lost on the judge's view of the facts, not on subtle points of law. Judges also know that if they do decide a substantial point of law in one case, that decision can determine the results in many others. And even if large numbers of the public don't care for the new twist in the law, there may be countless reasons why Parliament will not legislate on the matter. So some judges, on and off the bench, join in the debate. If they do, they may not readily persuade the other protagonists that their pronouncements are disinterested. They must hope to advance the argument not by reason of their authority but by the authority of their reasons.

Now I began by asking what judges do; and I shall not attempt a complete answer. But a fair summary might be this: a judge listens to other people giving evidence, which is extracted from them by lawyers who share with the judge a common understanding of the rules of evidence. Then the lawyers present arguments about what the evidence establishes, and bring to the attention of the judge such relevant rules of law as their own researches have discovered and invite the judge to give their clients the remedies they seek. The judge hears both sides. He passes all the material over his own well-calibrated mind, satisfies himself how the law applies to the established facts, and pronounces judgment which determines the rights and liabilities of the litigants. In short, he makes such decisions as are necessary in the light of the matters presented to him to declare which litigant wins and which loses. If several judges sit together, hearing cases on appeal, the facts are usually put before them in some pre-packaged form, and their real task is to consider if the law has been properly applied in the court below. So Appeal Court judges are routinely concerned with questions of law, sometimes abstruse, frequently intricate, occasionally entirely novel and seldom of great public interest or moment. But all the decisions of courts result from an inter-play between particular facts precisely established in evidence, and law derived from Acts of Parliament or from the Common Law.

Now it might be thought that if that is all there is to it, there should really be no problems. Alas, that is not all there is to it. First of all, though in a perfect world it should not matter, some advocates are better than others, and many a sow's ear is made to look like a silk purse, to judge or jury alike. Secondly, the law does not have the quality of a railway timetable with predetermined answers to all the questions that human life, man's wickedness and the intricacies of commerce can throw up. One of history's greatest lawgivers, the Emperor Justinian, promulgated a Code of Law in the belief that it contained all the answers; he prohibited any commentary upon it in the hope that by preventing interpretation of its provisions the law would remain clear. It was a vain hope. The law, as laid down in a code, or in a statute or in a thousand eloquently reasoned opinions, is no more capable of providing all the answers than a piano is capable of providing music. The piano needs the pianist, and any two pianists, even with the same score, may produce very different music.

Most cases that are fought to a finish are fought because, within the context of the rules, there is much to be said for both sides. Such cases are seldom hopeless till they're finished. One of Scotland's greatest judges, Lord Macmillan, believed that in most cases that were appealed it would be possible to decide the issue either way with reasonable legal justification. Even on pure matters of law, today's heresy is tomorrow's orthodoxy. That which is blindingly obvious to one judge is seen by another as logically unsound. So, in the case about the snail in the ginger beer, a principle of law which one Appeal Court judge characterised as 'little short of outrageous', was described by a Lord of Appeal as 'a proposition which I venture to say no one in Scotland or England who was not a lawyer would for one moment doubt', only to hear two other Lords of Appeal disagree with him.

Owen McIntyre
Institutions, Sources and Key Principles of European Community
Law (unpublished Paper, 1995)

The establishment of the European Community, by international treaty, has created a new legal order which, in conjunction with the member States' legal systems, makes binding law creating enforceable rights and binding obligations in respect of State parties and individuals. Community legislation can be directly effective, i.e. it can create individual rights without or irrespective of national implementing measures (Case 41/74: *Van Duyn* v *Home Office*). All Community law enjoys supremacy over national law and will prevail where any conflict arises (Case 6/64: *Costa* v *ENEL*).

History
The devastation wrought by the Second World War created the political impetus for close, formalised European integration. Not only was it necessary to rebuild the shattered European economies but it was hoped that new co-operative institutional structures would make conflict in Europe less likely in the future. Earlier calls for European Unity had been made, including the 1924 Coudenhove-Kalergi, Pan-European Union proposal and the 1930 proposal that the European members of the League of Nations should form a federated union, but these had largely been ignored. Also, the need for international co-operation in many spheres of activity, such as that of nuclear power, had become obvious, and the concept of regionalism, i.e. that small localised groups of nations could co-operate more effectively than large global groups, was growing in popularity. Three separate, yet closely related, economic organisations (the ECSC, EURATOM, and the EEC) were established by international treaties. The three Communities had originally only held two institutions in common, the European Parliament and the European Court of Justice, but the three sets of institutions were merged by the 1965 Merger Treaty which provided for a single Commission and a single Council of Ministers to administer all three Communities.

The first of these, the European Coal and Steel Community (ECSC), established under the 1951 Treaty of Paris, has established a common market for coal and steel products and aims to make European coal and steel industry sectors more efficient by reducing protectionism. The ECSC Treaty is due to expire in 2001 and it is envisaged that its functions will come under the EEC Treaty. Secondly, the European Atomic Energy Authority (EURATOM), established under the 1957 European Atomic Energy Treaty, seeks to create a specialist market for atomic energy. It aims to promote research and disseminate technical information, to establish uniform safety standards, to promote investment, to maintain regular supplies of nuclear fuels, and to ensure that nuclear materials are not diverted for aims other than peaceful purposes. The most important organisation, the European Economic Community (EEC), established under the 1957 Treaty of Rome, is concerned primarily with the creation of a European common market for all economic sectors not covered by the other two treaties.

Article 2 of the Treaty originally identified four objectives for the common market:

— the promotion of harmonious economic development throughout the Community;
— continuous and balanced economic expansion among the member States;
— the raising of standards of living among the population of the Community; and
— the development of closer relations among the member States.

Article 3 laid down instructions as to how the common market is to be established and the objectives achieved, including, *inter alia*:

— the elimination of customs duties (Articles 12–17), quantitive restrictions on imports and exports (Articles 30–37), measures having equivalent effect (Articles 95–99);
— the establishment of a common customs tariff (Articles 18–29) and of a common commercial policy towards third countries (Articles 110–116);
— the abolition, between member States, of obstacles to freedom of movement for persons (Articles 48–51), for services (Articles 59–66, and for capital (Articles 67–73), and to the right of establishment (Articles 52–58);
— the adoption of a common agriculture policy and a common transport policy;
— the creation of a Community competition policy;
— the approximation of the laws of the member States to the extent required for the proper functioning of the common market.

However, progress on the completion of a common market had been very slow and a 1985 Commission White Paper '*Completing the Internal Market*' called for the re-evaluation of the organisational structure and general objectives of the Community and also set out a programme, timetable and list of legislative measures required to complete the internal market by 31 December 1992. This led to the negotiation and adoption of the Single European Act, an international treaty which amended the founding treaties of the Community with a view to facilitating the internal market by giving the Community institutions more power to effect the removal of physical, technical and fiscal barriers. Amendments to the treaties included, *inter alia*:

— the inauguration of the internal market programme designed for completion by 1992 (Article 8A EC Treaty);
— the introduction of majority voting in the Council of Ministers for the enactment of certain measures (Article 100A EC Treaty);
— the creation of the co-operation procedure for the participation of the European Parliament in the Community legislative process (Articles 7(2), 49, 100A(1) EC Treaty);
— the grant of authority to the Council of Ministers to create a Court of First Instance (Article 168 EC Treaty);
— the addition of new Community objectives to the Treaty, including co-operation in economic and monetary policy and the preservation, protection and improvement of the environment (Article 130 R-T).

The European Community has evolved from a group of supranational organisations concerned primarily with economic co-operation into a political, economic, and monetary union which is concerned with issues ranging from social (i.e. industrial relations) policy to foreign policy. The European Union (EC) was brought into being by the 1992 Treaty on European Union (TEU) which was signed at Maastricht in February 1992 and entered into force in October 1993. The TEU contains provisions amending all three founding treaties (Titles II-IV), provisions on a Common Foreign Policy and Security Policy (Title V) and on Co-operation in the Fields of Justice and Home Affairs (Title VI). It also contains a number of supplementary protocols and agreements including the Agreement on Social Policy to which the UK has secured a derogation. However, the 'European Union' is an umbrella term which refers to three separate areas of activity or 'pillars':

— existing EC activities and competences (as amended);
— intergovernmental co-ordination of foreign policy and common external defence; and

— political intergovernmental co-operation in internal affairs.

Article L of the TEU provides that only the first pillar should fall within the Community legal order and that the Court of Justice has only jurisdiction over matters contained within the original founding treaties, as amended.

The EEC Treaty (now officially known as the EC Treaty) remains very much at the heart of the TEU which forms the constitution of the new European Union. However, in Title I, the TEU lays down new general principles for EC action. The most important of these are the principles of subsidiarity and proportionality contained in Article 3B of the EC Treaty (as inserted by Article G(5) TEU). The objectives and legal competences of the EC have been considerably expanded by the amendments made to the Treaty of Rome by both the Single European Act and the Maastricht Treaty. The number of activities listed in Article 3 has risen from the original 11 to 20 and objectives now include, *inter alia*, the improvement of employment conditions and the health and safety of workers (Article 118A), the achievement of equal pay as between men and women (Article 119), the provision of social security for migrant workers (Article 121), and the protection of consumers (Article 129A).

Community Institutions
Three of the institutions comprising the EC have legislative powers: the Council of Ministers, the Commission and the European Parliament. Originally, the Parliament's role was mainly an advisory and supervisory one but successive Treaty amendments have conferred upon the Parliament significant new legislative powers.

(1)   The Council of Ministers
The Council is made up of ministers of the national governments, so it is here that national interests are represented. The ministers change according to the issues being discussed. For example, when dealing with financial matters the Council will consist of the finance ministers of the member States while on farming issues it will be the agriculture ministers. The Presidency of the Council of Ministers, and therefore of the Community, is held for six months and rotates among each of the member States. The Council is the main legislator of the Community and it is here that the final decision lies with regard to EC legislative measures. To adopt a provision, the Council once had to vote unanimously, but this procedure proved to be very slow and inefficient and so now it more usually acts by means of a qualified majority. When voting by qualified majority the votes of each country are weighted according to each country's relative size and influence. The Council very rarely acts by simple majority and unanimity will usually still be required in matters of great importance, for example, the admission of a new member State to the Community. Also, where a vital interest of a member State is threatened that State may, under a convention known as the Luxembourg Accords, veto the offending measures, thus effectively requiring unanimity.

The twice yearly summit meetings held between the Heads of Government of the Member States together with the President of the Commission are referred to as the European Council. The European Council attempts to resolve matters which have proven problematic in the Council of Ministers and sets the agenda for the development of Community policies.

(2)   The Commission
The EC Commission consists of 20 members or Commissioners, each, rather like a government minister, with responsibility for a particular area of activity. The civil

servants working within the Commission are divided into Directorates-General which roughly mirror national government departments. By convention, at least one Commissioner comes from each member State with the five largest countries, i.e. Britain, Germany, France, Italy and Spain, each sending two. However, Commissioners are appointed by their member States on the grounds of their general competence and are expected to act at all times with complete independence. They are required to perform their duties solely in the interests of the Communities and must never take instructions from any national government or other body. Therefore it is through the Commission that the supra-national character of the Communities finds expression.

The Commission has three main functions. Firstly, it serves as the guardian or 'watchdog of the treaties' and ensures that all Community law obligations, originating either from Treaty provisions or secondary legislation, have been satisfied by both member States and private legal persons, (usually commercial undertakings). Regarding member States' obligations, it ensures that secondary legislation has been fully implemented and that Treaty obligations are observed and applied correctly by member States . . .

The Commission also has a significant law-making role under the Treaty of Rome, which confers upon it the power to make regulations, issue directives, take decisions or deliver opinions, together with the Council . . .

Thirdly, the Commission acts as the civil service of the Community and is responsible for a wide range of functions, including its day-to-day running and the administration of all Community funds. In this capacity it is required to publish an annual general report on the activities of the Community.

(3)   The European Parliament (Assembly)

The members of the European Parliament have been directly elected since 1979. The number of representatives returned from each member State are in vague proportion to the population of the State. The Parliament still has no direct power to make law but its advisory role and its powers to influence the legislative process have increased significantly in recent years.

(4)   The Court of Justice

The European Court of Justice is the dispute settlement mechanism of the Community and consists of 15 judges, assisted by 8 advocates-general, who act as independant arbiters making reasoned submissions on cases brought before the court. Each member State provides at least one judge, who must possess the qualifications required for appointment to the highest judicial offices in their respective countries, but again their independence and impartiality must be beyond doubt (Article 167). The appointment of the judges and advocates-general is by mutual agreement among the governments of member States, for a period of six years (Article 166). The principal function of the Court is to ensure the observance of law in the interpretation and application of the Treaties and measures made under the Treaties. The Court has a very varied jurisdictional competence and hears disputes between member states, between Community institutions and member states, between the Communities and their officials, between member States and private persons or commercial concerns, and between private persons themselves in relation to questions on the interpretation and application of Community law which arises before national courts. The Court also hears appeals for a declaration that, in violation of the Treaty, the Council or Commission failed to act, appeals for the annulment of legal acts of the Council and Commission, claims for damages arising from the non-contractual liability of the Communities, and claims arising from contracts concluded by or on behalf of the

Communities. It also delivers opinions on whether agreements entered into by the Communities are compatible with the Treaties. Under Article 177, the ECJ hands down preliminary rulings on the interpretation of the Treaties and on the validity and interpretation of acts of the Community institutions on questions referred to it by the national courts. This process facilitates the uniform application of Community law by the national courts of all member States. The Decisions of the ECJ are not subject to the doctrine of '*stare decisis*' but tend to be followed, especially where they concern the interpretation of the Treaties or secondary legislation. Only one judgement is given by the ECJ and no dissenting views are expressed. Also, the judgments do not contain *obiter dicta*. The workload of the ECJ has increased tremendously since its establishment and so the judges may now sit in chambers of up to five judges to hear cases.

Main Sources of Community Law

(1) Treaties

The treaties establishing the three Communities, the EEC, ECSC and Euratom treaties, are 'self-executing' and become law on ratification by the member States. Generally there can be no derogation from the obligations imposed by them. Treaties agreed by the Community with third States or international organisations become included in the concept of 'Community treaties'. The Treaties are generally referred to as 'primary' sources of Community law and comprise the constitutions of the three Communities. They not only form the legal basis of the Community institutions but also lay down the powers which can be exercised by those institutions and the procedures under which they must operate.

(2) Acts of the Institutions (Secondary Legislation)

The term 'secondary legislation' covers all laws passed by the main legislative bodies, the Council and Commission. All such law is made under the authority of and derives its legitimacy from provisions of the treaties. There are 5 types of acts listed under Article 189 of the Treaty:

(a) Regulations — these have general application and are binding in their entirety and directly applicable in all member States. Regulations often apply to administrative matters. An example is Reg 1210/90, which established the European Environment Agency.

(b) Directives — these are binding on the member State to which they are addressed and only as to the result to be achieved, not the means of achievement. Therefore States often must enact national legislation to comply. Most EC legislation takes this form as member States prefer autonomy over which measures to implement. A directive cannot be relied upon in national courts unless it has 'direct effect', which will normally require its wording to be very precise. An example of a directive having direct effect is the Equal Treatment Directive 76/207 (Case 152/84: *Marshall* v *Southampton and South West Hampshire Area Health Authority*).

(c) Decisions — a decision is binding only on those to whom it is addressed, i.e. groups or individuals. It is a binding act with the force of law and does not require implementation in order to take effect. A decision will normally take the form of a Commission ruling.

(d) & (e) Recommendations and Opinions — neither of these measures are binding but only persuasive. However, they may be issued by the Council or Commission on any matter at any time and carry considerable political and moral weight.

(3) Case Law of the European Court of Justice

Although the European Court of Justice does not operate under a doctrine of binding precedents and is not bound to follow its own decisions, it is unlikely to depart from previous decisions without strong reasons. This is especially true where it has interpreted a treaty or legislative provision or decided on the relative weight of different provisions. The ECJ has handed down many ground-breaking decisions, establishing for example, the direct effectiveness of Directives, the supremacy of Community law, and the Community's mandate to legislate for the protection of the environment.

Key Features of Community Law

(1) Subsidiarity
The principle was introduced in its modern form by encyclical 'Quadragesimo Anno', proclaimed by Pope Pius XI on 15 May 1931. It was recently further developed in encyclical 'Centesimus Annus' of 1 May 1991 by Pope John Paul II. In the context of the Catholic Church it can be seen as a Neo-Aristotelian, Aquinian view of the need for structures to take account of societal pluralism and to fit reality without curtailing its varied potential. The principle upholds the notion of the primacy of the human being over social structures.

During negotiation of the TEU, which again amends the Treaty of Rome and aims to facilitate the setting up of a political, economic and monetary union, the import-ance of the principle of subsidiarity was stressed by parties fearful of the increased centralization of power in the Community. The principle has thus been inserted into the Treaty as a fundamental principle of Community law, applying to all areas. It is formulated in Art 3B:

> The Community shall act within the limits of the powers conferred upon it by this Treaty and of the objectives assigned to it therein.
>
> In areas which do not fall within its exclusive competence, the Community shall take action, in accordance with the principle of subsidiarity, only and in so far as the objectives of the proposed action cannot be sufficiently achieved by the member States and can therefore, by reason of the scale or effects of the proposed action, be better achieved by the Community.
>
> Any action by the Community shall not go beyond what is necessary to achieve the objectives of this Treaty.

. . .

Regarding the justiciability of the principle as formulated in the TEU, most commen-tators agree that it could not be enforced judicially. Many grounds are advanced for this argument. For one thing, it is pointed out that the Treaty does not give a limited list of subject matters which fall within the competence of the Community. Instead, it sets the objectives to be attained. Also, nowhere in the Treaty are member States given the opportunity to seek preventative judicial review, allowing them to bring before the European Court of Justice any act by the Council infringing one of its competences. Subsequent judicial review may be sought under Art 173 of the Treaty but it can be argued that if the authors of the TEU envisaged the principle as being justiciable they would have provided for prior review. . . .

(2) Proportionality
The principle of proportionality, or intensity, provides a useful check to the unhar-monious unilateral exercise of their competences by the Member States. It also has a role in assessing the lawfulness of Community measures. This principle is derived from German administrative law and reflects an applicatiion of Aristotelian distribu-tive justice to Community law. In outline, the principle seeks to ensure a proportion-ate relationship between means and ends in legislative measures.

It is generally accepted that to establish the proportionality of a measure three distinct tests must be applied:

— the measure must be appropriately aimed at a legitimate objective;
— the measure must be necessary with no less restrictive means of achieving the objective available;
— the measure must be proportionate, in that any injury or restriction caused should be offset by the benefits gained (by the public or community) without the measure being discriminatory.

With regard to the validity of a Community measure, under the principle it is necessary to establish firstly that the means it employs to achieve an aim correspond to the aim, secondly that they are necessary for its achievement; and thirdly that it does not disproportionately burden any party/sector or disproportionately affect any of the Community's general objectives. If the measure is disproportionate to a substantial degree its legality may be adversely affected as in Case 114/76: *Bela-Muhle Josef Bergmann KG* v *Grows-Farm GmbH*, (the Skimmed-Milk Powder case). Art 3B, which introduces subsidiarity into the Treaty, expressly applies the principle of proportionality to Community action: 'Any action by the Community shall not go beyond what is necessary to achieve the objectives of this Treaty'.

With regard to the unilateral adoption of measures by the member States, the same principle applies and would seem to represent the outer limit of member State competence. Art 36 of the Treaty applies the principle to measures restricting the movement of pharmaceuticals: '. . . national rules or practices which do restrict imports of pharmaceutical products or are capable of doing so are only compatible with the Treaty to the extent to which they are necessary for the effective protection of health and life of humans'. Case 120/78: *Rewe-Zentral AG* v *Bundesmonopolverwaltung fur Branntwein*, (the Cassis de Dijon case), introduced the principle to a wide range of areas in which the Community and the member States have concurrent competences. In Case 302/86: *Commission* v *Denmark*, (the Danish Bottle case), the Court applied the proportionality test to a national measure for environmental protection which effectively created a barrier to trade between member States. . . .

(3)   Direct Effect
The doctrine of direct effect has been developed by the Court of Justice to ensure that parties can rely upon provisions of Community law despite the fact that these provisions have not been properly implemented by means of national measures. In order for Community provisions to be capable of direct effect they must exhibit certain characteristics:

— the content of the provision must be clear and precise;
— the provision must be self-executing (i.e. non-discretionary);
— the provision must not contain any conditions or qualifications or be contingent on any further occurence or event.

Under Article 189, a Regulation is of 'general application . . . binding in its entirety and directly applicable in all member States'. Therefore, Regulations are intended to take immediate effect and require no further implementation through national measures.

Direct effect is of greatest importance in the case of directives. Under Article 189, a directive is '. . . binding as to the result to be achieved, upon each member State to which it is addressed, but shall leave to the national authorities the choice of form and methods'. Directives are not, therefore, directly applicable. However, where a member State has not properly implemented the provisions of a directive by the specified date set down in the directive, an individual may seek to rely directly (by means of the ECJ or national courts) on any rights conferred under the directive and the member State may not rely on its non-implementation as grounds for denying these rights. In Case 9/70: *Grand* v *Finanzamt Traunstein*, the ECJ held that '. . . the effectiveness of such a measure (in this case a Council Decision) would be weakened if the nationals of that State could not invoke it in the courts and the national courts could not take it into consideration as part of Community law'. In Case 41/74: *Van Duyn* v *Home Office*, the ECJ established that the doctrine of direct effect could be applied to a directive in allowing the plaintiff to invoke Article 3 of Directive 64/221 on the co-ordination of special measures concerning the movement and residence of foreign nationals.

The provisions of a directive can only be vertically directly effective, i.e. they may only be relied upon as against a member State (as opposed to private individuals). However, the ECJ has broadly interpreted the concept of 'the state or an emanation thereof'. In Case 188/89: *Foster* v *British Gas*, it held that a directive may be enforced against 'a body, whatever its legal form, which has been made responsible, pursuant to a measure adopted by the State, for providing a public service under the control of the State and has for that purpose special powers beyond those which result from the normal rules applicable in relations between individuals'.

The ECJ has managed to ameliorate the harshness of the distinction between vertical/horizontal direct effect in two main ways. Firstly, in Case 14/83: *Von Colson* v *Land Nordrhein-Westfalen* (which concerned a claim against the prison service) and Case 79/83: *Harz* v *Deutsche Tradex GmbH* (involving a private company) it concentrated on Art. 5 EC Treaty instead of on the vertical/horizontal direct effect of the Equal Treatment Directive (76/207). Art. 5 requires States to 'take all appropriate measures' to ensure fulfilment of their Community obligations. Thus the ECJ held that member States' courts are bound to interpret national law in such a way as to ensure that the objectives of the Directive are achieved. Therefore, Community law, though not directly effective, may be applied indirectly as domestic law by means of interpretation — 'indirect effect'! In Case 106/89: *Marleasing SA* v *La Comercial Internacional de Alimentacion SA*, the ECJ further developed this approach. In this case Spain had not implemented Directive 68/151 on the protection of company members and third parties. The ECJ reiterated the view that a Directive cannot impose obligations on private parties and that national courts must as far as possible interpret national law in the light of the wording and purpose of the Directive in order to achieve the result pursued by the Directive. It concluded, without qualification, that the Spanish court was required to interpret domestic law so as to ensure achievement of the Directive's objectives and that it was not necessary to the application of the Von Colson principle that the relevant national measure should have been introduced for the purpose of complying with the Directive, nor even that a national measure should have been specifically introduced at all.

Secondly, in Cases 6&9/90: *Francovich* v *Italy*, the ECJ held that although Directive 80/987, on the payment of employees' wages arrears on the insolvency of an employer, was not sufficiently clear to be directly effective against the State, Italy's obligation to implement the Directive, arising from Art. 5 of the EC Treaty, required the State to compensate individuals for damage suffered as a result of failure to implement if certain conditions were satisfied:

(a)   the Directive involved rights conferred on individuals,

(b) the content of those rights could be indentified on the basis of the provisions of the Directive, and

(c) there was a casual link between the State's failure to implement and the damage suffered by the persons affected.

In the UK the House of Lords has held that UK courts must grant interim relief against the Crown where this was necessary to protect individuals' Community rights — *R* v *Secretary of State for Transport, ex parte Factortame (No 2)* [1991] 1 All ER 106.

(4) Supremacy

The EC Treaty is silent on whether national or Community law is to take precedence in the event of conflict. With the development of the doctrine of direct effect it became even more important to clarify this question. The matter was left to the courts of member States though the ECJ has also had occasion to express its view on the issue. In Case 26/62: '*Van Gend en Loos*', the ECJ stated that 'the Community constitutes a new legal order in international law, for whose benefit the States have limited their sovereign rights, albeit within limited fields'. In Case 6/64: *Costa* v *ENEL*, the ECJ went further, stating that:

'The reception, within the laws of each member State, of provisions having a Community source, and more particularly of the terms and of the spirit of the Treaty, has as a corollary the impossibility, for the member State, to give preference to unilateral and subsequent measures against a legal order accepted by them on the basis of reciprocity. . . . The transfer, by member States, from their national orders in favour of the Community order of the rights and obligations arising from the Treaty, carries with it a clear limitation of their sovereign right upon which a subsequent unilateral law, incompatible with the aims of the Community, cannot prevail'. In Case 11/70: the *Internationale Handelsgesellschaft* case, the ECJ allowed an EC Regulation to prevail over provisions of the German constitution, saying that 'the law born from the Treaty [cannot] have the courts opposing to it rules of national law of any nature whatsoever . . .'

In the following excerpt Cowan Ervine gives an outline of the operation of the small claims procedure in Scotland. In the rest of the article he outlines the equivalent schemes in England and Wales and Northern Ireland and evaluates the three schemes.

C. Ervine, 'The Importance of Small Claims Courts in the Resolution of Consumer Disputes in the United Kingdom' [1995] *Consumer LJ*, p. 24

. . .

Scotland was the last of the United Kingdom law districts to introduce a small claims scheme on November 30, 1988. (In 1979 a simplified procedure for dealing with disputes involving relatively small sums, the summary cause, had been introduced into the Sheriff Court, the equivalent of the county courts in other parts of the United Kingdom, but it was not a small claims scheme in the modern meaning of that term. As the Royal Commission on Legal Services in Scotland (see *Report Vol. 1*, Cmnd 7846, HMSO Edinburgh, 1980, the *Hughes Report*) accepted, it was too expensive and too complex and there was a need for a proper small claims procedure capable of being used by individuals on their own.) The present procedure was preceded by an experimental scheme in Dundee Sheriff Court which was supported both financially and morally by the European Commission. (For details of the operation of this scheme see Ervine, 'Small Claims: Recent Developments in Scotland' (1986) 9 *Journal of Consumer Policy* 191.)

The statutory basis of the Scottish small claims procedure is to be found in amendments made to the Sheriff Courts (Scotland) Act 1971 by section 18 of the Law Reform (Miscellaneous Provisions) (Scotland) Act 1985. The details of the scheme are found in the Act of Sederunt (Small Claims Rules) 1988 and a small claim is defined in the Small Claims (Scotland) Order 1988.

The effect of the legislation is that small claims are actions for the payment of money, the recovery of movable property, or the enforcement of an obligation where not more than £750 is claimed. Excluded from this definition are actions of aliment and actions of defamation. However, actions which are not small claims only because their value exceeds £750 may be dealt with as small claims provided both parties agree. It will be seen that this definition covers a very wide range of claims and will include most types of consumer claim. It is also important to note that, unlike England and Wales, all actions for less than £750 within the definition must be brought under the small claims procedure whether or not they are disputed. As a result, a high proportion of claims are debt collection actions.

A small claim is made by completing a form known as a summons settting out the names and addresses of the person making the claim and the person sued, as well as a brief account of what is claimed. This form together with the appropriate fee is lodged with the sheriff clerk, the official responsible for the administration of the sheriff court. Where the claimant is not a partnership or company the sheriff clerk may be requested to serve the summons. Where the person sued intends to dispute the claim this intention should be indicated by completing and returning the appropriate part of the summons. In a disputed case the next step is the preliminary hearing which usually takes place within six to eight weeks of the issuing of the summons. The function of this hearing (which is conducted by the sheriff, the equivalent of the English or Welsh County Court Judge as there is no equivalent to the district judge in Scotland) is to ascertain from the parties or their representatives what the disputed issues are and to note them on the summons. Thereafter, it is no longer necessary to satisfy the sheriff on any issue which had not been noted as a disputed issue. In some cases sufficient facts may be admitted to permit the sheriff to decide the case at this stage. In most cases a full hearing is arranged for a date usually six to nine weeks later.

The full hearing, like the preliminary hearing, is held in public 'in such manner as the sheriff considers best suited to the clarification of the issue before him: and shall so far as practicable, be conducted in an informal manner' (Small Claims rule 19.) To assist lay people to present their own cases the legislation creating the small claims procedure dispenses with the rules relating to the admissibility or corroboration of evidence. The parties may represent themselves or be represented by a solicitor, an advocate, or anyone else. The only controls on non-professional representatives are that they should have the authority of the party they claim to represent, and be regarded as suitable by the sheriff. In practice, trading standards officers, staff of advice agencies and relatives have acted as representives.

As another way of removing a perceived obstacle to using the courts the normal rules about legal expenses which normally result in the losing party having to meet the expenses of the winner have been abrogated. Where a claim has been defended and the parties have acted reasonably no expenses of any kind are payable where the amount of claim does not exceed £200. Where the claim does exceed £200 an award of expenses is limited to £75. (See the Small Claims (Scotland) Order 1988, art. 4 and Small Claims rule 26.) These rules do not apply to appeals which are only permitted on a point of law and only to the Sheriff Principal. (Scotland is divided into six sheriffdoms the senior judge in each of which is known as the sheriff principal and deals mainly with appeals from the sheriffs within his sheriffdom.) Legal aid is not available for small claims except in the event of an appeal.

In the first year of the operation of the small claims procedure there were almost 74,000 small claims of which only 16 per cent went to a full hearing. In 1990 the number of small claims rose to just over 87,000 and in 1991 to 88,500 before dropping to 79,395 in 1992. (*Civil Judicial Statistics Scotland 1989–1992*) Scottish Courts Administration, Edinburgh).

CHAPTER TWO
TYPES OF BUSINESS ORGANISATION

COMPANIES ACT 1989
A COMPANY'S CAPACITY AND RELATED MATTERS

108   A company's capacity and the power of the directors to bind it
In Chapter III of Part I of the Companies Act 1985 (a company's capacity, formalities of carrying on business), for section 35 substitute—

A company's capacity not limited by its memorandum

35(1)   The validity of an act done by a company shall not be called into question on the ground of lack of capacity by reason of anything in the company's memorandum.

35(2)   A member of a company may bring proceedings to restrain the doing of an act which but for subsection (1) would be beyond the company's capacity; but no such proceedings shall lie in respect of an act to be done in fulfilment of a legal obligation arising from a previous act of the company.

35(3)   It remains the duty of the directors to observe any limitations on their powers flowing from the company's memorandum; and action by the directors which but for subsection (1) would be beyond the company's capacity may only be ratified by the company by special resolution.

A resolution ratifying such action shall not affect any liability incurred by the directors or any other person; relief from any such liability must be agreed to separately by special resolution.

35(4)   The operation of this section is restricted by section 30B(1) of the Charities Act 1960 and section 112(3) of the Companies Act 1989 in relation to companies which are charities; and section 322A below (invalidity of certain transactions to which directors or their associates are parties) has effect notwithstanding this section.

Power of directors to bind the company

35A(1)   In favour of a person dealing with a company in good faith, the power of the board of the directors to bind the company, or authorise others to do so, shall be deemed to be free of any limitation under the company's constitution.

35A(2)   For this purpose—

(a)   a person 'deals with' a company if he is a party to any transaction or other act to which the company is a party;

(b)   a person shall not be regarded as acting in bad faith by reason only of his knowing that an act is beyond the powers of the directors under the company's constitution; and

(c)   a person shall be presumed to have acted in good faith unless the contrary is proved.

35A(3)   The references above to limitations on the directors' powers under the company's constitution include limitations deriving—

(a)   from a resolution of the company in general meeting or a meeting of any class of shareholders, or

(b)   from any agreement between the members of the company or of any class of shareholders.

35A(4)   Subsection (1) does not affect any right of a member of the company to bring proceedings to restrain the doing of an act which is beyond the powers of the directors; but no such proceedings shall lie in respect of an act to be done in fulfilment of a legal obligation arising from a previous act of the company.

35A(5)   Nor does that subsection affect any liability incurred by the directors, or any other person, by reason of the directors exceeding their powers.

35A(6)   The operation of this section is restricted by section 30B(1) of the Charities Act 1960 and section 112(3) of the Companies Act 1989 in relation to companies which are charities; and section 322A below (invalidity of certain transactions to which directors or their associates are parties) has effect notwithstanding this section.

No duty to enquire as to capacity of company or authority of directors

35B   A party to a transaction with a company is not bound to enquire as to whether it is permitted by the company's memorandum or as to any limitation on the powers of the board of directors to bind the company or others to do so.

109   Invalidity of certain transactions involving directors
In Part X of the Companies Act 1985 (enforcement of fair dealing by directors), after section 322 insert—

Invalidity of certain transactions involving directors, etc.

322A(1)   This section applies where a company enters into a transaction to which the parties include—

(a)   a director of the company or of its holding company, or

(b)   a person connected with such a director or a company with whom such a director is associated,
and the board of directors, in connection with the transaction, exceed any limitation on their powers under the company's constitution.

322A(2) The transaction is voidable at the instance of the company.

322A(3) Whether or not it is avoided, any such party to the transaction as is mentioned in subsection (1)(a) or (b), and any director of the company who authorised the transaction, is liable—

(a) to account to the company for any gain which he has made directly or indirectly by the transaction, and

(b) to indemnify the company for any loss or damage resulting from the transaction.

322A(4) Nothing in the above provisions shall be construed as excluding the operation of any other enactment or rule of law by virtue of which the transaction may be called in question or any liability to the company may arise.

322A(5) The transaction ceases to be voidable if—

(a) restitution of any money or other asset which was the subject-matter of the transaction is no longer possible, or

(b) the company is indemnified for any loss or damage resulting from the transaction, or

(c) rights acquired bona fide for value and without actual notice of the directors' exceeding their powers by a person who is not party to the transaction would be affected by the avoidance, or

(d) the transaction is ratified by the company in general meeting, by ordinary or special resolution or otherwise as the case may require.

322A(6) A person other than a director of the company is not liable under subsection (3) if he shows that at the time the transaction was entered into he did not know that the directors were exceeding their powers.

322A(7) This section does not affect the operation of section 35A in relation to any party to the transaction not within subsection (1)(a) or (b).

But where a transaction is voidable by virtue of this section and valid by virtue of that section in favour of such a person, the court may, on the application of that person or of the company, make such order affirming, severing or setting aside the transaction, on such terms, as appear to the court to be just.

322A(8) In this section 'transaction' includes any act; and the reference in subsection (1) to limitations under the company's constitution includes limitations deriving—

(a) from a resolution of the company in general meeting or a meeting of any class of shareholders, or

(b) from any agreement between the members of the company or of any class of shareholders.

110   Statement of company's objects

(1) In Chapter I of Part I of the Companies Act 1985 (company formation), after section 3 (forms of memorandum) insert—

'Statement of company's objects: general commercial company

3A Where the company's memorandum states that the object of the company is to carry on business as a general commercial company—

(a) the object of the company is to carry on any trade or business whatsoever, and
(b) the company has power to do all such things as are incidental or conducive to the carrying on of any trade or business by it.'

(2) In the same Chapter, for section 4 (resolution to alter objects) substitute—

'Resolution to alter objects

4(1) A company may by special resolution alter its memorandum with respect to the statement of the company's objects.

4(2) If an application is made under the following section, an alteration does not have effect except in so far as it is confirmed by the court.'

Note
See 2.2.3 and 2.3.1 above where these provisions are discussed.

COMPANIES ACT 1985

459 Order on application of company member
(1) A member of a company may apply to the court by petition for an order under this Part on the ground that the company's affairs are being or have been conducted in a manner which is unfairly prejudicial to the interests of the members generally or of some part of the members (including at least himself) or that any actual or proposed act or omission of the company (including an act or omission on its behalf) is or would be so prejudicial.
(2) The provisions of this Part apply to a person who is not a member of a company but to whom shares in the company have been transferred or transmitted by operation of law, as those provisions apply to a member of the company; and references to a member or members are to be construed accordingly.

Notes
(1) Why do you consider it appropriate to compromise 'majority rule' by such a provision?
(2) Who do you think might benefit from s.459? (See *Re A Company* [1986] BCLC 382).
(3) The following excerpt discusses a range of important provisions relating to the relationship between shareholders and those in control of companies (see 2.3.1).

**Lilian Miles, 'UK Company Shareholder Protection
— a Call for Reform'**
The Company Lawyer, **vol. 15, no 7, 202**

Introduction
Most shareholders regard the company as a place in which they can invest their money and expect a return in the form of a dividend at the end of the day. They provide the

capital while the power to run the company is delegated to directors. It is therefore important that directors should be competent and efficient so that shareholders' interests are advanced. When the need arises, the exercise of powers by directors should also be regulated so that they perform their job effectively and not abuse their position. This is especially significant in large companies where the ownership of shares is so widely dispersed that any group of shareholders will find it difficult to control what the directors do. Here, the function of the general meeting as a forum where shareholders make decisions which concern the company is greatly diminished, Instead it is the management who holds the reigns. This article aims to evaluate the effectiveness of UK law in protecting its company shareholders and discusses whether the law is adequate.

Company directors in this country have considerable discretion in conducting the business of the company. The relationship between the directors and the company in general meeting is largely based on the articles of association which empower the directors, to, *inter alia*, make policy decisions, enter into contracts or transactions with third parties, carry out the day-to-day business of the company and take appropriate action when the life of the company is in danger. (See e.g. art. 70 Table A. Besides authorising the directors to conduct the affairs of the company, articles of association also provide that directors are liable in the event that they fail to carry out their duties properly.)

Common law principles

To a large extent, the UK controls the behaviour of directors and sets a standard of conduct for them through the common law. For example the common law principle that directors owe certain fiduciary duties to the company is well established. These include a duty to act *bona fide* in the interests of the company, (*Re Roith* [1967] 1 WLR 432) a duty not to exercise their powers for an improper purpose, (*Hogg* v *Cramphorn* [1967] Ch 254) a duty to account for all profits (there are two conflicting views, one an absolute principle, the other which argues that it should not matter that the director makes a profit if the company is unable to take up the contract: *Regal Hastings* v *Gulliver* [1942] 1 All ER 378, *Peso Silver Mines* v *Cropper* (1965) 54 WWR 329) and a duty not to put themselves in a position whereby their interests conflict with the interests of the company (*Aberdeen Railway* v *Blaikie Bros* (1854) 2 Eq Rep 1281). In the event that directors breach these fiduciary duties, they will be liable to account for any personal gain made at the expense of the company or to indemnify the company for any loss caused by their misconduct.

Statutory regulation

In addition to these common law principles, directors must observe various statutory rules as directors in the company. (See e.g. Companies Act 1985, Pt X.) These provide a safeguard against any abuse of powers or attempts to make a personal gain at the expense of the company. Many of these rules, although clear in their purpose, are extremely technical. It is, for example, unlawful to pay a director compensation for loss of office or upon his retirement unless the particulars have been ratified by shareholders (Companies Act 1985, ss. 312–316). Again, a director who is in any way interested in a contract with the company must declare the nature of this interest to the whole board. (Companies Act 1985, s. 317. The criticism is that the director need only disclose his interest to the board of directors and not the shareholders. The problem is that the board of directors may consist of friends who would then approve his interest.) Directors are prevented from granting to themselves long-term contracts of service, and for this reason no director may enter into an agreement to work for the company which exceeds five years, unless first approved by the shareholders (Companies Act 1985, s. 319).

The Company Directors Disqualification Act 1986 provides that the directors may be disqualified from the company management under certain circumstances. The court may make an order disqualifying any director and also ban him from being associated with the running of any other company if he has been convicted of an indictable offence (normally associated with an offence against a company) (s. 2), persistently been in default under company legislation (s. 3), where he has become unfit for his duty as a director (s. 6) or where he has been found guilty of fraudulent trading (s. 10).

Directors who engage in wrongful or fraudulent trading in accordance with ss 213–214 Insolvency Act 1986 will be held liable to contribute to the assets of the company. Directors who continue the business of the company with an intent to defraud creditors of the company when, to their knowledge, there was no reasonable prospect of the company ever paying back its debts, or where they continue to trade when the company is known to be insolvent, will thus come within the Act. (Fraudulent trading under s. 213 is also a criminal offence under s. 458 of the Companies Act, while wrongful trading is only a civil wrong.) The liquidators of the company will apply to the court for an order declaring that the directors are liable to contribute to the company's assets. (Fraudulent trading under s. 213 is also a criminal offence under Companies Act 1985, s. 458, while wrongful trading is only a civil wrong. In both cases only the company liquidator may make an application against the directors.) In other circumstances, the court may make an order compelling them to put right affairs which have been conducted in such a way so as to unfairly prejudice members of the company (Companies Act 1985, s. 459). This would include instances where directors misappropriated company property (*Re London School of Electronics Ltd* [1986] Ch 211), or where they awarded themselves excessive remuneration (*Re Cumuna* [1986] BCLC 430, CA), failed to pay dividends to shareholders or engaged in self-dealing.

Directors knowingly in possession of unpublished price-sensitive information obtained by virtue of their position as directors are prohibited both from using that information to deal in the shares of the company or from communicating that information to anyone else. The Company Securities (Insider Dealing) Act 1985 makes such action a criminal offence on the basis that corporate confidence must be protected to ensure that insiders do not gain from information which is not yet available to the public. This is especially significant as directors invariably have a direct interest in the affairs of the company.

There exist statutory provisions which enable shareholders to remove directors from office (Companies Act 1985, s. 303). Others empower minority shareholders to bring an action against the director in the name of the company in order that the defaulting directors may make good any losses caused to these minority shareholders or to the company. (Common law exceptions to the majority rule in *Foss* v *Harbottle* include instances where there was a fraud on the minority and the minority could prove that the majority who had done wrong were also in control or where the act committed was clearly illegal or where a personal right has been infringed.) Still others provide that the company may be wound up if the need arises and there are various grounds upon which the life of the company may be brought to an end. (Insolvency Act 1986, s. 122(1)(g). This almost always occurs when there is a destruction of a personal underlying relationship between and among the shareholders. See *Ebrahimi* v *West-bourne Galleries* [1983] AC 360.)

Codes of Practice
Besides common law and statutory principles there exist also voluntary codes of practice. For example the UK City Code (which contains ten General Principles and

38 Rules which should be observed when companies are in the process of a takeover), administered by the Panel on Takeover and Mergers, contains standards of good commercial behaviour applying in relation to takeovers and mergers. There are provisions relating to such matters as the timetabling of the offer to take over, protection of shareholders who are hostile to the takeover or merger, provisions prohibiting insider dealing in the shares of both companies and control over undesirable defensive tactics by the target company. The main objective of the Code is to ensure that shareholders in the target company are treated equally and fairly and are given all the information they need in order to decide whether or not to accept the bid. Directors are required to observe the rules embodied in the City Code, and expected to carry out the takeover in the light of the Code.

Effectiveness of the current law

The important question is the effectiveness of these diverse provisions in preventing the abuse of power by company directors. How adequately are interests of shareholders protected?

Company directors have easy access to unpublished price-sensitive information which they can use to deal in the shares of the company. The present state of the law is unsatisfactory in that there is no helpful definition of 'price-sensitive information'. Section 10 of the Company Securities (Insider Dealing) Act 1985 limits it to information not of a general nature, but specific information relating to or of concern to the company. Although confidential information relating to the announcement of takeover bids, or a definite increase in the profits of the company, or an extension of management plans come within the definition, the nature of other circumstances is still very much a question of fact and it is difficult for anyone to state precisely in what circumstances liability will arise. It is also extremely difficult to measure the 'price sensitivity' of any information. Share prices fluctuate for more than one reason. It is thus difficult to say with any certainty that in any instance it was caused by a particular piece of information made generally known. In addition the Act demands that the insider must *know* that the information he holds is 'price sensitive' (s. 1 of the Act). To prove this, however, is an arduous task. It is therefore not surprising that the DTI has on average, only one successful prosecution a year (See JM Naylor (1990) 'The Use of Criminal Sanctions by UK and US Authorities for Insider Trading: How Can the two Systems Learn from Each Other?' (1990) 11 Co Law 57) although insider trading is rife. The Act only imposes a criminal penalty on the guilty director (s. 8 of the Act), it does not compensate the victims. The difficulty for shareholders is that not only their directors abuse their confidence in them, the latter have also made a personal profit as a result of this abuse.

A well-established company law principle is that wrong is done to a company by the directors, the only person who can bring an action against them to remedy the wrong is the company itself (*Foss* v *Harbottle* (1843) 2 Hare 461). It is not up to individual shareholders to commence action against the directors to put right the wrong. (This eliminates wasteful and vexatious litigation by individual and troublesome minorities and reinforces the democratic principle in companies.) There are very few exceptions to this general principle (where the act committed was illegal, or where a personal right was infringed, or where there was a fraud on the minority). Even if he comes within one of these, the minority shareholder is not entitled to personal damages. Rather, the courts will simply make a declaration that the directors have acted to the detriment of minority shareholders. Indeed, in a recent decision (*Smith* v *Croft* [1988] Ch 114) the courts even held that a minority shareholder, although having *locus standi* to sue, should not be permitted to proceed if the majority of the minority shareholders did not wish the proceedings to continue. There is a great likelihood that proceedings may be delayed as the court tries to decide if the majority of disinterested shareholders really is independent of the wrongdoers. Where it is important to put a stop to the wrongdoing, this is surely not desirable. One thus questions the enthusiasm of the UK courts in protecting both the views and interests of the minority shareholders. (For a different judicial attitude, see Sealy (1989) 10 Co Law 52 'The Rule in *Foss* v *Harbottle*: the Australian Experience.')

An alternative course for the minority shareholder is an action under s. 459 of the Companies Act 1985 (as amended) whereby he can petition the court to make a declaration that the affairs of the company have been conducted in a way unfairly prejudicial to the interests of members generally or at least some part of its members (including himself). (Prior to the 1989 amendment, unfairly prejudicial conduct (as defined by the 1985 Act) had to affect a part of, as opposed to the whole of the membership. The conduct must also be discriminatory.) The amendment is invaluable to the minority shareholder as it removes the need to show clear discriminatory conduct against himself, it is enough to show that the act complained of is unfairly prejudicial to the interests of members generally. (For an analysis on the new s. 459 see Griffin, 'The Statutory Protection of Minority Shareholders: Section 459 of the Companies Act 1985', (1992) 13 Co Law 83.) In theory therefore, it is easier for an action under the new section to proceed. Any comfort derived by this opening in the law quickly vanishes, however, when the shareholder steps into court. He will find a reluctance amongst the judiciary to interfere with the management of the company. UK courts have shown a very cautious approach in so far as imposing a standard of care on directors is concerned. Short of very clear fraud and a malicious exercise of power, they seldom overturn decisions taken by directors although they may have turned out to be disastrous. While it is understandable that the differences in sizes, complexity and the varying degree of involvement of directors in the company in different economic climates make it difficult for the courts to impose their decisions on the directors, it seems that they take an unduly restrictive attitude toward protection of minority shareholders (Redmond-Cooper (1988) 9 Co Law 169, 'Management Deficiencies and Judicial Intervention, A Comparative Analysis'. This article compares the different attitudes between the English and French courts.) Under s. 459 therefore, the court usually orders that the minority shareholder's shares be bought at a fair price, and thus puts him in a position where he no longer needs to complain. This however, does not necessarily put a stop to the wrongdoing in the company.

The City Code on Takeovers and Mergers, as we have seen, is only a voluntary code. Given the common occurrence of takeovers and mergers in the UK, it is perhaps surprising that they are subject to virtually no legal regulation. Compliance with the principles under the Code is not mandatory and depends ultimately on the willingness of the parties to co-operate. The Panel's primary sanction on directors who have breached the spirit of the Code is a public or private reprimand or as a last resort, a deprivation of the facilities of the Stock Exchange. It has, however, no power to investigate the affairs of the company or bring the offender to court. The fact that the Panel has to depend on the Stock Exchange to impose sanctions on the offending company also means that it has no direct control over the sanctions imposed. The Stock Exchange may well take a less severe view of the offence. (For a comprehensive treatment of the subject see Hurst (1984) 5 Co Law, 161, 'Self Regulation v Legal Regulation'.) The courts are equally unenthusiastic. In *R* v *Panel of Takeovers and Mergers* [1987] 2 WLR 699 they held that any decision of the Panel in relation to a takeover is liable to be judicially reviewed. Where the life of the company is at stake, and when speed and flexibility are most important, this will surely result in a delay which will hamper effective regulation of a takeover.

Last but not least, shareholders take a passive interest in the affairs of the company. They are absent from meetings and prefer to delegate their voting powers to the board of directors. The existence of this proxy voting machinery gives directors a fair amount of power to change the direction of the general votes. One survey conducted among British companies showed that the average length of annual general meetings amounted to no more than 23 minutes (Midgley [1974] 114 Lloyds Bank Review 24). Shareholder control over what directors can or cannot do is thus reduced . . .

INSOLVENCY ACT 1986

213 Fraudulent trading
(1) If in the course of the winding up of a company it appears that any business of the company has been carried on with intent to defraud creditors of the company or creditors of any other person, or for any fraudulent purpose, the following has effect.

(2) The court, on the application of the liquidator may declare that any persons who were knowingly parties to the carrying on of the business in the manner above-mentioned are to be liable to make such contributions (if any) to the company's assets as the court thinks proper.

214 Wrongful trading
(1) Subject to subsection (3) below, if in the course of the winding up of a company it appears that subsection (2) of this section applies in relation to a person who is or has been a director of the company, the court, on the application of the liquidator, may declare that that person is to be liable to make such contribution (if any) to the company's assets as the court thinks proper.

(2) This subsection applies in relation to a person if—

(a) the company has gone into insolvent liquidation,

(b) at some time before the commencement of the winding up of the company, that person knew or ought to have concluded that there was no reasonable prospect that the company would avoid going into insolvent liquidation, and

(c) that person was a director of the company at that time; but the court shall not make a declaration under this section in any case where the time mentioned in paragraph (b) above was before 28th April 1986.

(3) The court shall not make a declaration under this section with respect to any person if it is satisfied that after the condition specified in subsection (2)(b) was first satisfied in relation to him that person took every step with a view to minimising the potential loss to the company's creditors as (assuming him to have known that there was no reasonable prospect that the company would avoid going into insolvent liquidation) he ought to have taken.

(4) For the purposes of subsections (2) and (3), the facts which a director of a company ought to know or ascertain, the conclusions which he ought to reach and the steps which he ought to take are those which would be known or ascertained, or reached or taken, by a reasonably diligent person having both—

(a) the general knowledge, skill and experience that may reasonably be expected of a person carrying out the same functions as are carried out by that director in relation to the company, and

(b) the general knowledge, skill and experience that that director has.

(5)   The reference in subsection (4) to the functions carried out in relation to a company by a director of the company includes any functions which he does not carry out but which have been entrusted to him.

(6)   For the purposes of this section a company goes into insolvent liquidation if it goes into liquidation at a time when its assets are insufficient for the payment of its debts and other liabilities and the expenses of the winding up.

(7)   In this section 'director' includes a shadow director.

(8)   This section is without prejudice to section 213.

Note

The following article discusses proposed reforms to security over moveable property (see 2.3.2).

John Murray QC 'Security over Moveable Property'
(1995) 5 SLT 31

Professor Murray describes the two current DTI consultation papers, on which representations are invited by 28 February 1995, and highlights some of the issues arising from the proposals.

The Department of Trade and Industry has now published two documents touching (to some extent) on the same subject matter. One is on *Security over Moveable Property in Scotland*, the other on *Registration of Company Charges in Great Britain*. The first is termed a consultation paper, the second a consultative document, but nothing appears to turn on that. Both demand attention from all interested parties in Scotland.

Security over Moveable property in Scotland

The background to the Scottish paper is that over the last three decades perceived deficiencies in the present law as to security (both in Scotland and Great Britain as a whole) have led to three reports suggesting, by various methods, reform of that law. The latest of these, *A Review of Security Interest in Property*, by Professor A L Diamond in 1989, recommended a scheme for a new law of security over moveables, heavily based on art. 9 of the American Uniform Commercial Code for both Scotland and England and Wales although separate provisions for Scotland would be necessary. Following public consultation it emerged that in England and Wales a majority were against substantial reform, whereas in Scotland there was seen to be a need for reform. In light of the Scottish response, it was decided that, for Scotland only, a draft Bill should be prepared with assistance from an advisory panel. The object of preparing a draft Bill at this stage is to focus the attention of consultees on the type of legislation that might be expected to follow in any ultimate reform.

The initial approach

The first task was to identify the main perceived deficiencies in the present law of Scotland. The first was that it is simply not possible to create a non-possessory fixed security over corporeal moveable property (with a few statutory exceptions such as ships). The second was the practical difficulties involved in the granting of securities over incorporeal moveable property (for example the requirements of intimation). By the term 'fixed security' is meant one which is fully effective in reespect of the property subject to it, as opposed to a floating charge which is only effective as a fixed security if the charge has attached the relevant property.

The proposals for the reform put forward in earlier reports were for a form of security with characteristics akin to those provided by art 9 of the Uniform Commercial Code. One problem with a security of that type is that although it has many characteristics in common with the floating charge as that exists in Scots law, it is a fixed security from the time of its creation. This could result in major creditors obtaining an unduly strong security to the disadvantage of unsecured creditors, and seemed undesirable for that reason. The introduction of the notice filing procedure to create a perfected right in security would have required, at least in the case of companies, a system of dual registration which would have been difficult to operate unless the whole basis of registration of company charges in Great Britain were to be altered. The approach adopted in the present paper is to seek to build on the existing law and address particular weaknesses in that law. In the event, what is proposed is an extension of the law relative to floating charges and the creation of a new fixed security over moveable property, hereafter referred to as 'moveable security'.

The extended floating charge

At present only an 'incorporated company' may grant a floating charge under Scots law. 'Incorporated company' includes industrial and provident societies as well as foreign companies. The concept of the floating charge has become well understood in its operation in Scotland and can apply to any property of the company. It is now proposed that the facility to grant a floating charge should be extended to all other persons but with the significant exception that a floating charge in the case of a person other than a company should only be permitted to secure an obligation arising *in the course of business* and only over *moveable property*. Excepted from the scope of the charge would be any 'consumer goods' of the granter, property exempt from poinding under the Debtors (Scotland) Act 1987, s. 16 and property held on trust.

Land would be excluded because of the complications for domestic conveyancing which would otherwise tend to arise. One major question for consultation is whether companies should continue to be able to grant floating charges over land or whether they also should be restricted to moveables, leaving land to be the subject of fixed security.

Moveable security

This new form of security, which is to be in addition to the existing modes whereby security over moveables can be created, should be available over all or any part of the moveable property of the granter as widely defined, including receivables. The principal exceptions would be consumer goods, tools of trade and property held in trust. The power to grant the moveable security should be restricted to the securing of debts or obligations arising in the course of a business. It should be especially noted that in this case a fixed security would be granted over receivables which are the property of the granter at the time when the security is granted or which he subsequently acquires. But this is the exception to the general rule that the moveable security is limited to the property existing at the date of creation. Nor does it extend to proceeds of sale or disposal of secured property. One question to be considered is whether the moveable security extends not only to the property initially subject thereto, but also to the 'fruit' of such property. For example, should calves on birth become subject to the security having been granted over their dams, or where the security is over shares in a company should it extend to a bonus issue in respect of those shares? On creation the moveable security will be a fixed security and will have priority over any diligence which is effected thereafter.

Creation of the securities

The simplest way of ensuring that the extended floating charge would have public recognition appears to be the registration of prescribed particulars relating to that charge in a public register as part of the process of creation (similar, in essence, to the registration of a deed in the Register of Sasines as creating a real right). If that were to be done it seems appropriate to treat all floating charges equally and make the creation of a floating charge by companies also dependent on public registration. This would involve a change from the existing law for companies whereby the floating charge becomes effective as a security right provided registration takes place within 21 days of creation. What is now proposed is that in all cases the floating charge should be created when the grantor has executed a deed bearing to grant such a floating charge and the prescribed particulars have been registered, the time of registration being the date of presentation of the relevant particulars. For the moveable security to be created there would require to be an execution of a document stating it grants a moveable security, and registration of the prescribed particulars of that moveable security again under the same time provision. A single register of security interests should be established, to be divided into two parts, one for the floating charge and one for the moveable security. It is proposed that the Registrar of Companies should be the registrar of security interests.

All floating charges would be entered in that part of the register relating to floating charges. This leaves the question of entry in a register of company charges in the case of a company. It seems clear that as the law stands there would have to be an entry in that register. What is proposed is that on registration of the particulars of the security as either a floating charge or a moveable security by a Scottish company in the register of security interests, the registrar should be obliged to enter a copy of those in the register of company charges. Where the company in question is registered in Englang and Wales, the registrar should be obliged to send a copy of the particulars to that registrar who in turn should be under a duty to enter the particulars in the register of company charges kept by him. The company itself would not require to register particulars of such securities under the Companies Act 1985, s. 395. Since the transfer of the relevant particulars of floating charges and moveable securities would be automatic so far as the parties are concerned, s. 410 of the Companies Act 1985 would be irrelevant for such purposes. Nor would there be any need for the registrar to issue 'conclusive certificates' under ss. 418 or 401 of the Companies Act as to satisfaction of the requirements of Part XII of the Companies Act 1985. Registration in the case of a company would be met by the registration of the prescribed particulars in the register of security interests. In order to achieve these results it is proposed that the entry in the register of security interests should be a conclusive statement of the matters contained therein for all purposes. Since it is to be conclusive, the form containing the prescribed particulars should be signed by both grantor and creditor. Any deficiencies in the form could be rectified by the parties or if necessary by the court.

Remedies

At present a receiver has to be appointed under a floating charge to enable the holder to exercise his security rights. It is proposed that the same should apply to any floating charge granted under the extended provision. However, there may be cases where the property subject to the charge is only one part of the property held by the debtor which is subject to securities. The powers of the receiver under the present law are restricted to the property subject to the charge. There are, or may be, occasions when this will create difficulties in realising the property of a debtor to best advantage. For example if the business is an hotel business and the floating charge extends to the moveables and the hotel building is the subject of a standard security, the separation of the two may mean that it is not possible to realise the whole to best advantage. It is proposed that where the holder of the floating charge is also the creditor in a standard security, then the receiver may be appointed to exercise powers over the whole subjects where that has been so specified in his instrument of appointment.

Where a moveable security has been created, it is proposed that a receiver should be appointable with the same general rights, powers, duties and obligations as a receiver under a floating charge. This, however, should not be the only means whereby a creditor can realise a security. The holder of a moveable security should be able to require the granter to deliver the property or transfer the rights in the property to him for realisation. If the granter does not comply then the creditor may apply to the court for an appropriate order. To cover the case where no receiver is appointed, the order of priority of distribution for the distribution of funds recovered by the security creditor through disposal of such property will be set out in statute. It should be noted that the proposed order of payment, by contrast with that which would apply in a receivership, relates to secured creditors and does not include preferential creditors (see cl 19 of the Bill).

Questions arising
Questions both of principle and detail arise in connection with these proposals. Part of the paper sets out those on which views are especially invited. Space permits the mention of only a few. Should companies continue to be permitted to create floating charges over heritable property? If floating charges are to be as widely available as proposed, is the present policy that on attachment the holder's rights are subject to the rights of any person who has 'effectually executed diligence', but that such diligence does not include a bare arrestment, appropriate? If not, should effectually executed diligence be given a statutory definition? Should it be possible to appoint a receiver over part only of the property subject to the charges? Other questions will have occurred to the reader of this brief summary, and many others to those who study the Bill. . . .

T. E. Cooke and Andrew Hicks,
'Wrongful Trading—Predicting Insolvency'
1993 JBL 338

Introduction
As to the standard expected of the director in question in predicting insolvent liquidation, he is to be judged on 'the general knowledge, skill and experience that may reasonably be expected of a person carrying our the same functions as are carried out by that director in relation to the company'. (Insolvency Act 1986, s. 214 (4)(*a*). More will, of course, be expected of a director in a larger company with sophisticated accounting procedures and equipment (*Re Produce Marketing Ltd.* (No. 2) [1989] BCLC 520, at 550bc). Furthermore, if his general knowledge, skill and experience exceeds that required for the job, then he is expected to discharge his responsibilities in accordance with those skills. (Insolvency Act 1986, s. 214 (4)(*b*). He is thus judged according to the appropriate standard expected either for the job or of that individual, which ever is the higher.

Of particular importance, therefore, is that inadequate expertise necessary for a particular job does not excuse a director from failing to reach the inevitable conclusion. It is also worth noting that as individual directors will be judged by differing standards, the moment at which each individual should have reached the conclusion may differ. For example, a finance directors' liability may run from an earlier time than a non-executive directors'.

The cases—management information
The cases reported to date all seem to have been reasonably obvious cases of wrongful trading. The courts have, therefore, not been unduly troubled by any theoretical

approach to predicting business failure. For example, in *Re Purpoint Ltd.*, [1991] BCLC 491, a relatively late point in time was chosen as the liability date when increasing trading losses led to a cash-flow crisis. In *Re DKG Contractors Ltd*, (1990) BCC 903, when a supplier refused further deliveries, the court concluded that if proper financial controls had been instituted, the prediction of insolvent liquidation would have become clear. In the case of *Re Produce Marketing Consortium Ltd* (No 2) (see above), the liability point was pushed back to 14 months prior to liquidation. The date selected was the last time at which accounts, portraying a disastrous position, should have been, but were not, received and filed with the Registrar in compliance with the Companies Act 1985.

The early indications are, therefore, that the courts are likely to select a crisis point when the director should have recognised the inevitable. An indication of difficulties may include the loss of a major customer, a supplier refusing credit, or the loss of key employees. Evidence of advice from professionals that insolvent liquidation is unavoidable would also seem to assure the case against directors.

The time at which financial information becomes, or should have become, available that would lead to a prediction of insolvent liquidation, is an obvious time for liability to begin. The Act is clear that 'the facts which a director of a company ought to know or ascertain' (Insolvency Act 1986, s. 214(4)) are those which a diligent person in that job or with the expertise of that individual ought to have ascertained. Ignorance is no excuse and clearly the accounting information required by the Companies Act 1985 is an absolute minimum of deemed knowledge. In *Produce Marketing*, the court's selection of the last time for filing annual accounts as the liability point seems relatively indulgent. This point was selected even though 'Trial balances were made by Mr Murphy at roughly monthly intervals of these three ledgers' ([1989] BCLC 520 at p. 526a.). In *Re DKG Contractors Ltd*, warning signs should have led the directors to institute some kind of financial control and their failure to do so at that time fixed the liability point.

Directors cannot, however, assume from *Produce Marketing* that they need only produce and draw inferences from annual statutory accounts. The courts may expect a very much higher level of information according to legal, accounting or commercial standards. Section 221 of the Companies Act 1985 requires companies to keep accounting records sufficient to 'disclose with reasonable accuracy, at any time, the financial position of the company at that time', in particular containing day-to-day entries of transactions and a record of assets and liabilities. Listed companies are obliged to report half-yearly figures and some of them report quarterly. It is clearly arguable that directors of certain companies, particularly large enterprises, should ensure the production of monthly management accounts. (The Institute of Directors' *Guide to Boardroom Practice*; *Companies in Financial Difficulties*, states Guideline (1) as 'Directors of a company must at all times have up-to-date and accurate financial information . . .'; clearly an influential professional standard for directors.) Where such information would have assisted the prediction of insolvent liquidation, directors will be potentially liable from that time. It remains to be seen, therefore, precisely what accounting information courts will expect or deem directors to have. Clearly a liquidator should call expert evidence so as to establish the minimum management accounts that the director, according to the standard required of him, should have had produced and should have drawn conclusions from.

Management information is, therefore, the key to proper decision-making in business. The level of information that the courts will expect directors to obtain is accordingly a major aspect of the standard of expertise required of them. The courts will, therefore, have to assess what information should have been available to directors on the basis of evidence of current business and accounting practice and as legally required.

Assuming that such information is available, the courts have to consider, given the expertise required of the director in question, whether he should have concluded that insolvent liquidation was inevitable. What expertise is expected of particular directors in assessing information again may be primarily a matter of expert evidence. However, to date, the courts seem to have taken a common-sense plain man's approach to these decisions. Case involving large companies requiring a higher degree of management expertise may elicit a more technical approach to deciding what level of skill directors should have in making major commercial decisions, such as predicting insolvency.

Warning signs and professional advice
It is, of course, arguable that when warning signs of financial difficulty are apparent, directors should as a very minimum seek professsional advice. (*Op. cit.*, Guideline (2) says, 'Directors of a company in financial difficulties should seek competent professional advice'.) This would then make the directors' expertise less relevant from then on as it may in effect be superseded by the advice they receive or should have received. If properly informed and competent advice is favourable, directors may presumably proceed safely for the time being at least. But if it is not favourable, liability probably is fixed immediately. If they should have, but did not, seek advice at a time when that date would have been unfavourable, then liability is again probably fixed.

It could be argued, therefore, that in many cases the question of directors' expertise is primarily relevant in considering whether they should have recognised the warning signs and obtained professional advice. In many instances, warning signs are reasonably obvious. Courts may, therefore, fix liability by asking when was the earliest point after warning signs of financial difficulty were reasonably apparent that professional advice would have predicted insolvency? Such an approach would thus fix an early date for liability based on a professional level of expertise in predicting insolvency. Just as directors are deemed to know certain information, they may be deemed to have received formal advice that warning signs should have led them to obtain.

More difficult is to attempt to push the liability point to an earlier time when financial difficulty was less immediate and warning signs less obvious. Insolvency may be predicted long before a cash-flow crisis leads to an actual failure to pay current debts. In *Re Purpoint Ltd*, ([1991] BCLC 491 at p. 498) Vinelott J commented that he felt some doubt whether a reasonably prudent director should have allowed the company to begin trading at all: it had no capital base, it relied entirely on borrowing and the business it had taken on had previously been unprofitable. But, he said, to conclude that the director should have predicted losses from the very start would impose too high a test. The director was entitled to believe that his skills and contacts could turn the business around. The courts may thus tend to give directors the benefit of the doubt and not choose too early a time for liability to run.

However, the wording of section 214, which shifts the onus onto the directors to show that they properly protected the interests of the creditors, is very wide. Bad decision-making in expanding too fast, taking on excessive debt, underpricing a major contract; all might lead an experienced business man to conclude from an early time that commercial failure and insolvent liquidation are almost inevitable.

A similar point was raised by the Institute of Directors that the section could cover, for example, the situation of overtrading. (Institute of Directors, *Guide to Boardroom Practice No. 6; Directors' Personal Liabilities* (1986) at para. 4.34.) Where a board makes a bad commercial decision which ensures that the company's demand for working capital outstrips its capacity to generate or raise cash in the short-term, corporate failure is probably predictable. Should the directors of such a company have concluded that in taking the decision there was then no reasonable prospect of avoiding insolvency? While the section is intended to encourage directors to minimise losses when insolvency appears inevitable, it could also possibly catch directors guilty of major commercial misjudgement. It is, as yet, early days in predicting how the courts will act in response to this situation, but Vinelott J's approach suggests that too stringent a test will not be applied.

Nevertheless, it is arguable that the courts should expect a high objective standard in predicting insolvency and push back the commencement of liability to a relatively early date. The directors then have the opportunity to show that they did take full account of the creditors' interests, on the assumption that they knew that insolvent liquidation was inevitable. Unless such a robust approach is taken, the purpose of the legislation will not be achieved.

To do this, the courts will have to assess evidence brought by a liquidator as to available 'theories' in predicting insolvency. Clearly there is extensive informal management expertise available that can be called in evidence to show that a serious business error should have led to the inevitable conclusion. More general theories are not so well-known, but they are reasonably well-developed and capable of objectively predicting insolvency. . . .

CHAPTER THREE
CONTRACT

There follows an extract from the decision in *Avintair Ltd* v *Ryder Airline Services Ltd*, where the issue of consensus in idem is in question (see 3.2.3.2 in the text).

AVINTAIR v RYDER AIRLINE SERVICES LTD
1993 SCLR 576

Facts

A director of the pursuers had discussions with representatives of the defenders about assistance which the pursuers could provide for the defenders in the obtaining of contracts with an airline. Thereafter one of the defenders' representatives confirmed that the pursuers were to act for the defenders but it was agreed that the rate of commission would be a matter for further negotiation. The pursuers then did some lobbying on behalf of the defenders while negotiations continued as to the rate of commission to be paid. The defenders proposed a rate which was substantiallly less than that which had been proposed by the pursuers. Thereafter the defenders purported to decline the pursuers' offer to work on their behalf. The pursuers raised an action for declarator of the existence of a contract between the parties and to the effect that the pursuers were entitled to reasonable remuneration for their work. They also concluded for count reckoning and payment. The defenders argued that the pursuers had failed to aver the essentials of a completed contract as there had been no agreement about the rate of commission. The pursuers argued that there was a completed contract including an implied condition to the effect that they would be entitled to a reasonable rate of commission. In rejecting the pursuers' argument and dismissing the action as irrelevant the Lord Ordinary issued an opinion from which the following extracts are taken.

Lord Sutherland

In this action the pursuers seek declaration of the existence of a contract between the parties whereby the pursuers acted for the defenders as aviation consultants in relation to the obtaining for the defenders of contracts for engine overhaul and similar work from Pakistan International Airways and that the pursuers are entitled to reasonable remuneration for their work assessed at commission rates as set out in the first conclusion. The second conclusion is for count reckoning and payment and the third conclusion is for payment of £200,000 or such other sum as may be found due as the true balance on said account. Although the third conclusion does not contain the words 'failing an accounting', it is clear from the pursuers' third plea-in-law that this is how the conclusion should be interpreted. The case came on procedure roll on the defenders' motion that the action should be dismissed on the ground that the pursuers' pleadings do not disclose the existence of the contract as contended for and, in any event, even if there was a contract between the parties, there is no relevant basis averred for ascertainment of the price.

The pursuers aver that on or about 13th February 1990 one of their directors, Mr Husain, spoke to a manager of the defenders in order to discuss assistance that the pursuers could provide for the defenders in the obtaining of contracts with Pakistan International Airways. Thereafter there was contact between Mr Husain and Mr Allan, the marketing manager of the defenders. On 23rd May 1990 Mr Husain and Mr Allan had a three-hour meeting when the services offered by the pursuers were discussed and the pursuers made clear that payment for their services would be on a commission basis. They proposed certain rates of commission. Mr Allan confirmed that the pursuers were to act for the defenders but it was agreed that the rate of the commission would be a matter of further negotiation. Thereafter it is averred certain lobbying was done by the pursuers on the defenders' behalf and during this period the parties continued negotiations as to the rate of the remuneration to be paid. On 18th June 1990 Mr Allan proposed certain rates of payment which were substantially less than those which had been proposed by the pursuers. On 26th June 1990 the pursuers restated their proposals for commission which did not differ from the proposals originally made on 23rd May. Eventually on 16th August 1990 the defenders purported to decline the pursuers' offer of working on their behalf. . .

In my opinion in this case the facts do not establish that there was consensus in idem between the parties and accordingly there was no concluded contract. It is true that on 23rd May 1990 the pursuers aver that Mr Allan confirmed that the pursuers were to act for the defenders and it is also averred that at later stages the defenders were aware that the pursuers were making efforts on their behalf and these efforts were actively encouraged by the defenders. It is, however, equally clear that the rate of commission which the pursuers were to be paid was never a matter of agreement and indeed the gulf between the parties was a fairly substantial one. The rates of commission proposed by the pursuers were about 50 per cent above those proposed by the defenders and as the pursuers in their third conclusion estimated the amount of commission due to be in the region of £200,000, even on the basis of the defenders' rates of commission it is obvious that a fairly substantial sum was involved in the negotiations. I entirely accept that in a contract for services it may not be necessary to discuss price at all and in that situation there will be an implied term that the provider of the services will be entitled to reasonable remuneration. If necessary, the amount of that remuneration can be left to the court to adjust (see Gloag on the Contract, p. 294). Had there been no discussion in the present case between the parties about the rate of commission, I would have been satisfied that the pursuers averred enough to show that a concluded contract was entered into which included a term that the pursuers would be entitled to a reasonable rate of commission. As it was, however, there was a dispute between the parties from the very start as to what the rate of remuneration would be and, as I have indicated, the dispute was not about some trivial sum. It is quite clear that there was no consensus in idem between the parties on the matter of the rate of remuneration and it is equally clear in my view that this was a matter of considerable importance to the implementation of the alleged contract. This is not a case such as *Neilson* v *Stewart*, 1991 SLT 523, where the time for repayment of the loan was a collateral issue, nor is it a case like *R. & J. Dempster Ltd* v *Motherwell Bridge & Engineering Co. Ltd*, 1964 SC 308, where parties specifically agreed that the fixing of the price should be deferred until such time as the steel was actually delivered during the course of the following three years, it not being possible to fix the price at any earlier date. The cases referred to by counsel for the pursuers were cases in which there was no dispute that the pursuers were entitled to remuneration and the only questions were either whether the pursuers' efforts had led to a sale or as to what constituted reasonable remuneration in the circumstances. In the present case the fixing of the rate of remuneration was clearly a matter in the forefront of the parties' minds and I regard it in the circumstances of this contract as being an essential part of any contractual terms. The pursuers' agreement that they are entitled to fall back on an implied term will, in my opinion not do. An implied term means precisely what it says, namely that the parties are assumed to have included in their contractual arrangements a term that the provider of services would be entitled to reasonable remuneration. The reason why that term is applied in the contract is because the parties have not, in the course of their entering into contractual agreements, negotiated any different term. Where, however, the parties are actively negotiating as to what constitutes a reasonable rate of remuneration, it cannot be said that they have entered into a firm contract with an implied term that the remuneration shall be left to be fixed perhaps by the court at a later stage. If that had been the position there would be no need for the proposals and counter-proposals which were in fact made during the whole course of the negotiations in this case. On the whole matter I am satisfied that the alleged contract never got beyond the stage of negotiation on a vital matter, that accordingly there was no consensus in idem between the parties and that therefore the pursuers' claim for declarator must fail.

CARLILL v CARBOLIC SMOKE BALL CO
[1893] IQB 256

Facts
The defendants, who were the proprietors and vendors of a medical preparation called 'The Carbolic Smoke Ball', inserted in the *Pall Mall Gazette* of 13 November 1891, and in other newspapers, the following advertisement:

£100 reward will be paid by the Carbolic Smoke Ball Company to any person who contracts the increasing epidemic influenza, colds, or any disease caused by taking cold, after having used the ball three times daily for two weeks according to the printed directions supplied with each ball. £1000 is deposited with the Alliance Bank, Regent Street, shewing our sincerity in the matter.

During the last epidemic of influenza many thousand carbolic smoke balls were sold as preventives against this disease, and in no ascertained case was the disease contracted by those using the carbolic smoke ball.

One carbolic smoke ball will last a family several months, making it the cheapest remedy in the world at the price, 10*s.*, post free. The ball can be refilled at a cost of 5*s.* Address, Carbolic Smoke Ball Company, 27, Princes Street, Hanover Square, London.

The plaintiff, a lady, on the faith of this advertisement, bought one of the balls at a chemist's, and used it as directed, three times a day, from 20 November 1891 to 17 January 1892, when she was attacked by influenza. Hawkins J held that she was entitled to recover the £100. The defendants appealed.

Lindley LJ

. . . . I will begin by referring to two points which were raised in the Court below. I refer to them simply for the purpose of dismissing them. First, it is said no action will lie upon this contract because it is a policy. You have only to look at the advertisement to dismiss that suggestion. Then it was said that it is a bet. Hawkins J came to the conclusion that nobody every dreamt of a bet, and that the transaction had nothing whatever in common with a bet. I so entirely agree with him that I pass over this contention also as not worth serious attention.

Then, what is left? The first observation I will make is that we are not dealing with any inference of fact. We are dealing with an express promise to pay £100 in certain events. Read the advertisement how you will, and twist it about as you will, here is a distinct promise expressed in language which is perfectly unmistakable — '£100 reward will be paid by the Carbolic Smoke Ball Company to any person who contracts the influenza after having used the ball three times daily for two weeks according to the printed directions supplied with each ball'.

We must first consider whether this was intended to be a promise at all, or whether it was a mere puff which meant nothing. Was it a mere puff? My answer to that question is No, and I base my answer upon this passage: '£1000 is deposited with the Alliance Bank, shewing our sincerity in the matter'. Now, for what was that money deposited or that statement made except to negative the suggestion that this was a mere puff and meant nothing at all? The deposit is called in aid by the advertiser as proof of his sincerity in the matter — that is, the sincerity of his promise to pay this £100 in the event which he has specified. I say this for the purpose of giving point to the observation that we are not inferring a promise; there is the promise, as plain as words can make it.

Then it is contended that it is not binding. In the first place, it is said that it is not made with anybody in particular. Now that point is common to the words of this advertisement and to the words of all other advertisements offering rewards. They are offers to anybody who performs the conditions named in the advertisement, and anybody who does perform the condition accepts the offer. In point of law this advertisement is an offer to pay £100 to anybody who will perform these conditions, and the performance of the conditions is the acceptance of the offer. That rests upon a string of authorities, the earliest of which is *Williams* v *Carwardine*, which has been followed by many other decisions upon advertisements offering rewards.

But then it is said 'Supposing that the performance of the conditions is an acceptance of the offer, that acceptance ought to have been notified'. Unquestionably, as a general proposition, when an offer is made, it is necessary in order to make a binding contract, not only that it should be accepted, but that the acceptance should be notified. But is that so in cases of this kind? I apprehend that they are an exception to that rule, or, if not an exception, they are open to the observation that the notification of the acceptance need not precede the performance. This offer is a continuing offer. It was never revoked, and if notice of acceptance is required — which I doubt very much, for I rather think the true view is that which was expressed and explained by Lord Blackburn in the case of *Brogden* v *Metropolitan Ry Co* — if notice of acceptance is required, the person who makes the offer gets the notice of acceptance contemporaneously with his notice of the performance of the condition. If he gets notice of the acceptance before his offer is revoked, that in principle is all you want. I, however, think that the true view, in a case of this kind, is that the person who makes the offer shews by his language and from the nature of the transaction that he does not expect and does not require notice of the acceptance apart from notice of the performance.

We, therefore, find here all the elements which are necessary to form a binding contract enforceable in point of law, subject to two observations. First of all it is said that this advertisement is so vague that you cannot really construe it as a promise — that the vagueness of the language shews that a legal promise was never intended or contemplated. The language is vague and uncertain in some respects, and particularly in this, that the £100 is to be paid to any person who contracts the increasing epidemic after having used the balls three times daily for two weeks. It is said, When are they to be used? According to the language of the advertisement no time is fixed, and, construing the offer most strongly against the person who has made it, one might infer that any time was meant. I do not think that was meant, and to hold the contrary would be pushing too far the doctrine of taking language most strongly against the person using it. I do not think that business people or reasonable people would understand the words as meaning that if you took a smoke ball and used it three times daily for two weeks you were to be guaranteed against influenza for the rest of your life, and I think it would be pushing the language of the advertisement too far to construe it as meaning that. But if it does not mean that, what does it mean? It is for the defendants to shew what it does mean; and it strikes me that there are two, and possibly three, reasonable constructions to be put on this advertisement, any one of which will answer the purpose of the plaintiff. Possibly it may be limited to persons catching the 'increasing epidemic' (that is, the then prevailing epidemic), or any colds or diseases caused by taking cold, during the prevalence of the increasing epidemic. That is one suggestion; but it does not commend itself to me. Another suggested meaning is that you are warranted free from catching this epidemic, or colds or other diseases caused by taking cold, whilst you are using this remedy after using it for two weeks. If that is the meaning, the plaintiff is right, for she used the remedy for two weeks and went on using it till she got the epidemic. Another meaning, and the one which I rather prefer, is that the reward is offered to any person who contracts the epidemic or other disease within a reasonable time after having used the smoke ball. Then it is asked, What is a reasonable time? It has been suggested that there is no standard of reasonableness; that it depends upon the reasonable time for a germ to develop! I do not feel pressed by that. It strikes me that a reasonable time may be ascertained in a business sense and in a sense satisfactory to a lawyer, in this way; find out from a chemist what the ingredients are; find out from a skilled physician how long the effect of such ingredients on the system could be reasonably expected to endure so as to protect a person from an epidemic or cold, and in that way you will get a standard to be laid before a jury, or a judge without a jury, by which they might exercise their judgment as to what a reasonable time would be. It strikes me, I confess, that the true construction of this advertisement is that £100 will be paid to anybody who uses this smoke ball three times daily for two weeks according to the printed directions, and who gets the influenza or cold or other diseases caused by taking cold within a reasonable time after so using it; and if that is the true construction, it is enough for the plaintiff.

Notes

(1) Why does the advertisement in Carlill's case create legal relations whereas most advertisements do not?

(2) At what moment did the contract come into existence?

(3) If the smoke ball had been bought by Carlill's friend and loaned to her, would it have made any difference to the result of this action?

(4) If the Smoke Ball Co published an advertisement on 8 December 1892 in all the newspapers in which the original offer had appeared saying that the offer was now withdrawn, and Henry, who had been using the smoke ball regularly since 20 November, contracted influenza on 10 December, would the company be liable?

(5) If Carlill had used the smoke ball three times daily for two weeks without knowing anything about the advertisement offering the reward, and had then caught

influenza and learned of the advertisement through her doctor, could she have recovered the £100?

(6) Did the company promise that Carlill would not catch influenza? Were they in breach of contract when she did?

HOLWELL SECURITIES LTD v HUGHES
[1974] 1 All ER 161

Lawton LJ

The issue in this appeal was clear. Did the plaintiffs exercise an option to purchase the premises knowns as 571 High Road, Wembley, by posting a letter to the defendant which he never received? The answer to this problem can be reached by two paths: the short one and the roundabout one. Both, in my judgment, are satisfactory but the roundabout one has some paths leading off it which can lead the traveller after legal truth astray. The plaintiffs, I think, took one of these paths. I propose in this judgment to start by taking the short path and then to survey the other.

It is a truism of the law relating to options that the grantee must comply strictly with the conditions stipulated for exercise: *see Hare v Nicoll*. It follows that the first task of the court is to find out what was stipulated: the instrument of grant has to be construed. It is a formal document which must have been drafted by someone familiar with conveyancing practice. From its layout and content it is likely to have been based on a precedent in the Encyclopaedia of Forms and Precedents. It follows, so it seems to me, that the words and phrases in it should be given precise meanings whenever possible and that words which are in common use amongst conveyancers should be construed in the way they use such words.

The material parts of the option clause are as follows: 'The said option shall be exercisable by notice in writing to the Intending Vendor at any time within six months from the date hereof . . .' In my judgment, the phrase 'notice in writing' is of importance in this context. Conveyancers are familiar with it and frequently use it. It occurs in many sections of the Law of Property Act 1925; for examples, see ss. 36(2), 136, 146 and 196. In the option clauses under consideration the draftsman used the phrase in connection with the exercise of the option but in other parts of the agreement he was content to use such phrases as 'agreed in writing' (see cl. 4) and 'if required in writing' (see cl. 8(a)). Should any inference be drawn from the use of the word 'notice'? In my judgment, Yes. Its derivation is from the Latin word for knowing. A notice is a means of making something known. The Shorter Oxford English Dictionary gives as the primary meanings of the word: 'Intimation, information, intelligence, warning . . . formal intimation or warning of something.' If a notice is to be of any value it must be an intimation to someone. A notice which cannot impinge on anyone's mind is not functioning as such.

Now in this case, the 'notice in writing' was to be one 'to the Intending Vendor'. It was to be an intimation to him that the grantee had exercised the option: he was the one who was to be fixed with the information contained in the writing. He never was, because the letter carrying the information went astray. The plaintiffs were unable to do what the agreement said they were to do, namely, fix the defendant with knowledge that they had decided to buy his property. If this construction of the option clause is correct, there is no room for the application of any rule of law relating to the acceptance of offers by posting letters since the option agreement stipulated what had to be done to exercise the option. On this ground alone I would dismiss the appeal.

I turn now to what I have called the roundabout path to the same result. Counsel for the plaintiffs submitted that the option was exercised when the letter was posted, as the rule relating to the acceptance of offers by post did apply. The foundation of his argument was that the parties to this agreement must have contemplated that the option might be, and probably would be, exercised by means of a letter sent through the post. I agree. This, submitted counsel, was enough to bring the rule into operation. I do not agree. In *Henthorn v Fraser* Lord Herschell stated the rule as follows:

> Where the circumstances are such that it must have been within the contemplation of the parties that, according to the ordinary usages of mankind, the post might be used as a means of communicating the acceptance of an offer, the acceptance is complete as soon as it is posted.

It was applied by Farwell J in *Bruner v Moore* to an option to purchase patent rights. The option agreement, which was in writing, was silent as to the manner in which it was to be exercised. The grantee purported to do so by a letter and a telegram.

Does the rule apply in *all* cases where one party makes an offer which both he and the person with whom he was dealing must have expected the post to be used as a means of accepting it? In my judgment, it does not. First; it does not apply when the express terms of the offer specify that the acceptance must reach the offeror. The public nowadays are familiar with this exception to the general rule through their handling of football pool coupons. Secondly, it probably does not operate if its application would produce manifest inconvenience and absurdity. This is the opinion set out in Cheshire and Fifoot's *Law of Contract*. It was the opinion of Bramwell B as is seen by his judgment in *British & American Telegraph Co v Colson*, and his opinion is worthy of consideration even though the decision in that case was overruled by this court in *Household Fire and Carriage Accident Insurance Co Ltd v Grant*. The illustrations of inconvenience and absurdity which Bramwell B gave are as apt today as they were then. Is a stockbroker who is holding shares to the orders of his client liable in damages because he did not sell in a falling market in accordance with the instructions in a letter which was posted but never received? Before the passing of the Law Reform (Miscellaneous Provisions) Act 1970 (which abolished actions for breach of promise of marriage), would a young soldier ordered overseas have been bound in contract to marry a girl to whom he had proposed by letter, asking her to let him have an answer before he left and she had replied affirmatively in good time but the letter had never reached him? In my judgment, the factors of inconvenience and absurdity are but illustrations of a wider principle, namely, that the rule does not apply if, having regard to all the circumstances, including the nature of the subject-matter under consideration, the negotiating parties cannot have intended that there should be a binding agreement until the party accepting an offer or exercising an option had in fact communicated the acceptance or exercise to the other. In my judgment, when this principle is applied to the facts of this case it becomes clear that the parties cannot have intended that the posting of a letter should constitute the exercise of the option.

The option agreement was one to which s. 196 of the Law of Property Act 1925 applied: [s. 196(3)] is in these terms:

> The provisions of this section shall extend to notices required to be served by any instrument affecting property executed or coming into operation after the commencement of this Act unless a contrary intention appears.

The option agreement was an instrument affecting property. A notice in writing had to be given to exercise the option. Giving a notice means the same as serving a notice: *see Re 88 Berkeley Road*. The object of this subsection was to enable conveyancers to omit from instruments affecting property stipulations as to the giving of notices if they were prepared to accept the statutory ones. As there was nothing in the option agreement to a contrary effect, the statutory stipulations applied in this case. [Section 196(4)] is in these terms:

> Any notice required or authorised by this Act to be served shall also be sufficiently served, if it is sent by post in a registered letter addressed to the lessee, lessor, mortgagee, mortgagor, or other person to be served, by name, at the aforesaid place of abode or business, office, or counting-house, and if that letter is not returned through the post-office undelivered; and that service shall be deemed to be made at the time at which the registered letter would in the ordinary course be delivered.

The object of this subsection, as also of [s. 196(3)], is to specify circumstances in which proof of actual knowledge may be dispensed with. This follows from the use of the phrase 'any notice . . . shall also be sufficiently served . . .' If the submissions of counsel for the plaintiffs are well-founded, a letter sent by ordinary post the evening before the option expired would have amounted to an exercise of it; but a registered letter posted at the same time and arriving in the ordinary course of post, which would be after the expiration of the option, would not have been an exercise. The parties to the option agreement cannot have intended any such absurd result to follow. When the provisions of s. 196(4) are read into the agreement, as they have to be, the only reasonable inference is that the parties intended that the vendor should be fixed with actual knowledge of the exercise of the option save in the circumstances envisaged in the subsection. This, in my judgment, was enough to exclude the rule.

I would dismiss the appeal.

Notes

(1) What should I say if I do not wish an acceptance of my offer to take effect when posted? (Note the proposal to change the rules — 3.3.3.3 above.)

(2) Can you think of any commercial situations in which such an intention is commonly expressed?

(3) The following is as extract from an article by Hector MacQueen on the important commercial role played by gratuitous promises (see 3.4 in the text).

'Constitution and Proof of Gratuitous Obligations' by Hector MacQueen 1986 SLT 1

In Scotland the concept of promise seems to permit avoidance of the difficulties which have so troubled the English courts and textbook writers. But it has yet to be fully recognised how useful the concept might be in the commercial context. Indeed the discussion of gratuitous obligations has been bedevilled by the consideration of trivial examples such as the promise of a reward for walking to York, and by the belief that: 'The commonest purpose of a unilateral promise is probably to make a gift, benefit a person or a charity, or to reward services performed not under contract or to an extent not contractually exigible' (Walker, *Contracts* (2nd ed.), para. 2.13.). But in fact many unilateral undertakings are given in the business world and are normally treated there as binding. The courts have dealt with grants of options for the purchase of heritage and promises to hold offers open for acceptance for a stated period as obligatory (see *Littlejohn v Hadwen* (1882) 20 SLR 5; *Stone v MacDonald*, 1979 SLT 288), so fulfilling the reasonable expectations of those making and receiving such statements. Another example may be found in the letter of credit issued by a banker where the parties to an international sale of goods arrange for payment through a bank by means of a documentary credit transaction. The letter of credit is an undertaking by the buyer's banker to pay the seller upon presentation of the documents which represent the goods. It is fundamental to such an arrangement that the banker cannot withdraw the credit; the legal basis for this has never been clear in England, but in Scotland can clearly be found in the binding conditional promise (Gow, *Mercantile Law*, p. 471, n. 98).

Further examples of unilateral undertakings in commercial surroundings may be found by examining some of the English cases on unilateral contracts. The most recent is the decision of the House of Lords in *Harvela Investments Ltd v Royal Trust Co of Canada* [1985] 2 All ER 966. The Royal Trust Company invited bids for certain shares and stated that the highest offer would be accepted. Lord Diplock, with whom the other law lords agreed, held (at p. 969) that this statement constituted a unilateral contract binding on the company when communicated to prospective offerors for the shares. It is not clear from Lord Diplock's opinion how this is to be reconciled with the basic requirements of acceptance and consideration in the English law of contract, but the recognition of the statement's obligatory nature is quite apparent. In *British Steel Corp v Cleveland Bridge and Engineering Co* [1984] 1 All ER 504, Robert Goff J suggested that a letter of intent might be treated as a unilateral contract. Letters of intent, which are in common use in the construction and engineering industries, are responses to tenders for work stating that the sender proposes to award the contract to the recipient. Normally such letters do not amount to acceptances of the tender, because they make it clear that details of the contract have still to be worked out; their purpose is to assure the tenderer of the contract and to enable him to start preparing for it, for instance by setting up any necessary sub-contracts. It is common for the tenderer to start the contractual work on the basis of the letter of intent alone (see S. N. Ball (1983) 99 LQR 572). So the problem may occasionally arise that the parties are ultimately unable to agree upon the main contract and with it the question of remuneration for work done under the letter of intent. Although quasi-contractual remedies were used in the *British Steel* case, Robert Goff J did say (at p. 510) that in this situation there might be 'what is sometimes called an "if" contract, i.e. a contract under which A requests B to carry out a certain performance and promises B that, if he does so, he will receive a certain performance in return, usually remuneration for his performance'; but he held that there was no such contract in the case before him because he felt it 'repugnant to common sense and the commercial realities' to find the parties bound contractually when the letter of intent was expressly sent pending a formal contract. Finally, 'requirements contracts' where A agrees to supply B with goods as and when he requires them, may be cosidered. Here A is under an obligation to supply the goods but B is free to make orders or not as he pleases. In England this situation is usually treated as a standing offer by A, accepted and so becoming obligatory only when B makes an order (Cheshire and Fifoot, *Contract* (10th ed.), pp. 40–41). But again the familiar difficulty arises: if A is only offering he can withdraw at any time between orders, which is contrary to the commercial understanding of such arrangements.

The Scottish concept of gratuitous obligations and in particular the promise seems usefully and naturally applicable to all these situations, always provided that there is appropriate writing. I have already discussed this point in connection with the *Harvela* case before it went to the House of Lords (1985 SLT (News) 187 at p. 188); a statement that the highest bid will be accepted would clearly be an enforceable promise in Scots law not requiring any acceptance or consideration. Similarly a Scottish court might not have had the same difficulty as Robert Goff J in holding the senders of a letter of intent bound thereby as a promise to pay for work done before the formation of the main contract. This solution would avoid the need to depend upon remedies of unjust enrichment whose scope in Scots law is so uncertain and has the added attraction of giving the letter of intent some status in the law which matches their undoubted importance in the commercial world. (For inconclusive comments on letters of intent in Scots law, see *Uniroyal Ltd* v *Miller & Co Ltd*, 1985 SLT 101 at p. 107.) With regard to requirements contracts, Scots law would be able to fulfil the expectations of the parties either by holding that gratuitous contract had been formed ab initio, binding A only but covering all subsequent orders made by B, or alternatively by finding that A had promised to accept orders made by B, with each order thereafter being the subject of a separate contract.

SAMPLE TERMS AND CONDITIONS IN COMMERCIAL CONTRACTS

Note

Consider in relation to these clauses:

(a)   the aim you believe each clause is attempting to achieve;

(b)   the impact, if any, which any of the provisions of the Unfair Contract Terms Act 1977 (reproduced below) might have on each clause;

(c)   in the light of this and/or for any other legal or commercial reasons would you advise re-drafting of any clauses? If so, along what lines?

Time of performance

(a)   Time shall not be of the essence of this contract in so far as it concerns the delivery of goods. The sellers shall not be liable for any loss or damage howsoever arising from the failure to deliver by any date specified either by this contract or by any collateral agreement, representation or arrangement made by the sellers or their servants or agents, whether oral or in writing.

(b)   The times given by us for the delivery of goods or the completion of any installation shall run from the commencement date. The times are given as the best estimates we can give and are based upon current commitments and conditions but are subject to our ability to obtain any necessary outside supplies. We are to be under no liability for loss in respect of any failure to deliver or complete within the estimated time nor shall the customer be entitled to rescind the contract on this account unless on or after the expiry of the estimated time the customer gives written notice to us of a reasonable period within which he requires the goods to be delivered or the installation to be completed as the case may be.

(c)   We make every effort to meet delivery dates but we shall be under no liability for failure to deliver on a specified date or within a specified period.

(d)   The sellers will use their best endeavours to secure delivery of the goods on the estimated delivery dates from time to time furnished, but they do not guarantee time of delivery, nor shall they be liable for any damages or claims of any kind in respect of delay in delivery.

(e)   Whilst every effort will be made to avoid delay no responsibility is undertaken for meeting any specific delivery dates given in this contract, which have been inserted for guidance only. Accordingly, no liability will be accepted for any direct or indirect loss which may be caused by delayed delivery.

Conditional enforcement

(a)   Any claims in respect of errors on our invoice or non-delivery damage or shortage of goods shall not be accepted by us unless notified in writing to us within 7 days of the date of the invoice.

(b)   We shall be under no liability in respect of defects or failures unless:—

(i)   such defect or failure is notified to us in writing within 30 days after delivery and any goods in respect of which no such notification is given to us shall be deemed to be in all respects in accordance with the contract and the buyer shall be bound to accept and pay for the same accordingly;

(ii)   in respect of goods or parts not of our manufacture our responsibility shall be limited to any benefits we may receive under any guarantee given by the supplier of such goods or parts; and

(iii)   the user conditions and the operational/maintenance instructions laid down by us have been strictly complied with and no alterations, modifications or repairs have been made to the goods before we examine them.

(c)   The carrier shall not be liable for:

(1)   Loss from a parcel, package or container or from an unpacked consignment or for damage to a consignment or any part of a consignment unless he is advised thereof in writing otherwise than upon a consignment note or delivery note within three days, and the claim is made in writing within seven days, after the termination of transit;

(2)   Loss, misdelivery or non-delivery of the whole of a consignment or of any separate parcel, package or container forming part of a consignment unless he is advised of the loss, misdelivery or nondelivery in writing otherwise than upon a consignment note or delivery document within 28 days, and the claim is made in writing with 42 days, after the commencement of transit.

Provided that if the trader proves that:

(i)   it was not reasonably possible for the trader to advise the carrier or make a claim in writing within the time limit available, and,

(ii)   such advice or claim was given or made within a reasonable time, the carrier shall not have the benefit of the exclusion of liability afforded by this condition.

(b)   We shall be under no liability in respect of any such defects or failures unless:—

(i)   such defect or failure is notified to us in writing within 30 days after delivery and any goods in respect of which no such notification is given to us shall be deemed to be in all respects in accordance with the contract and the buyer shall be bound to accept and pay for the same accordingly;

(ii)   in respect of goods or parts not of our manufacture our responsibility shall be limited to any benefits we may receive under any guarantee given by the supplier or such goods or parts; and

(iii)   the user conditions and the operational/maintenance instruction laid down by us have been strictly complied with and no alterations, modifications or repairs have been made to the goods before we examine them.

Excluding or limiting conditions and warranties in contracts for the sale of goods

(a)   All conditions, warranties, terms, undertakings and obligations implied by statute, common law, custom, trade usage or otherwise (including, without prejudice to the generality of the foregoing, any implied condition, warranty or undertaking as to correspondence of the goods with any contract description given, merchantable quality or fitness for any particular purpose) are hereby wholly excluded.

(b)   The goods are sold as seen [as described in clause . . . hereof] and no [other] contractual description is attached or ascribed to them. They are further sold with all faults, imperfections and errors of description [but only in so far as such or any description has been attached to the goods in accordance with the terms of this clause] and, without prejudice to the generality of the foregoing, those terms which would otherwise be implied by virtue of the Sale of Goods Act 1979, ss.13 and 15 are hereby excluded.

(c) All defects have been drawn to the attention of the buyer and the buyer acknowledges that this is so. Further, the seller offers no opinion as to the suitability of the goods for any particular purpose and the buyer acknowledges that he does not rely on the seller's skill or judgement: [The buyer further acknowledges that he has examined the sample of the goods sold under the contract and finds them free from defect].

(d) Our liability under these conditions is in lieu and to the exclusion of all other warranties, conditions or obligations imposed or implied by statute or otherwise including but not limited to those in relation to the quality or description of the goods or their fitness for any particular purpose and all liability for any direct or indirect or consequential loss including loss of profit, goodwill or anticipated savings (howsoever arising) is hereby expressly excluded subject always to the provisions of the Unfair Contract Terms Act 1977, ss.16 and 20 and having regard to our willingness to exchange, repair or replace defective goods under clause . . . above;

'CONTRACTS BETWEEN BUSINESSMEN'
BY BEALE AND DUGDALE
(1975) 2 Br J Law & Soc 45

Formation

The attitudes of firms towards problems of formation provide an indication of their awareness of and concern about the process of contract law, and illustrate the conscious nature of the decision whether or not to plan in detail. The degree of planning is in part likely to be determined by the process of formation adopted. Contracts formed as a result of detailed negotiation were comparatively rare. They were usually to be found only where the goods to be supplied were expensive and complex, for instance complete aircraft, aero engines or machinery worth more than £50,000, and the risks were thus sufficient to justify the time and trouble, particularly as the sale of a finished product of this type would often be to a customer outside the trade who would not know or accept the usual practices. The negotiated contracts were often many pages in length and contained detailed planning of both the primary obligations and the mechanisms for adjustment. However even in such contracts planning might not be complete. Some details might be left vague, either consciously because the parties had decided that it was not worth negotiating certain areas of conflict, or unconsciously: managing directors might draw up 'heads of agreement' unwittingly leaving many areas vague. Research and development contracts provided a special problem for by their very nature they required some areas to be left unnegotiated in order to provide for future eventualities.

At the other extreme were contracts made informally by telephone or simple exchange of letters. Here only the primary obligations would be planned expressly but the parties to such contracts often held unexpressed assumptions about the way in which obligations would be adjusted or enforced, relying either upon trade custom or a 'gentlemen's agreement' with the other contracting party. The informal formation process was deliberately adopted only by a minority of firms who either were not prepared to create sufficient office capacity to deal with much paper work or who felt able to place faith in the other contracting party because of the market conditions. Often such firms were doing nearly all their business locally and there was close and continuous personal contact with their customers and suppliers; this would be more important to them than safeguarding an individual exchange which was usually of low value anyway.

The majority of firms intended to make their contracts by the use of forms containing standard conditions of sale or purchase. Usually these forms would have the main primary obligations (item, price, delivery date and perhaps terms of payment) typed on the front, while terms providing for adjustment, contingencies and so on would be printed on the back — hence they were commonly referred to as 'back of order' conditions.

When one set of conditions has been accepted by both seller and buyer as governing their exchange then in law a contract on the basis of those conditions has been formed. It was common for buyers of component parts or raw materials to accept sellers' conditions; occasionally sellers would accept the buyer's terms. It was clear that this was not done, however, with any conscious aim of ensuring that there would be a legally enforceable, fully-planned contract. It was partly the product of market power: a buyer faced with short supply might be forced to accept the seller's terms while we found sellers accepting buyers' terms only when selling to very powerful concerns susch as a nationalized industry. But it may also be explained by the difficulty in drafting uniform purchase conditions to suit a wide variety of different purchases, and the generally greater prestige and time given to sales, for the firm will be known by its product.

More usually each party attempted to get its 'back of order' conditions accepted by the other. Under commercial pressure this system might break down — salesmen trying to meet targets might enter informal contracts without bothering with their terms or engineers more concerned about production than purchasing arrangements might unthinkingly accept the other party's terms. The significance of what was being done was not always appreciated by the officer concerned despite occasional lectures complete with instructive cartoons provided by purchasing officers. Firms seemed to consider that it was difficult to prevent this sort of breakdown but the majority of contracts were made by each party using his 'back of order' conditions.

This meant that in many cases one party's conditions would not be fully accepted by the other, but the parties would instead exchange conditions. Typically the seller would issue to the purchaser a quotation form backed with his standard conditions, the buyer would reply with an order form with his conditions, and the seller would then acknowledge the order and in doing so refer again to his conditions. This stage would normally complete the exchange. Inevitably the seller's and buyer's conditions would conflict and indeed this was contemplated for most forms contained a condition to the effect that in the case of a conflict that set of conditions would override the other.

The legal effect of such an exchange of conflicting forms is not entirely clear but it seems most likely that no enforceable contract results: each communication, providing it refers clearly to the standard conditions, is an offer which is refused and replaced by another on different terms, the last one (the seller's acknowledgement') remaining an unaccepted offer. If however the other party later does something recognizing the existence of a contract, such as telephoning the seller to press for delivery, he may be held to have accepted that offer, so that the last set of conditions sent may win the day.

There was considerable awareness of the fact that in many cases an exchange of conditions would not necessarily lead to an enforceable contract, and some that the last set of conditions might prevail; one legal adviser had prepared a 'confirmation of order' form to be used to 'get his firm's conditions in last' when buying as well as when selling. But most firms seemed unconcerned about the failure to make a contract. They usually tried to ensure that they referred to their conditions in any written communications, which would prevent the letter 'accepting' the other party's terms, but no more, and some were not even concerned with that.

What did concern all the firms who contracted by this method was to reach a clear understanding on particularly important points or ones on which any difficulty was anticipated. Of course in every exchange certain items would be agreed expressly, if only the item and the price, and in some cases the 'back of order' would never be looked at. In others however almost every major difference would be followed up and settled, and in the majority of cases at least a few of the more important items dealt with in the standard conditions would be discussed and agreed. Usually these were the same items that would be the subject of detailed discussion if a contract were specifically negotiated, or at the other extreme which would be mentioned if a contract were made formally by 'phone or letter; for instance payment terms or warranty periods, and whether the price was fixed or open.

In commercial terms therefore the result of an exchange of 'back of order' conditions did not offer a complete contrast to a negotiated contract on the one hand or an informal exchange of letters on the other: the number of issues planned would vary enormously, but there would be definite agreement on certain of them. Legal enforceability seemed secondary to reaching a common understanding. But even this was not always considered necessary. Frequently we were told that the other party's 'back of order' conditions would be scrutinized but no objection would be raised unless some unusual term was found: for instance, many sellers did not mind what the buyer's order contained on the question of delay provided it did not attempt to impose liquidated damages. The implication seems to be that provided the two sets of conditions contained terms commonly found in the trade a sufficient basis would exist to enable any dispute to be settled without difficulty: even common understanding did not have to be very precise.

As far as the legal enforceability of agreements is concerned, two qualifications should be made to what has been said. First it is possible that enforceable contracts were created by the exchange of standard conditions more frequently than our analysis above suggests. A court faced with a clearly unresolved conflict of terms on the one hand but a clear intention to contract on the other *might* decide that there was a contract containing those terms which had been agreed, and dismiss the remainder of the conditions. Therefore positive planning on particular issues even while using standard terms may have legal as well as commercial significance. Secondly we were told of signs of a gradual change in attitude towards tightening up procedures and creating legally enforceable agreements. For instance we came across several examples of purchasing departments who for years had bought from their main suppliers on 'back of order' conditions now negotiating standing supply contracts to govern future orders. This may be entirely explicable by the recent inflation and economic troubles which make it desirable to have clear agreement on such matters as price increases and delays, but we were told by several representatives that it was the result of a new professionalism among young managers, many of whom have studied contract law.

The following two cases consider the reasonableness test in situations where there is exemption of liability for breach of the implied terms of the Sale of Goods Act 1979 (see 3.11.6.2 above).

UNFAIR CONTRACT TERMS ACT 1977, PART II

15. Scope of Part II

. . .

(2) Subject to subsection (3) below, sections 16 to 18 of this Act apply to any contract only to the extent that the contract —

    (a) relates to the transfer of the ownership or possession of goods from one person to another (with or without work having been done on them);

    (b) constitutes a contract of service or apprenticeship;

(c)   relates to services of whatever kind, including (without prejudice to the foregoing generality) carriage, deposit and pledge, care and custody, mandate, agency, loan and services relating to the use of land;

(d)   relates to the liability of an occupier of land to persons entering upon or using that land;

(e)   relates to a grant of any right or permission to enter upon or use land not amounting to an estate or interest in the land.

(3)   Notwithstanding anything in subsection (2) above, sections 16 to 18 —

(a)   do not apply to any contract to the extent that the contract —

(i)   is a contract of insurance (including a contract to pay an annuity on human life);

(ii)   relates to the formation, constitution or dissolution of any body corporate or unincorporated association or partnership;

(b)   apply to —

a contract of marine salvage or towage;

a charter party of a ship or hovercraft;

a contract for the carriage of goods by ship or hovercraft; or,

a contract to which subsection (4) below relates;

only to the extent that —

(i)   both parties deal or hold themselves out as dealing in the course of a business (and then only in so far as the contract purports to exclude or restrict liability for breach of duty in respect of death or personal injury); or

(ii)   the contract is a consumer contract (and then only in favour of the consumer).

(4)   This subsection relates to a contract in pursuance of which goods are carried by ship or hovercraft and which either —

(a)   specifies ship or hovercraft as the means of carriage over part of the journey to be covered; or

(b)   makes no provision as to the means of carriage and does not exclude ship or hovercraft as that means;

in so far as the contract operates for and in relation to the carriage of the goods by that means.

Note

The following provision amends sections 15 and 16. Students are encouraged to consider precisely how it affects each part of ss 15 and 16.

LAW REFORM (MISCELLANEOUS PROVISIONS) ACT 1990, SECTION 68

Amendment of Unfair Contract Terms Act 1977

(1)   The Unfair Contract Terms Act 1977 shall be amended in accordance with this section.

(2)   In section 15(1) (scope of Part II), the words 'applies only to contracts,' shall cease to have effect.

(3)   In section 16 (liability for breach of duty)—

(a)   in subsection (1)—

(i)   at the beginning there shall be inserted the words 'Subject to subsection (1A) below,';

(ii)   after the word 'contract' in the first place where it occurs there shall be inserted ', or a provision of a notice given to persons generally or to particular persons,';

(iii)   after the word 'term' in the second place where it occurs there shall be inserted 'or provision'; and

(iv)   at the end of paragraph (b) there shall be inserted the words 'or, as the case may be, if it is not fair and reasonable to allow reliance on the provision';
(b)   after subsection (1) there shall be inserted the following subsection—
'(1A)   Nothing in paragraph (b) of subsection (1) above shall be taken as implying that a provision of a notice has effect in circumstances where, apart from that paragraph, it would not have effect.';
and
(c)   in subsection (3)—
(i)   after the word 'contract' there shall be inserted 'or a provision of a notice';
and
(ii)   after the word 'term' in the second place where it occurs there shall be inserted 'or provision.'
(4)   In section 24 (the 'reasonableness' test)—
(a)   after subsection (2) there shall be inserted the following subsection—
'(2A)   In determining for the purposes of this Part of this Act whether it is fair and reasonable to allow reliance on a provision of a notice (not being a notice having contractual effect), regard shall be had to all the circumstances obtaining when the liablity arose or (but for the provision) would have arisen.';
(b)   in subsection (3)—
(i)   after the word 'contract' in the first place where it occurs there shall be inserted 'or a provision of a notice';
(ii)   after the word 'contract' in the second place where it occurs there shall be inserted 'or whether it is fair and reasonable to allow reliance on the provision';
(iii)   after the word 'above' there shall be inserted 'in the case of a term in a contract'; and
(iv)   in paragraph (a), after the word 'term' there shall be inserted 'or provision'; . . .

UNFAIR CONTRACT TERMS ACT 1977

16.   Liability for breach of duty

(1)   Where a term of a contract purports to exclude or restrict liability for breach of duty arising in the course of any business or from the occupation of any premises used for business purposes of the occupier, that term —
(a)   shall be void in any case where such exclusion or restriction is in respect of death or personal injury;
(b)   shall, in any other case, have no effect if it was not fair and reasonable to incorporate the term in the contract. . . .

17.   Control of unreasonable exemptions in consumer or standard form contracts

(1)   Any term of a contract which is a consumer contract or a standard form contract shall have no effect for the purpose of enabling a party to the contract —
(a)   who is in breach of a contractual obligation, to exclude or restrict any liability of his to the consumer or customer in respect of the breach;
(b)   in respect of a contractual obligation, to render no performance, or to render a performance substantially different from that which the consumer or customer reasonably expected from the contract;
if it was not fair and reasonable to incorporate the term in the contract.
(2)   In this section 'customer' means a party to a standard form contract who deals on the basis of written standard terms of business of the other party to the contract who himself deals in the course of a business.

18. Unreasonable indemnity clauses in consumer contracts

(1)   Any term of a contract which is a consumer contract shall have no effect for the purpose of making the consumer indemnify another person (whether a party to the contract or not) in respect of liability which that other person may incur as a result of breach of duty or breach of contract, if it was not fair and reasonable to incorporate the term in the contract.

(2)   In this section 'liability' means liability arising in the course of any business or from the occupation of any premises used for business purposes of the occupier.

19. 'Guarantee' of consumer goods

(1)   This section applies to a guarantee —

(a)   in relation to goods which are of a type ordinarily supplied for private use or consumption; and

(b)   which is not a guarantee given by one party to the other party to a contract under or in pursuance of which the ownership or possession of the goods to which the guarantee relates is transferred.

(2)   A term of a guarantee to which this section applies shall be void in so far as it purports to exclude or restrict liability for loss or damage (including death or personal injury) —

(a)   arising from the goods proving defective while —

(i)   in use otherwise than exclusively for the purposes of a business; or

(ii)   in the possession of a person for such use; and

(b)   resulting from the breach of duty of a person concerned in the manufacture or distribution of the goods.

(3)   For the purposes of this section, any document is a guarantee if it contains or purports to contain some promise or assurance (however worded or presented) that defects will be made good by complete or partial replacement, or by repair, monetary compensation or otherwise.

20. Obligations implied by law in sale and hire-purchase contracts

(1)   Any term of a contract which purports to exclude or restrict liability for breach of the obligations arising from —

(a)   section 12 of the Sale of Goods Act 1979 (seller's implied undertakings as to title etc.);

(b)   section 8 of the Supply of Goods (Implied Terms) Act 1973 (implied terms as to title in hire-purchase agreements);

shall be void.

(2)   Any term of a contract which purports to exclude or restrict liability for breach of the obligations arising from —

(a)   section 13, 14 or 15 of the said Act of 1979 (seller's implied undertakings as to conformity of goods with description or sample, or as to their quality or fitness for a particular purpose);

(b)   section 9, 10 or 11 of the said Act of 1973 (the corresponding provisions in relation to hire-purchase),

shall —

(i)   in the case of a consumer contract, be void against the consumer;

(ii)   in any other case, have no effect if it was not fair and reasonable to incorporate the term in the contract.

21. Obligations implied by law in other contracts for the supply of goods

(1)   Any term of a contract to which this section applies purporting to exclude or restrict liability for breach of an obligation —

(a)   such as is referred to in subsection (3)(a) below —
    (i)   in the case of a consumer contract, shall be void against the consumer, and
    (ii)   in any other case, shall have no effect if it was not fair and reasonable to incorporate the term in the contract;
(b)   such as is referred to in subsection (3)(b) below, shall have no effect if it was not fair and reasonable to incorporate the term in the contract.

(2)   This section applies to any contract to the extent that it relates to any such matter as is referred to in section 15(2)(a) of this Act, but does not apply to —
(a)   a contract of sale of goods or a hire-purchase agreement; or
(b)   a charterparty of a ship or hovercraft unless it is a consumer contract (and then only in favour of the consumer).

(3)   An obligation referred to in this subsection is an obligation incurred under a contract in the course of a business and arising by implication of law from the nature of the contract which relates —
(a)   to the correspondence of goods with description or sample, or to the quality or fitness of goods for any particular purpose; or
(b)   to any right to transfer ownership or possession of goods, or to the enjoyment of quiet possession of goods.

(4)   Nothing in this section applies to the supply of goods on a redemption of trading stamps within the Trading Stamps Act 1964.

22.   Consequence of breach

For the avoidance of doubt, where any provision of this Part of this Act requires that the incorporation of a term in a contract must be fair and reasonable for that term to have effect —
(a)   if that requirement is satisfied, the term may be given effect to notwithstanding that the contract has been terminated in consequence of breach of that contract;
(b)   for the term to be given effect to, that requirement must be satisfied even where a party who is entitled to rescind the contract elects not to rescind it.

23.   Evasion by means of secondary contract

Any term of any contract shall be void which purports to exclude or restrict, or has the effect of excluding or restricting —
(a)   the exercise, by a party to any other contract, of any right or remedy which arises in respect of that other contract in consequence of breach of duty, or of obligation, liability for which could not by virtue of the provisions of this Part of this Act be excluded or restricted by a term of that other contract;
(b)   the application of the provisions of this Part of this Act in respect of that or any other contract.

24.   The 'reasonableness' test

(1)   In determining for the purposes of this Part of this Act whether it was fair and reasonable to incorporate a term in a contract, regard shall be had only to the circumstances which were, or ought reasonably to have been, known to or in the contemplation of the parties to the contract at the time the contract was made.

(2)   In determining for the purposes of section 20 or 21 of this Act whether it was fair and reasonable to incorporate a term in a contract, regard shall be had in particular to the matters specified in Schedule 2 to this Act; but this subsection shall not prevent a court or arbiter from holding, in accordance with any rule of law, that a term which purports to exclude or restrict any relevant liability is not a term of the contract.

(3)   Where a term in a contract purports to restrict liability to a specified sum of money, and the question arises for the purposes of this Part of this Act whether it was fair and reasonable to incorporate the term in the contract, then, without prejudice to subsection (2) above, regard shall be had in particular to —

(a)   the resources which the party seeking to rely on that term could expect to be available to him for the purpose of meeting the liability should it arise;

(b)   how far it was open to that party to cover himself by insurance.

(4)   The onus of proving that it was fair and reasonable to incorporate a term in a contract shall lie on the party so contending.

25.   Interpretation of Part II

(1)   In this Part of this Act —

'breach of duty' means the breach —

(a)   of any obligation, arising from the express or implied terms of a contract, to take reasonable care or exercise reasonable skill in the performance of the contract;

(b)   of any common law duty to take reasonable care or exercise reasonable skill;

(c)   of the duty of reasonable care imposed by section 2(1) of the Occupiers' Liability (Scotland) Act 1960;

'business' includes a profession and the activities of any government department or local or public authority;

'consumer' has the meaning assigned to that expression in the definition in this section of 'consumer contract';

'consumer contract' means a contract (not being a contract of sale by auction or competitive tender) in which —

(a)   one party to the contract deals, and the other party to the contract ('the consumer') does not deal or hold himself out as dealing, in the course of a business, and

(b)   in the case of a contract such as is mentioned in section 15(2)(a) of this Act, the goods are of a type ordinarily supplied for private use or consumption;

and for the purposes of this Part of this Act the onus of proving that a contract is not to be regarded as a consumer contract shall lie on the party so contending;

'goods' has the same meaning as in the Sale of Goods Act 1979;

'hire-purchase agreement' has the same meaning as in section 189(1) of the Consumer Credit Act 1974;

'personal injury' includes any disease and any impairment of physical or mental condition.

(2)   In relation to any breach of duty or obligation, it is immaterial for any purpose of this Part of this Act whether the act or omission giving rise to that breach was inadvertent or intentional, or whether liability for it arises directly or vicariously.

(3)   In this Part of this Act, any reference to excluding or restricting any liability includes —

(a)   making the liability or its enforcement subject to any restrictive or onerous conditions;

(b)   excluding or restricting any right or remedy in respect of the liability, or subjecting a person to any prejudice in consequence of his pursuing any such right or remedy;

(c)   excluding or restricting any rule of evidence or procedure;

(d)   excluding or restricting any liability by reference to a notice having contractual effect,

but does not include an agreement to submit any question to arbitration.

(4)   In subsection (3)(d) above 'notice' includes an announcement, whether or not in writing, and any other communication or pretended communication.

(5)   In sections 15 and 16 and 19 to 21 of this Act, any reference to excluding or restricting liability for breach of an obligation or duty shall include a reference to excluding or restricting the obligation or duty itself.

The following extract considers the application of s. 17 of UCTA

Chris Willett, 'Fairness of Standard Terms and Conditions: Thorn Security Ltd v Matthew Hall Ltd' Scottish Business Law Bulletin (1995 Bus. L.B., 13.3)

. . . There remains considerable uncertainty as to the precise scope of section 17(1)(b). It is clear that it applies to both consumer and commercial sales. It is also clear that an important prerequisite to the application of the reasonableness test is that the term is offering something falling short of the reasonable expectations of the consumer or customer. This means that courts must come to a judgment as to what are the reasonable expectations of the consumer or customer, a judgment which must be reached by reference to the transaction as a whole. This raises a difficult question in itself, i.e. as to how exactly to determine the reasonable expectations of parties to a contract (see discussion by Willett in *Unfair Terms in Consumer Contracts,* forthcoming 1995).

An equally difficult question is raised by the phrase 'to render a performance'. This clearly covers the sort of term which openly waters down the obligations which a supplier of goods and services would owe normally. But what about the situation where the party relying on the standard terms is able formally to present his intentions in ways which may appear to be defining the obligations of the *other* party. In addition, given that it is the reasonable expectations of the *consumer* or *customer* which must have been compromised, what if it is the seller or supplier of the product or service who is complaining about the other party's terms? Can the seller or supplier be a customer when it comes to the obligations owed to him by the buyer?

Questions such as these are obviously important for sellers/suppliers and consumers/ business customers. They have, perhaps, become slightly less important for consumers and those who supply them with goods and services. This is because of the European Directive on Unfair Terms in Consumer Contracts which was adopted in April 1993. It was to have been implemented by December 31, 1994, a process taking place via regulations made under the European Communities Act 1972 (see Willett, *Unfair Terms in Consumer Contracts,* forthcoming 1995, and Willett, 'Unfair Terms in Consumer Contracts' (1994) Consumer Law Journal, Vol 2, No.4).

The Directive introduces a test of unfairness which is applicable to all terms (except price and main subject matter) in consumer contracts. In other words, the Directive will apply irrespective of the scope of application of UCTA, section 17, so that the latter is of slightly less importance in consumer contracts (although it still, along with the common law, provides an important control over price and main subject matter terms).

The recent case of *Thorn Security Ltd* v *Matthew Hall Ltd,* 1994 GWD 35–2047, raises questions both about incorporation of terms and the application of UCTA section 17 (1)(b).

Facts
T contracted to supply M with certain specialised equipment. There were a number of areas of dispute; however, the issue which is most legally significant was the dispute over T's right to interim payments. This entitlement was allegedly based upon a term

in their purchase orders which said 'Payment by end of month following month of invoice'. M claimed that their standard conditions applied, incorporating a term which said that 'the Supplier shall not invoice the Purchaser until performance of this Contract has been completed'. T responded that M's terms had not, by reasonable intimation, been incorporated into the contract, and that even if it had, it was subject to the reasonableness test under section 17(1)(b) in that it enabled M to render no performance or one substantially different from that reasonably expected (see section 17, above).

The sheriff decided that if the term was incorporated then it was not fair and reasonable under section 17. On appeal the sheriff principal decided that the incorporation question should go to a proof for more complete appraisal of the factual circumstances in the context of the rules.(The facts available in the reports are fairly limited and it would be difficult at this stage to predict what view will ultimately be taken on this matter.) The sheriff principal went on to say that section 17(1) did not apply to the term because the term did not relate to the performance proffered by M, but to the performance demanded of T (i.e. that they only submit invoices until the contract was complete). The sheriff principal also said that he saw section 17(1) as being there to control those terms which seek to exempt the party relying on them from some sort of contractual performance.

Comment
First of all, it is quite clear that section 17(1)(b) only controls terms which seek to place some restriction upon the contractual performance being offered by the party relying upon the term. Secondly, it is clear that for section 17(1)(b) to apply to M's term, it must be their performance which is being excused in some way or which falls below the reasonable expectations of T. Thirdly, however, the sheriff seems to have given an overly formalistic reading to section 17(1)(b) in concluding that the term did not relate to M's performance (i.e. their payment obligation), but rather to T's performance of their invoicing procedures. The bottom line is that these procedures and how they were exercised were being used as a means of controlling/restricting the extend of the payment obligation being offered by M. I do not believe, especially in the context of UCTA, that Parliament intended such formalistic readings to be made as have been made by the sheriff principal. However, there is another twist. Although a formalistic reading would be a bad precedent for UCTA generally, I do not believe that an alternative reading would have changed the final result on section 17(1)(b). Even if we do relate the terms to M's performance and say that it falls below reasonably expected performance, section 17 clearly relates to the reasonable expectation of the 'consumer or customer'.

It seems unlikely that the party providing the service (T) can be regarded as the 'customer', unless we give a broad meaning to customer which sees one party always as the customer of the other when an obligation is owed. If T is not a customer then section 17(1)(b) does not apply to the term and it must be looked at purely on its common law merits, i.e. the question goes back to incorporation and construction.

Although there is no space here to develop these points it is likely that the English equivalent of section 17 (section 3) does not apply only where it is the customer's expectation which is affected, but rather where either party's expectation is affected by the other's written standard terms. In addition, the general principles of contract being prepared by the European Contract Commission will introduce a fairness test for commercial contracts which can apply in favour of either party (see discussion in Willett (ed.), *Fairness in Contract* (forthcoming, 1995). This seems a more sensible approach in commercial contracts where a customer may be very capable of asserting onerous terms especially in respect of his obligation to pay, take delivery etc.

Where consumer contracts are concerned the issues are different, in that the consumer will rarely be asserting his or her own written terms. This is an important reason why in consumer contracts, section 17 and section 3 and the recent Directive on Unfair Terms in Consumer Contracts can only be invoked in favour of consumers. Only when asserting one's own terms is there usually the opportunity to depart from the legal, social and customary norms which make up the reasonable expectations of the other party.

GEORGE MITCHELL v FINNEY LOCK SEEDS LTD
[1983] 2 All ER 737 HL

Facts
The defendant seedsmen contracted to supply the plaintiff farmers with Dutch winter cabbage seed for £192. An invoice contained a clause limiting liability for defective seed to the contract price. The seed was unmerchantable and the wrong type and the plaintiffs claimed £63,000 for their lost crop. On an appeal by the seedsmen, the House of Lords had to consider *inter alia* whether the limitation clause satisfied a test of reasonableness.

Lord Bridge
But for the purpose of deciding this appeal I find it unnecessary to express a concluded view on this question.

My Lords, at long last I turn to the application of the statutory language to the circumstances of the case. Of the particular matters to which attention is directed by [the Sale of Goods Act 1979, s. 55(5)(a) to (e)] only those in paras (a) to (c) are relevant. As to para (c), the respondents [the farmers] admittedly knew of the relevant condition (they had dealt with the appellants for many years) and, if they had read it, particularly cl. 2, they would, I think, as laymen rather than lawyers, have had no difficulty in understanding what it said. This and the magnitude of the damages claimed in proportion to the price of the seeds sold are factors which weigh in the scales in the appellants' favour.

The question of relative bargaining strength under para (a) and of the opportunity to buy seeds without a limitation of the seedsman's liability under para (b) were interrelated. The evidence was that a similar limitation of liability was universally embodied in the terms of trade between seedsmen and farmers and had been so for very many years. The limitation had never been negotiated between representative bodies but, on the other hand, had not been the subject of any protest by the National Farmers' Union. These factors, if considered in isolation, might have been equivocal. The decisive factor however, appears from the evidence of four witnesses called for the appellants, two independent seedsmen, the chairman of the appellant company, and a director of a sister company (both being wholly-owned subsidiaries of the same parent). They said that it had always been their practice, unsuccessfully attempted in the instant case, to negotiate settlements of farmers' claims for damages in excess of the price of the seeds, if they thought that the claims were 'genuine' and 'justified'. This evidence indicated a clear recognition by seedsmen in general, and the appellants in particular, that reliance on the limitation of liability imposed by the relevant condition would not be fair or reasonable.

Two further factors, if more were needed, weigh the scales in favour of the respondents. The supply of autumn, instead of winter, cabbage seed was due to the negligence of the appellants' sister company. Irrespective of its quality, the autumn variety supplied could not, according to the appellants' own evidence, be grown commercially in East Lothian. Finally, as the trial judge found, seedsmen could insure against the risk of crop failure caused by supply of the wrong variety of seeds without materially increasing the price of seeds.

My Lords, even if I felt doubts about the statutory issue, I should not, for the reasons explained earlier, think it right to interfere with the unanimous original decision of that issue by the Court of Appeal. As it is, I feel no such doubts. If I were making the original decision, I should conclude without hesitation that it would not be fair or reasonable to allow the appellants to rely on the contractual limitation of their liability.

I would dismiss the appeal.

Notes

(1)   The Sale of Goods Act, s. 55 is very similar to the Unfair Contract Terms Act 1977, sch.2 in the factors which are to be looked at in determining reasonableness (see 3.11.5.1 in the text). Why do you think Lord Bridge chose to look at (a), (b) and (c)? Was his application of them logical? When would it be appropriate to look at (d) and (e)?

(2)   One significant difference between s. 55 and the Unfair Contract Terms Act 1977, s. 24(2) is that the latter requires the court to consider the reasonableness of incorporating the clause in the contract whereas s. 55 asks whether it was reasonable to rely on the clause. Given that George Mitchell was decided on s. 55, do you think that this diminishes its precedent value?

KNIGHT MACHINERY (HOLDINGS) LTD v RENNIE
1995 SLT 166

Opinion of the Court

This appeal against an interlocutor pronounced by the learned sheriff principal at Inverness on 29 January 1993 arises out of a dispute between the parties relating to a contract for the sale by the appellants to the respondent of a Ryobi 2700CD printing machine. In terms of the contract such a machine was sold by the appellants to the respondent on 21 September 1988 and delivered on 6 February 1989. It did not perform satisfactorily and in October 1989 the respondent wrote to the appellants his rejection of it. In this action the appellants sue him for the unpaid balance of the price; he counterclaims for repayment of what he has paid towards the price and also for damages.

In the pleadings there were many issues between the parties; but most of these have been resolved as a result of the proof which the sheriff heard or as a result of subsequent agreement between the parties as to the basis upon which this court should proceed. The appellants invited this court to conclude that the sheriff's findings in fact, contained in his interlocutor of 17 September 1992, were correct and that the inferences drawn by the sheriff, and expressed as findings in law in the same interlocutor, were the correct inferences to be drawn from those facts. The respondent invites the court to hold that the sheriff principal was correct to make the alterations which he effected to the findings in fact and to substitute his inferences for those of the sheriff, all as shown in the sheriff principal's interlocutor of 29 January 1993.

We need not rehearse the findings in fact; but the effect of the agreed approach of the parties may be summarised as follows. The appellants sold the machine to the respondent by contract dated 21 September 1988. The sale was governed by a written, standard form contract. The machine was delivered on 6 February 1989. Mr Gibson, one of the appellants' engineers, attended the respondent's premises on 6 February 1989 when the machine was installed. He supervised its installation and spent some two and a half days commissioning the machine and giving training to those who were to operate it. After he departed problems arose with the operation of the machine and those problems persisted throughout the following months. The respondent finally decided to reject the machine in October 1989. During the intervening period many attempts were made to discover the cause or causes of the machine's malfunctioning and various remedies were devised, prescribed and attempted. None of these attempts discovered any cause for the malfunctioning and none of the attempted remedies removed it. The sheriff concluded that the machine as sold was not reasonably fit for its purpose and was not of merchantable quality. On this basis of fact the respondent would have been entitled to succeed; for s. 14 of the Sale of Goods Act 1979 implies a condition in circumstances such as those under review, 'that the goods supplied under the contract are of merchantable quality'. However, cl 5 (c) of the conditions of sale of the contract was in the following terms: [his Lordship quoted the terms of cl 5 (c) set out supra and continued:]

There is no dispute that the respondent sent the appellants no notice in writing within the seven day period. Accordingly it follows that if cl 5(c) applies the respondent's purported rejection some months later would fall to be treated as ineffectual.

It is clear, however, that since s. 20 (2) of the Unfair Contract Terms Act 1977 came into force a contractual term such as that contained in cl 5 (c) can be elided. That subsection provides that: 'Any term of a contract which purports to exclude or restrict liability for breach of the obligations arising from . . . section . . . 14 . . . of the [Sale of Goods Act 1979] shall . . . have no effect if it was not fair and reasonable to incorporate the term in the contract.'

The effect of s. 24(4) of the Unfair Contract Terms Act 1977 is to place the onus on the appellants to prove that it was fair and reasonable to incorporate cl 5 (c) into the parties' contract. Section 24(2) of the 1977 Act provides that 'In determining for the purposes of section 20 . . . of this Act whether it was fair and reasonable to incorporate a term in a contract regard shall be had in particular to the matters specified in Schedule 2 to this Act.'

For the purposes of the present case the relevant matters, or 'guidelines', for application of the reasonableness test contained in Sched 2 are those numbered (c) and (d). Paragraph (c) reads: 'whether the customer knew or ought reasonably to have known of the existence and extent of the term'.

On that matter, both the sheriff and the sheriff principal concluded that the respondent ought reasonably to have known of the existence and extent of cl 5 (c); that conclusion is not challenged. Paragraph (d) reads: 'where the term excludes or restricts any relevant liability if some condition is not complied with, whether it was reasonable at the time of the contract to expect that compliance with that condition would be practicable'.

Accordingly, the real issue is whether or not, having regard to the onus upon them, the appellants have established that it was fair and reasonable to incorporate cl 5 (c) into the contract at the time of the contract, namely 21 September 1988. Both parties to this appeal accepted that, notwithstanding the express provision contained in cl 17 of the contract, the relevant applicable law was Scots law.

The appellants submitted that they had established that it was fair and reasonable to incorporate cl 5 (c) in the contract. The sheriff principal's approach was flawed. He had asked if the appellants had shown that it was practicable for the respondent to give notice within seven days of delivery of the machine; but held that that depended on what it was of which notice had to be given. Contrary to the sheriff's view, which was that notice required to be given of any problems in the operation of the machine, the sheriff principal concluded on his analysis of the clause that it envisaged the giving of notice 'of a defect which would entitle the buyer to reject the goods'; although the machine had been found (by the sheriff) to have suffered from such a defect, the sheriff principal held that it had not been practicable to give notice of that defect within seven days because no one supposed that such problems as were encountered in the first few days of operation were indicative of anything other than a temporary and remediable difficulty, and that it was only much later that it was reasonable to conclude that the machine was affected by a radical defect. On this basis the sheriff principal had concluded that it was not fair and reasonable to incorporate cl 5 (c) on the contract.

The sheriff principal's error, it was submitted, lay in his construction of the clause and in particular in his conclusion as to what was to be included in a cl 5 (c) notice. The business purpose of the clause was to enable dealers such as the appellants to know where they stood as soon as reasonably possible; so the clause provided that in the circumstances specified in it the buyer should be 'deemed' to have accepted the goods even although he had not in fact accepted them. The clause did not automatically deprive a buyer of his right to reject. Accordingly the notice which the clause envisaged was simply a notice saying, in effect, ' We are having trouble with your machine'. This was the approach taken by the sheriff, and the sheriff principal had been wrong to take the different approach which he had taken. The sheriff principal had a responsibility to refrain from interfering with the sheriff's decision unless it proceeded upon some erroneous principle or was plainly wrong: *George Mitchell Ltd* v *Finney Lock* [1983] 2 AC, per Lord Bridge of Harwich at p 816. On the facts, it was evident that problems did manifest themselves from the very start; and as both parties at the proof had treated the delivery, installation and operation of this machine as being quite typical of what would happen on and after delivery in all cases it was legitimate to look at the actual events and to regard them as a guide which might assist in evaluating reasonableness as at the date of the sale, in September 1988. It was not unreasonable to include a clause which imposed on the buyer the responsibility of inspecting the machine and of giving written notice within seven days of any problems encountered in its operation, all with a view to avoid the deemed effect of cl 5 (c). All that was required was that the notice had to be a genuine notice given in good faith and giving intimation of one or more real problems encountered in its operation. If, contrary to this submission, the sheriff principal had adopted the correct approach in construing what a cl 5 (c) notice had to contain, it was not submitted that he had erred in going on to conclude that it would not have been fair and reasonable to include such a clause in the contract of sale. Findings in fact 17 and 18 were conclusive of the matter in the appellants' favour, provided the approach taken by the sheriff to the requirements of cl 5 (c) was the correct approach.

For the respondent it was submitted that the appellants were in effect putting a substantial gloss on the word 'notice' in cl 5 (c) by requiring the notice to be genuine, based upon a real problem and in some way objectively sound. But the contract itself was silent as to what the notice should contain and consequently the bald requirement to give 'notice' was, in this context, at best ambiguous and at worst meaningless. The Unfair Contract Terms Act 1977 was designed for exempting provisions whose meaning was clear: per Kerr LJ in *George Mitchell Ltd* v *Finney Lock Seeds Ltd* [1983] 1 QB at p 314. The meaning of the clause in relation to the vital matter of notice was not in the least clear. Furthermore the clause was designed to take away the rights of the buyer and to afford additional protection to the sellers; the sellers were the author of the clause in a standard form contract and the contra proferentem rule applied. If the sellers desiderated a notice they must specify what was meant by that and in particular what the notice was supposed to contain. The ambiguity was demonstrated by the different views taken by the sheriff and the sheriff principal as to what the clause envisaged. The sheriff principal had provided a rational basis for his view; but even without adopting the sheriff principal's construction the court could properly conclude that it was not fair and reasonable to include in the contract a clause such as cl 5 (c) when its meaning was not at all plain. Turning to the facts in the present case, it was submitted that the appellants throughout the proof had been at pains to demonstrate that there never had been any radical defect in the machine and that any problems that had been encountered had derived from its not being operated properly. Thus the appellants were hardly in a position to submit that the respondent could have discovered some radical defect within a seven day period. Furthermore, at the time of delivery, the appellants had sent their own engineer and he had spent some two and a half days installing, demonstrating and operating the machine without there being any hint of any defect. Even if the findings in fact did yield the inference that some problems had begun to manifest themselves early enough to make it possible for them to be intimated within the prescibed period, it was absurd to expect that the buyer, operating a new machine which the sellers' engineer had made to work effectively, would draw any conclusion from the manifestation of minor problems other than that there were teething or settling-in problems, or problems deriving not from the machine itself but from the inexperience of operators new to the machine. The whole evidence, reflected in the findings in fact, demonstrated that problems of the kind which appeared in the early days of the machine's operation were problems that manifested themselves from time to time with any such machine. It could not be reasonable to insert in the contract a clause which deprived the buyer of his right to reject simply because he failed to give to the seller notice in writing of defective performance at a time at which no reasonable buyer would have concluded that the machine was significantly, permanently or irremediably defective. The sheriff's approach to the whole matter had been flawed because he had failed to analyse the clause or had tried to discover what the clause envisaged by 'notice'. The burden in relation to the reasonableness question lay upon the appellants; they had failed to discharge it. The sheriff principal's interlocutor should be affirmed. Essentially, however, the appellants must fail because the clause was so vague that no businessman could possibly understand what it was that he was supposed to give notice of within seven days, if the machine appeared to be giving nothing more than minor settling-in problems. The appeal should be refused.

The intention of s. 20(2) of the Unfair Contract Terms Act 1977 is to prevent a party to a contract from contracting out of liability for breach of obligations arising from certain terms and undertakings implied by statute, unless he is able to establish that when the contract was entered into it was fair and reasonable to incorporate in the contract the term limiting his liability for such breach. The onus rests upon the party who seeks to found upon such a term. The reasonableness judgment is one to be made objectively by the court having regard to the circumstances of the particular case and to the guidelines prescribed by s. 24(2) of and Sched 2 to the Act. The very width of the matters listed in Sched 2 appears to us to be indicative of the court's responsibility to look critically at any provision which is conceived wholly in the interests of the author of the words of the contract and at the expense of the other party's rights derived from statute. The least that can be expected of such a term before it can pass the reasonableness test is that the meaning of the term should be clear and unambiguous.

In the present case the court has to decide whether or not the appellants have shown that when the contract was entered into it was reasonable to expect that it would be practicable for the respondent to give the necessary, valid notice within seven days of delivery of the machine. But that issue cannot be resolved until it is discovered what the notice was supposed to contain and on what it had to be based. In this regard, in our opinion, the sheriff principal's approach is correct because he recognises that the clause has to be construed in order to define the obligation it seeks to lay upon the buyer; by contrast the sheriff does not expressly address himself to the construction issue. In our view, it is quite possible to read the clause literally and say that it simply provides for the sending by the buyer of a written notice which does no more than intimate that he is exercising his right to continue to found upon his statutory right to reject. Such a notice might read: 'Having inspected the goods delivered on (date) I give you notice in terms of cl 5 (c) that I am reserving all my legal rights'.

But the appellants reject the literal construction and do not construe the clause in this way. They maintain that such a construction would render the clause nugatory, because, even if the machine appeared to be functioning perfectly, and buyer could — to the possible prejudice of the seller — elide the deeming provision in the clause simply by sending out a formal written notice. Accordingly, they maintain that the clause necessarily implies that there must be some genuine objective basis for the buyer to believe that the machine is not functioning perfectly and that the notice must be based upon or derived from that objective reality, must be sent in good faith and be in such terms as to alert the sellers to the general nature of the apparent malfunction or of the observed results of malfunctioning. This construction is not exactly the same as that adopted by the sheriff and it is wholly different from that adopted by the sheriff principal. Its most obvious weakness is that it is not a literal construction and it is only tenuously related to the concepts of acceptance and rejection, the very condition implied by the Sale of Goods Act 1979 and expressly mentioned in cl 5(c); it is, of course, this relationship which the sheriff principal regarded as most significant. In addition, however, it is subject to the comment that, this being a commercial contract, if the appellants had intended that the character of the notice desiderated should be what their counsel now contend for, they could easily have said so in words that were clear, explicit and intelligible in that sense to the reasonable businessman.

At the other end of the spectrum of possibilities is that identified by the sheriff principal, namely that the notice must identify 'a defect which *would* entitle the buyer to reject the goods' (emphasis added). As we have already observed, this construction has the merit that it is clearly related to the statutory rights which the clause seeks to make forfeit and it is one which appears apt in relation to circumstances of the kind obtaining in this case. There may well be other possible constructions but none was canvassed in argument before us.

In our opinion this clause has no clear, business sense. The businessman buying such a machine cannot tell from the clause what the notice is to contain, on what it is to be based, and whether or not he should send such a notice when he encounters what appear to be fairly typical, apparently minor, possibly temporary, probably remediable problems, particularly when he has no means of determining whether they are symptomatic of some defect in the machine or simply of maladroitness in those attempting to operate it or are perhaps related to the emulsions, inks, papers or other materials being used in the operation of the machine or to some combination of such factors. That being so, we consider that prima facie it would not be reasonable at the time of the contract to expect that it would be practicable for the buyer to send a written notice to the sellers within seven days of delivery of the machine in circumstances such as could reasonably be expected to obtain in this type of contract in relation to this type of machine. Different considerations might apply in the event that inspection or commissioning of the machine were likely to reveal that it was incomplete or materially and obviously defective.

In our view, the reasonableness judgment in this particular case falls to be made against the general background of facts which have been found by the sheriff. The sheriff principal did not make any significantly different judgment on the basic facts from that made by the sheriff. We refer, in particular, to the passage in the sheriff's note where he described condition 5(c) 'somewhat draconian' and goes on: 'the evidence does indicate that problems with emulsification arose within a few days or within the first week of operation of the machine. Unhappily for the defender he and his printers being reasonable men and having dealt successfully with the occasional incidence of emulsification and similar problems in the past with other integrated dampening machines decided that problems with the 2700 were merely internal 'settling in' problems and nothing of a potentially troublesome nature long term' (1993 SLT (Sh Ct) at p 67C–D).

This passage briefly summarises what is clear from the full findings in fact, namely that the respondent's workmen were new to the machine and they encountered some problems some time after the appellants' engineer had departed, but that the problems encountered were of a kind encountered with many such machines and were of such a character that they were normally remediable without great difficulty. The sheriff principal has proposed adding a passage to findings in fact 46. That finding reads: "46. There was nothing mechanically wrong with the Ryobi 2700CD machine which could be discovered by the pursuers' engineers. The emulsification and similar problems which the defender and his printers experienced with the machine were not due to operator error'.

We emphasise the first sentence of this finding, which demonstrates that even the appellants' engineers could discover no defect in the machine immediately after or weeks and months after delivery, which is why no doubt the appellants took the position at the proof (though it was rejected by the sheriff) that the problems were caused by the respondent's operators. However, the additional passage proposed by the sheriff principal reads: 'Such problems are not uncommon, and this was known to those engaged in the printing trade, including the pursuers and the defender'. The appellants did not object to this addition and we think it is important. We consider that on the facts established, including this addition, the sheriff principal was well entitled to go on and modify finding 47 in the way indicated and in particular to add to it the passage: 'It was not reasonable at the time of the contract to expect that compliance by the defender with the rquirement to give notice of that defect within seven days of the delivery of the machine would be practicable'.

The sheriff, in failing to draw this inference, was plainly wrong; and his error flowed from his failure to analyse the clause in question to discover what it desiderated and to go on to consider whether or not it was practicable for the buyer to do what was provided for in the clause. In our view, however, it is appropriate, in order to express more clearly our view of the circumstances, to amend finding 47, by prefacing the finding with the words, 'Having regard to the whole circumstances,'. We shall make that addition to the findings in fact.

On the whole matter, therefore, we refuse the appeal and uphold the interlocutor of the sheriff principal but with the addition to finding in fact 47 specified above.

Note
There follows a discussion of the 'good faith' aspect of the test of unfairness which is contained in the Unfair Terms in Consumer Contract Regulations which implement the Unfair Terms Directive (see 3.11.8 in the text).

**Extract from
'Unfair Terms in Consumer Contracts', forthcoming, 1996
C. Willett**

Terms are unfair if they, 'contrary to the requirements of good faith cause a significant imbalance in the rights and obligations arising under the contract to the detriment of the consumer' (Regulation 4(1)). I am assuming 'significant imbalance' and 'detriment' to refer to the substantive nature of the terms. So that the wider an exclusion of liability or the wider a discretion vesting in a supplier, the greater imbalance and detriment. But what of the good faith aspect of the test?

. . . Good faith is a concept which is traditionally associated with differet aspects of the contractual relationship from negotiation, through performance and enforcement; Brownsword, Two 'Concepts of Good Faith'; (1994) 7 JCL 197; Storme, 'The Validity and Contents' in Hartkamp et al. (eds) (1994) *Towards a European Civil Code*, ch. 10; Lando, 'Performance and Remedies in the Law of Contracts'; in Hartkamp et al, ibid., ch. 11.). It seems that for our present purposes we can rule out the possibility that good faith involves analysis of the performance or enforcement of consumer standard form contracts. If we reflect upon the test it is clear that we are concerned with a situation in which the lack of good faith is contributory to *the term* causing significant imbalance to the detriment of the consumer and thus making the term unfair. Given that a term is unfair based upon the circumstances existing at the time of making the contract it is clear that performance and enforcement issues are not relevant.

To the extent that good faith might be about bargaining environment issues what might its content be? As I have argued if an enquiry of this sort is to take place at all it is logical for it to examine the extent to which the problem of consumer choice is addressed. After all it is the perception that consumers are not really choosing or consenting to standard terms which makes us think of them as potentially unfair . . .

It seems reasonable to suggest that meaningful choice in the bargaining environment implies

(1)   awareness of the risks which are on the table, and
(2)   the ability to use this knowledge to make a choice or negotiate over the risks.

The second requirement is principally to do with the consumer's bargaining strength, the choices offered by the market etc. (see further below). However the first requirement is about the transparency of the terms. This clearly encompasses the plainness and intelligibility of the language, size of print and the extent to which the term was drawn to the consumer's attention. If substantive unfairness is about departure from certain fairness norms/reasonable expectations then a term which effects such a departure must presumably stand a greater chance of being fair the more its presence and implications are made clear. The UK courts have shown themselves willing to consider the size, legibility and intelligibility of print under the UCTA reasonableness test. (See *Wight* v *BRB* [1983] CL424 and *The Zinnia* [1984] 2 Lloyds Rep. 210.) Indeed the UCTA reasonableness guidelines refer to the extent to which the party burdened by the clause was aware of the existence and extent of the clause [see above at 3.11.5.1], although strictly speaking these guidelines are only for use in commercial contracts under ss. 6 and 7 of UCTA.

It is interesting, however, that criteria such as these are not mentioned explicitly in the guidance on good faith given in schedule 2 to the regulations. Nevertheless for the reasons I have given above I would suggest that the plainness and intelligibility of language, and the steps taken to draw terms to a consumer's attention are very important aspects of good faith.

. . .

But what of the second requirement of meaningful choice, i.e., the ability to use knowledge of the terms to make a choice between terms or to negotiate for a change in terms? Even if the first requirement (i.e. awareness of risks) is satisfied for some consumers, this may not be sufficient to force the supplier market to engage in bargaining or to offer choices between terms (thereby satisfying the second require-ment). The UK courts look at both of these issues under the UCTA reasonableness test [see 3.11.1.6 above]. The UK courts appear to mistrust normal market forces to provoke choices. The courts choose, rather, to say that lack of a good choice or alternative weighs against the term being reasonable. It seems likely that the good faith aspect of the test, with its connotations of respect for the interests of the other party (see below), would place at least as much stress on the choice/available alternatives issue. Enhanced choice as a condition of fairness also accords well with Directive's goal to create confident consumers in order to aid the completion of the single market.

Good Faith in the Preamble [Schedule 2 to the UK Regulations]
There is, in fact, guidance in the preamble to the Directive as to the criteria to be taken into account in deciding whether there has been good faith, which is said to involve an 'overall evaluation of the different interests involved; in making an assessment of good faith, particular regard shall be had to the strengths of the bargaining position of the parties, whether the consumer had an inducement to agree to the term and whether the goods or services were sold or supplied to the special order of the consumer; where as the requirement of good faith may be satisfied by the seller or supplier where he deals fairly and equitably with the other party whose legitimate interests he has to take into account'. (Recital 16) [now contained in Schedule 2 of the UK Regulations].

Three of the criteria mentioned have clearly been taken from Schedule 2 of UCTA (see above at 3.11.1.5) in an attempt to make the UK feel more comfortable about the nature of the test. The DTI had consistently been uncomfortable about the use of concepts such as good faith, imbalance and detriment, feeling that they were alien to common law jurisprudence. The attempt in the preamble to make the UK government feel comfortable indicates that whatever the terminology may mean on the continent, there is an intention to delegate a fair degree of autonomy in the way in which the test is applied. We could deduce from this that the Commission is unlikely to argue to vigorously over the detailed application of the test.

The three criteria which have been taken from Schedule 2 relate partly to the dynamics of the bargaining environment and partly to the substantive balance of the contract. What were the parties' relative bargaining strengths at the time when the contract was made? In other words could the consumer have been expected to look after his own interests in the face of a harsh term? This may include consideration of the transparency of the term (to the extent that if a term cannot be understood it is difficult to bargain over it); and the choices offered by the supplier or others in the market. (see above). Both of these affect the extent to which the consumer is in a position to bargain for better terms. If these issues are not considered under the heading of bargaining strength they must be considered under the 'overall evaluation of the different interests' or elsewhere under the good faith test as they are clearly crucial to the issue of consumer choice.

Did the consumer receive an inducement to agree to the term? Such an inducement might be taken to have balanced the substantive burdens effected by the term in question. It might also indicate a bargaining environment in which there was actually some give and take. The suspicion of many consumer contracts lies in the idea that there hasn't been real agreement or bargaining.

Did the supplier make the goods to the special order of the consumer? If he did then again it may indicate a generally more active bargaining environment in which the consumer was more aware than average what to expect, what could be argued over etc. Further it might be that the extra demands substantively resting on the supplier justify more limited liability on his part.

No mention is made of the other three criteria included on Schedule 2 of UCTA or of any of the other specific criteria which are looked at in decisions under UCTA. However the Preamble defines good faith as being 'an overall evaluation of the different interests involved' saying that 'particular regard' is to be had to the three criteria already mentioned. The overall evaluation of different interests appears then to be shorthand for the Article 3 test.

The overall evaluation of different interests clearly encompasses an analysis of the substantive risk allocations in the context of the bargaining environment. This presumably overlaps with the ideas of imbalance and detriment. A less clear issue is whether the 'overall evaluation' also encompasses issues such as who is the best insurer, and what will be the impact on suppliers and consumers generally of holding the term to be fair or unfair.

The UCTA reasonableness test pays close attention to the question as to who was best placed to insure — this is in part simply another way of asking who should bear the risk in question. However it also involves consideration of the impact on the market generally of disallowing the term in question. (See *Smith* v *Bush* [1989] 2 All ER 514.) Will it mean that the insurance or other burden upon the supplier is such that the cost is passed back to consumers in the form of significantly higher prices? It seems hard to exclude this sort of consideration from an 'overall evaluation of the different interests involved' unless we say that the different interests involved are only those of the two parties to the contract.

Of course insurance may not, in itself, be such an important issue where terms other than exemption clauses are concerned. The issue with exemption clauses is that one of the parties expects compensation for a loss which he perceives has resulted from defective performance. Insurance by one of the parties is a typical way to cover such a loss. A term which gives a supplier some form of discretion (e.g. a discretion vesting in an insurance company to discontinue a claim) is hardly the sort of thing which one would be insured against. Indeed it may not even be an actual exercise of the discretion which is being objected to, but rather the unfairness residing in the *power* to do so. Here, the question of insurance is irrelevant. The interests of the parties are definable much more in terms of supplier interests to operate efficiently and effectively as he sees fit, versus consumer interests in security within the relationship.

The final part of the Preamble discussion of good faith says that,

> the requirement of good faith may be satisfied by the seller or supplier where he deals fairly and equitably with the other party whose legitimate interests he has to take into account.

This raises very interesting questions.

It could simply be another way of saying that the terms in question are being tested against a standard which involves examining the various interests involved including those of the consumer in not being substantively overburdened and/or having some choice/bargaining options. It could however imply a particular and distinct consumer interest in the whole equation, i.e. a new factor on top of the ones discussed, this being that suppliers take some positive steps to safeguard the consumers. This might mean that issues such as transparency and choice at the bargaining stage are to be given special importance in deciding upon unfairness, i.e. the supplier must show that he took special steps either to highlight the existence and perhaps explain the implications of an onerous clause and/or to offer alternative terms, or point the consumer in the direction of other suppliers who could offer alternative terms. This interpretation implies a very high requirement of fairness, higher even than that required by the Courts in UCTA cases. If this is correct all of the criteria and the overall approach are affected in a way which makes it more difficult for terms to be held fair. There is of course another interpretation of this last part of the Preamble discussion of good faith. This is that the supplier need merely act fairly and equitably by subjective standards which a supplier might apply to the presentation of standard forms to consumers. However this approach cannot be correct if good faith is about the degree of real choice which the consumer had, and associated questions of bargaining strength and transparency; and if it is about respect for the consumer's legitimate substantive interests as defined by various legal norms/reasonable expectations. These are objective questions. What sorts of choices were available? What were the bargaining strengths of the parties? How transparent were the terms? They cannot be answered by asking whether the supplier felt subjectively that he was offering a choice or that his terms were transparent.

Note
There follow three extracts which discuss codes of practice and redress systems in the financial services sector. The first extract outlines the key provisions of the Banking Code of Practice.

ELLINGER AND LOMNICKA, MODERN BANKING LAW (1994)

6. THE BANKING CODE

An important project, which enjoyed the support of the banking ombudsman, was the promulgation of the Good Banking Code, observed by banks, building societies, and card issuers when dealing with customers. The Code, which appeared in its final form in December 1991, was prepared by the British Bankers' Association, the Building Societies Association, and the Association for Payment Clearing Services. It came into effect on 16 March 1992.

The object of the Code is to promote good banking practice. To ensure that the Code deals with new problems surfacing from time to time, it is to be reviewed at least once every two years.

The Code is divided into two parts. Part A deals with aspects of the ordinary services provided to customers, such as current accounts, overdrafts, bankers' references and various services provided by banks. Part B is addressed to banks that provide services by means of plastic cards.

Specific provisions of the Code are to be dealt with where relevant. But it is important to note, at this stage, the four governing principles of the Code. The first of these is to 'set out the standard of good banking practice which banks, building societies and card issuers will follow in their dealings with customers'. The second is that such institutions 'will act fairly and reasonably in all their dealings with their customers'. The third principle is that the institutions in question 'will help customers to understand how their accounts operate and will seek to give them a good understanding of banking services'. The last principle emphasizes the need to 'maintain confidence in the security and integrity of banking and card payment systems'. It further recognizes that, to protect both customers and the institutions involved, the systems and technology need to be reliable. The Code further recognizes the need for providing certain information to customers and prospective customers.

The specific matters dealt with in Part A of the Code — entitled 'Customers, their Banks and Building Societies' — can be summarized as follows. First, banks are expected to satisfy themselves of the identity of a person who seeks to open an account with them. The object of this requirement — which gives effect to existing banking practice — is to safeguard against fraud and the misuse of the banking system. Secondly, the Code seeks to ensure that the general terms and conditions, executed by a customer when the account is opened, are written in a plain language and provide a balanced view of the relationship of banker and customer. Variations of such terms have to be notified to the customer within a reasonable time before they come into effect and, when substantial changes are introduced, customers have to be given a consolidation of the variations introduced within a period of twelve months. Thirdly, customers have to be provided with details of charges levied by banks and of interest rates applicable to their accounts.

An innovative principle of the Code is the requirement that banks establish their own internal procedures for the proper handling of customers' complaints. Customers have to be notified of the existence of this procedure and, where a customer seeks to make use of it, have to advise him of the steps to be taken. In addition, banks and building societies subscribing to the Code have to belong either to the Banking and Building Societies Ombudsman Scheme or to the Finance Houses Conciliation and Arbitration Scheme. Customers have to be given details of the applicable scheme by means such as leaflets or notices displayed at branches.

The remaining provisions of the Code cover aspects of banking secrecy and of bankers' references. They also provide certain additional disclosure requirements applicable to services such as lending and foreign exchange and in situations where individuals propose to issue guarantees or to provide a security to the bank. Customers must, in addition, be given information on the manner in which their accounts are to be operated, including such details as their right to withdraw funds or to countermand payment of a cheque.

Notes

(1)   The commitment to plain language of terms and conditions will help to satisfy Regulation 6 of the Unfair Terms Regulations (see 3.11.8 above and see Willett, 'Plain Language in Consumer Contracts', *SCOLAG Bulletin*, February 1995). It will also help to make terms fair under Regulation 4(1). The commitment to notify consumers of variations in terms seems to imply that a term giving a right to vary terms is acceptable as long as notification is given. However, it may well be that a term is unfair under Regulation 4(1) if it does not require valid reasons to exist for variation.

(2)   The following extract considers the role of the Statement of Insurance Practice in mitigating the 'pro-insurer' nature of insurance contract law.

'Do Insurers Know Best?'
By Ian Cadogan and Richard Lewis
1992, *Anglo-American Law Review*, p. 123

It is widely acknowledged that the 'law of insurance contains a number of doctrines which can in theory operate against the interests of the innocent insured person.' The courts on numerous occasions have accused the law of operating harshly and of favouring the insurer. This view has been endorsed by academic lawyers, the Law Commission and consumer organizations. Even insurance companies themselves recognize the potential unfairness of the law and have admitted that 'in practice they do not take advantage of their full legal rights'.

Parliament has taken an interest in the manner in which insurance companies have operated ever since 1870. But the major area to escape reform is the insurance contract itself. The explanation often put forward to justify this is that the insurance industry has been prepared to regulate itself. In recent times the Statements of Insurance Practice have provided the most noticeable examples of such self-regulation. These take the form of two documents drafted by the Association of British Insurers (ABI) with one relating to general insurance and the other to long-term business. They were forced upon the insurance industry as the price of keeping insurance contracts out of the otherwise wide scope of the Unfair Contract Terms Act 1977. Introduced in the same year as that Act, the Statements aim to mitigate the severity of the law and set out 'normal insurance practice' to be followed by the 839 registered UK insurance companies in their dealings with policyholders. It has been claimed that the Statements work well in practice. Certainly as will be seen, they represent an improvement upon the strict law of insurance. . . .

The Present Law and its Defects

The contract of insurance in theory is governed by the same rules which form the general law of contract. However, during its long history the insurance contract has developed so many principles of its own that some refer to the 'law of insurance'. Two of these particular principles applicable only to the law of insurance are frequently cited as examples of doctrines capable of producing harsh results. These are the rules relating to the duty of disclosure and those applicable in the event of a breach of warranty.

(a)   The Duty of Disclosure

Insurance contracts are recognized by the courts as contracts of '*uberrimae fidei*': in contrast to the rule of '*caveat emptor*' the insurance contract requires a buyer to disclose all material facts and it does not allow him to keep silent. The duty extends beyond those matters covered by questions upon the proposal form. If the proposer fails to disclose a material fact it makes the policy voidable at the option of the insurer, entitling him to avoid the contract *ab initio* and to refuse the payment of any claim.

The case of *Lambert* v *Co-operative Insurance Society Ltd* was described by the Court of Appeal as showing 'the unsatisfactory state of the law'. Here, Mrs Lambert's claim for lost jewellery was refused because of her failure to disclose her husband's conviction for dishonesty, even though the proposal form contained no question about this matter. This duty of disclosure, when taken together with the test applied to determine whether a fact is material, may result in the absurd situation whereby the insured must possess clairvoyant powers to discover what a reasonable insurer would regard as material.

(b)   Breach of Warranty

The law relating to the use of warranties can be criticized as unfair because where there is a breach of contract the insurer is allowed to repudiate no matter how trivial that breach may be, and regardless of the materiality of the term to the loss caused. In addition, it has been all too easy to create warranties either by using a 'basis of the contract clause', or by drafting a question very specifically such that its answer must be taken to give rise to a warranty. This has meant the courts have been forced to make decisions in favour of insurers upon what they have agreed to be technical and harsh grounds. For example, in *Dawsons Ltd* v *Bonnin*, the information contained on the proposal form indicated a lorry was garaged in Glasgow city centre, whereas in fact it was garaged on a farm on the city's outskirts. This did not present a greater risk for the insurance company — indeed had the correct facts been disclosed, no additional premium would have been charged. However, because the proposal form contained a 'basis of the contract clause' it meant that any untruth would make the contract voidable at the option of the insurer. As a result the House of Lords reluctantly upheld the insurers' decision to repudiate a claim for breach of warranty.

Quite clearly, the strict application of these rules may result in unfairness. In recent years attempts have been made without any success to reform the law. In 1978 the Government, prompted by an EC draft directive, asked the Law Commission to report on insurance contract law. Their report published in 1980 indentified various mischiefs in the present. . . .

[Applicability and Principles of the Statement of Practice]
The Statement applies only to policyholders insured in their private capacity. . . . Nevertheless, it seems that in practice the protection given by the Statements is sometimes extended to commercial policies. However, the survey showed that insurers were keen to safeguard their discretion here, and only wanted to extend the protection given by the Statements when they thought it appropriate to do so.

The Law Commission proposals would have applied to all contracts of insurance except for 'Marine, Aviation and Transport' policies. Throughout their report the Commission highlighted the defects of the law by referring to cases involving both private and commercial policyholders. Whilst it is welcome that the Statements protect policyholders in Mrs Lambert's position from the unsatisfactory state of the law, there would appear to be no justification for imposing that law upon a company such as Dawsons Ltd.

(b)   Proposal Forms
This is the longest section in the Statement, reflecting the fact that this is the area where the policyholder needs most protection.

■ Section 1(a) states that:

> The declaration at the foot of the proposal form should be restricted to completion according to the proposer's knowledge and belief.

The effect of this is to make the 'basis of the contract clause' ineffective. It thus resolves the unfairness whereby an insurer could avoid liability if any answer on the proposal form was incorrect. In practice, the survey showed that this provision was complied with. However, the fact that insurers are only required to amend their policies in relation to private insurance means that the 'basis of contract clause' continues to be used in commercial proposal forms.

■ Section 1(b) did not appear in the original 1977 Statement. It states that:

> Neither the proposal form nor the policy shall contain any provision converting the statements as to past or present fact in the proposal form into warranties. But insurers require specific warranties about matters which are material to the risk.

This means that whilst the use of warranties is permitted, they must be connected specifically to a risk material for that type of policy. Forte is of the opinion that whilst there is 'nothing inherently improper in wanting to create a warranty, it is essential that they can clearly be understood by the insured'. He expresses concern that 'where specific warranties are created, a proposer will not be aware of the effect'. In this respect the Statement of Practice can be criticized for not implementing the Law Commission's proposal that warranties should be contained in the policy document itself. The insurers surveyed responded to this by suggesting that, in the vast majority of cases, warranties deriving from answers to proposal forms are in fact incorporated in the policy document by means of a written endorsement. Nevertheless, the Statement does not reflect this general practice. Where warranties are created they should be confirmed in writing.

■ Section 1(c) states that:

> If not included in the declaration, prominently displayed on the proposal form should be a statement:
> (i)   drawing the attention of the proposer to the consequence of failure to disclose all material facts, explained as those facts an insurer would regard as likely to influence the acceptance and assessment of the proposal;
> (ii)   a warning that if the proposer is in any doubt about facts considered material, he should disclose them.

This is effectively a declaration of the common law regarding the duty of disclosure. Whilst all insurers interviewed complied with this requirement, the manner in which they did so varied considerably. For example, one insurer incorporated the following within the declaration section at the foot of the proposal form:

> Failure to disclose facts that an insurer would regard as likely to influence the acceptance and assessment of a Proposal may render the insurance invalid — if in doubt whether facts are material they should be disclosed.

This should be contrasted with the much clearer warning given by another company. In a section headed 'IMPORTANT' and typed in bold print, the company says:

> Failure to disclose a material fact may render the contract void. The questions in this proposal deal with those matters which we have found generally to be material, but because no list of questions can be exhaustive, you must ensure that any information known to you which could influence an acceptance or assessment of the risk is disclosed. If you are in any doubt whether a fact is material then it should be disclosed.

Although the first sentence does not provide much help or guidance to the average proposer, the second represents a genuine attempt to explain the extent of the duty of disclosure, and it draws attention to the fact that truthful answers to questions may not necessarily discharge it.

The Law Commission called for 'clear and explicit warnings . . . presented in a prominent manner' and the Statements certainly follow this recommendation. If an insurer fails to comply it may mean that, in some cases, the first time the policyholder will become fully aware of the extent of the duty of disclosure is when the insurer refuses his claim and explains the duty in a letter in layman's terms. However, it is clearly also in an insurer's interest that the proposer should disclose all material facts in the proposal form in order not only to determine what premium to charge, but also to avoid costly correspondence at the claims stage.

■ Section 1(d) states:

> Those matters which insurers have generally found to be material will be the subject of clear questions in proposal forms.

An insurance company is free to decide which questions to include on its forms. In practice, the areas upon which questions are asked are largely determined by the underwriting and claims departments, although constraints are often imposed by marketing departments upon the number of questions which can be asked. Adverse claims' experience may result in the inclusion of a question. For example, following a number of claims where valuable equipment inside cars had contributed to losses, one company's motor proposal form now asks about the value of radios, cassettes, compact disc players and car telephones.

Whether insurers always comply with the requirement of asking 'clear questions' is doubtful. Vaguely worded questions may lead to a materially inaccurate answer. For example, household insurance proposals often ask:

Is the home in a good state of repair and will it be so maintained?

This is a question of opinion to which there may be no easy answer. Other questions are unclear. For example.

Is the home free from any sign of damage by flood, subsidence, heave or landslip and not in an area which has a history of such damage?

This question includes technical words such as 'heave and landslip' and the vague term 'area.' Such usage is surprising in view of s. 1(e) which states:

So far as is practicable insurers will avoid asking questions which would require expert knowledge beyond that which the proposer could reasonably be expected to possess or obtain or which would require a value judgment on the part of the proposer.

Hodgin points out that whilst the basic thrust of the section is an attempt to help the proposer, the phrase 'so far as is practicable' must surely have an important limiting effect. He goes on to highlight the absurdity which may arise when an insurer is able to ask technical questions for which the insured lacks the technical knowledge to answer.

Note

The Unfair Terms Directive and the UK Regulations implementing it apply to insurance contracts. The approach taken by sections 1(c) and 1(d) in the above Statement of Practice is likely to help terms pass the unfairness test, which is greatly concerned with terms being transparent as to their meaning and implications (see excerpt from Willett, above).

Philip Rawlings and Chris Willett,
'Ombudsman Schemes in the United Kingdom's Financial Sector: The Insurance Ombudsman, the Banking Ombudsman, and the Building Societies Ombudsman'

Journal of Consumer Policy 17: 307–333, 1994

THE INSURANCE OMBUDSMAN BUREAU

The Origins of the Scheme

The contract of insurance has long been a source of complaints from academics, the courts, the Law Commission and consumer groups (Birds, 1982, 1987; Law Commission, 1980; Lewis, 1985). The key problem is that consumers normally lack the bargaining strength to be able to negotiate a change in the standard form contracts which insurance companies use. That lack of strength is not balanced by doctrines of fairness or inequality of bargaining power which might enable the consumer to challenge the contract in a court (although see Birds, 1988). Moreover, the weakness of the bargaining position of the consumer is exacerbated by the view which the common law has of insurance contracts as ones in which the insured is obliged to disclose all 'material facts' to the insurer: that is, facts which a prudent insurer would deem relevant, whether or not the insurer asks questions on the proposal form which might elicit such facts (*Lambert* v *Cooperative Insurance Society Ltd.*, Birds, 1988; Matthews, 1987; Merkin & McGee, 1989). However, insurance companies have claimed that they do not take advantage of their full legal rights (Cadogan & Lewis, 1992: Law Commission, 1980), and, indeed, it may be that pressure on insurance companies not to do so will increase as the single market in financial services may enable consumers to deal with non-United Kingdom companies on more favourable terms.

The insurance industry successfully opposed being covered by the Unfair Contract Terms Act 1977 (schedule 1, para. 1(a); Willett & O'Donnell, 1991; Woodroffe & Lowe, 1991) and later avoided the impact of the Law Commission's (1980) proposals on contracts. Instead, it adopted less severe measures (Cadogan & Lewis, 1992), including the Statements of Insurance Practice in 1977. These were revised in 1981 and became the Statements of General and Long-term Insurance Practice in 1986 (Ellis & Wiltshire, 1990). Although a voluntary code of practice, it is a condition of membership of the Association of British Insurers (A.B.I.) that an insurer complies with the Statements. In broad terms, the Statements seek to prevent insurance companies from relying unfairly on the insured's duty to disclose all material facts.

There are certain problems with the Statements. First, the A.B.I. did not set up any proactive mechanism for monitoring compliance; Instead it relies on complaints that a company has failed to comply, so, although all insurance companies claim to adhere to the Statements, there is no adequate way of knowing whether or not this is true (Cadogan & Lewis, 1992). Second, the directives on the provision of insurance services in the European Community leave regulation in the hands of a company's home state and do not, in general, allow host states to impose conditions; as a result, it will be impossible to require companies from outside the United Kingdom to adopt the Statements, although, of course, commercial pressures may force adoption. The third problem is that the Statements mainly cover warranties and disclosures, and do not require fair dealing in other aspects of the relationship between the insurer and the insured. It is unclear whether or not European Community law will repair some of these defects. The Unfair Terms in Consumer Contracts Directive, which might have been used to require minimum standards of fairness in insurance contracts, may, by virtue of Article 4, be found not to cover many of the terms in insurance contracts. This is because Article 4 excludes from the fairness criteria of the directive terms defining the main subject matter of the contract. The insurance industry is likely to argue that virtally all terms in an insurance contract fall into this category (Willett, 1993). [Article 4(1) is implemented in the UK by Regulation 3(1) of the Unfair Terms Regulations (see 3.11.8 above).]

Aside from the Statements of Insurance Practice, some of the difficulties faced by consumers as a result of the complexities and apparent unfairness of insurance law have been addressed by the creation of the Insurance Ombudsman Bureau (I.O.B.). It was established as a voluntary scheme in 1981 on the initiative of three major insurance companies, although, as with the Office of the Banking Ombudsman, in the background was the possibility of a statutory scheme being introduced as part of a package of regulatory measures passed in the late 1970s and early 1980s (Birds & Graham, 1988). By 1990 over 300 companies had joined the scheme (Birds & Graham, 1988; Hodgin, 1989, 1992; Thomas, 1988; Wilson, 1990). Initially, there was concern within the industry that the I.O.B. might become a champion of the consumers, and so in 1982 a rival scheme was set up — the Personal Insurance

Arbitration Scheme. However, experience showed this fear to have been exaggerated, and the I.O.B. gained dominance (Merkin & McGee, 1989). There are also complaints mechanisms run by the A.B.I. and Lloyd's of London.

The Structure of the Scheme

The I.O.B. has a full-time staff, and it also has the power to commission others to undertake research and investigations. The costs are met by levies on those who are members of the scheme, so that the service is free to consumers. The I.O.B. is subject to the supervision of the Board and the Council. The Council appoints the Ombudsman. In an effort to ensure the independence of the scheme, only two of the Council's ten members are linked to insurance companies.

The I.O.B. is based on a Memorandum and Articles of Association which set out its objectives. These are to receive from private individuals complaints or disputes over insurance policies issued in the United Kingdom, where the internal complaints mechanisms have been exhausted. It may conciliate or adjudicate on such disputes and may make awards up to £100,000. Members are bound by the award and have no right of appeal; consumers, on the other hand, are not so bound, and, if dissatisfied, may pursue their grievances through the courts. Since the scheme is based on contract and membership is voluntary, the High Court has recently ruled that it is not a body operating in the public — as opposed to the private — domain, and, therefore, its awards are not subject to judicial review (*R v Insurance Ombudsman Bureau and Another, Ex parte Aegon Life Assurance Ltd*). This decision is likely to affect insurers more than consumers, since it cuts off their only avenue of challenge to an award made by the I.O.B.

The Standards Used

Paragraph 2(d) of the terms of reference sets out the criteria which guide the I.O.B's decisions:

> The Ombudsman may, in relation to any complaint, dispute or claim comprised in a reference, make an award against any member named in such reference and in making any award he shall have regard to the terms of the contract, and act in conformity with any applicable rule of law or relevant practical authority, with general principles of good insurance practice, with these terms of reference and with the statement of insurance practice and codes of practice issued from time to time by the Association of British Insurers and the Life Offices Associations but shall not otherwise be bound by any previous decision made by him or any predecessor in his Office. In determining what are the principles of good insurance practice he should where he considers it appropriate consult with the industry (Insurance Ombudsman Bureau, 1992).

The criteria set out in this paragraph are not particularly clear, and, as such, leave it open to the Ombudsman to place stress where he or she considers appropriate. However, the focus seems to be on the current state of both the law as it would regulate the contract and the practice of the industry, as informed by the Statements of Practice and by the view of the industry. Given the perception that the current law and practice are unfair we might expect the Ombudsman to be simply providing improved — that is, cheaper — access to unfair law and practice. However, the current Ombudsman has made it clear that where law and/or the contract come into conflict with fairness, he will tend to give priority to fairness. In his 1989 Report he said, 'I am . . . entitled to reach a fair and common sense conclusion whatever may be the strict legal position' (cited in Ellis & Wiltshire, 1990). Speaking of case law, he added that he will, 'mitigate the implications of ancient decisions which appear unjust in the light of modern times. I do not consider it similarly justifiable to disregard recent case law' (cited in Ellis & Wiltshire, 1990). In practice, then, the I.O.B. has often sought to introduce fairness norms that hold insurers responsible for things for which, in both law and insurance practice, they would not normally be held responsible.

Where appropiate the I.O.B. has applied the reasonableness criteria set out in the Unfair Contract Terms Act (Willett & O'Donnell, 1991; Woodroffe & Lowe, 1991). They have been used by the I.O.B. to determine the acceptability of attempts to avoid the responsibility which the consumer — with no knowledge of insurance law — might reasonably anticipate the insurer would bear. More specifically, the I.O.B. has ignored or mitigated rules of law which are regarded as operating against consumer expectations in particular cases. For instance, because an intermediary is deemed in law to be the agent of the insured person rather than the insurer, an insurance company is not normally held legally liable for the negligence of such an intermediary: so, for instance, there is no legal liability for negligent misrepresentations made by an intermediary about the benefits offered under an insurance policy (Hodgin, 1987). This has long been criticized (Law Reform Committee, 1957; *Roberts* v *Plaisted*), but it has been the I.O.B. that has given practical effect to these criticisms. The Ombudsman noted in the 1989 Report:

> Pending legislation it seems impossible to assume that the legal positions will necessarily produce an equitable outcome. Accordingly, I am prepared, in appropriate cases, to hold insurers responsible for the defaults of intermediaries (Hodgin, 1992, p. 4).

To take another example, although the Statements of Practice require insurers to be more explicit about the duty on the insured to disclose all material facts, it is still possible that a customer will fail to disclose them and may thereby invalidate the policy. The I.O.B. declared in 1984, that

> a member of the lay public cannot be expected to have the same understanding of what is 'material' as a proposer for commercial insurance . . . The underwriter should decide what information he really needs to assess the risk, and what he can do without. He can then ask for specific relevant information in the proposal form (Merkin & McGee, 1989, p. A.5.8–03).

Similarly, where circumstances have altered, but the insured has failed to notify the insurer, then to avoid a total loss of benefits in all such cases, the I.O.B. has adopted an approach which seeks to allocate the losses according to a 'proportionality principle'.

> the basic solution adopted as equitable was that the claim should be met proportionately taking into account the relative amounts of the actual premium and the appropriate premium. For example in one case had the business use of a house (seasonal bed and breakfast) been disclosed the premium would have been increased by approximately one quarter (say, from £100 to £125). The proportionality solution meant that the insurer should be liable for 80% of the claim (because £100 is 80% of £125). Similar results have been reached with motoring policies where increased premium rates (e.g. in the light of the policyholder's claim record) are easily ascertainable (Insurance Ombudsman Bureau, 1989, para. 2.17).

Alongside these notions of substantive fairness, the I.O.B. has also tried to introduce procedural fairness in the way in which insurers investigate claims. For instance, having considered several cases in which trained nurses, posing as counsellors, called on people who had claimed for disabilities in order to verify those claims, the I.O.B. ruled that the nature of any inquiry must be made clear to the insured at the outset. In cases where this has not been done, the I.O.B. has been prepared to make an award for the 'upset and distress' caused, even where no actual financial loss has been suffered.

The insurance industry's initial fears that the I.O.B. would be a consumer's champion have, apparently, largely subsided, either because the Bureau is seen as being independent or because most complaints against insurers actually fail. Nevertheless, the I.O.B. has developed concepts of both substantive and procedural fairness. There seem to be two linked reasons for the I.O.B. adopting these approaches. First, the unfair nature of insurance contract law and the lack of statutory regulation of the contract mean that there is a wide gulf in the definitions of the insurer's responsibility between, on the one hand, the formal, legal rules and, on the other hand, the notion of what might fairly accord with reasonable consumer expectations. Second, the reason that this gulf is being actively closed seems to lie in the fact that the insurers have always sought to avoid statutory regulation of the insurance contract. To a large extent, they have been successful in this goal, but, as has been mentioned, there is an acute awareness that the industry has been strongly criticized and that, unless such criticism is taken seriously, there might be legislation (Law Commission, 1980; Law Reform Committee, 1957).

BLYTH v SCOTTISH LIBERAL CLUB
(1982) SC 140

Facts
The pursuer was dismissed for two breaches of his contract with the defendants. These were failing to turn up for a meeting and refusing to take minutes at another meeting. It was held that this was a material breach of his contractual obligation as managing secretary. It made no difference that he was ignorant of his obligation to carry out his duties as requested.

Lord Wheatley
Despite the extensive controversies canvassed in the pleadings and in the evidence the issue in the reclaiming motion was simply this: It being conceded by the pursuer that the Lord Ordinary's finding that he had been in breach of his contract of service with the defenders in two respects could not be impugned, were these material breaches of the contract sufficient to warrant his dismissal from his job and thus negate his action of damages for breach of contract? In these circumstances I do not consider it necessary to rehearse the history of events leading up to and surrounding this limited issue, since that history has been fully set out by the Lord Ordinary in his opinion for the purpose of the wider issues with which he had to deal . . .

The two instances of admitted breach of contract on the part of the pursuer were (1) despite an express instruction to attend a meeting of the review committee on 8 August 1977 he refused to so so; and (2) despite express instructions from the chairman of the club to take minutes of a meeting of the management committee on 12 September 1977 which he was attending he refused to do so. The Lord Ordinary has held that these were cases of wilful disobedience in important and material respects which entitled the defenders to terminate the pursuer's contract. He accordingly found in favour of the defenders. In order to assess properly the extent of the materiality of these refusals it is necessary to go deeper into their significance than a view of them taken in isolation might suggest. Despite the fact that the defenders had made it abundantly plain that in their view it was part of his contract of service that he was obliged to carry out these duties he steadfastly maintained that these duties were not comprehended in his contract as managing secretary. I do not require to go into this matter because it is now accepted that they were comprehended in his contract. As events had materialised they were virtually the only duties which were left for him to perform in return for the salary which the defenders were obliged to pay to him under the contract. When asked what other tasks the pursuer might then have to perform under his contract, his senior counsel could only suggest forwarding members' mail and seeing to the security of the club premises. As matters stood, the club was still in existence and its affairs were being run by the management committee. How the future of the club could be best determined was the function of the review committee, and it is perhaps not without significance that at an earlier stage in the club's crisis a similar review committee for development had been serviced by the pursuer without question.

In the course of the debate under reference to selected cases various concepts and various phrases were developed to provide a test for materiality of the breach in this context. It seemed to me at times that there was a danger of getting bogged down in a mire of semantics. For present purposes I take the view that the well known test expounded by Lord President Dunedin in *Wade v Waldon* 1909 SC 571 at p. 576 and cited in Gloag on *Contract* (2nd ed.) at p. 602 is the apposite one:

It is familiar law, and quite well settled by decisions, that in any contract which contains multifarious stipulations there are some which go so to the root of the contract that a breach of those stipulations entitles the party pleading the breach to declare that the contract is at an end. There are others which do not go to the root of the contract, but which are part of the contract and which would give rise, if broken, to an action of damages.

In the state of affairs of the club at the time when the breaches took place I can think of nothing which would strike more at the root of the contract than the refusal by the pursuer to service the review committee and to carry out orders in connection with the affairs of the management committee. Once it is accepted that those were duties which the pursuer was obliged to carry out under his contract, and were virtually the only ones at the time, the Lord Ordinary's finding on the materiality of the breaches is prima facie clearly confirmed.

Pursuers' counsel maintained, however, that the question of materiality had to be considered in the light of all the circumstances of the case. On that approach, it was said, the breaches took on a lesser significance, tapered from major to minor and were insufficient to warrant the pursuer's dismissal. In the very forefront of this line of approach was the contention that the pursuer, albeit mistakenly as it turned out, had proceeded in the bona fide belief that the said work which he was instructed to do did not fall within the four corners of his contract. Reference was made to the cases of *Spettabile Consorzio Veneziano de Armamento di Navigazione* v *Northumberland Shipbuilding Co Ltd* [1919] 88 KB 1194, *Rubel Bronze and Metal Co.* v *Vos* [1918] 1 KB 315, *Sweet & Maxwell* v *Universal News* [1964] 2 QB 699, and *Woodar Investment Development Limited* v *Wimpey Construction U.K. Limited* [1980] 1 WLR 277 (in selected passages) which were claimed to buttress the proposition that in view of this bona fide if mistaken belief the pursuer's refusals although breaches of the contract were not material ones in the circumstances. This was reinforced by the fact that the pursuer was pursuing the line which he took on the scope and limit of his contractual duties fortified by legal advice. I do not propose to go into these cases for the reason that, whatever the position may be in respect of bona fide belief when dealing with an anticipatory breach of contract, there is no room for that doctrine when the breach is an instant and actual one. The position here can be conveniently summarised by reference to a passage in the speech of Lord Keith of Kinkel at p. 296G in *Woodar Ltd* supra where his Lordship said:

> I would accept without hesitation the statement of Lord Denning MR in *Federal Commerce & Navigation Co. Ltd.* v *Molena Alpha Inc.* [1978] 1 QB 927, 929 that a party who breaks a contract cannot excuse himself by saying that he did it on the advice of his lawyers, or that he was under an honest misapprehension. If in the present case the time for performance had passed while the appellants were still maintaining these positions based on the erroneous interpretation of condition E(a)(iii), they would have been in breach of contract and liable in damages accordingly.

I appreciate that a refusal to carry out an order may be a question of circumstances and degree — *Laws* v *London Chronicle (Indicator Newspapers) Ltd* [1959] 1 WLR 698 — but when as previously noted the refusals which are now accepted as breaches of contract relate to what was virtually the only duties left for him to do in return for his salary, and the two committees to which they related were the lifelines to the club's then existence and future destiny, I cannot conceive of anything more material in the circumstances. I accordingly reject this contention.

I now turn to consider a number of other matters which were said to support this 'minor breach' approach and to give my observations thereon. It was said that these matters clearly showed that the pursuer never had any intention of terminating the contract, as would require to be established if a breach of contract was to be sustained. I feel that these can be dealt with shortly since I have taken the view that where, as here, there is an instant and flagrant breach of contract, attitudes taken at earlier stages might explain but cannot temper an action which instantly strikes at the whole root of the contractual relationship. (1) It was argued that the last thing which the pursuer wanted to do was to repudiate the contract — that it was clear that he wanted the contract to continue, but on his interpretation of it. The comment that this sits strangely with his raising of the present action is tempered by the explanation that this was an expedient to obtain security by way of an inhibition for the damages which he was claiming for breach of contract. But his interpretation of the contract involved the securing of a fresh contract in relation to the work which he erroneously maintained did not fall within the original contract. (2) The pursuer was understandably perturbed about the assurance of employment being restricted to twelve months when he had a five years contract, and his unanswered claim for a further assurance was reasonable. While his anxiety was understandable, he did not legally require any further assurance — he had his contract which he was entitled to enforce. (3) It was argued that the pursuer kept giving way, and was eventually prepared to carry out his disputed work with the review committee if the club would accept this as 'without prejudice' to his claim that it did not fall within the contract. There was no need for the pursuer to await the acceptance of this 'without prejudice' offer. He could have carried out the work required of him on such a stated basis without breaching the contract if he was wrong and without prejudice to his claim if he was right. (4) It was submitted that if the disputed work did not fall within the contract there was no work to do, and, under reference to several authorities, failure by the employer to provide work for the employee constituted a breach of contract. I do not require to deal with that point of law since that factual situation did not arise. Prior to and at the time of the pursuer's breach of contract there was work for him to do in return for his salary, namely the work which it is now conceded he was required but refused to do. (5) It was then argued that the materiality test had to be considered in the light of all the duties which the pursuer had to perform when he first entered the contract, and should not be restricted to those which remained at the time when the breach occurred. This, in my opinion, is an untenable proposition. The duties which might properly be required from a managing secretary of a club will normally vary according to circumstances. Some additional ones may accrue, others may disappear. The test is whether any new duties fall within the general work of a managing secretary. Virtually all the other duties had disappeared by the time the pursuer's refusals created the breaches, which, as previously mentioned, constituted a refusal to do what was virtually all that he was then being paid to do. (6) It was suggested that the defenders had sought and succeeded in placing the pursuer into a position where he was forced or induced to do something which would entitle them to hold that he had repudiated the contract, thus enabling them to escape the inevitable claim for damages which the pursuer would have against them in respect of any unfulfilled duty during the currency of the five year contract. I have two observations to make on this. In the first place, the parties were admittedly taking up entrenched positions with regard to the scope of the contract. The breaking point was the two matters on which the issue now centres. The defenders were taking the view that these duties fell within the contract, and made this plain repeatedly, both verbally and in correspondence. The pursuer, by the same methods, made it clear that they did not, and indeed he wanted a new and separate contract in respect of them. It is now conceded that the defenders were right and that the pursuer was wrong in refusing to carry out the explicit orders. That being the situation, I cannot see how the pursuer's submissions can be sustained. Secondly, on the question of motive, it is noteworthy that when the Lord Ordinary dealt with this subject his animadversion related not to the defenders but to the pursuer. He observed . . . that when the pursuer wrote his letter of 3 June 1977 to the chairman of the club all that he was interested in was his claim against the club for damages, and that this had been his concern since some time earlier. The Lord Ordinary went on to say: 'By this time, every letter which he wrote and every action which he took was designed to assist him in the prosecution of his claim which he felt he had against the club. I should also add that the letter contains various allegations against the committee which, on the whole, I regard as unjustified.' It is perhaps necessary to note in this regard that when the pursuer, supported by Mr Roberts, asserted in evidence that at the interview at which he was appointed he was assured, in answer to his question, that he would not be expected to take minutes of meetings as that would be the responsibility of the honorary secretary, his evidence was not believed by the Lord Ordinary.

In all these circumstances I am satisfied that nothing that was advanced by the pursuer's counsel has any impact upon or in any way diminishes the effect of the materiality of the breaches of the contract by the pursuer, and that it has not been demonstrated that the Lord Ordinary was not entitled to reach the conclusion which he did. I appreciate the anxiety which the pursuer felt when he realised that the position which he had secured and which he thought would give him security until he reached retirement age was seemingly coming to a premature end. But he had his contract, and he had the inhibition and later the deposited money as a security for any damages to which he was entitled. All he had to do was to keep his side of the contract. Whether through anxiety, stubbornness or impetuosity or all three, he tried to force the issue, and in the process he lost the security which he was so anxious to secure. He no doubt must feel doubly disappointed in view of the fact that his claim for compensation for unfair dismissal was upheld by the industrial tribunal and the

Employment Appeal Tribunal and yet his claim for damages for breach of contract has failed in the courts of law. It must be pointed out in fairness that the facts before the respective bodies were different. In this court case it has been established, and was accepted before this Appeal Court, that while the contract was still extant the pursuer was in breach of his contractual duties in two respects which have been held to have been materaial and struck at the root of his contract. The industrial tribunal's decision under a statutory code was based on a finding that the pursuer's refusal to do what the defenders asked him to do stemmed from their failure to give him a proper assurance about their intentions in relation to his contract, and so acted unreasonably. Different criteria were applied and these produced the different decisions.

In all the circumstances I am of the opinion that the reclaiming motion should be refused and that the Lord Ordinary's interlocutor reclaimed against should be affirmed. I so move your Lordships.

DUNLOP PNEUMATIC TYRE CO LTD v NEW GARAGE & MOTOR CO LTD
[1915] AC 79

Lord Dunedin

My Lords, we had the benefit of a full and satisfactory argument, and a citation of the very numerous cases which have been decided on this branch of the law. The matter has been handled, and at no distant date, in the Courts of highest resort. I particularly refer to the *Clydebank Case* in your Lordships' House and the cases of *Public Works Commissioner* v *Hills* and *Webster* v *Bosanquet* in the Privy Council. In both of these cases many of the previous cases were considered. In view of that fact, and of the number of the authorities available, I do not think it advisable to attempt any detailed review of the various cases, but I shall content myself with stating succinctly the various propositions which I think are deducible from the decisions which rank as authoritative: —

1.   Though the parties to a contract who use the words 'penalty' or 'liquidated damages' may prima facie be supposed to mean what they say, yet the expression used is not conclusive. The Court must find out whether the payment stipulated is in truth a penalty or liquidated damages. This doctrine may be said to be found passim in nearly every case.

2.   The essence of a penalty is a payment of money stipulated as in terrorem of the offending party; the essence of liquidated damages is a genuine covenanted pre-estimate of damage (*Clydebank Engineering and Shipbuilding Co.* v *Don Jose Ramos Yzquierdo y Castaneda*).

3.   The question whether a sum stipulated is penalty or liquidated damages is a question of construction to be decided upon the terms and inherent circumstances of each particular contract, judged of as at the time of the making of the contract, not as at the time of the breach (*Public Works Commissioner* v *Hills* and *Webster* v *Bosanquet*).

4.   To assist this task of construction various tests have been suggested, which if applicable to the case under consideration may prove helpful, or even conclusive. Such are:

(a)   It will be held to be penalty if the sum stipulated for is extravagant and unconscionable in amount in comparison with the greatest loss that could conceivably be proved to have followed from the breach. (Illustration given by Lord Halsbury in *Clydebank Case.*)

(b)   It will be held to be a penalty if the breach consists only in not paying a sum of money, and the sum stipulated is a sum greater than the sum which ought to have been paid (*Kemble* v *Farren*). This though one of the most ancient instances is truly a corollary to the last test. Whether it had its historical origin in the doctrine of the common law that when A promised to pay B a sum of money on a certain day and did not do so, B could only recover the sum with, in certain cases, interest, but could never recover further damages for non-timeous payment, or whether it was a survival of the time when equity reformed unconscionable bargains merely because they were unconscionable, — a subject which much exercised Jessel MR in *Wallis* v *Smith* — is probably more interesting than material.

(c)   There is a presumption (but no more) that it is penalty when 'a single lump sum is made payable by way of compensation, on the occurrence of one or more or all of several events, some of which may occasion serious and others but trifling damage' (Lord Watson in *Lord Elphinstone* v *Monkland Iron and Coal Co.*).

On the other hand:

(d)   It is no obstacle to the sum stipulated being a genuine pre-estimate of damage, that the consequences of the breach are such as to make precise pre-estimation almost an impossibility. On the contrary, that is just the situation when it is probable that pre-estimated damage was the true bargain between the parties (*Clydebank Case*, Lord Halsbury; *Webster* v *Bosanquet*, Lord Mersey).

Turning now to the facts of the case, it is evident that the damage apprehended by the appellants owing to the breaking of the agreement was an indirect and not a direct damage. So long as they got their price from the respondents for each article sold, it could not matter to them directly what the respondents did with it. Indirectly it did. Accordingly, the agreement is headed 'Price Maintenance Agreement', and the way in which the appellants would be damaged if prices were cut is clearly explained in evidence by Mr. Baisley, and no successful attempt is made to controvert that evidence. But though damage as a whole from such a practice would be certain, yet damage from any one sale would be impossible to forecast. It is just, therefore, one of those cases where it seems quite reasonable for parties to contract that they should estimate that damage at a certain figure, and provided that figure is not extravagant there would seem no reason to suspect that it is not truly a bargain to assess damages, but rather a penalty to be held in terrorem.

The argument of the respondents was really based on two heads. They overpressed, in my judgment, the dictum of Lord Watson in *Lord Elphinstone's Case*, reading it as if he had said that the matter was conclusive, instead of saying, as he did, that it raised a presumption, and they relied strongly on the case of *Willson* v *Love*.

Now, in the first place, I have considerable doubt whether the stipulated payment here can fairly be said to deal with breaches, 'some of which' — I am quoting Lord Watson's words — 'may occasion serious and others but trifling damage'. As a mere matter of construction, I doubt whether clause 5 applies to anything but sales below price. But I will assume that it does. None the less the mischief, as I have already pointed out, is an indirect mischief, and I see no data on which, as a matter of construction, I could settle in my own mind that the indirect damage from selling a cover would differ in magnitude from the indirect damage from selling a tube; or that the indirect damage from a cutting-price sale would differ from the indirect damage from supply at a full price to a hostile, because prohibited, agent. You cannot weigh such things in a chemical balance. The character of the agricultural land which was ruined by slag heaps in *Elphinstone's Case* was not all the same, but no objection was raised by Lord Watson to applying an overhead rate per acre, the sum not being in itself unconscionable.

I think *Elphinstone's Case*, or rather the dicta in it, do go this length, that if there are various breaches to which one indiscriminate sum to be paid in breach is applied, then the strength of the chain must be taken at its weakest link. If you can clearly see that the loss on one particular breach could never amount to the stipulated sum, then you may come to the conclusion that the sum is penalty. But further than this it does not go; so, for the reasons already stated, I do not think the present case forms an instance of what I have just expressed.

As regards *Willson's Case*, I do not think it material to consider whether it was well decided on the facts. For it was decided on the view of the facts that the manurial value of straw and of hay were known ascertainable quantities as at the time of the bargain, and radically different, so that the damage resulting from the want of one could never be the same as the damage resulting from the want of the other.

Added to that, the parties there had said 'penalty', and the effort was to make out that that really meant liquidated damages; and lastly, if my view of the facts in the present case is correct, then Rigby LJ would have agreed with me, for the last words of his judgment are as follows:

> On the other hand it is stated that, when the damages caused by a breach of contract are incapable of being ascertained, the sum made by the contract payable on such a breach is to be regarded as liquidated damages. The question arises, What is meant in this statement by the expression 'incapable of being ascertained'? In their proper sense the words appear to refer to a case where no rule or measure of damages is available for the guidance of a jury as to the amount of the damages, and a judge would have to tell them they must fix the amount as best they can.

To arrive at the indirect damage in this case, supposing no sum had been stipulated, that is just what a judge would, in my opinion, have had to do.

On the whole matter, therefore, I go with the opinion of Kennedy LJ, and I move your Lordships that the appeal be allowed, and judgment given for the sum as brought out by the Master, the appellants to have their costs in this House and in the Courts below.

Note

A library's terms and conditions of lending state 'each book retained beyond the agreed loan period will be charged at 20p per day for the first week and at 40p per day thereafter'. Is this a penalty clause? Would it make any difference if the figures had been £1 and £2 respectively?

CHAPTER FOUR
DELICTUAL RIGHTS AND DUTIES

In the following extract Jane Stapleton discusses various criteria that might be relevant in deciding whether there should be a duty of care in delict (or in England, tort).

JANE STAPLETON, 'IN RESTRAINT OF TORT'
in Birks (ed.), *The Frontiers of Liability*
vol. 2, p. 90

. . .

Insurance

Recently I have heard appellate judges informally describe the currect incremental approach to tort claims as a reaction to the insurance background of such claims. One impression given is that in certain cases, denying a duty of care is justified because it will not leave future victims uncompensated because they have or could have insured the particular loss. But this argument is as flawed as the earlier reliance by some advocates of *expansion* of liability on the argument that future defendants will not be crippled by the relevant liability because they are or could be insured against that loss. If tort law is to retain an appearance of coherence as a private law mechanism for the vindication of an individual plaintiff's rights against an individual defendant it must be that, as Justice Stephen of the Australian High Court implied, insurance may follow liability but liability need not follow insurance.

Any intended moral or economic incentives of liability are already weakened where insurance exists but predicating the existence of liability on the existence or availability of insurance cuts away any grounds for such incentives. The concept of negligence liability is posited on the defendant's conduct being wrong, a 'wrong', and it is morally incoherent for such a judgement to hinge on the availability of first party insurance to his victim. Just as if liability is treated simply as a gateway to an insurance pool, it fails to provide a reason why anyone ever should lose a tort claim. If liability is denied because the plaintiff could get first party insurance it penalises the cautious and would severely limit the scope of tort recovery since such insurance is available against many forms of actionable loss. The liability of one particular individual to another must be based on reasons other than insurance.

The presence or absence of insurance certainly affects who sues and is sued, but it should not determine who is liable to whom, any more than the wealth or poverty of the parties does. It is certainly not a legitimate factor for inclusion in any agenda of countervailing concerns militating against tort liability.

(c)   The 'correct' spheres of tort and contract: linear liability
Underlying the reining in of liability in negligence seems to be a concern that it had begun to encroach on the legitimate sphere of contract. Thus to grant protection to the plaintiff in *Junior Books* was seen as tantamount to providing it with a warranty of quality for which it had not paid the defendant. The most obvious objection to this is that the very *nature* of tort protection is that it is awarded even where the plaintiff had not paid the defendant for it. Mrs Donoghue was in effect given the protection of a warranty of safety without paying for it. Moreover, in the context of *Junior Books* to say that warranties of quality are the province of contract is mere assertion. A better reason for opposition to that decision needs to be found.

In fact there is, underlying the 'warranty' argument against *Junior Books*, a much stronger and far more general dichotomy, one which does not correspond with the line of privity but is often confused with it, and one which provides a more convincing basis for criticism of that and other expansionary cases. This is the choice the law of obligations has when faced with a sequence of dealings or potential dealings. On the one hand, the law might prefer to simplify the relevant obligations of the parties by imposing them in a linear form. The first party would owe an obligation only to the party next in sequence and that party's obligations in turn would only be owed to the next and so on. In other words, the eventual victim, the plaintiff, would be prevented from leapfrogging a party with whom it had had dealings or could have had dealings in order to sue a distant party. This form of liability is most well known in contract where it is secured by the doctrine of privity. However it is a major and widespread misconception to see this form of liability arrangement as synonymous with a contractual vision of law. It is a form of arrangement also available in tort law. It is a form of arrangement also available in tort law: a tort plaintiff may be refused a claim against a distant party even though the plaintiff does not have (nor reasonably could have had) a contract with another intermediate party so that any protection the plaintiff could fall back on when faced with this refusal is at most a *tort* obligation owed by, say, that intermediate party. Although not yet explicitly recognised in UK law, the 'learned intermediary' doctrine in the US is a good example of this. This doctrine states that so long as the drug manufacturer adequately warns the GP of the products risks, it has discharged its duty to warn and is not liable to a patient injured by the product, who is therefore forced to concentrate his claim, be it in tort or contract, against the GP. The deployment by US *tort* law of this linear form of liability rests on the wholly tenable assumption that patients are far more likely to have been influenced by GP advice than by package inserts from manufacturers. In other product contexts where this assumption about the intermediary's role fails, the law may then revert to the alternative strategy of imposing obligations on manufacturers to distant victims regardless of whether, for example, the manufacturer had adequately warned the intermediary.

Intermediary not a co-tortfeasor
The preferable basis of the criticism of *Junior Books*, then, is that sometimes a linear arrangement of liability may be justified and that, on the facts of that case, this was the situation there. Such a linear arrangement may be justifed even where the intermediary is not negligent. In *Junior Books* the argument would be that given the circumstances it was not unfair to require the commercial plaintiff to seek protection from the party with which it had directly dealt, that is, the main contractor. Instead of relying on bald and unconvincing assertions that warranties of quality are the province of contract not tort, appellate court would be better advised to defend their criticism of *Junior Books* by explaining why, in certain circumstances, it is preferable to channel liability through the sequence of dealings of the parties than to allow the victim to leapfrog the party it had or could have dealt with and sue the negligent creator of the defective property directly. Care would have to be taken here. The 'explanation' cannot simply be the assertion that it is unfair for the defendant subcontractor to have to face obligations other than those owed to parties in privity with him, for this is the privity fallacy.

But reasons can be found here just as they could in the learned intermediary context. The most convincing reason in the circumstances of *Junior Books* is that the plaintiff had had an *appropriate* opportunity to protect itself, either in its dealings with the main contractor or by dealing directly with the sub-contractor. Instead, then, of deriving from the opposition to *Junior Books* a denial of *all* claims against the creator of defective acquired property with respect to its quality, the more convincing deduction is a countervailing factor to liability which refers to the adequacy of the appropriate alternative means of protection available to the plaintiff. Not all avenues of protection are 'appropriate' in this sense. First party insurance, for example, is not. In *Junior Books* the alternative means of protection of bargaining with the contractors were 'appropriate' because this (unlike insurance) would have been likely to generate adequate deterrence incentives on sub-contractors.

Distinctive advantages would follow if appellate courts abandoned their reliance on assertions that certain types of obligation are the province of contract and determined whether a plaintiff should be granted the protection of a tort obligation from a distant defendant on the basis of whether the plaintiff had had an appropriate opportunity to protect itself in its dealings, or potential dealings, with another suitable party. First, some case law would be more intelligible: for example the decision in *Smith* v *Bush* would be compatible with opposition to the decision in *Junior Books*. Secondly, there would be no risk of the reasoning collapsing into some version of the privity fallacy. Thirdly, adequacy of appropriate alternative means of protection is part of a much bigger picture. It is relevant in all situations not just in cases where there is a sequence of parties; and it is an important and effective constraint on the growth of tort law. In particular it would help us to find the demarcation line between plaintiffs to whom the law grants protection not bargained for, and plaintiffs to whom no such help is to be given. It is now appreciated that in many areas this line does not correspond with the no privity/privity line. Plaintiffs technically linked by privity with the defendant may still be given protection while plaintiffs who are strangers to the defendant may yet be refused tort protection. Privity is not the appropriate organising principle here.

Appropriate Alternative Means of Protection
Elsewhere I have noted that imbedded in past caselaw on economic loss there is a concern not to assist plaintiffs who had *certain* alternative means of protection and some recent dicta and caselaw have confirmed the importance of this particular hurdle in both tripartite and bilateral cases. Thus in the recent Canadian case of *Norsk* the powerful dissent of La Forest et al. used this argument to find against the plaintiff in a situation analogous to that of the *Mineral Transporter* case: the plaintiff, who relied on the integrity of the property of a party with whom it had a contractual relationship, suffered economic loss as the result of physical damage caused to that property by the negligence of the defendant. The plaintiff is regarded [on this view] as having in its contractual relationship with the property owner, real (not just nominal) and adequate means of protecting itself from the relevant risk, while appropriately feeding back into a relevant chain of dealings adequate deterrence incentives. Its claim, if any, should therefore be against that party who in turn has a claim against the negligent injurer of the property. . . . (see 4.3.3.2 above).

The following case concerns the range of people to whom a 'negligent misstatement duty of care' might be owed. It provides a good example of the current judicial approach in Scotland, and the reading given by the Scottish judiciary to the mainly English cases.

DAWN A. SMITH v ROSS CARTER
1994 SCLR 539

Facts
The pursuer and a friend (H.A.) bought a flat in Edinburgh. Prior to the purchase the defender, a surveyor who was a friend of H.A., agreed with her that he would, without any charge, inspect the property and submit a report on his inspection to a building society. The pursuer was not a party to this agreement and the defender knew nothing of her involvement in the purchase of the flat. Before completion of the missives for the flat the defender submitted an oral report to H.A. This contained no adverse comments on the state of the flat and, the pursuer averred, the purchase proceeded relying on its terms, The pursuer claimed that the flat had defects which the defender should have discovered in the course of his inspection. She raised an action against him in which she concluded for damages on the ground of his negligence. The defender pleaded that the action was irrelevant as he had owed the pursuer no duty of care. After debate the Lord Ordinary held that the ambit of the defender's duty of care could not be established without evidence being led and allowed a proof before answer, reserving the defender's plea to the relevancy. His opinion, so far as dealing with the question of duty care, was in the following terms.

Lord McCluskey
This case arises out of the purchase by the pursuer and a friend, Helen Alison Aitchison, of a flat in Blackwood Crescent, Edinburgh. The seller was one Elaine Webster and the missives were concluded on 25th June 1990. The purchase price was

£39,500 and the purchasers took entry in August 1990. The purchase of the flat was funded by a loan of £39,500 advanced to the purchasers by the Alliance & Leicester Building Society. Before the offer to purchase was made, the defender, who is a chartered surveyor by profession, agreed, apparently without charge, to inspect the property and to arrange for a written report based on his inspection to be submitted to that building society. Despite the wording of certain averments it is now accepted by the pursuer that the arrangements whereby the defender agreed to inspect the property and to submit a report were made between the defender and Ms Aitchison; the pursuer was not a party to those arrangements and it is not suggested that the defender was informed that she might be involved in the purchasing of the flat. In the written report which the defender prepared for submission to the building society it was stated that the property was found to be in a satisfactory condition. The written report made no mention of any internal structural alterations having been carried out within the flat. The report valued the property at £42,000. However, at the time of the defender's inspection, significant internal alterations had been carried out within the flat. Load-bearing walls had been removed to effect the alterations and it is averred that the alterations had been carried out without building warrant and that they 'do not comply with relevant building regulations'. It is averred by the pursuer that the written report was submitted to the building society 'subsequent to the conclusion of [the] missives'. However, before receiving the written report and concluding the bargain, the said Ms Aitchison had received a verbal report from the defender about the property. The verbal report contained a valuation of £42,000. It is also averred in relation to that verbal report:

> He mentioned in passing that some alterations might have been carried [out] to the flat but said nothing more. He made no adverse comment when giving his verbal report. He said nothing which indicated to the said Alison Aitchison that the carrying out of alterations was of particular significance or was information which she ought to pass on to her solicitors. The said Alison Aitchison attached no significance to what had been said in passing about the possible alterations and did not communicate what the defender had said to the pursuer or the said solicitors. The pursuer and the said solicitors when concluding the said missives relied upon the said valuation and the absence of any adverse comment on the part of the defender in his verbal report.

The solicitors referred to are those who acted for the pursuer and Ms Aitchinson.

In these circumstances, which are narrated on the basis of the pursuer's pleadings, which are taken pro veritate for the purpose of this debate, the pursuer now maintains that the defender was negligent in the carrying out and reporting upon his inspection of the property and that that negligence resulted in a breach of duty owed by the defender to the pursuer. The pursuer also makes certain averments in support of her conclusion for damages in the sum of £5,000.

. . . counsel for both parties were agreed that the principal issue before the court in the present procedure roll debate was the issue as to whether or not it had been relevantly averred that the defender owed any duty to the pursuer. . . . Both parties sought a decision on the main point and, for this purpose, it was accepted that the pursuer at no stage had any direct dealings whatsoever with the defender; the defender's only dealings in relation to the inspection and report were dealings with Ms Aitchinson.

[Counsel for the defender] submitted that the pursuer's pleadings disclosed no duty of care owed by the defender to the pursuer. In particular he referred to the averments which appeared to focus this issue, in article 8 . . . . They read:

At the material time the defender knew or ought to have known that the purpose of his inspection and valuation of the property was to enable a particular prospective purchaser, whether acting alone or along with others, to decide whether to purchase the property and if so at what price. He knew or ought to have known that any report given by him would be relied on by the said Alison Aitchison and anyone interested in purchasing the property with her as well as by any building society to whom he submitted or caused to be submitted a written report to enable the said Alison Aitchison and anyone interested in purchasing the property with her as well as by any building society to whom he submitted or caused to be submitted a written report to enable the said Alison Aitchison and anyone interested in purchasing the property with her to obtain loan finance. The defender in the whole circumstances owed a duty of care to inter alios Alison Aitchison and the pursuer, who was purchasing the property with her.

This, it was submitted, was an unusual case in that valuers were ordinarily instructed not by the prospective purchaser but by the building society or by agents on behalf of the building society. It was accepted that no instructions emanated from the pursuer and that the defender did not know anything of the pursuer. There was, it was submitted, no authority for the existence of a duty of care owed by the defender to the pursuer in these circumstances. This was illustrated by reference to the speeches in *Smith* v *Bush (Eric S.)* [1990] 1 AC 831 and *Caparo Industries plc* v *Dickman* [1990] 2 AC 605. It was submitted, if a professional person supplied another person with a report or certificate or similar document containing a professional assessment and judgment about the thing reported upon and that other person suffered economic loss as a result of acting in reliance upon the report, he could not claim that the author of the report had owed him a duty of care in the preparing of it unless, when he prepared it, the author of the report knew that that other would rely upon it. 'Neighbourhood', in the *Donoghue* v *Stevenson* sense, depended upon knowledge that the other so rely. No duty arose until the person preparing the report was made aware of the other person's potential reliance upon it. Thus it was clear that a person such as the present pursuer, of whom the defender knew nothing when preparing the report or reporting verbally, was not a person to whom the defender owed any duty of care in its preparation. It was not suggested that the necessary knowledge had to extend to the precise identity of the other; what was essential was that the pursuer had to show that, when he made the report, the defender knew or ought to have known that the pursuer was a person who would be likely to act in reliance upon it. Any other rule would result in an *Ultramares* 'liability in an indeterminate amount for an indeterminate time to an indeterminate class' (see *Ultramares Corporation* v *Touche* (1931) 255 NY Rep 170, per Cardozo CJ). *Caparo Industries plc* v *Dickman* illustrated the need for precision in determining the limits of liability for statements which came into the hands of persons with whom the maker of the statements which came into the hands of persons with whom the maker of the statement had no contractual or other direct relationship.

In reply on this main issue [counsel] for the pursuer submitted that his averments were relevant for inquiry. There was, he said, no precise line defined by law between cases where a duty of care could be said to exist and cases where it could be affirmed that no such duty existed. The important thing was to look at the particular circumstances averred. What was averred here was that the defender had accepted an instruction, as a surveyor, to inspect and put a valuation upon a particular house in contemplation of the purchase of that house by Ms Aitchison. It was that very transaction which subsequently took place, albeit the pursuer joined Ms Aitchison as an equal purchaser and acquired a pro indiviso title. It could not be said as a matter of law that the defender owed a duty to Ms Aitchison in relation to this transaction but owed no duty to her co-purchaser. There could be no question of an *Ultramares* type of indeterminate liability in the present case. The duty was owed only to any person or persons who might rely upon the report for the particular transaction which Ms Aitchison had in contemplation when she commissioned the report. There was no hint that the defender would have approached the task in any different manner if he had been informed of the pursuer's potential interest in the transaction. The court should not readily reach a conclusion that the pursuer was not included within the ambit of the duty of care when it was conceded that Ms Aitchison, being a person who the defender could reasonably foresee would rely upon the accuracy of his report, was a person to whom the duty was owed. The identification of the actual purchaser could never be an essential prerequisite of liability. Nor was direct contact between the person relying and the person issuing the report essential. These propositions were illustrated by the two cases referred to and by the many authorities quoted in the speeches in those cases. In particular in the *Hedley Bryne & Co. Ltd* [v *Heller & Partners Ltd* [1964] AC 465] case there discussed the bankers did not know the identity of the possible investor. The *Caparo Industries plc* v *Dickman* case did not itself provide an answer in the present case; but it did set out the approach that had to be taken. [Counsel for the pursuer] then provided detailed references to the speech of Lord Oliver of Aylmerton to demonstrate (a) that knowledge of the actual identity of the person was not necessary; (b) that the court could look not only at the actual knowledge of the defender but at such knowledge as would be attributed to a reasonable person placed as he was placed; and (c) that, therefore, the necessary relationship giving rise to a duty of care might typically be held to exist where (i) the precise purpose of the advice, namely to assist in the making of a decision about a specified commercial transaction, was made known to the adviser; (ii) the adviser was in a position to know that his advice might be shown to or shared with others for use for that very purpose; and (iii) that the advice would be likely to be acted upon for that known purpose without independent inquiry by the person receiving it. These were broad propositions only and all the speeches demonstrated that the court had to look at a number of matters, including foreseeability of damage, proximity and the overriding issue as to whether or not it was 'just and reasonable that the law could impose a duty of a given scope upon the one party for the benefit of the other', per Lord Bridge of Harwich at p. 618 in *Caparo Industries plc* v *Dickman*. Here, given that the transaction from which the pursuer averred she had suffered loss was the very transaction for which the report was prepared, and given that the pursuer was simply a person who had joined Ms Aitchison in that transaction — a not uncommon situation — the circumstances pointed strongly to the existence of a duty. It could hardly be said that the addition of the pursuer to Ms Aitchison as a person to whom the duty was owed would be likely to give rise to any significant additional liability on the part of a negligent surveyor, if indeed ther could be any addition at all. He was liable for such loss as fell to be assessed prima facie by reference to the difference between the market values of the property before and after the discovery that alterations had been carried out without due warrant. Thus the extension of the duty to include the pursuer neither enlarged the loss nor did it alter the content of the duty itself; it in no way had a bearing upon how a surveyor would carry out the task. At the very least, it could not be said at this stage that no such duty could exist in such circumstances. In reply on the point relating to additional liability or loss, [counsel for the defender] drew attention to an averment in article 9 of the condescendence where the pursuer appeared to be claiming solatium. It reads, 'She has suffered and will suffer material inconvenience.' This, it was submitted, was an averment that suggested that the potential liability could be extended if strangers joined in the transaction after the report had been prepared.

The test of relevancy is to be found in *Jamieson* v *Jamieson*, 1952 SC (HL) 44 in the speech of Lord Normand.

The true proposition is that an action will not be dismissed as irrelevant unless it must necessarily fail even if all the pursuer's averments are proved.

In my opinion, in the light of the decisions in the cases referred to and the other cases quoted by Lord Bridge of Harwich in his speech in *Caparo Industries plc* v *Dickman* at p. 617, resulting in the overruling of *Anns* v *Merton London Borough Council* [1978] AC 728, it is very difficult to dismiss as irrelevant a claim for damages for economic loss arising out of alleged carelessness in the preparation by a professional person of a report on the ground that no duty of care was owed to the person suffering the loss, except where it is absolutely clear on the pursuer's pleadings that no such duty could have been owed. It does not appear to me that that exacting test can be met in the present case. I am not prepared to affirm as a matter of general law that, in all circumstances, a surveyor who is instructed by an individual to carry out an inspection of property which that individual is considering buying owes no duty in the preparation and submission of his report of the inspection to any person who may join with the prospective purchaser in effecting the purchase. It cannot be uncommon for one person such as a relative or a friend who has some relevant experience in the property market to be acting as the undisclosed agent for another or as the spokesperson for a group interested in a possible property transaction; but not every such agent or spokesperson would consider that it was necessary to reveal to all and sundry who else was interested in the particular transaction. Indeed it might be that the precise interest of the others might not be fully known at the early stages, for example, when the professional person is invited to report. It is a very important feature of the present case that the transaction which it is said gave rise to the pursuer's loss is the very transaction which the defender is averred to have had in contemplation when he accepted instructions to make the report. The transaction in question was one in which Ms Aitchison would enter into a contract to purchase the property. She did. Nothing in the present case suggested that including the pursuer within the ambit of the duty of care would give rise to an *Ultramares* type of indeterminate liability, which the courts have always resisted. Indeed prima facie the liability will be exactly the same, albeit there may be more than one person entitled to a share of the damages that reflect that liability. In this respect it appears to me that, given the concession by counsel for the pursuer that the true measure of loss is prima facie to be made by reference to differences in the market value, it follows that the claim that the pursuer has suffered and will suffer material inconvenience is not an admissible claim, but I shall deal with that later. I am not able to affirm that a surveyor, when invited by one person to provide him with a report for the purposes of considering the wisdom of a particular house-purchase transaction, owes no duty of care to persons who might join with the known prospective purchaser in effecting the purchase. It is therefore necessary to reserve any judgment on the main question of ambit of the duty of care, so far as affecting this particular case, until after a proof before answer.

The following extract considers certain implications of the restrictive approach to certain types of economic losses (see 4.3.2 above).

MacQueen, 'The Future of Liability for Defective Buildings: the Law After : *Murphy* v *Brentwood D.C.* 1990 SLT 337'

Collateral warranties and duty of care agreements

A recurring theme in House of Lords judgments in economic loss cases is that such loss can only be recovered between contracting parties (see in *Murphy*, Lord Keith at

p. 427 and Lord Bridge at p. 436). As the House has denied negligence recovery in respect of defective buildings to developers and commercial occupiers, so it has become common for such parties to insist upon the provision by architects, engineers, contractors and subcontractors of so called collateral warranties or duty of care agreements, by which contractual obligations at least equivalent to those formerly imposed in negligence are undertaken by the grantors in respect of their contribution to the project. The warranties are collateral because they run alongside the often complex structure of contracts under which the actual construction work is carried out. The obligations undertaken may go further than those under the principal contracts, having the effect of guaranteeing that the building will be fit for its purpose, rather than merely requiring care and skill. A typical clause will state that no deleterious materials will be used; unless carefully confined, such clauses have the potential to go well beyond the scope of any negligence liability at common law. In the absence of provision to the contrary, the warranty may be assigned by the grantee, opening up liability to subsequent occupiers unknown to the grantor at any stage during his involvement at the project. All this means that contractual liability for defective buildings could reach even more widely than did negligence liability, and there is nothing in *Murphy* to prevent that.

PRESCRIPTION AND LIMITATION (SCOTLAND) ACT 1973

6. Extinction of obligations by prescriptive periods of five years

(1) If, after the appropriate date, an obligation to which this section applies has subsisted for a continuous period of five years —

    (a) without any relevant claim having been made in relation to the obligation, and

    (b) without the subsistence of the obligation having been relevantly acknowledged;

then as from the expiration of that period the obligation shall be extinguished:

17. Actions in respect of personal injuries not resulting in death

(1) This section applies to an action of damages where the damages claimed consist of or include damages in respect of personal injuries, being an action (other than an action to which section 18 of this Act applies) brought by the person who sustained the injuries or any other person.

(2) Subject to subsection (3) below and section 19A of this Act, no action to which this section applies shall be brought unless it is commenced within a period of 3 years after —

    (a) the date on which the injuries were sustained or, where the act or omission to which the injuries were attributable was a continuing one, that date or the date on which the act or omission ceased, whichever is the later; or

    (b) the date (if later than any date mentioned in paragraph (a) above) on which the pursuer in the action became, or on which, in the opinion of the court, it would have been reasonably practicable for him in all the circumstances to become, aware of all the following facts —

        (i) that the injuries in question were sufficiently serious to justify his bringing an action of damages on the assumption that the person against whom the action was brought did not dispute liability and was able to satisfy a decree;

        (ii) that the injuries were attributable in whole or in part to an act or omission; and

        (iii) that the defender was a person to whose act or omission the injuries were attributable in whole or in part or the employer or principal of such a person.

(3)   In the computation of the period specified in subsection (2) above there shall be disregarded any time during which the person who sustained the injuries was under legal disability by reason of nonage or unsoundness of mind.

18.   Actions where death has resulted from personal injuries

(1)   This section applies to any action in which, following the death of any person from personal injuries, damages are claimed in respect of the injuries or the death.

(2)   Subject to subsections (3) and (4) below and section 19A of this Act, no action to which this section applies shall be brought unless it is commenced within a period of 3 years after —

(a)   the date of death of the deceased; or

(b)   the date (if later than the date of death) on which the pursuer in the action became, or on which, in the opinion of the court, it would have been reasonably practicable for him in all the circumstances to become, aware of both of the following facts —

(i)   that the injuries of the deceased were attributable in whole or in part to an act or omission; and

(ii)   that the defender was a person to whose act or omission the injuries were attributable in whole or in part or the employer or principal of such a person.

(3)   Where the pursuer is a relative of the deceased, there shall be disregarded in the computation of the period specified in subsection (2) above any time during which the relative was under legal disability by reason of nonage or unsoundness of mind.

(4)   Subject to section 19A of this Act, where an action of damages has not been brought by or on behalf of a person who has sustained personal injuries within the period specified in section 17(2) of this Act and that person subsequently dies in consequence of those injuries, no action to which this section applies shall be brought in respect of those injuries or the death from those injuries.

22A.   Ten years' prescription of obligations under the Consumer Protection Act 1987

(1)   An obligation arising from liability under section 2 of the 1987 Act (to make reparation for damage caused wholly or partly by a defect in a product) shall be extinguished if a period of 10 years has expired from the relevant time, unless a relevant claim was made within that period and has not been finally disposed of, and no such obligation shall come into existence after the expiration of the said period.

(2)   If, at the expiration of the period of 10 years mentioned in subsection (1) above, a relevant claim has been made but has not been finally disposed of, the obligation to which the claim relates shall be extinguished when the claim is finally disposed of.

(3)   In this section a claim is finally disposed of when —

(a)   a decision disposing of the claim has been made against which no appeal is competent;

(b)   an appeal against such a decision is competent with leave, and the time limit for leave has expired and no application has been made or leave has been refused;

(c)   leave to appeal against such a decision is granted or is not required, and no appeal is made within the time limit for appeal; or

(d)   the claim is abandoned;

'relevant claim' in relation to an obligation means a claim made by or on behalf of the creditor for implement or part implement of the obligation, being a claim made —

(a)   in appropriate proceedings within the meaning of section 4(2) of this Act; or

(b)   by the presentation of, or the concurring in, a petition for sequestration or by the submission of a claim under section 22 or 48 of the Bankruptcy (Scotland) Act 1985; or

(c)   by the presentation of, or the concurring in, a petition for the winding up of a company or by the submission of a claim in a liquidation in accordance with the rules made under section 411 of the Insolvency Act 1986;
'relevant time' has the meaning given in section 4(2) of the 1987 Act.

(4)   Where a relevant claim is made in an arbitration, and the nature of the claim has been stated in a preliminary notice (within the meaning of section 4(4) of this Act) relating to that arbitration, the date when the notice is served shall be taken for those purposes to be the date of the making of the claim.

22B.   Three year limitation of actions under the Consumer Protection Act 1987

(1)   This section shall apply to an action to enforce an obligation arising from liability under section 2 of the 1987 Act (to make reparation for damage caused wholly or partly by a defect in a product), except where section 22C of this Act applies.

(2)   Subject to subsection (4) below, an action to which this section applies shall not be competent unless it is commenced within the period of 3 years after the earliest date on which the person seeking to bring (or a person who could at an earlier date have brought) the action was aware, or on which, in the opinion of the court, it was reasonably practicable for him in all the circumstances to become aware, of all the facts mentioned in subsection (3) below.

(3)   The facts referred to in subsection (2) above are —

    (a)   that there was a defect in a product;

    (b)   that the damage was caused or partly caused by the defect;

    (c)   that the damage was sufficiently serious to justify the pursuer (or other person referred to in subsection (2) above) in bringing an action to which this section applies on the assumption that the defender did not dispute liability and was able to satisfy a decree;

    (d)   that the defender was a person liable for the damage under the said section 2.

(4)   In the computation of the period of 3 years mentioned in subsection (2) above, there shall be disregarded any period during which the person seeking to bring the action was under legal disability by reason of nonage or unsoundness of mind.

(5)   The facts mentioned in subsection (3) above do not include knowledge of whether particular facts and circumstances would or would not, as a matter of law, result in liability for damage under the said section 2.

(6)   Where a person would be entitled, but for this section, to bring an action for reparation other than one in which the damages claimed are confined to damages for loss of or damage to property, the court may, if it seems to it equitable to do so, allow him to bring the action notwithstanding this section.

22C.   Actions under the Consumer Protection Act 1987 where death has resulted from personal injuries

(1)   This section shall apply to an action to enforce an obligation arising from liability under section 2 of the 1987 Act (to make reparation for damage caused wholly or partly by a defect in a product) where a person has died from personal injuries and the damages claimed include damages for those personal injuries or that death.

(2)   Subject to subsection (4) below, an action to which this section applies shall not be competent unless it is commenced within the period of 3 years after the later of —

    (a)   the date of death of the injured person;

    (b)   the earliest date on which the person seeking to make (or a person who could at an earlier date have made) the claim was aware, or on which, in the opinion of the court, it was reasonably practicable for him in all the circumstances to become aware —

    (i)   that there was a defect in the product;

    (ii)   that the injuries of the deceased were caused (or partly caused) by the defect; and

    (iii)   that the defender was a person liable for the damage under the said section 2.

(3)   Where the person seeking to make the claim is a relative of the deceased, there shall be disregarded in the computation of the period mentioned in subsection (2) above any period during which that relative was under legal disability by reason of nonage or unsoundness of mind.

(4)   Where an action to which section 22B of this Act applies has not been brought within the period mentioned in subsection (2) of that section and the person subsequently dies in consequence of his injuries, an action to which this section applies shall not be competent in respect of those injuries or that death.

(5)   Where a person would be entitled, but for this section, to bring an action for reparation other than one in which the damages claimed are confined to damages for loss of or damage to property, the court may, if it seems to it equitable to do so, allow him to bring the action notwithstanding this section.

(6)   In this section 'relative' has the same meaning as in the Damages (Scotland) Act 1976.

(7)   For the purposes of subsection (2)(b) above there shall be disregarded knowledge of whether particular facts and circumstances would or would not, as a matter of law, result in liability for damage under the said section 2.

Notes

(1)   Section 6 applies *inter alia* to obligations arising from a breach of contract or from the commission of a delict which does not cause personal injury or death (see *Miller* v *City of Glasgow DC* 1989 SLT 44). For a fuller discussion of the concepts of 'relevant claim' and obligations being 'relevantly acknowledged' see Gloag and Henderson, 'Introduction to the Law of Scotland', at p. 190 *et seq.*

(2)   Sections 17 and 18 were substituted by the Prescription and Limitation (Scotland) Act 1984, s. 2.

(3)   Sections 17 and 18 cover liability for breaches of contract or the commission of delicts which cause personal injury or death. The 'three-year rule' is qualified by s. 18(2) by reference to s. 19A, which gives the court power to disregard lapse of time where it is equitable to do so. When do you think such a power might be exercised?

(4)   Sections 22A to 22C were added by the Consumer Protection Act 1987 and apply to all actions arising under that Act.

RHM BAKERIES (SCOTLAND) LTD v STRATHCLYDE REGIONAL COUNCIL
1985 SLT 3

Lord Fraser of Tullybelton

This appeal raises a question as to the principle on which the owner or occupier of land in Scotland (the defender) is liable at common law for damage to his neighbour's land caused by an agency, in this case sewage, which escapes from an artificial work on the defender's land.

The appellants (defenders), are a local authority responsible for sewerage in a large area of Scotland including Glasgow. I shall refer to them as 'the local authority'. The respondents (pursuers) are a company which operates a bakery in Paton Street, Glasgow. I shall refer to them as 'R.H.M.' On 28 September 1978, there was heavy rainfall in Glasgow and R.H.M.'s bakery in Paton Street was flooded. The cause of the flooding was that a main brick sewer in Paton Street, which was under the operation and control of the local authority, had collapsed about a fortnight earlier and had not been repaired, so that on 28 September it did not effectively drain the area. The precise cause of the collapse is not known. The case has been argued throughout, on both sides, on the footing that the bakery was flooded not only by rainwater from the street, but also, and indeed mainly, by sewage from the blocked sewer, although that is not specifically averred. R.H.M. claim damages from the local authority at common law and also under the provisions of the Sewerage (Scotland) Act 1968. In their common law case, they do not aver that the damage to their bakery was caused by any fault on the part of the local authority, either in failing to take reasonable care to maintain the sewer, or in failing to repair it promptly after it had collapsed, or in any other way. Their case at common law on record is that the flooding was, or possibly was caused by, a nuisance for which the local authority are 'strictly liable'. Their case under the Sewerage (Scotland) Act 1968 is that by s. 2 of that Act the local authority were under a duty to maintain the sewer, and that 'said duty [was] absolute'. A faint attempt was made by counsel for R.H.M. to argue that his pleadings were sufficient to found a case of fault at least by relying on the brocard *res ipsa loquitur*. In my opinion the attempt was hopeless on the pleadings as they stand, and we were not moved to allow them to be amended. The pleadings are not well drawn. Nevertheless, inelegant as the pleadings are, the judgments of both courts below show that there has never been any doubt about the issues between the parties. The first issue is, and has always been, whether the local authority are liable at common law for the damage caused by flooding, even if it occurred without fault on their part, or whether they are only liable if they were to some extent at fault.

The doubt about whether culpa is the essential basis in Scots law for the liability of the proprietor of land to a neighbour arises from the fact that the English decision in *Rylands* v *Fletcher* has sometimes been referred to as if it were authoritative in Scotland. In my opinion, with all respect to eminent judges who have referred to it in that way, it has no place in Scots law, and the suggestion that it has, is a heresy which ought to be extirpated. The facts in *Rylands* v *Fletcher* were very similar to those in *Kerr* v *Earl of Orkney*, which had been decided 10 years earlier but which does not seem to have been referred to in the argument. In *Rylands* v *Fletcher* this House applied a rule of strict libility to the duties owed by a landowner to his neighbours. The rule was stated at its highest by Lord Cranworth at p. 340. It is not necessary for the present purpose to inquire fully into the historical reasons for applying that rule although it appears from Vol. 8 of Sir William Holdsworth's *A History of English Law* (2nd edn 1937) at pp. 446, 465, that it was based on the medieval principle that a man acts at his peril, and incurs absolute liability for damage caused by an act which comes within one of the forms of action, even though the damage is the result of pure accident. That principle which is (or was in 1868) still applicable to acts which infringed another person's possession of land never formed part of Scots law, where liability has, I think, always depended on culpa.

OCCUPIERS' LIABILITY (SCOTLAND) ACT 1960

2. Extent of occupier's duty to show care

(1) The care which an occupier of premises is required, by reason of his occupation or control of the premises, to show towards a person entering thereon in

respect of dangers which are due to the state of the premises or to anything done or omitted to be done on them and for which the occupier is in law responsible shall, except in so far as he is entitled to and does extend, restrict, modify or exclude by agreement his obligations towards that person, be such care as in all the circumstances of the case is reasonable to see that that person will not suffer injury or damage by reason of any such danger.

(2) Nothing in the foregoing subsection shall relieve an occupier of premises of any duty to show in any particular case any higher standard of care which in that case is incumbent on him by virtue of any enactment or rule of law imposing special standards of care on particular classes of persons.

(3) Nothing in the foregoing provisions of this Act shall be held to impose on an occupier any obligation to a person entering on his premises in respect of risks which that person has willingly accepted as his; and any question whether a risk was so accepted shall be decided on the same principles as in other cases in which one person owes to another a duty to show care.

Note
Fred contracts with Joe (an electrician) to refit his shop. Joe places a sign reading 'Danger' outside a cupboard where there are exposed wires. Pat, a nosey customer of Fred's, ignores the notice and opens the door. There is an explosion and Pat is injured. Is Fred liable under the Occupiers' Liability (Scotland) Act 1960? (See 3.10.6.1 and 4.10.1.2 above.)

CHAPTER FIVE
THE LAW OF AGENCY

The materials that follow can only highlight a few of the issues raised by the agency relationship. They concentrate on the creation of the relationship and on the question of the agent's authority. In the first case we can see that the courts will apply strict rules in deciding whether an agent/principal relationship exists at all. A similarly strict approach is taken on when ratification may occur. Lord President Dunedin's surprisingly colloquial 'heads I win, tails you lose' explains why.

GOODALL v BILSLAND
1909 SC 1152

Lord President Dunedin
This was a mandate which, upon its terms, limited Mr Kyle's authority — I will not say limited, but never gave Mr Kyle authority — to do more than appear at the Licensing Court, and . . . consequently, when he lodged an appeal in these parties' names, he did an entirely unauthorised act.

Well, now, what is the result of that? I think the result is that there were in law no proceedings at all, because what the Act [Licensing (Scotland) Act 1903, s. 22] says is . . . 'it shall be lawful . . . to appeal . . . to the next Court of Appeal from such Licensing Court: Provided always that such appeal shall be lodged with the clerk to such Court of Appeal within ten days after such proceeding. . . .' Now, it is certain that within ten days of such proceeding there was no note of appeal lodged by the persons qualified. . . . The only thing that was done was that a note of appeal was lodged for them by an unauthorised person, Mr Kyle. . . .

Now, it is said, and it was argued very strenuously, that although Mr Kyle had no authority when he lodged the appeal his proceedings were homologated afterwards.

Now, it is first of all necessary to see exactly what homologation in this case means. Homologation in this case means that, after the whole thing was over and when this case of reduction was raised, then the parties in whose names the appeal was taken are asked, in the action of reduction, whether they approved of everything that Mr Kyle did, and they said, 'Oh, certainly we do'. Well, that is homologation of a very easy character. It is homologation — I am afraid it is not a very judicial expression, but it expresses it better than any other phrase — of the 'heads I win tails you lose' character, because it is homologation after you perfectly well know that the case has been decided in your favour . . . .

It seems to me that the gentleman here who got his licence was entitled to hold that licence unless within the ten days a note of appeal was lodged by a person authorised to lodge that note of appeal; that no such person was here in this case; and that consequently the whole proceedings were *funditus* null and void.

Note

(1)   *Goodall* v *Bilsland* illustrates not only that power of attorney or mandate will be strictly construed by the courts but additionally that it is not enough that the agent acts in time; (where there is as here a time limit) the principal must ratify in time also, for the ratification to be effective (see also *Dibbins* v *Dibbins* [1896] 2 Ch 348).

The case below highlights a potential problem for those who supply goods, services or finance to 'company directors' in pre-incorporation contracts. The Companies Act 1985, s. 36 will be of assistance, however.

TINNEVELLY SUGAR REFINING CO LTD v MIRLEES, WATSON AND YARYAN CO LTD
(1894) 21 R 1009

Facts
Darley and Butler, acting on behalf of a then unincorporated company (the pursuers), entered into a contract with the defenders for the supply of machinery. The company, by then incorporated, raised an action for damages on the grounds that the machinery was defective.

Lord President Robertson
The pursuers of this action are the Tinnevelly Sugar Refining Company, Limited, with consent and concurrence of Messrs Darley & Butler for all right and interest they may have in the premises. The fact that Messrs Darley & Butler thus appear, not merely as consenting to the instance of the company, but as themselves pursuers, has no practical importance; for in this action of damages no averment is made that that firm has suffered damage. The action is therefore the action of the Tinnevelly Company Limited.

Now, against this action the defenders' first plea is, 'No title to sue.' . . .

The company was registered on 29 July 1890, and accordingly was not in existence at the date of the contract. It is therefore legally impossible that the contract can bind the company, unless the company since its registration, has in some way acquired the rights and submitted itself to the obligations of the contract. Accordingly, the defenders are in the right when they say that the question is, Do the pursuers set forth, on this record, anything done by the company itself which has this result? I have carefully examined the condescendence, and must answer this question in the negative. . . .

They begin by saying that when Darley & Butler contracted with the defenders they were acting, and were known by the defenders to be acting, as agents for the Tinnevelly Company. This is the basis of the pursuers' case. It is in law an untenable position, for Darley & Butler could not be the agents of a non-existent company. I should infer from the record that the persons acting for the company had not realised this. Accordingly, it is quite consistent with the record to suppose that the persons acting for the company were unaware that if the company was to take the place of Darley & Butler it require, that is to say, the shareholders or their executive required, consciously to do so. In place of any such overt action on the part of the company things were allowed to rest on the original contract between Darley & Butler and the defenders, which was erroneously believed to bind the company. . . .

Well, now, the law applicable to such a case seems to be tolerably clear. First of all, where there is no principal there can be no agent; there having been no Tinnevelly Company at the date of this contract, Darley & Butler were not agents of that company in entering into the contract. The next point is that, in order to bind the company to a contract not incumbent on it, it is necessary that the company should voluntarily so contract; and it is not equivalent to this if the company merely acts as if, contrary to the fact, the contract had from the beginning been obligatory on it . . .

I am for finding that the pursuers have not set forth on record any title in the Tinnevelly Sugar Refining Company, Limited, to sue.

Note
(1) What type of danger does this decision highlight for people setting up in business as a registered company? See 2.3.2 above.

Lawton LJ says in the case below that the commercial agent has a precarious existence, depending as he does on his principal for his remuneration. Usually this will present no problem, but a not uncommon scenario is where the agent 'sets up' the contract (as requested by the principal), the principal is then unwilling or unable to contract and is also unwilling (or unable) to pay the agent's fee or commission. This is an issue that should ideally be agreed at the formation of the principal–agent relationship. In the absence of such agreement the case below may give some guidance.

ALPHA TRADING LTD v DUNNSHAW-PATTEN LTD
[1981] 1 All ER 482

Facts
The plaintiffs and the defendants were international traders who entered into a contract whereby in consideration of the plaintiffs introducing to the defendants a buyer for 10,000 tonnes of cement at $49.50 per tonne the defendants agreed to pay the plaintiffs commission on the sale at the rate of $1.50 per tonne and also to make certain other payments. The plaintiffs duly introduced a buyer for the cement and the defendants and the buyer entered into a contract for the quantity and at the price envisaged. The buyer opened a letter of credit and the defendants provided the buyer with a 3 per cent performance bond but, the defendants later being unable or unwilling to provide the cement, the contract of sale was never implemented and the buyer was released from its obligation to pay the purchase price. The plaintiffs claimed to be entitled to be paid the commission agreed under the agency contract or, alternatively, damages for breach of an implied term in the agency contract that the defendants would not break their contract with the buyer and thereby deprive the

plaintiffs of the commission. The defendants denied that any term was to be implied in the agency contract and contended that the commission only became payable if the purchase price became payable, and since it had not they were not liable for the commission. The judge rejected the plaintiffs' direct claim for commission but held that there was an implied term in the agency contract that the defendants would not break their contract with the buyer and that the plaintiffs were entitled to damages for breach of that implied term. The defendants appealed.

Templeman LJ

The agents claim damages on the grounds that the vendors are in breach of an implied term in the contract between the agents and the vendors, an implied term that the vendors would perform their contract with the purchaser so as to become entitled to the purchase price out of which the commission was to be paid.

The vendors deny that any term is to be implied. By repudiating their contract with the purchaser, they painlessly released themselves from their contract with the agents.

Counsel for the defendant vendors submitted that there was no room or necessity for any implied term. The commission was only payable out of the purchase price paid by the purchaser. The purchase price was never paid. Therefore, the commission never became payable.

In the present case, the agents performed their part of their bargain with the vendors by providing a purchaser who was ready and willing to contract with the vendors. The vendors utilised and took advantage of the services provided by the agents by entering into a contract with the purchaser on terms acceptable to the vendors and, no doubt, designed and intended by the vendors to produce a profit for themselves.

In my judgment, it is necessary to imply a term to prevent the vendors from making use of the agents' services without being under any liability to the agents to ensure, so far as the vendors were concerned, that the agents then received the stipulated reward for the agents' services, which were supplied to and utilised by the vendors. An agent does not provide services and agree to accept and postpone payment for his services restricted to the purchase price on terms that the vendor, who accepts, exploits and makes use of the agent's services, is free to deprive the agent of the reward promised for the services of the agent if the vendor thinks fit to do so. If there was no implied term in the present case, the vendors could have sold their cement to the purchaser provided by the agents if the market price of cement went down, thus increasing the benefit of the contract with the purchaser so far as the vendors were concerned.

Counsel for the defendants relied on *Luxor (Eastbourne) Ltd v Cooper* . . . In that case the House of Lords held that a promise to pay a commission on completion of a sale did not imply an obligation on the vendor to enter into any contract for sale. The position would have been different if the vendor, as in the present case, not only received the benefit of the agent's work in finding a purchaser but also made use of the agent's services by entering into a contract which bound that purchaser for the benefit of the vendor on terms acceptable to and dictated by the vendor.

Lord Wright said that the result is different 'if the negotiations between the vendor and the purchaser have been duly concluded and a binding executory agreement has been achieved'. . . . It is true that he then refers to specific performance which was relevant to the facts in the *Luxor* case, which dealt with real property. For myself, I can see no sensible distinction between an agency contract relating to the sale of real property and other agency contracts for present purposes.

Similarly, Lord Wright said that different considerations would apply if a contract had been entered into. He said . . .

It cannot have been contemplated that, when a binding contract with the purchaser has been made on the agent's mediation, the principal can, as between himself and the agent, break that contract without breaking his contract with the agent.

Adapting those words to the present circumstances, it cannot have been contemplated that when a binding contract with the purchaser had been made on the agents' mediation, the vendors, as principals, could as between themselves and the agents break that contract with the purchaser without breaking their contract with the agents.

The result which I have reached is consistent with the dicta of Lord Wright in the *Luxor* case, and also with the decision of Rowlatt J in *Vulcan Car Agency Ltd* v *Fiat Motors Ltd* (1915) 32 TLR 73. The result is also consistent with the dissenting judgment of Scrutton LJ, later upheld by the House of Lords, in *George Trollope & Sons* v *Martyn Brothers* [1934] 2 KB 436 at 445-446, and with the observations of Denning LJ in *Dennis Reed Ltd* v *Goody* [1950] 1 All ER 919 at 923, [1950] 2 KB 277 at 285 . . .

. . . In the present case, I can see no uncertainty, no difficulty and no hardship in implying a term that, if the principal enters into a contract with a third party procured by the agents, then the principal agrees that he will not deprive the agent of his commission by committing a breach of the contract which releases the third party from his obligation to pay the purchase price which is the sole agreed source of the agent's commission.

In my judgment, it is necessary to imply a term in the present case because no agent would agree and no principal would attempt to insist that the principal should be able to take the benefit of the agent's work and the advantages of the contract with the third party and yet retain the right to defeat the agent's claim for commission by breaking his contractual obligations to the third party.

I would dismiss the appeal.

Note
How might this decision affect someone who uses the services of an estate agent to sell his property? It has become increasingly common to use the services of an estate agent to sell property. Once the agent has introduced prospective purchasers there may be a temptation to 'edge out' the agent and deal directly with the purchaser. The main aim is, of course, to avoid paying the agent's commission. As we saw above, whether this will succeed will depend on the terms of the contract. The courts will usually take the view that the agent (in the absence of contrary contractual provision) will be entitled to be paid if the sale was achieved through his efforts. The case below is an example of an agent claiming payment, although not involved in the ultimate sale.

WALKER, FRASER AND STEELE v FRASER'S TRUSTEES
1910 SC 222

Facts
The pursuers were employed by one Fraser to sell his estate. A prospective purchaser, Scott, who had enquired after another property, was also sent details of Fraser's estate.

Three years later Scott specifically asked for details of Fraser's estate but in spite of the pursuers' urgings, he made no move to purchase it. The following year Scott, who had advertised for a property, received details of the Fraser estate, from Fraser, in response to his advertisement. Scott subsequently bought the estate. Walker, Fraser and Steele claimed the commission on the sale.

Lord Dundas
Shortly put, I think the test is whether or not the ultimate sale of Balfunning was brought about, or materially contributed to, by actings of the pursuers, as authorised agents of the defender. Actual introduction of the purchaser to the seller is not a necessary element in a case of this sort; it is enough if the agents introduce the purchaser to the estate, and by their efforts contribute in a substantial degree to the sale. A careful consideration of the evidence leads me to hold that the pursuers have sufficiently complied with the test indicated. . . .

It was through the pursuers that Mr Scott first really got into touch with this estate, and got full information and particulars about it; and that they did not effect an actual introduction between him and the defender was only due to the facts that Mr Scott did not permit them to disclose his name in any way, and that he did not choose, at the pursuers' invitation, to submit an offer. It seems to me that the facts of this case bring it well within the region in which property agents have been found entitled to a commission upon a resulting sale. I think the fair inference to be drawn by the Court, viewing the matter as a jury, from the evidence, is that the pursuers' exertions, as duly authorised agents in the matter for the defender, did to a sufficient extent contribute to the ultimate purchase of the estate by Mr Scott. We should therefore, in my judgment, give decree for the pursuers.

Note
(1)   Do you think that the pursuers had, as Lord Dundas said, 'contributed in a substantial degree to the sale'?

One reason for using an agent is that the principal cannot physically carry out a particular task (as in *Copland* below), or because the principal lacks some specialist skill needed for the task (as in *Chaudry*). In either case the agent will be expected to exercise reasonable care. This will apply whether or not the agent is paid, as can be seen from the two cases below.

COPLAND v BROGAN
1916 SC 277

The Lord Justice-Clerk (Scott-Dickson) (at p. 282)
With regard to the English authorities which have been quoted, I have difficulty in accepting them as being in conformity with the law of Scotland, and I do not agree that the same rule of law as applies to gratuitous obligations under English law can be held as applying in this case. According to Bell's *Principles*, there is an obligation on the depositary to 'keep the thing with reasonable care,' and the editor of the last edition of that work states that reasonable care in the case of a gratuitous depositary means 'such care as a man of common prudence generally exercises about his own property of like description.' Now, the packet having gone astray while it was in the defender's custody, the *onus*, in my opinion, rests on him to explain how this happened or at least to show that he exercised the necessary reasonable care. Here the explanation given did not, in my opinion, sufficiently discharge the defender of responsibility for the loss of the packet. The consequences would be most unfortunate if we were to hold that it did. On the defender's own statements, and on the other evidence in the case, there is enough to shew that the defender, in executing his commission, did not exercise the care which a prudent man would have taken with regard to a valuable packet of this kind.

CHAUDHRY v PRABHAKAR AND ANOTHER
[1988] 3 All ER 718

Stuart-Smith LJ
I cannot accept this. The degree of skill and care owed by a gratuitous agent is stated to be — 'such skill and care as persons ordinarily exercise in their own affairs or, where the agent has expressly or impliedly held himself out to his principal as possessing skill adequate to the performance of a particular undertaking, such skill and care as would normally be shown by one possessing that skill'.

. . . For my part I would prefer to state an agent's duty and care as that which may reasonably be expected of him in all circumstances.

Note
(1) From what Stuart-Smith LJ says it would seem that the liability of gratuitous agents is very similar in Scotland and England. 'Gross negligence', which seemed to be a requirement before there would be liability in England, seems to have been dispensed with in this case. There seems to be little difference between Stuart-Smith's person exercising the degree of skill that persons ordinarily do and Scott-Dickson's 'man of common prudence'.

The nature and extent of the agent's authority is at the heart of the relationship between principal and agent, principal and third party, agent and third party. It was said in *Laing* v *Provincial Homes Investment Co* 1909 SC 812, that whether or not an agent has particular authority is a question of fact in each case. Of the different types of authority (actual, ostensible, presumed) ostensible probably causes the most difficulty. The case that follows indicate judicial thinking on the matter, while the article by Reynolds gives an academic analysis.

INTERNATIONAL SPONGE IMPORTERS LTD v WATT & SONS
1911 SC(HL)57

Facts
A commercial traveller employed by the pursuers had over many years sold sponges to the defenders who were saddlers. Payment was supposed to be made direct to the pursuers but was on occasion paid by crossed cheque in favour of the pursuers to the traveller. The sponges were sold on six months' credit. The traveller, Cohen, hatched a fraudulent scheme in association with two other employees. He on several occasions persuaded the defender to pay him either by cheque made out to himself or on one occasion in gold and notes. He justified this to the defenders by representing to them that immediate payment in one of these forms would entitle them to a 'specially cheap' price. The monies paid to Cohen were never remitted to the pursuers. The pursuers invoices stated that the only acceptable means of payment was by crossed cheque made out to themselves. When the fraud came to light the pursuers sought to recover the sum defrauded from the defenders.

Lord Chancellor
. . . It is a peculiar case. The Sponge Company employed an agent named Cohen, who proved to be a rogue. His authority was to carry round with him parcels of sponges, to sell them and fix the price, to deliver them, and to receive cheques in payment. He had dealt with Messrs Watt for a considerable time, and generally — nearly always in fact — Messrs Watt paid for the sponges they bought by crossed

cheque payable to Cohen's principals. In 1904, however, if not earlier, Cohen commenced a system of fraud. He sold and delivered sponges to Messrs Watt as before, but on four occasions he induced them to pay at once, either by open cheque payable to Cohen or by coin and notes, and then embezzled the money. The International Sponge Company now say that these four transactions were beyond Cohen's authority, and this action relates to three of the transactions. . . .

It is clear that Cohen had no actual authority to receive in payment for sponges anything except crossed cheques in favour of the pursuers. It is not, however, established that Messrs Watt had express notice that, while he might receive payment, such payment could only be in the way of crossed cheque in the pursuers' favour. There is a printed direction in the form of account usually rendered, relating both to payment by cheque and to the form of receipt. It is, however, partly equivocal, for it admits of a construction which allows of payment in cash, and in such case would dispense with the prescribed form of receipt. Still I am impressed by Mr Buckmaster's argument that, whatever the notice may be, Messrs Watt had no right to pay so large a sum as £120 in notes or gold, as they did on one occasion, or to pay by open cheque payable to Cohen, as they did in the three incriminated transactions, because that was not in the ordinary course of business. And the excuses invented by Cohen to induce the defenders to pay in that way were flimsy enough. I should be very sorry to affirm as a general proposition that such payments to a traveller are to be upheld.

What determines me, though not without doubt, in upholding these payments in the present case is this. The good faith and integrity of Messrs Watt are undisputed and indisputable. Cohen occupied a position of fuller authority than is usual. The only limit of his actual authority was as to the kind of cheque he might receive. And, finally, it is clear that on one occasion, a year or so before the last transactions, Messrs Watt had paid by open cheque payable to Cohen, and, though the attention of the Sponge Company was drawn to the sale and a question arose about it between them and Messrs Watt, yet it was allowed to stand and no objection was taken.

In the same way, the later transactions passed at the time without complaint or objection, and it was only after Cohen's dishonesty had been discovered that, on investigation of his frauds, the responsible managers of the pursuers' business found that their traveller had sold and delivered these sponges and received payment for them himself.

No doubt the reason of this protracted oversight was that the pursuers were the victims of a conspiracy among their own staff. Books had been falsified, auditors deceived, and documents concealed, so that the responsible managers were not aware of Cohen's dishonest dealings or of his departure from his instructions. But the same conspiracy which cheated them had also the result of misleading the defenders, Messrs Watt, and causing them to act as though Cohen was entitled to receive payment in the manner in which they made it.

Lord Shaw

. . . In short, I do not doubt that not only did Messrs Watt & Sons in good faith believe, but they were warranted in believing, that the trusted agent of the appellants had power to take the best terms for goods delivered, — that is to say, cash, or its equivalent, namely, a cheque in his favour which could be cashed on the spot.

Note

This case is an example of the ostensible authority of the agent where the fraud was similar.

Reynolds, 'The Ultimate Apparent Authority'
(1994) LQR 110 21

An agent binds his principal in contract when he acts within his actual authority. He may also bind his principal under the doctrine of apparent authority. This doctrine, which may depend on estoppel but is probably better based on the same reasoning as that which holds contracting parties to the objective appearances of intention which they create, is said to depend on a manifestation (or 'holding out') by the principal to the third party that the agent has authority. The third party is normally entitled to assume that the agent has the authority which the acts of the principal suggest that the agent has; where the agent is put in a particular position, he may be assumed to have the authority which would normally be implied for a person in that position. But this is not so if the third party knows or is to be taken as knowing (a controversial point in the doctrine) that the authority has in fact been withheld.

In cases of the second type (authority which would normally be implied) the third party is not always protected simply in accordance with his own expectations, reasonable though they may have been. In many cases he is only entitled to rely on the agent having the authority which would normally be implied *between principal and agent* in the circumstances; and of what would normally be implied he may, as a person outside that form of activity, be ignorant. Thus in the rather harsh case of *British Bank of the Middle East* v *Sun Life Insurance Co. of Canada Ltd* [1983] 2 Lloyd's Rep 9 a third party was dealing with an insurance agent who had no authority to give guarantees on behalf of his company but nevertheless did so. The third party sent an inquiry to the 'General Manager' of the company in London as to whether the agent was authorised. There was no 'General Manager' but the letter was answered by a person who signed himself as 'Branch Manager'. Without having any authority to do so he confirmed the authority of the first agent. Persons like him would normally have no authority to bind their company in such a case; the company was not bound. The unlucky third party may have been imprudent in acting on a letter from a different person than that to whom it had been addressed, but quite reasonably had no knowledge of practice within insurance companies. Not all cases are solved by calling evidence as to what persons in such a position normally do: but some are.

The principal's manifestation may and often does itself come via an agent if that agent has actual authority to indicate authority in another, and despite a case in the High Court of Australia to the contrary (*Crabtree-Vickers* v *Australian Direct Mail Advertising Pty Ltd* (1975) 133 CLR 72), it would seem on principle that that other agent's authority may also be apparent, provided that that authority can in the end be traced back to the principal himself or another agent with actual authority.

One limit however is always stated: the manifestation must come from the principal. The agent's statement, express or implied, that he has authority is not sufficient. Otherwise an agent could simply give himself authority.

This rule cannot however be absolute. There may be cases where the agent only has authority in certain circumstances: only the agent knows whether they have arisen. The third party may be entitled to rely on the agent's statement, express or implied, that they have. Thus the master of a ship has no authority to sign for goods not on board. There was old authority that if he signs for goods not on board he did not bind the owner even as against a third party who had no way of knowing: *Grant* v *Norway* (1851) 10 CB 665. This has long been regarded as unsatisfactory and is now reversed by statute (Carriage of Goods by Sea Act 1992, s.4); nowadays one would say that the master has authority to say whether the goods are on board. Again, a solicitor may purport to do something on behalf of his firm, such as give a guarantee on behalf of a client, which would be normal for a solicitor if certain background facts were true, for example that the firm was holding money for the client. The third party may be entitled to rely on the express or implied assertion of the solicitor that such background facts exist: *United Bank of Kuwait v Hammoud, City Trust Ltd v Levy* [1988] 1 WLR 1051.

But where the third party knows that the agent would not normally have authority, and there is *nothing* beyond the agent's own false assertion that he has authority, it is assumed that the principal is not bound. This was restated fairly clearly by the House of Lords in *Armagas Ltd v Mundogas SA (The Ocean Frost)* [1986] 1 AC 717 (where it was also held that the principal could not be liable in deceit either in such circmstances).

In the *First Energy (U.K.) Ltd v Hungarian International Bank Ltd* [1993] 2 Lloyd's Rep 194 a 'Senior Manager' of the bank in Manchester was arranging *ad hoc* finance for a client pending approval of a more general facility. He had done this once already, and the decision had been communicated in a letter carrying two signatures. The client knew that the Senior Manager himself had no authority to agree to such an arrangement. The Senior Manager subsequently wrote and signed (alone) a letter which was interpreted as an offer of such a loan and as indicating approval of the transaction from above. The transaction had not been approved and the bank repudiated it. The Court Appeal unanimously held the bank liable on the basis that though the manager had no authority and was not thought to have authority to grant the loan himself, he had at least apparent authority to notify the customer that the loan had been approved.

The decision is difficult to reconcile with *The Ocean Frost* (it in fact raises again a suggestion made at first instance in that case by Staughton J [1985] 1 Lloyd's Rep 1 at pp. 14–15, apparently disapproved by the Court of Appeal: [1986] AC 730–731 at pp. 748, 758–759). But since three members of the present Court of Appeal were able to distinguish the House of Lords decision (largely on the ground that the actual question did not arise for resolution) it obviously can be done. So for a commentator the question is whether the decision is one to be welcomed or not.

It is heavily based on the desirability of third parties in commercial situations being able to rely on letters such as that written. There must be many who do this: indeed, to question such assurances is rude and may also be risky. It is also known to be difficult to ascertain the limits of authority of bank officials. On the other hand, to allow a person known to have no authority in effect to give himself authority by wrongly purporting to notify a decision of someone else that the act is authorised is virtually to abandon the idea that the doctrine of apparent authority rests on manifestation by the principal. A number of American cases deal with agents who purport to go and telephone to obtain authority and then report that they have got it. The third party has usually failed. Perhaps the best is *Owners Loan Corporation v Thornburgh* 106 P 2d 511 (SC Okl 1940), where the court said:

Apparent authority loses all of its apparency when the third party knows that actual authority is lacking (at p. 512).

and later

When an agent by express words represents to a third person that the principal has consented and has therefore given his authority to close the deal, he is saying no more than what he would imply or infer anyway by the mere offer to transact for his principal, unaccompanied by such words, for of course an offer or an agreement by one representing himself to be an agent includes his accompanying representation of authority. Else he would not hold himself out as agent (at p. 514).

The reasoning that an agent has authority to *sign letters* indicating that a transaction is authorised is perhaps slightly different; but it has the same effect if generalised. The *Restatement, Second, Agency* allows effect to a representation by an agent that he has authority only in special circumstances: see section 170; and this approach appears to be supported by Lord Keith of Kinkel in *The Ocean Frost:* see p. 779. On orthodox reasoning a person in the position of the borrower (who had already had one loan authorised by two signatures) should have asked for a letter from higher up in the organisation.

Perhaps this case is to be regarded as exceptional on the facts. The person concerned, despite the absence of authority, seems to have held a position of considerable importance in a fairly small organisation apparently unknown to the court; and perhaps reasoning can be based on the general corporate conduct of the defendant. But there is little in the judgments to suggest that the court saw the case as a special one. If the reasoning is correct, some modification of the existing theoretical basis of apparent authority may in the end be needed. That may be appropriate: some think the *Sun Life* case harsh, for the reasons given above. Lord Wilberforce suggested wider reasoning in agency contexts more than 20 years ago (*Branwhite* v *Worcester Works Finance Ltd* [1969] 1 AC 552 at p. 587). But such a development would require the disavowal of *The Ocean Frost* (unless, as seems unlikely, the case is to be confined to deceit), which refuses to apply tort vicarious liability reasoning to an agency situation. And it would leave the basis of apparent authority reasoning open to new offers.

CHAPTER SIX
THE LAW RELATING TO THE SALE AND SUPPLY OF GOODS

First there are some cases on various important aspects of s. 14 SGA on the quality and fitness for purpose of goods.

The following case considers the element of s. 14(2) of the SGA (now s. 14(2)(c) of SSGA) which allows the seller to escape his liability for merchantable (now satisfactory) quality obligation where defects are pointed out to the buyer.

TURNOCK v FORTUNE
1989 SLT (Sh Ct) 32

Facts

The purchaser of a motor vehicle raised an action of damages against the seller, contending that a vehicle had not been of merchantable quality in that it had been unroadworthy at the time of purchase. The evidence before the court disclosed that the vehicle had been subject to 19 defects of varying degrees of gravity. Few if any of those defects had been specifically drawn to the purchaser's attention. What had been drawn to his attention, however, was that the car had been in an accident, that a firm of car dealers had rejected it because it had been extensively damaged, and that the car was being offered at less than half its price in good condition. Additionally, the purchaser had the benefit of advice from the sales manager of the car dealer not to buy the car because it had been in a bad accident. A question arose as to whether that advice was tantamount to a warning that the car was unroadworthy. The sheriff having held that s. 14(2)(a) of the Act was applicable (i.e. that there was no implied condition as to merchantable quality because the defects were drawn to the buyer's attention). The purchaser appealed to the sheriff principal.

Held

That to bring the case within s. 14(2)(a) the unroadworthiness of the car had to be specifically drawn to the attention of the purchaser; that the sales manager's warning against buying the car could not be considered as tantamount to a warning that the car was unroadworthy; and that therefore an implied term that the goods supplied under the contract were of merchantable quality had been imported into the contract; and, there being no question but that the seller was in breach of that implied term, the pursuer was entitled to decree; and appeal allowed and decree granted accordingly.

Sheriff Principal Sir W F O'Brien QC

No attempt was made to argue that the vehicle was of merchantable quality within the meaning of s. 14(6), and the solicitor for the respondent gave up an argument that the appellant's examination of the car brought him within exception (b) of s. 14(2). The single issue in the appeal is whether or not exception (a) applies to the facts of this case, i.e. whether the relevant defects were specifically drawn to the appellant's attention before the contract was made.

The defects in the vehicle are listed in Mr Doherty's report . . . Nineteen defects were enumerated of varying degrees of gravity. Mr Doherty's conclusion was that the vehicle was not in a roadworthy condition at the time of the sale. Few if any of the 19 defects were specifically drawn to the appellant's attention. What was drawn to his attention was (i) that the car had been in an accident, (ii) that it had been offered for sale to the Western Automobile Co Ltd, and Mr Richardson of that company had rejected it because it had been extensively damaged, and (iii) that the car was being offered at less than half its price in good condition. Additionally the appellant had the benefit of Mr Richardson's strong advice not to buy the car because it had been in a bad accident.

The solicitor for the appellant pointed out that Mr Richardson was not a skilled mechanic, but I do not see how that can matter if he drew the appellant's attention to the relevant defects. The solicitor for the appellant emphasised that these had to be drawn specifically to the buyer's attention. I cannot think that this meant that each of the 19 defects had to be drawn to the appellant's attention in a case where the one defect which matters was that the car was not roadworthy. The respondent was unaware of this, and did not himself bring it to the notice of the appellant.

If Mr Richardson had expressly warned the appellant that the car was unroadworthy, that would in my opinion have been enough, albeit the warning came from a third party and not from the seller. I have considered whether Mr Richardson's warning against buying the car was tantamount to a warning that the car was unroadworthy. It could well be interpreted as a warning that the car was not safe to drive.

I have, however, come to the conclusion that Mr Richardson's warning did not bring enough to the attention of the appellant. To bring the case within exception (a) to s. 14(2) the unroadworthiness of the car had to be specifically drawn to his attention. I cannot construe the facts as amounting to this. The appellant ignored a warning not to buy the car because it had been extensively damaged in an accident, perhaps in the hope that the bargain price which he was paying would make it worth while paying for repairs found later to be necessary. I cannot assume that he would have ignored a specific warning that the car was unroadworthy, i.e. a warning which would have called for immediate and probably expensive repairs before putting the car on the road.

It follows from this that a condition as to the car being of merchantable quality within the meaning of the Act was imported into the contract, and there is no question that the respondent was in breach of it. The solicitor for the respondent did not dispute that the car was unroadworthy at the time of the sale, and submitted no argument to the effect that, if a breach of the condition was proved, reparation was not an appropriate remedy. Nor did he suggest that the damages claimed were wrongly assessed. I have accordingly granted decree for the sum sued for.

Comment

Consider the following hypothetical statements in a seller's conditions of sale or on a delivery note.

(1) 'The buyer acknowledges that there are no defects of substance in the goods'.
(2) 'This car is sold as seen'.

Do you think that these statements would effectively negate the seller's obligation to provide goods of satisfactory quality?

The following case considers the fitness for purpose and quality obligation. Issues considered are the importance of reliance on the seller (required under s. 14(3) and the role of examination in s. 14(2) (see 6.6.3).

GRANT v AUSTRALIAN KNITTING MILLS
[1936] AC 85

Facts

The appellant contracted dermatitis as the result of wearing a woollen garment which, when purchased from the retailers, was in a defective condition owing to the presence of excess sulphites which had been negligently left in it in the process of manufacture. He claimed damages against both retailers and manufacturers.

Held

That the retailers were liable in contract for the breach of implied warranty or condition of fitness for purpose and merchantable quality under the South Australia Sale of Goods Act, s. 14(1) and (2) (identical with the relevant provision for Great Britain).

The presence of the deleterious chemical in the garment was a hidden and latent defect, and could not be detected by any examination that could reasonably be made; nothing happened between the making of the garment and its being worn to change its condition; and the garment was made by the manufacturers for the purpose of being worn exactly as it was worn in fact by the appellant.

Further those facts established a duty to take care as between the manufacturers and the appellant for the breach of which the manufacturers were liable in tort. The principle of *Donoghue v Stevenson* 1932 SC 31 (HL) was applied. It can be applied only where the defect is hidden and unknown to the customer or consumer.

The liability in tort was independent of any question of contract.

Lord Wright

So far as concerns the retailers, Mr Greene conceded that if it were held that the garments contained improper chemicals and caused the disease, the retailers were liable for breach of implied warranty, or rather condition, under s. 14 of the South Australia Sale of Goods Act, 1895. . . . The section is in the following terms:

14. Subject to the provisions of this Act, and of any Statute in that behalf, there is no implied warranty or condition as to the quality or fitness for any particular purpose of goods supplied under a contract of sale, except as follows —

I.   Where the buyer, expressly or by implication, makes known to the seller the particular purpose for which the goods are required, so as to show that the buyer relies on the seller's skill or judgment, and the goods are of a description which it is in the course of the seller's business to supply (whether he be the manufacturer or not), there is an implied condition that the goods shall be reasonably fit for such purpose: Provided that in the case of a contract for the sale of a specified article under its patent or other trade name, there is no implied condition as to its fitness for any particular purpose:

II.   Where goods are bought by description from a seller who deals in goods of that description (whether he be the manufacturer or not), there is an implied condition that the goods shall be of merchantable quality: Provided that if the buyer has examined the goods, there shall be no implied condition as regards defects which such examination ought to have revealed:

III.   An implied warranty or condition as to quality or fitness for a particular purpose may be annexed by the usage of trade:

IV.   An express warranty or condition does not negative a warranty or condition implied by this Act unless inconsistent therewith.

He limited his admission to liability under exception (ii), but their Lordships are of opinion that liability is made out under both exception (i) and exception (ii) to s. 14, and feel that they should so state out of deference to the conflicting views expressed in the Court below. Section 14 begins by a general enunciation of the old rule of *caveat emptor*, and proceeds to state by way of exception the two implied conditions by which it has been said the old rule has been changed to the rule of *caveat venditor*: the change has been rendered necessary by the conditions of modern commerce and trade. . . . There are numerous cases on the section, but as these were cited below it is not necessary to detail them again. The first exception, if its terms are satisfied, entitles the buyer to the benefit of an implied condition that the goods are reasonably fit for the purpose for which the goods are supplied, but only if that purpose is made known to the seller 'so as to show that the buyer relies on the seller's skill or judgment.' It is clear that the reliance must be brought home to the mind of the seller, expressly or by implication. The reliance will seldom be express: it will usually arise by implication from the circumstances: thus to take a case like that in question, of a purchase from a retailer, the reliance will be in general inferred from the fact that a buyer goes to the shop in the confidence that the tradesman has selected his stock with skill and judgment: the retailer need know nothing about the process of manufacture: it is immaterial whether he be manufacturer or not: the main inducement to deal with a good retail shop is the expectation that the tradesman will have bought the right goods of a good make: the goods sold must be, as they were in the present case, goods of a description which it is in the course of the seller's business to supply: there is no need to specify in terms the particular purpose for which the buyer requires the goods, which is none the less the particular purpose within the meaning of the section, because it is the only purpose for which any one would ordinarily want the goods. In this case the garments were naturally intended, and only intended, to be worn next the skin. The proviso does not apply to a case like the sale of Golden Fleece make such as is here in question, because Golden Fleece is neither a patent nor a trade name within the meaning of the proviso to exception (i). With great deference to Dixon J, their Lordships think that the requirements of exception (i) were complied with. The conversation at the shop in which the appellant discussed questions of price and of the different makes did not affect the fact that he was substantially relying on the retailers to supply him with a correct article.

The second exception in a case like this in truth overlaps in its application the first exception; whatever else merchantable may mean, it does mean that the article sold, if only meant for one particular use in ordinary course, is fit for that use; merchantable does not mean that the thing is saleable in the market simply because it looks all right; it is not merchantable in that event if it has defects unfitting it for its only proper use but not apparent on ordinary examination: that is clear from the proviso, which shows that the implied condition only applies to defects not reasonably discoverable to the buyer on such examination as he made or could make. The appellant was satisfied by the appearance of the underpants; he could not detect, and had no reason to suspect, the hidden presence of the sulphites: the garments were saleable in the sense that the appellant, or any one similarly situated and who did not know of their defect, would readily buy them: but they were not merchantable in the statutory sense because their defect rendered them unfit to be worn next the skin. It may be that after sufficient washing that defect would have disappeared: but the statute requires the goods to be merchantable in the state in which they were sold and delivered; in this connection a defect which could easily be cured is as serious as a defect that would not yield to treatment. The proviso to exception (ii) does not apply where, as in this case, no examination that the buyer could or would normally have made would have revealed the defect. In effect, the implied condition of being fit for the particular purpose for which they are required, and the implied condition of being merchantable, produce in cases of this type the same result. It may also be pointed out that there is a sale by description even though the buyer is buying something displayed before him on the counter: a thing is sold by description, though it is specific, so long as it is sold not merely as the specific thing but as a thing corresponding to a description, e.g., woollen under-garments, a hot-water bottle, a second-hand reaping machine, to select a few obvious illustrations.

The retailers, accordingly, in their Lordships' judgment are liable in contract: so far as they are concerned, no question of negligence is relevant to the liability in contract.

Note

There are two ways in which examination of goods may be important in relation to rights and remedies surrounding the implied terms. First, as discussed in *Grant*, in relation to whether an examination *which actually took place ought to have discovered a defect*, so meaning there is no obligation of quality under s. 14. This rule is contained in the new s. 14(2)(c) of the SGA. The second way in which examination may be relevant is in the context of the right to reject and whether it is lost by acceptance under s. 35 (see 6.6.5 and Ong below in Cases and Materials for Chapter six). Here the existence of the obligation and its breach are clear. What is at issue is whether, *after the contract*, a reasonable opportunity for examination has been made available. This is a factor in deciding whether the buyer has lost his right to reject.

The main point about the following case is that the s. 14(2) quality obligation is not intended to cover a situation where the goods are simply not those ordered, i.e. they are of a different type or description.

McCALLUM v MASON
1956 SC 50

Facts

A nurseryman purchased from a manufacturer a quantity of a proprietary fertiliser to which a percentage of magnesium sulphate was to be added. This mixture had been recommended to him by the seller for application to his tomato crop as a remedy for soil deficiency. Two bags purporting to contain the mixture were delivered to him and paid for. Some of the mixture was applied to the tomato plants, which deteriorated and died. In the following year more of the mixture was applied to healthy tomato plants and healthy chrysanthemum plants, and these also died. A sample of the mixture was subsequently analysed and was found to contain sodium chlorate instead of magnesium sulphate. The purchaser brought an action of damages for breach of contract against the seller under the SGA, s. 14(1) and (2) (now s. 14(3) and s. 14(2) respectively), averring that the defender had failed to supply goods which were reasonably fit for the purpose for which they were required and that he had failed to supply goods of merchantable quality.

Lord Thomson

As to s. 14(1) it is agreed that he is entitled to a proof before answer so far as the 1952 tomato crop is concerned. But I do not see how, on the pursuer's averments as to the purpose of the purchase and the precise evil which it was sought to remedy, he can possibly found on that subsection for any other crop. The mixture was supplied on the footing that it was all to be used in 1952 and to remedy a set of circumstances existing in 1952. There was no consideration given to subsequent years or different crops whether the circumstances and the treatment might be different.

Accordingly so far as the 1953 tomato crop and the chrysanthemums are concerned, the pursuer falls back on s. 14(2) and the implied condition that the goods supplied shall be of merchantable quality. He says that the mixture was not of that quality. The scope of this subsection, however, is limited to the case where the goods tendered are damaged to some extent or are defective in quality but not so much that they can no longer be said to correspond with the description. The buyer gets goods of the sort described in the contract but they are for some reason or another sub-standard. In s. 13 the goods are not what was ordered; in s. 14(2) the buyer gets the kind of goods he ordered but they are defective. It seems to me therefore that, where, as here, the pursuer says that having ordered fertiliser he got weed-killer, he is far from s. 14(2). Section 14(2) operates where what he got is still capable of being described as fertiliser but on account of some defect it is not of such quality as a reasonable buyer would regard as satisfying the contract, assuming him to be aware of the true facts. . . . As Lord Justice-Clerk Inglis put it in *Jaffe* v *Ritchie*, at p. 249: 'The terms "bad quality", "defect", "insufficiency", do not apply to a case in which the goods offered are of a different description from those about which the parties contracted. There, there is a clear failure to perform the express words of the contract, and we do not need to imply anything.

In my view, then, the pursuer on his averments is not in a position to bring himself within the scope of s. 14(2).

MILLARS OF FALKIRK v TURPIE
1976 SLT 66

Lord President Emslie

There is no doubt that the question of whether an article sold is of 'merchantable quality' or is 'reasonably fit' for a relevant purpose in terms of s. 14(3) is a question of fact, once the court has correctly understood the meaning of these expressions. Support for this view is, I think, to be found in the opinion of Roskill LJ in *Cehave N.V* v *Bremer m.b.H.* [1975] 3 WLR 447 at p. 468. In this case, bearing in mind that the defender has throughout relied upon showing that the new car was not of 'merchantable quality' and has at no time argued that if he failed so to show he could be in any stronger or different position under s. 14(3), the sheriff approached his judgment by appreciating perfectly correctly the meaning of the expression 'merchantable quality' in s. 14(2). It is now defined as follows: 'Goods of any kind are of merchantable quality within the meaning of this Act if they are as fit for the purpose or purposes for which goods of that kind are commonly bought as it is reasonable to expect having regard to any description applied to them, the price (if relevant) and all the other relevant circumstances'. With Lord Denning MR in *Cehave* I am of opinion that this definition is the best that has yet been devised, and that in any particular case in which the question of merchantable quality arises it is to be answered as a commercial man would be likely to answer it having regard to the various matters mentioned in the statutory definition. As I read his note, the sheriff has approached the question in precisely this way and in light of all the relevant circumstances upon which his judgment proceeded, and which I have already set out, he reached the conclusion that the car sold to the defender was of merchantable quality and reasonably fit for the purpose which a new motor car is designed to serve. In my opinion he was entitled to reach that conclusion on the facts of this case and I would not quarrel with that conclusion. I have in mind particularly that the relevant circumstances included these: (i) the defect was a minor one which could readily and very easily be cured at very small cost; (ii) the pursuers were willing and anxious to cure the defect; (iii) the defect was obvious and the risk of the car being driven long enough to create some danger if the steering unexpectedly ceased to be assisted was slight; (iv) many new cars have, on delivery to a purchaser, some defects, and it was not exceptional for a new car to be delivered in the condition in which the defender's car was delivered.

There follows an excerpt from the decision in *Rogers v Parish (Scarborough) Ltd* [1987] 2 All ER 232 at 233, which clearly shows that even under the old s. 14(2) the courts were willing to look beyond whether a car was capable of going from point A to point B, and is free of serious defects.

ROGERS AND ANOTHER v PARISH (SCARBOROUGH) LTD AND OTHERS
[1987] 2 All ER 232

Mustill LJ

This is an appeal by the plaintiffs against a judgment given in favour of two defendants by his Honour Judge Herrod QC sitting as a judge of the High Court in Leeds. The first plaintiff is a Yorkshire businessman; the first defendants are motor dealers with the franchise for the sale of Range Rovers; and the second defendants are a finance house. During May 1980 two Range Rovers were delivered by the manufacturers to the first defendants' premises. The particulars of their registration numbers are immaterial; it is sufficient to say that one of the vehicles was coloured green and the other yellow.

For a number of months the vehicles were stored in an open compound. Afterwards they were moved to showrooms indoors, It proved necessary as a consequence of their prolonged storage to clean up some rust on the wheels of the vehicles and to touch up the paintwork to take account of some minor damage during delivery.

On 6 November 1981 the green Range Rover was sold under a conditional sale agreement to the plaintiffs. The transaction took a conventional shape, the vehicle being sold by the dealers to the second defendants and then resold by the latter to the plaintiffs. It was an express term of the sale agreement by the finance house to the plaintiffs that:

7.(a) The Seller supplies the Goods to the Buyer for his use with the benefit . . . of the following which are implied by statute . . . (ii) a condition that the Goods are of merchantable quality . . . (d) Nothing in this agreement does or will affect the statutory rights of the Buyer in respect of the Goods . . .

It appears that at the time of the sale, or perhaps at the time of delivery under the sale, the first plaintiff was handed a warranty document. This document, so far as material to the present dispute, reads as follows:

Should any part of the vehicle require repair or replacement as a result of a manufacturing or material defect within twelve months from the date on which the vehicle was handed over to the first owner, the part will be repaired or replaced completely free of charge by your authorised Dealer, regardless of any change of ownership during the period covered. Any part so repaired or replaced will benefit from these arrangements for the balance of the period applicable to the vehicle . . .

After certain exclusions the document went on as follows: 'Your statutory rights and obligations as against the supplier are not in any way affected by this statement.'

The warranty document also prescribed a procedure which the purchaser was to follow if he wished to take advantage of the warranty, and this included a liberty to take the vehicle to another franchised dealer if it was inconvenient to return it to the vendor for repair. It does not appear from the documents before us whether this warranty was signed or precisely what its contractual status was intended to be, but primarily at least it must have constituted an engagement by the manufacturers collateral to the sale contract itself.

The price at which the vehicle was sold was some £16,000. After a few weeks' use it proved unsatisfactory and was returned by the plaintiffs to the dealers. By agreement between the parties a yellow vehicle of the same type was substituted for the original subject matter of the sale. The parties were thereafter content to have their relationship governed by the same contractual terms as had applied to the original purchase and sale. All the proceedings in the present action have gone forward on that basis.

Unfortunately it proved that the yellow vehicle was no more satisfactory than its predecessor. It is now known, as the judge found in his judgment, that by the time the vehicle was sold to the plaintiffs it had deteriorated to the extent that oil seals at vital junctions were no longer sound and that the defective seals permitted the loss of significant quantities of oil. It also proved to be the case that the engine and the gearbox of the vehicle had defects at the time of sale. After a series of inspections and attempts at repair it was found as late as June 1982, some six months after the delivery of the second vehicle, that the engine was still misfiring at all road speeds and that excessive noise was emitting from the gearbox and the transfer box. In addition the vehicle was suffering, as the judge has found, from substantial defects as regards the bodywork. In all the condition of the vehicle was such that, as the judge has found, 'It must be said that the defects to the engine, the gearbox and the bodywork reflect great discredit on the inspection procedures at the Land Rover factory'.

As I have already said, the vehicle had been subjected to a number of inspections during the months following its delivery and also to attempts to put it right. During this period the first plaintiff had been able to drive it for upwards of 5,500 miles, albeit in a manner which gave him no satisfaction. In the end, however, he lost patience, and during May 1982 he gave notice to the dealers that the car was rejected. We are told that thereafter it has remained in the possession of the plaintiffs since the defendants were unwilling to take it back.

In due course the plaintiffs instituted the present action against both the dealers as first defendants and the finance house as second defendants. The latter were plainly parties to a direct contract of sale with the plaintiffs. The position of the first defendants might be more complex, but they are content to have the issue of liability dealt with on the basis that they are in privity with the plaintiffs and that their liabilities are to be assessed in precisely the same manner.

In these circumstances two questions arise: first whether the defendants were in breach of an express promise that the vehicle was new; and second whether they were in breach of an express or implied promise that the car would be in merchantable condition. I say 'express or implied' because there was, as I have already indicated, an express promise by the second defendants. In the event, however, both the defendants and the plaintiffs have been content to treat this case as if it were governed by the provisions relating to implied terms created by s. 14 of the Sale of Goods Act 1979, and in particular by the definition of the words 'merchantable quality' which are to be found in s. 14(6) of that Act.

It is convenient to deal first with the contention that the goods were unmerchantable at the time of delivery and that the plaintiffs were accordingly entitled to reject them. An implied term as to merchantability has been governed by statute, the Sale of Goods Act, since 1893. It was however subject to important modification by the Supply of Goods (Implied Terms) Act 1973, as regards both a change in the wording of s. 14(2) itself and the addition of a new definition of merchantable quality. These were re-enacted with a minor alteration as regards the definition in s. 14 of the 1979 Act, the material parts of which read as follows:

> . . . (2) Where the seller sells goods in the course of a business, there is an implied condition that the goods supplied under the contract are of merchantable quality, except that there is no such condition — (a) as regards defects specifically drawn to the buyer's attention before the contract is made: or (b) if the buyer examines the goods before the contract is made, as regards defects which that examination ought to reveal . . .
>
> (6) Goods of any kind are of merchantable quality within the meaning of subsection (2) above if they are as fit for the purpose or purposes for which goods of that kind are commonly bought as it is reasonable to expect having regard to any description applied to them, the price (if relevant) and all the other relevant circumstances . . .

In the course of argument before us our attention was drawn to various expressions of opinion in cases decided before the enactment of the 1973 legislation as to the precise significance of the term 'merchantable quality'. In my judgment this is not a practice to be encouraged. The 1973 Act was an amending Act and it cannot be assumed that the new definition was included simply because the draftsman saw a convenient opportunity to reproduce in more felicitous and economical terms the gist of the speeches and judgments previously delivered. The language of s. 14(6) is clear and free from technicality, and it should be sufficient in the great majority of cases to enable the fact-finding judge to arrive at a decision without exploring the intricacies of the prior law. In my judgment the present is not one of those exceptional cases where it may be necessary to have recourse to the former decisions in order to give a full meaning to the words of a s. 14(6), and I propose to concentrate on the words of the subsection.

Against this background we must look to see how the matter was dealt with by the judge at first instance. He said:

> I do not take the view that any of the defects in this case were such as to render the vehicle unroadworthy, unusable or unfit for any of the normal purposes for which a Range Rover might be used. It is true that there were a number of defects on this vehicle at the time of sale and delivery, defects which manifested themselves very shortly after the plaintiffs took delery, and defects which must have been infuriating

to the plaintiffs. However, the defects were capable of repair, and the defendants attempted to repair them at no cost to the plaintiffs. When those repairs did not meet with the plaintiffs' approval the vehicle was returned to the factory, it was examined and further work was then done on it by the first defendants. Ultimately, by the time the vehicle was examined by the Automobile Association inspector on 28 April 1982, all repairs had been carried out to an acceptable standard, and the mechanical performance was within the manufacturers' tolerances. Some of the defects did recur by 9 June 1982, but the fact that these defects had been satisfactorily dealt with on one occasion can only mean that they were susceptible to further repair, and if the first plaintiff had lost confidence in the ability of the first defendants to repair his vehicle his proper remedy was to take it to some other Range Rover dealer, as he was entitled to do under the terms of the vehicle warranty. I do not take the view that this is one of the so-called 'congeries of defects' cases, which destroy the workable character of a machine. Indeed, the very fact that during the first six months of its life the plaintiffs were able to use the vehicle for a distance in excess of 5,000 miles demonstrates that it had plenty of use. Accordingly, the plaintiffs must also fail in their allegations that the vehicle was not of merchantable quality and unfit for the purposes for which it was required.

If the approach to the problem adopted by the judge was correct, this court shold be slow indeed to interfere with the conclusion which he reached, since it seems to me that the intent of s. 14(6) was to make an issue of merchantable quality into very much a jury question. In the present case however I feel bound to say that the approach adopted by the judge was not correct. In the first place, he did not expressly direct himself in accordance with s. 14(6) and indeed did not mention the subsection in his judgment, possibly because it was given less prominence at the trial than during the argument before us.

This in itself could not be conclusive, for the judge could in fact have applied s. 14(6) correctly, without saying so in so many words. There are two respects in which the judge in my opinion applied a test which was not that of s. 14(6). In the passage already quoted he gave much weight to the fact that the defects were capable of repair and that the defendants had in some measure been able to repair them. Yet the fact that a defect is repairable does not prevent it from making the res venditur unmerchantable if it is of a sufficient degree (see *Lee* v *York Coach and Marine* [1977] RTR 35). The fact, if it was a fact, that the defect had been repaired at the instance of the purchaser, which in the present case does not appear to be so, might well have had an important bearing on whether the purchaser had by his conduct lost his right to reject, but it cannot in my view be material to the question of merchantability, which falls to be judged at the moment of delivery. Furthermore, the judge applied the test of whether the defects had destroyed the workable character of the car. No doubt this echoed an argument smilar to the one deveoped before us that, if a vehicle is capable of starting and being driven in safety from one poiint to the next on public roads and on whatever other surfaces the car is supposed to be able to negotiate, it must necessarily be merchantable. I can only say that this proposition appears to have no relation to the broad test propounded by s. 14(6) even if, in certain particular circumstances, the correct inference would be that no more could be expected of the goods sold.

This being so, I think it legitimate to look at the whole issue afresh with direct reference to the words of s. 14(6). Starting with the purpose for which 'goods of that kind' are commonly bought, one would include in respect of any passenger vehicle not merely the buyer's purpose of driving the car from one place to another but of doing so with the appropriate degree of comfort, ease of handling and reliability and, one may add, of pride in the vehicle's outward and interior appearance. What is the appropriate degree and what relative weight is to be attached to one characteristic of the car rather than another will depend on the market at which the car is aimed.

To identify the relevant expectation one must look at the factors listed in the subsection. First, the description applied to the goods. In the present case the vehicle was sold as new. Deficiencies which might be acceptable in a secondhand vehicle were not to be expected in one purchased as new. Next, the description 'Range Rover' would conjure up a particular set of expectations, not the same as those relating to an ordinary saloon car, as to the balance between performance, handling, comfort and resilience. The factor of price was also significant. At more than £16,000 this vehicle was, if not at the top end of the scale, well above the level of the ordinary family saloon. The buyer was entitled to value for his money.

With these factors in mind, can it be said that the Range Rover as delivered was as fit for the purpose as the buyer could reasonably expect? The point does not admit of elaborate discussion. I can only say that to my mind the defects in engine, gearbox and bodywork, the existence of which is no longer in dispute, clearly demand a negative answer.

It is, however, also necessary to deal with an argument based on the fact that the vehicle was sold with the benefit of a manufacturers' warranty, a fact which was relied on to show that the buyer was required to take in his stride to a certain degree at least the type of defects which would otherwise have amounted to a breach of contract. Speaking for myself, I am far from satisfied that this argument is open to the defendants at all, having regard to the express disclaimer in the contract of sale, and also in the warranty, of any intenton to vary the buyer's rights at common law and also having regard to s 6 of the Unfair Contract Terms Act 1977. Nor am I convinced that this objection can satisfactorily be answered by saying that the argument founded on the warranty operates not to deprive the buyer of his common law rights but rather as a relevant circumstance for the purposes of s. 14(6) operating simply to diminish the reasonable expectations of the buyer.

Moreover, I am not clear about the logic underlying the argument. Assume that on an accurate balancing of all the relevant circumstances it could be said that the buyer of a new Range Rover could reasonably expect it to have certain qualities and that accordingly he has a contractual right to receive a vehicle possessing those qualities and to recover damages, including damages for any consequential loss, if it does not possess them. Can it really be right to say that the reasonable buyer would expect less of his new Range Rover with a warranty than without one? Surely the warranty is an addition to the buyer's rights, not a subtraction from them, and, it may be noted, only a circumscribed addition since it lasts for a limited period and does not compensate the buyer for consequential loss and inconvenience. If the defendants are right the buyer would be well advised to leave his guarantee behind in the showroom. This cannot be what the manufacturers and dealers intend or what their customers reasonably understand.

Assume, however, tha I am wrong in all this and that the presence of the warranty did in some degree have the effect of diminishing the standard of expectation and hence the vendor's required standard of performance. Even so, I can only say that, after rebalancing the relevant circumstances, I would again conclude that these defects lie well outside the range of expectation and that the vehicle was not merchantable.

In the light of this conclusion the question whether the vehicle was 'new' when delivered becomes academic. Since the general issue may be of some importance to the motor trade and was not fully explored in argument before us I would say only that on the particular facts of this case I would not differ from the conclusion of the judge that the vehicle was properly described as 'new'.

Finally, I should mention that the defendants sought to contend, on the argument of the appeal, that even if there had been a breach of s. 14 the first plaintiff had, by his conduct, precluded himself from rejecting the car. This point was not pleaded by either defendant, nor was it mentioned in the judgment in the court below or in either defendant's respondent's notice. Since the argument could not in any event have been explored by this court in the absence of findings about the entire course of dealings between the parties between the dates of delivery and rejection we considered it inappropriate to allow this matter to be raised before us.

In the result I would allow the appeal. I would wish to hear submissions in due course on the appropriate form of order.

The following article discusses the different approaches of the UK courts to the buyer's right to reject defective goods under s. 14 of the SGA (as it was before it was amended by the Sale and Supply of Goods Act 1994). The new provision expressly states that in considering when a reasonable time has elapsed, the courts must decide whether there has been a reasonable opportunity for examination. This must involve consideration of whether the defect was latent or patent, and is therefore nearer to the approach which the Scottish courts seem to have taken to the old s. 14 anyway. Indeed, as Ong shows, the latency or patency of the defect appears to be regarded as an extremely important factor by the Scottish courts.

A Comparative Study of the Buyer's Right of Rejection: Dennis Ong, Barrister, Scots Law Times, 24 November 1989

This article makes a comparative study between the English and Scottish judicial approaches to the question of the buyer's right of rejection for defective goods under the Sale of Goods Act 1979, and considers critically whether one approach should be followed in preference to the other.

Introduction
Although important differences exist between English and Scottish law under the Sale of Goods Act 1979 (see generally the Law Commission and the Scottish Law Commission report, *Sale and Supply of Goods*), the provision of the buyer's right of rejection under the Act in both jurisdictions is identical. The buyer's right of rejection is an important and often effective remedy against a seller who supplies the buyer with defective goods, that is goods which are of unmerchantable quality and/or unfit for their purpose. Upon a successful plea of the right of rejection, the buyer is relieved of his imprudent bargain and is then able to recover the full purchase price which he paid for the goods. The buyer can then start anew. On the other hand, if the buyer loses his statutory right of rejection he will be relegated to a claim in damages and perhaps plagued with the uncertain prospect that future faults may develop in the goods.

This article begins with a comparative study of the English and Scottish judicial approaches respectively, followed by a critical assessment of the dichotomous approaches, and concludes with a choice between the two approaches.

The English approach
The High Court of England was recently afforded the opportunity of considering the buyer's right of rejection in *Bernstein v Pamson Motors (Golders Green) Ltd* [1987] 2 All ER 220. The plaintiff purchased from the defendant a new Nissan Laurel car at a

not insubstantial price of £ 8,000. The car was duly delivered on 7 December 1984. The plaintiff was ill over Christmas of 1984 and thus unable to make any use of the car. After he recovered he made one or two short trips in order to get used to the fairly sophisticated controls. It was not, however, until 3 January 1985 that the plaintiff decided to make his 'first proper trip' which involved travelling on a motorway. Whilst en route, an unusual noise began to be heard from the engine. The plaintiff pulled onto the hard shoulder and switched the engine off. The car had then done some 140-odd miles. The car could not be restarted, and was in fact towed away by the emergency services. The following day, the plaintiff wrote to the defendants and rejected the car, alleging it to be of unmerchantable quality. Later inspection revealed that a piece of sealant had entered the lubrication system (most likely during assembly but in any case present at the moment of delivery) and lodged itself in the restrictor, thus starving the camshaft of oil and causing the engine to seize up. The car was eventually repaired and found as good as new (save for two minor imperfections; but query also if the car could be so described if there were potential knock-on effects). But the plaintiff was adamant (this was judicially commented on, but appears to be no more than the attitude which a plaintiff has to adopt if he is not to run the risk of losing his right of rejection under s. 35 of the Act), and demanded refund of his money following his rejection of 3 January 1985. Two issues emerged for determination before Rougier J. First, whether the inherent defect rendered the car of unmerchantable quality, an issue not examined here. Secondly, if so, whether the plaintiff had properly exercised his right to reject the car. This in turn depended on whether the plaintiff had had the car for a reasonable time so as to have accepted the car in law, thus losing his right to reject it. In a reserved judgment, Rougier J concluded that the car was not of merchantable quality and then proceeded to consider the question of rejection. He held that the plaintiff was deemed in law to have accepted the car under s. 35 of the Sale of Goods Act because there had been a lapse of a reasonable time. The plaintiff therefore lost his right to reject the car and had to be content with damages. . . .

In his judgment, the nature of the particular defect, discovered ex post facto, and the speed with which it might have been discovered, were irrelevant to the question of reasonable time in s. 35 as drafted [1987] 2 All ER at p. 230). Therefore, in his view it did not matter whether the defect was patent or latent since the nature of the defect was an irrelevant consideration.

The Scottish approach
As early as 1885, a Scottish case which preceded the Sale of Goods legislation, considered the nature of the defect as a relevant fact in deciding whether a reasonable time had elapsed for rejecting the goods. In *James Carter & Co* v *Campbell* (1885) 12 R 1075 the pursuer had bought from the defender a certain quantity of 'oats clear of barley'. The pursuer did not examine the oats on arrival, but his son made a cursory examination and found nothing amiss. The oats were sown but it was found that a quantity of barley grew alongside the oats, the proportion being about 4 per cent of barley. The pursuer sought to reject the goods on the basis that they did not conform to the contract. The Court of Session found the defender in breach of contract, but refused the pursuer his remedy because he had failed timeously to reject the goods. The court held that a reasonable examination of the goods would have revealed the disconformity of the goods to the contract. Lord Adam said (at p. 1082): 'It may be that the objection to the article is latent, and that no amount of examination would discover it — we have seen examples of that in such cases as that of turnip seed, or where the defect, as in the case of machinery, would not become visible until the

article was used. In such cases, of course, the purchaser would not be bound to return the goods at once. But here there can be no doubt that the defect would have been discovered if a careful examination had been made, and it is also clear that no proper examination was made.'

In the post-1893 case of *Hyslop* v *Shirlaw* (1905) 7 F 875 the distinction between patent and latent defects was again brought up. The pursuer in that case sought to reject certain paintings some 18 months after he had bought them from the defender on account that they were not genuine (cf. *Leaf* v *International Galleries*). The pursuer sought to argue that the defect in that case was latent so that the time after which rejection must be timeous was the discovery of the defect some one and a half years after the date of purchase. The defender on the other hand did not seek to disagree with the premise that a reasonable time in the case of a latent defect meant the date the defect was discovered. Rather he argued that the defect in question was patent, and not latent so that the defect 'could have been just as easily discovered at the date of the delivery as eighteen months after'. The court decided that the genuineness of the painting (or the lack of it) amounted to a patent defect because the 'pursuer could have found out all he knows now had he thought of taking reasonable diligence at that time' (per Lord Justice-Clerk Macdonald at p. 880). Therefore, a lapse of 18 months was far more than a reasonable time. Lord Kyllachy opined on the position of latent defects (at p. 882): 'He is not ... in the position of a person who has by accident discovered, perhaps years afterwards, something justifying rescission which could only have been discovered by accident. That is, of course, a different case altogether.'

Flynn v *Scott*, 1949 SLT 399; 1949 SC 442, a decision of Lord Mackintosh in the Outer House, appears to suggest that the right of rejection has to be exercised within a few days after the defect has been discovered, if it is not to be lost completely. The pursuer bought a secondhand motor van from the defender on 10 June 1948 for the purpose of his business as a haulage contractor. On 17 June the van loaded with some goods, broke down during the commencement of the journey. There was no evidence tendered by the pursuer of what use, if any, had been made of the van between the date of purchase and the date the van broke down. Be that as it may, the pursuer did not intimate rejection of the van until 8 July, some three weeks after the breakdown. Lord Mackintosh went on to say that 'if the remedy of rejection was going to be exercised by the pursuer, he was bound . . . to intimate this to the seller within a very few days after the 17th June' (1949 SLT at p. 401). In his judgment no mention was made of the nature of the defect, but we can fairly assume that whatever the nature, the pursuer became aware of the defect on 17 June and it was that date which Lord Mackintosh was prepared to use in computing what was a reasonable time.

The Scottish cases demonstrate quite convincingly that their approach of differentiating between latent and patent defects comes closer to reality and fairness than the English approach as epitomised by Rougier J in *Bernstein*. In addition, and apart from principle, there is nothing contained in the Sale of Goods Act which prevents the trial judge from so differentiating. It is submitted that there is much the English judges can learn from their Scottish counterparts, and it is hoped that when the opportunity does present itself, the English judges would review both the Scottish and English cases and be persuaded by the view, as the author is, that the former approach comes closer not only to the spirit and intendment of Parliament but also to justice and fairness.

MACLEOD v KERR AND ANOTHER
1965 SC 253

Facts

A motor car held by the procurator fiscal (Macleod) was the subject of a dispute as to ownership. Kerr, the original owner of the car, had advertised it for sale and, on

12 February, a man, Galloway, purporting to be L. Craig bought by writing out a cheque for £375 and signing it in that name. Kerr gave Galloway the registration book and allowed him to drive the car away. On the next day, he discovered that the cheque book had been stolen and informed the police. On 14 February, Galloway, purporting to be Kerr, sold the car to Gibson at Gibson's garage. Gibson purchased the car in good faith and without any knowledge of any defect in Galloway's title. The procurator fiscal raised an action of multiple poinding to establish who owned the car.

Lord Carmont
The stolen cheque was, therefore, used in furtherance of a fraudulent transaction so as to obtain delivery of the car from Kerr. The fact that the cheque was stolen did not result in a theft of the car, delivery of which had been obtained from Kerr. The use of a stolen cheque and Galloway's obtaining of delivery of the car from Kerr by passing off the cheque as his own, by Galloway, did not bring about a theft of the car from Kerr, but the fraudulent obtaining by Galloway of possession of the car from Kerr. This approach to the case is entirely different from that taken by the sheriff-substitute and no *vitium reale* tainted the car. Until the fraudulent transaction was set aside, Galloway was in a position to pass, by sale, the property in the car which he (Galloway) had fraudulently obtained provided the sale was to an innocent third party. The defender, George Gibson, was such an innocent third party. He bought it on 14 February and paid Galloway £185 for it. In acquiring the car when he did, from Galloway in the open market without any notice of a taint, Gibson acquired the ownership of the car albeit through a fraudulent person.

The suggestion that because Kerr notified the police of the fraud which had been used against him so as to get him to part with the car to Galloway (alias 'L. Craig') was enough to prevent Gibson from acquiring ownership through the fraudulent seller to him, has no validity or bearing on the result of this case. The matter would, of course, have been different if Kerr had notified Gibson of what had happened in regard to his (Kerr's) car before Gibson had acquired it from the seller to him.

I agree with your Lordships that the Interlocutor of the sheriff-substitute should be reversed and that Gibson's claim to be ranked and preferred to the car should be sustained.

Lord Guthrie
The contract, having been induced by fraud, was voidable, not void. Therefore it conferred a title to the car on Galloway, who could transfer the ownership of it to a purchaser in good faith until his title was avoided.

It was argued for Mr Kerr that the title of Galloway was avoided on 13 February, the day before the car was acquired by Mr Gibson, because on 13 February Mr Kerr had notified the police of the transaction. There is neither averment nor plea to found this contention, which was not put before the sheriff-substitute. In any event it is wholly unsound, since an invocation of the powers of the criminal authorities cannot possibly be the avoidance of a contract entered into under the civil law.

CAR AND UNIVERSAL FINANCE CO LTD v CALDWELL
[1965] 1 QB 525

Facts
The facts in this case were broadly similar to those of *Macleod* v *Kerr*, although the car in question passed through several sets of hands after being acquired from Caldwell. After having discovered that the cheque would not be honoured Caldwell

(like Kerr) immediately informed the police and the AA who said they would try and find the car. Caldwell sought the return of the car from the plaintiffs on the grounds that his action in informing the police and AA constituted avoidance of the contract with the con-man.

Lord Denning

This case raises the familiar question which of two innocent persons is to suffer for the fraud of a third? [His Lordship referred to the facts and continued:] The principal question in this case is whether Caldwell did succeed in avoiding the sale by the steps which he took of going to the bank, the police and the AA, before the rogue sold the car. It is said by Mr Tapp, for the plaintiffs, that a man from whom goods have been obtained by false pretences cannot avoid the transaction unless he does an act which unequivocally shows his election to avoid it; and furthermore, communicates his election to the other side, that is to the other party to the contract. The avoidance does not, it is said, take place until it is communicated. In this case, therefore, the avoidance did not take place on the morning of 13 January when Caldwell went to the police. It would not take place until Caldwell discovered Norris [the original purchaser] and Foster (the later purchaser) and communicated his election to them. . . .

I would ask this simple question: How is a man in the position of Caldwell ever to be able to rescind the contract when a fraudulent person absconds as Norris did here? If his right to rescind is to be a real right, when the rogue absconds, it must be sufficient if he does all that he can in the circumstances unequivocally to make it known. It is not sufficient for him, of course, to keep it in his own mind or write down a note in his own private sitting room. However, conduct such as we have here, namely, telling the bank, the police and the AA, 'Find this car if you possibly can. Get it back. It is mine', seems to me an unequivocal act of rescission.

Lord Upjohn

If one party, by absconding, deliberately puts it out of the power of the other to communicate his intention to rescind which he knows the other will almost certainly want to do, I do not think he can any longer insist on his right to be made aware of the election to determine the contract. In these circumstances communication is a useless formality. I think that the law must allow the innocent party to exercise his right of rescission otherwise than by communication or repossession. To hold otherwise would be to allow a fraudulent contracting party by his very fraud to prevent the innocent party from exercising his undoubted right. I would hold that in circumstances such as these the innocent party may evince his intention to disaffirm the contract by overt means falling short of communication or repossession.

Comment

Whose views do you think are correct, those of the Court of Session in *Macleod* or those of the Queen's Bench in *Caldwell?* In either case there will of course be a loser. The issue raised by the foregoing extracts (i.e. whether a voidable contract has been successfully set aside) often follows the distinct question as to whether the original contract is void or voidable (see 3.12.3 in the text for a discussion of this problem).

BUYERS' AND SELLERS' REMEDIES FOR BREACH OF DUTIES OF DELIVERY, ACCEPTANCE AND PAYMENT SALE OF GOODS ACT 1979: PARTS V AND VI

38 Unpaid seller defined

(1) The seller of goods is an unpaid seller within the meaning of this Act —

    (a)   when the whole of the price has not been paid or tendered;

    (b)   when a bill of exchange or other negotiable instrument has been received as conditional payment and the condition on which it was received has not been fulfilled by reason of the dishonour of the instrument or otherwise.

(2)   In this part of this Act 'seller' includes any person who is in the position of a seller, as, for instance, an agent of the seller to whom the bill of lading has been indorsed, or a consignor or agent who has himself paid (or is directly responsible for) the price.

Note
Section 38(1)(b) would cover situations where the seller has taken a cheque as payment and it has not been honoured by the bank.

39 Unpaid seller's rights
(1)   Subject to this and any other Act, notwithstanding that the property in the goods may have passed to the buyer, the unpaid seller of goods, as such, has by implication of law —

    (a)   a lien on the goods or right to retain them for the price while he is in possession of them;

    (b)   in case of the insolvency of the buyer, a right of stopping the goods in transit after he has parted with the possession of them;

    (c)   a right of re-sale as limited by this Act.

(2)   Where the property in goods has not passed to the buyer, the unpaid seller has (in addition to his other remedies) a right of withholding delivery similar to and co-extensive with his rights of lien or retention and stoppage in transit where the property has passed to the buyer.

41 Seller's lien
(1)   Subject to this Act, the unpaid seller of goods who is in possession of them is entitled to retain possession of them until payment or tender of the price in the following cases:—

    (a)   where the goods have been sold without any stipulation as to credit;

    (b)   where the goods have been sold on credit, but the term of credit has expired;

    (c)   where the buyer becomes insolvent.

(2)   The seller may exercise his lien or right of retention, notwithstanding that he is in possession of the goods as agent or bailee or custodier for the buyer.

Note
An insolvent buyer is defined by s. 61(4) as someone who has ceased to pay his debts in the ordinary course of business, or cannot pay them as they fall due.

Part delivery
Where an unpaid seller has made part delivery of the goods, he may exercise his lien or right of retention on the remainder, unless such part delivery has been made under such circumstances as to show an agreement to waive the lien or right of retention.

43 Termination of lien
(1)   The unpaid seller of goods loses his lien or right of retention in respect of them:

    (a)   when he delivers the goods to a carrier or other bailee or custodier for the purpose of transmission to the buyer without reserving the right of disposal of the goods;

(b)   when the buyer or his agent lawfully obtains possession of the goods;

(c)   by waiver of the lien or right of retention.

(2)   An unpaid seller of goods who has a lien or right of retention in respect of them does not lose his lien or right of retention by reason only that he has obtained judgment or decree for the price of the goods.

44   Right of stoppage in transit

Subject to this Act, when the buyer of goods becomes insolvent, the unpaid seller who has parted with the possession of the goods has the right of stopping them in transit, that is to say, he may resume possession of the goods as long as they are in course of transit and may retain them until payment or tender of the price.

45   Duration of transit

(1)   Goods are deemed to be in course of transit from the time when they are delivered to a carrier or other bailee or custodier for the purpose of transmission to the buyer, until the buyer or his agent in that behalf takes delivery of them from the carrier or other bailee or custodier.

(2)   If the buyer or his agent in that behalf obtains delivery of the goods before their arrival at the appointed destination, the transit is at an end.

(3)   If, after the arrival of the goods at the appointed destination, the carrier or other bailee or custodier acknowledges to the buyer or his agent that he holds the goods on his behalf and continues in possession of them as bailee or custodier for the buyer or his agent, the transit is at an end, and it is immaterial that a further destination for the goods may have been indicated by the buyer.

(4)   If the goods are rejected by the buyer, and the carrier or other bailee or custodier continues in possession of them, the transit is not deemed to be at an end, even if the seller has refused to receive them back.

(5)   When goods are delivered to a ship chartered by the buyer it is a question depending on the circumstances of the particular case, whether they are in the possession of the master as a carrier or as agent to the buyer.

(6)   Where the carrier or other bailee or custodier wrongfully refuses to deliver the goods to the buyer or his agent in that behalf, the transit is deemed to be at an end.

(7)   Where part delivery of the goods has been made to the buyer or his agent in that behalf, the remainder of the goods may be stopped in transit, unless such part delivery has been made under such circumstances as to show an agreement to give up possession of the whole of the goods.

46   How stoppage in transit is effective

(1)   The unpaid seller may exercise his right of stoppage in transit either by taking actual possession of the goods or by giving notice of his claim to the carrier or other bailee or custodier in whose possession the goods are.

(2)   The notice may be given either to the person in actual possession of the goods or to his principal.

(3)   If given to the principal, the notice is ineffective unless given at such time and under such circumstances that the principal, by the exercise of reasonable diligence, may communicate it to his servant or agent in time to prevent a delivery to the buyer.

(4)   When notice of stoppage in transit is given by the seller to the carrier or other bailee or custodier in possession of the goods, he must re-deliver the goods to, or according to the directions of, the seller; and the expenses of the re-delivery must be borne by the seller.

47   Effect of sub-sale etc. by buyer

(1)   Subject to this Act, the unpaid seller's right of lien or retention or stoppage in transit is not affected by any sale or other disposition of the goods which the buyer may have made, unless the seller has assented to it.

(2)   Where a document of title to goods has been lawfully transferred to any person as buyer or owner of the goods and that person transfers the document to a person who takes it in good faith and for valuable consideration, then:

(a)   if the last-mentioned transfer was by way of sale the unpaid seller's right of lien or retention or stoppage in transit is defeated; and

(b)   if the last-mentioned transfer was made by way of pledge or other disposition for value, the unpaid seller's right of lien or retention or stoppage in transit can only be exercised subject to the rights of the transferee.

48   Rescission: and resale by seller

(1)   Subject to this section, a contract of sale is not rescinded by the mere exercise by an unpaid seller of his right or lien or retention or stoppage in transit.

(2)   Where an unpaid seller who has exercised his right of lien or retention or stoppage in transit resells the goods, the buyer acquires a good title to them as against the original buyer.

(3)   Where the goods are of a perishable nature, or where the unpaid seller gives notice to the buyer of his intention to resell and the buyer does not, within a reasonable time, pay or tender the price, the unpaid seller may resell the goods and recover from the original buyer damages for any loss occasioned by his breach of contract.

(4)   Where the seller expressly reserves the right of resale in case the buyer should make default, and on the buyer making default resells the goods, the original contract of sale is rescinded, but without prejudice to any claim the seller may have for damages.

Note

The right of resale is not automatic, it is as limited by the Act (s. 39(1)(c)).

It is questionable how effective these remedies are. In most transactions the seller will have parted with the possession of the goods (if not the property also). Lien resale will be remedies unavailable to him and the opportunity to exercise stoppage in transit may be limited. It is submitted that the use of some suspensive condition would be a better safeguard for the unpaid seller.

49   Action for price

(1)   Where, under a contract of sale, the property in the goods has passed to the buyer and he wrongfully neglects or refuses to pay for the goods according to the terms of the contract, the seller may maintain an action against him for the price of goods.

(2)   Where, under a contract of sale, the price is payable on a day certain irrespective of delivery and the buyer wrongfully neglects or refuses to pay such a price, the seller may maintain an action for the price, although the property in the goods has not passed and the goods have not been appropriated to the contract.

(3)   Nothing in this section prejudices the right of the seller in Scotland to recover interest on the price from the date of tender of the goods, or from the date on which the price was payable, as the case may be.

50   Damages for non-acceptance

(1)   Where the buyer wrongfully neglects or refuses to accept and pay for the goods, the seller may maintain an action against him for damages for non-acceptance.

(2)   The measure of damages is the estimated loss directly and naturally resulting, in the ordinary course of events, from the buyer's breach of contract.

(3) Where there is an available market for the goods in question, the measure of damages is prima facie to be ascertained by the difference between the contract price and the market or current price at the time or times when the goods ought to have been accepted or (if no time was fixed for acceptance) at the time of the refusal to accept.

CHAPTER SEVEN
CONSUMER CREDIT

One of the most intractable problems for creditors was having some security over goods. One of the more successful (and longest lasting) solutions has been hire-purchase. The inability (or unwillingness) of the ordinary debtor to understand the true legal nature of the contract can be seen in the case below. (See also *Muirhead and Turnbull* v *Dickson* (1905) 7F 686).

HELBY v MATTHEWS
[1895] AC 471

Facts

The appellant was the owner of a piano, of which he had given possession to one Brewster, under an agreement in writing of 23 December 1892. On 22 April 1893, Brewster, improperly and without the consent of the appellant, pledged the piano with the respondent pawn brokers, as security for an advance. The appellant, upon discovering this, demanded the piano from the respondents, and on their refusing to deliver it, brought an action for its return. The defence set up by the respondents was that they had received the piano from Brewster in good faith, and without notice of any claim on the part of the appellant, and that Brewster having 'bought or agreed to buy' it from him they were protected by the Factors Act 1889 . . . s. 9.

The agreement was in the following terms:

This agreement made the . . . between Charles Helby . . . (hereinafter called the 'owner'), of the one part, and Charles Brewster . . . (hereinafter called the 'hirer'), of the other part witnesseth that the owner agrees at the request of the hirer to let on hire to the hirer a pianoforte. . . . And in consideration thereof the hirer agrees as follows:— 1. To pay the owner, on the 23rd day of December 1892 a rent or hire instalment of ten shillings sixpence (10s. 6d.); and 10s. 6d. on 23 of each succeeding month. 2. To keep and preserve the said instrument from injury (damage by fire included). 3. To keep the said instrument in the hirer's own custody at the above-named address, and not to remove the same (or permit or suffer the same to be removed) without the owner's previous consent in writing. 4. That if the hirer do not duly perform this agreement, the owner may (without prejudice to his rights under this agreement) terminate the hiring and retake possession of the said instrument. And for that purpose leave and licence is hereby given to the owner (or agent and servant, or any other person employed by owner) to enter any premises occupied by the hirer, or of which the hirer is tenant, to retake possession of the said instrument, without being liable to any suit, action, indictment, or other proceeding by the hirer, or any one claiming under said hirer. 5. That if the hiring should be terminated by the hirer (under clause A below), and the said instrument be returned to the owner, the hirer shall remain liable to the owner for arrears of hire up to the date of such return, and shall not on any ground whatever be entitled to any allowance, credit, return, or set-off for payments previously made. The owner agrees:

A. That the hirer may terminate the hiring by delivering up to the owner the said instrument.

B. If the hirer shall punctually pay the full sum of £18 10s. by 10s. 6d. at date of signing, and by 36 monthly instalments of 10s. 6d. in advance as aforesaid, the said instrument shall become the sole and absolute property of the hirer.

C. Unless and until the full sum of £18 18s. be paid, the said instrument shall be and continue to be the sole property of the owner.

The Factors Act 1889, s. 9 provided that:

Where a person, having bought or agreed to buy goods, obtains with the consent of the seller possession of the goods or the documents of title to the goods, the delivery or transfer, by that person or by a mercantile agent acting for him, of the goods or documents of title, under any sale, pledge, or other disposition thereof, or under any agreement for sale, pledge, or other disposition thereof, to any person receiving the same in good faith and without notice of any lien or other right of the original seller in respect of the goods, shall have the same effect as if the person making the delivery or transfer were a mercantile agent in possession of the goods or documents of title with the consent of the owner.

Lord Shand
My Lords, I am also of the same opinion. The right of the defendant to refuse delivery of the piano in question under [the Factors Act, s. 9] depends on his being able to show that Brewster in whose possession it was had either bought it or agreed to buy it from Mr. Helby the plaintiff and appellant, and the decision of this question depends entirely on the true construction of the agreement between the plaintiff and Brewster under which the latter got possession of the instrument. It is true that by that agreement Brewster undertook to pay to the appellant not only a first instalment of 10s. 6d. described as a 'rent or hire instalment', but to pay the same amount on the 23rd of each succeeding month and that it was provided that on the payment of 36 monthly instalments the piano should become his property. If these stipulations had been unqualified there would have been an absolute obligation or agreement by Brewster to acquire the instrument in property, and by purchase, although the instalments were described as for rent or hire. . . . But the whole obligations by Brewster were qualified by the stipulation: 'That the hirer may terminate the hiring by delivering up to the owner the said instrument'. This provision appears to me to make it clear that there was no purchase and no agreement to purchase. The hirer need not continue the hiring a day longer than he desired; and he need not allow the transaction to become one of purchase unless he desired to do so.

An agreement to purchase would infer an obligation to pay a price, the payment of which could be enforced by action, while here it is plain that no action for any balance of the alleged price could be maintained if Brewster thought fit at any time to return the instrument to its owner. The substance of the transaction was a hiring of the piano for the use of which monthly instalments were to be paid with a provision that the arrangement might ultimately result in a purchase, but that this should be entirely at the option of the hirer, and should depend entirely on his thinking fit to make payment of 36 monthly instalments. The contract of hiring only was to cease at his option on the instrument being returned to the owner.

It was maintained that under the general words of undertaking to pay future instalments there was an agreement to purchase within the meaning of the Factors Act, although there was power to resolve the agreement or to bring it to an end by returning the instrument. It seems to me to be very difficult to hold that even if in form the agreement could be correctly thus described this would satisfy the provision of the Factors Act which it has been forcibly maintained requires an absolute obligation to purchase and pay a price, or, at least, an obligation which is not merely dependent on the will or wish of the alleged purchaser.

In this case, however, I think there was an agreement of hiring only with an option to the hirer to become the purchaser; and that although there was an obligation to sell if the hirer should avail himself of the right of option to purchase, there was no obligation or agreement to purchase. I cannot hold that there is such an agreement on the part of one who having the beneficial use of the property of another agrees to pay instalments described as rent or hire instalments, and which he is entitled to treat as payments for hire only, because it is also stipulated that by continuing to make the payments for a certain time he shall acquire the property, he having at the same time the power at any moment and at his own will by returning the property to the owner to put an end to any obligation to pay any further instalments.

Note

Helby v *Matthews* signified judicial approval of what we know as hire-purchase. In spite of the fact that almost all individuals who enter into hire-purchase contracts as hirers have no wish to hire the goods that are the subject of the contract, that is the legal reality. Goods cannot be 'bought on hire-purchase', at least not until the final hire payment has been made and the option to purchase exercised. The Crowther Committee acknowledged that the legal form of hire-purchase contracts is a legal fiction and Lord Denning said in *Bridge* v *Campbell Discount Co* [1962] 1 All ER (at p. 398) 'My Lords, in order to determine this case it is as well to remember the nature of a hire purchase contract. It is in effect though not in law, a mortgage of goods.'

ELLIOTT v DIRECTOR GENERAL OF FAIR TRADING
[1980] 1 WLR 977 (DC)

In an attempt to boost their sales, Elliott & Sons, shoe retailers, mailed to selected members of the public an envelope containing advertising literature relating to the Elliott Credit Account Card and a card which had the appearance of a bank credit card. The front of the card said: 'Elliott Shoe Account', and on the back there was a box for the holder's signature and the words: 'This credit card is valid for immediate use. The sole requirement is your signature and means of identification. Credit is immediately available if you have a bank account'. The Director General of Fair Trading instituted proceedings against the company alleging that the cards were sent contrary to the 1974 Act, s. 51(1). The central issue in the case was whether the cards were credit tokens within the meaning of the Act. In the magistrates' court the company was found guilty of a contravention of s. 51(1) and appealed to the Divisional Court. In the Divisional Court counsel for the company argued that the word 'undertakes' in s. 14(1) implied that there was a need for a contractual agreement, i.e. making an offer capable of being accepted so as to impose upon the trader a legally binding obligation to supply to the consumer goods on offer. Taking this one step further, counsel argued that since the production of the card did not entitle the customer to a supply of goods on credit, but only to apply for a credit card when he signed an agreement, the card was not a credit card; the card was not valid for immediate use, the sole requirement was not a signature, and credit was not immediately available since, in order to get credit, a customer would have to fill in a direct debiting mandate to his bank.

However, the Divisional Court did not accept these arguments. There was no need, they said, for a contractual agreement to exist. One looked at the card and asked, whether on its face or its back, the company undertook on the production of it that cash or goods would be supplied. The fact that none of the statements on the card was true did not prevent it being a credit token within the Act. The court found that the card in this case did fall within the meaning of s. 51(1) and that the company was guilty of a contravention of that subsection.

Lender's Liability

In many cases goods will be supplied by one party (e.g., a garage) and the credit for the goods by another party (e.g., a finance company). Section 75 of the 1974 Act makes both of these parties potentially liable in the event of breach of contract, misrepresentation, etc. Section 75 does not cover the classic hire-purchase contract because the supplier of the goods and of the credit will be the same person (the finance company) (although s. 56 will apply). *UDT* v *Taylor* (below) is concened with liability of the lender under s. 75. Creditors have expressed the view that the liability imposed on them is unduly burdensome and are seeking to have the section repealed.

UNITED DOMINIONS TRUST LTD v TAYLOR
1980 SLT 28

Facts

A finance company lent money to the purchaser of a motor car, and subsequently raised an action against him for payment of the balance of the loan and interest, in terms of the agreement between them. The defender averred that he had rescinded the contract beween himself and the supplier on the ground of the latter's misrepresentation as to the condition of the motor car and on the ground of their breach of the contract with him. It was not disputed that the whole transaction was a debtor–creditor–supplier agreement in terms of s. 11(1)(b) and 12(b) of the said Act. The defender contended that the words 'any claim against the supplier' in s. 75(1) included a claim of rescission of the contract with the supplier. The pursuers contended that there were two contracts and that the ground of rescission of the contract with the supplier, namely, misrepresentation and breach of contract, could only apply to that contract, and that there was therefore no 'like claim against the creditor' in respect that the contract of loan had not been induced by misrepresentation or breach of contract.

Sheriff Principal R. Reid, Q.C.

The pursuers made a loan to the defender for the purchase of a motor car from a supplier, who is not a party to the action. The defender avers that the car was represented to him as being in good condition, roadworthy and fit for use on public roads and that it was none of these things. He has intimated the alleged misrepresentation and breach of contract to the supplier and the pursuers and has refused to pay the monthly instalments of loan repayment as they fall due. In the present action the pursuers sue for the balance of the loan and interest. The defender has pleaded the supplier's misrepresentation and breach of contract as a defence to the action and contends that he is entitled to do so under the terms of s. 75(1) of the Consumer Credit Act 1974 which is in the following terms:

If the debtor under a debtor-creditor-supplier agreement falling within section 12(b) or (e) has, in relation to a transaction financed by the agreement, any claim against the supplier in respect of a misrepresentation or breach of contract, he shall have a like claim against the creditor, who, with the supplier, shall accordingly be jointly and severally liable to the debtor.

The pursuers admit that the agreement with them is covered by the Consumer Credit Act 1974 and the parties' agents were agreed that the whole transaction was a debtor-creditor-supplier agreement in terms of s. 11(1) (b) and 12(b) of the Act.

In opening the appeal the defender argued that he had relevantly averred that the contract had been rescinded on the ground of the supplier's misrepresentation and breach of contract and that, by virtue of s. 75(1), the rescission affected both the contract of sale with the supplier and the contract of loan with the pursuers. The question, according to the appellant, was whether the words 'any claim against the supplier' included a claim of rescission of the contract with the supplier and the answer he proposed was that, as a matter of ordinary English usage, they plainly did. The pursuers' reply to this argument was that there were two contracts and that the grounds of rescission of the contract with the supplier, namely, misrepresentation and breach of contract, could only apply to that contract. These grounds could not constitute 'a like claim against the creditor' because there was no question of the contract of loan having been induced by misrepresentation or of there being a breach of contract in relation to it. The pursuers' agent also presented the wider argument that s. 75(1) was intended to enable the debtor to exercise claims against the creditor, such as claims for restitution or damages, but not to plead a right as a defence to an action by a creditor because the claims referred to in the subsection were limited to those whose enforcement would make the creditor jointly and severally liable with the supplier to the pursuer. The pursuers' agent accepted that there would be anomalous results if these limited rights were exercised while the loan contract remained operative but he contended that these difficulties arose from the wording of the subsection.

I do not agree with the pursuers' argument. The subject-matter of the section is 'any claim against the supplier in respect of a misrepresentation or breach of contract'. the claims which leap to mind as being open in these circumstances are claims to rescind the contract, to claim restitution of any sums paid to the supplier and to claim any damage which the debtor has sustained. It would be odd, to say the least, if the right to rescind was not available against the creditor and the right to restitution, which depends on rescission, was available. The section goes on to provide that, where such claims against the supplier exist, the debtor shall have 'a like claim against the creditor'. The section does not require that the claim against the creditor shall be justifiable on like grounds to the claim against the supplier, merely that it shall be the same sort of claim. The words 'a like claim' are thus wide enough to include a claim for rescission although the creditor has given no grounds for rescission of the loan contract.

This view of the subsection has been confirmed by a consideration of other provisions of the Act, particularly as they relate to debtor-creditor-supplier agreements. The long title of the Act narrates *inter alia* that the Act establishes a new system of licensing and other control of traders concerned with the provision of credit and their transactions. A reading of the Act discloses that it has created a completely new system of classifications and remedies to take effect whenever consumer credit is associated with the contracts of sale and hire. These statutory remedies have been superimposed on existing contractual remedies. One of the innovations of the Act is to treat two or more contracts which are economically part of one credit transaction as transactions which are legally linked. Where these linked transactions contain two contracts the fate of each contract depends on the other, even where the parties to the contracts are different. This approach leaves no room for the idea of privity of contract which is fundamental to the common law of contract. It is for that reason that I am unable to agree with the learned sheriff's use of the principle of privity of contract to throw light on the meaning of the subsection.

The present contract between the parties is agreed to be a debtor-creditor-supplier agreement under the Act, i.e. a consumer credit agreement regulated by the Act of the type in which credit is given for a restricted purpose or use in a transaction between a debtor and the supplier (who is not also the creditor) and made by the creditor under pre-existing arrangements between himself and the supplier (ss. 11(1)(b) and 12(b)). In such circumstances the contract of sale between the debtor and the supplier is a transaction linked to the credit agreement (s. 19(1)(b)). Withdrawal from the credit agreement operates as withdrawal from the contract of sale and cancellation of the credit agreement has a similar effect on the contract of sale (ss. 57(1), 69(1)); and there are other circumstances in which a credit agreement and the transaction linked to it stand or fall together (see Goode on *Consumer Credit Act 1974*, para. 19.9). All these are instances of cases in which events affecting the credit agreement operate also in the transaction linked to it. In precisely the same way s. 75(1) ensures that rescission of the contract of sale shall operate as rescission of a credit agreement linked to it where both form part of a debtor–creditor–supplier agreement.

Note

Sheriff Principal Reid's reasoning in this case has been doubted by some (*Stephenson*, (1987) *Consumer Credit Act*, Collins, p. 115). Are there public policy reasons, however, why Taylor should be allowed to act as he did?

CHAPTER EIGHT
THE LAW OF EMPLOYMENT

We saw in the text that the distinction between contracts of employment and self-employment is a fundamental one. Employers will generally be liable for the delictual acts of employees, but rarely for those of the self-employed. Even if it is established that the negligent act has been caused by an employee, the employer (more correctly his insurer) may seek to avoid liability by arguing that the employee was not within the 'scope of his employment' at the time. This is the issue in the first three cases. The issue of liability for employees when travelling to, during or from work, is obviously one that has a potential impact on very many employers. The first case considers liability for employees who are 'loaned' or hired out by one employer to another while the other concerns the employee's liability while the employee is travelling to or from work.

MERSEY DOCKS AND HARBOUR BOARD v COGGINS
& GRIFFITH LTD
[1947] AC 162

Facts

A harbour authority let a mobile crane to a firm of stevedores for loading a ship, providing a craneman who was employed and paid and liable to be dismissed by it, though the general hiring conditions stipulated that cranemen so provided should be the servants of the hirers. In the course of the operation he injured a third person by negligently driving the crane. At the time the stevedores had the immediate direction and control of the operation of picking up and moving each piece of cargo but had no power to direct how the crane should be worked or the controls manipulated. The injured person sued the harbour authority and the stevedores for damages.

Held

That the harbour authority, as general permanent employer, was liable, not having discharged the heavy burden of proof so as to shift to the stevedores its prima facie responsibility for the negligence of the craneman, who in the manner of his driving was exercising the discretion it had vested in him. The question who was the employer responsible for his negligence was not determined by any agreement between the harbour authority and the stevedores.

Lord Macmillan

My Lords, the only question for your Lordships' determination is whether on the principle of *respondeat superior*, the responsibility for the negligence of the driver of the crane lies with the stevedores or with the appellant board, whom the plaintiff sued alternatively. The answer depends on whether the driver was acting as the servant of the stevedores or as the servant of the appellant board when he set the crane in motion. That the crane driver was in general the servant of the appellant board is indisputable. The appellant board engaged him, paid him, prescribed the jobs he should undertake and alone could dismiss him. The letting out of cranes on hire to stevedores for the purpose of loading and unloading vessels is a regular branch of the appellant board's business. In printed regulations and rates issued by the appellant board the cranes are described as 'available for general use on the dock estate at Liverpool and Birkenhead' and as regards portable cranes the stipulated rates vary according as they are provided 'with board's driver' or 'without board's driver'. Prima facie therefore it was as the servant of the appellant board that Newall was driving the crane when it struck the plaintiff. But it is always open to an employer to show, if he can, that he has for a particular purpose or on a particular occasion temporarily transferred the services of one of his general servants to another party so as to constitute him *pro hac vice* the servant of that other party with consequent liability for his negligent acts. The burden is on the general employer to establish that such a transference has been effected. Agreeing as I do with the trial judge and the Court of Appeal, I am of opinion that, on the facts of the present case, Newall was never so transferred from the service and control of the appellant board to the service and control of the stevedores as to render the stevedores answerable for the manner in which he carried on his work of driving the crane. The stevedores were entitled to tell him where to go, what parcels to lift and where to take them, that is to say, they could direct him as to what they wanted him to do; but they had no authority to tell him how he was to handle the crane in doing his work. In driving the crane, which was the appellant board's property confided to his charge, he was acting as the servant of the appellant board, not as the servant of the stevedores. It was not in consequence of any order of the stevedores that he negligently ran down the plaintiff; it was in consequence of his negligence in driving the crane, that is to say, in performing the work which he was employed by the appellant board to do.

SMITH v STAGES AND ANOTHER
[1989] 1 All ER 833

Facts

The employee was employed by the employers as a peripatetic lagger to install insulation at power stations. In August 1977 he was working on a power station in the Midlands when he was taken off that job and sent with another employee, the first defendant, to carry out an urgent job on a power station in Wales. The two employees were paid eight hours' pay for the travelling time to Wales and eight hours' pay for the journey back, as well as the equivalent of the rail fare for the journey, although no stipulation was made as to the mode of travel. The two employees travelled to Wales in the first defendant's car and stayed a week in Wales while working on the power station there. At the end of the job, after working for 19 hours without sleep in order to finish the job, they decided to drive straight back to the Midlands. On the way back the car, driven by the first defendant, left the road and crashed through a brick wall. The employee was seriously injured and he brought an action against the first defendant, who was uninsured, and against the employers alleging that they were vicariously liable for the first defendant's negligence since he had been acting in the course of his employment while driving the two employees back to the Midlands. The employee subsequently died from unrelated causes and his widow continued the action on behalf of his estate. The judge held that the accident had been caused by the first defendant's negligence but further held that the employers were not liable because he had not been acting in the course of his employment at the time of the accident. On appeal, the Court of Appeal reversed his decision and held that the employers were vicariously liable for the first defendant's negligence. The employers appealed to the House of Lords.

Held
An employee who for a short time was required by his employer to work at a different place of work some distance away from his usual place of work was acting in the course of his employment when returning to his ordinary residence after completing the temporary work if he travelled back to his ordinary residence in the employer's time, which he would be doing if he was paid wages (and not merely a travelling allowance) for the time travelled notwithstanding that the time and mode of travel were left to his discretion. Accordingly, since the employees had been paid while driving back to the Midlands they had been travelling in the employers' time and the employers were vicariously liable for the first defendant's negligence. The appeal would therefore be dismissed.

Per curiam. An employee travelling on the highway will be acting in the course of his employment if, and only if, he is at the material time going about his employer's business. The duty to turn up for work must not be confused with the concept of already being 'on duty' while travelling to it.

Lord Lowry
. . . If the employers cannot succeed, they seek in the alternative as much certainty as the common law and your Lordships' House can give them in a field which can too easily provide wasteful and expensive opportunities for conflict between the insurers, on the one hand, of motorists alleged to have caused damage by negligence and, on the other, of employers who are sought, by reason of someone's allegedly negligent driving, to be rendered vicariously liable for (and sometimes to) one of their employees.

The paramount rule is that an employee travelling on the highway will be acting in the course of his employment if, and only if, he is at the material time going about his employer's business. One must not confuse the duty to turn up for one's work with the concept of already being 'on duty' while travelling to it.

It is impossible to provide for every eventuality and foolish, without the benefit of argument, to make the attempt, but some prima facie propositions may be stated with reasonable confidence. (1) An employee travelling from his ordinary residence to his regular place of work, whatever the means of transport and even if it is provided by the employer, is not on duty and is not acting in the course of his employment, but, if he is obliged by his contract of service to use the employer's transport, he will normally, in the absence of an express condition to the contrary, be regarded as acting in the course of his employment while doing so. (2) Travelling in the employer's time between workplaces (one of which may be the regular workplace) or in the course of a peripatetic occupation, whether accompanied by goods or tools or simply in order to reach a succession of workplaces (as an inspector of gas meters might do), will be in the course of the employment. (3) Receipt of wages (though not receipt of a travelling allowance) will indicate that the employee is travelling in the employer's time and for his benefit and is acting in the course of his employment, and in such a case the fact that the employee may have discretion as to the mode and time of travelling will not take the journey out of the course of his employment. (4) An employee travelling *in the employer's time* from his ordinary residence to a workplace other than this regular workplace or in the course of a peripatetic occupation or to the scene of an emergency (such as a fire, an accident or a mechanical breakdown of plant) will be acting in the course of his employment. (5) A deviation from or interruption of a journey undertaken in the course of employment (unless the deviation or interruption is merely incidental to the journey) will for the time being (which may include an overnight interruption) take the employee out of the course of his employment. (6) Return journeys are to be treated on the same footing as outward journeys.

All the foregoing propositions are subject to any express arrangements between the employer and the employee or those representing his interests. They are not, I would add, intended to define the position of salaried employees, with regard to whom the touchstone of payment made in the employer's time is not generally significant.

Note

(1)   Before undertaking the return journey the employees had worked 19 hours without sleep. With a couple of exceptions (lorry and bus drivers) there is no provision as to the maximum length of a working day. Do you think there should be? What do you think of the argument that an employer who allows his employees to work exceptionally long hours is in breach of his common law duty of care by not providing a safe system of work?

It is unfortunate that the question of whether a worker is an employee or self-employed has been left to the uncertainty of the courts. They have grappled with the problem as best they could (with a few exceptions) and it seems that they are prepared to take a very broad look at the relationship in reaching a decision. The multifactorial test in general use today, which seeks to determine whether the employee really is in business on his own account, has, arguably, Scottish parents, as the case below shows.

PARK v WILSONS AND CLYDE COAL COMPANY LTD
1928 SC 121

Facts

A brusher and his partner contracted with the colliery company to drive a stonemine in one of their pits, and as permitted by the contract personally engaged two miners to help with the work. In the course of the work the brusher and one of the miners were injured through an explosion of shots which certain shot firers in the employment of the colliery company had left unexploded during earlier operations. In actions of damages brought by the injured men, the defenders denied liability in respect of the pursuers, averring that they were servants of the company and that the accident was due to the act of their fellow servants. This was the defence of common employment which was an English import into the common law. Under it an employee could not recover damages from an employer if the injury had been caused by a fellow employee. It was finally abolished by the Law Reform (Personal Injuries) Act 1948.

Lord Moncrieff

The principal facts which in former cases have been held to be relevant and to invite inquiry appear to be four in number. The law will affirm that the relation of master and servant exists in a case in which he who claims to be master (1) selects and engages the employee as his servant; (2) pays the wages; (3) controls and directs the manner of the doing of the work; and (4) exercises the right of dismissal. If it be established in evidence that all these facts are present or are accepted by the parties as present in any particular relation between men, the law will affirm that the parties are related as master and servant. The four elements are, however, in my opinion, of unequal importance. The relation of master and servant may survive even in a case in which a servant has been lent by his master in order that he may act *pro hac vice* as servant of another. In such circumstances there may be delegation of control. In like manner it is established in the cases that payment of wages may be made by some other party than the master without breach of the contract of service.

Note

Lord Moncrieff's dicta about the master/servant relationship surviving when the servant is lent out by the master to be the servant of another predates the decision in *Mersey Docks and Harbour Board* v *Coggins and Griffith Ltd* by many years.

The employment contract need not be in writing. Most employees do, however, have the right to a written statement of the major terms of the contract. The statement (which is not a contract itself) now has to be given within two months of the start of the employment (TURERA 1993 adopting EC Directive 91/533, Proof of Employment Relationship).

EMPLOYMENT PROTECTION (CONSOLIDATION) ACT 1978

1 Written particulars of terms of employment

(1) Not later than thirteen weeks after the beginning of an employee's employment with an employer, the employer shall give to the employee a written statement in accordance with the following provisions of this section.

(2) An employer shall in a statement under this section —
(a) identify the parties;
(b) specify the date when the employment began;
(c) specify the date on which the employee's period of continuous employment began (taking into account any employment with a previous employer which counts towards that period).

(3) A statement under this section shall contain the following particulars of the terms of employment as at a specified date not more than one week before the statement is given, that is to say—
(a) the scale or rate of remuneration, or the method of calculating remuneration,

(b)   the intervals at which remuneration is paid (that is, whether weekly or monthly or by some other period),

(c)   any terms and conditions relating to hours of work (including any terms and conditions relating to normal working hours),

(d)   any terms and conditions relating to —

(i)   entitlement to holidays, including public holidays, and holiday pay (the particulars given being sufficient to enable the employee's entitlement, including any entitlement to accrued holiday pay on the termination of employment, to be precisely calculated),

(ii)   incapacity for work due to sickness or injury, including any provision for sick pay,

(iii)   pensions and pension schemes,

(e)   the length of notice which the employee is obliged to give and entitled to receive to determine his contract of employment, and

(f)   the title of the job which the employee is employed to do:

Provided that paragraph (d)(iii) shall not apply to the employees of any body or authority if the employees' pension rights depend on the terms of a pension scheme established under any provision contained in or having effect under an Act of Parliament and the body or authority are required by any such provision to give to new employees information concerning their pension rights, or concerning the determination of questions affecting their pension rights.

(4)   Subject to subsection (5), every statement given to an employee under this section shall include a note —

(a)   specifying any disciplinary rules applicable to the employee, or referring to a document which is reasonably accessible to the employee and which specifies such rules,

(b)   specifying, by description or otherwise —

(i)   a person to whom the employee can apply if he is dissatisfied with any disciplinary decision relating to him; and

(ii)   a person to whom the employee can apply for the purpose of seeking redress of any grievance relating to his employment,

and the manner in which any such application should be made;

(c)   where there are further steps consequent upon any such application explaining those steps or referring to a document which is reasonably accessible to the employee and which explains them; and

(d)   stating whether a contracting-out certificate is in force for the employment in respect of which the statement is given.

(5)   The provisions of paragraphs (a) to (c) of subsection (4) shall not apply to rules, disciplinary decisions, grievances or procedures relating to health or safety at work.

(6)   The definition of week given by section 153(1) does not apply for the purposes of this section.

Notes

(1)   Why is it important to know the date employment began (s.1(2)(b)) and the date continuous employment began (s.1(2)(c))?

(2)   Since TURERA 1993 amended the EPCA 1978 provisions employers have to provide the following additional information:

(a)   the place of work;

(b)   where the employee is required (or permitted) to work in various places, an indication of that fact and the address of the employer;

(c)   any collective agreement which directly affects the terms and conditions of employment of the individual employee (including the identity of the parties by whom such collective agreements were made);

(d)   where the employment is not intended to be permanent the period of the expected duration of the contract;

(e)   where the employee is to work outside the UK for a period of one month certain additional information.

(2)   The written particulars contain provision for a mobility clause (see 8.3.2 above). This one seems to be broad in its terms. Do you think it would be upheld by the courts? Do you think it involves an element of sex discrimination? (See 8.6.12).

(3)   In an action by an employee for breach of duty of care by the employer one of the main defences is that of remoteness i.e. the loss or injury was not reasonably forseeable as a consequence of the negligent act or omission. The case below discusses this issue albeit not in an employer/employee setting.

Generally speaking, ex-employees face no legal difficulties if they wish to go into competition with their former employer. There may, be a problem however, if in doing so they use trade secrets, particularly if the ex-employee is subject to a restraint of trade clause. The case below is the most authoritative statement of the law on this topic.

FACCENDA CHICKEN LTD v FOWLER AND OTHERS
[1987] Ch 117

Facts
The plaintiff company was engaged in the business of marketing fresh chickens. In 1973 it employed F as its sales manager and at his suggestion adopted a method of selling fresh chickens from refrigerated vans which travelled through particular routes within a defined area. Each van salesman received sales information regarding the customers' names and addresses, the general limits of the routes, the quantity and quality of goods sold and the prices charged. In November 1980 F left the plaintiff's employment and subsequently set up his own business of selling fresh chickens from refrigerated vans. He conducted his business in the same area as the plaintiff, his vans operated on the same routes as the plaintiff's and he served the same type of customers. Five of the plaintiff's van salesmen and three other employees left the plaintiff's employment and joined F's business. None of the former employees was subject to an express agreement restricting his or her services after leaving the plaintiff's employment. The plaintiff brought an action against F and the other former employees claiming (i) damages for breach of their contracts of employment in using the plaintiff's sales information to the disadvantage or detriment of the plaintiff and (ii) damages for conspiracy to injure the plaintiff's goodwill by abuse of confidential information. The judge dismissed the action on the grounds that, although the defendants had made use of the sales information for the purpose of the new business, that did not involve any breach of contract by F and the other employees or provide evidence of an actionable conspiracy. The plaintiff appealed to the Court of Appeal, contending that any information about prices charged to individual customers was confidential and that, since the information about prices formed part of the package of sales information, the whole package should be regarded as confidential.

Held
(1)   The duty of fidelity owed by an employee to a former employer was not as great as the duty implied in the employee's contract of employment and owed during

the subsistence of the employment, when use or disclosure of confidential information, even though it did not amount to a trade secret, would be a breach of the duty of good faith. Accordingly, confidential information concerning an employer's business acquired by an employee in the course of his service could be used by the employee after his employment had ceased unless the information was classed as a trade secret or was so confidential that it required the same protection as a trade secret. Furthermore, an employer could not restrict the use or disclosure of confidential information by a restrictive covenant in the employee's contract of employment unless the information sought to be protected was a trade secret or equivalent to a trade secret.

(2) In order to determine whether information was a trade secret or equivalent to a trade secret it was necessary to have regard to (a) the nature of the employment, for example whether the status of the employee was such that he regularly handled confidential information and recognised it as such or whether the information was only handled by a restricted number of employees, (b) the nature of the information itself, (c) whether the employer had stressed the confidentiality of the information to the employee and (d) whether the relevant information could easily be isolated from other non-confidential information which was part of the same package of information. Applying those tests, it was clear that neither the sales information as a whole nor the information about prices charged by the plaintiffs fell within the classes of confidential information which an employee was bound by an implied term of his contract not to use or disclose after his employment had ceased.

Per curiam. The general duty of good faith owed by an employee to his employer during the currency of his employment will be broken if the employer makes, copies or deliberately memorises a list of the employer's customers for use after his employment has ceased, notwithstanding that, except in special circumstances, there is no general restriction on ex-employees canvassing or doing business with customers of former employers.

Neil LJ

In these two appeals it will be necessary to consider the interaction of three separate legal concepts. (1) The duty of an employee during the period of his employment to act with good faith towards his employer; this duty is sometimes called the duty of fidelity. (2) The duty of an employee not to use or disclose after his employment has ceased any confidential information which he has obtained during his employment about his employer's affairs. (3) The prima facie right of any person to use and to exploit for the purpose of earning his living all the skill, experience and knowledge which he has at his disposal, including skill, experience and knowledge which he has acquired in the course of previous periods of employment. . . . In the course of his submissions in support of the appeal counsel for Faccenda Chicken Ltd took us on an instructive and valuable tour of many of the cases dealing with the law of confidence in the context of the relationship between employer and employee and also referred us to some of the cases on restrictive covenants.

It is not necessary, however, for us for the purpose of this judgment to travel this ground again. It is sufficient to set out what we understand to be the relevant principles of law. Having considered the cases to which we were referred, we would venture to state these principles as follows.

(1) Where the parties are, or have been, linked by a contract of employment, the obligations of the employee are to be determined by the contract between him and his employer: cf *Vokes Ltd* v *Heather* (1945) 62 RPC 135 at 141.

(2) In the absence of any express term, the obligations of the employee in respect of the use and disclosure of information are the subject of implied terms.

(3) While the employee remains in the employment of the employer the obligations are included in the implied term which imposes a duty of good faith or fidelity on the employee. For the purpose of the present appeal it is not necessary to consider the precise limits of this implied term, but it may be noted: (a) that the extent of the duty of good faith will vary according to the nature of the contract (see *Vokes Ltd* v *Heather*); (b) that the duty of good faith will be broken if an employee makes or copies a list of the customers of the employer for use after his employment ends or deliberately memorises such a list, even though, except in special circumstances, there is no general restriction on an ex-employee canvassing or doing business with customers of his former employer (see *Robb* v *Green* [1895-9] All ER 1053 and *Wessex Dairies Ltd* v *Smith* [1935] All ER 75).

(4) The implied term which imposes an obligation on the employee as to his conduct after the determination of the employment is more restricted in its scope than that which imposes a general duty of good faith. It is clear that the obligation not to use or disclose information may cover secret processes of manufacture such as chemical formulae (see *Amber Size and Chemical Co Ltd* v *Menzel* [1913] 2 Ch 239), or designs or special methods of construction (see *Reid Sigrist Ltd* v *Moss Mechanism Ltd* (1932) 49 RPC 461), and other information which is of a sufficiently high degree of confidentiality as to amount to a trade secret.

The obligation does not extend, however, to cover all information which is given to or acquired by the employee while in his employment, and in particular may not cover information which is only 'confidential' in the sense that an unauthorised disclosure of such information to a third party while the employment subsisted would be a clear breach of the duty of good faith.

This distinction is clearly set out in the judgment of Cross J in *Printers and Finishers Ltd* v *Holloway* [1964] 3 All ER 731 where he had to consider whether an ex-employee should be restrained by injunction from making use of his recollection of the contents of certain written printing instructions which had been made available to him when he was working in his former employers' flock printing factory. In his judgment, delivered on 29 April 1964 (not reported on this point in the Weekly Law Reports), Cross J said ([1964] 3 All ER 731 at 738n):

In this connexion one must bear in mind that not all information which is given to a servant in confidence and which it would be a breach of his duty for him to disclose to another person during his employment is a trade secret which he can be prevented from using for his own advantage after the employment is over, even though he has entered into no express covenant with regard to the matter in hand. For example, the printing instructions were handed to [the first defendant] to be used by him during his employment exclusively for the plaintiffs' benefit. It would have been a breach of duty on his part to divulge any of the contents to a stranger while he was employed, but many of these instructions are not really 'trade secrets' at all. [The first defendant] was not, indeed, entitled to take a copy of the instructions away with him; but insofar as the instructions cannot be called 'trade secrets' and he carried them in his head, he is entitled to use them for his own benefit or the benefit of any future employer.

The same distinction is to be found in *E Worsley & Co Ltd* v *Cooper* [1939] 1 All ER 290, where it was held that the defendant was entitled, after he had ceased to be employed, to make use of his knowledge of the source of the paper supplied to his previous employer. In our view it is quite plain that this knowledge was nevertheless 'confidential' in the sense that it would have been a breach of the duty of good faith for the employee, while the employment subsisted, to have used it for his own purposes or to have disclosed it to a competitor of his employer.

(5) In order to determine whether any particular item of information falls within the implied term so as to prevent its use or disclosure by an employee after his employment has ceased, it is necessary to consider all the circumstances of the case. We are satisfied that the following matters are among those to which attention must be paid. (a) The nature of the employment. Thus employment in a capacity where 'confidential' material is habitually handled may impose a high obligation of confidentiality because the employee can be expected to realise its sensitive nature to a greater extent than if he were employed in a capacity where such material reaches him only occasionally or incidentally. (b) The nature of the information itself. In our judgment the information will only be protected if it can properly be classed as a trade secret or as material which, while not properly to be described as a trade secret, is in all the circumstances of such a highly confidential nature as to require the same protection as a trade secret *eo nomine*. The restrictive covenant cases demonstrate that a covenant will not be upheld on the basis of the status of the information which might be disclosed by the former employee if he is not restrained unless it can be regarded as a trade secret or the equivalent of a trade secret.

It is clearly impossible to provide a list of matters which will qualify as trade secrets or their equivalent. Secret processes of manufacture provide obvious examples, but innumerable other pieces of information are *capable* of being trade secrets, though the secrecy of some information may be only short-lived. In addition, the fact that the circulation of certain information is restricted to a limited number of individuals may throw light on the status of the information and its degree of confidentiality. (c) Whether the employer impressed on the employee the confidentiality of the information. Thus, though an employer cannot prevent the use or disclosure *merely* by telling the employee that certain information is confidential, the attitude of the employer towards the information provides evidence which may assist in determining whether or not the information can properly be regarded as a trade secret. It is to be observed that in *E Worsley & Co Ltd* v *Cooper* [1939] 1 All ER, Morton J (at p. 307) attached significance to the fact that no warning had been given to the defendant that the source from which the paper came was to be treated as confidential. (d) Whether the relevant information can be easily isolated from the other information which the employee is free to use or disclose. . . .

These then are the principles of law which we consider to be applicable to a case such as the present one. We would wish to leave open, however, for further examination on some other occasion the question whether additional protection should be afforded to an employer where the former employee is not seeking to earn his living by making use of the body of skill, knowledge and experience which he has acquired in the course of his career, but is merely selling to a third party information which he acquired in confidence in the course of his former employment.

Note
How do you think this reasoning squares with the decisions on restraint of trade generally (see 3.9.3 above)?

The next case demonstrates the importance that is placed on following correct procedures in dismissal cases. There have been decisions since, however, which would seem to regard minor breaches of procedure as unimportant (*Eclipse Blinds* v *Wright* [1992] IRLR 133, *Fuller* v *Lloyds Bank* [1991] IRLR 337). Employers are, however, still advised to follow correct procedure.

POLKEY v A E DAYTON SERVICES LTD
[1987] 3 All ER 974

Facts

The employee was one of four drivers employed by the company. The company decided to replace the van drivers with two van salesmen and a representative. Only one van driver was considered suitable for transfer to the new duties, and it was then decided that the other three including Polkey would have to be made redundant. Without prior warning, the employee was called into the branch manager's office and informed that he had been made redundant. He was handed a redundancy letter setting out the payments due to him and sent home. On his complaint that he had been unfairly dismissed because he had been made redundant without any consultation, the industrial tribunal held that the employers had been in breach of their obligation to consult the employee under the provisions of the code of practice. They went on however to consider whether, if there had been any consultation, the result would have been any different, concluded that the result would have been the same and dismissed the employee's complaint. The employee appealed, contending that the industrial tribunal had applied the wrong test in inquiring whether the employee would have been made redundant if he had been consulted. The employee appealed to the House of Lords.

Lord Bridge

My Lords, I have had the advantage of reading in draft the speech of my noble and learned friend the Lord Chancellor and I agree with it. I add some short observations of my own because of the importance of the case.

Employers contesting a claim of unfair dismissal will commonly advance as their reason for dismissal one of the reasons specifically recognised as valid by section 57(2)(a), (b) and (c) of the Employment Protection (Consolidation) Act 1978. These, put shortly, are: (a) that the employee could not do his job properly; (b) that he had been guilty of misconduct; (c) that he was redundant. But an employer having prima facie grounds to dismiss for one of these reasons will in the great majority of cases not act reasonably in treating the reason as a sufficient reason for dismissal unless and until he has taken the steps, conveniently classified in most of the authorities as 'procedural', which are necessary in the circumstances of the case to justify that course of action. Thus, in the case of incapacity, the employer will normally not act reasonably unless he gives the employee fair warning and an opportunity to mend his ways and show that he can do the job; in the case of misconduct, the employer will normally not act reasonably unless he investigates the complaint of misconduct fully and fairly and hears whatever the employee wishes to say in his defence or in explanation or mitigation; in the case of redundancy, the employer will normally not act reasonably unless he warns and consults any employees affected or their representative, adopts a fair basis on which to select for redundancy and takes such steps as may be reasonable to avoid or minimise redundancy by redeployment within his own organisation. If an employer has failed to take the appropriate procedural steps in any particular case, the one question the industrial tribunal is *not* permitted to ask in applying the test of reasonableness posed by section 57(3) is the hypothetical question whether it would have made any difference to the outcome if the appropriate procedural steps had been taken. On the true construction of section 57(3) this question is simply irrelevant. It is quite a different matter if the tribunal is able to conclude that the employer himself, at the time of dismissal, acted reasonably in taking the view that, in the exceptional circumstances of the particular case, the procedural steps normally appropriate would have been futile, could not have altered the decision to dismiss and therefore could be dispensed with. In such a case the test of reasonableness under section 57(3) may be satisfied.

My Lords, I think these conclusions are fully justified by the cogent reasoning of Browne-Wilkinson J in *Sillifant* v *Powell Duffryn Timber Ltd* [1983] IRLR 91 to which my noble and learned friend the Lord Chancellor has already drawn attention.

If it is held that taking the appropriate steps which the employer failed to take before dismissing the employee would not have affected the outcome, this will often lead to the result that the employee, though unfairly dismissed, will recover no compensation or, in the case of redundancy, no compensation in excess of his redundancy payment. Thus in *Earl* v *Slater & Wheeler (Airlyne) Ltd* [1973] 1 WLR 51 the employee was held to have been unfairly dismissed, but nevertheless lost his appeal to the National Industrial Relations Court because his misconduct disentitled him to any award of compensation, which was at that time the only effective remedy. But in spite of this the application of the so-called *British Labour Pump* principle [1979] ICR 347 tends to distort the operation of the employment protection legislation in two important ways. First, as was pointed out by Browne-Wilkinson J in *Sillifant's* case, if the industrial tribunal, in considering whether the employer who has omitted to take the appropriate procedural steps acted reasonably or unreasonably in treating his reason as a sufficient reason for dismissal, poses for itself the hypothetical question whether the result would have been any different if the appropriate procedural steps had been taken, it can only answer that question on a balance of probabilities. Accordingly, applying the *British Labour Pump* principle, if the answer is that it probably would have made no difference, the employee's unfair dismissal claim fails. But if the likely effect of taking the appropriate procedural steps is only considered, as it should be, at the stage of assessing compensation, the position is quite different. In that situation, as Browne-Wilkinson J put it in *Sillifant's* case, at p. 96:

> There is no need for an 'all or nothing' decision. If the industrial tribunal thinks there is a doubt whether or not the employee would have been dismissed, this element can be reflected by reducing the normal amount of compensation by a percentage representing the chance that the employee would still have lost his employment.

The second consideration is perhaps of particular importance in redundancy cases. An industrial tribunal may conclude, as in the instant case, that the appropriate procedural steps would not have avoided the employee's dismissal as redundant. But if, as your Lordships now hold, that conclusion does not defeat his claim of unfair dismissal, the industrial tribunal, apart from any question of compensation, will also have to consider whether to make any order under section 69 of the Act of 1978. It is noteworthy that an industrial tribunal may, if it thinks fit, make an order for re-engagement under that section and in so doing exercise a very wide discretion as to the terms of the order. In a case where an industrial tribunal held that dismissal on the ground of redundancy would have been inevitable at the time when it took place even if the appropriate procedural steps had been taken, I do not, as at present advised, think this would necessarily preclude a discretionary order for re-engagement on suitable terms, if the altered circumstances considered by the tribunal at the date of the hearing were thought to justify it.

For these reasons and for those given by my noble and learned friend the Lord Chancellor I would allow the appeal and remit the case to be heard by another industrial tribunal.

Hayward (below) was one of the first and most significant of the equal pay for work of equal value cases.

HAYWARD v CAMMELL LAIRD SHIPBUILDERS LTD
[1988] 2 All ER 257

Facts

The appellant was employed as a cook in a canteen at the respondents' shipyard. She claimed that her work was of equal value to that of three male employees, namely a painter, a joiner and an insulation engineer, and that she was entitled under s. 1(2) of the Equal Pay Act 1970 to equal pay to the men because a 'term' of her contract was less favourable than a term of a similar kind in the contracts of her male comparators. The respondents conceded that her basic pay and overtime rates were less favourable than those of the male comparators but claimed that, looking at the contracts as a whole and taking into account such factors as sickness benefits and meal breaks, she was treated as favourably as the men. The industrial tribunal held that the appellant was not entitled to relief in respect of specific terms of her contract if her contract, considered as a whole, was as favourable as the men's contracts. The appellant's appeals to the Employment Appeal Tribunal and then to the Court of Appeal were dismissed. She appealed to the House of Lords.

Held

Where a term of a woman's contract of employment was less favourable than a term of a similar kind in the contract of a man employed by the same employer and doing work of equal value she was entitled, under s. 1(2) to parity as regards that term irrespective of whether she was as favourably treated as the man when the whole of both contracts were compared. Furthermore, for the purpose of such a comparison a 'term' of a contract denoted a distinct provision or part of a contract which could be compared with a similar provision in another contract, and in relation to pay a 'term' referred to particular provisions regarding pay, such as basic pay, overtime and bonuses etc, and not to the overall remuneration package. Since the appropriate comparison to be made was between the basic pay and overtime rates of the appellant and her male comparators her appeal would be allowed and the case remitted to the industrial tribunal to determine the merits on the basis of such a comparison.

Article 1 of EC Council Directive 75/117, which requires that the 'principle of equal pay' be implemented by the 'elimination of all discrimination on grounds of sex with regard to all aspects and conditions of remuneration' is to be interpreted as requiring each aspect to be considered and discrimination existing in any aspect to be eliminated irrespective of the other aspects.

Lord Goff

Section 1(2) is subdivided into three paragraphs: the first, (a), being concerned with like work, the second, (b), with work rated as equivalent, and the third, (c), with work of equal value. Each of these paragraphs makes provision for two alternative situations, (i) where any term of the woman's contract is (or becomes) less favourable to her than a term of a similar kind in the male comparator's contract, and (ii) where the woman's contract does not include a term corresponding to a term benefiting the male comparator included in his contract. I will call the first situation the case of the less favourable term, and the second situation the case of the absent term.

In considering the question of construction, it is plain that we have to consider it in relation both to the case of the less favourable term and the case of the absent term, for the same policy considerations must underlie each. Furthermore, I find it easier to approach the problem by considering first the case of the absent term, because the provisions of sub-para (ii) of each paragraph are in simpler terms than those of sub-para (i), and are therefore easier to construe.

What does sub-para (ii) in each case provide? It provides that if the woman's contract does not include a term corresponding to a term benefiting the male comparator included in his contract, her contract shall be treated as including such a term. Next, what does such a provision mean? If I look at the words used, and give them their natural and ordinary meaning, they mean quite simply that one looks at the man's contract and at the woman's contract, and if one finds in the man's contract a term benefiting him which is not included in the woman's contract, then that term is treated as included in hers. On this simple and literal approach, the words 'benefiting that man' mean precisely what they say, that the term must be one which is beneficial to him, as opposed to being burdensome. So if, for example, the man's contract contains a term that he is to be provided with the use of a car, and the woman's contract does not include such a term, then her contract is to be treated as including such a term.

It is obvious that this approach cannot be reconciled with the approach favoured by the Court of Appeal, because it does not require, or indeed permit, the court to look at the overall contractual position of each party, or even to look at their overall position as regards one particular matter, for example, 'pay' in the wide sense adopted by the Court of Appeal. To achieve that result, it would be necessary, in sub-para (ii), to construe the word 'term' as referring to the totality of the relevant contractual provisions relating to a particular subject matter, for example, 'pay', or, alternatively, to construe the words 'benefiting that man' as importing the necessity of a comparison in relation to the totality of the relevant contractual provisions concerning a particular subject matter and then for a conclusion to be reached that, on balance, the man has thereby benefited. The latter construction I find impossible to derive from the words of the statute; and, to be fair, I do not think that there is any evidence that it would have found favour with the Court of Appeal. But what of the former, which is consistent with the judgment of the Court of Appeal? Again, I find myself unable to accept it. First, it would mean that the situation of the absent term must be confined only to those cases where there was *no* provision relating, for example, to pay, or, I suppose, to overtime, or to some other wholly distinct topic. I cannot think that that was the intention of the legislature. In common sense terms, it means that sub-para (ii) would hardly ever be relevant at all; certainly, since every contract of employment makes some provision for 'pay' in the broad sense adopted by the Court of Appeal, sub-para (ii) would never be relevant in relation to pay or any other form of remuneration in cash or in kind or in the form of other benefits. I find this proposition to be startling. Second, it imposes on the word 'term' a meaning which I myself do not regard as its natural or ordinary meaning. If a contract contains provisions relating to (1) basic pay, (2) benefits in kind such as the use of a car, (3) cash bonuses, and (4) sickness benefits, it would never occur to me to lump all these together as one 'term' of the contract, simply because they can all together be considered as providing for the total 'remuneration' for the services to be performed under the contract. In truth, these would include a number of different terms; and in my opinion it does unacceptable violence to the words of the statute to construe the word 'term' in sub-para (ii) as embracing collectively all these different terms.

It is against the background of this reasoning in relation to the case of the absent term, that I turn to sub-para (i) and the case of the less favourable term. Here the Court of Appeal was able to build its construction on the basis of a reference, in the sub-paragraph, to 'a term of a similar kind' in the male comparator's contract. It considered that these words referred necessarily to a term relating to the same overall subject matter, in particular pay, and that the question whether the relevant term in the woman's contract was less favourable than that in the man's contract could only sensibly be considered by comparing all the provisions relating to this subject matter in the contracts of each. From this it derived the broad meaning of the word 'term' which I have described.

For my part, I cannot accept this reasoning. Suppose that there is a term in a woman's contract which provides that she is to be paid £x per hour, and that there is a term in the male comparator's contract that he is to be paid £y per hour, y being greater than x. On the natural and ordinary meaning of the words in the statute, there is, in my opinion, in such a case, a term of the woman's contract which is less favourable to her than a term of a similar kind in the male comparator's contract, and that would be so even if there was some other provision in her contract which conferred on her a benefit (which fell within her overall 'remuneration') which the man was not entitled to receive under his contract, such as, for example, the use of a car. I do not consider that the words 'a term of a similar kind' are capable of constituting a basis for building the construction of the word 'term' favoured by the Court of Appeal. Again, in my opinion, the words mean precisely what they say. You look at the two contracts; you ask yourself the common sense question, is there in each contract a term of a similar kind, i.e. a term making a comparable provision for the same subject matter; if there is, then you compare the two, and if, on that comparison, the term of the woman's contract proves to be less favourable than the term of the man's contract then the term in the woman's contract is to be treated as modified so as to make it not less favourable. I am, of course, much fortified in this approach in that it appears to me to be consistent with the only construction of sub-para (ii), concerned with the case of the absent term, which I find to be acceptable. But, in addition, I feel that the Court of Appeal's attempt to introduce the element of overall comparison placed it firmly, or rather infirmly, on a slippery slope; because, once it departed from the natural and ordinary meaning of the word 'term', it in reality found it impossible to control the ambit of the comparison which it considered to be required. For almost any, indeed perhaps any, benefit will fall within 'pay' in the very wide sense favoured by it, in which event it is difficult to segregate any sensible meaning of the word 'term'.

Now I fully appreciate that this construction of s. 1(2) will always lead, where the section is held to apply, to enhancement of the relevant term in the woman's contract. Likewise, it will in the converse case lead to enhancement of the relevant term in the man's contract. This appears to me to be the effect of the philosophy underlying the subsection. I also appreciate that this may, in some cases, lead to what has been called mutual enhancement or leap-frogging, as terms of the woman's contract and the man's contract are both, so to speak, upgraded to bring them into line with each other. It is this effect which was found to be so offensive by both the Employment Appeal Tribunal and the Court of Appeal. They viewed with dismay the possibility of equality being achieved only by mutual enhancement, and not by an overall consideration of the respective contractual terms of both the man and the woman, at least in relation to a particular subject matter such as overall remuneration, considering that mutual enhancement transcended the underlying philosophy of the 1970 Act and that it could have a profoundly inflationary effect.

To these fears there are, I consider, two different answers on two different levels. The first answer is that given by counsel for the appellant, which is that the employer must, where he can, have recourse to s. 1(3). I, for my part, see great force in this argument. I am, however, a little troubled about embarking on any deep discussion of the meaning and effect of the subsection in the present case. First, we were told that no reliance was placed on the subsection in this case, so that its effect has no direct bearing on your Lordship's decision in this appeal. Second, and for the same reason, we have before us no concrete facts on which to consider the application of the subsection in the context of the present case. Third, it appears that the construction of the subsection has caused, and indeed is causing, very considerable difficulty; to substantiate this, I need only refer to the helpful discussion in Pannick, *Sex Discrimination Law* (1985) pp 105-114. Even so, I do not think that it would be right in the present case to ignore the possible impact of s. 1(3). I propose however only to make these observations. First, it must be right, when construing the subsection, to have regard both to the statutory context, and in particular to the effect of the neighbouring s. 1(2); and it must also be right to have regard to the philosophy underlying the whole legislation. If regard is to be had to these, then, as counsel for the appellant suggests, s. 1(3) could indeed have the effect, in appropriate cases, of preventing the mutual enhancement which was so much feared by the Court of Appeal in the present case. An example may be derived from the recent decision of the Employment Appeal Tribunal in *Reed Packaging Ltd* v *Boozer* (1988) Times, 28 March, decided after the argument before your Lordships' House in the present case. In that case the tribunal held that different pay structures for the woman and her male comparator, wholly devoid of discrimination on the ground of sex, could constitute a material fact which is not the difference of sex, within s. 1(3). I must not be taken as stating that the particular case was correctly decided, since its correctness is not in issue before your Lordships' House in the present case: I use it only for the purpose of illustration. Of course, s. 1(3) must not be used so as to promote either direct or indirect discrimination (cf *Clay Cross (Quarry Services) Ltd* v *Fletcher* [1979] 1 All ER 474). So where, for example, there is direct or indirect discrimination embedded in the two relevant pay structures of the woman and her male comparator, it would appear that s. 1(3) cannot be invoked by the employer. In such a case, it may be that the effect of the statute, as I would construe it, is that it is capable of leading to mutual enhancement of the contractual terms of the man and the woman; though I entertain some doubt whether some of the examples considered in the course of argument are likely to arise in practice.

This brings me to my second answer, which is that, if the construction of s. 1(2) which I prefer does not accord with the true intention of Parliament, then the appropriate course for Parliament is to amend the legislation to bring it into line with its true intention. In the meanwhile, however, the decision of your Lordships' House may have the salutary effect of drawing to the attention of employers and trade unions the absolute need for ensuring that the pay structures for various groups of employees do not contain any element of sex discrimination, direct or indirect, because otherwise s. 1(3) will not be available to mitigate the effects which s.1(2), in its present form, is capable of producing on its own.

For these reasons, I would allow the appeal.

Note

(1)   Lord Goff says the Employment Appeal Tribunal and the Court of Appeal found the effect of mutual enhancement or leapfrogging as offensive, and profoundly inflationary. This was indeed the view taken by many employers of this decision. Cammell Laird did not use s. 1(3) as a defence. If they had done so, do you think they would have been successful in defeating Ms Hayward's claim? See Lord Mackay at p. 261.

One of the defences to an equal pay claim is that the reason for the difference in pay is a genuine material factor which has nothing to do with sex. *Rainey* (below) is an example of this defence. The decision in *Rainey* has, however, been somewhat diluted by *Enderby* v *Frenchay Health Authority* [1993] IRLR 591, where the ECJ said that market forces could not operate as a blanket defence to claims of sex discrimination as to pay. The employer must be able to justify the different pay rates on objectively justified economic grounds (which will include the state of the employment market).

RAINEY v GREATER GLASGOW HEALTH BOARD
[1987] AC 224

Facts
In 1979 the Scottish health department decided to discontinue the specialist prosthetic service provided by private contractors and to engage full-time prosthetists to be employed within the national health service on the appropriate civil service pay scale. However, in order to recruit prosthetists from the private contractors for the new service the department offered to prosthetists employed by the private contractors the option of entering the national health service on the civil service scale or on the basis of the pay and conditions offered by the private contractors, such pay being considerably higher than that paid under the civil service scale. Twenty prosthetists, including C, all of whom happened to be men, employed by the private contractors opted to join the national health service on the private sector pay and conditions. The appellant, a woman, later entered the employment of the national health service direct as a prosthetist and was paid according to the appropriate civil service scale. Because of the disparity between her pay and that of C, whose qualifications and experience were broadly similar, the appellant applied to an industrial tribunal under the Equal Pay Act 1970 for a declaration that she was entitled to the same pay as C. At the date of the tribunal hearing C was being paid £10,085 and the appellant £7,295. The tribunal dismissed the appellant's application on the ground that the difference in salary between the appellant and C was 'genuinely due to a material difference (other than difference of sex) between her case and his' and therefore the equality requirements of the 1970 Act were excluded by s. 1(3) of that Act. On appeal, both the Employment Appeal Tribunal and the Court of Session upheld that decision. The appellant appealed to the House of Lords, contending that only a difference relating to the personal circumstances of the two employees, such as their respective skills, experience or training, could be a 'material difference' for the purposes of s. 1(3).

Held
On the true construction of s. 1(3) a 'material difference' between a male and a female employee which had the effect of excluding the equality requirements of the 1970 Act was not restricted to the circumstances or qualities personal to the employees concerned but embraced all the significant and relevant circumstances, including, where relevant, differences connected with economic factors affecting the efficient running of the employer's business. Since there had been sound reasons for offering C and other prosthetists employed by the private contractors more than the civil service rates of pay in order to attract them to enter national health service employment, effectively C was being paid more than the norm rather than the appellant being paid less. Furthermore, the fact that the appellant was a woman and C a man was fortuitous. It followed that there was a material difference between the appellant's case and C's for the purpose of s. 1(3) and therefore the equality provisions of that Act did not apply. The appeal would accordingly be dismissed.

Lord Keith
In the present case the difference between the case of the appellant and that of Mr Crumlin is that the former is a person who entered the national health service at

Belvidere Hospital direct while the latter is a person who entered it from employment with a private contractor. The fact that one is a woman and the other a man is an accident. The findings of the industrial tribunal make it clear that the new prosthetic service could never have been established within a reasonable time if Mr Crumlin and others like him had not been offered a scale of remuneration no less favourable than that which they were then enjoying. That was undoubtedly a good and objectively justified ground for offering him that scale of remuneration. But it was argued for the appellant that it did not constitute a good and objectively justified reason for paying the appellant and other direct entrants a lower scale of remuneration. This aspect does not appear to have been specifically considered by either of the tribunals or by their Lordships of the First Division, apart from Lord Grieve, who said ([1985] IRLR 414 at 425):

> I accept that the facts which provided the evidence before both Tribunals were sufficient to explain why Mr Crumlin (and his colleagues) were paid on a scale equivalent to that which they had been receiving while employed in the private sector, but in my opinion that evidence is not sufficient to explain why, when the National [Health] Service door was opened to the appellant (and other prosthetists not previously employed in the private sector) the appellant (and her fellow prosthetists) were paid on a lower scale. In the absence of a reasonable explanation as to why the appellant was paid on a lower scale than Mr Crumlin I am of opinion that the respondents have not discharged the onus placed upon them by s. 1(3) of the 1970 Act, and that the majority of the Employment Appeal Tribunal were not entitled on the facts before them to conclude that they had.

The position in 1980 was that all national health service employees were paid on the Whitley Council scale, and that the Whitley Council negotiating machinery applied to them. The prosthetic service was intended to be a branch of the national health service. It is therefore easy to see that from the administrative point of view it would have been highly anomalous and inconvenient if prosthetists alone, over the whole tract of future time for which the prosthetic service would endure, were to have been subject to a different salary scale and different negotiating machinery. It is significant that a large part of the difference which has opened up between the appellant's salary and Mr Crumlin's is due to the different negotiating machinery. Accordingly, there were sound objectively justified administrative reasons, in my view, for placing prosthetists in general, men and women alike, on the Whitley Council scale and subjecting them to its negotiating machinery. There is no suggestion that it was unreasonable to place them on the particular point on the Whitley Council scale which was in fact selected, ascertained by reference to the position of medical physics technicians and entirely regardless of sex. It is in any event the fact that the general scale of remuneration for prosthetists was laid down accordingly by the Secretary of State. It was not a question of the appellant being paid less than the norm but of Mr Crumlin being paid more. He was paid more because of the necessity to attract him and other privately employed prosthetists into forming the nucleus of the new service.

I am therefore of the opinion that the grounds founded on by the respondents as constituting the material difference between the appellant's case and that of Mr Crumlin were capable in law of constituting a relevant difference for purposes of s. 1(3) of the 1970 Act, and that on the facts found by the industrial tribunal they were objectively justified.

Counsel for the appellant put forward an argument based on s. 1(1)(b) of the Sex Discrimination Act 1975 (with which the 1970 Act is to be read as one: see *Shields* v *E Coomes (Holdings) Ltd* [1979] 1 All ER 456 at 463, which is in these terms:

A person discriminates against a woman in any circumstances relevant for the purposes of any provision of this Act if . . . (b) he applies to her a requirement or condition which he applies or would apply equally to a man but — (i) which is such that the proportion of women who can comply with it is considerably smaller than the proportion of men who can comply with it, and (ii) which he cannot show to be justifiable irrespective of the sex of the person to whom it is applied, and (iii) which is to her detriment because she cannot comply with it.

This provision has the effect of prohibiting indirect discrimination between women and men. In my opinion it does not, for present purposes, add anything to s. 1(3) of the 1970 Act, since, on the view which I have taken as to the proper construction of the latter, a difference which demonstrated unjustified indirect discrimination would not discharge the onus placed on the employer. Further, there would not appear to be any material distinction in principle between the need to demonstrate objectively justified grounds of difference for purposes of s. 1(3) and the need to justify a requirement or condition under s. 1(1)(b)(ii) of the 1975 Act. It is therefore unnecessary to consider the argument further.
My Lords, for these reasons I would dismiss the appeal with costs.

Some surveys have claimed that 60 per cent of women have been the victims of sexual harassment at work. The decision in *Bracebridge* (below) indicates that there need not be a sustained campaign (as in *Porcelli* v *Strathclyde Regional Council*), but that one single act will suffice. The act need not be physical but could consist of a remark, e.g., about a woman's breasts (*Insitu Cleaning* v *Meads* [1995] IRLR 4).

BRACEBRIDGE ENGINEERING LTD v DARBY
[1990] IRLR 3

Facts
Mrs Darby had been employed for 13 years by the appellants, a small company with some dozen staff. On 11 November 1987, she was about to wash her hands before finishing her shift when she was grabbed by her chargehand (Mr Daly) and the works manager (Mr Smith) and taken to the works manager's office. The lights were put out and Mr Smith picked up her legs and put them around him. She tried to get away but was threatened with a written warning for leaving early. Mr Daly then put his hands between her legs and touched her private parts remarking 'you've got a big one'. She was eventually able to open the door and run out. The following morning Mrs Darby complained to the general manager, Miss Reynolds. However, as both Mr Daly and Mr Smith denied the incident, Miss Reynolds decided that no steps should be taken.
Mrs Darby regarded this as wholly unsatisfactory and resigned a week later on grounds of her treatment. She complained that she had been constructively dismissed and unlawfully discriminated against on grounds of sex. An industrial tribunal upheld both complaints. It awarded £3,900 compensation for unfair dismissal and £150 compensation for sex discrimination. The employers appealed against both the finding of sex discrimination and of unfair dismissal.

Held
The industrial tribunal had not erred in finding that the respondent had been unlawfully discriminated against by the appellant employers, contrary to the Sex Discrimination Act, s. 6(2)(b) by reason of having been sexually harassed by her chargehand and works manager.

The industrial tribunal was entitled to find that a single act of sexual harassment was a 'detriment' to the complainant within the meaning of s. 6(2)(b), notwithstanding the dictionary definition of 'harassment' as a continuing course of conduct. A single incident of sexual harassment, provided it is sufficiently serious, clearly falls within the proper intention and meaning of the statute as it is an act of discrimination against a woman because she is a woman.

Nor had the industrial tribunal erred in finding that the 'detriment' suffered by the respondent was in the context of her employment so as to fall within s. 6(2)(b) since the harassers, the complainant's chargehand and works manager, were involved in disciplinary supervision.

Similarly, the industrial tribunal had correctly concluded that the acts perpetrated by the harassers were acts committed in the course of their employment since they were engaged in exercising, or in the course of exercising, a disciplinary and supervisory function.

The industrial tribunal had correctly concluded that the respondent employee was entitled to resign and treat herself as having been constructively dismissed by reason of the employers' failure to treat her allegation of sexual harassment seriously.

The implied contractual term relating to mutual trust, confidence and support is an extremely important one for female staff in a case such as the present where sexual discrimination and investigation are concerned. Given its findings of fact that the respondent had been greatly upset and suffered shock and trauma as a result of the incident and that she complained that the incident had not been treated with the seriousness and the gravity with which it should, the only conclusion to which the industrial tribunal could have come was that there had been a constructive dismissal.

Wood J
To deal with the sex discrimination issue first. The allegation was that there had been a breach of the provisions of s. 6(2)(b) and s. 1 of the 1975 Act. The Act complained of was alleged to fall within this wording in s. 6(2)(b):

It is unlawful for a person, in the case of a woman employed by him at an establishment in Great Britain, to discriminate against her . . . (b) by dismissing her, or subjecting her to any other detriment.

The detriment and the discrimination is being treated less favourably within the definitions sections. The tribunal found that this assault upon her, the incident in the office, was a detriment and that within the wording of s. 6(2)(b).

The first point taken by Mr de Mello for the appellant company before us is that this was a single act, a single incident and it cannot properly be described as sexual harassment. He referred us to the definition in the Shorter Oxford English Dictionary. It seems to us that 'sexual harassment' is a phrase which can embody a whole number of notions. It would seem that whether or not harassment is a continuing course of conduct, there was here an act which was an act of discrimination against a woman because she was a woman, and it was a most unpleasant one, and one which in our judgment clearly falls within the proper intention and meaning of the Act. We would deplore any argument that could be raised that merely because it was a single incident — provided it is sufficiently serious, I think one must say that — that it could not fall within the wording of the subsection.

The second point taken is that the detriment needs to be in the context of employment. The wording of s. 6(2)(b) has been the subject of a number of cases. One of the issues which ultimately will have to be decided is whether there is any sort of limitation to those words at the end of that phrase. Although not strictly necessary for the decision, that part of the section was considered in *De Souza* v *Automobile Association* [1986] IRLR 103 by the Court of Appeal presided over by Lord Justice May. It is unnecessary for us to deal with the difficult point of construction on the Act as it is drafted, although we are quite satisfied that sexual harassment as it is called should fall within the Act as to whether — and to what extent — detriment must be connected with the employment or the termination or disciplinary aspects of employment, because in this case it is abundantly clear that Mr Smith and Mr Daly were involved in what might be termed disciplinary supervision. When one looks at the judgment of Lord MacDonald at first instance in the case of *Porcelli* v *Strathclyde Regional Council* [1984] IRLR 467, he expressed the view that in connection with that subsection the action being taken could be:

suspension, warning, enforced transfer, etc all of which would be to the detriment of the female employee although open to an employer under her contract of service in a genuine case not associated with sexual harassment.

A reading of his judgment indicates clearly that the background circumstances of this case would fall within the understanding. Although Lord Justice May felt in *De Souza* that Lord MacDonald had been a little restricted in his view, it is unnecessary for us to decide whether that was necessary to the decision in *De Souza* because this case clearly falls within the words used by Lord MacDonald. We therefore reject the suggestion that this was not sufficiently connected in the present case with the employment context.

The third point taken by Mr de Mello was that the acts perpetrated by Mr Smith and Mr Daly were not acts committed in the course of their employment. He emphasises the importance of considering the phrase 'course of their employment' from two aspects. First he submits that the presence of the existence of s. 41 of the Act emphasises that there is provided a defence to employers for acts which are either not within the course of employment or when under s. 41(3) there is a defence; a statutory defence that the employers have done all that is reasonably practicable to prevent the act of discrimination which is the subject matter of the proceedings. But secondly he submits that on a proper understanding of s. 6 itself, and in particular s. 6, the whole ambit of the provisions of that subsection are in the employment context, and therefore unless the act was committed in the course of the employment, it might very well not come within subsection 2. As anyone knows the problems of that phrase have been the subject of consideration by the courts and academics over many years.

The two lay members sitting with me with their experience of the workings in industry both on the shop floor and generally, have no doubt that in the picture which they envisage here, this act was perpetrated in the course of the employment of these two men. We accept the findings of fact of the tribunal, and are satisfied that the findings here fall on the correct side of the law upon the principles laid down in the authorities which have been cited. These men were involved in carrying out their functions as part of their employment. It follows therefore that so far as the points taken and argued on the Sexual Discrimination Act we find that there is no flaw in the way in which the tribunal dealt with this matter and the learned chairman directed the tribunal upon it. That part of this appeal fails.

There is however the second limb. The second limb is the issue of constructive dismissal.

The findings of fact were that this lady, Mrs Darby, had clearly been greatly upset and suffered shock and trauma as a result of this extremely unpleasant incident in the office of the chargehand. She made her complaint that it had not been treated with the seriousness and the gravity which it should. The tribunal found on the facts that there had been a breach of that term. Thereafter the question would have been 'had it been accepted as repudiation?' and that followed a week later when Mrs Darby left. Thirdly, they decided was it a reasonable period of time in which she had to make up her mind. It seems again to those sitting with me with experience of situations such as this, that it was evidently reasonable that she should be allowed a week in which to decide about it, the more especially as she might have been waiting for the chairman, Mr Reynolds, to return and he did not return until just after she had left. In the circumstances, therefore, if properly directed we have no doubt that the only conclusion to which the tribunal could have come on its finding of fact was that there had been a constructive dismissal.

Note

(1)   This case is a good illustration of the type of conduct which will entitle the employee to regard herself as dismissed by virtue of 'constructive dismissal'. It also discusses the issue of the employer's vicarious liability for his employees when acting in the course of their employment. What implied duty is the employer in breach of here?

The Times leader of 5 March 1994 hailed the decision below as a profound judgment and said that it gave Britain its first taste of a constitutional court. In the wake of this decision employment protection laws on redundancy payment and unfair dismissal rights have been extended (the Employment Protection (Part-Time Employees) Regulations 1995, SI 1995 No 31).

R v SECRETARY OF STATE FOR EMPLOYMENT EX PARTE EQUAL OPPORTUNITIES COMMISSION AND ANOTHER
[1994) IRLR 176

Facts

On 21 March 1990, the Equal Opportunities Commission (EOC) wrote to the Secretary of State for Employment referring to the provision of the EPCA 1978 concerning redundancy pay and compensation for unfair dismissal, and expressing the view that the hours thresholds for these rights constituted indirect discrimination against women employees, contrary to Community law. The EOC argued that, as nearly 90 per cent of employees working fewer than 16 hours are women, the statutory provisins were contrary to Article 119 of the Treaty of Rome, which lays down the principle of equal pay for equal work; the 'Equal Pay' Directive (75/117/EEC), which provides further detail on the right to equal pay; and the 'Equal Treatment' Directive (76/207/EEC), which prohibits discrimination in working conditions, including the conditions governing dismissal.

On 23 April 1990, the Minister replied, stating that he did not accept that the legislation was in breach of EC law and had no plans to change the statutory thresholds. The EOC applied to the High Court for judicial reveiw.

The High Court held that statutory redundancy pay and unfair dismissal compensation fell within the definition of pay under EC law, and that the provisions were indirectly discriminatory because of their adverse effect on women. However, it was held that the Government was able to justify the provisions on grounds of social policy. The Court accepted the government's argument that to remove or reduce the hours threshold would place additional burdens on employers and lead to fewer job opportunities for those wishing to work less than 16 hours per week. The EOC's appeal against this decision was rejected by a majority of the Court of Appeal, on the grounds that the EOC did not have standing to bring proceedings against the Secretary of State and that judicial review was not the appropriate mechanism for determining whether the UK is in the breach of EC law. In the Court's view what the EOC should do is support test cases in industrial tribunals. The House of Lords allowed the EOC's appeal. Having decided, *inter alia*, that the EOC had *locus standi* to bring the proceedings, their Lordships held that the hours threshold was not capable of objective justification.

Lord Keith of Kinkel

The original reason for the threshold provisions of the Act of 1978 appears to have been the veiw that part time workers were less committed than full time workers to the undertaking which employed them. In this letter of 23 April 1990 the Secretaty of State stated that their purpose was to ensure that a fair balance was struck between the interests of employers and employees. These grounds are not now founded on as objective justification for the thresholds. It is now claimed that the thresholds have the effect that more part time employment is available than would be the case if employers were liable for redundancy pay and compensation for unfair dismissal to employees who worked less than 8 hours a week or between 8 and 16 hours a week for under five years. It is contended that if employers were under that liability they would be inclined to employ less part time workers and more full time workers, to the disadvantage of the former.

The bringing about of an increase in the availability of part time work is properly to be regarded as a beneficial social policy aim and it cannot be said that it is not a necessary aim. The question is whether the threshold provisions of the Act of 1978 have been shown, by reference to objective factors, to be suitable and requisite for achieving that aim. As regards suitability for achieving the aim in question, it is to be noted that the purpose of the thresholds is said to be to reduce the costs to employers of employing part time workers. The same result, however, would follow from a situation where the basic rate of pay for part time workers was less than the basic rate for full time workers. No distinction in principle can properly be made between direct and indirect labour costs. While in certain circumstances an employer might be justified in paying full time workers a higher rate than part time workers in order to secure the more efficient use of his machinery (see *Jenkins* v *Kingsgate (Clothing Production) Ltd* [1981] ICR 715) that would be a special and limited state of affairs. Legislation which permitted a differential of that kind nationwide would present a very different aspect and considering that the great majority of part time workers are women would surely constitute a gross breach of the principle of equal pay and could not possibly be regarded as a suitable means of achieving an increase in part time employment. Similar considerations apply to legislation which reduces the indirect cost of employing part time labour. Then as to the threshold provisions being requisite to achieve the stated aim, the question is whether on the evidence before the Divisional Court they have been proved actually to result in greater availability of part time work than would be the case without them. In my opinion that question must be answered in the negative. The evidence for the Secretary of State consisted principally of an affidavit by an official in the Department of Employment which set out the views of the Department but did not contain anything capable of being regarded as factual evidence demonstrating the correctness of these views. One of the exhibits to the affidavit was a report with draft Directives prepared by the Social Affairs Commissioner of the European Commission in 1990. This covered a wide

range of employment benefits and advantages, including redundancy pay and compensation for unfair dismissal, but proposed a qualifying threshold for those benefits
of 8 hours of work per week. The basis for that was stated to be the elimination of
disproportionate administrative costs and regard to employers' economic needs.
These are not the grounds of justification relied on by the Secretary of State. The
evidence put in by the EOC consisted in large measure in a Report of the House of
Commons Employment Committee in 1990 and a Report of the House of Lords
Select Committee on the European Communities on Part-Time and Temporary
Employment in 1990. These revealed a diversity of views upon the effect of the
threshold provisions on part time work, employers' organisations being of the opinion
that their removal would reduce the amount available with trade union representatives
and some employers and acadamics in the industrial relations field taking the opposite
view. It also appeared that no other member state of the European Community, apart
from the Republic of Ireland, had legislation providing for similar thresholds. The
Republic of Ireland, where statute at one time provided for an 18-hour per week
threshold, had recently introduced legislation reducing this to 8 hours. In the
Netherlands the proportion of the workforce in part time employment was in 1988
29.8 per cent and in Denmark 25.5 per cent, neither country having any thresholds
similiar to those in the Act of 1978. In France legislation was introduced in 1982
providing for part time workers to have the same rights as full time, yet between 1983
and 1988 part time work in that country increased by 36.6 per cent, compared with
an increase of 26.1 per cent over the same period in the United Kingdom. While
various explanations were suggested on behalf of the Secretary of State for these
statistics, there is no means of ascertaining whether these explanations have any
validity. The fact is, however, that the proportion of part time employees in the
national workforce is much less than the proportion of full time employees, their
weekly remuneration is necessarily much lower, and the number of them made
redundant or unfairly dismissed in any year is not likely to be unduly large. The
conclusion must be that no objective justification for the thresholds in the Act of 1978
has been established.

A subsidiary issue of substance in the appeal is whether or not compensation for
unfair dismissal is 'pay' within the meaning of Article 119 of the Treaty and the Equal
Pay Directive. The definition of 'pay' in Article 119 has been set out above. In
Arbeiterwohlfahrt der Stadt Berlin ev v *Botel* [1992] IRLR 423, at p 425, the European
court of Justice said:

> 12.   According to the case law of the court . . . the concept of 'pay' within the
> meaning of article 119 of the Treaty comprises any consideration whether in cash
> or in kind, whether immediate or future, provided that the employee receives it,
> albeit indirectly, in respect of his employment from his employer, whether under a
> contract of employment, legislative provisions or made ex gratia by the employer.

In *Barber* v *Guardian Royal Exchange Assurance Group* [1990] ICR 616 the Court held
that redundancy pay was 'pay' within the meaning of Article 119 on the ground
(paragraph 18 of the judgment at p. 668) that receipt of it arose 'by reason of the
existence of the employment relationship'. There is much to be said in favour of the
view that compensation for unfair dismissal is of a comparable nature, but the
European Court of Justice has not yet pronounced upon this issue, and there may be
a question whether the answer to it can properly be held to be acte clair, or whether
resolution of it would require a reference to the European Court under Article 177 of
the Treaty.

Such a reference is in any event, however, unnecessary for the disposal of the present appeal. Discrimination as regards the right to compensation for unfair dismissal, if not objectively justified, is clearly in contravention of the Equal Treatment Directive.

In the light of the foregoing I am of the opinion that the appeal by the EOC should be allowed and that declarations should be made in the following terms:

(1)   That the provisions of the Employment Protection (Consolidation) Act 1978 whereby employees who work for fewer than sixteen hours per week are subject to different conditions in respect to qualification for redundancy pay from those which apply to employees who work for sixteen hours per week or more are incompatible with Article 119 of the Treaty of Rome and the Council Directive 75/117/EEC of 10 February 1975.

(2)   That the provisions of the Employment Protection (Consolidation) Act 1978 whereby employees who work for fewer than sixteen hours per week are subject to different conditions in respect of the right to compensation for unfair dismissal from those which apply to employees who work for sixteen hours per week or more are incompatible with the Council Directive 76/207/EEC of 9 February 1976.

It remains to note that the EOC proposed that the House should grant a declaration to the effect that the Secretary of State is in breach of those provisions of the Equal Treatment Directive which require Member States to introduce measures to abolish any laws contrary to the principle of equal treatment. The purpose of such a declaration was said to be to enable part time workers who were employed otherwise than by the State or an emanation of the State, and who had been deprived of the right to obtain compensation for unfair dismissal by the restrictive thresholds in the Act of 1978, to take proceedings against the United Kingdom for compensation, founding upon the decision of the European Court of Justice in *Francovich* v *Italian Republic* [1992] IRLR 84. In my opinion it would be quite inappropriate to make any such declaration. If there is any individual who believes that he or she has a good claim to compensation under the *Francovich* principle, it is the Attorney-General who would be defendant in any proceedings directed to enforcing it, and the issues raised would not necessarily be identical with any of those which arise in the present appeal.

The *Webb* case (below) would seem to reaffirm the principle that discrimination on grounds of pregnancy or maternity amounts to sex discrimination as only a woman is affected. Rubenstein says it sounds the death knell for the 'sick man' defence (but see *Brown* v *Rentokil* [1995] IRLR 211). Note that pregnancy dismissals are now unlawful under TURERA 1993.

WEBB v EMO AIR CARGO (UK) LTD
[1994] IRLR 482

Facts
The respondent firm had 16 employees. It had an import department of four staff, including an import operations clerk, Mrs Stewart. In June 1987, it became known that Mrs Stewart was pregnant and would be taking maternity leave at the end of the year. Mrs Webb was taken on as an import operations clerk on July 1. It was recognised that she would need six months' training from Mrs Stewart and would then be able to act as her temporary replacement. It was anticipated that Mrs Webb would probably stay in employment when Mrs Stewart returned.

Several weeks after starting work, however, Mrs Webb discovered that she was pregnant and so informed the employers. The employers took the view that they had no alternative but to dismiss her. She complained that she had been discriminated against on grounds of sex.

Held

The House of Lords held that the appellant's dismissal did not constitute unlawful direct discrimination since a hypothetical man required for the same purpose who would also be unavailable at the material time would have been treated similarly. The case was remitted to the ECJ for them to determine whether a dismissal in these circumstances was discriminatory under EC law.

Decision

Article 2(1) of the Directive states that 'the principle of equal treatment shall mean that there shall be no discrimination whatsoever on grounds of sex either directly or indirectly by reference in particular to marital or family status'. Under Article 5(1), 'application of the principle of equal treatment with regard to working conditions, including the conditions governing dismissal, means that men and women shall be guaranteed the same conditions without discrimination on grounds of sex'.

As the Court ruled in paragraph 13 of its judgment in *Handels-og Kontorfunktionoerernes Forbund i Danmark*, C–179/88 [1991] IRLR 31 (hereinafter 'the *Hertz* judgment') and confirmed in paragraph 15 of its judgment in *Habermann-Beltermann*, C–421/92 [1994] IRLR 364, the dismissal of a female worker on account of pregnancy constitutes direct discrimination on grounds of sex.

Furthermore, by reserving to Member States the right to retain or introduce provisions which are intended to protect women in connection with 'pregnancy and maternity', Article 2(3) of Directive 76/207 recognises the legitimacy, in terms of the principle of equal treatment, first, of protecting a woman's biological condition during and after pregnancy and, second, of protecting the special relationship between a woman and her child over the period which follows pregnancy and childbirth (*Habermann-Beltermann* . . . and *Hoffmann* v *Barmer Ersatzkasse*, 184/83 [1984] ECR 3047 . . .).

In view of the harmful effects which the risk of dismissal may have on the physical and mental state of women who are pregnant, have recently given birth or are breastfeeding, including the particularly serious risk that pregnant women may be prompted voluntarily to terminate their pregnancy, the Community legislature subsequently provided, pursuant to Article 10 of Council Directive 92/85/EEC of 19 October 1992 on the introduction of measures to encourage improvements in the safety and health at work of pregnant workers and workers who have recently given birth or are breastfeeding (OJ 1992 348, p. 1), for special protection to be given to women, by prohibiting dismissal during the period from the beginning of their pregnancy to the end of their maternity leave.

Furthermore, Article 10 of Directive 92/85 provides that there is to be no exception to, or derogation from, the prohibition on the dismissal of pregnant women during that period, save in exceptional cases not connected with their condition.

The answer to the question submitted by the House of Lords, which concerns Directive 76/207, must take account of that general context.

First, in response to the House of Lords' inquiry, there can be no question of comparing the situation of a woman who finds herself incapable, by reason of pregnancy discovered very shortly after the conclusion of the employment contract, of performing the task for which she was recruited with that of a man similarly incapable for medical or other reasons.

As Mrs Webb rightly argues, pregnancy is not in any way comparable with a pathological condition, and even less so with unavailability for work on non-medical grounds, both of which are situations that may justify the dismissal of a woman without discriminating on grounds of sex. Moreover, in the Hertz judgment, cited above, the Court drew a clear distinction between pregnancy and illness, even where the illness is attributable to pregnancy but manifests itself after the maternity leave. As the Court pointed out (in paragraph 16), there is no reason to distinguish such an illness from any other illness.

Furthermore, contrary to the submission of the United Kingdom, dismissal of a pregnant woman recruited for an indefinite period cannot be justified on grounds relating to her inability to fulfil a fundamental condition of her employment contract. The availability of an employee is necessarily, for the employer, a precondition for the proper performance of the employment contract. However, the protection afforded by Community law to a woman during pregnancy and after childbirth cannot be dependent on whether her presence at work during maternity is essential to the proper functioning of the undertaking in which she is employed. Any contrary interpretation would render ineffective the provisions of the Directive.

In circumstances such as those of Mrs Webb, termination of a contract for an indefinite period on grounds of the woman's pregnancy cannot be justified by the fact that she is prevented, on a purely temporary basis, from performing the work for which she has been engaged (see the judgment in *Habermann-Beltermann* . . . and paragraphs 10 and 11 of the Advocate-General's Opinion in this case).

The fact that the main proceedings concern a woman who was initially recruited to replace another employee during the latter's maternity leave but who was herself found to be pregnant shortly after her recruitment cannot affect the answer to be given to the national court.

Accordingly, the answer to the question submitted must be that Article 2(1) read with Article 5(1) of Directive 76/207 precludes dismissal of an employee who is recruited for an unlimited term with a view, initially, to replacing another employee during the latter's maternity leave and who cannot do so because, shortly after recruitment, she is herself found to be pregnant.

CHAPTER NINE
ADMINISTRATIVE & CRIMINAL REGULATION OF BUSINESS

TRADE DESCRIPTIONS ACT
1968

1 Prohibition of false trade descriptions

(1)   Any person who, in the course of a trade or business, —

(a)   applies a false trade description to any goods; or

(b)   supplies or offers to supply any goods to which a false trade description is applied;

shall, subject to the provisions of this Act, be guilty of an offence.

(2)   Sections 2 to 6 of this Act shall have effect for the purposes of this section and for the interpretation of expressions used in this section, wherever they occur in this Act.

2 Trade description

(1)   A trade description is an indication, direct or indirect, and by whatever means given, of any of the following matters with respect to any goods or parts of goods, that is to say —

(a) quantity, size or guage;
(b) method of manufacture, production, processing or reconditioning;
(c) composition;
(d) fitness for purpose, strength, performance, behaviour or accuracy;
(e) any physical characteristics not included in the preceding paragraphs;
(f) testing by any person and results thereof;
(g) approval by any person or conformity with a type approved by any person;
(h) place or date of manufacture, production, processing or reconditioning;
(i) person by whom manufactured, produced, processed or reconditioned;
(j) other history, including previous ownership or use.

Note
Can you think of statements in different business contexts which fall into the above categories?

3 False trade description
(1) A false trade description is a trade description which is false to a material degree.

(2) A trade description which, though not false, is misleading, that is to say, likely to be taken for such an indication of any of the matters specified in section 2 of this Act as would be false to a material degree, shall be deemed to be a false trade description.

(3) Anything which, though not a trade description, is likely to be taken for an indication of any of those matters and, as such an indication, would be false to a material degree, shall be deemed to be false trade description.

(4) A false indication, or anything likely to be taken as an indication which would be false, that any goods comply with a standard specified or recognised by any person or implied by the approval of any person shall be deemed to be a false trade description, if there is no such person or no standard so specified, recognised or implied.

4 Applying a trade description to goods
(1) A person applies a trade description to goods if he —
    (a) affixes or annexes it to or in any manner marks it on or incorporates it with
—
        (i) the goods themselves, or
        (ii) anything in, on or with which the goods are supplied; or
    (b) places the goods in, on or with anything which the trade description has been affixed or annexed to, marked on or incorporated with, or places any such thing with the goods; or
    (c) uses the trade description in any manner likely to be taken as referring to the goods.

(2) An oral statement may amount to the use of a trade description.

(3) Where goods are supplied in pursuance of a request in which a trade description is used and the circumstances are such as to make it reasonable to infer that the goods are supplied as goods corresponding to that trade description, the person supplying the goods shall be deemed to have applied that trade description to the goods.

5 Trade descriptions used in advertisements
(1) The following provisions of this section shall have effect where in an advertisement a trade description is used in relation to any class of goods.

(2)   The trade description shall be taken as referring to all goods of the class, whether or not in existence at the time the advertisement is published —

(a)   for the purpose of determining whether an offence has been committed under paragraph (a) of section 1(1) of this Act; and

(b)   where goods of the class are supplied or offered to be supplied by a person publishing or displaying the advertisement, also for the purpose of determining whether an offence has been committed under paragraph (b) of the said section 1(1).

(3)   In determining for the purposes of this section whether any goods are of a class to which a trade description used in an advertisement relates regard shall be had not only to the form and content of the advertisement but also to the time, place, manner and frequency of its publication and all other matters making it likely or unlikely that a person to whom the goods are supplied would think of the goods as belonging to the class in relation to which the trade description is used in the advertisement.

6   Offer to supply

A person exposing goods for supply or having goods in his possession for supply shall be deemed to offer to supply them.

Note

Why do you think Parliament considered it necessary to say explicitly that possession of goods is tantamount to offering to supply them in this context? (See 3.1.3. above.)

14   False or misleading statements as to services, etc.

(1)   It shall be an offence for any person in the course of any trade or business —

(a)   to make a statement which he knows to be false; or

(b)   recklessly to make a statement which is false;

as to any of the following matters, that is to say, —

(i)   the provision in the course of any trade or business of any services, accommodation or facilities;

(ii)   the nature of any services, accommodation or facilities provided in the course of any trade or business;

(iii)   the time at which, manner in which or persons by whom any services, accommodation or facilities are so provided;

(iv)   the examination, approval or evaluation by any person of any services, accommodation or facilities so provided; or

(v)   the location or amenities of any accommodation so provided.

Note

Can you think of examples of statements which would fall into the above categories in the context of (a) hotels and (b) the motor trade?

24   Defence of mistake, accident, etc.

(1)   In any proceedings for an offence under this Act it shall, subject to subsection (2) of this section, be a defence for the person charged to prove —

(a)   that the commission of the offence was due to a mistake or to reliance on information supplied to him or to the act or default of another person, an accident or some other cause beyond his control; and

(b)   that he took all reasonable precautions and exercised all due diligence to avoid the commission of such an offence by himself or any person under his control.

(2)   If in any case the defence provided by the last foregoing subsection involves the allegation that the commission of the offence was due to the act or default of

another person or to reliance on information supplied by another person, the person charged shall not, without leave of the court, be entitled to rely on that defence unless, within a period ending seven clear days before the hearing, he has served on the prosecutor a notice in writing giving such information identifying or assisting in the identification of that other person as was then in his possession.

(3)   In any proceedings for an offence under this Act of supplying or offering to supply goods to which a false trade description is applied it shall be a defence for the person charged to prove that he did not know, and could not with reasonable diligence have ascertained, that the goods did not conform to the description or that the description had been applied to the goods.

25   Innocent publication of advertisement

In proceedings for an offence under this Act committed by the publication of an advertisement it shall be a defence for the person charged to prove that he is a person whose business it is to publish or arrange for the publication of advertisements and that he received the advertisement for publication in the ordinary course of business and did not know and had no reason to suspect that its publication would amount to an offence under this Act.

CONSUMER PROTECTION ACT
1987

10   The general safety requirement

(1)   A person shall be guilty of an offence if he —
(a)   supplies any consumer goods which fail to comply with the general safety requirement;
(b)   offers or agrees to supply any such goods; or
(c)   exposes or possesses any such goods for supply.

(2)   For the purposes of this section consumer goods fail to comply with the general safety requirement if they are not reasonably safe having regard to all the circumstances, including —
(a)   the manner in which, and purposes for which, the goods are being or would be marketed, the get-up of the goods, the use of any mark in relation to the goods and any instructions or warnings which are given or would be given with respect to the keeping, use or consumption of the goods;
(b)   any standards of safety published by any person either for goods of a description which applies to the goods in question or for matters relating to goods of that description; and
(c)   the existence of any means by which it would have been reasonable (taking into account the cost, likelihood and extent of any improvement) for the goods to have been made safer.

(3)   For the purposes of this section consumer goods shall not be regarded as failing to comply with the general safety requirement in respect of —
(a)   anything which is shown to be attributable to compliance with any require-ment imposed by or under any enactment or with any Community obligation;
(b)   any failure to do more in relation to any matter than is required by —
(i)   any safety regulations imposing requirements with respect to that matter;
(ii)   any standards of safety approved for the purposes of this subsection by or under any such regulations and imposing requirements with respect to that matter;
(iii)   any provision of any enactment or subordinate legislation imposing such requirements with respect to that matter as are designated for the purposes of this subsection by any such regulations.

(4)   In any proceedings against any person for an offence under this section in respect of any goods it shall be a defence for that person to show —

(a)   that he reasonably believed that the goods would not be used or consumed in the United Kingdom; or

(b)   that the following conditions are satisfied, that is to say —

(i)   that he supplied the goods, offered or agreed to supply them or, as the case may be, exposed or possessed them for supply in the course of carrying on a retail business; and

(ii)   that, at the time he supplied the goods or offered or agreed to supply them or exposed or possessed them for supply, he neither knew nor had reasonable grounds for believing that the goods failed to comply with the general safety requirement; or

(c)   that the terms on which he supplied the goods or agreed or offered to supply them or, in the case of goods which he exposed or possessed for supply, the terms on which he intended to supply them —

(i)   indicated that the goods were not supplied or to be supplied as new goods; and

(ii)   provided for, or contemplated, the acquisition of an interest in the goods by the persons supplied or to be supplied.

(5)   For the purposes of subsection (4)(b) above goods are supplied in the course of carrying on a retail business if —

(a)   whether or not they are themselves acquired for a person's private use or consumption, they are supplied in the course of carrying on a business of making a supply of consumer goods available to persons who generally acquire them for private use or consumption; and

(b)   the descriptions of goods the supply of which is made available in the course of that business do not, to a significant extent, include manufactured or imported goods which have not previously been supplied in the United Kingdom.

(6)   A person guilty of an offence under this section shall be liable on summary conviction to imprisonment for a term not exceeding six months or to a fine not exceeding level 5 on the standard scale or to both.

(7)   In this section 'consumer goods' means any goods which are ordinarily intended for private use or consumption, not being —

(a)   growing crops or things comprised in land by virtue of being attached to it;

(b)   water, food, feeding stuff or fertiliser;

(c)   gas which is, is to be or has been supplied by a person authorised to supply it by or under section 6, 7 or 8 of the Gas Act 1986 (authorisation of supply of gas through pipes);

(d)   aircraft (other than hang-gliders) or motor vehicles;

(e)   controlled drugs or licensed medicinal products;

(f)   tobacco.

Note

For a discussion of the general safety requirement see Weatherill, 'Unsafe Goods: Protecting the Consumer and Protecting the Diligent Trader', (1990) *Journal of Business Law*, 36.

20   Offence of giving misleading indication

(1)   Subject to the following provisions of this Part, a person shall be guilty of an offence if, in the course of any business of his, he gives (by any means whatever) to any consumers an indication which is misleading as to the price at which any goods, services, accommodation or facilities are available (whether generally or from particular persons).

(2)   Subject as aforesaid, a person shall be guilty of an offence if —

(a)   in the course of any business of his, he has given an indication to any consumers which, after it was given, has become misleading as mentioned in subsection (1) above; and

(b)   some or all of those consumers might reasonably be expected to rely on the indication at a time after it has become misleading; and

(c)   he fails to take all such steps as are reasonable to prevent those consumers from relying on the indication.

(3)   For the purposes of this section it shall be immaterial —

(a)   whether the person who gives or gave the indication is or was acting on his own behalf or on behalf of another;

(b)   whether or not that person is the person, or included among the persons, from whom the goods, services, accommodation or facilities are available; and

(c)   whether the indication is or has become misleading in relation to all the consumers to whom it is or was given or only in relation to some of them.

(4)   A person guilty of an offence under subsection (1) or (2) above shall be liable —

(a)   on conviction on indictment, to a fine;

(b)   on summary conviction, to a fine not exceeding the statutory maximum.

(5)   No prosecution for an offence under subsection (1) or (2) above shall be brought after whichever is the earlier of the following, that is to say —

(a)   the end of the period of three years beginning with the day on which the offence was committed; and

(b)   the end of the period of one year beginning with the day on which the person bringing the prosecution discovered that the offence had been committed.

21   Meaning of 'misleading'

(1)   For the purposes of section 20 above an indication given to any consumers is misleading as to a price if what is conveyed by the indication, or what those consumers might reasonably be expected to infer from the indication or any omission from it, includes any of the following, that is to say —

(a)   that the price is less than in fact it is;

(b)   that the applicability of the price does not depend on facts or circumstances on which its applicability does in fact depend;

(c)   that the price covers matters in respect of which an additional charge is in fact made;

(d)   that a person who in fact has no such expectation —

(i)   expects the price to be increased or reduced (whether or not at a particular time or by a particular amount); or

(ii)   expects the price, or the price as increased or reduced, to be maintained (whether or not for a particular period); or

(e)   that the facts or circumstances by reference to which the consumers might reasonably be expected to judge the validity of any relevant comparison made or implied by the indication are not what in fact they are.

(2)   For the purposes of section 20 above, an indication given to any consumers is misleading as to a method of determining a price if what is conveyed by the indication, or what those consumers might reasonably be expected to infer from the indication or any omission from it, includes any of the following, that is to say —

(a)   that the method is not what in fact it is;

(b)   that the applicability of the method does not depend on facts or circumstances on which its applicability does in fact depend;

(c)   that the method takes into account matters in respect of which an additional charge will in fact be made;

(d) that a person who in fact has no such expectation —
    (i) expects the method to be altered (whether or not at a particular time or in a particular respect); or
    (ii) expects the method, or that method as altered, to remain unaltered (whether or not for a particular period); or
(e) that the facts or circumstances by reference to which the consumers might reasonably be expected to judge the validity of any relevant comparison made or implied by the indication are not what in fact they are.

(3) For the purposes of subsections (1)(e) and (2)(e) above a comparison is a relevant comparison in relation to a price or method of determining a price if it is made between that price or that method, or any price which has been or may be determined by that method, and —
(a) any price or value which is stated or implied to be, to have been or to be likely to be attributed or attributable to the goods, services, accommodation or facilities in question or to any other goods, services, accommodation or facilities; or
(b) any method, or other method, which is stated or implied to be, to have been or to be likely to be applied or applicable for the determination of the price or value of the goods, services, accommodation or facilities in question or of the price or value of any other goods, services, accommodation or facilities.

Note
Consider advertising and marketing practices which might be covered by the above provisions. (See also the Code of Practice which has been issued. For a brief explanation see 9.2.2.1.)

24 Defences
(1) In any proceedings against a person for an offence under subsection (1) or (2) of section 20 above in respect of any indication it shall be a defence for that person to show that his acts or omissions were authorised for the purposes of this subsection by [pricing regulations made under this Act].

(2) In proceedings against a person for an offence under subsection (1) or (2) of section 20 above in respect of an indication published in a book, newspaper, magazine, film or radio or television broadcast or in a programme included in a cable programme service, it shall be a defence for that person to show that the indication was not contained in an advertisement.

(3) In proceedings against a person for an offence under subsection (1) or (2) of section 20 above in respect of an indication published in an advertisement it shall be a defence for that person to show that —
(a) he is a person who carries on a business of publishing or arranging for the publication of advertisements;
(b) he received the advertisement for publication in the ordinary course of that business; and
(c) at the time of publication he did not know and had no grounds for suspecting that the publication would involve the commission of the offence.

(4) In any proceedings against a person for an offence under subsection (1) of section 20 above in respect of any indication, it shall be a defence for that person to show that —
(a) the indication did not relate to the availability from him of any goods, services, accommodation or facilities;
(b) a price had been recommended to every person from whom the goods, services, accommodation or facilities were indicated as being available;

(c)   the indication related to that price and was misleading as to that price only by reason of a failure by any person to follow the recommendation; and

(d)   it was reasonable for the person who gave the indication to assume that the recommendation was for the most part being followed.

Note

Section 24(2) would exonerate a pop artist who misquoted the price of his latest album while conducting a radio or television interview. Section 24(3) would exonerate the advertiser who innocently conveys a misleading price. Section 24(4) is obviously intended to cover manufacturers who recommend prices but cannot monitor them on a continual basis.

Note

The following extract discusses a recent decision on s. 20 of the Consumer Protection Act 1987.

PRICING OFFENCES AND STATUTORY INTERPRETATION AFTER *PEPPER* v *HART*

COLIN SCOTT,
1993 JBL 490

The House of Lords recently handed down its decision in *Warwickshire County Council v Johnson* in what appears to be the first case taken under the pricing provisions of the Consumer Protection Act 1987 to the House. The case is of considerable interest because it reveals continuing tensions in the interpretation of consumer protection legislation between a functional consumer protection perspective and a more traditional criminal law agenda. It is arguable that the case also demonstrates a tendency, seen in both the Divisional Court and the House of Lords, to decide cases without full reference to relevant case law. The case has considerable wider interest, as it appears to be the first occasion on which the House has taken advantage of its own decision in *Pepper (Inspector of Taxes)* v *Hart* to the effect that it is permissible, in limited circumstances, for a court to have regard to *Hansard* to determine the correct interpretation of legislation. The application of *Pepper* v *Hart* in the case, and in two subsequent House of Lords decisions, tends to suggest that *Hansard* may be consulted by the courts to settle questions of statutory interpretation with greater frequency than might have been anticipated.

Warwickshire County Council v *Johnson* concerned an employee of Dixons, the major retail electrical chain. The appellant was the manager of one of Dixons' stores in Stratford-on-Avon. He had put out a notice on the street claiming, 'We will beat any TV, HiFi and Video price by £20 on the spot', which was in accordance with company policy. A consumer saw the notice and subsequently saw a particular brand and type of TV, which Dixons sold, for sale at another electrical retailers for £159.95. The consumer took the defendant to see this set and demanded to be sold the same model, normally sold by Dixons at £179.95, for £139.95. The defendant refused to sell it at the reduced price. The consumer reported the matter to the respondent trading standards department, which decided to lay an information before the justices alleging that he had committed an offence under section 20(1) of the Consumer Protection Act 1987. The Magistrates acquitted the defendant on the ground that the notice was not misleading, but they also held that the defendant was properly described as acting 'in the course of a business of his', as required under section 20(1) of the Act.

The Divisional Court allowed an appeal by the prosecuting trading standards department, holding that the notice was misleading, and upholding the view of the justices that an employee could properly be prosecuted under section 20 of the Act. The court certified two points of law of general public importance. The first certified question considered by the House was

Whether for the purposes of section 20(1) of the Consumer Protection Act 1987 a statement, which in itself is not misleading on the face of it, can be rendered misleading by virtue of the fact that, even in the absence of evidence to show a general practice or intention to dishonour the offer contained therein, on one occasion the person making the statement declined to enter into the contract within the terms of the statement.

The second certified question considered by the House was: 'Whether for the purpose of section 20(2)(a) of the Consumer Protection Act 1987 an employed branch manager who fails to comply with a price indication so that this same is regarded as misleading does so "in the course of any business of his".'

With regard to the first question, the House approved the decision of the Divisional Court that a notice could be rendered misleading by a refusal to honour it, without even making reference to the statute. The conceptual problem with the notice was that at the time it had been put out, it represented the correct position, that Dixons would beat any price in town by £20 for an identical product. It was only the subsequent actions of the branch manager in refusing to honour the terms of the notice that rendered it misleading. Lord Roskill, giving a judgment with which all the other members of the House agreed, said that there could be no doubt that the consumer was misled by the notice, which was correctly characterised in the Divisional Court as a continuing offer '[W]hether it is misleading or not can only be tested by somebody taking up the offer. It was misleading because [the appellant] did not in accordance with the terms of the notice beat any TV, hi-fi, video price by £20 on the spot'. It would appear that Lord Roskill was self-consciously pursuing a policy-driven interpretation of the offence, because he went on to say that to hold that the notice was not misleading 'would be seriously to restrict the efficacy of this part of the consumer protection legislation. Seemingly innocent notices could be put up and then when such notices were followed by a refusal to honour them by a person acting in the course of his business no offence would be committed'. It seems strange that in reaching this decision Lord Roskill did not take advantage of the considerable jurisprudence on when statements or prices may be misleading under the Trade Descriptions Act 1968.

The second certified question, concerning the interpretation of the words 'in the course of any business of his', was dealt with at great length by Lord Roskill. The basic question seems to be whether the possessive form 'his' refers to business in the sense of ownership or control of a commercial concern, or rather does it refer to the activities, affairs or occupation of the defendant, as in 'What's his business?' The Divisional Court had construed the phrase in the latter sense. This interpretation is supported by the definition of 'business' in the Act to include trade or profession. However, having regard to the provisions under section 11 of the Trade Descriptions Act, which part III of the Consumer Protection Act 1987 replaced, it would appear that the rather peculiar wording of section 20 of the 1987 Act was intended explicitly to prevent the conviction of employees for pricing offences. Under section 11 of the 1968 Act it was fairly clear that both an employer and an employee could be strictly liable for a pricing offence. This remains the position for offences under section 1 of the Trade Descriptions Act 1968 of giving false or misleading trade descriptions in relation to goods. Having regard to the quite deliberate phrasing, and in particular the contrast between the phrasing of the Act and the earlier provisions of the Trade Descriptions Act 1968, Lord Roskill said that the phrase must refer to a business of which the defendant is 'either the owner or in which he has a controlling interest'. Lord Roskill noted that some of their Lordships had found it strange 'that the person actually responsible for what happened, as the appellant clearly was, should be immune from conviction', but nevertheless concluded that this could be the only correct interpretation of the words. He thus answered the second certified question No, though with some misgivings. The reason for the misgivings may be identified as the tension between the legislative policy not to permit prosecutions of employees, and the traditional criminal law perspective which seeks to attribute responsibility to those whose actions constitute the commission of an offence. The Divisional Court appears to have given in to the criminal law perspective, ignoring the policy of the legislation as clearly expressed in the words of the Act, and so the House of Lords took up the invitation of the appellant to interpret the words according to the policy of the legislation. . . .

Note
The following extract discusses the implementation of the Product Safety Directive in the UK. It will be policed by Trading Standards Officers.

Peter Cartwright
'Product Safety and Consumer Protection'
1995, 58 MLR, 222

. . . The latest legislation to deal with unsafe products is contained in the General Product Safety Regulations 1994 (hereafter 'the Regulations') which implement Council Directive 92/59 (hereafter 'the Directive'). The UK has had general criminal legislation on product safety since 1987, when section 10(1) of the Consumer Protection Act introduced a general safety duty (see below) for consumer goods. Some Member States, however, had no criminal measures, while others adopted horizontal measures with different levels of protection. This disparity created barriers to trade and distorted competition within the internal market, leaving the Community to adopt, in the new Directive, a requirement for all Member States, to provide a minimum standard of protection. Since it is extremely difficult to adopt community legislation for all existing and future products, the solution adopted was a broad and horizontal legislative framework, and although the Directive is directed at the free movement of goods, it seeks also to ensure a high level of protection of health and safety as required by Article 100a(e) EC. The Regulations amend the existing UK law to ensure compliance with the Directive. . . .

'Safe product'
The regulations adopt the economic concept of optimal safety in the definition of a safe product, which corresponds with the approach of the UK in the 1987 Act. The UK Government, for example, emphasised that 'safety policy must reflect a judgment on the degree to which the community as a whole is prepared for pay for additional safety,' and rejected 'suggestions which would involve major interference with the normal processes of manufacture and trade and so put up unduly the prices consumers have to pay for their products.'

Section 10(2) of the 1987 Act provides that consumer goods fail to comply with the general safety requirement if they are not reasonably safe having regard to all the circumstances. Regulation 2(1) takes a similar approach, stating that:

'Safe product' means any product which, under normal or reasonably foreseeable conditions of use, including duration, does not present any risk, or only the minimum risks compatible with the product's use, considered as acceptable and consistent with a high level of protection for the health and safety of persons.

Regulation 2(1) then states that certain factors are to be taken into account. These include the product's characteristics, effects on other products where it is reasonably foreseeable that it will be used with other products, presentation, labelling, instructions for use and disposal, and any other indication of information provided by the producer. It also includes the categories of consumer at serious risk when using the product, in particular children. The Regulation then states that 'the fact that higher levels of safety may be obtained or other products presenting a lesser degree of risk may be availible shall not of itself cause the product to be considered other than a safe product.'

The phrase 'minimum risk compatible with the product's use' is the key to the test of a product's safety, but may cause some concern. Clearly, the Regulations seek a balance between protecting consumers and allowing them some choice about levels of safety. The difficulty in determining socially acceptable levels of safety has been emphasised, and it is important to remember the costs to consumers of not having products available at all, or availalbe only at a high cost because of the expense of making them sufficiently safe. Products are not expected to be free from any risk, but free from undue risk. Different groups will have different views as to when a risk is unacceptable, which varies not just between cultures and periods of time, but also between different income groups.

It is particularly notable that, while factors such as the composition and presentation of a product are to be considered when judging if a product is reasonably safe, there is no reference in the Regulation to the cost of the product. It is recognised that a product is not automatically unsafe because of the existence of safer similar products (which may, of course, be more expensive), but price is not stipulated as a matter to be considered. The Regulation may, however, be wide enough to allow this. This would, of course, be judged against the degree of risk presented by the product. It seems that the Regulations are there to set out the minimum acceptable risk that a product may present, and it is hoped that the courts will not set the standard so high as to take too many products out of the range for poorer consumers.

Another difficulty is that of drawing a balance between consumer choice and the protection of 'a few careless consumers' who may be more likely than most to be injured. Many products present a risk if used carelessly, and the Regulations refer to the 'reasonably foreseeable conditions of use.' It appears that a product must present the minimum acceptable risk, both when used normally and when used abnormally but foreseeably. There will presumably be occasions where the careless but foreseeable act of the consumer will not lead to liability; this ought to be dealt with as a question of causation. . . .

Index